UNDER THE EDITORSHIP OF

Leonard Carmichael

SECRETARY, SMITHSONIAN INSTITUTION

FORMERLY PRESIDENT, TUFTS COLLEGE, AND

DIRECTOR, TUFTS RESEARCH LABORATORY

OF SENSORY PSYCHOLOGY AND PHYSIOLOGY

The Evolution and Growth

of Human Behavior

A REVISION OF *Psychological Development*

NORMAN L. MUNN · BOWDOIN COLLEGE

HOUGHTON MIFFLIN COMPANY · *Boston*

New York · Chicago · Dallas · Atlanta · San Francisco

The Riverside Press Cambridge

To my Mother

Nothing gives a better insight into the working of the mind than the study of the development of behaviour through the different animal species, and from the birth of the child up to maturity. It is not merely the bald facts acquired in such a study that are of value, but the attitude that it induces. The man who has heard the beginning of a story is ipso facto a more reliable judge of the credibility of the ending than the man who has come in at the middle.

Victoria Hazlitt, *Infant Psychology*
(Cambridge University Press)

Editor's Introduction

Anyone who is interested in understanding the nature of the adult human mind can learn a great deal from a study of the evolution of mental processes in the animal series and the growth of such functions in the individual. Both of these topics are effectively considered in this thoroughgoing revision of the author's *Psychological Development* (1938).

The importance of Dr. Munn's treatment of the science of genetics in his earlier book was immediately recognized. This significant treatment has now been amplified and brought up to date. The great progress of research in genetic psychology during the past seventeen years has made this new presentation even more valuable than its excellent predecessor. Indeed, a knowledge of genetics is more important for the psychologist today than it was two decades ago, for psychologists in increasing numbers are recognizing the large part that hereditary factors play in the determination of the processes that underlie the development of adult mental life. Dr. Munn has performed a remarkable service to scholarship in summarizing the most important old and new experimental and observational studies which contribute to a basic understanding of the growth of the mind. He is never content, however, merely to report the findings of investigations, but with great skill he fits ideas together, giving his readers a modern, factual, and above all coherent picture of how the mind develops.

In considering the growth of intellectual capacity in the individual, the part played by symbolic processes is especially important. No one today would attempt a serious understanding of adult human anatomy without a knowledge of the evolution of bodily structures, as disclosed in the study of comparative anatomy, and of the growth of organ systems as described in embryology. The same racial and individual biological and historical approach is certainly equally important for anyone who wishes to understand in a fundamental way the complex and subtle processes that make up adult human mental reactions. Dr. Munn has treated this topic most adequately.

The new volume will be found useful in a number of courses in psychology. Students of the social sciences, of child development, of education, and of psychiatry will also find it of great professional value. Like its predecessor it is an unusual achievement. It is written so that the advanced expert will find it valuable, and yet its statements are so clear that it can advantageously be used as a textbook by a student who is at the beginning of his serious study of modern scientific psychology.

LEONARD CARMICHAEL

Preface

Human behavior is what it is because we are end products of the evolutionary process and because we grow in an environment having characteristically human aspects. The human baby, with inherent human potentialities, is thrown into an environment saturated with the accumulations of man's cultural past — implements, ways of doing things, language, and ideologies. In many obvious as well as subtle ways, the individual is gradually molded by this cultural heritage, focused as it is in his parents and in others charged with the responsibility for making him behave like a human being. A child thus grows physically and culturally at the same time. The growth process is one in which biological and cultural influences are integrally related. The end product is an organism possessing not only a human body but also a human nature.

This book, like its predecessor, *Psychological Development*, surveys the entire psychological development of human beings. It deals with the evolution of human psychological characteristics and also with their growth and decline during individual life. This is the area of *genetic psychology*, which is defined by Warren's *Dictionary of Psychology* as the "systematic study of mental phenomena and behavior by the genetic method, i.e., in terms of the origin and historic unfolding of mental life and responsive activity in the individual, or in the organic series."

Although the overall plan of the book remains essentially the same as before, the great amount of significant research that has been carried on in the whole field of human development and behavior has of course necessitated many changes within that original framework. A brief survey of the more extensive revisions follows. Chapter 2 has been revised in the light of recent developments in the field of genetics, though it still owes much to the help originally given by Dr. P. W. Whiting. Chapters 3, 4, and 5, which deal primarily with psychological evolution, take cognizance of recent research on unlearned behavior (including work by the Lorenz-Tinbergen group), on sensory evolution, and on the evolution of intelligence. In addition to tracing developments culminating in the higher symbolic processes of human beings, these chapters suggest some of the important methods involved in the study of child development. Child development is covered more directly, however, by ten chapters which trace the growth of various psychological processes from conception to puberty. The first of these, Chapter 6, dealing with prenatal development, has been rewritten to take cognizance of new findings, but it still owes much to Dr. Davenport Hooker, not only because he provided helpful criticisms of my initial efforts in this field, but because most of the new findings have come from his laboratory. Portions of Chapter 7 have been rewritten to provide a more meaningful presentation of relevant learning theory. Chapters 8–12 incorporate much new material, particularly in the areas of perceptual aspects and language development, where recent research and theory have suggested also the need for a somewhat different orientation. Chapter 13 has been expanded to take into consideration the influence of social conditions. Social perception and other aspects of social development in children are now dealt with in a separate chapter. Another full chapter is devoted to the growth of personality in children, with increased attention to the results of projective studies and to motivational aspects of personality. The final chapter, which traces the growth of personality from adolescence to adulthood, and then the changes wrought by old age, has also been rewritten and greatly enlarged.

The field covered by this book is so broad and the literature so extensive that an exhaustive treatment would prove too cumbersome for instructional purposes. It has thus been necessary to delimit topics and studies with which to illustrate them. In making a selection of research material, therefore, my aim has been to consider only the most relevant, the most representative, and the most recent studies. The overall approach however, is eclectic. There has been no attempt to delimit in terms of any one systematic viewpoint.

Dr. Leonard Carmichael, who helped me plan the original edition and constructively criticized my efforts, has again given me the benefit of his advice. I am also indebted to Edith Lemon and Audrey Ainsworth for stenographic assistance, and to my wife for her help and encouragement. Finally, thanks are due to the authors and publishers who kindly granted me permission to borrow from their publications, and to the investigators who provided me with reprints and photographs; specific acknowledgments of such courtesies appear at appropriate places throughout the book.

NORMAN L. MUNN

Brunswick, Maine

Contents

Contents

1

The Nature of Genetic or Developmental Psychology

STUDENTS often confuse genetic psychology with genetics. This confusion stems from use of the term "genetic," which refers to origins, and also from the fact that geneticists and genetic psychologists have a mutual interest in the contributions of heredity and environment to the origin and development of organisms. Actually, the overlap between these two fields is small. They are decidedly different in emphasis and scope.

Genetics emphasizes the inborn characteristics of organisms, those properties which are determined primarily by heredity. Environment is considered, but only as a limiting or modifying influence upon what is primarily inborn. The mechanisms of hereditary transmission are of focal interest. Even when geneticists turn to the organism itself, they pay closer attention to structure than to function, or behavior. When a genetic psychologist seeks information about hereditary transmission, as did the author in writing Chapter 2, he naturally turns to the research of geneticists. But he is interested in chromosomes and genes, in mutations and sex determination, and in the other topics of a typical text on genetics only insofar as these help to explain the origin and development of psychological processes. Thus, except that it has a place in the literature of psychology, the term "genetic psychology" might well give way to "developmental psychology," a term which would not be confused with genetics.

Genetic psychologists are interested in the origin and development of psychological processes in (1) animals ranging from the simplest to the most complex and (2) individual organisms from the time of conception until senescence. The first of these ranges of interest involves different types (or *phyla*) of animals and is for this reason often referred to as *phylogenetic* psychology. The development involved is phyletic, or racial, as compared with individual. The second range of interest, dealing with individual growth, is known as *ontogenetic* psychology because the term *ontogeny*, as used by biologists, deals with the development of the individual organism in contradistinction to *phylogeny*, which deals with racial development, that is, the evolution of species. In both fields of genetic psychology the predominant interest is man. The trend of behavioral development from lower organisms to man is interesting in itself, but we look back down the long road that evolution has traversed because, above all else, we want to see how we came to be what we are. Similarly, we might investigate the behavioral development of any individual animal, but we most often study the human organism, following it from infancy through

1

adolescence and old age. Even when we do trace the development of some other organism we are usually looking for principles which will aid our understanding of human development.

Origins of Phylogenetic Psychology

Phylogenetic psychology began as an adjunct to the evolutionary biology of the latter half of the nineteenth century. With the publication in 1859 of Darwin's *Origin of Species*, doubt concerning man's relationship with other animals was considerably dissipated. By a painstaking accumulation of data Darwin demonstrated that the structural and many of the behavioral traits of man may be interpreted in the light of their prehuman origins. He regarded human traits as the culmination of developments initiated in lower animals. In a later book, Darwin (1873) suggested that many aspects of human emotional expression are meaningless unless one considers them as vestiges of similar emotional reactions in prehuman ancestors. Man's incipient or overt baring of the canine teeth during rage, for example, was traced to the snarling gestures made by many prehuman animals. In a somewhat similar vein both Darwin (1871) and Spencer (1855) accounted for many other processes of human behavior. Even the ability to reason, once regarded as an exclusively human possession, was claimed to be the culmination of essentially similar abilities evidenced earlier in the animal series.

Interest in the psychological evolution of animals led to the publication in 1883 of Romanes' *Animal Intelligence*, which may possibly be called the first book on comparative psychology.* In this book Romanes

---

* Comparative psychology is now sometimes regarded as synonymous with animal psychology. Strictly speaking, however, animal psychology is comparative only when, as in comparative anatomy, different stages or levels of development are compared. It is phylogenetic when comparison of one form with another is for the purpose of disclosing developmental trends.

collected and systematized most of the available information on the psychology of animals. Successive discussions dealt with the psychology of mollusks, ants, bees, wasps, termites, spiders, scorpions, fish, batrachians, reptiles, birds, mammals, rodents, elephants, cats, foxes, wolves, jackals, dogs, monkeys, apes, and baboons. Most of the material was anecdotal. Romanes' prime interest was in discovering evidence for mental evolution. Anthropomorphic speculations and observed facts were given equal weight. By anthropomorphic speculation is meant the tendency to read human traits into animals. As a typical example of the prevailing tendency to humanize animals, let us take Romanes' personal report on the psychology of a domesticated monkey. He [1]* says:

Another trait in the psychology of this animal which is worth observing was his quietness of manner toward my mother. With me, and indeed with everyone else, his movements were unrestrained, and generally monkey-like; but with her he was always as gentle as a kitten: he appeared to know that her age and infirmities rendered boisterousness on his part unacceptable.

Other observations reported by Romanes are of a similar nature. Many of them were contributed by persons who wrote to the author concerning remarkable feats performed by their pets.

A reaction against the humanizing of animals came from another comparative psychologist, C. Lloyd Morgan. Morgan (1894) stressed the need for separation of the facts of animal behavior from speculation concerning the psychological bases of these facts. He pointed out, moreover, that psychologists, by tentatively accepting the simplest rather than the most highly speculative type of interpretation, should counteract the prevalent tendency to humanize animals. Morgan's principle of parsimony, which is now rather

---

* These numbers refer to notes and references listed at the end of each chapter. The historically important works referred to in this chapter by dates are listed separately at the end of the chapter.

generally accepted by psychologists, reads as follows: [2]

In no case may we interpret an action as the outcome of the exercise of a higher psychical faculty, if it can be interpreted as the outcome of the exercise of one which stands lower in the psychological scale.

Let us apply this principle to the responses of the above-mentioned monkey. According to Morgan, one should seek the simplest explanation consonant with the facts. Perhaps the mother, being old and inactive, failed to feed the animal or to play with it as frequently as did other members of the household. If observations of the circumstances surrounding the monkey's training showed this supposition to be correct, one might interpret its apparent consideration of age as mere absence of response in the presence of one who failed to play with it or to minister to its needs. The same type of reaction would perhaps be exhibited in the presence of some *young* person who similarly failed to feed or play with the monkey.

Following the appearance of Morgan's contribution, anecdotes about the psychological feats of animals were given less than their former credence. There was a growing trend in the direction of experimental observation of animal behavior, a movement stimulated by the experiments of Lubbock (1883, 1888) and Morgan (1894, 1896) on discrimination and learning. (Figure 1.) In 1898 Thorndike was investigating animal learning at Columbia University. Independently, Small (1899, 1900) and Kline (1899) were working on similar investigations at Clark University. These studies stimulated development of a science of animal behavior. It was Hobhouse (1901), however, who did most to crystallize the efforts of men like Lubbock, Romanes, and Morgan to found a science dealing with *psychological evolution* in animals. His *Mind in Evolution* is the first comprehensive discussion of the data and problems of phylogenetic psychology. In it, Hobhouse traced the evolution of instincts, habits, and higher processes from the simplest organisms to man. Many of Hobhouse's conclusions were supported by his own experiments on a wide variety of animals. (Figure 2.) Some of these experiments are similar to those performed later by Gestalt psychologists.

During the last fifty years, much American animal psychology has centered upon the rat; so much so that this animal has even been accused of leading psychologists away from comparative and phylogenetic research. [3] It has indeed become a "tool" for the investigation of psychological processes and underlying neural and physiological mechanisms. Nevertheless, in this country and abroad, many psychologists have greatly extended our information on comparative psychology. The significance of their findings for the study of psychological evolution may be gathered from Chapters 3 to 5, which deal with unlearned behavior and the development of intelligence.

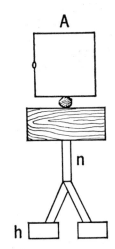

Figure 1. An Early Ant Maze

Lubbock used this maze to investigate how ants recover stolen larvae. Coming from its nest at *A*, the ant reached the strip of paper *n* and was then confronted with two further strips, one leading to the larvae at *h* and the other to an empty piece of glass. Various control experiments demonstrated that, although some ants may have used vision, most of them followed an odor trail. (From J. Lubbock, *Ants, Bees, and Wasps*, New York: Appleton, 1888, p. 167.)

Figure 2. Problem Solving in a Monkey

In order to reach food on the table it was necessary for the monkey to push a box into position, stand upon it, and stretch, as illustrated. This was learned after several false moves. Hobhouse said that "the animal judged, from memory or otherwise, that a certain arrangement would help him, and set about to make that arrangement." (After L. T. Hobhouse, *Mind in Evolution*, New York: Macmillan, 1901. From p. 287, 3d ed., 1926.)

Ontogenetic Psychology

Ontogenetic psychology has always been closely affiliated with biological interests. In this respect its history is similar to that of phylogenetic psychology. The earliest published observations on psychological development in children were those of Tiedemann (1787). These were the only observations on the psychological aspects of child development published in scientific journals until 1876, when Taine's study of the acquisition of language in a child appeared. About a year later, Darwin published his biographical sketch of an infant's development. It was Preyer's (1882) *Die Seele des Kindes*,[4] however, which provided the greatest stimulation for development of modern ontogenetic psychology. This book reported observations on the development of sensory, intellectual, and voluntary processes in a child. Although Preyer did not use the careful experimental methods of current psychology, his observations have in many instances been verified by later workers. Preyer was also a pioneer investigator of prenatal behavior in animals.[5]

Following the appearance of Preyer's book on child development many similar investigations were undertaken. One of the best known of these is the biographical study of a baby reported by Shinn (1900). Like the anecdotal method in phylogenetic psychology, however, the biographical method of investigating child development gradually gave way to a systematic observational and experimental type of approach which involved large numbers of cases instead of single individuals.

In addition to the above-mentioned trend in ontogenetic psychology, there was another which developed in close contact with evolutionary biology. Biologists had observed that many structural characters of animals lower in the scale of evolution are exhibited in the prenatal development of the human individual. During the early embryonic period, such characters as gill slits, a yolk sac, and a tail appear for a short time and then disappear or become transformed into typically human organs. These were regarded as recapitulations in ontogenetic development of the racial history or phylogeny of the individual. Some individuals were observed to possess outmoded structures, such as a tail at birth. Such structures were regarded as atavistic.[6]

The idea that individual biological development mirrors the biological history of the race was not confined to structural characters. A few biologists, stimulated by the doctrine of recapitulation, claimed that many of the early responses of the human child are recapitulations in ontogeny of phylogenetic behavior patterns. The reflex grasping of the newborn, for example, was regarded as evidence of the individual's primate ancestry. (Figure 3.) While useful to the arboreal ancestors of man, the grasping reflex was said to have no human usefulness. Buckman [7] claimed that it is their "monkey ancestry" which makes children like to do such things as climb trees and jump up and down when excited. The same idea has been invoked in the case of children who walk on all fours like apes. Hřdlicka,[8] a famous anthropologist, made a special study of running on all fours and other apelike behavior of children. He

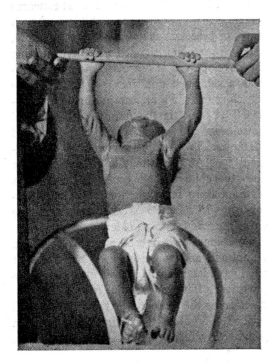

Figure 3. The Grasping Reflex

Some babies can support their weight at birth, even with one hand. This baby was one month old when the picture was taken. (After F. L. Goodenough in her *Developmental Psychology*. Photo from the *Journal of Heredity*.)

also utilized the concept of recapitulation, as illustrated by the following quotation:

It seems just to conclude that just as the human child before birth recapitulates, more or less, various phases of its physical ancestry, so the child after birth recapitulates and uses for a time various phases of its prehuman ancestral behavior.

G. Stanley Hall and his students at Clark University applied the doctrine of recapitulation to child development as previous workers had done. However, they did not restrict it to phylogenetically derived behavior. Hall, following the tradition of the German psychologist, Herbart, believed that the *cultural* as well as the phylogenetic stages of development are mirrored, as it were, in the development of the individual. Cultural recapitulation was invoked to explain why children manifest different types of play as they grow older. In its play, the child was assumed to pass through stages representing the cultural epochs of human progress. Thus, Hall [9] says:

I regard play as the motor habits and spirit of the past of the race, persisting in the present, as rudimentary functions sometimes of and always akin to rudimentary organs. The best index and guide to the stated activities of adults in past ages is found in the instinctive, untaught, and non-imitative plays of children. . . . Thus we rehearse the activities of our ancestors, back we know not how far, and repeat their life work in summative and adumbrated ways. It is reminiscence, albeit unconsciously, of our line of descent, and each is the key to the other.

Early nomadic and asocial reactions of the child were thus regarded as recapitulations in individual development of the nomadic and asocial epochs of human cultural evolution. This idea, because it found no biological support, was eventually rejected by the majority of psychologists, but only after it had stimulated a large number of fruitful researches on child development. It also helped to bring about a closer affiliation between psychology and anthropology.

Much of the research initiated in connection with the idea of cultural recapitulation was of a questionnaire variety. Questionnaires were used to ascertain the fundamental interests and activities of children. Such studies set the pattern for much of the later work on child development. Most of these researches are reported in the *Pedagogical Seminary*, a journal founded by Hall in 1891 as an avenue for the publication of genetic investigations.[10] Hall stimulated the development of a genetic psychology in other ways. His two-volume work on *Adolescence* pointed out the importance of this stage of development for the integration of personality. In his old age, Hall paid particular attention to the psychology of senescence; his *Senescence* was published in 1923, one year before his death at the age of eighty.

Since the days of G. Stanley Hall there has been a rapid expansion in all aspects of ontogenetic psychology. Investigations of child development have been facilitated by the establishment of many clinics and institutes of child welfare, both in this country and abroad. Much of the research on child development was at first normative. That is to say, its primary aim was to discover what psychological accomplishments are to be expected, or are to be considered normal, at different age levels throughout childhood. The norms especially sought after were for sensorimotor development, intelligence, and language. Now that vast amounts of normative information have accumulated and are being used in various practical ways, the emphasis is shifting to studies of causal and functional factors in psychological development, and especially to those involved in the development of character, personality, and mental health. With this shift of emphasis, more attention than ever before is being given to such factors as parent-child and other interpersonal relations. There has also, since Hall's time, been a great expansion of interest in and research on adolescent psychology. The aim has always been to understand this period of growth so that the adjustment of adolescents may be rendered less difficult. Interest in later maturity, old age, and se-

nescence, the third aspect of Hall's ontogenetic psychology, was not widespread until recent years. Now this aspect is undergoing a rapid expansion, chiefly because the age of the population is increasing so much as to raise many problems of adjustment, for both old people and those who are responsible for their welfare. When G. Stanley Hall wrote his *Senescence*, the average life expectancy in the United States was a little less than 60 years; now it is almost 70.

The Problem of Consciousness

Any historical introduction to the field of genetic psychology would be incomplete without some mention of an issue which confronted early genetic psychologists, but which many present-day investigators tacitly ignore. The issue is that of consciousness. It concerns the existence in animals and children of such states or processes as *sensations, images, ideas*, and *feelings*. Not satisfied with investigating the development of *behavior*, some psychologists asked such questions as: "When does consciousness first appear in the animal series?" "What is the nature of this initial consciousness?" "Does consciousness aid the animal in its adjustment to the environment?" "At what stage of its development does the child become conscious?" "What is the nature and function of human consciousness?" "How does consciousness change as the individual grows older?"

Consciousness is beyond direct observation. In animals and young children one does not even have language as a basis for inferring its presence. Titchener, who regarded introspection as the basic method of psychological science, recognized the difficulty of having a genetic psychology of conscious experience. He [11] said:

Only by looking inward can we gain knowledge of mental processes; only by looking inward under standard conditions can we make our knowledge scientific. Even when we are examining a mind as if it were an object in the outside world — when we are trying to understand the mental processes of a child or a dog or an insect as shown by conduct and action, the outward signs of mental processes — we must always fall back upon experimental introspection. For our own mind is our only means of interpreting the mind of another organism; we cannot imagine processes in another mind that we do not find in our own. Experimental introspection is thus our one reliable method of knowing ourselves; it is the sole gateway to psychology.

Any answer to questions on the nature of consciousness in animals and in children who do not speak would have to be based, then, upon inferences derived from reading our own experiences into their reactions as Titchener has suggested. Absence of speech makes the inferences more hazardous than they might otherwise be. Nevertheless, some animal psychologists have inferred the nature of conscious processes in animals. Yerkes, after positing certain structural and functional correlates of consciousness, said that the sea-anemone "probably possesses consciousness of the sensory discriminative grade, but . . . no signs of either intelligent or rational consciousness." [12] Washburn [13] also believed that such inferences might prove of value to a scientific psychology:

We know not where consciousness begins in the animal world. We know where it surely resides — in ourselves; we know where it exists beyond a reasonable doubt — in those animals of structure resembling ourselves which rapidly adapt themselves to the lessons of experience. Beyond this point, for all we know, it may reside in simpler and simpler forms until we reach the lowest of living beings.

Essentially similar inferences have been presented in connection with child psychology. Peterson and Rainey,[14] for example, say that the baby "comes into the world with a small store of experience and associated feelings and a shadowy consciousness."

The difficulty with such inferences is that one has no possible way of checking their accuracy. They remain on the level of sheer speculation. When other sciences make inferences, they devise means of verifying them objectively. When such verification is not forthcoming, the inferences are discarded. The impossibility of checking the validity of inferences concerning consciousness, even in adults who can give a verbal report of their experiences, led many psychologists to confine their investigation to observable behavior.[15] They undertook to investigate behavior (language and non-language) without reference to what it may imply concerning consciousness. The student of behavior does not, of course, deny that consciousness exists. It may exist even in the amoeba. He claims, however, that since it is beyond direct observation, and inferences regarding it cannot be checked, consciousness must remain outside the sphere of scientific psychology. Thus envisaged, the science of psychology is a science of behavior and genetic psychology is the scientific investigation of behavioral development.

The chief aim of genetic psychologists, whether or not they indulge in inferences concerning consciousness, is to discover principles which underlie the development of behavior in the phylogenetic series and in the individual. They believe that determination of these principles will lead to a better understanding of adult human behavior. In this connection, note the statement by Victoria Hazlitt at the beginning of this volume.

The Genetic Method of Investigation

Genetic psychology differs from other branches of the science of behavior more in its viewpoint than in its precise method of investigation. Any person who studies behavior in such a manner as to disclose its developmental aspects may be regarded as a genetic psychologist.

The essential respect in which this field differs from that of animal psychology, for example, is that, rather than observing a given cross-section or level of behavior for its own sake, it seeks to discover the *trend of development* represented by this in relation to other cross-sections. Similarly, the genetic psychologist's interest in the behavior of an individual organism at any given time is in terms of what has preceded and what follows, or is likely to follow, this particular level of development. In investigating the behavior of a monkey, for example, genetic psychologists may turn their attention to either or to both of the following problems. They may study the phylogenetic significance of the animal's behavior, seeking to understand it in terms of the responses of animals lower and higher in the evolutionary scale. On the other hand, they may direct their investigation to the ontogenetic significance of the behavior, asking such questions as, "How is this behavior related to the level of development attained by the monkey's sensory, neural, and motor structures?" and "In what way is the animal's behavior related to its past activities and specific training?"

Ideally, a genetic psychologist would observe the growth of behavior as it takes place. Actually, however, his investigation must usually be confined to levels or cross-sections. The gaps which separate levels are filled in, much as we connect the points on a graph in order to see the trend of the facts represented. The genetic method is, in general, similar to that of the time-lapse photographer who, by photographing an organism at various closely related stages of development and then running the pictures through a projector with appropriate spatial and temporal succession, obtains a representation of continuous growth. The closest approach to observation of continuous growth is to observe the *same* organism at successive age levels. This, the *longitudinal* approach, is given further consideration at various places throughout this book. It necessarily deals with stages, or cross-sections, rather than with the entire process of growth, for it is only rarely that an organism can be continually observed. Another approach, known generally as the *cross-sectional*, involves different groups of individuals rather than the same individual. One may, for example, have a cross-section of five-year-olds, a cross-section of six-year-olds, and so on, with the different age groups comprising different individuals. This approach is often used in the study of child development, as will be seen when we get to that area of genetic psychology. The trend of development for an individual can be ascertained only by use of the longitudinal approach, but general trends may be gauged by use of either approach. In the latter instance, it is necessary to have large representative groups (either of individuals studied longitudinally or of individuals in each cross-section); otherwise individual variations might obscure general trends.

As we proceed with a discussion of the facts of genetic psychology, it will become apparent that there are many gaps in our knowledge, some of which cannot readily be filled. Several stages of behavioral development, both phylogenetic and ontogenetic, have received and are at present receiving inadequate attention from investigators. This inadequacy is particularly evident in the phylogenetic field where comparative psychologists have failed to provide methods adequate to compare the behavior of phyla and species of different degrees of complexity.[16] If animals are to be ranked in terms of their ability to adapt themselves, as we rank human beings in intelligence, the tests of adaptability must be comparable for the phyla and species compared and must at the same time measure all of the significant aspects of the animals' reaction repertoire. The development of such tests is a task which taxes the ingenuity of investigators in this field.

It is quite obvious that the method of genetic psychology, like that of other sciences, must be analytical. One cannot adequately investigate all levels and aspects of behavior simultaneously. Genetic psychologists must turn their attention to one level or to one aspect of behavior at a time. After the analysis is complete and the significant aspects of behavioral development have been disclosed, they may then observe the whole pattern of behavior with better understanding than would have been possible without an analytical approach. Thus we observe the development of sensory processes, neglecting for the moment the motor processes which are developing concomitantly. Sometimes we concentrate on a particular level of development, such, in phylogenetic psychology, as the unicellular, mammalian, or primate, and in ontogenetic psychology, as infancy, adolescence, or adulthood. There is no implication, however, that one process develops independently of other processes or that *discrete* stages of development actually exist. As a matter of fact, the degree to which the various psychological processes and levels of development are interdependent is in itself an important problem which genetic psychologists are investigating.

Affiliations of Genetic Psychology

The behavior of living organisms is the most complex phenomenon known to science. In order to comprehend it, one is forced to seek technological assistance and supplementary data from the more fundamental sciences of mathematics, physics, chemistry, and biology. Mathematics, especially in its statistical phase, facilitates the analysis of those problems of genetic psychology which deal with individual differences, the interdependence of different psychological developments, and fundamental biopsychological functions. Physics and chemistry, through biophysics and biochemistry, contribute to our knowledge of organic functions such as nervous activity, glandular activity, cellular differentiation, and the like. The various branches of zoology also contribute important data. Thus the protozoologist informs us concerning the structures and functions of the simplest living organisms; the geneticist offers information about the mechanisms of inheritance and evolution; the naturalist gathers data on the behavior of animals in their normal habitat; and the embryologist investigates the early stages of individual development.

Genetic psychology is closely affiliated, also, with social sciences such as anthropology and sociology. Knowledge of the earliest human beings and of their transition from savagery to civilized activity comes from the anthropologist. Such information is important not only for an understanding of the change from beastlike to human behavior, but also for an appreciation of the cultural milieu in which personality develops. From sociology are obtained data concerning the nature of the individual's social contacts and the significance of these for the development of such aspects of personality as social habits and attitudes.

Genetic psychology is closely associated with other branches of psychology. The study of behavioral evolution, as suggested earlier, obtains valuable supplementation from animal and comparative psychology. Investigations of individual development are likewise aided by child, abnormal, and social psychology.

Besides contributing to the methodology of phylogenetic psychology, animal psychology offers fundamental information relating to such functions of the organism as discrimination, motivation, and learning. It is from comparative psychology, however, that the phylogenetic psychologist obtains the most immediate aid. This is because comparative psychologists study behavior at different levels of evolution.

When they both deal with the development of behavior in children, child psychology and ontogenetic psychology are similar in aim and content. As was pointed out earlier, however, ontogenetic psychology is not necessarily restricted to human behavioral development. It may deal with the development of behavior in a member of any species. Child psychology, furthermore, is not necessarily ontogenetic. Many child psychologists are concerned more with the psychological care and training of children than with the development of behavior as such. In carrying out this aim they may, of course, contribute to the solution of developmental problems. In turn, solution of their practical problems of guidance is frequently facilitated by application of the findings of genetic psychology.

The solution of problems of personality development is aided by investigations of abnormal and social behavior. Indeed, abnormal and social psychology are often approached in a genetic manner. The abnormal psychologist, in addition to describing the chief behavioral anomalies, may attempt to discover their origin and mode of development. We then have a genetic abnormal psychology. Social psychologists also frequently use genetic methodology in tracing development of the individual's social functions. Even when they do not use genetic methods, social psychologists obtain much data of supplementary interest to us. The nature of social control and social interaction in general, since it bears upon the socialization of individuals, touches the ontogenetic sphere.

Genetic psychology is thus an eclectic field of investigation, gathering data which will help in the solution of its problems wherever such are available. It serves as a point of focus, so to speak, for the genetically significant findings of all other fields of study. These fields are in themselves genetic when their problems are approached developmentally.

Problems of Genetic Psychology

Many phylogenetic and ontogenetic problems are intimately related to findings of the science of heredity. It was therefore deemed advisable to begin this presentation with a brief summary of pertinent genetic discoveries. These bear upon such problems of genetic psychology as the following: the origin, development, and mode of transmission of unlearned forms of behavior, tropistic, reflex, and instinctive; the possibility of inheriting acquired behavior; the influence of heredity upon individual development; and the role of inheritance in the determination of individual differences in psychological development. Correlative with the inheritance factor in development is that of environment.

Hence a discussion of the nature and significance of environmental conditions is presented in connection with our consideration of inheritance. Special attention is given to the relation between inherent and environmental factors in racial and individual development. Since it plays so important a role in the development of personality, the cultural environment is also considered.

The phylogenesis of unlearned behavior raises many interesting problems. Some of these concern the nature, origin, mode of transmission, and adjustmental significance of unlearned reactions. One may ask to what degree man's adjustment is dependent on unlearned responses like instincts. This question raises many phylogenetic and ontogenetic problems which the genetic psychologist attempts to solve. The evolution of intelligent behavior raises such problems as the following: What is the nature of intelligence? Upon what structures does it depend? How has it changed as organisms have developed from the simplest to the most complex? What is its significance for adjustment?

Psychological development in the individual raises several questions of considerable importance to psychology in general. Some of these refer to the role of maturation and exercise, or specific training, in the development of behavior; the saltatory (abrupt) versus the gradual nature of behavioral development; and the mode of origin of behavior patterns. The last-mentioned problem, brought to the front by the German school of Gestalt psychology, concerns the question as to whether behavior patterns exist from the first or whether they are derived from integration of originally discrete units such as reflexes. Our discussion of fetal development deals with these problems in some detail. Another chapter, concerned with such basic developmental functions as maturation, conditioning, and learning, also bears upon some of these problems. Succeeding chapters trace development in the human individual of sensory processes; spatially coordinated behavior;

motor processes; symbolic processes, including memory, imaginative activities, concepts, reasoning, language, and intelligence as measured by standard tests; emotional behavior; and social behavior and personality. The final chapter discusses changes in social behavior and personality during adolescence, adulthood, and senescence.

When the end of this book is reached, we shall have traced the development of fundamental psychological processes in animals ranging from the unicellular organisms to man and, in the human individual, from conception until senescence. Our survey will have covered the chief problems, facts, and principles of genetic psychology, as these are now known.

Summary and Conclusions

Genetic psychology has emerged in close association with developments within the field of biology. The doctrine of evolution pointed to a psychological relation between man and other animals, thus stimulating the development of a body of knowledge and a sphere of investigation known as phylogenetic psychology. The phylogenetic problem is, in general, that of investigating psychological development in animals ranging from the simplest to the most complex forms. Ontogenetic psychology, which studies the development of psychological processes in individual members of a species, received its chief impetus from the early biographical observations of behavioral development in infancy and from the biological theory of recapitulation. The aim of both fields of genetic psychology is to discover the principles which underlie psychological development. Genetic psychologists believe that a knowledge of the evolution of psychological processes in animals and of the development of these processes in individuals will facilitate our understanding of adult human behavior.

We have seen that the genetic method is one which discloses trends or lines of development. It does this by investigating cross-sections or levels of development at sufficiently close temporal intervals.

Genetic psychology is eclectic, borrowing supplementary technological and factual material from the mathematical, physical, biological, and social sciences. It is also closely affiliated with other branches of psychology. Phylogenetic investigation is related to animal and comparative psychology, while ontogenetic investigation is closely associated with the fields of child, abnormal, and social psychology.

Phylogenetic psychologists study the evolution of unlearned and intelligent behavior in animals ranging from the unicellular organisms to man. Ontogenetic psychologists, on the other hand, investigate the nature and bases of behavioral development from conception until birth; the subsequent development of sensory, motor, symbolic, and emotional processes; and the nature and development of social behavior and personality.

REFERENCES

1. Romanes, G. J., *Animal Intelligence.* New York: Appleton-Century-Crofts, 1883. Quotation is from the 8th ed., pp. 496–497.
2. Morgan, C. L., *Introduction to Comparative Psychology* (2d ed.). London: Scott, 1909, p. 53.
3. Beach, F. A. "The Snark Was a Boojum," *Amer. Psychologist*, 1950, *5*, 115–124.
4. *The Mind of the Child*, 2 vols. (trans. H. W. Brown). New York: Appleton, 1888–1889.
5. *Specielle Physiologie des Embryo: Unter-suchungen über die Lebenserscheinungen vor der Geburt.* Leipzig, Grieben, 1885.
6. See especially H. Klaatsch, *The Evolution and Progress of Mankind*, Stokes, 1923, pp. 38 ff., or D. D. Whitney, *Family Treasures*, Cattell, 1942, p. 274.
7. Buckman, S. S., "Babies and Monkeys," *Pop. Sci. Mo.*, 1895, *46*, 371–388.
8. Hřdlicka, A., *Children Who Run On All Fours.* New York: McGraw-Hill, 1931, p. 93.

9. Hall, G. S., *Adolescence: Its Psychology and Its Relations to Physiology, Anthropology, Sociology, Sex, Crime, Religion, and Education.* New York: Appleton-Century-Crofts, 1904, vol. I, p. 202.
10. This journal is now published at Provincetown, Massachusetts, by the Journal Press. Its present title, under the editorship of Carl Murchison, is the *Journal of Genetic Psychology.* It has been expanded in scope and is supplemented by the *Genetic Psychology Monographs.*
11. Titchener, E. B., *A Primer of Psychology*, 1903, p. 32. By permission of The Macmillan Company, publishers.
12. Yerkes, R. M., "Animal Psychology and the Criteria of the Psychic," *J. Phil.*, 1905, *2*, 141–149, p. 145.

13. Washburn, M. F., *The Animal Mind* (3d ed.), 1926, p. 33. By permission of The Macmillan Company, publishers.
14. Peterson, F., and L. H. Rainey, "The Beginning of Mind in the Newborn," *Bull. Lying-in Hospital* [New York], 1910, *7*, 121.
15. See especially J. B. Watson, *Behavior: An Introduction to Comparative Psychology.* New York: Holt, 1914, Chapter 1.
16. See the discussion by A. F. McBride and D. O. Hebb, "Behavior of the Captive Bottle-Nose Dolphin," *J. Comp. & Physiol. Psychol.*, 1948, *41*, 111–123. This paper deals with some of the problems involved in deciding whether a particular animal form, in this case the dolphin, is more or less intelligent than other animals.

HISTORICALLY IMPORTANT PUBLICATIONS ON GENETIC PSYCHOLOGY

Darwin, C., *The Origin of Species.* London: Murray, 1859.

Darwin, C., *The Descent of Man.* London: Murray, 1871.

Darwin, C., *Expression of Emotion in Man and Animals.* New York: Appleton, 1873.

Darwin, C., "A Biographical Sketch of an Infant," *Mind*, 1877, *2*, 285–294.

Hall, G. S., "The Contents of Children's Minds on Entering School," *Ped. Sem.*, 1891, *1*, 139–173.

Hall, G. S., *Adolescence*, 2 vols. New York: Appleton, 1904.

Hall, G. S., *Senescence.* New York: Appleton, 1923.

Hobhouse, L. T., *Mind in Evolution.* New York: Macmillan, 1901; (2d ed. 1915; 3d ed. 1926).

Kirkpatrick, E. A., *Genetic Psychology.* New York: Macmillan, 1909.

Kline, L. W., "Methods in Animal Psychology." *Amer. J. Psychol.*, 1899, *10*, 256–279.

Lubbock, J., *On the Senses, Instincts, and Intelligence of Animals, with Special Reference to Insects.* New York: Appleton, 1883.

Lubbock, J., *Ants, Bees, and Wasps.* New York: Appleton, 1888.

Morgan, C. L., *Introduction to Comparative Psychology.* London: Scott, 1894.

Morgan, C. L., *Habit and Instinct.* London: Arnold, 1896.

Preyer, W., *Die Seele des Kindes.* Leipzig: Fernan, 1882. (*The Mind of the Child*, 2 vols. New York: Appleton, 1888–1899.)

Romanes, G. J., *Animal Intelligence.* New York: Appleton, 1883.

Shinn, N. W., *The Biography of a Baby.* Boston: Houghton Mifflin, 1900.

Small, W. S., "Notes on the Psychic Development of the Young White Rat," *Amer. J. Psychol.*, 1899, *11*, 80–100.

Small, W. S., "An Experimental Study of the Mental Processes of the Rat." *Amer. J. Psychol.*, 1900, *11*, 135–165.

Spencer, H., *Principles of Psychology*, 2 vols. New York: Appleton, 1855.

Taine, H., "Note sur l'Acquisition du Langage chez les Enfants et dans l'Espèce Humaine," *Rev. Phil.*, 1876, *1*, 3–23. (Translated in *Mind*, 1877, *2*, 252–257.)

Thorndike, E. L., "Animal Intelligence," *Psych. Rev. Monog. Suppl.*, 1898, *2*, No. 8.

Tiedemann, D., "Beobachtungen über die Entwicklung der Seelenfähigkeiten bei Kindern," 1789. (See translation by C. Murchison and S. Langer in *Ped. Sem.*, 1927, *34*, 205–230.)

2

Foundations of Development

GENETIC psychology is not genetics. Nevertheless the developmental psychologist is interested in many aspects of life which for their full explanation require a knowledge of what geneticists have learned about the origin and growth of organisms. This is because psychological evolution, and also psychological development in individuals, involves the emergence of structures under the joint influence of hereditary factors and internal and external environmental conditions.

Sensitivity evolves with the evolution of structures responsive to stimulating aspects of the environment. As visual, auditory, and other specialized receptors arise, the organism is better attuned to its surroundings, hence can be influenced by environmental details and can more readily adjust its behavior to changing circumstances. Motor dexterity, or facility in moving around in and changing the environment, is also basically structural. It depends upon cues provided by the receptors, but its expression demands flexible motor organs like joints, tendons, and muscles. Most organisms are equipped from the start with certain behavior patterns which depend upon inherently connected structures. Reflexes and complex inborn patterns of behavior like those sometimes called "instincts" have such a basis. These unlearned modes of adjustment depend upon inborn nervous connections which route impulses over pre-established channels from receptors to effectors; that is, to muscles and glands. Their evolution, to be discussed in the next chapter, requires an understanding of certain aspects of genetics.

The evolution of ability to profit from past experience, to learn new modes of adjustment, to remember, to think, and to reason, is also at base structural. It depends upon receptors (for information), effectors (for execution), but above all upon central nervous structures, especially those of the brain (for retention, elaboration, and direction). Thus psychological evolution is at every stage concomitant with, and indeed dependent upon, structural evolution. Patterns of response and capacities which appear for the first time in the evolution of animals are all functions of emerging structures and structural integrations. An understanding of how any structure originates and undergoes evolutionary change requires some knowledge of hereditary factors (genes) as well as of how these change (as in mutations). We also need some appreciation of how the genes influence internal and external environmental conditions, and in turn are limited in action and effects by them. Without a knowledge of such things we could not begin to understand the production of new structures, new species, and

13

phylogenetically novel reactions and capacities.

The foundations of psychological development in individuals are also structural, and thus likewise dependent upon hereditary factors and environmental influences. An individual gets structures characteristic of his species. He also gets the characteristic reflexes or instincts and the characteristic capacities for further development. His growth from birth to maturity, and even his decline in later years, is to a considerable extent determined by heredity. A rat grows to maturity in a few months. At three years, if it still survives, it is old and decrepit. Its level of psychological achievement, even under the most stimulating conditions, is insignificant compared with that of a child of the same chronological age. These differences between a child and a rat are almost completely due to a difference in their genes. Even within a species there are great individual differences in the rate and upper limits of development. This is true at all levels of evolution, although the range of differences seems to grow larger as the higher levels are reached. No animal shows so great a range of individual differences as does the human being. In these things, too, heredity plays a very important role. We shall observe, however, that environment plays an increasingly important part in the production of individual differences as organisms become better endowed to sense environmental changes and to react to them. In a sense, racial inheritance to a large extent determines how significant the environment, and especially the social aspects of it, will be in producing individual differences. The rat is oblivious to the aspects of the environment which, at the human level, do so much to shape individual differences and similarities in attitudes, personality, and character.

In human beings, tradition, cultural transmission, or what is often called "social inheritance" has from earliest times done much to change what we have inherited from previous generations of human and animal ancestry. The development of thought processes and of language as a means of communication made man in many respects the arbiter of his own further evolution and gave him the power, within biologically restricted limits, to mold individuals to suit his own purposes. We recognize this fact when we see how different genetically similar people can be when they are reared in widely different cultures and subjected to this or that political pressure. For these reasons our discussion of developmental foundations must not stop with hereditary mechanisms, or indeed with the internal and external environments in which these most directly operate, but must go on to take cognizance of how, at the human level, development is further influenced by cultural factors.

The Origin and Characteristics of Living Organisms

The manner in which living organisms originated is not known. Certain scientists assert that protoplasm, the substance of which all living cells are composed, resulted from a fortuitous combination of inorganic elements during some remote period when the earth was much warmer than it is at present. They point out, in partial support of this belief, that analysis of living organisms discloses the existence within their cells of such elements as carbon, hydrogen, oxygen, nitrogen, sulphur, phosphorus, chlorine, sodium, potassium, calcium, magnesium, and iron. These elements are so complexly arranged in protoplasm, however, that their synthesis in the biochemist's test-tube has not been accomplished. Other scientists, looking upon the origin of life as an inexplicable riddle, prefer to ignore the issue. No matter what their attitude concerning the origin of life may be, however, biologists believe that all existing organisms have genetic affiliations with those original organisms which were able to survive and reproduce. Explanation of the multiplication and differentiation of these primitive organisms to form present-day types with their characteristic patterns of behavior resides in hereditary processes and their relation to environmental conditions.

Existing animals range from those comprising a single cell to those which possess billions of cells. Regardless of its ultimate complexity, however, each organism typically begins life as a single cell. After they have reached a certain size, unicellular organisms, like *Amoeba*, divide to form two or more separate individuals. Under normal conditions, they do not attain the multicellular state. In multicellular organisms the original cell, or ovum, splits into two cells which usually cohere instead of separating. These divide again to form a four-celled organism. Multiplication continues in this way until a creature having billions of cells may be formed.

In many organisms the process of cell division and multiplication is begun without introduction of a sexual factor. Reproduction of this nature is designated as asexual. In other organisms, and especially those of the higher phyla, the process of multiplication is begun soon after the ovum is fertilized. Sexual reproduction is present in all the higher phyla. Our discussion of hereditary mechanisms deals only with this type of reproduction.

Characteristics of cells

Regardless of the animal in which they are found and their location within its body, all typical cells possess certain characteristics. A schematic cell is shown in Figure 4. It will be observed that the cell contains a nucleus,

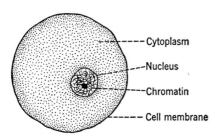

Figure 4. Schematic Diagram of a Typical Cell

cytoplasm, and a cell membrane. Within the nucleus is a substance known, because of its susceptibility to staining, as chromatin. During cell division the chromatin separates into structures known as chromosomes. These, as we shall observe in more detail later, are arranged in pairs. They are observed as dark bodies of various shapes and sizes which differ in number and characteristics from one species to another, but which are alike in members of the same species. Chromosomes carry the determiners of hereditary traits.

The cytoplasm is a relatively clear substance separated from the nucleus by the nuclear membrane. As we shall observe in subsequent discussions, the cytoplasm and the chromosomes cooperate, as it were, to produce the many different kinds of cells which compose the total organism. Each cell is separated from others by means of the cell membrane.

The initial cells from which an individual develops are approximately spherical in shape. Others derived from these undergo differentiation which makes them diverge markedly from this shape. Some are polygonal, others ovoid, others elongated into thin threads, and so on.

Duplication of chromosomes in production of body cells

Within a species, all cells except those involved in reproduction normally possess the same complement of chromosomes. This is due to the fact that, during division of the original and subsequent cells, there is a mechanism which leads to doubling of the number of chromosomes (making temporarily four of each kind) and the passing of a complete set (two of each kind) to the daughter cells. This mechanism is known as *mitosis*. The chief processes involved are illustrated in Figure 5.

Certain details of interest to the geneticist need not concern us here. Note, however, that the chromatin separates into threadlike structures known as *chromonemata* (*A*). These split lengthwise (*B*), then thicken and

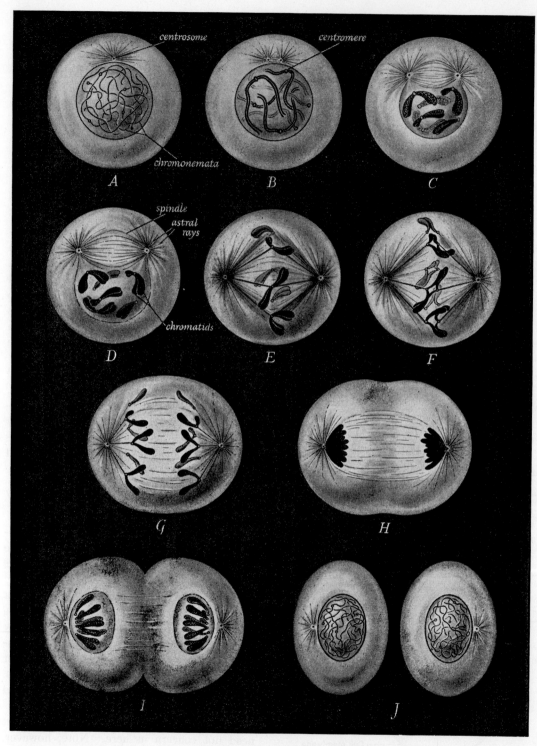

Figure 5. Diagrams Illustrating Mitosis

The technical terminology of genetics which is used to designate these stages has been omitted here.   If the reader wishes to do so, he may get this from the original illustration in A. M. Winchester, *Genetics*, Boston: Houghton Mifflin, 1951, p. 36.

form pairs of half-chromosomes called *chromatids* (*C–E*). At a later stage, two identical chromosomes are derived from each chromatid. Observe that each of these half-chromosomes has a *centromere* which seems to hold them together. In each of them, moreover, the centromere has a different position. Thus different chromosomes may be identified. Eventually (*F*) the centromere also divides, and attached spindles direct each resultant centromere, and its chromosome, to opposite poles of the cell. Now, for every original chromosome, we have two. As the members of each new pair go to opposite poles (*G–H*), the cell itself begins to divide and, finally, there are two cells (*I–J*). In this illustration, for purposes of simplicity, only six chromosomes (three pairs) are represented.

The process of mitosis is repeated again and again until the requisite number of cells has been formed. It is through this process that the fertilized ovum reproduces itself. The fertilized human ovum has 48 chromosomes (24 pairs) and these are duplicated in every subsequent body cell. Mature reproductive cells, on the other hand, have only 24 single chromosomes. How this happens will now be considered.

Halving of chromosomes in production of germ cells

When an individual approaches puberty there is a marked change in the nature of the cells which are to function in reproduction. These cells, originally like those of the body, are set aside in the testes of the male and in the ovaries of the female during an early stage of development. There they lie dormant until around the time of puberty. They then begin to multiply and undergo germ cell maturation, the process known as *meiosis*. This is illustrated in Figure 6, which represents the origin of sperms and ova.

The onset of meiosis is marked by a pairing off of homologous chromosomes. That is to say, each chromosome of a given kind takes its place at the side of its partner. Each chromosome then splits lengthwise to form

identical chromonemata, as in Figure 6, *A*. These structures are held together by their centromere. The chromonemata then line up (*B*) and separate as two cells form (*C*). Note that the identical chromonemata are still attached, since their centromere has not divided. The homologous chromosomes, however, have been separated. In the next stage (*D*), the chromonemata line up and, as their centromeres now separate, two chromosomes are produced. They migrate to opposite poles of the cell. Each cell then divides (*E*) to form a total of four spermatids. These modify to form the sperms (*F*). Thus, in spermatogenesis, each parent cell gives rise to four sperms. In maturation of ova (at right) the general process is like that described for spermatogenesis. Note, however, that three of the four cells fail to develop fully. These are called polar bodies. Only the fully developed cell may be fertilized. The small cells at the edge of the ovum in Figure 8 are polar bodies.

The process of meiosis guarantees that each individual will have the proper number of chromosomes. Each human ovum or sperm has only 24 chromosomes. At fertilization the full complement of 48 is restored. It will be seen that a particular sperm gets only one-half of the father's chromosomes and an ovum only one-half of the mother's.

Whether a chromosome which the father contributes to the ovum from which a new individual will form came to him from his father or mother (the new individual's paternal grandfather or grandmother) is determined in so complex a way that it can at present only be referred to as resulting from chance. Moreover, which particular sperm fertilizes a given ovum is also determined by chance. The laws of inheritance are laws based upon the "chance" assortment of chromosomes within the sperm and ova and the "chance" association of sperms and ova at fertilization.

Although 48 chromosomes are involved in human inheritance, we can illustrate the random assortment of chromosomes in meiosis

SPERMATOGENESIS — (IN ANIMALS) — OOGENESIS

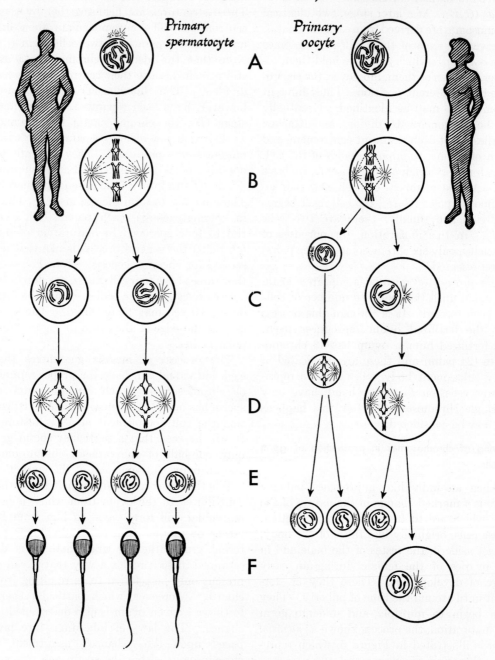

Figure 6. Spermatogenesis

This diagram illustrates the process of meiosis as described in the text. It shows how, in an organism assumed to have six chromosomes (three pairs), the sperms and ova would come to have only three (one member of each original pair). (From A. M. Winchester, *Genetics*, Boston: Houghton Mifflin, 1951, p. 49.)

and fertilization by reference to Figure 7, which assumes the involvement of only six chromosomes, or three pairs.

The fertilized cell

Organisms which reproduce sexually begin their existence as illustrated in Figure 8. The diagram represents an ovum which has just been impregnated by a sperm cell, or spermatozoon. The three polar bodies are shown on its outer edge. One will note that nothing but the head, or nucleus, of the spermatozoon enters the ovum. The tail, which serves merely to propel the nucleus until it penetrates the membrane of the ovum, remains outside and disappears. After entering the ovum, the sperm nucleus absorbs moisture from the cytoplasm. Then it approaches and finally merges with the nucleus of the ovum. The resulting nucleus contains the double

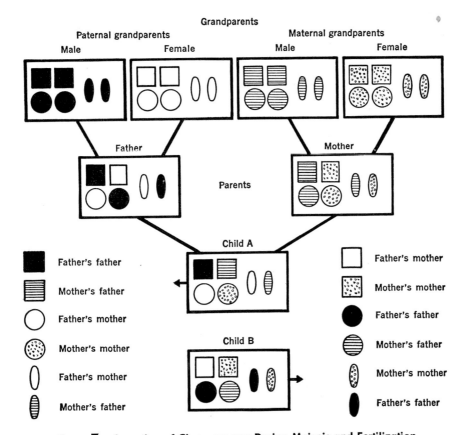

Figure 7. Assorting of Chromosomes During Meiosis and Fertilization

Only six instead of the 48 human chromosomes are shown. The chromosomes passed on by the parents of the children represented here are derived from the grandparental pool, the father having one-half of his parents' chromosomes and the mother one-half of those of her parents. The parents of children A and B likewise contribute one-half of their chromosomes. Which of their chromosomes will go to make up this half is determined at meiosis and at fertilization. Meiosis halves the chromosomes, in the "chance" manner mentioned in the text, determining, so to speak, which particular chromosomes will be in a particular sperm or ovum. Different sperms and ova will have different combinations from the parental pool. But which of the many sperms and ova will unite to form the new individual is again a matter of "chance." Thus the combinations shown for these children result from both factors. (From N. L. Munn, *Psychology*, 2d ed, Boston: Houghton Mifflin, 1951, p. 95.)

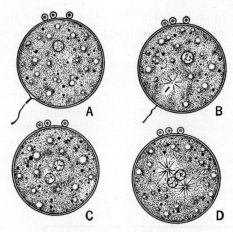

Figure 8. Fertilization

(Reproduced from T. H. Morgan, *Embryology and Genetics*, 1934, p. 28, by permission of Columbia University Press.)

(complete) set of chromosomes. Thus, in the case of human sperm and ova, each contains 24 chromosomes. When fertilization has been consummated, 48 chromosomes are present. The mere fact that chromosomes are the only parts of a cell halved in number during production of germ cells and restored to the full number at fertilization strongly suggests that they determine inherited traits.

The sperm and ova are usually referred to as *gametes* while the fertilized ovum is designated as a *zygote*. The zygote soon undergoes mitotic division, forming two cells. These divide to form four cells, the four cells to form eight, and so on. As far as the chromosomes are concerned, all cells derived from the zygote, except the mature reproductive cells which develop at puberty, are identically constituted. On the other hand, the cytoplasmic constitution of cells beyond the first few may vary considerably. At first there is sheer multiplication, but later the cells begin to differentiate as well as multiply. In this way the various structures of the body are formed. The process of cellular differentiation is to be discussed later. It may be said at this point, however, that differentiation is determined by the chromosomes and the various environmental influences to which

the growing cells are subjected. These influences, while they ordinarily do not change the constitution of the chromosomes, place definite limitations upon their determining properties. As we shall observe later, the chromosomes are themselves internally differentiated. Each chromosome contains factors (genes) or groups of factors associated with the determination of each hereditary trait.

Before discussing hereditary transmission, it may be advisable to consider the constituents of the fertilized ovum, or zygote, in closer detail. We have pointed out that each zygote contains 24 pairs of chromosomes. All these chromosomes contribute to the various traits of an organism. However, there are pairs which contain alternative factors for brown or blue eyes, for curly or straight hair, and so on. Frequently these factors are alike in each member of a pair of chromosomes; that is, they are both concerned with the determination of blue eyes, both concerned with the determination of brown eyes, and so on. In these instances the organism is said to be *homozygous* for eye-color. The zygote from which it developed, and all subsequent body cells, have homogeneous determiners for eye-color. On the other hand, the factor in one chromosome may be so constituted as to produce brown eyes; that in the other, blue eyes. When such a situation is present, the organism is said to be *heterozygous* for eye-color. The zygote from which it develops has heterogeneous determiners for eye-color.

Thus the individual's inherited traits will depend upon the constitution of the chromosomes present in the fertilized ovum. If the factors for determination of a given trait are alike, the resultant trait is clearly indicated. For example, two factors for blue eyes produce blue eyes; two for brown eyes, brown eyes. If the individual is heterozygous for a given trait, however, *dominance* and *recessiveness* need to be considered before one can predict the resultant character. The factor for brown eyes is dominant, that for blue eyes recessive. If these diverse factors occur in a zygote, the individual will have brown eyes. The factor for blue will, as far as the individual's somatic characters are concerned, be non-effective, although it may be transmitted to offspring. Where dominance is not present, something approximating an intermediate trait may appear. In Andalusian fowls, for example, the factors which determine color of plumage are neither dominant nor recessive. Hence, when a factor for white plumage is paired with one for black plumage, the individual has slate-blue plumage, representing what appears to be a compromise between the diverse traits. As we shall observe later, many factors are involved in the determination of some inherited traits.

Hereditary Transmission

Many, and perhaps all, biologically inherited traits are transmitted in accordance with principles discovered by Mendel. Mendel did not know about chromosomes. Later, when these structures were discovered, they were found to be assorted in accordance with the principles discovered by Mendel for assortment of observable bodily traits. We have already considered facts relating to assortment of chromosomes. These are: (1) One member of each pair of chromosomes comes from the individual's father, while the other member comes from the individual's mother. (2) Whether given chromosomes contributed by the father shall come from *his* father or mother is determined by "chance." Likewise, a given chromosome contributed by the mother may come from either her father or mother. (3) This chance assortment of chromosomes occurs during the processes of meiosis and fertilization. (4) If given factors in two homologous chromosomes are identical, the trait which appears will be that represented by each. (5) If given factors in two homologous chromosomes are dissimilar in determining properties, the trait which appears will depend upon the presence or absence of dominance. Should one of these factors be dominant, the trait for which it is

the fundamental determiner will appear. Should neither factor be dominant, an intermediate or seemingly blended trait will appear. In the following discussion a number of typical examples will be presented in order that the student may gain a working knowledge of the ways in which these principles apply.

Inheritance involving a pair of factors without dominance

Let us take, as our first example, a case lacking dominance. When a homozygous white and a homozygous black Andalusian fowl are crossed, all of the offspring will be slate blue. Letting *bb* represent the paired factors for black and *ww* the paired factors for white present in the respective parents, it will readily be seen that each offspring must possess the factor combination *bw*. This is the only possible combination of factors. The germ cell of one parent must contain the factor *b* while that of the other must contain the factor *w*. Fertilization brings the diverse factors together in the combination *bw*. Since neither factor is dominant, the color of the hybrid, or first filial (F_1) generation, will be slate blue. If hybrids (*bw*) are crossed, the possible combinations of factors are *bb*, *bw*, *wb*, and *ww*, as illustrated in Figure 9. It will be observed that plumage color of progeny resulting from this cross occurs in the proportion one black to two slate blue to one white. This does not mean that out of four animals resulting from such a cross, there will necessarily be one black, two slate blue, and one white. It means that when large numbers are involved, the 1 : 2 : 1 ratio will hold.

If the black members of the F_2 generation are mated, all offspring of this cross will be black, since only one combination of factors can result. Each parent, being homozygous for black, has the factor combination *bb*. Hence the only combination possible in the fertilized ovum is *bb*. Likewise, crossing white individuals will produce white offspring having the factor combination *ww*. When the slate blue animals are crossed, however, the

SLATE BLUE
Male
Sperm Cells

		b	w
SLATE BLUE Female Ova	w	bw Slate blue	ww White
	b	bb Black	wb Slate blue

Figure 9. **Possible Combinations of the Factors b and w in a Cross Between Hybrids**

The father produces two differently constituted types of sperm cell, or gamete, one containing the b factor and the other the w factor. Likewise, the mother produces ova, or gametes, with either the b or the w factor. In the upper left-hand section of the figure, it is assumed that the sperm containing the b factor has fertilized an ovum containing the w factor. In the upper right-hand section, a sperm containing the w factor is represented as having fertilized an ovum containing the w factor. In the lower left-hand section a sperm containing the b factor is assumed to have fertilized an ovum containing a b factor. The remaining section gives the other possible combination, a sperm containing the factor w having fertilized an ovum containing the factor b. Since neither factor is dominant, the heterozygous individuals will be slate blue. The ratio is one black: two slate blue: one white.

ratio of one black to two slate blue to one white will again be produced. Figure 10 helps in visualizing what we have said concerning inheritance of traits dependent upon a pair of factors when dominance is absent.

Inheritance involving a pair of factors with dominance

Let us now take an illustration involving dominance of a trait which depends upon a pair of factors. Guinea pigs may have either rough or smooth coats. When a rough is crossed with a smooth, and both parents are homozygous for the traits in question, the hybrids will all have rough coats. When the hybrids are crossed, however, rough and smooth coats appear in the ratio of three to one. This is because the factor for rough coat is dominant, that for smooth coat recessive. Whenever a factor for roughness appears in a zygote, the coat will be rough. The only possibility of obtaining a smooth coat is to get the factor combination in which both factors are for smoothness. If we represent the factor for roughness by a capital R (capitals are customarily used for dominant

characters) and the factor for smoothness by the letter r (lower-case letters are customarily used for recessive characters), then the homozygous rough has the factors RR and the homozygous smooth the factors rr. It is obvious that a cross between an RR and an rr animal can produce only one factor combination, namely Rr. Since rough is dominant, all having this combination of factors will be rough-coated. When two Rr guinea pigs are crossed, however, the possible combinations are RR, Rr, rR, and rr. (The principles of combination are the same as those illustrated in Figure 9.) There will be three rough-coated animals to one smooth-coated. Crosses between homozygous roughs will produce roughs only. Likewise, crosses between homozygous smooths will produce offspring all of whom are smooth. Crosses between heterozygous (hybrid) animals will again produce the ratio of three roughs to one smooth.

Dihybrid and trihybrid crosses

Our illustrations, so far, have concerned crosses in which a given trait dependent upon

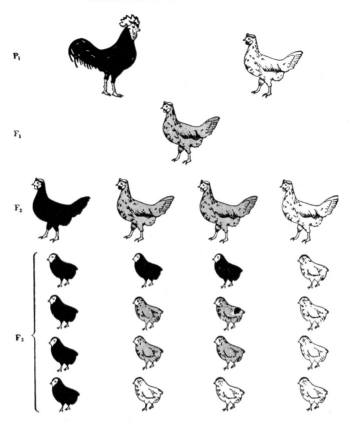

Figure 10. Summary of the Results Obtained in Crossing Black and White Andalusian Fowls

(After E. W. Sinnott, C. L. Dunn, and Th. Dobzhansky, *Principles of Genetics*, 4th ed., New York: McGraw-Hill, 1950, p. 37.)

a single pair of factors has been followed. Such crosses are known as *monohybrid*. We shall now turn our attention to a *dihybrid* cross, one involving two traits and two pairs of factors. The following illustration will suit our purposes admirably. A gray mouse which runs in normal fashion is mated with a white mouse which progresses by whirling or making waltzing movements. Both mice are homozygous for the traits in question. Grayness and running, furthermore, are dominant characters. Thus the genetic constitution of the homozygous gray runner with respect to color and type of progression is *GGRR*. The white whirler, on the other hand, has the combination *ggrr*.

The hybrids will be gray runners, since all must receive *GgRr* (see Fig. 11), and *G* and *R* are dominant. A cross between hybrids will produce gray runners, gray waltzers, white runners, and white waltzers in the ratio, respectively of 9:3:3:1. How these results are derived is apparent in Figure 11, which the reader should examine thoughtfully. It is interesting from the standpoint of psychology to note that this special form of behavior (that is, the structures on which it depends) can be shown to be inherited in precisely the same manner as hair color.

Two-factor ratios are modified by the presence or absence of dominance. When polled red and horn white cattle are mated, all the offspring are polled roan. The F_2 generation, however, has six types of individual in the ratio 3:6:3:1:2:1. The 9:3:3:1 ratio fails to appear because the factor for red is not dominant. When neither of the two factors is dominant, a 1:2:2:4:1:2:1:2:1 ratio results. Such a ratio is obtained when red-flowered, broad-leaved snapdragons are crossed with white-flowered, narrow-leaved snapdragons. By following the procedure shown in Figure 11, one can see why these modified ratios result from dihybrid crosses when only one trait is dominant and when neither is dominant. Other modifications of the two-factor ratio have been discovered, but space forbids our discussing them here.

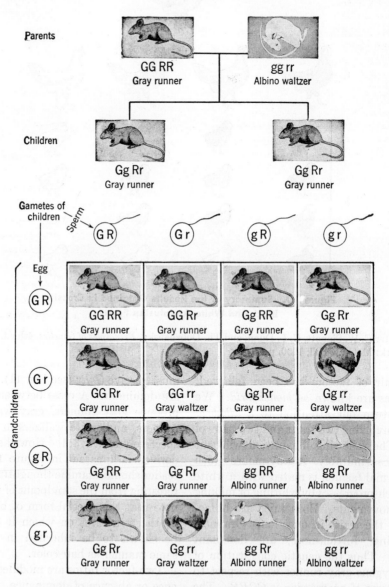

Figure 11. Inheritance of Whirling and Albinism in Mice

(From C. L. Dunn, *Heredity and Variation*, The University Society, New York, 1932, p. 33. Reproduced by permission of The University Society.)

As one follows more than two traits, the ratios become increasingly complicated. The usual ratio from a trihybrid cross, for example, is 27:9:9:9:3:3:3:1. As in the case of dihybrid crosses, there are various modified ratios.

In the examples discussed above, we have considered inheritance of separate traits, each specific trait due to a pair of factors. For example, although two pairs of factors are involved in the color and mode of locomotion evidenced by mice, each pair of factors concerns a different trait. We are now going to consider some single traits (like pigmentation of the skin in human beings) which depend upon more than one pair of factors, the various pairs of factors here combining their effects to produce the given trait.

Inheritance involving multiple factors

Combinations of independent pairs of factors, as we have observed, yield definite classes of individuals. For example: Andalusian fowls are black, slate blue, or white in a 1:2:1 ratio; guinea pigs are smooth or rough in a ratio of 3:1; mice are gray runners, gray waltzers, white runners, or white waltzers in the ratio of 9:3:3:1. In such cases, individuals fail to evidence all intermediate traits. Many inherited traits are, however, distributed in continuous series. Take, for example, skin color produced by Negro-white intermarriage. It is impossible to classify the progeny into definite types on the basis of skin color. From the lightest to the darkest there is a gradation involving indiscriminable increments. Many other observable traits of plants and animals present a similar picture. Snyder[1] points out, as a matter of fact, that the most fundamental and deepseated qualities of a race tend to be distributed in a continuous rather than in a discontinuous manner. They are represented by a *frequency distribution curve* rather than by a simple ratio or a series of classifications. Is one, in order to account for the hereditary transmission of such traits, forced to forsake the principles of factor combination discussed above? The answer is "No." There is every reason for supposing that the same basic principles which account for transmission of other hereditary traits are applicable here. One has to suppose, however, that hereditary differences represented by a frequency curve are produced by multiple factors. Usually these factors appear to have cumulative (or blended) effects, although dominance and recessiveness may in some instances be involved. For illustrative purposes we shall discuss the inheritance of skin color in progeny of Negro-white crosses, and of certain behavior characteristics, namely, maze-learning ability and vigor (general activity level) in white rats. The explanation of these phenomena in terms of multiple factor determination will be given.

The skin color resulting from Negro-white crosses is assumed by Davenport to depend upon two pairs of factors working in a cumulative (rather than in a dominant-recessive) manner. Let S and T represent factors producing pigment, and s and t factors, paired with the above, which produce no pigment but have a "blending" effect when combined with S and T. The combination $SSTT$ would produce the blackest skin and $sstt$ the whitest. Combinations like $SSTt$ and $SsTT$ would produce dark brown skin and combinations like $Sstt$ and $ssTt$ would produce light-brown skin. Medium-brown skin would result from combinations like $SsTt$, and $SStt$. Snyder, from whom the illustration is taken, indicates that carefully collected family histories tend to support this two-factor explanation of the skin color of Negro-white progeny.

An animal like the rat is far superior to human beings for investigations on inheritance. Rats may be obtained in large numbers, they may be mated in accordance with experimental requirements, they have large numbers of progeny in a given litter, they reproduce frequently, and one can control their environment in a manner not possible with human subjects.

Tryon[2] gave each member of an unselected

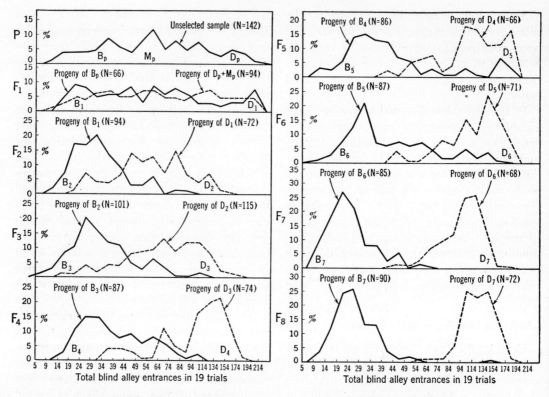

Figure 12. Effects of Selective Breeding on Individual Differences in the Maze-Learning Ability of Rats Reared in a Uniform Environment

Maze-learning ability is inferred from the total number of errors (blind alley entrances) exhibited in the course of 19 trials on the maze. The curves are to be read as follows: P represents the parental generation. In this generation (comprising 142 unselected rats), the fewest number of errors per rat was approximately 7, the largest number over 214. The most frequent error score was approximately 60. This score was made by about 12 per cent of the rats. The height of the curve at any point thus represents the percentage of the rats making a given score. The curves for each filial generation are to be interpreted in a similar way. Note that all curves are continuous. No clear-cut classes of rats can be differentiated. No ratio is apparent. *Bp*, bright parents; *Dp*, dull parents; *Mp*, parents making a median error score (i.e., parents of median brightness). (From R. C. Tryon. Reprinted by permission from *Comparative Psychology*, ed. by F. A. Moss. Copyright, 1942, Prentice-Hall, Inc., New York City.)

group of white rats 19 trials on a maze * All the animals had been reared in a comparable environment and all of them were given comparable treatment during the experiment. Thus individual differences are attributable to hereditary factors. A frequency distribution curve for the group of 142 unselected

rats is shown in Figure 12. One will observe that maze-learning ability is measured in terms of the total errors (blind alley entrances) of an animal, the brightest animal making fewest errors and the dullest most errors. Errors range in number from about 7 to more than 214. Instead of being divided into discrete groups, each making a given number or a given range of errors, the animals distribute themselves continuously from the

---

* Refer to Figure 48 for an illustration of a maze. The maze used by Tryon was of the complex multiple-T variety.

most bright to the most dull. The number of errors which appeared most frequently was approximately 60. To obtain his F_1 generation, Tryon mated bright rats with bright ones and dull rats with those making a median number of errors. One will observe that the animals resulting from these two crosses exhibited errors throughout approximately the same range as did the parental generation. The distribution curves are of approximately similar shape. The F_2 generation was produced by mating dull rats with dull and bright rats with bright. Note that the two curves (B_2 and D_2) for the F_2 generation differ considerably. None of the progeny resulting from the dull cross made as few errors as some progeny of the bright cross. On the other hand, the progeny of dull rats achieved higher error scores than did any progeny of the bright ones. The modal scores for the two distributions are also dissimilar.

In successive generations until the eighth, Tryon followed the procedure of selection outlined above. In each generation the frequency distribution curves for errors became more distinct. In the F_7 and F_8 generations, the frequency distribution curves for progeny of bright and dull rats show very little overlapping. By selective breeding within a constant environment, two "races" of rats had been produced, a bright and a dull "race." Within each of these "races," differences in maze-learning ability were still distributed in a continuous rather than a discontinuous series. There were no distinct classes of "bright" or of "dull" rats.

Crossing "bright" and "dull" strains, Tryon[3] obtained a distribution in which most rats performed at an intermediate level. The distribution, although of narrower range, was somewhat similar to that of the original sample, as illustrated in Figure 12, $P.*$

* Heron[4] also attempted to differentiate strains of bright and dull rats, but except at early stages of the experiment there was no clear differentiation. Later research with Tryon's animals suggests that the two strains differ in characteristics more specific than general learning ability, or general brightness and dullness. Searle,[5] for instance, compared the reactions of

Tryon assumes that maze-learning ability in a constant environment is produced by a number of hereditary factors. One of the factors, A for example, may exist in two degrees of expression, A and a. It is assumed that a rat of homozygous constitution AA is brighter than a rat of homozygous constitution aa. A rat with heterozygous constitution Aa is assumed to lie between the two extremes, being of average ability as far as this single pair of factors is concerned. No dominance is assumed to exist. If one assumes that there are many factors determining maze-learning ability, and that each pair of factors functions in a manner comparable with that just described for A and a, the constitution of an individual rat of the highest degree of brightness may be written as follows: $AABBCCDD$.... The dullest possible rat would have the constitution $aabbccdd$. ... An average rat would have the genetic constitution $AaBbCcDd$.... The next to the brightest rat might have the factor combination $AaBBCCDD$...; the next to dullest, the combination $Aabbccdd$.... All possible combinations of the different pairs of factors would produce all of the individual differences in maze-learning ability evidenced in the parental stock. By mating bright rats with bright, one is gradually sorting out the $abcd$ ...factors in favor of the $ABCD$...; by mating dull with dull, one is, on the other hand, producing individuals with a preponderance of the factors $abcd$.... Obviously, if the above assumptions are correct, mating of dull with bright rats should produce rats with factor combinations approximating $AaBb$-$CcDd$.... As Tryon points out, if many

Tryon's bright and dull strains in a wide range of learning situations as well as situations calculated to test emotionality, motivation, discrimination, and other traits. The bright group was not generally superior. It was superior in some situations and not others; all of which implies that, although there is an inherent difference between Tryon's strains, it is specific to a certain maze situation. Moreover, the difference may be in part motivational or sensory, or a combination of these factors, rather than in learning ability as such.

factors are involved in determination of a trait (we have assumed four or more in the above illustrations), the resulting distribution for all degrees of individual differences in the trait will approximate a normal (bell-shaped) distribution curve. This is actually what one finds when a sufficient number of individuals is represented in the curve.*

In experiments involving selective breeding of rats in a fairly constant environment it has been possible to develop relatively active and inactive strains,[6] relatively emotional and non-emotional strains,[7] and strains relatively susceptible or non-susceptible to epileptoid seizures produced by high-pitched sounds.[8] In one strain of mice, these audiogenic seizures, as they are called, are to a high degree lethal.[9] That is to say, most of the animals which respond to the sound die during the seizure. In all these instances, the genetic factors are too complex to fall into any clearly recognizable Mendelian ratios. Whether any or all of them involve multiple factors, such as seem to be present in Tryon's animals, remains to be seen.

How can one ascertain the number of factors involved in hereditary determination of individual differences in a given trait? Snyder [10] points out that examination of extreme variations of a trait exhibited by the F_2 generation gives us a clue as to the number of factors involved. For example, when a single pair of factors is involved, one individual out of every four in the F_2 generation will exhibit a trait as extreme as that of either parent. In other words, one out of four of our Andalusian fowls was as dark as the black parent, and one out of four was as light as the white parent. The possible combinations of a pair of factors, Aa, for example, gives this result. Likewise, two pairs of factors when combined in all possible ways would yield, in the F_2 generation, one extreme individual out of every 16. When three pairs of factors are

* Differences of environmental origin are distributed in a similar fashion; hence normality of a distribution curve has no genetic significance unless the environment, as in the above experiment, is constant.

involved, the F_2 generation will have one out of every 64 individuals as extreme as either parent. Should ten pairs of factors be involved, there would be an individual as extreme as either parent in every 1,048,576 progeny. Thus, as the number of factors increases, the proportion of offspring having traits as extreme as either parent becomes exceedingly small. A small sampling of individuals would not be likely to produce extreme variations. If extremely large numbers of cases were involved, observations such as the above would suggest the number of factors determining a given trait.

Human traits thought to be related to such multiple-factor inheritance are differences in intelligence, in shape of head, in bodily conformation, in special constellations of abilities such as musical talent, and in longevity. Human vigor, like that of rats, may in part depend upon multiple factors.

Sex Determination and Related Phenomena

Numerous studies have shown that sex is inherited in a manner comparable with other traits. Whether an individual shall be male or female is determined by the combinations of chromosomes present in the fertilized zygote. In *Drosophila*, a small fruit fly, there are, as illustrated in Figure 13, three pairs of chromosomes which are alike in each sex. In addition to these three pairs, however, the female has a pair of chromosomes designated by the letter X. The male, on the other hand, has but one X chromosome. It also has a chromosome, designated by the letter Y, which does not appear in females.

The human male and female possess 23 pairs of chromosomes (autosomes) in common. In addition, the female has two X chromosomes and the male an X and a Y chromosome. Since the female possesses two X chromosomes, one of these will, during the process of meiosis, go to each ovum. Half of the male sperm, however, will receive an X chromosome and half of them a Y chromosome. If the ovum is fertilized by a sperm

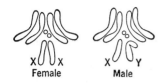

Female   Male

Figure 13. The Chromosomes of Drosophila Melanogaster

The X and Y chromosomes are those in which the sexes differ. (After Morgan, Bridges, and Sturtevant.)

carrying the X chromosome, two X chromosomes will be present and the individual will, other things equal, be female. If, on the other hand, a sperm with the Y chromosome fertilizes an ovum, the zygote must contain an X and a Y chromosome and the individual will probably be male. The individual's fifty-fifty chance of receiving an X or a Y chromosome from the father produces, other things being equal, the ratio of approximately one male to one female.

In most organisms possessing a Y chromosome, this structure exerts no known effect. The presence of one or two X chromosomes is thus the most important difference in the chromosomal constitution of the sexes. Chromosomes other than the X and Y are referred to as autosomes. It is believed that sex determination, rather than depending upon X chromosomes alone, results from a balance between the influence of factors (genes) in the X chromosomes and factors in the autosomes. When two X chromosomes are present, the *genic balance* is usually thrown in a direction requisite to the production of female characters; when only a single X chromosome is present, the genic balance is usually thrown in a direction which leads to production of male characters. Unusual types of interaction of X chromosomes and autosomes occasionally produce intersexes, that is, masculine females and effeminate males. All degrees of masculinity and femininity are genetically possible.

Glandular functions, determined by the genic balance and by various environmental conditions to be discussed later, are intimately involved in the production of differences in sexual structures. In other words, the genic balance and environmental conditions lead to the formation of certain kinds of glandular tissue and secretions therefrom. These secretions exert a controlling influence upon the further development of sex structures and of related sexual functions.

Sex-linked characters

Sometimes a given trait fails to appear in females, but appears in males resulting from a given cross. In *Drosophila*, a very convenient organism for such studies, a cross between white-eyed males and homozygous red-eyed females produces red-eyed males and red-eyed females. A cross between these produces red-eyed males and females and white-eyed males. *No females are white-eyed.* There are three red-eyed flies to one white-eyed, but all white-eyed animals are male. Such a trait is said to be sex-linked. This results from the fact that the chief determiners of eye-color reside in X chromosomes and that a determiner for white eyes is recessive to a determiner for red eyes. The white-eyed male has one Y and one X chromosome, the X chromosome carrying a recessive factor for eye-color. This factor may be designated by r. The red-eyed female has two X chromosomes. If she is homozygous for eye-color, both of the factors associated with determination of eye-color may be designated as RR. If she is heterozygous for eye-color, one factor is R and the other r. In the cross mentioned above, the male factors are rY and the female RR. In the F_1 generation the combinations RY and Rr result. All progeny, male or female, have red eyes. In the F_2 generation, however, the combinations shown in Figure 14 result. One will note that every female receives at least one dominant factor whereas one-half of the males receive a recessive factor and thus have white eyes. White-eyed females may, of course, be produced by crossing heterozygous females with white-eyed males.

A human sex-linked trait of especial interest to psychologists is red-green color blindness.

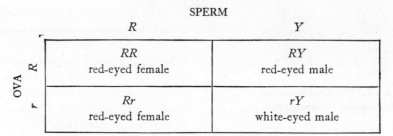

Figure **14.** Sex-Linked Eye-Color in an F$_2$ Generation of Drosophila

This is a weakness in the ability to perceive red and green under conditions where these colors are equivalent in brightness value. It is found in approximately one boy in ten or twelve and in only one girl in a hundred. The explanation is similar to that given above for eye-color in *Drosophila*. If the mother is color blind, all of her sons are also color blind. Usually all of her daughters are normal. This is because the factor for color vision is located in the X chromosome, because the normal factor is dominant, and because the male receives but one X chromosome, the daughters two. Since the normal or C factor is dominant, a color-blind female must have two "bad" factors for color vision, or cc. Each ovum will thus contain a c factor. If the father is normal, the factor combination of the girls, with respect to color vision, will be Cc. A dominant factor (C) comes from the father, and normal color vision results. Every boy, on the other hand, must receive a factor for color blindness (c) with no "normal" factor to counteract its influence. He receives an X and a Y chromosome, but only the X chromosome, which comes from his mother, contains a factor for color vision. Hence he must be color blind. These facts explain why a color-blind woman must have sons all of whom are color blind and may have daughters with normal color vision.

Should the father and mother both be color blind, the daughters as well as the sons will be color blind. The daughters will receive a c factor from the mother and another c factor from the father. Should the mother have normal color vision with the factor combina-

tion CC, and the father color blindness (with the factor c), both sons and daughters will be normal. The daughters will receive a C factor from the mother and a c factor from the father. The sons will receive a C factor from the mother. On the other hand, the mother might possess normal color vision with the factor combination Cc. If the father were color blind, carrying only the c factor, the daughters would have an equal chance of receiving the combinations Cc and cc. The latter combination would, of course, lead to color blindness. If the father should be normal, however, he would carry the factor C, and all the daughters would have normal vision. They would receive the combination Cc or the combination CC. The boys would have an equal chance of receiving the C or c from the mother. In other words, they would possess an equal chance of having normal color vision or of having red-green color blindness.

Among other sex-linked traits known to be inherited by human beings are hemophilia (lack of normal blood coagulation), optic atrophy, and absence of sweat glands. Snyder [11] reports that twenty such sex-linked traits have been identified in human beings. In each case, females rarely have the anomaly.

Sex-influenced and sex-limited factors

Sometimes a trait differs in frequency among males and females, and yet is not assorted in the sex-linked fashion considered above. Examples of human *sex-influenced* traits are inherited baldness and a certain kind of white forelock. These traits are determined by the fact that a given factor is dominant when it appears in males and recessive when it appears in females. For example, the factor (B) for baldness is dominant in males, recessive in females. The factor combination Bb thus produces bald men and non-bald women. Women inherit baldness only when the BB combination is present. White forelock is thought to be similarly determined.

Sex-limited factors are normally expressed in one sex and not in the other, expression depending, apparently, upon the influence of sex hormones. Snyder [12] indicates that beardedness in men is probably a sex-limited factor. Its expression appears to depend upon the presence of male rather than female hormones. Although females have the same number of hairs possessed by males, the female hairs remain undeveloped due to absence of the male sex hormones, presence of the ovarian hormones, or both. Snyder is of the opinion that other secondary sex characters may likewise depend upon sex-limited factors.

Genes

Until the present we have merely referred to hereditary transmission as dependent upon factors carried by the chromosomes and assorted as the traits are assorted. Although we have suggested that the factors are designated as *genes*, or determiners of inherited traits, we have considered neither the nature of the genes nor the evidence for their existence.

While chromosomes are readily visible under the microscope, being distinguishable in terms of size and shape, their internal composition had not, until recently, been directly observed. That the chromosomes consist of differentiable parts, or genes, was first inferred from certain phenomena of hereditary transmission. We shall briefly consider these phenomena at this point.

Studies of inheritance in *Drosophila* demonstrate that while some traits are assorted at random, others tend to stick together, coming out of a cross as they go into it. The most reasonable explanation of this is that the randomly assorted traits depend upon factors in *different* chromosomes (which, as we have previously observed, are randomly assorted) while the *linked* traits depend upon different factors in the same chromosome. An example of linkage is given in the following illustration, which is based upon data reported by Snyder.[13]

In experiments on linkage, geneticists must resort to the back-cross. That is, they must mate individuals heterozygous for the linked factors with those which are doubly recessive. *Black body and long wings and gray body and vestigial wings* are, for example, linked traits. Gray body and long wings are dominant traits designated, respectively, by the letters B and V. Black body and vestigial wings are recessive, designated by b and v. A linkage experiment involving these traits is begun by crossing flies which possess the factor combination $bbVV$ (black body and long wings) with flies having the factor combination $BBvv$ (gray body and vestigial wings). The progeny of this cross will, of course, all possess the factor combination $BbVv$ and hence a gray body and long wings. These heterozygous gray-bodied long-winged flies are then back-crossed, i.e., mated with flies having the double recessive combination $bbvv$ and hence a black body and vestigial wings. As one can readily observe by making a checkerboard diagram and indicating the types of zygote resulting from possible combinations of the germ cells involved, random assortment of the factors in this back-cross would produce four types of individuals in a 1:1:1:1 ratio. Actually, however, such a ratio fails to appear. If dihybrid males are crossed with recessive females only *two* kinds of progeny result, namely, flies with *black body and long wings* and flies with *gray body and vestigial wings*. The ratio is 1:1. Linkage of the factors b with V and B with v accounts for this result. If linkage is complete, half of the germ cells of the heterozygous ($BbVv$) flies have the factor combination bV and half the combination Bv (random assortment would have produced BV, bV, Bv, and bv). The only kind of germ cell in the doubly recessive flies is, of course, bv. Thus only two kinds of zygote are possible from the back-cross, namely (bV)(bv) and (Bv)(bv). These produce 50 per cent black long-winged and 50 per cent gray vestigial-winged flies.

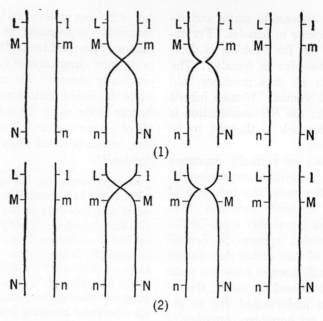

Figure 15. Diagram to Illustrate Crossover Phenomena

The lines represent chromosomes, the letters homologous parts (genes) of the chromosomes. Crossing over takes place during germ-cell maturation when homologous chromosomes may be seen to twist around each other. The twisting may take place at any point. It may occur at several points simultaneously. One will note that, when the two chromosomes of a pair separate to go each to a different germ cell, there has been an exchange of parts. Note also that the possibility of the genes L and M being transferred to different chromosomes is much less than that of either of these being separated from N. In other words, the percentage of crossing over evidenced by L and M would be much less than that evidenced by L or M and N. There would be a slightly greater percentage of crossing over between L and N than between M and N, the reason being that the distance between the genes M and N is smaller than that between L and N. (After Snyder.)

This illustrates complete linkage. There are no recombinations, crossovers, in the male. If dihybrid females are crossed with recessive males, linkage is incomplete. About 16 per cent of the offspring are crossovers showing the combinations $BbVv$ or $bbvv$. Some linked traits exhibit such crossovers in a much smaller percentage of cases than in the present instance; others exhibit them in a higher percentage than that indicated in the above example. These facts are of great significance for inferences concerning the internal differentiation of chromosomes. But how, if the linked traits are determined by parts of the same chromosome, can linkage ever fail to appear?

It is assumed that each of the linked traits is determined by a different part of a chromosome * and that, during meiosis, when the chromosomes of a pair are twisting around each other preparatory to going each to a different germ cell (see Figure 6,B), an exchange of chromosome material takes place. This phenomenon, called *crossing over* of chromosome parts, is illustrated diagrammatically in Figure 15. As indicated in this figure, parts of a chromosome that are widely sep-

* By means of experiments which we cannot discuss here, it has been discovered that there are, in *Drosophila*, as many linkage groups as chromosome pairs. The chromosome determining each set of linked factors has also been identified. Chromosome II determines the linkage discussed above.

arated will cross over frequently, while those which are close together in the chromosome will tend to be separated very infrequently. One can now readily see that the percentage of new associations (crossovers) is an index of the relative position of the genes along the chromosome.

Knowledge of the chromosomes in which given linkage groups occur and of the relative frequency with which given genes within these chromosomes exhibit new linkages has enabled geneticists to prove (inferentially) that chromosomes are divisible into parts and that each part plays a peculiar role in the determination of hereditary characters. Geneticists have been able, on the basis of such inferential evidence, to make maps which indicate the approximate location of the genes within each of *Drosophila's* chromosomes. They have concluded that a chromosome consists of many genes, strung along it "like beads on a thread." Each gene is thought to have peculiar chemical properties which enable it, through its effect upon cytoplasm, to play a role in the determination of hereditary traits.

There is now additional evidence that chromosomes are internally differentiated in some such manner as that indicated above. Indeed, differentiations are visible under the microscope. Ordinary chromosomes are too small for separate structures to be observed within them. However, the salivary gland cells of *Drosophila* are very much enlarged and the chromosomes within their nuclei are approximately 150 times the usual size. Except in magnitude, however, these chromosomes are like those of other body cells. The size of the salivary-gland chromosomes is such that differentiations not observable in other chromosomes are clearly seen under the microscope. Dark and light bands show up along their entire length, as illustrated in Figure 16, which also shows the differentiation made evident by the electron microscope. There is still much discussion as to the exact location of the genes in such representations of the giant salivary glands.

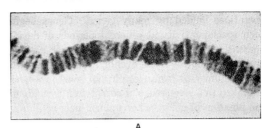

A

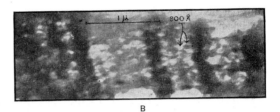

B

Figure 16. A Portion of Salivary Gland Chromosome

This is one of the giant salivary gland chromosomes of the fruit fly. *A* shows such a chromosome under a high-powered microscope. *B* is not a photograph but an electron micrograph of a very small portion of a salivary gland chromosome. The differentiations, enlarged here 26,000 times, are believed to be, or to contain, genes. (From D. C. Pease and R. F. Baker, "Chromosomes, Genes, and the Electron Microscope," *Science*, 1949, *109*, 9.)

As indicated above, the genes are thought to affect the cytoplasm which surrounds them by exerting a chemical influence upon it. For this reason, geneticists sometimes refer to genes as "packets of chemicals." They appear to consist of enzymes which, like other catalysts, affect chemical reactions without themselves undergoing changes. It was at one time thought that each gene plays a particular part in the determination of one trait, but not in the determination of others. This particulate conception of the function of genes has now given way to a concept of genic balance very well expressed by East [14] in the following quotation:

Genes vary greatly in the importance of their activities during ontogeny, and various specimens might be dispensed with were it not that this would cause disharmony in the machine as a whole. The activity of each gene is effective on numerous characters; and each character is the end effect of the operations guided by many genes. Genes begin their special activity at different periods of development, and may take active parts over periods of varying length. At all events, it has been shown that in numerous instances physiological processes are taken to a given stage of completion by a given combination of genes, whereupon a new combination takes charge and pushes the process further, to a point where still another set takes command. Thus one may think of a developmental process as a serial affair much like the building of a motor car, with specialist genes directing each step.

Mutations

Mutations are inherited bodily changes brought about by alterations of chromosomes and genes. To understand the significance of such phenomena one need only consider the fact that germ cells are relatively impervious to ordinary environmental influence. Many changes may be wrought in an organism during its lifetime, such as increased muscular development, physical anomalies, and so on, yet there is no evidence that these are transmitted to offspring by means of inheritance. For example, Jews have practiced circumcision for thousands of years, yet there is no evidence that any related hereditary changes have taken place. Upon the basis of such evidence, supplemented by laboratory experiments with hundreds of generations of *Drosophila*, biologists claim that germ cells are beyond the influence of ordinary environmental conditions; that they are passed on unchanged from parent to offspring.

Although the germ cells are apparently uninfluenced by training, acquired degeneracy, and the like, they sometimes undergo "spontaneous" alterations in their internal constitution. That is to say, new characters sometimes appear suddenly and are thereafter inherited by offspring of the affected individuals. Since these sudden changes are inheritable in the usual way, it is assumed that they have been brought about by changes in the chromosomes or in the genes. In their experiments with *Drosophila*, geneticists have observed that new and inheritable characters

appear in about one out of every five to ten thousand individuals. These characters involve new wing structures, absence of wings, changes in bristle formations, absence of eyes or changes in their structure, and the like. In some instances it appears that chromosomes have been altered in number or in character. In other instances it seems that the constitution of single genes or groups of closely associated genes has been affected directly. Changes in the chromosomes as such are known as chromosome mutations; those in the genes as gene mutations.

Chromosome mutations are believed to result from some chance slip in the ordinarily smooth-running process of cell division. Instead of going to different cells, homologous chromosomes sometimes "stick together" and go to the same cell. In this case one cell may be deprived of chromosomes while the other has extra ones. One such phenomenon, known as non-disjunction of chromosomes, is illustrated in Figure 17. Chromosome division in normal mitosis is shown in the upper diagrams (A–C). The chromosomes A, a, B, and b are equally distributed in each cell. The mutation is illustrated in A'–C'. It will be observed that the chromosome B is absent in one cell and duplicated in the other. Thus one cell will be deprived of a set of genes, while the other will have an extra set. Sometimes part of a chromosome is added to one cell, and as it were, subtracted from another. Other chromosome mutations have been observed in which the entire group of chromosomes had been doubled, tripled, or quadrupled.

If these anomalous cells become sperm or ova and are involved in the conception of a new individual, some unusual change in structure may occur. Such changes are prone to appear, of course, when close inbreeding takes place, since two germ cells possessing similar mutated chromosomes are more likely to unite under these circumstances than under those of diverse breeding. Very frequently, if either the ovum or the sperm is normal, the anomalous characters fail to appear.

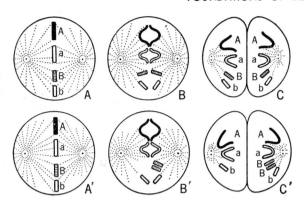

Figure 17. A Type of Chromosome Mutation

(From W. R. Coe, "Mutation and Environment," in *Organic Adaptation to Environment*, New Haven: Yale University Press, 1924.)

Chromosome mutations are thought to be of small significance for structural evolution because, since the genes remain unchanged in constitution, being merely arranged in new combinations, no entirely new or radically changed structures appear in the species. Changes in size, in presence or absence of certain structures already present in the species, and similar anomalies alone result from chromosome mutation. Most of the mutations in *Drosophila*, involving such changes as new wing formation, bristle characters, and eye structures, are believed to depend upon direct changes in genes. Thus a new wing structure is thought to depend upon change in the chemical make-up of a gene in chromosome II. The altered gene would be in the region of chromosome II which is concerned with wing formation. The gene is transmitted in its changed state since, by selective breeding, a race of flies having the changed character may be produced.

As we have already indicated, gene mutations appear with apparent spontaneity in about one out of every five to ten thousand fruit flies bred in the laboratory. At an altitude of 14,000 feet, where the frequency of cosmic rays is fifteen times as great as at sea level, there are three times as many mutations as have been found in laboratory studies.[15] However, it has been shown by Muller and others that the greatest incidence of mutations occurs when the germ cells are bombarded with X-rays. Under these conditions the mutation process may be speeded up.

The mutations thus produced are similar to those which arise with apparent spontaneity. Most of the mutations studied in animals and in man (one example is shown in Figure 18) are of such a nature as to be regarded as abnormal. But many mutations may produce no visible effects; and some of the effects, under certain environmental conditions, may be beneficial to the organisms concerned. We shall return to this question in a later consideration of the phylogeny of unlearned behavior.

The Nature and Significance of Environmental Conditions

The general phenomena of inheritance have been discussed, but we have largely ignored the influence exerted by the environment in directing and limiting the functions of the genes. It will be recalled that the environment has been assumed in the above discussions to be relatively constant, a phenomenon which rarely occurs in nature. Actually, inherent and environmental factors are reciprocally associated in the production of the organism's many traits.

Although environmental conditions rarely produce inherently transmissible changes in the organism, they do markedly influence individual development. Organisms with the same sets of genes may differ as a result of developing in diverse environments. It was for this reason that we assumed the presence

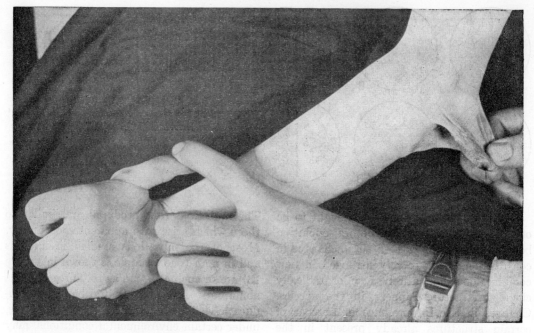

Figure 18. One of Many Obvious Human Mutations

The gene mutation has here produced multiple effects, including extreme looseness of the joints, looseness and elasticity of the skin, fragility of blood vessels, and susceptibility to hemorrhages in the skin. (From A. M. Winchester, *Genetics*, Boston: Houghton Mifflin, 1951, p. 234. Photo by M. T. Eliegelman and Sture M. Johnson.)

of a constant environment in our consideration of the mechanisms of inheritance. In the following pages we shall observe what may happen when heredity is constant and environmental conditions are variable.

Our conception of what is implied by the term "environment" will of course depend upon whether we take the chromosome, the single cell, or the total organism as a point of reference. Customarily the term is used to represent conditions external to the organism. If the chromosomes are taken as a reference point, however, certain conditions within the organism are to be regarded as environmental. These intra-organic conditions, as Marquis [16] has suggested, may for purposes of analysis be differentiated into two kinds, intracellular and intercellular. These will be discussed in turn. We shall then consider the influence of conditions external to the organism.

Intracellular conditions

Such conditions are functions of the cytoplasm and other materials of the cell which surround the chromosomes. (See Figure 19.) Jennings[17] has pointed out that the cytoplasm is structurally transformed under the influence of the genes. The maternal genes produce a structural transformation of the cytoplasm even before fertilization has taken place.

It has been observed that cells which contain identical genes, but diverse cytoplasmic structures, differ in their ultimate characters. The ovum of the sea-urchin, for example, has a noticeable differentiation of its cytoplasm. When the ovum divides to form two cells, this differentiation is maintained in each cell. The genes are also identical with those of the original cell. These two cells with identical cytoplasmic differentiation and identical genes

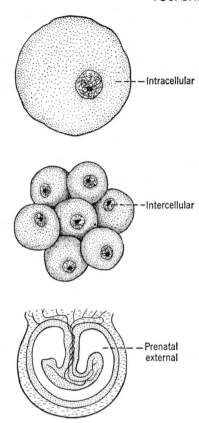
— Intracellular

— Intercellular

— Prenatal
external

Figure 19.   The Prenatal Environments

(From N. L. Munn, *Psychology*, 2d ed., Boston: Houghton Mifflin, 1951, p. 97.)

may, if caused to separate, develop into a pair of normal organisms which are identical in structure. At the four-celled stage there is again complete duplication of cytoplasmic differentiation and genes. Hence the four cells may, when separated, also become complete and structurally identical animals. At the eight-celled stage, however, while the genes are still alike in each cell, the differentiation of the cytoplasm is no longer similar to that in earlier stages. Some cells have the cytoplasmic structure which appeared in the upper half of the original cell; others, that which appeared in the lower half. Separation of these cells does not lead to the development of normal animals. If they develop at all, the organisms are lacking in certain struc-

tures which normally develop from the missing cytoplasmic parts.

This and similar evidence shows that identical sets of genes may produce different structures, depending upon the intracellular environment, especially the cytoplasm which surrounds them and with which they must work to produce the characteristic structures of the organism. That both the genes and the cytoplasm are necessary for development is shown by the fact that either of these alone fails to produce an organism. That the genes play a determining role, and the cytoplasm a limiting one, is suggested by an experiment performed by Boveri.[18]   He demonstrated that the structures produced are those characteristic of the genes rather than of the cytoplasm. When the nucleus was removed from the ovum of one species of sea-urchin and replaced by the sperm cell of another species, the resulting individuals possessed structures comparable with those of the species from which the sperm cells (the genes) had come.

Intercellular conditions

The intercellular conditions are produced by cells which surround a cell which is taken as a point of reference. When the initial cell divides to form a pair of cells, each of these influences the further development of the other. The cells multiply, and eventually there exists a ball of them, as shown in Figure 19. The cells contain identical genes, but they differ in cytoplasmic structure and in location with respect to each other. In the following discussion we shall consider the role played by the location of a cell with respect to other cells. Summarizing the results of numerous embryological experiments, Jennings [19] says:

In the mass of small cells, what part of the later individual will, in the usual course, be produced by each portion can be predicted with certainty. A certain set of cells can be pointed out as those that will produce the brain, certain others will produce eyes, others the spinal cord, the skin, the alimentary canal, and so on. It appears as if everything were fixed and determined; as if the fate of every cell were dependent merely on what genes or what kind of cytoplasm it contains. But experimental study shows that this is not the case. If, in these early stages, from the region that is to produce the skin, a portion is removed and transplanted to the region that is to produce the brain, then the fate of the transplanted cells is changed. They alter their development, and become part of the brain instead of part of the skin. Or if the reverse transplantation is made, cells that would have formed a part of the brain alter their development and become part of the skin. What the cells become depends on their surroundings; on what the cells about them are becoming. Their development takes such a course as to fit into the general pattern; such a course that they produce structures which are fitted to the position in which they find themselves.

Such transformations of cells or groups of cells is brought about by mechanical pressure and by chemical and electrical properties of the developing tissues. It appears that certain regions of the organism exert dominance over cells in other regions. The central nervous system, which is first evidenced as a groove, dominates even remote parts of the organism. The head end, especially, serves as an "organizing center" and has a marked effect upon development of even remote cells. There appears to be a hierarchy of such centers, with the head exerting the greatest dominance. Child [20] speaks of these as centers of dominant polarity and of their influence upon neighboring cells as evidencing a physiological gradient such that the closer a cell is to the center of dominance, the greater the influence of this center upon its development. If, instead of moving groups of cells to new locations, one moves the center of dominance itself, the cells surrounding this center may accordingly be transformed.

It should be pointed out, however, that such results as we have discussed above appear only when the cells involved are in a primitive stage of development. If cells are transplanted after differentiation has gone too far, they tend to maintain the chief characteristics normal to their former location.

Another intercellular condition which arises early in the development of the individual is that associated with glandular functions. When the endocrine glands appear, secretions (hormones) which may influence the further development of the entire organism are poured into the blood stream. It will be recalled that we discussed the influence of sex hormones in determination of sex-limited traits.

Hoskins, [21] an outstanding investigator of endocrine functions, points out that although we know very little about the influence of hormones on prenatal development, such factors are undoubtedly important. Much of our information concerning the influence exerted by the endocrines comes from clinical observations. Something goes wrong with glandular functioning, and the organism is accordingly malformed. For example, when the thyroid gland fails to function appropriately in infancy the individual may have the anomaly known as cretinism. The cretin is stunted, pot-bellied, and, among a number of other things, mentally deficient. If given sufficiently early in development, thyroid extracts may clear up the anomaly.

All these considerations indicate that cells possessing the same genes may develop markedly different structures, depending upon the conditions which surround them during the early period of their growth. Under normal circumstances, of course, the position that each cell shall occupy and the time and way in which it will be influenced by glandular secretions is determined by preceding conditions. The sequence is somewhat as follows: The maternal cytoplasm is differentiated under the influence of the maternal genes, the genes from the sperm enter and merge with those of the ovum, the cell divides to form two, these to form four, and so on. As the cells multiply, since the space in which they can develop is limited, some are developed on the inside of the mass, others on the outside. This leads to the setting up of complex mechanical, chemical, and even electrical relationships between the cells. Certain regions, due to these chemical and electrical properties associated with their growth, soon come to dominate, as it were, development of cells in more and more remote regions. At a certain time the glandular contributions make their appearance and exert a further influence upon the development of the organism. This sequence of events is alike for all normal members of a species. It is initiated by the genes of the mother and father of the individual. Nevertheless, the process is one in which the genes and the cytoplasm and the conditions surrounding them are integrally related. Only under experimental or anomalous circumstances can the intracellular and intercellular conditions be isolated in a manner that shows the limitations which they may at any given time place upon the functioning of the genes.

External conditions

Conditions external to the organism differ rather widely before and after birth; hence it is customary to differentiate between the prenatal and the postnatal environments. Under normal circumstances the *prenatal* environment (Figure 19) is relatively constant and, like the intra-organic conditions, is characteristic for members of a given species. As Marquis [22] points out:

The mass of evidence from embryology indicates that the external environment of the embryo (except in the possible case of extreme variations causing teratosis) is constant and, within a range of variation maintained by the parent, has little specific influence in producing individual differences. In the tissue fluid of humans, there is a constancy of temperature, oxygen, salt balance, osmotic pressure, and hydrogen-ion concentration which is unequalled in the developmental environment of any other form. But besides this definite, constant environment, there is provision that other stimuli will have little influence except in so far as they are reflected indirectly in the tissue fluid of the mother.

Despite its relative constancy under normal conditions, however, the environment immediately external to the embryo or fetus may be modified, accidentally or experimentally, in such a manner as to effect significant alterations in structure or in the rate of development. Mechanical constriction due to abnormal position of the fetus, malnutrition or unusual glandular conditions in the mother, may produce such anomalous developments. Some of our information concerning the influence of changes in the external environment of the very young organism comes from experiments with larvae. Stockard,[23] for example, has shown that the larvae of a marine fish, *Fundulus*, which normally become fish with two eyes, will develop but one eye if subjected to certain unusual solutions of magnesium salts in sea-water.

The influence of glandular products introduced from outside the organism is shown in two interesting experiments, one with tadpoles and the other with young rats. Gudernatsch [24] fed thyroid tissue to tadpoles. This caused them to metamorphose at a much earlier age than usual. Tadpoles metamorphosed to form frogs as small as flies, whereas in the normal course of events they should, after about three years, have become bull frogs.* Although this does not, strictly speaking, involve an alteration in the prenatal environment, the conditions are somewhat comparable with those of an organism receiving its hormones through the placenta from the mother instead of ingesting them directly. Evidence that glandular products residing in the mother influence the development of the unborn organism comes from an experiment by Rowntree, Clark, and Hanson [25] on white rats. Rats born to mothers that had received a daily injection of 1 cc. of thymus extract were significantly larger than those delivered by normal animals. Their precocity was also evidenced for as long as sixty days after birth. They were much larger and heavier than normal rats, their teeth erupted earlier, their sexual development was precocious, and so on. The ultimate size of the rats was not greater than

* But the metamorphosed frogs do not survive. In a repetition of this experiment the writer found that the frogs died soon after metamorphosis had occurred, a result also reported by Gudernatsch.

normal; hence only the *rate* of development was affected by the excess glandular substance.

It has been customary to attribute all congenital defects to bad heredity, either in the mother or in the child or in both. However, experiments on the prenatal environment such as we have just discussed show that not all congenital developments are necessarily due to inherent factors. Moss and Hunt [26] point out:

As we know so little about the injuries which occur in intra-uterine life, we have built up an hypothesis that when a child is born with gross deformities, those deformities are due to defects in the germ plasm and are hereditary rather than environmental. It is the opinion of the writers, however, that as our knowledge increases concerning the intra-uterine period, many of the congenital defects will be taken out of the hereditary group and explained on the grounds of environmental influences during the prenatal period.

The *postnatal* environment, unlike the prenatal, is obviously quite variable from one individual to another. It includes not only inorganic and organic surroundings, as such, but also the social and cultural significance which, as it were, has become attached to these during the history of the race. That this environment is an important factor in development no one can doubt. However, the relative influence of heredity and of the external environment is frequently debated. In the following discussion we shall consider some data which bear upon this problem.

The Continued Integral Relation of Heredity and Environment After Birth

Inherent and environmental conditions are integrally related after as well as before birth. Only accidental or experimentally produced variations in one condition while the other is held constant can enable us to differentiate between their respective effects. Differentiation of inherent and environmental influences is, however, more difficult after than before birth. This is because both the organism and the environment to whose influence it is susceptible have increased tremendously in complexity and in variability. Controlled observation, except in rather rare instances, such as we shall discuss presently, is out of the question.

The influence of the external environment is often quite specific, as, for example, when learning of a particular skill is accomplished, or when malfunction is elicited by lack of adequate nourishment or by externally introduced toxins. On the other hand, the carry-over of an inherent factor to postnatal life is evidenced by the fact that organisms develop certain structures and behavior in the absence of training or opportunities to imitate. Furthermore, they differ in learning ability, in susceptibility to toxins, and in every known trait. Such differences often occur in instances where it is impossible to explain them on environmental grounds alone.

The complexity of this problem of attempting to differentiate between the influence of heredity and the influence of environmental conditions after the individual has begun to develop, and especially after birth, has led some psychologists to doubt the advisability of attempting such a differentiation. For example, Carmichael [27] says:

The fact as it appears to the present writer is that no distinction can be expediently made at any given moment in the behavior of the individual, after the fertilized egg has once begun to develop, between that which is native and that which is acquired. The so-called hereditary factors can only be acquired in response to an environment, and likewise the so-called acquired factors can only be secured by a modification of already existing structure, which in the last analysis is hereditary structure.

What Carmichael says is undoubtedly true if we confine our considerations to development of *a particular individual*. If differences between individuals are considered, however, the relative influence of heredity and of environment in producing such differences often becomes clearly apparent. A partial resolution of the problem is achieved by investigations in which heredity is held constant while environmental conditions are varied, or vice versa.

Identical twins, since they possess identical genes and similar prenatal conditions of development, are often used in studies of the relative influence of hereditary and environmental conditions upon determination of individual differences. Such twins resemble each other very closely not only in physical traits (Figure 20) but also in motor skills, learning ability, and intelligence.

Newman, Freeman, and Holzinger [28] compared the differences between identical twins reared together and the differences between those adopted at an early age and reared in diverse environments. Measurements of physical characteristics, of intelligence, and of aspects of personality were used in the comparisons. Fifty pairs of identical twins, both members of which were reared in the same home, showed extremely slight differences in physique. Greater differences were found for I.Q. (intelligence quotient). The

Figure 20. Three Sets of Identical Twins

The identical twin brothers married identical twin sisters, and one couple had the identical twin girls. The boy was born to the other couple. (From A. Scheinfeld, *You and Heredity*, new ed., Philadelphia: Lippincott, 1950, facing page 134.)

average difference in I.Q. for identical twins reared together was 5.35 points. The differences ranged from 0 to 20 points. Nineteen pairs of identical twins, the members of which were reared apart, exhibited slight changes in some physical characteristics such as weight and condition of teeth. In most of the important physical traits, however, similarity was obvious, despite diversity of environment for periods of about eleven to forty years. Differences in I.Q. were slightly greater than those for identical twins reared in the same home. The average difference was 8.21, 2.86 points greater than that between identical twins reared together. This difference is statistically significant. The differences ranged from 1 to 24 points. Personality differences were in many instances quite large. These results indicate that when heredity is constant, as in identical twins, diverse environments produce differences in physique, intelligence, and personality.[29]

Whether the I.Q. differences produced by environmental diversity are to be regarded as large or small depends upon one's inclination to give greater weight to heredity or to environment. Newman, Freeman, and Holzinger point out the complexity of this problem of assigning different weights to heredity and environment. As far as psychological traits are concerned, no clear-cut decision can be based upon the above results. The investigators agree with Jennings' dictum that "what heredity can do environment can also do." This dictum does not hold for many physical characteristics, although it holds, apparently, for small differences in I.Q. and for large differences in personality.

One cannot forget the results on maze learning and on activity level in rats. These experiments show that marked differences in learning ability and in activity are produced *in a constant environment* by variation of genes. Such differences cannot be produced by holding heredity constant and varying the rats' environment any more than variations in environment alone can produce the large variety of plants and animals.

While heredity and environment are both significant for determination of racial and individual differences, there are definite limits placed by one upon the other.

The Social and Cultural Environment

Most organisms are influenced in various ways by the presence of others of their kind. As we go up the scale of evolution, however, we find that the influence of the group becomes increasingly significant. The highest organisms are dependent upon others for sustenance. If they are not fed and protected by others they die. In this respect, man is the most helpless of all. He is, on the other hand, especially sensitive to social influences. From the precepts and examples of others, he soon acquires the language of his group and its other skills and attitudes as well. The sum-total of all such acquisitions is what we call *culture*.

The impact of culture upon the personality of human beings has attracted a great deal of attention in recent years. Observations of development in a wide range of cultures has suggested that many human characteristics once thought to be universal and hereditary in origin are actually due to culural influences. What was once called "human nature" actually differs a great deal from one culture to another. Thus the Oedipus complex*, thought by Freud to be universal and inborn, was shown by Malinowski [30] to be absent among Trobriand Islanders. Its widespread appearance in societies like our own is due to the father-son relationship found in these societies. The so-called "acquisitive instinct" and the "instinct of pugnacity," once stressed by McDougall as aspects of human nature, are likewise absent in some societies with traditions unlike our own.[31] Marked aggressiveness characterizes the individual of certain societies but not of others, and there is some evidence that its presence or absence

* This is the tendency for males to have a strong attachment for the mother and jealousy of the father

is related to the mother-infant relationship during the nursing period.[32] Attitudes, concepts, and modes of thought also tend to bear a cultural stamp.

These influences upon individual development are so important that geneticists, whose prime concern is with heredity, are themselves drawing attention to them. Thus Dunn and Dobzhansky,[33] in a discussion of "cultural inheritance" have the following to say:

Certain biologists have contended that human personalities and even cultures are to all intents and purposes determined by biological heredity, environment being of little consequence. Certain cultural anthropologists, whose business it is to study and compare different cultures, answered by claiming that man is entirely a creature of his culture, and that his biological heredity stops at the surface of his skin. Thus we have heard in recent years that the Japanese character is set by the early and severe toilet training of Japanese babies; while Russians are what they are because of the swaddling of infants which was practiced in Russia (and, incidentally, in many European countries). All that needs to be said about such theories is that they fail to take into account this well-established fact: Man's personality, as well as his physical traits, results from a process of development in which both heredity and environment play important parts.

This is not the place to consider cultural influences in detail, especially since they receive attention at appropriate places during our discussion of psychological development in children. It is important, however, to recognize at the outset that cultural aspects of the social environment play an important role in the development of human beings. Unless the impact of culture upon development is recognized, one runs the risk of attributing to heredity alone certain uniformities of human behavior which result from common cultural influences. One also runs the danger of supposing that differences between nations and races are necessarily hereditary in origin.

Summary and Conclusions

Regardless of its ultimate complexity, every organism begins life as a single cell. In multicellular organisms the initial cell usually divides to form two, these divide to form four, and so on until a mass of cells is produced. Billions of cells are derived in this manner from a fertilized ovum. After the first few cells have appeared, differentiation as well as multiplication is evidenced. Such differentiation produces the structures of the organism and thus the foundations of behavior. Differentiation is produced by the reciprocal action of two general conditions, the hereditary and the environmental.

In a relatively constant environment it is possible to trace the characteristic structures of organisms to the influence of the genes. These so-called "units" of inheritance are believed to be chemical agents having different locations with the chromosomes.

In animals which reproduce sexually, the initial cell (fertilized ovum) contains a number of chromosomes which are arranged in pairs and which differ in number and characteristics from one species to another. In man there are 48 (24 pairs). One member of each pair of chromosomes (and hence genes) comes from each parent. The chromosomes and genes are duplicated in all body cells and in all immature reproductive cells derived from the fertilized ovum. The process involved in such duplication of chromosomes and genes is called mitosis. The reproductive cells undergo a reduction of chromosomes at the time of puberty, one member of each pair going to each daughter cell. This process is known as meiosis. With fertilization the full complement of chromosomes is restored.

Mendel worked out certain principles which enable one to predict the structural characteristics of the offspring from parents of known inheritance. It can be shown that the principles discovered by him long before chromosomes were known to exist are accounted for by the possible combinations of chromosomes (and genes) in the fertilized ovum. For hereditary determination of a given trait, four chromosomes (with their genes) are potentially available, one from each of the grandparents of the individual. Which chromosome shall come from the father (his father's or mother's) and which from the mother (her father's or mother's) is determined by chance. It is this chance combination which accounts for Mendelian inheritance, the principal phenomena of which were discussed in this chapter.

Sex is also determined by genes. Human males possess an X and a Y chromosome and females two X chromosomes. Genic balance and glandular influences are important for sex determination. Traits are sometimes sex-linked, sex-influenced, or sex-limited. We have considered each of these phenomena. They relate to factors involved in sex determination.

Inherently transmissible changes in structure sometimes occur with apparent spontaneity and can be traced to alterations in the constitution of chromosomes and genes. These changes in inherent structure are known as mutations. Some of them (gene mutations), as we shall observe in the next chapter, may underlie the evolution of unlearned behavior. Although mutations occur with apparent spontaneity, they may be produced experimentally by subjecting the germ cells to X-rays. Such mutations have been produced in *Drosophila*. The frequency of their occurrence is much greater under the influence of X-rays than when brought about with apparent spontaneity.

Although the genes play a significant role in the determination of the characteristic structures of species and individuals, an optimum environment is requisite. Numerous experiments have shown that what a cell or an individual becomes does not depend upon the genes alone. For example, alterations in the intracellular conditions of development, comprising the cytoplasm and other substances which surround the chromosomes and genes, lead to the development of anomalous structures or to the death of the cell.

Likewise, the intercellular conditions — that is, the location of a cell with respect to other cells — play an important part in the development of the organism. If they are transplanted sufficiently early, cells will develop into structures appropriate to their new location rather than those appropriate to the former one, yet the genes have remained unaltered during the process. It can be shown, in this connection, that certain parts of the organism dominate the development of cells in other regions, their influence being proportional to the proximity of these cells. The central nervous system, and especially the head end, exerts such dominance. Secretions from the organism's own endocrine glands are intercellular factors which influence its development.

We have shown that the intra-organic conditions of development may, in the last analysis, be determined by the genes themselves, since it is these which start the orderly succession of developments leading to the production of a new individual. In any case, it is also obvious that the genes and their surrounding conditions are integrally related. Nothing is produced by cytoplasm and intercellular conditions without the genes, and nothing is produced by the genes without appropriate cytoplasmic and intercellular factors. Normally the intra-organic conditions of development are relatively constant.

The environment external to the organism may conveniently be differentiated into *prenatal* and *postnatal*. The prenatal environment, like the intra-organic conditions discussed above, is, under normal circumstances, relatively constant for different members of a species and for a given individual from time to time. However, it is possible to show that accidental or experimentally produced alterations in the immediate environment of the very young organism effect marked changes in its structures and in its rate of development. Glandular, nutritional, and mechanical factors are significant in this connection.

During the prenatal stage of development

it is not possible for the external environment of the parent to have any specific influence upon the growing organism. The external environment has a significant and quite specific influence after birth. Nevertheless, experiments with identical twins have shown that these individuals, possessing the same inheritance and closely similar prenatal conditions of development, are similar in physical characteristics and in intelligence even when reared in diverse environments. These results show that despite wide differences in postnatal conditions of development, individuals with the same inheritance and prenatal conditions tend to retain a large degree of the similarity present at birth. Experiments with animals have also shown that marked differences in behavior occur in a constant postnatal environment, the differences being associated with the combinations of genes transmitted to the individual by its parents. In a constant environment one may produce dull and bright or active and inactive "races" of rats merely by determining the nature of the genes received.

In the light of the above evidence, one must conclude that the characteristic structures upon which the behavior of species and individuals depends is determined by the genes in association with the intracellular, intercellular, and external conditions of development. Disturbance of any one of these factors, inherent or environmental, may produce anomalous structures and behavior. So integrally related are inherent and environmental conditions that it is impossible, except under controlled experimental conditions, to differentiate between their respective contributions to the development of an organism.

The differentiating influence of the environment becomes increasingly great as one goes from lower animals to man. The more complex the organism, the more susceptible it is to these differentiating effects. While one might with some degree of confidence state that two or more rats have the *same* environment, one could hardly make such a claim for two or more human beings. Even within a given family, one child will react to certain aspects of the environment and another child to others. Likewise, exactly the same object may arouse a much wider diversity of responses in human beings than in lower organisms.

The differences between men and other animals are attributable almost entirely to differences in genes. Differentiations within a species, however, are normally due to differences in genes and in environment. In other words, one cannot make a man out of a rat by variation of environment, but one can make somewhat different kinds of men and different kinds of rats in this way. Furthermore, an environmental diversity can produce greater differences in men than in rats. This is because men (owing to the inheritance of better sensory, neural, and motor equipment, as well as to language and cultural transmission) respond more readily than rats to changes in their environment. Heredity and environment are thus integrally related at every point.

These considerations should be clearly understood by the reader, for we shall frequently refer to them in later discussions of the phylogeny of unlearned behavior, of the ontogenesis of human behavior, and of individual differences in various psychological traits.

REFERENCES

1. Snyder, L. H., *The Principles of Heredity* (3d ed.). Boston: Heath, 1946, p. 179.
2. Tryon, R. C., "Individual Differences," in F. A. Moss (ed.), *Comparative Psychology* (rev. ed.). New York: Prentice-Hall, 1942, pp. 330–365.
3. Tryon, R. C., "Genetic Differences in Maze-Learning Ability in Rats," *39th Annual Yearbook, National Society for the Study of Education*, 1940, 111–119.
4. Heron, W. T., "The Inheritance of Maze-Learning Ability in Rats," *J. Comp. Psychol.*,

1935, *19*, 77–89; and "The Inheritance of Brightness and Dullness in Maze-Learning Ability in the Rat," *J. Genet. Psychol.*, 1941, *59*, 41–49.

5. Searle, L. V., "The Organization of Hereditary Maze-Brightness and Maze-Dullness," *Genet. Psychol. Monog.*, 1949, *39*, 279–325.

6. Rundquist, E. A., "Inheritance of Spontaneous Activity in Rats," *J. Comp. Psychol.*, 1933, *16*, 415–438. See also E. G. Brody, "Genetic Basis of Spontaneous Activity in the Albino Rat," *Comp. Psychol. Monog.*, 1942, *17*, No. 5, 1–24.

7. Hall, C. S., "The Inheritance of Emotionality," *Sigma Xi Quart.*, 1938, *26*, 17–27, 37; and "The Genetics of Behavior," in S. S. Stevens (ed.), *Handbook of Experimental Psychology*. New York: Wiley, 1951, pp. 308–309.

8. Maier, N. R. F., "Studies of Abnormal Behavior in the Rat. XIV. Strain Differences in the Inheritance of Susceptibility to Convulsions," *J. Comp. Psychol.*, 1943, *35*, 327–335. Maier, N. R. F. and N. M. Glaser, "Studies of Abnormal Behavior in the Rat. V. The Inheritance of the 'Neurotic Pattern,'" *J. Comp. Psychol.*, 1940, *30*, 413–418. Also see W. J. Griffiths, "Transmission of Convulsions in the White Rat," *J. Comp. Psychol.*, 1942, *34*, 263–277.

9. Hall, C. S., "Genetic Differences in Fatal Audiogenic Seizures Between Two Inbred Strains of House Mice," *J. Heredity*, 1947, *38*, 2–6.

10. Snyder, L. H., *The Principles of Heredity* (3d ed.). Boston: Heath, 1946, p. 84.

11. *Ibid.*, p. 84.

12. *Ibid.*, p. 135.

13. *Ibid.*, pp. 138–149.

14. East, E. M., "Genetic Aspects of Certain Problems of Evolution," *Amer. Nat.*, 1936, *70*, 143–158. Quotation from p. 151.

15. Shull, A. F., *Heredity* (4th ed.). New York: McGraw-Hill, 1948, pp. 153–154.

16. Marquis, D. G., "The Criterion of Innate Behavior," *Psych. Rev.*, 1930, *37*, 334–349.

17. Jennings, H. S., *The Biological Basis of Human Nature*. New York: Norton, 1930.

18. Reported by H. E. Walter, *Genetics*. New York: Macmillan, 1914, p. 32.

19. Jennings, *op. cit.*, pp. 93–94.

20. Child, C. M., *The Origin and Development of the Nervous System from a Physiological Viewpoint*. Chicago: University of Chicago Press, 1921.

21. Hoskins, R. G., *Endocrinology*. New York: Norton, 1941, pp. 369–371. Also see B. H. Willier, T. F. Gallagher, and F. C. Koch, "The Modification of Sex Development in the Chick Embryo by Male and Female Sex Hormones," *Physiol. Zool.*, 1937, *10*, 101–122.

22. Marquis, *op. cit.*, p. 341.

23. Stockard, C. R., "The Artificial Production of a Single Median Eye in the Fish Embryo by Means of Sea-Water Solutions of Magnesium Chloride." *J. Comp. Neur. & Psychol.*, 1909, *17*, 191–192.

24. Gudernatsch, J. F., "Feeding Experiments on Tadpoles," *Arch. Entw. Mech.*, 1913, *35*, 457–483.

25. Rowntree, L. G., J. H. Clark, and A. M. Hanson, "The Biological Effects of Thymus Extract (Hanson)," *Science*, 1934, *80*, 274–275.

26. Moss, F. A., and T. Hunt, *Foundations of Abnormal Psychology*. New York: Prentice-Hall, 1932, p. 429.

27. Carmichael, L., "Heredity and Environment: Are They Antithetical?" *J. Abn. & Soc. Psychol.*, 1925, *20*, 257.

28. Newman, H. H., F. N. Freeman, and K. J. Holzinger, *Twins: A Study of Heredity and Environment*. Chicago: University of Chicago Press, 1937.

29. Scheinfeld, A., *You and Heredity* (new ed.). Philadelphia: Lippincott, 1950. On pp. 422–423 there is a discussion of additional cases of identical twins reared apart and also of similarities and differences in human quadruplets and in the Dionnes.

30. Malinowski, B., *Sex and Repression in Savage Society*. New York: Harcourt, Brace, 1927.

31. See especially Margaret Mead's *Cooperation and Competition Among Primitive Peoples*, New York: McGraw-Hill, 1937; and *Sex and Temperament in Three Primitive Societies*, New York: Morrow, 1935.

32. Mead, M., *Sex and Temperament in Three Primitive Societies*. New York: Morrow, 1935.

33. Dunn, L. C., and Th. Dobzhansky, *Heredity, Race and Society* (rev. ed.). New York: New American Library, 1952, pp. 36–37.

SUGGESTIONS FOR FURTHER READING

Anastasi, A., and J. P. Foley, *Differential Psychology* (rev. ed.). New York: Macmillan, 1949, Chapter 4.

Dunn, L. C. (ed.), *Genetics in the 20th Century.* New York: Macmillan, 1951.

Dunn, L. C., and Th. Dobzhansky, *Heredity, Race and Society.* New York: New American Library (A Mentor Book), 1952.

Fuller, J. L., "Nature and Nurture: A Modern Synthesis," *Doubleday Papers in Psychology.* New York, 1954, No. 4, 1–40.

Hall, C. S., "The Genetics of Behavior," Chapter 9 in S. S. Stevens (ed.), *Handbook of Experimental Psychology.* New York: Wiley, 1951.

Kalmus, H., *Genetics.* London: Penguin Books, 1950.

Scheinfeld, A., *You and Heredity* (new ed.). Philadelphia: Lippincott, 1950.

Shull, A. F., *Heredity* (4th ed.). New York: McGraw-Hill, 1948.

Snyder, L. H., *The Principles of Heredity* (3d ed.). Boston: Heath, 1946.

Winchester, A. M., *Genetics.* Boston, Houghton Mifflin, 1951.

3

Unlearned Behavior

ALL animals display certain relatively stereotyped responses which do not require specific training for their first appearance. These responses are from one point of view phylogenetic; they represent the individual's racial heritage. Some of them develop before birth and others later, but their pattern is determined in large measure by the racial genes. We refer to such responses as "unlearned" to distinguish them from habits, which differ a great deal from one individual to another and which depend upon such modes of learning as practice, training, and observation of similar behavior in others.

In the present chapter we attempt to answer certain questions regarding unlearned behavior. What are the criteria of such behavior? What experimental techniques are required in its investigation? How may unlearned reactions be differentiated and classified? What is their relation to the physiological needs which every organism has and which must be satisfied if an optimal adjustment to its world is to be achieved? What are these physiological needs? What, if any, inborn patterns of behavior are provided for their satisfaction? How do innate patterns of behavior originate, and how are they transmitted to future generations? How do unlearned reactions function in the individual's adjustment? What stimuli or stimulus patterns activate or release them? Does man have the same physiological needs as other organisms? Is he, like other animals, equipped with unlearned reactions? These and many related questions are of interest to genetic psychologists who turn their attention to unlearned behavior.

An organism, as we have suggested, behaves in a certain way for various reasons. One reason is that its structures (sense organs, nervous system, muscles, and skeletal make-up) are conducive to certain kinds of behavior (such as walking, flying, manipulating). Structures differ greatly from one species to another. Even within a given species, they differ in certain respects with age. Their functioning at any time is also dependent upon what has happened during the lifetime of the individual, including what it has learned. This is represented in modifications of the nervous system. Structures and structural integrations are initially determined, as we have already pointed out, by the reciprocal action of the genes and the conditions which surround them. When responses appear as a function of structures, and integrations of these structures, developed before birth, they are usually regarded as unlearned.* Other general terms frequently applied to such behavior are "innate," "na-

* Later we shall be called upon to question this assumption, since there is evidence that some learning may occur before birth.

tive," and "congenital." When these behavior patterns are *racial* in origin (that is, relics of our animal rather than our individual human ancestry), they are said to be "tropistic," "reflex," or "instinctive," depending upon their characteristics. Not all unlearned behavior occurs at birth, however, or even soon after. Sexual responses, for example, await the delayed development of certain necessary structures, particularly the sex glands. When behavior patterns are observed to result from such delayed structural growth, and can be demonstrated as independent of specific environmental influences such as training or observation of the performance of others, they are likewise designated as unlearned, regardless of the age at which they appear. The process which underlies their development is referred to as "maturation." On the other hand, behavior produced by structural changes which depend upon specific environmental influences is said to be "acquired" or "learned."

As we have already pointed out, the appearance of structures and of the behavior which depends upon them has both inherent and environmental sources. Hence it is not as easy to differentiate between learned and unlearned aspects as the above discussion might imply. For this reason some psychologists have questioned the utility, and even the possibility, of distinguishing between learned or acquired behavior on the one hand and unlearned or innate behavior on the other. The behavior of a given organism is, they claim, dependent upon both inherent and environmental conditions, and these conditions are inseparable after fertilization has taken place. In our previous discussion of this question, however, we demonstrated that it is sometimes possible experimentally to hold inherent conditions constant while the influence of environmental conditions is observed. Likewise, constant environmental conditions may be maintained while one observes the effect of different inherent factors. Similar techniques, when applied to behavior, enable investigators to discover which re-

actions occur primarily as a function of inherent factors and which occur primarily as a function of environmental conditions such as training and imitation. We shall discuss such techniques later.

General Criteria

There have been many attempts to differentiate between learned and unlearned behavior on a purely rational and observational basis without resort to experimental controls such as those just mentioned. Thus the *universality* of a behavior pattern within a species has been said to indicate its unlearnedness and its dependence upon the racial genes. Likewise the *sequential development* of certain behavior patterns has been used as a criterion of their innateness. Some authors have claimed, also, that the *peculiar adaptiveness* of certain acts argues for their phylogenetic origin. We shall briefly consider and critically evaluate each of these criteria before discussing experimental approaches to the problems of unlearned behavior.

Universality

Phylogenetically derived behavior must be present in all normal members of a species. This is because it depends upon the possession by each individual of similar genes and early conditions of development. However, the mere universality of a response is no guarantee of its unlearnedness. Some responses are exhibited by all normal members of the group because they depend upon a common type of motivation, a common form of structure, and subjection to a common type of environmental influence. Such responses are acquired as the most adequate ones under the circumstances. To illustrate this fact we shall consider some observations made upon white rats.

Fernberger [1] reports data on rats crowded together in large cages, 250 to 400 in a cage. The rats were placed in the cages while too young to have acquired from their parents the behavior about to be described. Fernberger observed that the animals jump up and hang by their teeth from the wire mesh of the cages. They sleep in such a position without disturbance from the milling mass of animals below them. To the observer these rats appear to be dead. Without the crowding of a large number of animals into a small space, no such reaction appears. Fernberger regards this as an excellent example of unlearned behavior requiring a set of peculiar circumstances for its appearance, namely, a cage constructed of wire mesh, together with crowded conditions.

It is likely, however, that the universality of this response under these conditions can be explained in terms of the structure of the animal, a need for sleep, and a consequent learning of the most adequate means of escaping an "intolerable" situation. The rats are biologically similar. They possess in common a certain form of dental structure, a certain ability to climb or jump upwards, and a need for sleep. These biological similarities are, to be sure, a function of racial inheritance and racial conditions of development, but they do not determine the precise behavior of hanging by the teeth from wire mesh. In order to understand this behavior one must take cognizance of the conditions of elicitation. The wire mesh of the cage is such that the teeth may be hooked over it. Furthermore, it is sufficiently high to enable the rat to hang clear of other animals. In addition, the situation is such that necessary sleep is impossible without escape from the crowd. In the light of these considerations it is quite reasonable to suppose that each rat will attempt this and that means of escape. If hanging from the wire mesh by means of the teeth is the only, or the most adequate, way of escape, each rat will eventually acquire it. The stereotypy of the response, moreover, depends upon the rats' structure and the relation of this structure to the nature of the situation. In the present situation, teeth and wire mesh are perhaps the most significantly related factors.

In situations comparable with the above, many reactions are frequently possible. All individuals may acquire one of them because it is most adequate or, in the case of human beings, because it is sanctioned by the group. The *unlearned* aspects of the behavior are the structure of the organism and the need for sleep, nourishment, warmth, or the like. The expression of these factors takes the form of an *acquired* behavior pattern. This pattern tends to be alike in all members of the species (1) when it is the only adequate one, (2) when it is the most adequate one, or (3) where group pressure demands that it, of all the possible patterns, be the one acquired. Such acquired behavior patterns, when they appear in all or most members of a species, are designated as universal habits, or *coenotropes*. They are thus differentiated from phylogenetically derived responses which represent, in other words, the innate behavioral heritage of the species.

From the above considerations it should be apparent that the universality of a response, while suggestive, is not an indubitable indication of its unlearnedness.

Sequentiality

Sometimes patterns of reaction emerge gradually, the various aspects appearing in accordance with a rather definite schedule which differs from one species to another, but which is quite similar for all normal members of a given species. Such a sequence is often regarded as indicative of the unlearnedness of the behavior in question.[2]

Where the environment of the organism is either constant or variable in a non-sequential manner, and yet the development of behavior follows a rather definite sequence like that described, there is no other alternative than to regard the behavior, in its essential aspects at least, as unlearned. Prenatal behavior often fulfills these conditions. In the case of behavior which develops after birth, however, it is necessary to prove that environmental factors are ineffective, as far as determination of the sequence is concerned, before concluding that the responses are unlearned. Locomotion in the human infant, for example, can hardly be regarded as unlearned *merely* because it develops in accordance with a rather definite schedule. It is necessary to show that the stimulation received by the child from adults and other children follows no correlated sequence. Several experiments with animals have demonstrated that, even in isolation, the normal sequences and ultimate patterns appear. But the proof does not come from the sequential nature of the behavioral development alone, or even primarily. Rather it comes from the fact that all possibilities of learning the behavior have been removed. This is tantamount to saying that behavior is unlearned when it is proved, by analysis or experimental control of environmental conditions, to be unlearned.

Hence, like that of universality, the criterion of sequential development is not, in itself, a sure indication of the unlearnedness of a response. Many *learned* activities follow a sequence, later developments depending upon mastery of earlier stages in a developmental hierarchy. Furthermore, some responses which are demonstrably unlearned do not show an externally evident sequence of development, and thus would not be indicated by the use of this criterion. They appear suddenly and are almost perfect in function from the beginning. Many responses of insects exemplify this statement. The sexual response in some mammals is of a similar character.

Peculiar adaptiveness

It has been suggested on many occasions that unlearned behavior has a peculiar adaptiveness; that it evidences a wisdom which transcends that which the animal conceivably can have. Many examples of such adaptiveness are to be found in the literature, and especially in that which deals with the behavior of insects.

Apparently in order that its larvae may have fresh meat, as well as a warm substance on which to develop, the wasp *Ammophila* stings and paralyzes a caterpillar. She then lays her eggs upon the helpless, yet living, creature. Paralysis is effected by stinging the caterpillar in appropriate places along its spinal ganglion.* Hingston [3] says that:

In this act we see the wisdom of instinct developed to an amazing degree. For the wasp behaves as if she understood the internal anatomy of her victim. She not only injects her poison into its nervous system, but actually strikes the one spot in that system which can cause the kind of paralysis she requires.

It is hardly possible that these organisms could learn complicated and well-adapted acts of such a nature. For this reason many have regarded the behavior as unlearned, as instinctive. Hingston says of the behavior of *Ammophila*, for example:

Thus we see how wise Instinct can be. Indeed it may be said to surpass Intelligence in the knowledge that it seems to possess.... As the race is more stable and enduring than the individual, so is the wisdom of racial origin more perfect than that which the individual acquires.

Peculiar adaptiveness such as that discussed above is, if it can be substantiated, good presumptive evidence of the unlearned nature of a response. However, this criterion is of restricted usefulness in differentiating learned and unlearned behavior. Many unlearned responses are clearly not adaptive in a teleological sense. Take, for example, the flight of moths and other insects into a flame. The response is, from the point of view of survival, extremely maladapted, nevertheless unlearned. Furthermore, learned responses sometimes involve a high degree of adaptiveness. This is particularly true in the higher organisms.

As we have pointed out several times already, the surest indication that a response is unlearned is its appearance when all opportunity for learning it has been eliminated. Such elimination does not always require the relatively artificial experiments of the laboratory. In many instances nature itself has

* This interpretation has been questioned by some. It appears that the animal frequently misses ganglia.

provided requisite controls. Take, for example, pollination behavior of the yucca moth. Stone [4] analyzes this behavior and points out its obvious unlearnedness. He says:

After eating some of the tender ovules, the larvae cut holes through the ovary, spin webs, descend to the ground, burrow beneath its surface, and pass the winter there in the pupal state, from which they emerge at the time the yucca is in flower. The adult does not partake of the pollen which it gathers and probably obtains no nourishment at all from the plant while performing this round of complicated activities. Finding the flower is itself an unlearned response, a type of chemotropism so common among insects. *The adult insect does not learn this complicated routine of acts through imitation of its parents, long since dead, or contemporaries either, for its visual receptors do not provide the kind of vision necessary to the human's concept of visual. Action systems of the larvae are totally unlike those of adults, and the activities are even performed with different appendages; the body of this selfsame larva that descended the silken thread to bury itself in the ground is differentiated and resynthesized during the resting state; finally, a prolonged interval of time, the winter season, intervenes between the last act of the larva and the first of the adult. In view of these facts, no concept of memory or transfer of training that is supported by experimental evidence can be invoked to account for the behavior of the yucca moth.*

Responses in many insects may be analyzed on a similar basis. Such analysis is also possible in higher animals than insects. If, for example, one stimulates with a galvanic current animals which could have received no such stimulation during the earlier course of their development, and a definitely predictable response occurs, he is safe in assuming that the response is unlearned. Likewise, the pupil of the eye is not stimulated by light until the time of birth. Hence a response which occurs the first time light strikes the pupil must be unlearned. If such responses are present in every normal member of the species, moreover, it is fairly safe to assume that they represent phylogenetic influences; that they are determined by the genes and conditions of development characteristic of the race from which the individual is derived.

When such controls as we have mentioned are absent in nature, one who wishes to differentiate between learned and unlearned reactions must produce such conditions experimentally. Methods used to test for the unlearnedness of behavior will now be considered.

Experimental Evidence for Unlearned Behavior

Two experimental procedures are widely used in the attempt to identify unlearned responses. Both achieve the same goal, which is to eliminate all possibility of acquiring the response in question. If the response fails to occur under these conditions, one assumes that it is normally acquired. If, however, it still appears, one assumes that it is unlearned.

The *isolation method* segregates an animal from stimulation which might in any way lead to acquisition of the response in question. This may involve segregation from more mature fellows (social isolation) or it may, in addition, involve removal from non-social conditions of a kind calculated to arouse and stimulate practice of the response. The other method, often used in combination with the first, involves actual *prevention of activity* relevant to the response under consideration. This may be achieved by placing the animal in a cast or other restraining device, or by anesthetizing it.

In their essential aspects both of these methods comprise (1) separation of similarly constituted animals into two or more groups, one group developing normally while the others develop under controlled conditions, and (2) testing of the groups reared under controlled conditions at a time when members of the normal group are showing the response. If the segregated or restrained animals exhibit some aspects of the response and not others, as often happens in such experiments, the learned and unlearned aspects can be distinguished.

Consideration of a few representative experiments will serve to illustrate the above methods and to indicate typical outcomes. Experiments illustrating the isolation method are considered first.

Several investigators [5] have used the isolation method to study the development of mating behavior in white rats. Both the male and the female mating patterns have been carefully observed under normal conditions, sometimes by use of slow-motion photography. Thus the normal responses are well known. All normal males react very much alike. The same is true of females. We also know that mating normally occurs for the first time at puberty (around the beginning of the third month of life) and that females are responsive to male advances only on every fourth or fifth day, the day of heat. The problem, then, is to see whether the typical mating patterns are exhibited by rats reared in isolation from infancy until the time of puberty. Each isolated rat, when it reaches puberty, is placed with a receptive animal of the opposite sex. Usually, under such circumstances, the mating pattern typical of normally reared rats is soon elicited. The different investigators agree that this pattern is an outcome of structural growth and that previous relevant experience is not necessary for its appearance. This outcome is especially interesting since, in chimpanzees and men, structural growth is not sufficient to produce a uniform pattern and the different patterns which appear from one individual to another are greatly dependent upon what has been learned.[6]

Maternal behavior in rats is also clearly patterned. The maternal pattern, which includes care of the young at birth, nest-building, retrieving, and nursing, is quite similar whether or not the rat has had other litters and whether or not it has had any opportunity to observe this behavior beyond the time of its own infancy.[7]

The pecking response in chicks has been subjected to intensive study. Spalding [8] first called attention to the accuracy of pecking. He claimed that a high level of accuracy is maintained even when chicks are blindfolded or kept in a darkened basket from the time of hatching. Research on the pecking response is worthy of our attention for two reasons. In the first place, it provides an interesting and worthwhile study in method. In the second place, it shows how innate and learned aspects of behavior are sometimes coexistent and interrelated in a behavior pattern which, to cursory observation, seems completely unlearned.

Another analysis of pecking behavior, more careful than that carried out by Spalding, led Breed [9] to conclude that pecking is not initially very accurate. Three reactions are quite clearly involved; namely, striking the grain, seizing it, and swallowing. Sometimes the chick attempts to strike, but misses. Sometimes it strikes, but fails to seize the grain. Sometimes it strikes and seizes, but fails to swallow. If one considers the series of acts culminating in that of swallowing a grain, the initial accuracy is only 15 per cent. However, the accuracy of the striking-seizing-swallowing sequence increases with practice. The increase in accuracy is rapid at first, then slow. After 25 days of practice, the maximum accuracy is about 84 per cent.

The question which now arises is this: What would happen if chicks were prevented from pecking at visual objects until they were, say, three, four, or five days old? Would the older chicks have a higher initial accuracy than the younger ones? Would they improve more or less rapidly than chicks allowed to peck at visual objects from the time of hatching? If the older chicks were more accurate and if they improved faster than younger chicks, this would argue for maturation as the basis of improved accuracy. But if the opposite were true, then the improvement could be attributed to learning. This issue, as framed by Shepard and Breed,[10] involves the relative influence of "maturation and use in the development of an instinct."

Experiments on pecking have been carried out by many investigators,[11] but only the typical and comprehensive study of Cruze[12] will be considered in detail here. Like the earlier investigators, Cruze reared his chicks in darkness so that no visually initiated pecking could occur until the chicks were tested. The chicks were fed by placing small pellets in their mouths. They were given water with a medicine dropper. Different groups were kept under these conditions for periods ranging from 24 to 120 hours after hatching. The various experimental conditions are indicated in Table 1. Hunger was kept constant by giving the same amount of food each day regardless of whether it was placed in the bill by hand in the darkroom or whether it was obtained by pecking under natural conditions, as in the tests. During the test a chick was placed on a well-lighted table and one piece of grain at a time was placed before it. Each test was separated from the preceding one by a period of 24 hours. There was an attempt to equate all the chicks in everything except the period of isolation and the amount of practice allowed in the tests.

The average number of reactions culminating in swallowing, in each of the daily tests, is shown in Figure 21. These results, which are analyzed more fully in the legend, show that there is a low initial accuracy, a rapid improvement in accuracy with age, and a *faster* improvement in older than in younger chicks. These results substantiate those of earlier investigators. They suggest that maturation is a potent factor in development of the pecking response. However, it is interesting to ask what might happen if the pecks allowed in each test were reduced to a relatively small number. In other words, what influence is exerted by daily practice? All the chicks represented in the figure were given 25 pecks in each daily test. After the initial test period, however, they fed naturally. Each subsequent test period merely sampled the degree of accuracy so far attained. Much of the improvement might have been influenced by practice not involved in the tests. It was for this reason that Cruze also used groups (see Table 1) which remained in darkness between tests and were thus limited to 12 or 25 practice pecks. These groups did not attain a very high level of accuracy. Those with 25 pecks per day improved, but reached a level only one-half as accurate as that of the groups which fed naturally after the tests. The group with only 12 pecks per day exhibited almost no improvement in the striking-seizing-swallowing sequence. In a group given 12 pecks per day for 10 days, then 25 pecks thereafter, marked improvement followed the increased amount of practice. These results show that, although ma-

Table 1. Experimental Conditions for the Eight Groups of Chicks in Cruze's Investigation

Group	Number in each group	Age when taken from dark room (hours)	Number of pecks each test	Method of subsequent feeding
A	26	24	25	Natural
B	25	48	25	Natural
C	25	72	25	Natural
D	25	96	25	Natural
E	25	120	25	Natural
F	25	24	12	In dark 20 days
G	25	24	25	In dark 20 days
H	26	24	12 for 10 days, 25 for next 10	In dark 20 days

turation is important, learning is also involved.

Analysis of the results for separate aspects of the striking-seizing-swallowing sequence demonstrated quite clearly which aspects are instinctive and which learned. The fact that a small visual stimulus elicits pecking, even when seen for the first time, and that it does so in all chicks, shows that pecking is dependent upon inborn mechanisms and does

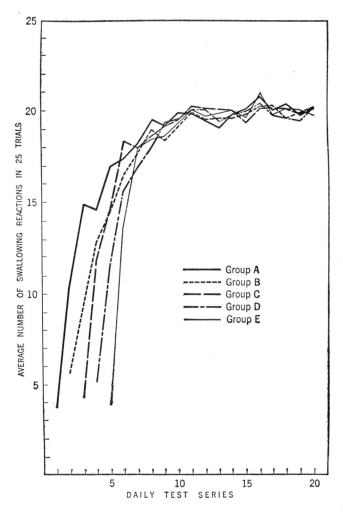

Figure 21. The Swallowing Reactions of Five Groups of Chicks Taking Their Initial Tests at One, Two, Three, Four, and Five Days, Respectively, After Hatching

All the chicks were reared and tested alike except that some were given their initial test at one day, some at two days, and so on. The curve shows that there is in each group a low initial accuracy and a rapid improvement. It also demonstrates that the *rate* of improvement in older chicks is faster than that in younger ones. For example, the one-day group (A) required 15 days to make its first score of 20 swallows out of 25 pecks, the two-day group (B) reached this score after ten days of practice, the three-day group (C) reached the same level of accuracy in 9 days, the four-day group (D) required 8 days, and the five-day group (E) required only 7 days. (From W. W. Cruze, "Maturation and Learning in Chicks," *J. Comp. Psychol.*, 1935, *19*, 386.)

not result from learning. But what we have been discussing is the *accuracy* with which a grain is struck, seized, and swallowed. Only two aspects of the sequence are instinctive, the accuracy of striking the pecked-at grain and swallowing. As illustrated in Figure 22, accuracy in striking a grain improved with age, even in the initial tests, where there had been no practice. Chicks given their first 25 pecks after 24 hours in the dark missed only six times. That is to say, out of 25 pecks they struck the grain 19 times. Chicks given their first pecks after 48 hours missed only four times. Finally, chicks given their first pecks after 120 hours of darkness hardly ever missed. Practice apparently had no influence on this reaction. Maturation alone brought complete, or almost complete, accuracy within a few days. Swallowing itself is a reflex. It is apparently not influenced by practice.

Once it had struck the grain, a chick might or might not seize it. Here practice was shown to play an important role. The striking-

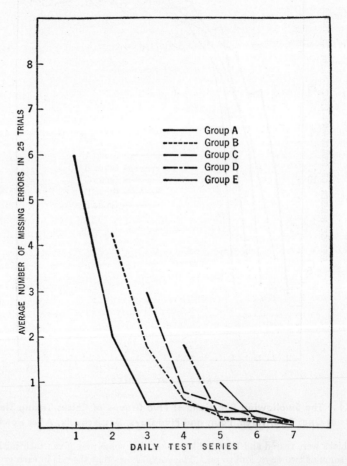

Figure 22. Missing Errors of Chicks Given Their First Opportunity to Peck When They Were, Respectively, One, Two, Three, Four, and Five Days Old

The data here represented indicate that the older the chick the greater the initial accuracy in hitting a grain. They also show that there is a rapid increase in accuracy with near elimination of errors at the fifth or sixth day. (From W. W. Cruze, "Maturation and Learning in Chicks," *J. Comp. Psychol.*, 1935, *19*, 391.)

seizing response improved with practice as did the total sequence previously discussed. Sometimes, having seized the grain, a chick dropped it before swallowing could occur. This response was similarly frequent in all groups; thus delayed pecking had no influence upon it.

That an instinct may lapse from disuse has also been demonstrated with the pecking response in chicks. Padilla [13] found that chicks prevented from pecking for eight days or longer subsequently fail to peck at single grains.

Further data on unlearned behavior are offered by Carmichael's [14] experiment. In this investigation tadpoles were completely immobilized until the time at which swimming normally occurs. Obtaining eggs of frogs and salamanders during the early stages of cell division, Carmichael kept them in his laboratory until the head and tail buds appeared. At this time, before the peripheral nervous system had developed and, of course, before any movement had yet appeared, the animals were separated into two groups. One group was placed in a dish of ordinary tap water. The other group was at the same time placed in a weak solution of chloretone. This drug, while it does not interfere with neuromuscular growth, produces complete immobilization. For the anesthetized animals, therefore, practice was impossible. These tadpoles remained in the chloretone solution until those in the tap water were swimming in a normal manner. They were then removed to tap water and stimulated with a rod, the time of their first reactions being noted. Their first movements appeared within from 6 to 25 minutes after removal from chloretone. Within 30 minutes both frog and salamander tadpoles were exhibiting a typical swimming reaction.

What happened during the period between removal from chloretone and the appearance of swimming? Did rapid learning occur during the interval? Was the delayed appearance of swimming due to a continuation of the effect of the chloretone, this requiring

about 30 minutes to wear off? In a further experiment, Carmichael [15] substantiated his former results and at the same time obtained an answer to these questions. He placed in the chloretone solution some tadpoles which had been raised in a normal manner and which had been swimming for some time. When these animals were returned to tap water they also required a period for the effects of the drug to wear off. Carmichael concluded from his experiments that development of swimming in these animals depends upon the interdependent action of inherent and environmental influences. However, there is no possibility that it could, in the usually accepted sense of the term, have been learned. It depended upon internal growth processes which are a function of the race and age of the animal.

Thinking that the above results, since they were obtained under abnormal conditions, might be anomalous, Carmichael [16] carried out a check experiment using the isolation method of control. A number of salamander eggs in the early stages were divided into three groups. One group was removed to a light-proof, sound-proof, and almost completely vibration-proof room. Another was placed in a quiet part of the laboratory, but where changes in light and sound were present. The third group was placed in the laboratory workshop where there was much vibration and other stimulation. After the two groups outside of the control room were swimming normally, Carmichael stimulated the isolated animals with a flashlight. He reports that their behavior, although they had been deprived of normal stimulation, was not noticeably different from that of the other two groups. Furthermore, these two groups could not be distinguished on the basis of their behavior despite the differences in stimulation.

The above experiments and several similar ones have demonstrated conclusively that unlearned behavior exists. The appearance of unlearned behavior depends upon structural organization achieved as a function of inner growth, or maturation. Maturation, as we shall note in more detail later, results from the interaction of genes and conditions of development discussed in the preceding chapter.

Differentiation of Unlearned Behavior

When the overt characteristics and underlying mechanisms of unlearned responses are considered, three types may roughly be differentiated. These are *tropistic*, *reflex*, and *instinctive*. Such responses tend to shade into each other. In fact, some psychologists refer to all unlearned responses as instinctive. Others speak of reflexes and instincts, including tropistic with instinctive behavior. Still others, like Loeb, regard all unlearned behavior as essentially tropistic in nature.

Tropistic behavior

Tropistic behavior has been defined in many ways. The term *tropism*, however, can best be understood in terms of its origin. In 1832 De Candolle applied the term *heliotropism* to the behavior shown by plants when they bend toward the sun or some other source of illumination. This orientation toward light was regarded as a necessary consequence of the chemical constitution of the plant and the nature of photic stimulation. The term *tropism* was later extended to certain unlearned and stereotyped reactions of animals to sources of stimulation. It was, moreover, no longer restricted to orientation toward light. A response elicited by the force of gravity was designated as *geotropic*, a response elicited by electrical stimulation as *galvanotropic*, a response elicited by stimulation associated with the direction of movement of currents as *rheotropic*, a response elicited by chemicals in contact with the body as *chemotropic*, and a response elicited by surfaces of contact as *stereotropic*. These responses are but a few of those designated as tropistic. A further differentiation between tropistic forms of behavior is in terms of their positive or negative nature. A response

which brings the animal closer to the source of stimulation is said to be positive, while that which involves withdrawal from the source of stimulation is said to be negative. Thus, approaching a light is positively heliotropic (or phototropic) behavior, and withdrawing from it is negatively heliotropic behavior.

Definitions of tropisms all stress (1) their unlearned nature, (2) the fact that their elicitation is controlled by the structure of the animal's body and the properties of the external stimuli rather than by volition, (3) the fact that they involve the entire organism rather than some part of it, and (4) the fact that they are orienting responses which involve approach to or withdrawal from a source of stimulation.

The best-known concept concerning the mechanism of tropistic behavior is Loeb's [17] theory of "local action" or "muscle-tension." Loeb regards tropistic responses as forced movements, that is, movements over which the animal has no control. They are determined by the structure of its body and the nature of the external stimulus. A good example is the galvanotropism of salamanders. A larval salamander is subjected for the first time in its life to an electric current running through its body from head to tail or from tail to head. When stimulated in this manner the animal assumes definitely predictable postures. If the current flows from head to tail the salamander is forced into the posture shown in Figure 23 A. The legs are pushed backwards, the head is bent forward, and the entire body assumes a convex posture. When the current flows from the other direction, however, the legs come forward, the head goes up, and the concavity shown in Figure 23 B is elicited.

In animals which possess bilateral symmetry, Loeb supposed that orientation is determined by unequal stimulation of the receptors and by correlated inequalities of muscular tension. According to this view, equal stimulation of symmetrically located receptors produces an equal degree of tension in the muscles with which they are associated.

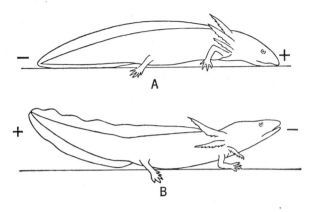

Figure 23. Forced Movements to an Electric Current in the Larval Salamander

(From J. Loeb, *Forced Movements, Tropisms, and Animal Conduct*, Philadelphia: Lippincott, 1918, p. 41.)

Since the affected muscles are also symmetrically located, the animal is forced to move in a straight line toward or away from the source of stimulation. When symmetrically located receptors are unequally stimulated, however, the unequal muscle-tension thereby produced forces the animal to orient until equal stimulation is restored.* Loeb believed that the behavior of asymmetrical animals may be explained in a somewhat comparable fashion. Absence of symmetry, according to Loeb, makes the analysis of behavior more difficult, but it does not change the fundamental principles involved. He assumed that all behavior is essentially tropistic, even in as complex an animal as man. He thought that man's great ability to learn, and especially his use of memory images, renders the tropistic character of his behavior only less evident than it would otherwise be.

* An analogy of the type of mechanism assumed by Loeb to explain tropistic behavior is John Hays Hammond's well-known automatic torpedo. On each side of the missile is a selenium cell. When these light-sensitive cells are equally stimulated by a source of illumination, they control mechanisms in the torpedo which drive it straight ahead. If the illumination is more intense on one side than on the other, however, the cell which receives greater stimulation sets in motion a steering device which turns the torpedo until the two sides are again equally stimulated. By alternations in its internal mechanisms, the torpedo may be made to back away from a source of illumination instead of approaching it. In other words, it may be made "negatively heliotropic." When the illumination is sufficiently weak, the torpedo comes to rest. Any other bilaterally symmetrical robot would also illustrate Loeb's idea.

Jennings[18] claimed that the behavior of simple organisms like *Amoeba* and *Paramecium* is too variable to fit Loeb's concept of tropisms. The behavior of these organisms, except in a few instances which seem to fit the tropistic envisagement, appears to be of a trial-and-error nature. Mast[19] has also critized Loeb's concept on a somewhat similar basis. Crozier and his collaborators at Harvard applied Loeb's tropistic envisagement to certain reactions of chickens, rats, guinea pigs, and other animals. For a review of this as well as other literature on tropisms, see Crozier and Hoagland[20]. Hunter[21] has argued that Crozier's envisagement of certain behavior of rats in terms of muscle-tension is too simple to fit the facts. Munn[22] has discussed this issue as it applies to rat behavior.

The literature contains many reports of behavior which seems to fit the muscle-tension envisagement. On the other hand, many responses are regarded as tropistic in a general sense, but not in the narrow sense implied by Loeb's concept. Many other unlearned forms of behavior do not appear to fit even a general tropistic classification. Some of them, like reflexes, involve a reaction primarily of some organ of the body rather than of the organism as a whole. Others are more than mere approach and withdrawal movements such as one finds in tropistic behavior. They involve movements nicely attuned to a changing situation both inside the organism and outside of it. The organism approaches, retreats,

surmounts an obstacle, or attacks another. No simple tropistic envisagement appears applicable in such instances. Many
forms of unlearned behavior are under the
control of physiological conditions such as
the presence or absence of hormones. External stimuli exert no control unless internal
physiological conditions are such as to render
the animal susceptible to their influence.
Loeb admitted the influence of such internal factors, and even pointed out where
reversal or other modification of tropisms
might take place as a result of satiation,
altered glandular conditions, and learning.

For the many unlearned responses which
do not seem to fit the tropistic envisagement,
other categories appear necessary. They are
the categories of reflex and instinct.

Reflex behavior

The reflex is an unlearned response which,
unlike tropisms, involves a *partial* reaction
of the organism to some rather specific form
of stimulation. It is not a diffuse orienting
reaction, but a *specific* one. It occurs in its
most characteristic form only in animals
which possess a synaptic nervous system.

The simplest organisms react to external
stimulation by approach, withdrawal, and
general orienting movements. Their reactions are mediated by relatively non-special-
ized protoplasm. Any part of the protoplasm
is susceptible to stimulation; any part of it
will conduct impulses aroused in adjacent
protoplasm; and any part of it possesses
motility. When the amoeba, for example, is
stimulated by some object in its surroundings
streaming movements are soon apparent.
The entire protoplasm seems to "flow" toward or away from the source of stimulation.
Stimulation of any part of the protoplasm
will elicit similar movements. All parts of the
animal possess motility. The reactions of
such animals are too diffuse and too slow to
be regarded as reflex.

Evolution has involved an increasing specialization of the primary functions of sensitivity, conductivity, and motility. Sensi-

tivity is eventually mediated by specialized
receptors. Conduction of impulses from the
source of stimulation to more remote parts of
the animal is performed by specialized nerve
fibers, connected by synapses, over which
impulses travel in only one direction. Likewise, motion is a specialized function of effectors. Specialization of these functions
and the structures which mediate them has
developed slowly. A relatively large amount
of specialization had to take place before true
reflexes made their appearance. The specialization of nervous structures and functions is
especially significant in this connection.

Several stages involved in the development
of the nervous system are illustrated in Figures 24–26. The muscles of some organisms
react directly to stimulation. Nervous mechanisms are not present and are not necessary
for muscular reaction, but reaction is slow
and diffuse. Gradually, however, nerve fibers
make their appearance and are associated
with the receptors at one end and the muscles
at the other. These fibers consist, at first, of
a diffuse network. Stimulation of any fiber
sends impulses to all parts of the animal,
which reacts in a generalized manner; there is
nothing in its behavior which corresponds to a
true reflex. Such responses are too slow and
too diffuse to be considered reflex. The jellyfish is a typical animal possessing the nerve-
net type of system. Such a system has been
designated by Parker [23] as *protoneuronic*. He
refers to the single fibers of the nerve-net as
protoneurons, since they are precursors of the
discrete nerve fibers, or neurons, connected
through synapses, which appear in animals
higher than the jellyfish.

The lowest organism in which reflex activity
clearly occurs is the sea-anemone, whose
nervous system is illustrated in Figure 24 *E*.
Here the nerve-net has been modified so that
a receptor is connected to a given muscle
through a relatively discrete nerve fiber.
Parker [24] says:

Such modifications of the nerve-net lead to conditions in which are realized the beginnings of un-
questionable reflex activity. In this form of

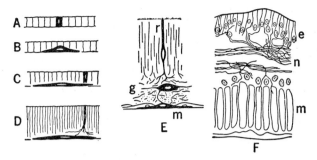

Figure 24. Stages in the Differentiation of the Neuromuscular Mechanism

A to *C*, hypothetic early stages: *A*, epithelial stage; *B*, muscle cell at the stage of the sponge; *C*, partially differentiated nerve cell in proximity to fully differentiated muscle cell. *D*, nerve and muscle cell of coelenterate stage; *E*, a type of receptor-effector system found in many parts of sea anemones, including not only receptors, *r*, with their nerve nets, and muscle cells, *m*, but also ganglion cells, *g*, in the nerve net; *F*, section at right angles to the sphincter of the bell of a jellyfish (Rhizostoma); *e*, epithelium of the subumbrellar surface; *n*, nervous layer; *m*, muscle layer. (After Parker. From S. W. Ranson and S. L. Clark, *The Anatomy of the Nervous System*, 8th ed., 1947, p. 2.)

response a definite motor or other efferent activity appears after the application of a specific stimulation. In other words, on the application of a definite stimulus not a diffuse response, but a highly particularized one appears.

Further specialization of the nervous system leads to neural organization such as that shown in Figures 25 and 26. Here we find clearly defined sensory and motor neurons.

The reflexes of vertebrates involve sensory-neural-motor patterns such as that illustrated in Figure 26. Stimulation of the receptor arouses an impulse in the adjacent sensory nerve-fiber. This impulse goes to the central nervous system where it is shunted to a motor nerve-fiber. The motor (or efferent) fiber carries the impulse to the muscle or other effector organ and a specific response occurs. In the simplest possible reflex of this type, only one synapse is involved. It lies between the sensory and motor neurons. Most reflexes are much more complex than this. Association neurons are located between the sensory and motor fibers. An impulse passing from a receptor in the limb to the association

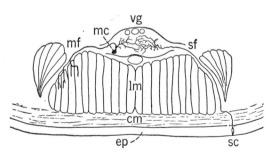

Figure 25. Transverse Section of the Ventral Chain and Surrounding Structures of an Earthworm

cm, circular muscles; *ep*, epidermis; *lm*, longitudinal muscles; *mc*, motor cell body; *mf*, motor nerve fiber; *sc*, sensory cell body; *sf*, sensory nerve fiber; *vg*, ventral ganglion. (From G. H. Parker, *The Elementary Nervous System*, Philadelphia: Lippincott, 1919, p. 18.)

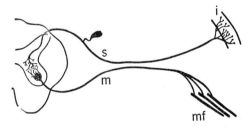

Figure 26. A Reflex Arc

Diagram of the primary sensory *s* and motor *m* neurons of the spinal cord of a vertebrate showing their connections with the integument *i* and the muscle fibers *mf*. (From Parker, *The Elementary Nervous System*, p. 17.)

neuron in the spinal cord may be transmitted to the brain or other parts of the organism as well as to the motor neuron which carries it to the effector. This tendency to involve the rest of the organism is, however, quite different from the diffuseness of response evident in a nerve-net system. The observable response, instead of being like that characteristic of the jellyfish and similar organisms, is quite specific. The arm is withdrawn, the eyelid closes, and so on.

It should be obvious that classification of reflexes is a well-nigh impossible task. Different stimuli arouse different reflexes. The nature of reflex activities differs for different animals. The reflexes present at any time, moreover, depend upon the organism's maturity. Many reflexes appear before birth; others make their appearance for a while and then disappear. Some of the most obvious human reflexes are discussed in Chapter 6.

Instinctive behavior

Instinctive behavior is partly characterized by the fact that it involves unlearned * co-ordinations of reflexes. Usually the instinc-

* In our discussion of heredity and environment it was pointed out that there is some question concerning the validity of any distinction between learned and unlearned behavior. The same question arises, obviously, in connection with any discussion of instinct. It is generally conceded as evident that tropistic behavior is unlearned; that it results from the physico-chemical properties of the organism and the properties of the stimulating conditions. Likewise, reflex behavior is regarded as obviously the result of stimulation passing over definite neural pathways connecting receptor and effector. Because of the relative simplicity of these forms of response the question concerning their unlearnedness seldom if ever arises. When we say, however, that *unlearned coordinations of reflexes* occur, a question arises as to the origin of the coordinations. Usually we assume that the nervous pathways subserving the reflexes are laid down in accordance with a certain plan, this plan being essentially the same as those involved in the physical integration of all structures of the body. Kuo,[26] however, has claimed that the term "instinct," as well as distinctions between learned and unlearned and inherited and acquired responses, should be discarded by psychologists. His objection is based principally upon the fact that behavior develops gradually, beginning long before birth, and that one level of coordination leads to another, until the complete pattern is present. He points out that the so-called instinctive patterns

tive act comprises a delicate adjustment to some situation, the adjustment involving many reflexes which work together in a highly integrated manner. In many instances instinctive behavior seems like a "chain" of reflexes, the elicitation of one reflex serving to discharge the next, and so on until the act has reached its consummation. For this reason, Watson [25] referred to instincts as series of "concatinated reflexes." He said, furthermore, that "the order of unfolding of the separate elements is a strictly heritable character."

Instinctive behavior, besides involving a coordination of reflexes, and thus differing from reflex behavior in terms of complexity, also differs from such behavior in that it is usually an adjustment involving the whole organism. In tropistic behavior, which likewise involves the entire organism, there is not the apparent flexibility and delicacy of adjustment that one finds in a typical instinctive response. In tropistic behavior the pattern is thoroughly stereotyped and relatively simple. In the instinctive response, however, there is, as it were, a "rough framework" rather than a completely worked-out pattern. Although stereotyped in its more general aspects, the instinctive response has sufficient variability to adapt the organism to changes in a situation. In building its nest,

do not appear suddenly, but that they have a long developmental history. Nowhere in this development, he claims, can one say which aspect is inherited or which acquired. Nor can one say that one aspect is unlearned, another learned. We have shown elsewhere (pp. 40–42), however, that despite the fact that inherent and environmental factors are normally so interwoven, it is possible under certain conditions to investigate, as it were, their separate influences. The entire controversy over instinct would perhaps be avoided were we to remember that the term is only descriptive of a certain kind of behavior; that it does not, nor is it intended to, *explain* the behavior in question. When we say that a coordination of reflexes is unlearned, we are merely pointing out that the coordination results from interaction of the genes and their immediate (uniform or uniformly changing) environment (i.e., from maturation) rather than from training or social stimulation. An explanation of how the integration occurs would require knowledge of the fundamental processes involved in neural integration.

for example, the bird follows a pattern characteristic of its kind. The oriole makes its typical hanging nest; the bluejay a much less elaborate depression composed of twigs. But these and other birds adapt their nests to different available locations and they often make appropriate use of different materials. Orioles usually build with plant fibers, but they will also use string or yarn. Even though the materials may differ, the nest has its characteristic shape. The fact that instinctive behavior is mediated by a complex nervous system, whereas tropistic behavior usually is not, may account for the great degree of variability and adaptability of the former.

Although animals without a receptor-effector nervous system have no reflexes and instincts, their only unlearned reactions being tropisms, this does not mean that animals with reflexes and instincts do not also react tropistically. We have already mentioned the tropistic reactions of rats and other mammals. However, in animals with a nervous system, tropistic reactions, while sometimes present, are much less evident than the more complex and variable instinctive responses. The existence of a complex nervous system also increases the modifiability of unlearned behavior. Tropisms may be modified as to direction, but instincts are modified in many ways, especially in the higher organisms.

Instincts are often internally controlled. One of the most significant differences between tropistic and reflex behavior on the one hand and instinctive behavior on the other is the fact that instinctive behavior is often internally driven or, as some would say, "goal-directed." It is peculiarly dependent upon "needs," "appetites," or blood chemistry. In a sense, therefore, instinctive behavior is to a large extent what Skinner [27] has called "operant" as against "respondent." In certain of its aspects it falls under the heading of "emitted behavior." Although stimuli of certain kinds are important in the arousal and maintenance of responses in an instinctive sequence, they are completely ineffective, with respect to such responses, unless internal physiological conditions are appropriate.

The mating response in rats is an excellent example of this internal drive aspect of instinctive behavior.[28] The mature female is not only unreceptive to male advances but actively rejects them unless she happens to be in the period of "heat," which occurs every fourth or fifth day. When in heat, on the other hand, she actively solicits mating and, upon appropriate stimulation from the male, places herself in a posture conducive to copulation. Many researches agree in showing that this receptivity to mating is associated with the presence of *estrin,* a hormone secreted into the blood stream by the ovaries. Ovariectomy eliminates sexual response and the grafting of ovaries or the injection of estrogenic hormones restores it. In the male, also, the presence of mating is correlated with gonadal hormone secretion. The androgenic hormone known as *testosterone* is crucial here. Castration leads to eventual elimination of mating behavior, but injections of testosterone restore it. Actually, as Beach and Holz [29] have shown, the male mating pattern matures even in rats gonadectomized soon after birth, but it is not elicited until, during the period of maturity, the rats are injected with testosterone and placed with a receptive female. In other words, the pattern is present neurologically, but two things are necessary for its arousal: (1) presence of the appropriate hormone, and (2) appropriate stimulation, as from a receptive female. Beach [30] has reviewed evidence which leads to the conclusion that sexual behavior in animals above the insect level is generally dependent upon the presence of gonadal hormones.

In rats, and perhaps in many other animals, maternal behavior is also peculiarly dependent upon internal physiological conditions. Several investigators [31] have shown that the rat which gives birth to a litter, even its first, goes through a sequence of activities which is characteristic of rats. Among these activities are removal of fetal membranes, unusually active nest-building, collecting the young in the nest, retrieving them when they crawl out, and hovering over them while they feed. Nest-building is normally decreased with an increase in temperature,[32] but the rat with a litter builds very actively regardless of temperature. This in itself shows how the effectiveness of an external condition may be altered by internal conditions. But what is particularly interesting in this connection is the dependence of the rat's maternal behavior upon hormones. Injection of *prolactin*, a gonadotropic hormone from the anterior pituitary gland, produces maternal behavior in virgin rats presented with a litter — rats which normally would fail to respond in a maternal way to young animals. Riddle, Lahr, and Bates [33] have concluded that several pituitary hormones influence the maternal drive, but that prolactin precipitates and regulates responses involved in the care and feeding of the young. The role of hormones in normally aroused maternal behavior is still under discussion, but the discussion takes for granted that hormones are involved. The question at issue is whether prolactin, or some other hormone, is indispensable.

There would be no point in enumerating all the forms of instinctive behavior in animals, even if this were possible. Actually, most of our knowledge concerning the initiation of such behavior is confined to sexual and maternal reactions. The fact that these have hormonal instigators should not lead us to gather that every instinctive response is initiated by hormones, or even by internal physiological conditions of some other sort. Singing in birds, as Metfessel [34] has demonstrated, is unlearned. Except where it is imitative, that is to say, initiated by the singing of some other bird, the song is apparently emitted. It is an expression of something inside the bird. But we do not know whether hormones or some other aspects of blood chemistry are involved.

Flying, swimming in aquatic animals, and other forms of locomotion in land animals are examples of instinctive behavior. These are utilized in the service of other forms of

motivation, such as food-getting, seeking a sexual partner, flight from danger, and so on. Flying, however, exemplifies a form of instinctive behavior which would not need to be initiated by internal factors. When a fully developed bird is launched, and begins to fall, the sensory consequences of falling may initiate the sequence of activities required in flight. Other locomotor activities may also be initiated by external stimuli, rather than (or in addition to) internal physiological conditions. Whether or not there is an internal physiological control, the external stimulating conditions are always important, not only in eliciting instinctive behavior but also in controlling the sequence of activities leading toward the consummatory response.

External control of instinctive behavior. What avenues of sensory stimulation are involved in particular instinctive activities? Questions of this nature are often answered by extirpating sense organs, anesthetizing parts of the body, or cutting nerve connections to sensory areas of the brain. Beach [35] demonstrated, for example, that mating in male rats is not dependent upon vision, hearing, smell, or tactual stimulation taken singly. He found, however, that rats deprived of several senses at the same time failed to copulate. Apparently what is necessarily involved is not any single form of stimulation but some pattern involving two or more senses.

A more direct approach to the problem of sensory stimulation is that used by the Lorenz-Tinbergen group of investigators in Europe and discussed in detail by Tinbergen.[36] The question asked is: "What aspect of the instinct-eliciting situation is essential in initiating the response?" The answer is sought by using dummies. Thus the gaping reaction of young thrushes is elicited * by models of the parent, provided that they are beyond a certain size and placed above the horizontal

---

* Tinbergen says that these models "release" rather than elicit the response. The reason for this will become clearer when we consider theoretical aspects of instinctive behavior, particularly the theoretical approach developed by Lorenz and Tinbergen.

plane passing through the nestling's eyes. Pecking at the parent's bill by chicks of the herring gull is also elicited by models of the head which have a red patch simulating that of the parent. Escape reactions of hens, ducks, and geese were elicited by dummy birds of prey flown overhead, but only if the model had a short neck. In many instances a dummy very different in certain respects from the actual animal, but having a certain specific characteristic of that animal, will elicit instinctive behavior where an otherwise perfect model does not do so. Take, for example, the model shown at the right in Figure 27. A highly detailed model — a model without, however, the swollen abdomen of a ripe stickleback — is much less effective in eliciting the male's courtship activities than is the crude model below, which does little beyond simulating the swollen abdomen. In addition to the swollen abdomen, female posturing is also important. A model which simulates this is more effective than a model which fails to simulate it. The female itself reacts primarily to the redness of the male's belly and to a peculiar zigzag pattern of movement. Models which simulate these aspects of the courting situation are maximally ef-

Figure 27. A Male Three-Spined Stickleback Courts a Crude Model of the Female

A model which faithfully simulates a female but which does not have the swollen abdomen of pregnancy is relatively ineffective. This model, which does not look much like a stickleback, but which has a swollen abdomen, is more effective than the other in eliciting courtship from the male. (From N. Tinbergen, *Social Behavior in Animals*, New York: Wiley, 1953, p. 27.)

fective in arousing the appropriate reactions of females.

Tinbergen, who speaks of the crucial stimulus aspects of each situation as "sign stimuli" and who also regards them as "releasing" rather than eliciting instinctive behavior, makes a point of the fact that animals are able to perceive other aspects of a situation even though their instinctive acts are not "released" by them. In other words, a male stickleback is said to be able to respond to other details of another male than the red belly, even though the red belly alone releases his instinctive fighting reactions.

Another point which requires mention, before we consider theoretical aspects, is that these "sign stimuli" are effective in "releasing" instinctive responses only under appropriate drive conditions. In the case of reproductive activities in the stickleback, as Tinbergen points out, even the most effective dummy in the reproductive season will have little or no effectiveness at other times.

Some theoretical issues. Why should a particular situation arouse one stereotyped unlearned pattern or sequence of reactions rather than some other, differing from one individual to another, as in the case of learned reactions? Writing some thirty years ago, Lashley [37] supposed that, in the case of reproductive behavior at least, hormones lower thresholds of response, thus facilitating the elicitation of relevant reaction patterns. At about the same time, Floyd Allport [38] suggested that instinctive reaction patterns are prepotent over others. He had in mind such facts as these: Scratching the saddle area of a dog causes him to raise his foot and scratch. But if a painful stimulus is simultaneously applied to the foot, withdrawal takes precedence over scratching. This is a matter of innate neural organization. Likewise, the sexual embrace of a male frog takes precedence over noxious stimulation. One can even transect the spinal cord above and below the shoulder region without terminating the embrace. These theories received only passing attention, and there was little interest in instinct theory until in recent years the Lorenz group, of which Tinbergen appears to be the leading spokesman, presented their highly speculative and controversial envisagement of mechanisms underlying the appearance of instinctive acts.

As presented by Tinbergen,[39] the theory posits a hierarchy of responses, beginning with appetitive behavior of a more or less general nature and culminating in specific consummatory acts. This behavioral hierarchy is said to be controlled by a hierarchical arrangement of neural centers. Impulses supposedly flow from higher to lower centers in the hierarchy. Overt expression is prevented by a hypothetical inhibitor, or block. This is removed, and the response "released," only when the adequate "sign stimulus" arouses (trigger-like) an "innate releasing mechanism." When this occurs at a higher center, releasing generalized responses (such as migration or prowling), a lower center is activated, perhaps leading to pursuit. This activates a still lower center, and so on, until the consummatory act is released. In the male stickleback, for instance, the consummatory act of passing through the nest and fertilizing the eggs deposited there by the female is preceded first by migration to shallow fresh water, then by various courting activities and fighting off of other males, and then by inducing the female to enter the nest. The sign stimulus, female in nest, releases the innate fertilizing mechanism and thus produces the consummatory act. There is much more detail to this theory, but these are its major aspects. It involves, as we see, several intervening variables. The most important of these is the construct of an innate releasing mechanism.

As we have already suggested, the theory is highly speculative and it has already been attacked on various grounds. Ginsberg,[40] while questioning the concept of instinct in general, accuses the Lorenz-Tinbergen group of various logical fallacies and particularly that of *ad hoc* postulation. He accuses them,

that is, of generalizing without restriction upon the basis of facts which could have other interpretations. There is actually no generally acceptable experimental proof of an internal block and an innate mechanism which releases it. The evidence which Tinbergen[41] himself advances could clearly have other interpretations. He says:

The strict dependence of an innate reaction on a certain set of sign stimuli leads to the conclusion that there must be a special neuro-sensory mechanism that releases the reaction and is responsible for its selective susceptibility to such a very special combination of sign stimuli. This mechanism is what we call the Innate Releasing Mechanism (IRM).

More specifically, he refers to the fact that a ripe stickleback, in posturing to the male, responds to his red belly and zigzag dance, but that later, in the nest, her spawning reaction, while still elicited by the male, is produced by thrusts of his snout against her rump, or thrusts of any hard object if similarly applied.

None of this seems sufficient evidence for positing such complicated constructs as the Lorenz-Tinbergen theory involves. It seems just as likely that organisms are equipped with innately organized neural mechanisms which are activated directly by appropriate stimuli. There is nothing remarkable about the fact that a free-swimming female stickleback responds to a red belly or a zigzag movement, or both, in a prescribed way, and in another situation (the nest) responds now just as specifically to other stimuli (proddings of the rump) in a different but equally prescribed way. Stimulus-response theory leaves many questions unanswered, but it does not raise as many apparently unanswerable questions as the theory under consideration. What is needed to establish any theory is the testing of its postulates experimentally. If the theory is correct, there should be one outcome; if not, another outcome. There has not, to the writer's knowledge, been any such test of any instinct theory.

The experiments of the Lorenz-Tinbergen

group are ingenious, and it is to the credit of this group that their researches cover such a wide range of animals. Thus, whatever the final verdict on their theory may be, their researches on the stimulus-aspects of instinctive behavior will doubtless stand as important contributions to our knowledge of unlearned behavior.

Needs and goals. Many internal conditions conducive to the appearance of instinctive reactions are, in the last analysis, innate. Discussions of instinctive behavior often make no distinction between these innate physiological conditions and patterns of response. The sex "need," "urge," or "appetite" and the associated patterns of expression are, for example, frequently considered together or separately as the sex instinct. Hunger and food getting are frequently referred to indiscriminately as instincts. Sometimes the physiological condition has been referred to as an internal "need," "urge," or "appetite," the term "instinct" being reserved for the pattern of behavior which alleviates the internal condition. The internal physiological condition is said to act as a "drive." It is customary to assume that, owing to the absence of something needed for the optimum functioning of the organism, an internal condition of tension, disequilibrium, or want is aroused. This condition forces the animal to become active, and the activity normally persists until the condition has been alleviated.

When such an internal "need" appears for the first time in the life of the organism there is no specific direction to the activity which follows. There is apparently nothing in the internal physiological condition as such which *guides* the animal in any particular direction or toward any particular object such as water, food, a member of the opposite sex, or the like. The internal "need" is merely an activating condition. During the initial random activity aroused by this condition the animal, if appropriate conditions or materials are available in its vicinity, eventually comes upon something which elicits the pat-

tern of behavior which, in turn, alleviates the "need." Rearousal of the internal condition and repetition of the conditions of alleviation will eventually introduce a *goal* element. That is, the conditions which at first aroused random activity will now arouse activity directed toward the alleviating situations. The animal is said to be *motivated*. We say that it is motivated by hunger because it apparently seeks food, by sex because it apparently seeks out a member of the opposite sex, and so forth. It is obvious that the internal condition, which, for want of a better term, we have designated as an internal "need," is unlearned. It is obvious, also, that the *direction* of activity aroused by this condition is learned. *The pattern of reflexes the elicitation of which alleviates the internal condition may, if it is unlearned, be designated as instinctive.* This pattern is aroused only when the appropriate internal physiological condition is present and the animal finds itself in an appropriate situation.

We shall now turn our attention to theories concerning the racial origins of unlearned behavior. These theories pertain especially to instinctive behavior, although similar principles also underlie the phylogenesis of tropistic and reflex behavior.

The Evolution of Unlearned Behavior

Since unlearned behavior is of racial rather than individual origin, its evolution is possible of adequate envisagement only in terms of the phenomena of inheritance. Any acceptable theory of the phylogenesis of unlearned behavior must accord with the known principles of genetics. Moreover, since patterns of unlearned behavior are characteristic of a species and dependent upon its structures and structural organization, an acceptable theory of the origin of species must be relevant in connection with attempts to discern how tropisms, reflexes, and instincts originated.

Before we consider theories which attempt to account for the evolution of different kinds of animals with their characteristic unlearned reactions and capacities we should correct a common misconception about the relation of the various phyla in the evolutionary scale. This is the idea that the phyla are arranged in linear order, in direct line of descent, with fishes, for example, giving rise to amphibians, amphibians to birds, birds to lower mammals, infraprimate mammals to monkeys, monkeys to apes, and apes to men. It is not correct to say, as many do, that man evolved from a monkey, or an ape. Actually the "scale" should be represented as a tree, with the many types of animals represented as branches. An extremely simplified version of such a tree is given in Figure 28. Men and apes are believed to have come from a common ancestor, a manlike ape or ape-like man. The modern types of both apes and men have had many ancestors which are now extinct.

There are four outstanding theories which attempt to account for the origin of species.

These are: the theory which stresses *inheritance of acquired characters;* the theory of *natural selection*, which stresses survival of the best-adapted individuals; the *mutation* theory, which regards new structures as dependent upon gene mutations, and the *theory of orthogenesis*, which assumes that there is an unfolding principle which underlies evolution. Each of these theories will be examined in terms of its adequacy in accounting for the evolution of unlearned behavior. We shall also consider the possibility that some of these theories, rather than being adequate in themselves, are mutually related.

Theories of unlearned behavior which involve the concept that acquired characters may be inherited

The theory of acquired characters assumes that functions performed by an organism over a long period of time affect its germ plasm in

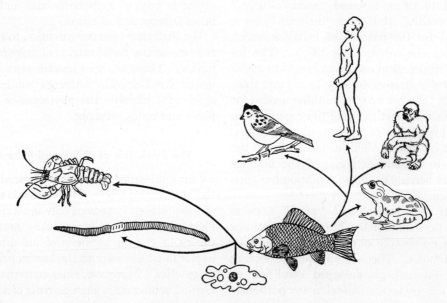

Figure 28. The Modern Conception of the Relation of Phyla in the Evolutionary Tree

Many of the lower varieties are of course missing from this figure, which is designed principally to represent the vertebrates, known technically as a subphyllum of the phylum chordata. Fishes, amphibia, birds, and mammals are classes within the subphyllum. Within the mammalian class the primates are referred to as an order. We belong to the sub-order anthropoid, family hominidae, genus homo, and species sapiens. (Redrawn from Figure 456 in Hunter and Hunter's *College Zoology*, Philadelphia: Saunders, 1949, p. 690.)

such a way that members of the next generation will inherit structures enabling them to
perform these functions with greater ease
than their parents. Lamarck claimed that
such effects are not evident until many generations have performed the same functions or
undergone the same structural changes. The
influence of somatic changes upon the germ
plasm was thus assumed to be minute and
accumulative rather than immediately apparent.

Two theories concerning the origin of
unlearned behavior are based upon this view.
One theory, that of *lapsed intelligence*, supposes that instincts are ancient habits, first
acquired by use of intelligence, but later becoming stereotyped or automatized and transmitted from generation to generation through
the mechanisms of inheritance. The other
theory, which may be designated as that of
innately associated reflexes, assumes that reflex activities which, owing to the nature of
the animal's adaptive behavior, are frequently
associated eventually become associated inherently. The theories differ in that one
places great emphasis upon the intelligent
nature of primeval adaptations, while the
other assumes merely that certain reflexes
will naturally tend to be associated during
adequate forms of adaptation.

The theory of lapsed intelligence has been
subjected to a large amount of criticism from
psychologists and biologists alike. In the
first place, it makes the unwarranted assumption that, phylogenetically, intelligent forms
of adaptation precede automatic and stereotyped forms. One would have to suppose,
in other words, that earlier species and the
earliest members of a given species were more
intelligent (that is, manifested a greater
flexibility of adjustment to their environment)
than the most recent ones. It is a well-known
fact that many acquired activities become
automatic from frequent performance. However, it is quite a different matter to suppose,
because of this, that the intelligent adaptations of early members of a species become
automatized in later members. In the second

place, if this theory were true one should
expect to find more unlearned forms of behavior in man than in other organisms. As we
shall observe presently, such is not the case.
Man has less unlearned behavior than any
other species. In the third place, there is no
evidence that habits acquired by individuals
can be transmitted to their offspring by inheritance. This criticism applies equally to
the lapsed intelligence and the inherently
associated reflex theories.

Although previous investigators [42] had
found no evidence that maze habits were
transmitted from trained rats to their offspring, McDougall [43] felt that a somewhat
different approach might yield evidence of
what he called "Lamarckian transmission."
He trained rats to escape from a water tank
via a dim alley, thereby avoiding the tetanizing shock received from a brightly illuminated
alley. Selected offspring, which McDougall
felt were chosen in random fashion, learned
the same problem. This was continued for
38 generations. The claim that Lamarckian
transmission occurred is based upon the fact
that, in successive generations, there was a
more or less general decrease in the average
number of trials required to learn the problem and in the average number of errors
made.

There have been several critical evalua-
tions of McDougall's experiment, [44] as well as
repetitions carried out under conditions calculated to remove imperfections of his procedure. One of these imperfections was the
failure to maintain, throughout the experiment, an untrained group comparable in other
respects with the trained animals. Three
Australian investigators (Agar, Drummond,
and Tiegs [45]) and Crew, [46] an English investigator, maintained and tested two groups, a
group derived from the trained stock and one
derived from the untrained stock. Actually,
in both of these experiments, the untrained
as well as the trained stock showed more or
less consistent improvement. If the untrained stock had not been utilized, there
might have been reason, as in McDougall's

experiment, for supposing that the offspring were inheriting something of what their parents had learned. But the animals tested in each generation were offspring of parents without training, so their improvement must have had some basis other than inheritance of acquired characteristics.

Agar, Drummond, and Tiegs think that, as an experiment of this kind continues over a long period, gradual changes in the conditions may occur and facilitate learning. This might be especially true with regard to the experimenter's skill in conducting the investigation. These investigators also suggest that there may be progressive changes in a stock of closely inbred rats, changes which may influence performance yet have nothing to do with ancestral habit formation. It is interesting to note, in this connection, that whereas Crew's trained stock dropped from an average of 32 errors in the first generation to 15 in the eighteenth generation, the eighteenth generation of rats from untrained stock made an average of only 12 errors. Clearly something apart from ancestral training was producing this result. The results obtained by Agar, Drummond, and Tiegs were similar for offspring of trained and untrained rats.

McDougall's experiment had other defects in addition to his failure to maintain a line of untrained controls. In selecting rats to produce the next generation, he took the animals which first came to the door of a cage as he opened it. In this way he could have been selecting the more active or even the brighter rats in successive generations. Many of the rats which made a large number of errors were sterilized by tetanizing shocks; hence these duller rats were prevented from contributing to the next generation. Runts were excluded, again with the possibility that the stock would thereby undergo improvement. These and other criticisms, of which Drew [47] has presented several, all point to the conclusion that there is no reliable evidence for the concept that habits acquired by one generation will be inherited in later generations.

In fact, geneticists have found no reliable evidence that *any* acquired traits are inherited. This is the crux of the recent controversy between the Soviet geneticist, Lysenko, and most other geneticists of the world, who regard his claims as utter nonsense. [48] The Soviet government, which officially sponsored Lysenko's views, has now withdrawn its support.

Natural selection and unlearned behavior

Darwin, [49] who is responsible for the theory of natural selection, summarized its chief points as follows:

If under changing conditions of life organic beings present individual differences in almost every part of their structure, and this cannot be disputed; if there be, owing to their geometrical rate of increase, a severe struggle for life at some age, season, or year, and this certainly cannot be disputed; then, considering the infinite complexity of the relations of all organic beings to each other and to their conditions of life, causing an infinite diversity in structure, constitution, and habits, to be advantageous to them, it would be a most extraordinary fact if no variations had ever occurred useful to each being's own welfare, in the same manner as so many variations have occurred useful to man. But if variations useful to any organic being ever do occur, assuredly individuals thus characterized will have the best chance of being preserved in the struggle for life; and from the strong principle of inheritance, these will tend to produce offspring similarly characterized. This principle of preservation, or the survival of the fittest, I have called natural selection. It leads to the improvement of each creature in relation to its organic and inorganic conditions of life; and consequently, in most cases, to what must be regarded as an advance in organization.

Thus the concept of natural selection assumes that variation will naturally occur in structure and behavior and that, in the struggle for existence, those having the most adaptive structures and behavior will alone survive and reproduce. It is assumed, furthermore, that those factors which made for survival in the parents will be inherited by the offspring.

In discussing the origin of instinctive patterns of behavior, more specifically Darwin again invoked the concept of variability. He supposed that any pattern of behavior, inherited or acquired, varies from one individual to another. Some variations, being more adaptive than others, would, according to this view, survive. Although he believed that habits may, under certain circumstances, be inherited in a Lamarckian sense, Darwin's chief stress was upon variability of behavior known already to be unlearned. He [50] said:

I have attempted to show that instincts vary slightly in a state of nature. No one will dispute that instincts are of the highest importance to each animal. Therefore, there is no real difficulty, under changing conditions of life, in natural selection accumulating to any extent slight modifications of instinct which are in any way useful.

In normal animal populations, a large number of individuals fail to survive. Even though organisms may breed in unrestricted fashion, their number remains approximately constant from year to year. However, the individuals who survive do not always transmit their own characteristics to their offspring in the manner posited by Darwin. Many of the characteristics which enable them to survive in the struggle for existence may be phenotypical rather than genotypical.* In other words, these structures and behavior patterns may not be represented in the germ cells in such a manner as to guarantee their future existence. One will recall the gray runners and white waltzers discussed on page 24. Only the homozygous ($GGRR$) animals bred true. Heterozygous animals ($GgRr$, etc.), although they looked and behaved like the homozygous ones, did not necessarily transmit their characteristics to their offspring. Some of the progeny were white waltzers and others gray waltzers, depending upon the nature of the matings involved. Thus survival of the animals better adapted

---

* Individuals are said to be genotypical when they are homozygous for the trait in question. Being homozygous, they have offspring like themselves, all of which breed true. Phenotypical organisms are those which, although they look alike, have a heterozygous constitution. Their offspring differ.

(assuming the running response to be better adapted than the waltzing one) would not insure progeny of equal adaptability. Furthermore, many of the characters of organisms which aid survival may be environmentally rather than genetically produced. We have already observed that habits acquired by parents are not transmissible to offspring. Hence selection of individuals who have acquired adequate modes of adjustment would not insure progeny with these modes of adjustment.

That selection of the best adapted does not mean selection of the *inherently best* individuals is shown by Johannsen's well-known experiment on beans. Size of beans from a pure (homozygous) line is distributed in accordance with the normal frequency curve. A few beans are small, a few are large, but most of them are intermediate in size. Johannsen found that it did not matter whether he selected small, medium, or large beans for the next generation. Beans of any size yielded something approximating the original distribution. Since all of the beans had identical genes for size, the differences must have been environmentally produced.

Of this experiment Morgan [51] says:

For the selection theory, whether artificial or natural, this discovery is of the first importance; for it shows positively that nothing can be accomplished by selecting variants due to environmental influences. This conclusion is in direct contradiction to the widespread belief that, since, by selection of different kinds of individuals in a *general* or mixed population the kinds of individuals produced in the next generation will be changed in the direction of the selection, this change will go on indefinitely. The apparent contradiction between this belief and Johannsen's conclusion is based . . . on the confusion between the variability due to the environment and that due to genetic differences.

Darwin's contemporaries seem to have understood that by selection of extreme individuals in any population the next generation would be moved in the direction of the selection. This is true, however, only when different genetic factors are present, and even there the process comes to an end as soon as these factors are sorted out. Nothing really new is accomplished, except that there are more of given kinds of individuals; but the limits of the original population are not transcended.

Thus selection of those individuals with the best-adapted variations in learned or unlearned behavior (or underlying structures) does not necessarily guarantee transmission of such behavior to further generations in the manner suggested by Darwin's theory. Nevertheless, environmental selection is of great significance in sorting out, as it were, new genetically determined traits when they do chance to appear. We have already observed that changes in the genes (mutations) occur with apparent spontaneity from time to time. Some mutations are more adaptive than others in enabling the organism to adjust to its environment. Mutations in individuals who survive are alone perpetuated. If mutations are such as to make for inadequate adjustment, the individuals in whom they reside may die and the mutations will, as it were, be lost.

Environmental selection is also important in that it produces isolation of certain individuals. Similar individuals may undergo similar mutations and, being isolated, inbreed. Inbreeding offers greater chances for the perpetuation of the mutations than would be possible were the mutated individuals to breed outside of their own immediate group. The strange fauna of an isolated region like Australia demonstrate the significance for evolution of the factors just mentioned.

Unlearned forms of behavior as dependent upon mutations

De Vries, the originator of the mutation theory of evolution, observed that a plant known as Lamarck's evening primrose produced what appeared to be a number of new species of primrose. Some of these "sports" bred true; that is, had offspring like themselves. This suggested that the new forms were genetically rather than environmentally produced; in other words, that they possessed altered genes.

Although the observations of De Vries (owing to the impurity of the genetic factors involved in his stock) were not conclusive proof of the evolution of species by chance sports, or mutations, the reality of such a process in nature cannot now be doubted. We have seen that mutations arise sporadically and with apparent spontaneity. It will be recalled that Morgan and his co-workers observed mutations in about one out of every five to ten thousand flies bred in their laboratories. They also observed that X-rays speed up the mutation process by about 150 times. It has also been suggested that cosmic rays, changes in temperature, and several other conditions may influence the rate at which mutations occur.

Some of the mutations observed in *Drosophila* are lethal; that is, they kill the flies possessing them. Other obvious mutations in *Drosophila* involve such structural changes as absence of wings or eyes, unusual eye-shape, unusual wing formations, changes in bristles, and so forth. Mutations have been observed in many plants and animals. It is also claimed that certain human anomalies are mutations. Among these are glandular anomalies, head shape, hair and skin color, blood constitution, and structural anomalies of body parts, including absence of feet, extra fingers and toes, and loose joints (see p. 36). Some mutations, as we have seen, involve new combinations of chromosomes or chromosome parts; others result from a change in the constitution of genes. *Gene mutations* are regarded as more significant for evolution than are the chromosome mutations, since they alone effect an alteration in the fundamental types of structure. Of great significance is the fact that mutations are transmitted according to the laws of Mendelian inheritance.

Most of the mutations so far observed have been deleterious and recessive. They have yielded structures which hinder rather than facilitate the organism's adjustment to its environment. A few of them might be regarded as adaptive under certain circumstances. A change in the nature of the organism's environment might render the mutant characters better adapted than the normal ones and, by aiding the survival of those possessing the new structures and modes of behavior lead to perpetuation of the mutations. As suggested above, isolation might also aid evolution of new structures and behavior by increasing the possibility that mutants would mate with mutants. Since most of the observed mutations are recessive they could have no effect unless individuals with similar mutated genes were mated.

East [52] claims that the most obvious mutations are probably of small consequence for evolution. He says:

Since any given character is the result of activities of numerous genes working both concurrently and serially, these activities must be harmonious if the organism concerned is to be favored in the struggle for existence. Three different effects of mutations are therefore conceivable: (a) the machinery may be stopped entirely because the new gene can not do essential work previously performed by the old gene, and the result is ordinarily lethal; (b) the machinery may be restricted in operation, getting a physiologically less complete end product; (c) the machinery may be diverted from its original manufacturing tendencies into the production of an end product different from the original.

The last-mentioned mutations are alone significant for constructive evolution. East believes that they are much more numerous than the destructive types; but, because the changes produced by them are small (although accumulative), they are not as readily apparent as the destructive mutations. East [53] says:

Formal solution of the more pressing evolutionary problems presented to the consideration of biologists from Darwin's time onward is possible . . . provided stress is laid almost exclusively upon constructive gene mutations fitting the pre-existing patterns of gene activity. Raw material of this type exists in quantity. It meets the requirements of physiology. It satisfies the demands of taxonomy. And it places orthogenesis on a sensible basis.

As far as we know at present, the only way in which structures and correlated behavior can change and be transmitted in the changed form to further generations is by mutations such as those mentioned by East. Thus the sole evolutionary principle of which we have any reliable evidence at the present time is that based upon mutations.

Orthogenesis and the evolution of unlearned behavior

The theory of orthogenesis assumes that there is an order in nature of which evolution is the unfolding. Supposedly the original form of life had within it potentialities for development along certain rather definitely prescribed lines, which were those followed in the evolution of species and their unlearned behavior. It is pointed out, in support of this theory, that animal forms have evolved by following a definite course; that is, they have gradually increased or decreased in size, steadily increased in complexity of brain structure, and so forth. It is often pointed out that this unfolding goes on regardless of whether the characters produced are adaptive or maladaptive. For example, the spiral character of a snail's shell is without any known adaptive value, yet it has gradually evolved as though predestined to achieve spiral form. The canine teeth of the sabretooth tiger continued to evolve in the direction of greater length even though, it is said, they eventually led to the animal's extinction. According to the orthogenetic theory the growth of the canine teeth was determined by a relentless unfolding principle and was quite unrelated to their adaptive value.

Many students of evolution have pointed out that progress such as that assumed by orthogenetic evolutionists may be illusory. Many characters which arise sporadically may be arranged into a series which gives the appearance of a gradually unfolding principle. Even if the principle of orthogenesis were established as a phenomenon in nature, one would still not have *explained* the evolution of species and their unlearned behavior. It would be necessary to find out how orthogenesis works to produce its progressive effects. The only way in which evolution is known definitely to occur today is, as we have indicated, through mutations. Some proponents of the orthogenetic theory have suggested, therefore, that orthogenesis may do its work by determining the direction of mutations. If any trend such as that posited by orthogenesis is involved, it may, of course, come from environmental selection of certain types of mutation and the extinction of others.

The interrelation of certain concepts of evolution

The preceding discussion of the evolution of unlearned behavior has indicated that of the four outstanding theories only one, the theory of evolution by mutation, is supported by reliable experimental evidence. In evolution by mutation, however, selection of certain mutant types and elimination of others is requisite.* This selection involves survival and reproduction of those organisms which possess the best-adapted structures and behavior patterns. Such selection is different from that posited by Darwin in his theory of natural selection. Darwin assumed that selection of somatic characters, that is, acquired structures and behavior, can lead to evolution of new forms. He did not know that selection must involve new inherent factors (mutations) if it is to control evolution.

It has often been pointed out, against the theory of evolution by mutations, that these alterations of genes and chromosomes produce types of structure and behavior which are less adaptive than the normal ones. This is true, in general, of mutations produced in the laboratory. On the other hand, many mutations may, as East has suggested, involve very slight changes in genic balance that are cumulative and that eventually lead to mark-

---

* Modern proponents of natural selection, like Huxley,[54] admit the evolutionary significance, or indispensability, of gene mutations but stress the role played by natural selection in favoring and, possibly, in encouraging mutations. They look upon the mutation theory of evolution as an explanation of the variations which Darwin recognized as basic to natural selection.

edly altered types. Certain changes in environmental influences might, under normal conditions of breeding, be such as to make the mutant types better adapted than the normal ones.

The Role of Unlearned Reactions in the Adjustments of Organisms

A review of the available literature on unlearned behavior in different phyla and species shows that as one goes from the lowest organisms to man there is a decreasing dependence upon unlearned patterns of reaction for adjustment. In general, it may be said that the unlearned reactions of animals which do not possess a nervous system of the receptor-effector type are tropistic in nature. In other words, they involve relatively simple orienting motions with respect to environmental conditions, the reactions depending in a direct way upon the physicochemical properties of the organism and those of its surroundings. This does not imply that all of the behavior of these animals is tropistic. Even in animals as low as *Amoeba* and *Paramecium*, changing internal states are of considerable consequence, and Jennings[55] suggests that many reactions are of a trial-and-error nature. It has also been shown, as we shall see later, that these organisms are capable of learning simple adaptive reactions. However, their most characteristic and prevalent activities appear to agree with a general tropistic envisagement. Many animals possessing a nervous system may have tropistic reactions. Such forms of behavior are particularly evident in insects. They may also appear in organisms as highly developed as the mammals. However, tropistic reactions in birds and mammals can be elicited in a clear-cut form only under peculiar stimulating conditions. Even then, the responses are unusually variable. As we go from the lower to the higher organisms it appears that tropistic reactions become fewer and at the same time less precise, that they comprise a smaller proportion of the animal's total repertoire of behavior, and that they become increasingly amenable to training.

All organisms above the sea anemone exhibit the particularized responses which have been designated as reflex. In general, the repertoire of reflex responses is enlarged as the nervous system increases in complexity. The more receptor-effector pathways exist, the more possibility for precise partial responses to appear. Reflex behavior is correlated, also, with the mobility of the animal's skeletal and muscular system. One would hardly expect a worm or a snake to have as great a variety of reflex responses as a rat, despite the existence of a complex nervous organization.

Most reflexes are readily modified by training. The pupillary response, for example, may be conditioned so that it appears upon the presentation of a wide variety of stimuli other than those which normally elicit it. If a buzzer is sounded at about the same time as light is flashed into the eye, and this association of buzzer and light is continued for a sufficient period of time, the buzzer will eventually elicit the response which previously appeared in response to the light alone. This is modification of a reflex from the point of view of the stimulus which may elicit the response. The response itself may also be modified. Winking when a puff of air is blown into the eye, or when an object is seen rapidly approaching the eye, may be reduced in magnitude and, in many instances, entirely eliminated. Many other reflexes are similarly modified. Most of the reflexes appear at birth. Others appear some time after birth. Some reflexes, like that of grasping in the human baby, may appear for a short time and then disappear. The newborn baby tightly grasps any object which stimulates its palm. Later on, however, the grasping response no longer automatically appears upon presentation of a stimulus which previously aroused it. Such responses will be discussed in more detail later (see Chapter 6).

While the number of reflexes increases as we approach the higher organisms, there is good evidence that just the opposite is true of the unlearned reflex patterns designated as instinctive. In organisms like the insects, instinctive behavior is quite prevalent. Many of the responses of these organisms, as the Peckhams,[56] Hingston,[57] and others have demonstrated, may be envisaged as chain reflexes. One reflex response leads to the arousal of the next, and so on until the activity in which the animal is engaged has reached its consummation. One example from Hingston illustrates the characteristic inflexibility and the chainlike nature of instinctive behavior as it often appears in insects. He says:

Psammophila tydei hunts caterpillars in the Himalayas. Her instinct possesses the following links: She finds a caterpillar, paralyzes it by stinging, drags it to a tunnel, lays an egg on it, finally closes the hole. Let us cut out the first two links. I take a caterpillar from a wasp's nest, one that has already been paralyzed and lies helpless as if it were dead. I give it to another wasp which is hunting about for prey. This is a valuable find for the wasp. She now has a victim already helpless. She need not waste her time or poison in stinging it. All she need do is drag it away. But the wasp could not recognize these advantages. She seized hold of the helpless caterpillar, pierced it with her sting in the orthodox manner eight successive times. Then she proceeded according to routine to crush her victim's head. Of course all such labor was useless. The stinging and crushing had already been done. That the caterpillar was helpless and made no resistance did not seem to matter to the wasp. She did not take advantage of what others had done for her. She had found a caterpillar, therefore she must sting it. That is the routine of her particular instinct. The paralyzed must again be paralyzed, the crushed head must again be crushed, before the next psychic step can follow, that is, the dragging of the victim to the nest.

Other instinctive reactions of insects manifest a much greater degree of variability (both from the point of view of the stimulus which elicits them and from the standpoint of the pattern of expression) than the above example might imply. However, the degree of variability and of modifiability is apparently small as compared with that of animals higher in the evolutionary scale. The fishes, amphibia, reptiles, birds, and lower mammals have a large number of instinctive responses, but there appears to be a tendency away from stereotypy and toward plasticity of behavior as the higher forms are approached.

This increase in the plasticity of behavior is to be interpreted in terms of changes taking place in the nervous system. In the nervous system of insects, for example, one finds that the course followed by a nerve impulse is relatively fixed. Neural impulses elicited by an external stimulus travel over predetermined pathways from receptor to effector, thus producing stereotyped behavior. There is relatively little opportunity for other than the innately determined course to be traversed by a given impulse. As the nervous system increases in complexity, however, there is increasingly less likelihood that a stimulus will lead to transmission of impulses in preformed functional pathways without affecting others. This increase in complexity of nervous structure is associated with the development of the cerebral cortex, which reaches its highest elaboration in man. Some idea of the complexity of cortical structure in higher mammals may be gathered from Figure 29. It has been calculated that there are approximately 9,200,000,000 nerve cells in the human cortex. As the cortex develops greater complexity, instinctive patterns of behavior become less apparent. The stereotyped unlearned patterns of behavior which do exist are served, as in lower organisms, by the structures of the spinal cord and brain stem. Herrick [58] says:

The functions of the cerebral cortex are still largely wrapped in mystery, but the evidence so far accumulated suggests that these functions are, so far as physiologically known, not different in kind from those of the other parts of the brain. It is, however, manifest that these functions are concerned with the individually acquired and especially the intelligently performed activities as distinguished from the fundamental reflex and instinctive processes whose mechanisms are innate.

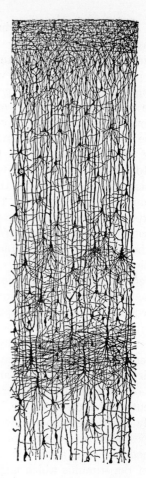

Figure 29. A Section of the Cerebral Cortex of a Human Infant

This view of the complexity of neural structure is tremendously oversimplified. It shows nerve cells and dendrites, but only a few of the axons. (After Cajal. From C. J. Herrick, *Introduction to Neurology*, Philadelphia: Saunders 1931, p. 321.)

It is almost impossible to find in man any evidence of the complex unlearned patterns of reflexes which have been designated as instinctive. As we shall observe later, the behavior of newborn human infants is characterized by some as undifferentiated mass activity. Man has, however, a number of fundamental physiological "needs" in common with lower organisms. While the physiological "needs" or "innate driving factors" in behavior have not changed a great deal from the lower organisms to man, the patterns of behavior which alleviate them have changed from stereotypy to extreme plasticity. Many of the reflexes still exist as essential unlearned aspects of behavior patterns, but the organization of these reflexes has become an individual more than a racial characteristic. This is because the existence of a cortex with its millions of neurons facilitates inhibition of reflexes, modification of reflexes, and organization of reflexes into patterns dictated, as it were, by individual experience rather than by inherently determined neural pathways.

Newborn infants of successively higher phyla become increasingly helpless. The insects are perfectly capable of taking care of themselves from the moment of birth. This is true, also, of organisms up to the level of the reptiles. In birds there is a period of helplessness after hatching, and such helplessness appears to increase in the mammals. Within mammals, helplessness gradually increases as the higher forms are approached. It culminates in the utter dependence of the human infant upon older members of his group. This, in itself, indicates a relative decrease in preformed nervous pathways. It is true, of course, that some development which follows birth is determined by maturation. Neural pathways continue to develop in a manner determined by the genes and the intracellular and intercellular environment. It is thus conceivable that some unlearned reflex patterns are formed after birth.

What has just been said is further supported by the fact that, in addition to being the most helpless of animals at birth, the human infant experiences a *longer* period of dependency than any other organism. It thus undergoes a much longer period of subjection to the modifying influences with which older individuals surround it. As a result of these influences and their relative uniformity within a group, most of the relatively universal stereotyped activities shown by human beings are coenotropes (see p. 50) rather than instincts.

Summary and Conclusions

There are three general criteria of unlearned behavior; namely, universality, sequentiality, and peculiar adaptiveness. It has been pointed out that neither singly nor together are these criteria indubitable indices of the unlearnedness of behavior. The only reliable index of the learned or unlearned nature of a response is its appearance under conditions which prevent the organism from observing it in others or from practicing it. A number of typical experimental techniques and the data yielded by them have been discussed. Analysis of such experimental findings forces us to conclude that behavior patterns may develop as a result of the interaction of genes and internal environmental conditions, or maturation. In other words, not all behavior requires practice or observation of others for its development.

We found that it is convenient to distinguish between three types of unlearned response, even though the differences are not always clearly defined. Tropistic behavior involves an unlearned orienting movement of the entire organism, the orientation being with respect to some external stimulus and being determined in a mechanical way by the nature of this stimulus and the physicochemical structure of the organism. Reflex behavior is an unlearned specific response of some part of the organism. Reflex responses are determined by the external stimulus and the narrowly prescribed neural pathway over which the nervous impulse travels from receptor to effector. Reflex behavior makes its first clear-cut appearance in animals which, like the sea anemone, possess a receptor-effector nervous system. Instinctive behavior involves an unlearned coordination of reflexes, the elicitation of which is in some instances peculiarly dependent upon internal physiological conditions. The presence of hormones of certain kinds is demonstrably associated with the presence, in some animals, at least, of mating and maternal behavior. Organisms are so constituted physiologically that optimum adjustment, and sometimes life itself, depends upon the satisfaction of what have been called, for want of a better name, "physiological needs." The presence of a condition of need often drives the animal to activity, hence the term "physiological drive" seems appropriate.

The physiological conditions associated with needs and drives energize or activate an organism, but they do not in themselves determine the direction taken in satisfying them. A hungry, thirsty, or sexually deprived animal does not know where to satisfy his need. He is activated to behave in various ways, to go in random directions, but the results of such activities demonstrate their appropriateness. His behavior becomes less random, as to direction, as he learns where his needs may be satisfied. The pattern of behavior elicited when the animal has placed itself in appropriate circumstances is usually such as to remove or alleviate the physiological condition which activates him. When the coordination of reflexes involved in the consummation of such activity is unlearned, it is designated instinctive. There are, however, some instincts which may not depend upon internal physiological conditions such as are involved in drives. Flying has been mentioned as a possible case in point. Perhaps falling, or the pull of gravity, provides the stimulus for this behavior pattern.

In recent years there has been a great deal of interest in those aspects of the external stimulating situation which arouse instinctive behavior, especially in animals below the mammalian level. Dummy animals have been used in such a way as to reveal which aspects of the stimulating situation are most effective in eliciting instinctive responses. Although an animal may be capable of responding to various aspects of the total situation, only certain restricted aspects are required to elicit the response. Thus we saw that the pregnant stickleback responds to the male's red belly and zigzag movements by exhibiting courtship behavior. Models having these characteristics, even though they do not closely resemble the male in other respects, are quite effective. Likewise, the male responds with typical courtship behavior to a distended abdomen. Such stimulating conditions are effective only when the physiological condition of the animal is also conducive to arousal of the behavior in question. While the facts revealed by such experiments seem well established, theories as to underlying mechanisms are highly speculative and their constructs need to be subjected to testing experiments.

There are several theories which attempt to show how new structures and unlearned behavior patterns evolve. It is apparent that gene mutations are basic to such evolution. The most acceptable theory combines gene mutations and natural selection, but natural selection is given significance, not as the originator of new characters, which depend upon gene mutations, but as determining which new characters shall survive and be transmitted to subsequent generations. There is no evidence for the theory that acquired characteristics are inherited. The principle of orthogenesis is descriptive rather than explanatory. Even the descriptive value of orthogenetic theories is questionable, since the "orthogenetic" sequences may be illusory.

Considering the role of unlearned behavior in organisms ranging from unicellular animals to man, we observed that stereotypy decreases and general plasticity of response increases as the higher forms are approached. The "original nature" of the human baby is, for example, the culmination of this trend in the direction of freedom from biological stereotypy. The complexity of its nervous system and the correlated plasticity of its behavior are unparalleled in the animal world. The brain assumes a high degree of dominance over the lower nervous structures which subserve reflex and instinctive responses. Innate patterns of behavior may still exist, although they are relatively hard to find. The organism is impelled to activity by the same "needs" that impel lower organisms, but the complexity of its brain gives it a greater ability to learn and to adjust to the environment in terms of past experience than is possible in lower organisms. To a lesser extent than in any other animals are human nervous pathways innately preformed so as to render possible the elicitation of the definite unlearned patterns of response designated as instinctive. In general, the higher one goes in the animal scale the more helpless is the individual at birth and the longer is its period of dependence. These facts, combined with those mentioned above, make the plasticity of reaction in the human being readily understandable.

In the newborn infant there are, as we shall see, many relatively simple unlearned responses. These are reflexes. It is highly doubtful whether there is anything here that one could call an "instinct." As we shall also observe in our discussion of child development, some unlearned responses develop during early childhood through the process known as "maturation." Whether any of these later-appearing responses is an instinct is also highly questionable.*

The flexibility of adjustment which we find in the higher organisms and which culminates in man will be discussed with greater thoroughness in the following chapters, which deal with the evolution of intelligent behavior.

---

* We are of course using the term "instinct" to represent a complex unlearned behavior pattern.

REFERENCES

1. Fernberger, S. W., "Unlearned Behavior of the Albino Rat," *Amer. J. Psychol.*, 1929, *41*, 343–344.

2. See especially M. M. Shirley, "A Motor Sequence Favors the Maturation Theory," *Psychol. Bull.*, 1931, *28*, 203–204.

3. Hingston, R. W. G., *Problems of Instinct and Intelligence.* New York: 1929, pp. 55, 68. By permission of The Macmillan Company, Publishers.

4. Stone, C. P., "Maturation and Instinctive Functions" in C. P. Stone (ed.), *Comparative Psychology* (3d ed.). New York: Prentice-Hall, 1951, p. 33. Italics not in the original.

5. See N. L. Munn, *Handbook of Psychological Research on the Rat.* Boston: Houghton Mifflin, 1950, pp. 16–31. This discusses the relevant research and gives the specific references.

6. See especially H. C. Bingham, "Sexual Development in Apes," *Comp. Psychol. Monogs.*, 1928, No. 23; and A. C. Kinsey, *et al.*, *Sexual Behavior in the Human Male* (Philadelphia: Saunders, 1948, Chapter 6) and *Sexual Behavior in the Human Female* (Philadelphia: Saunders, 1954, Chapter 13).

7. Munn, *op. cit.*, pp. 31–37. Here the relevant literature is summarized and the detailed references are given.

8. Spalding, D. A., "Instinct," *Macmillan's*, 1873, *27*, 282–293.

9. Breed, F. S., "The Development of Certain Instincts and Habits in Chicks," *Behavior Monographs*, 1911, *1*, No. 1.

10. Shepard, J. F., and F. S. Breed, "Maturation and Use in the Development of an Instinct," *J. Anim. Behav.*, 1913, *3*, 274–285.

11. See D. Moseley, "The Accuracy of the Pecking Response in Chicks," *J. Comp. Psychol.*, 1925, *5*, 75–97; C. Bird, "The Relative Importance of Maturation and Habit in the Development of an Instinct," *Ped. Sem.*, 1925; C. Bird, "The Effect of Maturation upon the Pecking Instinct of Chicks," *Ped. Sem.*, 1926, *33*, 212–234; C. Bird, "Maturation and Practice: Their Effects Upon the Feeding Reaction of Chicks," *J. Comp. Psychol.*, 1933, *16*, 343–366.

12. Cruze, W. W., "Maturation and Learning in Chicks," *J. Comp. Psychol.*, 1935, *19*, 371–409.

13. Padilla, S., "Further Studies on the Delayed Pecking of Chicks," *J. Comp. Psychol.*, 1935, *20*, 413–443.

14. Carmichael, L., "The Development of Behavior in Vertebrates Experimentally Removed from the Influence of External Stimulation," *Psych. Rev.*, 1926, *33*, 51–58.

15. Carmichael, L., "A Further Study of the Development of Behavior in Vertebrates Experi-

mentally Removed from the Influence of External Stimulation," *Psych. Rev.*, 1927, *34*, 34–47.

16. Carmichael, L., "A Further Experimental Study of the Development of Behavior," *Psych. Rev.*, 1928, *35*, 253–260.

17. Loeb, J., *Forced Movements, Tropisms, and Animal Conduct.* Philadelphia: Lippincott, 1918.

18. Jennings, H. S., *The Behavior of Lower Organisms.* New York: Columbia University Press, 1906.

19. Mast, S. O., *Light and the Behavior of Organisms.* New York: Wiley, 1911.

20. Crozier, W. J., and H. Hoagland, "The Study of Living Organisms," in C. Murchison, (ed.), *A Handbook of General Experimental Psychology.* Worcester: Clark University Press, 1934.

21. Hunter, W. S. "The Behavior of the White Rat on Inclined Planes," *Ped. Sem.*, 1927, *34*, 299–332; "The Mechanisms Involved in the Behavior of White Rats on Inclined Planes," *J. Gen. Psychol.*, 1931, *5*, 295–310.

22. Munn, *op. cit.*, pp. 41–48.

23. Parker, G. H., *The Elementary Nervous System.* Philadelphia: Lippincott, 1919.

24. *Ibid.*, p. 135.

25. Watson, J. B., *Behavior: An Introduction to Comparative Psychology.* New York: Holt, 1914.

26. Kuo, Z. Y., "Giving Up Instincts in Psychology," *J. Phil.*, 1921, *18*, 645–664; "How Are Our Instincts Acquired?" *Psych. Rev.*, 1922, *29*, 344–365; "A Psychology Without Heredity," *Psych. Rev.*, 1924, *31*, 427–448; "The Net Result of the Anti-Heredity Movement in Psychology," *Psych. Rev.*, 1929, *36*, 181–199; "The Genesis of the Cat's Responses to the Rat," *J. Comp. Psychol.*, 1930, *11*, 1–35; "Ontogeny of Embryonic Behavior in Aves. I. The Chronology and General Nature of the Behavior of the Chick Embryo," *J. Exper. Zool.*, 1932, *61*, 395–430; "II. The Mechanical Factors in the Various Stages Leading to Hatching," *J. Exper. Zool.*, 1932, *62*, 453–489; "III. The Structural and Environmental Factors in Embryonic Behavior," *J. Comp. Psychol.*, 1932, *13*, 245–271; "IV. The Influence of Embryonic Movements upon the Behavior after Hatching," *J. Comp. Psychol.*, 1932, *14*, 109–122; "V. The Reflex Concept in

the Light of Embryonic Behavior in Birds," *Psych. Rev.*, 1932, *39*, 499–515.

27. Skinner, B. F., *The Behavior of Organisms.* New York: Appleton-Century, 1938.

28. See Munn, *op. cit.*, pp. 16–31, for a review of the literature.

29. Beach, F. A., and A. M. Holz, "Mating Behavior of Male Rats Castrated at Various Ages and Injected with Androgen," *J. Exper. Zool.*, 1946, *101*, 91–142.

30. Beach, F. A., "Instinctive Behavior: Reproductive Activities," Chapter 12 in S. S. Stevens (ed.), *Handbook of Experimental Psychology.* New York: Wiley, 1951.

31. See especially B. P. Wiesner and N. M. Sheard, *Maternal Behavior in the Rat.* London: Oliver and Boyd, 1933. These activities are pictured in E. J. Farris and J. Q. Griffith (eds.), *The Rat in Laboratory Investigation* (rev. ed.). Philadelphia: Lippincott, 1949. Some of these illustrations are reproduced on page 32 of Munn, *op. cit.*

32. Kinder, E. F., "A Study of Nest-Building Activity in the Albino Rat," *J. Exper. Zool.*, 1927, *47*, 117–161.

33. Riddle, O., E. L. Lahr, and R. W. Bates, "The Role of Hormones in the Initiation of Maternal Behavior in Rats," *Am. J. Physiol.*, 1942, *137*, 299–317.

34. Metfessel, M., "Relationships of Heredity and Environment in Behavior," *J. Psychol.*, 1940, *10*, 177–198.

35. Beach, F. A., "Analysis of the Stimuli Adequate to Elicit Mating Behavior in the Sexually Inexperienced Rat," *J. Comp. Psychol.*, 1942, *33*, 163–207. See also F. A. Beach, "Experimental Studies of Sexual Behavior in Male Mammals," *J. Clin. Endocrinology*, 1944, *4*, 126–134.

36. Tinbergen, N., *The Study of Instinct.* London: Oxford University Press, 1951. Also see the articles by Lorenz, Tinbergen, and others in *Symposia of the Society for Experimental Biology.* New York: Academic Press, 1950, 175–384.

37. Lashley, K., "Physiological Analysis of the Libido," *Psych. Rev.*, 1924, *31*, 192–202.

38. Allport, F. H., *Social Psychology.* Boston: Houghton Mifflin, 1924.

39. Tinbergen, N., "The Hierarchical Organization of Nervous Mechanisms Underlying Instinctive Behaviour," *Symposium of the Society for Experimental Biology*, No. 4, 1950,

pp. 305–312. See also Tinbergen's *The Study of Instinct*. Oxford: Clarendon Press, 1951, Chapter 5.

40. Ginsberg, A., "A Reconstructive Analysis of the Concept of 'Instinct'," *J. Psychol.*, 1952, *33*, 235–277.

41. Tinbergen, N., *The Study of Instinct*. London: Oxford University Press, 1951, pp. 41–42.

42. This literature is summarized in Munn, *op. cit.*, pp. 38–39.

43. McDougall, W., "An Experiment for Testing of the Hypothesis of Lamarck," *Brit. J. Psychol.* (Gen. Sec.), 1929, *17*, 267–304; "Second Report on a Lamarckian Experiment," *Brit. J. Psychol.*, (Gen. Sec.), 1930, *20*, 201–218; "Une expérience lamarckienne à résultats positifs," *J. Psychol. Norm. Path.*, 1937, *34*, 413–425; "Fourth Report on a Lamarckian Experiment," *Brit. J. Psychol.*, 1938, *28*, 321–345, 365–395.

44. For a review of these experiments see Munn, *op. cit.*, pp. 38–39.

45. Agar, W. E., F. H. Drummond, and O. W. Tiegs, "A First Report on a Test of McDougall's Lamarckian Experiment on the Training of Rats," *J. Exper. Biol.*, 1935, *12*, 191–211; "Second Report on a Test of McDougall's Lamarckian Experiment on the Training of Rats," *J. Exper. Biol.*, 1942, *19*, 158–167.

46. Crew, F. A. E., "A Repetition of McDougall's Lamarckian Experiment." *J. Genetics*, 1936, *33*, 61–101.

47. Drew, G. C., "McDougall's Experiments on the Inheritance of Acquired Habits," *Nature*. London, 1939, 188–191.

48. See especially L. C. Dunn and Th. Dobzhansky, *Heredity, Race and Society*, New York: New American Library, 1952, pp. 103–106; or P. D. Strausbaugh and B. R. Weimer, *General Biology* (3d ed.), New York: Wiley, 1952, pp. 359–360.

49. Darwin, C., *Origin of Species* (6th London ed.). Murray, 1859, pp. 122–123.

50. *Ibid.*, p. 275.

51. Morgan, T. H., *The Scientific Basis of Evolution*. New York: Norton, 1932, pp. 95–96.

52. East, E. M., "Genetic Aspects of Certain Problems of Evolution," *Amer. Naturalist*, 1936, *70*, 153–154.

53. *Ibid.*, p. 158.

54. Huxley, J., "Genetics, Evolution, and Human Destiny," Chapter 26 in L. C. Dunn, *Genetics in the Twentieth Century*. New York: Macmillan, 1951.

55. Jennings, H. S., *The Behavior of Lower Organisms*. New York: Columbia University Press, 1906.

56. Peckham, G. W., and E. G. Peckham, *Wasps, Social and Solitary*. Boston: Houghton Mifflin, 1905.

57. Hingston, R. W. G., *Instinct and Intelligence*. New York: Macmillan, 1929, pp. 41–42.

58. Herrick, C. J. *Introduction to Neurology* (5th ed.). Philadelphia: Saunders, 1931, pp. 357–358.

SUGGESTIONS FOR FURTHER READING

Beach, F. A., "Instinctive Behavior: Reproductive Activities," in S. S. Stevens, (ed.), *Handbook of Experimental Psychology*. New York: Wiley, 1951.

Hebb, D. O., *The Organization of Behavior*. New York: Wiley, 1949, pp. 165–170.

Huxley, J., "Genetics, Evolution and Human Destiny," in L. C. Dunn, *Genetics in the 20th Century*. New York: Macmillan, 1951.

Lashley, K. S., "Experimental Analysis of Instinctive Behavior," *Psych. Rev.*, 1938, *45*, 445–471.

Morgan, C. T., and E. Stellar, *Physiological Psychology* (2d ed.). New York: McGraw-Hill, 1950, Chapters 18–20.

Munn, N. L., *A Handbook of Psychological Research on the Rat*. Boston: Houghton Mifflin, 1950, Chapter 2.

Stone, C. P., "Multiply, Vary, Let the Strongest Live and the Weakest Die — Charles Darwin," *Psychol. Bull.*, 1943, *40*, 1–24.

Stone, C. P., "Maturation and Instinctive Functions," in C. P. Stone, (ed.), *Comparative Psychology* (3d ed.). New York: Prentice-Hall, 1951.

Tinbergen, N., *The Study of Instinct*. London: Oxford University Press, 1951.

Tinbergen, N., *Social Behavior of Animals*. New York: Wiley, 1953, especially Chapters II and IV.

4

Evolution of Intelligent Behavior: Basic Processes

WHAT aspects of behavior lead us to regard it as intelligent, or to infer that the behaving organism is intelligent? If we should use the term "intelligence" with respect to unlearned responses, such as the more complicated instinctive behavior patterns found in insects and many other organisms, all of which evidence a high level of adaptiveness, it would have to be attributed to something outside of the individual animal.* But the intelligence of concern to us in this and the following chapter is attributed to the behaving organism. It is inferred from what this organism does when confronted by new situations, or from what it learns. Capacities for learning, and thus for acting intelligently, increase as we go up the scale from unicellular organisms to man. Any organism at a particular level, say that of the birds, is restricted in what it can learn, as compared with the individual at a higher level. This is a phylogenetic limitation which, like unlearned behavior, depends to a major extent upon inheritance. When we speak of bird intelligence, or mammalian intelligence, therefore, we are referring to something which is phylogenetically limited, yet something which, unlike tropistic, reflex,

or instinctive behavior, is also dependent upon what happens to the animal during its lifetime. With respect to unlearned behavior, moreover, all individuals of a similarly constituted group have a comparable repertoire. They all have the tropisms, reflexes, or instincts of their group. But with respect to intelligent behavior, in the sense in which we use the term, individuals of the group may show considerable variation. Some may acquire habits of adjustment which others do not acquire. Some may solve their problems in one way and some in another. While capacities for such adjustments are limited, at a particular level, the actual activities involved in adjustment are dependent upon the situations which an organism meets and the demands made upon it by these situations.

Most of our tests of animal intelligence call for the learning of new adjustments. Intelligence as a capacity characteristic of the particular animal, or of the group which it represents, is inferred from such behavioral facts as the following: Organisms differ in the quickness with which they learn. Some retain habits longer than others. Some, more readily than others, transfer to a new situation what they have learned elsewhere. Confronted by a new situation calling for adjustment, some organisms respond in a routine and ineffective manner while others quickly

---

* We have already (p. 73) discussed the idea that there is a predetermined unfolding plan in evolution — the concept of orthogenesis. Some writers see in this the expression of a "divine intelligence."

"size up" the situation and solve their problem. Some, as we shall see, show more ability than others to solve problems by reasoning, by "putting two and two together," by combining old habits in novel ways and thus solving a problem. It was with such things in mind that Edwards [1] defined intelligence in terms of variability, flexibility, or versatility.

Emphasis upon versatility is especially useful in that it gives us a definition which is as applicable to the behavior of unicellular organisms as to that of human beings. The former's very limited versatility marks it as of low intelligence. Increasing versatility culminates in man, the most intelligent of all creatures. Defining intelligence in terms of human characteristics, such as conceptual thinking and facility in use of language, would be of very limited phylogenetic significance. Such definitions would have little or no relevance below the human level. When we think in terms of versatility, however, man's conceptual and linguistic abilities are regarded as the end products of a versatility which had its beginnings in remote times and increased as the higher animals evolved.

We have insufficient evidence to decide whether the evolution of intelligence represents a continuous increase from lower to higher levels or whether there was discontinuity — whether new functions suddenly emerged. Language, and with it the influence of tradition, is possibly the clearest instance of discontinuity, but even this is dependent upon processes which appear in infrahuman forms — processes which, in several respects, approach language functions. Nissen [2] discusses this problem at length, pointing out that although modern biological theories might lead us to expect new behavioral mechanisms at various points along the phylogenetic scale, our behavioral data do not support this expectation.

Intelligent behavior depends upon various subsidiary functions. It is highly dependent upon the ability to *discriminate*, or differentiate, aspects of the environment. An animal without sense receptors, or in whom sensitivity was deficient, could have only a low order of intelligence because it would be unable to perceive what was going on around it. Even if it had the wherewithal to adjust, the animal could not know what to adjust to. In discussing the evolution of intelligent behavior we shall therefore give priority to sensory processes.

Intelligence also calls for *motor dexterity*. Some organisms have a low order of ability to move things around in their environment and to change their own position relative to aspects of it. Others have a high order of such ability. Birds and human beings, although through different mechanisms, can leave the earth itself. Some attention is thus given to the effectors, the muscles and related mechanisms whose evolution has increased the motor dexterity, both manipulatory and locomotor, of animals ranging from the lower vertebrates to man.

Neither good sensitivity nor good motor dexterity would mean much for the evolution of intelligence unless modifiability were possible. As we have seen, animals are intelligent to the degree that they are modified by what happens to them and to the degree that they retain and apply the modifications.

The evolution of sensitivity, motor dexterity, and learning ability is dependent upon nerves and brains as well as receptor and effector mechanisms. In any discussion of basic processes in the evolution of intelligent behavior one must therefore take cognizance of neural evolution.

For the highest types of learning, which involve the development and utilization of *symbolic processes*, the evolution of the cerebral cortex is especially significant. All animals have some degree of sensitivity, motor dexterity, and modifiability, but only those with a highly developed cerebral cortex possess the ability to utilize symbols — to do such things as recall objects or situations no longer present, to let words represent these, to think, and to reason. Man's cerebral cortex, and the psychological functions made possible by it, may actually change the nature and course of further human evolution.[3]

This chapter traces the evolution of sensory, motor, and nervous mechanisms and functions, including those of the cerebral cortex. The succeeding chapter deals with the evolution of learning ability and ends with a discussion of higher learning processes in which symbols play a predominant role.

How Sensory Processes Are Studied

The sensory capacities of animals may be gauged in several ways. One source of information, which always needs supplementation from behavior studies, is sense-organ structure. Studying the structure of an eye — its shape, the characteristics of its lens, and the microscopic features of its retina, for example — may tell us a great deal about the possibility that certain aspects of visual sensitivity are or are not present. The comparative anatomy of sense organs is often taken as an index of sensory evolution. Another source of information, although by no means a reliable one, is general observation of the behavior of animals in their native habitats. The responses of animals to sounds, for example, may indicate that they hear, but these responses usually tell us nothing very specific about the stimulus required for such behavior. Nor do they indicate how weak a sound the animal can hear. Likewise, an organism may seem to respond to color (wave length), but upon analysis of the stimulus responsible for the behavior, we may find that a colorless (achromatic) stimulus of the same brightness, or perhaps shape, is equally effective. Only careful experimental investigation, where the various aspects of the stimulus are varied at will, and the resulting behavior studied, is capable of discovering whether or not color vision is present. Comparative anatomy and naturalistic observations often suggest appropriate experimental studies and give insights as to how these should be carried out, but in themselves they are usually insufficient to establish the kind and degree of sensitivity present in an animal.

Experimental investigations

The methods used to investigate sensitivity in animals may, for convenience, be divided into three classes, the *direct method*, the *conditioned-response method*, and the *discrimination method*.

The direct method. This is so named because it requires no special training of the animal. Suppose, for example, that we wish to know whether the paramecium responds to light. We light one end of an aquarium and make the other end dark. Congregation of the animals at either end indicates that they differentiate light and darkness. If two brightnesses are involved, a differential response of the animals again indicates differential sensitivity. To take another example of the direct method, suppose that we want to know whether a certain animal is capable of responding to sound. We place it on a platform (stabilimeter) that wobbles at the slightest movement. Then we observe, through records of the movements, whether there is a different response to noise and its absence, or perhaps a different response to two different intensities or frequencies of sound. This method, as we shall observe in Chapter 8, has been used to investigate the visual, auditory, and olfactory sensitivity of human infants. Sometimes the animal's respiration, or some other physiological reaction is recorded. Then a difference in physiological response, elicited by different stimuli, is used as an index of sensitivity. In some instances investigators have recorded differential neural reactions (action currents) in the auditory, optic, and gustatory nerves. When different stimuli arouse different action currents there is presumptive evidence for differential sensitivity. Differences in general physiological reactions, in sense-organ reactions, and in neural activities do not, of course, guarantee that the stimuli which arouse these reactions are differentiated in everyday life, nor that the sensory differentiation is utilized by the animal in adjustment. All that these studies suggest, from this standpoint, is the possibility that the animal is capable of the respective sensory discriminations.

The conditioned-response method. This is also of somewhat limited value as an index of the degree to which an animal uses its sensory capacities in actual everyday adjustments. It can, however, be a highly sensitive indicator of sensory capacity. Actually, there are many variations of conditioned-response procedure. Among other things, these procedures vary in the following ways: (1) The animal may be free to move around, or its movements may be greatly restricted. (2) The response conditioned may be of the whole organism, or it may be a reflex or narrowly prescribed group of reflexes. (3) The animal's response may or may not be instru-

mental in obtaining a reward or in enabling the animal to escape punishment. From the standpoint of sensory discrimination, where we are merely interested in whether or not the organism makes a differential reaction and not in how quickly the conditioning occurs, these differences in methodology are of secondary concern.

An experiment on acquisition of the withdrawal response in dogs will serve to illustrate some essentials of the conditioned-response technique of investigating sensory processes. The general arrangement is shown in Figure 30. No withdrawal of the dog's foot is elicited by the onset of a tone of, let us say, 300 cycles per second. Electrical stimulation of the foot (unconditioned stimulus) elicits a withdrawal reaction (unconditioned response). The tone (conditioned stimulus) is now presented shortly before the shock occurs and

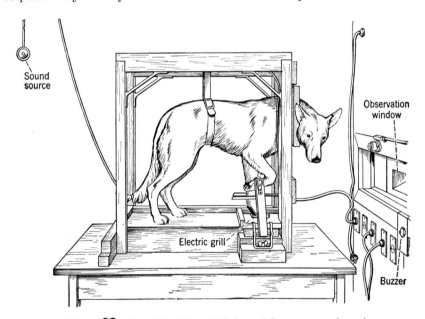

Figure 30. Conditioning a Withdrawal Response to Sound

A shock to the right foot produces withdrawal, which is recorded in a neighboring sound-proofed observation room. Initially the response is aroused only by the shock. During the course of the experiment, other stimuli which closely precede the shock become effective in eliciting the withdrawal reaction, even though shock is not present. We then say that withdrawal has been conditioned to the stimulus or stimuli involved. Sometimes the conditioned stimulus, in this case a tone, arouses anticipatory reactions like barking, struggling, or trembling. These, as well as actual withdrawal, indicate that conditioning has occurred. (After Culler.)

this tone-shock sequence is repeated until conditioning occurs or until it becomes apparent that further presentation would be fruitless. Evidence that the animal hears the tone is forthcoming when (1) it withdraws its foot to the tone — that is, before the shock comes on, or (2) it trembles, struggles, barks, or makes other responses to the tone which show that it anticipates the shock to follow. After this stage has been reached and stabilized, other tests are possible. The tone may be diminished in intensity until the animal no longer responds to it, thus indicating the lower threshold intensity. The frequency may be reduced, or increased, until the animal no longer responds. This shows the range of frequencies to which it is responsive. Or, if we wish to know how small a difference in frequencies is discriminated, we associate the shock with one frequency and not with another. In doing this we follow a random sequence of shock and no-shock tones. If the animal comes to respond to one tone and not to the other, we then know that the difference in frequency is discriminable. During subsequent tests we may reduce the frequency of the no-shock tone until the animal no longer makes a differential response. In this way we discover how small a difference in frequency it is capable of discriminating under these conditions. Differentiation of intensities may be tested in a similar fashion.

The discrimination method. There are many variations of discrimination procedure, depending upon the animal with which it is being used and the problem being investigated. All variations have certain features in common. They require the organism to select one out of two or more stimuli with which it is confronted. It is rewarded for selecting this stimulus and punished for selecting any other. The stimuli are always varied in left-right position in accordance with a chance order, so that the animal cannot learn to respond upon the basis of position, and they are always presented under conditions where extraneous stimuli cannot be used as cues for response. Thus, if color vision is being tested,

the colored areas to be discriminated are not only varied in position, but they are alike in shape, size, brightness, odor, and other characteristics. These controls, plus others after discrimination has occurred, are designed to make certain that color and nothing else is controlling the differential response. Controls subsequent to discrimination may involve variations in brightness, because stimuli which seem equally bright to the human eye may not be so for the animal. If brightness variation interferes with discrimination, then there is evidence that the response is not actually to color. Comparable controls are required when discrimination involves differentiation of other stimuli, such as odors and sounds.

One of the simplest discrimination procedures, first devised by Yerkes [4] for use with mice, but since adapted to a wide variety of animals including aquatic forms, is that illustrated in Figure 31. The walking or swim-

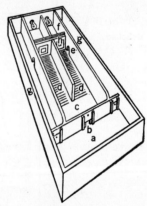

Figure 31. A Yerkes Sensory Discrimination Apparatus

This form of apparatus has been used to test the sensory processes of animals ranging from fishes to primates. *a*, entrance; *b*, door admitting animal to discrimination chamber; *c, d, d,* passages wired with electric grid; *e*, door to alleys *g, g,* leading back to entrance which also serves as a food box; *h*, frame holding visual stimuli; *f*, light box. Modifications of this apparatus have been used to test olfactory, cutaneous, auditory, and kinesthetic processes in addition to vision. (From K. S. Lashley, "Visual Discrimination of Size and Form in the Albino Rat," *J. Anim. Behav.,* 1912, *2*, 311.)

ming animal is confronted by two stimuli which differ from each other to some measurable degree. The experimenter arbitrarily decides which stimulus shall be selected by the animal. When the animal approaches this stimulus it is allowed to proceed unimpeded to the food chamber, where it receives its reward. But when the other stimulus is approached, a shock or some other punishment is administered. This may be confinement in one alley. As we have already indicated, the stimuli vary in right-left position and extraneous stimuli are eliminated or under control. We have implied, in this discussion, that hunger or escape from punishment, or a combination of these, provides the necessary motivation. Sometimes, however, the motive is to get out of the water as quickly as possible, to return to the home cage, or to get to an animal of the opposite sex. Hunger and shock are widely used because they are most easily controlled.

One difficulty with this method, as used by Yerkes and many later investigators, is that the animal may take a long time to learn what it is to do (even though it may be able to discriminate) and that it may not actually notice that the stimuli are somehow related to satisfaction of its needs. Use of this method gave grounds for supposing that rats are incapable of differentiating between such figures as circles and triangles, yet a modification of the method, which made the stimuli more obvious and forced the animal to respond directly to them, yielded very quick discrimination.[5]

With animals capable of jumping toward a stimulus, the modification devised by Lashley and illustrated in Figure 32 is especially useful as a means of investigating visual processes. After preliminary training in which the animal learns to jump through the open windows to obtain food, then to knock down cards placed over the apertures, the stimuli to be discriminated are placed on the cards. Whenever the animal hits the correct card, this falls and the animal is then able to obtain food from the platform behind the card. But

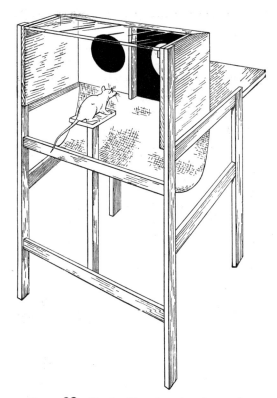

Figure 32. The Lashley Jumping Apparatus

When the animal jumps at the correct card, it falls and he obtains food on the platform beyond. The incorrect card, however, is locked from behind. If the rat jumps at this it fails to give, and he thus falls into the net below. The stimuli are alternated in right-left position as described in the text. (After Lashley.)

when the incorrect card is hit, it fails to give and the animal falls into a net below. Failure to reach food and the fall through space constitute punishment. Controls are similar to those already described.

There are two major reasons for the success of this modification. (1) Since the animal is forced to jump at the cards, it more readily notices the stimuli to be discriminated. (2) Reward and punishment are not delayed as in the Yerkes apparatus; they follow almost immediately after the animal has made its choice. One limitation of the jumping procedure is that it is suitable only for relatively small animals who can jump.

Several apparatuses have since been developed which have the above advantages but do not require jumping. One of these [6] is very much like the Yerkes apparatus in that the animal walks or runs through it, but the stimuli are placed on cards or doors through which the animal must push to reach the food beyond. If doors are used, these are usually hung from above and the animal pushes them open with its head. Pushing the incorrect door, or card, which is locked from behind, brings a shock. This device is adaptable for a wide variety of animals, of various sizes, and can also be used with aquatic organisms. Multiple forms have been devised [7] in which, after making its choice in one unit, the animal moves into another, and so on until the final unit, with food, is reached. Each incorrect response brings a shock, as in the single unit. Still another modification of the discrimination technique calls upon the animal, or child,

to press a pedal below the correct stimulus. Two or more boxes may be presented simultaneously. Pressing the correct pedal opens the door and makes accessible the food, or toy, within. Pressing the incorrect pedal, however, does not open the door. Moreover, through electrification of the pedal, a shock may be received. This kind of discrimination device has been used with cats, as illustrated in Figure 33, and also with monkeys, chimpanzees, and children. When food is used as a reward, all boxes are smeared with the odor so that this cannot provide a cue for correct discrimination. [8]

Although the illustrations given here apply especially to vision, various modifications of the discrimination technique have been used to test the other senses. When discrimination of auditory or olfactory stimuli is being studied, the animal may be placed in a

Figure 33. Testing Discrimination in the Cat

The animal is here being tested for brightness discrimination. It if presses the pedal below the correct stimulus, the cat gets food through the door, which opens immediately. But if the other pedal is pressed, the door fails to open. Sometimes the apparatus is electrified so that a shock is received whenever the incorrect pedal is pressed. The stimuli appear in a randomly arranged right-left sequence from trial to trial. Thus the brighter stimulus might be on the right in one trial, on the left in the next, and on the right in the next two, followed by one to three trials on the left. (Photo courtesy Karl U. Smith.) From C. P. Stone (Editor), *Comparative Psychology* (Third Edition). New York: Prentice-Hall, 1951, p. 319.

T-shaped or Y-shaped apparatus. It is then required to go in one direction or the other when it reaches the bifurcation from the central alley. It may be required to turn to the right when the sound, or odor, is present and to go to the left when the stimulus is absent. Or it may be required to go in one direction for one stimulus and in the other for the stimulus paired with it. A wrong turn brings punishment (shock or confinement) and a correct turn is rewarded. Controls are similar to those already discussed for the other discrimination methods. Cutaneous sensitivity may be tested by giving the animal a choice of smooth and rough paths, warm and cold paths, and so on.

This has not been an exhaustive discussion of the ways in which we gauge the sensory abilities of animals. Enough has been said, however, to provide a background for the following survey of the evolution of sensory processes in animals ranging from unicellular organisms to man. At the present stage of comparative psychology a survey of this kind can be no more than sketchy. Many different methods have been used and one cannot be sure that the results obtained with one method at a particular level are comparable with those obtained by another method at another level. The direct, or the conditioned-response, method might reveal sensitivity of a certain sort whereas the discrimination method might fail to reveal it. Another difficulty is that the sensitivity of most animals has never been tested by any method. Thus there are immense gaps in the data. All that our survey attempts to do, therefore, is to sketch trends as these are revealed by anatomical, naturalistic, and experimental information at present available.

Vision

Structural and functional data indicate that all animals are, in some degree, sensitive to light. In the lowest organisms there are no specialized receptors for vision, but the entire body is light-sensitive. The amoeba, when stimulated by a strong light, makes avoidance reactions of a slow and diffuse nature. Other lower organisms make similar responses to light. In certain of these organisms the appearance of an eye is foreshadowed by a spot of pigment, a part of the body-surface rendered especially sensitive to light. (See Figure 34 A.) A light-sensitive body surface or a pigment spot as such can indicate the presence, direction, and to some extent the intensity and movement of light. Eyes which indicate these things alone are of course elementary

Many lower organisms in which elementary functions are alone present often give the impression that they are able to discriminate color. When spectral light is thrown over an aquarium the animals frequently congregate in given regions. It is as though they possessed, as the case may be, a preference for red, for blue, for yellow, or the like. However, such differential reactions may be determined by the fact that wave-lengths of light possess different intensities in addition to their color aspects. It is to the intensity (associated with discrimination of brightness differences) rather than to wave length (associated with discrimination of color differences) that these organisms respond.

Eyes which indicate the size and shape of objects are called *eidoscopic*, or image-forming. Such eyes may be differentiated in terms of whether they are compound, of fixed focus, or of variable focus. Compound eyes (Figure 34 B) comprise a mosaic of many miniature "eyes" or ommatidia. Washburn suggests that this type of eye, found especially in crustaceans and insects, is probably little better than the simple pigment spot, allowing the organism to respond only to direction, intensity, and movement of light. It is claimed by others, however, that compound eyes are, in a sense, image-forming. As we shall observe presently (p. 93), there is evidence that animals with compound eyes are able visually to discriminate structural details. Eyes of fixed focus (Figure 34 C) project clear images on the retina only when

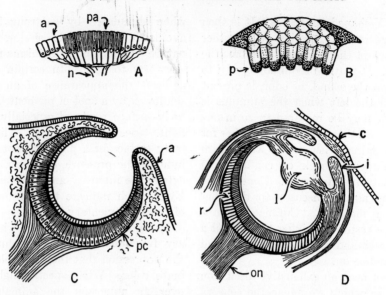

Figure 34. Evolution of the Eye

(*A*) Pigment spot. (After Conn.) (*B*) Compound eye of *Diadema setosum*. (After Sarasin.) (*C*) Fixed focus eye of Nautilus. (After Conn.) The cavity is filled with water. (*D*) Eye of variable focus possessed by the cuttlefish. (After Conn.) *a*, ordinary epithelial cells; *p*, pigment cups; *pa*, pigment particles; *pc*, pigment cells; *n*, nerve fibers; *on*, optic nerve; *c*, cornea; *i*, iris; *l*, lens; *r*, retina.

objects are at a given distance. Eyes with variable focus (Figure 34 *D*) have a lens whose shape and, in some instances, position can be altered so as to adjust to the variable distance of objects. These alterations in the curvature of the lens or in its distance from the retina are effected through muscular attachments.

Several factors other than those mentioned above are important in the evolution of visual functions. The refractive index of the lens and fluid media of the eye differs from one organism to another and has an influence upon discrimination of environmental details. Likewise, eyes may differ with respect to the existence of the fovea centralis. This is a pitlike depression in the retina. It is especially sensitive, and serves as the point of clearest vision. Discrimination of visual detail is possible outside of the fovea, but such discrimination becomes less clear as the periphery of the retina is approached. On the extreme periphery the shape of objects is in-

distinguishable. Thus, while a fovea may not be necessary for discrimination of shape, its existence is probably correlated with the clearest possible differentiation of visual details.

Another factor associated with the evolution of visual processes is the presence of rods and cones, specialized receptor endings which mediate, respectively, brightness and color vision. These structures, as they appear in the eyes of primates, are diagrammatically represented in Figure 35. There is good evidence that animals whose retinae contain no cones are color blind. In low illumination the rods are alone functional and no color is seen. Verrier's [9] study of the visual sense in vertebrates leads him to conclude that, in general, nocturnal animals lack cones, while diurnal animals possess both rods and cones.

Vision does not depend upon the structure of the eye alone. It is to a considerable extent dependent upon the position of the eyes and the nature of the optic nerves and their

Nerve impulse ————————➤

Light

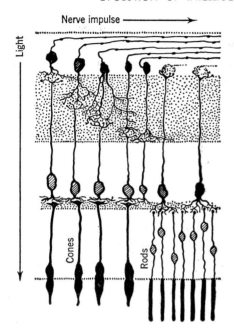

Cones

Rods

Figure 35. Diagram of a Section Through the Retina Showing Rods and Cones and Their Neural Connections

Light passes through the retina until it reaches a layer of pigment in close proximity to the rods and cones. It then stimulates the tips of the rods and cones, thereby arousing nerve impulses. These impulses are carried across the two indicated synapses to the optic nerve (shown as going to the right above). The optic nerve conveys these impulses to the thalamus. They are then relayed to the visual cortex. (After Cajal.)

connections in the brain stem and cortex. The position of the eyes, whether to the front of the head or to the side, is significant for binocular vision and reaction to tridimensional aspects of the environment. In all lower vertebrates the eyes are at the side of the head as shown in Figure 36 A. The optic tracts decussate, that is, cross to opposite sides of the brain, and each eye works as a separate unit. There are therefore two separate visual fields. At a higher level of evolution there is, as shown in Figure 36 B, partial representation of each eye on the *same* side of the brain. Some fibers from the right eye go to the left side, while others go to the right side, and similarly for the fibers of the

left eye. Thus a given side of the brain receives nerve impulses from both eyes. This renders possible some coordination of the functions of the two eyes. Furthermore, the eyes are closer together and, although binocular vision is not yet present, there is less of a gap between the two monocular fields than in lower vertebrates. In the higher vertebrates, including man, the eyes are close together in the front of the head and there is hemidecussation of the optic tracts. As shown in Figure 36 C, half of the fibers from the right eye go to the right half of the visual cortex, while the other fibers go to the left half. Hemidecussation involves fibers from the fovea as well as retinal fibers in general. Optimal coordination of the two eyes is present at this stage. Movements involved in accommodation of the lens, convergence of the eyes, and the like are coordinated. When such a visual mechanism evolves, binocular vision is possible for the first time. Instead of being restricted to a flat, bidimensional picture of its environment, the organism may now obtain a tridimensional view.

Going hand in hand with the developments in the optic mechanism which we have just sketched is an increasing elaboration of the brain stem and visual cortex. After the optic fibers cross, or partly cross, at the optic chiasma they go to the thalamus. Here they make synaptic connection with other fibers which find their ultimate locus in the lower rear part of the brain, known as the occipital cortex. The evolution of higher visual functions is associated with increasing elaboration of this region of the brain.

An analysis of such structural differentiations as were presented above, together with information gained from naturalistic and experimental observations, leads to the following conclusions concerning the status of vision in animals at successive levels of evolution. There is good evidence that all animals respond to light in terms of its *brightness*. It is possible, also, that all of them respond in some measure to *movement* of objects in the field of vision. Some organisms make no response to

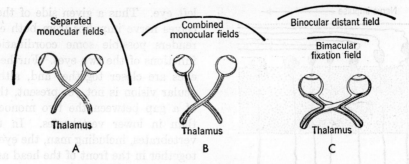

Figure **36.** Evolution of the Binocular Fixation Field

A. Diagram of the eyes and optic tracts at the stage in which there are separate monocular visual fields, absence of conjugate movements of the eyes, with total decussation of the fibers of the optic nerves. *B.* Diagram of the eyes and optic tracts at the stage in which there are combined monocular fields and some conjugate movements of the eyes, with subtotal decussation of the fibers of the optic nerves. *C.* Diagram of the eyes and optic tracts at the stage in which there are developed a binocular distant field, a bimacular (bi-foveal) fixation field, conjugate movements of the eyes, and himidecussation of general retinal and macular fibers of the optic nerves. (After F. W. Jones and S. D. Porteus, *The Matrix of the Mind,* University of Hawaii Press, pp. 297, 298, and 300.)

objects unless these move. In many animals the ability to discriminate movement has apparently developed to a high degree.

Discrimination of color

Reliable information about the ability of animals to discriminate color is difficult to obtain. This is because what seems to us to be color discrimination, that is, discrimination of wave-length differences, may have other bases. The objects of everyday life which have color characteristics often also differ in such aspects as shape, size, movement, and odor. If a bee shows any preference for a particular flower, its preference may be based upon some of these characteristics rather than color as such. But suppose we have established that the bee is discriminating what to us are the color aspects of the flower. Even here we are confronted with the possibility that the animal is color blind and, like a color-blind human being, is responding to brightness rather than wave length. Suppose that we set up an experiment in which the colors to be discriminated are equated in brightness for the human eye. That is, we take a red and a green which to our eye look equally bright. But again we are in difficulty for it has been established

that colors of equal brightness to our eye may not be equally bright to the animal's eye, and this discrepancy between human and animal may differ from one type of animal to another.

The surest way to discover whether or not an organism is responding to wave length is to arrange an experiment in which we equate the brightness of colors for its eye and then test to see whether it can discriminate between them. The details of this difficult procedure have been discussed elsewhere.[10] In most experiments in which the brightness factor has been controlled, a short cut has been taken. The brightness values of the colors have not been determined beforehand. However, attempts have been made to discover if brightness variations confuse the animal who has already discriminated, apparently on the basis of wave length. The colored stimuli have been varied in brightness over a wide range in the hope that there will be times when both are equally bright to the animal's eye. In some cases a color stimulus to which the animal has been responding has been presented in the midst of colorless stimuli covering a wide range of brightness. The latter procedure, illustrated in Figure 37, is especially adapted to research with animals

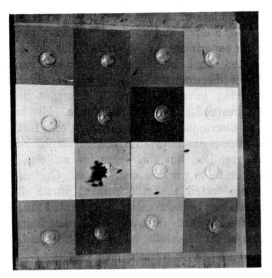

Figure 37. Bees Discriminate Blue from Shades of Gray

The blue card, on which the bees are seen to be congregated, was initially presented alone beneath a watch glass containing sweetened water. In the final tests, as illustrated here, the blue card was placed among cards having various shades of gray. It was moved in position, relative to the other cards, from trial to trial. The cards were all covered with a large sheet of glass and all of the watch glasses were empty, so that the response could not be based upon odor. When a red card was used, the bees failed to make the sort of discrimination illustrated here. They congregated on dark gray or black cards as well as the red one, thus suggesting red blindness. (From K. von Frisch, *Bees: Their Vision, Chemical Senses, and Language*, Ithaca: Cornell University Press, 1950, p. 7.)

which are not readily trained in the laboratory.

The above procedures are adequate providing the brightness steps are sufficiently small to provide a brightness confusion. If our tests cause the discrimination to break down — if the accuracy of response, for example, drops from around one hundred per cent to around a chance percentage — we know either of two things. That is, the animal may be responding to brightness, as a more obvious stimulus, and not to color as such, or it may be color blind. If we continue training, at the point of confusion, and the animal returns to a high level of accuracy, which is

not disturbed by further brightness variations, then we have good evidence of color discrimination. If the discrimination cannot be re-established, however, it is assumed either that the animal is color blind or that, if color vision is present, our method is inadequate to reveal it.

There is no evidence that any animals below the arthropods (crabs, bees, ants, etc.) discriminate in terms of wave length. Evidence for color vision in many of the arthropods is questionable because investigators have failed to make an adequate control of the brightness factor. Of the many studies with arthropods, those of von Frisch [11] on bees are especially worthy of mention. Using the method already described, von Frisch found that bees distinguish certain colors from grays of the same brightness but that they confuse red with black or dark gray. His own work, as well as that of others using similar methods, leads von Frisch to conclude that, while bees are red-blind, they distinguish the following colors from grays of the same brightness and from each other: yellow, blue-green, blue, and ultraviolet. The bee's spectrum, as compared with ours, thus appears to be shortened at the red end and lengthened at the ultraviolet end.

It is generally assumed that fish respond to color, and the use of colored flies by fishermen is based upon this assumption. However, the literature on color vision in fish, while extensive, is far from conclusive. In his excellent review of this literature, Walls [12] concludes that, although nine-tenths of the research needs repetition, especially to obtain more adequate control of the brightness factor, some fish have demonstrable color vision. The evidence for color vision in amphibians and reptiles is even weaker than that on fishes, again because of the inadequacy of brightness controls. Color vision in birds, however, has been very clearly established. Lashley,[13] using bantams, and Hamilton and Coleman,[14] using pigeons, have shown that these birds differentiate colors under conditions where the brightness of the stimuli is varied over a wide range, the positive stimulus sometimes being brighter and sometimes less bright than the negative one. Pumphrey,[15] who bases his discussion upon anatomical and behavioral data, believes that there is little difference between the color vision of birds and of human beings, either with respect to the colors differentiated or the spectral range. There is still doubt concerning the existence of color vision in some of the mammals, like the rat, cat, and dog. Rats respond to red on a wave-length basis, and there is some evidence that other colors are differentiated. This research has been reviewed elsewhere.[16] Much research needs to be done with other infraprimate mammals. Fox[17] refers to an unpublished experiment on horses in which they distinguished green and yellow from each other and from many shades of gray but failed to differentiate red and blue.

All the primates so far tested have demonstrated good ability to differentiate colors in terms of wave-length differences, although there is some evidence that Cebus monkeys are red-blind. The most extensive research on monkeys and chimpanzees has been done by Grether and by Grether and Malmo[18] who provide good summaries of the earlier literature. Some of Grether's investigations compare the color vision of chimpanzee and human subjects under comparable conditions. These studies reveal a basic similarity in human and chimpanzee color vision.

Discrimination of visual details

Arthropods are the lowest organisms which show unequivocal discrimination of visual details such as those involved in figures, forms, and patterns. Most of these possess compound eyes; hence it is assumed that their vision of objects is like a mosaic of the impressions made by separate parts. In any event it can be demonstrated experimentally that bees, wasps, and butterflies distinguish between a variety of patterns.[19] Bees were found by Hertz to discriminate between open or broken figures (like an X) and solid figures

(like a black circle) but not between an X and a Y or a circle and a square.[20] A very thorough experiment by Meesters[21] has demonstrated that sticklebacks, minnows, and dories discriminate between various figures differing in shape, such as triangles and squares and crosses and diamonds. His fish also discriminated differences in size. Little is known about detail vision in amphibians and reptiles, but their eyes are sufficiently elaborate to provide such vision. Casteel[22] demonstrated that the painted turtle discriminates between rather complicated visual patterns. Birds have very good discrimination of visual details, as shown by a number of experiments on hens and pigeons.[23] A controversial issue is whether the pigeon has as good detail vision as man. All the mammals so far tested have revealed that they are able to differentiate various geometrical and other figures. Among these animals are rats,[24] cats,[25] raccoons,[26] dogs,[27] and monkeys and apes.[28] Spence[29] obtained results which point to a similarity in the visual acuity of chimpanzees and human subjects.

It is generally believed that *stereoscopic vision* first appears at the primate level of evolution. Such a belief is based upon the fact that the structural requisites for such vision (see Figure 36 C) do not appear in animals below the primates.

In summary we may say that all animals respond to light in terms of brightness. All of them probably respond to movement of objects in the field of vision. Response to wave length (color) is present in some arthropods, like the bees, and probably also in fish, although the data are somewhat equivocal. Birds have very good color vision. Mammals below the primates may have color vision, but so far the evidence is not too conclusive. We know that rats respond to red, in terms of wave length, and there is evidence, although controversial, that they respond to certain other colors. Very little of any value is known of color vision in cats and dogs. Recent research suggests that horses may have color vision of a sort. All of the primates so far tested (monkeys and chimpanzees) have good color vision, possibly as good or almost as good as our own. Response to visual detail of a structural nature (as in figures and patterns) is present in various arthropods, including the bees, and possibly in all vertebrates, although the evidence for such vision in amphibians and reptiles is meager. Fish respond to figures, and so do birds and all the mammals so far tested. Such vision is especially good in the birds and the primates. Third-dimensional vision based upon retinal disparity (binocular vision) is probably absent below the primates.

Hearing

Like vision, hearing enables the organism to respond to environmental objects before they come into contact with the skin. Compared with vision, however, it gives relatively little information about the details of these objects. As the higher vertebrates are approached, auditory functions play an increasingly important role in the processes of communication.

All invertebrates except certain of the arthropods are devoid of auditory organs. Although these lower organisms are responsive to vibration applied at the skin, there is no evidence that they possess auditory sensitivity. Such sensitivity is probably a higher elaboration of the responses of the skin to vibratory stimulation. Some of the arthropods, like the crustacea, possess an organ known as a statocyst, which was once thought to be auditory in function. The statocyst is a small cavity into which hairs project. Grains of sand within the cavity shift their positions during certain kinds of movement, and by stimulating the hairs indicate to the organism the position of its body in space. This function is, however, equilibratory or static rather than auditory. Somewhat similar organs appear in vertebrates where, in structural connection with the auditory apparatus, they likewise serve an equilibratory function. In other arthropods such as grass-

hoppers, crickets, and katydids there exist complicated tympanal organs which resonate sympathetically when vibratory stimulation is set up in the air. Wever and Bray [30] found that the cricket's tympanal organ responds to frequencies ranging from 500 to 11,000 cycles per second. The katydid's upper limit is around 45,000 cycles.

The auditory structures of the vertebrates have evolved in close association with their organs of equilibrium. Figure 38 illustrates this relationship. It is believed that the cochlea of higher vertebrates has evolved from the lagena of the lower ones. Frisch and Stetter [31] demonstrated that the lagena and the saccule of minnows have an auditory function. When these were removed, the fish no longer responded to sounds, although equilibrium was undisturbed.

It is now becoming well known that, rather than being a silent world, the world of fishes,

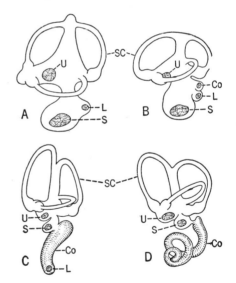

Figure 38. Evolution of the Inner Ear in Vertebrates

A, Fish. *B*, Frog. *C*, Bird. *D*. Mammal. *SC*, semicircular canals; *Co*, cochlea; *U*, *S*, and *L*, otoliths of the utricle, saccule, and lagena. (After von Frisch. From D. M. Purdy, "The Functions of the Receptors." Reprinted by permission from *Comparative Psychology*, first edition, ed. by F. A. Moss. Copyright, Prentice-Hall, Inc., New York City, p. 176.)

even those of the ocean depths, is full of sounds made by the fishes themselves. Whether or not these sounds have communicative significance is not known. Recent research discussed by Pumphrey [32] suggests that the lateral-line organs of fishes, as well as their inner ears, are responsive to sound. The evidence is physiological, being based upon the fact that microphonic potentials such as can be recorded from the cochlea are obtained from these organs.

The mammalian ear has various accessory structures in addition to those shown in Figure 38. These convey vibrations set up by external media from the outer to the inner ear, or cochlea. Such accessory structures are shown in Figure 39. In its essential characteristics, the human ear is like that of other mammals. The organ of Corti, which transmits stimulation received by the accessory apparatus to the auditory nerve, is diagrammed in Figure 40. When vibrations reach the oval window of the vestibular canal via the small bones of the middle ear, the fluid which fills this canal and the others is set in motion. This motion is conveyed through the basilar membrane to the hair cells of Corti. It is the motion of these hairs which gives rise to nerve impulses. Auditory nerve impulses are transmitted, via the cochlear branch of the auditory nerve, to lower brain centers and thence to the temporal area of the cortex. This is not the place, however, to enter into details of auditory theory. These are discussed by Wever.[33] An elementary account will be found in Munn.[34]

Response to noise is perhaps more primitive than that to tone. While many of the lower vertebrates respond to noises, there is much doubt concerning the ability of certain of them to respond to tone. The problem is complicated by the fact that, like different wave lengths of light, vibratory stimuli vary in purity and in intensity, the physical correlate of loudness. In order to be sure that an organism is responding to tone, one must control the intensity factor, requiring the animal to discriminate between different frequencies

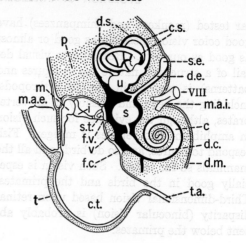

Figure 39. Diagram of a Typical Mammalian Ear

The diagram is that of a rabbit's ear. The external ear (*m.a.e.*) is seen to the left and it extends as far as the tympanic membrane, or ear drum, to which the bone *m* is attached. The middle ear extends from the ear drum to the oval window (*f.v.*) of the vestibule of the cochlea (*c*). It consists, essentially, of the three small bones known as the malleus (*m*), the incus (*i*), and the stapes (*s.t.*) as well as the air chamber to the eustachian (auditory) tube (*t.a.*). External air vibrations are transmitted to the tympanic membrane and cause it to vibrate. The three small bones transmit this vibration to the window of the vestibule and liquids which fill the cochlear canals are set in motion. The movements of these liquids activate fibers in the basilar membrane which, in turn, are connected with fibers of the VIIIth (auditory) nerve. The other structures shown in the diagram are *c.s.* semicircular canals; *c.t.* tympanic cavity; *d.c.* cochlear duct; *d.e.* endolymphic duct; *d.m.* dura mater; *d.s.* semicircular ducts; *f.c.* cochlear round window; *m.a.i.* internal acoustic meatus; *s*, sacculus; *s.e.* endolymphic sac; *u*, utriculus; *v*, vestibulum; VIII, acoustic nerve; *p* and *t*, bony structures. Reproduced by kind permission of the University of Toronto Press, publishers of Bensley, *Practical Anatomy of the Rabbit*, 6th ed., revised by Professor E. Horne Craigie.

equated in loudness for its ear, or to discriminate between them while their intensity varies over a wide range. Few investigators have taken cognizance of this fact; hence their results are equivocal. Another necessary precaution, which is hard to fulfill with water-living species, is that of preventing vibratory stimulation of non-auditory structures.

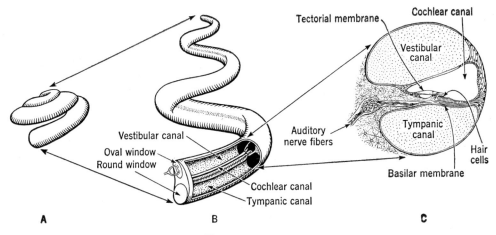

Figure 40. The Human Cochlea

In *A* the cochlea is coiled, as in the inner ear. This can be extended, as in *B*, to show the inner canals. A cross-section of the canals, as in *C*, shows the organ of Corti, with its hair cells and nervous outlets. (From N. L. Munn, *Psychology*, 2d ed., Boston: Houghton Mifflin, 1951, p. 458).

There is, as we have seen, evidence that some fish are able to respond to sounds, though they lack the complicated accessory apparatus and cochlear mechanism of mammals. Stetter [35] found that minnows discriminate between tones of 286 and 341 cycles under conditions where intensity is controlled. The evidence for tonal discrimination in the other lower vertebrates is not clear, but Kurodo,[36] who has done the most thorough work, obtained what appears to be good evidence of reaction to tone in lizards. Snakes, turtles, and similar vertebrates are believed to be entirely deaf. No experiment on these animals has given the least evidence that they can even hear noise. General observation would suggest that birds respond to tonal frequencies as well as to noise. An investigation by Wever and Bray [37] on electrical responses of the pigeon's cochlea suggests sensitivity to frequencies between 100 and 10,000 cycles.

All mammals respond to noise, and many of them have demonstrated ability to respond to and differentiate tones. Several investigators, whose work has been summarized elsewhere,[38] have demonstrated that rats respond to pure tones, that their upper limit is somewhere above 40,000 cycles compared with 20,000 cycles in ourselves, and that they are capable of differentiating pairs of tonal frequencies which are wide apart. Guinea pigs,[39] cats,[40] and dogs [41] also respond to tones. The upper limit in dogs, as in rats, is known to be high. In dogs it is at least as high as 35,000 cycles. The so-called "silent whistles" to which dogs respond, but which human beings cannot hear, have frequencies in this upper range. As is now well-known, bats both emit and respond to frequencies as high as 50,000 cycles. They use these frequencies in avoiding obstacles by echolocation.[42]

All the mammals so far tested have shown good ability to locate sounds. The typical procedure is to place before, or around, the animal a number of identical objects under conditions where a sound emitted by one object at a time can provide the only cue for successful response. Several of these experiments have been discussed by Katz.[43]

The auditory mechanisms of primates are very much like our own, and one might expect comparable auditory sensitivity. Monkeys, as Wendt [44] has shown, respond to pure tones within the human range, their acuity being better than human acuity at some frequencies and poorer at others. The upper limit is not known, since the highest frequency used was only 16,384 cycles. At the higher frequencies, however, monkeys apparently have better acuity than the human subjects. Elder's [45] experiment with chimpanzees shows that they respond to frequencies above the human range. Their upper limit is around 33,000 cycles. The results on acuity tests imply that chimpanzees have a better acuity than human subjects, but Elder feels that this is because his method favors chimpanzees. Yerkes [46] believes that although the acuity of the chimpanzee may be no better than ours, its sound world is probably richer than our own because of its ability to respond to the high frequencies emitted by many insects and other organisms, frequencies which are above our audible range.

The ability to respond to noise, which, as we have shown, is present in all mammals and in some of the lower vertebrates and invertebrates, is probably as important in general adjustment as is the more highly evolved ability to respond to tone. Tonal discrimination, however, becomes of outstanding importance in vocal communication.

The Other Senses

Vision and hearing are the most specialized senses and, for higher animals, the most important. It is perhaps for this reason that they have been so extensively studied that we know a great deal about them. The other senses which we shall now discuss are the proprioceptive (static and kinesthetic), the cutaneous (touch, temperature, pain), and the chemical (taste and smell). What little is known about these senses in animals can be dealt with briefly.

Proprioceptive processes

Most organisms possess static sensitivity

of some kind. In many of the arthropods equilibration is, as suggested above, mediated by the statocysts. In the vertebrates, static sensitivity depends upon the semicircular canals and the other non-auditory structures of the labyrinth. Hairs within the labyrinth are stimulated by movements of the liquid of the canals, and nerve impulses are sent to the cerebellum and to other lower brain centers. Associated with this receptor mechanism are vestibular reflexes which, in some organisms like members of the cat family, enable the animal to land on its feet even when it is dropped from various heights in a variety of different positions.

Kinesthetic sensitivity is mediated by sense organs located within the muscles, tendons, and joints. Impulses from these organs indicate the positions of the limbs and of other parts of the body. Little experimental work on kinesthesis has involved infrahuman subjects. However, rats have demonstrated good ability to discriminate the inclinations of planes when all stimuli other than static and kinesthetic are excluded.[47] Some rats discriminate a difference of one degree in the inclination of two inclined pathways. The researches of Crozier and others on geotropic reactions in invertebrates, lower vertebrates, and mammals (see pp. 59–60) indicate the existence of kinesthetic sensitivity in these organisms.

Cutaneous processes

All organisms are responsive to tactile stimulation, whether mechanical, electrical, or chemical. In mammals, hairs increase the susceptibility of tactual receptors to mechanical stimulation. Temperature sensitivity is probably present in all animals to some degree, although few experimental data are available. Experiments by Yoakum [48] on rats and squirrels indicate ability to discriminate temperatures differing by 10 to 16 degrees centigrade. The nest-building of rats, as Kinder [49] has shown, is controlled by temperature changes in their environment. Sensitivity to cutaneous injury probably exists to some degree in even the lowest animals.

The chemical senses

The entire surface of the body in lower forms, and specialized parts of the body in higher ones, are receptive to various forms of chemical stimulation applied directly. General chemical sensitivity is also found, to some extent, in all higher forms. All the vertebrates have, in addition to the common chemical sense, two specialized chemical senses. One of these, the gustatory, is mediated by specialized receptors (taste buds) in or around the mouth. The other chemical sense is that of olfaction. Specialized receptors for odorous stimuli are located in the nasal epithelium. Like vision and audition, olfactory sensitivity enables the organism to respond to distinct stimuli. The gustatory and olfactory senses, while they have their special receptor and nerve mechanisms, are closely allied in many respects. In air-living vertebrates it is relatively easy to test for the separate existence of taste and smell, but in those which reside in water the task becomes relatively difficult. Parker and Sheldon [50] have shown, nevertheless, that the catfish possesses both gustatory and olfactory sensitivity. There is good evidence that all true vertebrates possess both forms of sensitivity. Dogs are of course credited with good olfactory sensitivity. The olfactory sensitivity of rats, particularly from the standpoint of locating foodstuffs and finding their way through mazes is apparently quite good. Their taste sensitivity is also good, and it is used, in the cafeteria-feeding situation, to select needed foodstuffs. Pfaffman's [51] experiments have demonstrated that the gustatory nerve of the cat makes differential responses to acids and non-acids. The olfactory and gustatory senses of infrahuman primates have not been subjected to experimental study, but there is reason to believe that they are every bit as good as our own.

A number of investigators have placed particular significance upon the fact that the structures of the brain devoted to smell have gradually decreased in relative size from the lower vertebrates to the mammals and from the lower mammals to man. In some of the fishes one-third of the total brain tissue is olfactory in function. Higher mammals, however, have an extremely small "smell brain." As we shall observe later, the proportion of the brain given over to other sensory functions also becomes smaller as we go from the lower vertebrates to man.

Motor Dexterity

Animals exhibit various degrees of dexterity in locomotion and in manipulation. Locomotor dexterity enables an organism to orient and to travel in space. The degree of dexterity in such activity determines the facility with which objects or situations may be approached or avoided. It also underlies the ease and swiftness with which transportation may take place. Manipulatory dexterity, on the other hand, enables an animal to change aspects of its environment without the necessity of changing its own position relative to them.

Locomotor dexterity

From the lowest animals to man there is a wide range of locomotor dexterity. In this particular function man does not, biologically speaking, stand at the top. Certain of the arthropods, the birds, and some infrahuman mammals far exceed human beings in locomotor ability. They orient with a higher degree of adroitness than man and they travel faster.*

* It would lead us too far afield to trace the evolution of the different forms of locomotion from the lowest organisms up, interesting as this study would be. Maier and Schneirla, however, have given an excellent discussion of important stages in the evolution of locomotion from the amoeba to birds. Their discussion is not confined to a single chapter or group of chapters, but is scattered in various places throughout the book. The reader is referred especially to the

The most remarkable thing about human locomotion is the posture assumed. Whereas all other primates characteristically travel on all fours, man assumes the upright position. This change from walking on all fours to walking on the hind limbs alone has contributed immensely to the evolution of human intelligence. In the first place, an upright position enlarges the range of vision during locomotion. In the second place, upright locomotion releases the fore limbs for manipulation and makes possible a high degree of manual dexterity. In the third place, freedom of the fore limbs for manipulation releases the mouth from manipulatory activities such as moving objects, struggling, and other grosser reactions. A greater degree of flexibility of the facial and throat musculature is thus rendered possible and these structures may be used primarily for communicative activities. Hand in hand with this fundamental change in locomotion went alterations in the central nervous system. The increased dexterity resulting from man's upright position is thus a product of nervous as well as skeletal and muscular development. Some of the correlated changes in central neural mechanisms are discussed later in the present chapter.

Manipulatory dexterity

Manipulatory structures consist primarily of the mouth and appendages. Under manipulation are included (1) picking up food or other objects with the mouth or appendages, (2) use of the mouth or appendages in struggle, (3) use of the mouth or appendages in changing the position and relationship of objects, and (4) use of the mouth, appendages, or general musculature in signaling and other forms of communication.

It is impossible to say at which stage manip-

following pages: 14–16 (amoeba), 40–41 (hydra), 46–49 (medusa), 52–62 (brittle star), 64–73 (starfish), 79–82 (flatworm), 92–95 (earthworm), 105–107 (snail), 143–146 (insect), 203–208 (amphibian), 235–236 (bird).

ulatory ability was first evidenced. In a sense, it is exhibited to a low degree by unicellular organisms when these displace objects by moving their bodies against them. Many of the invertebrates and all of the vertebrates manipulate objects with their mouths. All mammals and some inframammalian animals manipulate aspects of their environment with their front appendages. Mammals as lowly as the rat can pull in objects on a string, pick up food or other objects, use chips to gather up water, push up the latch on a puzzle box, and so on, all by using the front appendages. From the rat to the primates, however, manual dexterity made great strides. Monkeys evidence a high degree of ability in manipulating instruments such as latches, bolts, sticks, and strings. They also exhibit fine finger prehension in grooming and in other activities. Chimpanzees demonstrate a still higher degree of dexterity. Not only do they stack boxes, manipulate strings, and use sticks to reach food, but Köhler,[52] and others since, have observed them fitting two sticks together in order to have a sufficiently long instrument with which to reach distant objects. At the Yerkes Laboratories of Comparative Psychobiology chimpanzees press on small push-buttons to get food from instruments used to test their sensory discrimination and reaction time. One frequently observes trained chimpanzees using knives, forks, spoons, and drinking utensils much as human beings use them. In many such activities, infrahuman primates are also quite dexterous with their toes. The ability of the higher primates to oppose the thumb to the fingers makes fine finger prehension possible, and this adds greatly to the dexterity with which objects may be manipulated. Monkeys are able to pick up small objects, even fleas, with finger-thumb opposition. Development of finer sensory discrimination and motor representation in the cortex has been associated with evolution of manual dexterity.

The evolution of manual dexterity has contributed to intelligent adaptation in several important respects. It has enabled the organism to explore and gain knowledge of unseen parts of its own body. It has increased, in many respects, the biological flexibility of food-getting, struggle, escape, courtship, and other vital reactions. It has enhanced the flexibility of gestural reactions involved in communication. It has made possible the use of tools and weapons to control the physical and social aspects of the environment. It has, in man alone, because of correlated cerebral superiority, led to the *invention* of tools and weapons. It has led man to the production, use, and control of fire. Finally, and also in man alone, it has made writing possible. This is of far-reaching consequence, for it makes possible transmission of man's accumulated experience without the need for direct social contacts.

Another motor superiority of man over lower organisms resides in his use of his mouth and throat, as well as his appendages, in communication. Other animals possess the mechanisms to produce sound, and they can make a wide variety of sounds and gestures, but man possesses a greater degree of flexibility in sound-producing and gestural mechanisms than any other organism. This superiority is, of course, partly dependent upon evolution of brain mechanisms. While animals below man can, by making sounds and gestures, signal * the approach of danger, make advances to members of the opposite sex, and the like, they are not, as far as one can tell, capable of true speech. This is a purely human accomplishment and it depends much more upon associative brain functions than upon manipulatory mechanisms as such.**

* We do not mean by use of the word "signal" that the animal intentionally uses its mouth, appendages, or general musculature to warn, court, and the like. Certain sounds and movements of the body, being frequently associated with certain situations involving danger, struggle, and courtship, become conditioned stimuli for the arousal of responses appropriate to these situations. They appear to be signals only in the sense that a light, in the conditioned-response experiment, signals the approaching electric shock.
** Animal language is given detailed consideration in Chapter 12.

The Role of Central Nervous Mechanisms

Some earlier stages in the evolution of the nervous system were discussed in Chapter 3. There our interest was chiefly in structures which preceded the appearance of the receptor-effector system. One will recall that this system comprises separate neurons functionally connected through synapses. Stimulation of a receptor sets up impulses which travel along the sensory nerve-fiber until they reach a synapse. Here the impulse may travel across the synapse to a motor fiber which in turn carries it to the muscle or gland. (See Figures 25 and 26, page 61.) This is the simplest possible synaptic nerve connection. In all vertebrates, and in many invertebrates, association neurons are involved. These are nerve-fibers between the sensory and motor neurons. A reflex arc involving three neurons has one such fiber. Normally, many association fibers are involved in a reflex activity. The most significant function of the association fibers is not transmission as such, but integration. The brain, which is both a terminus for sensory impulses from the brain stem and spinal cord and a sending station for motor impulses which travel down the spinal cord, has as its most important function the integration of various incoming and outgoing impulses. This function is carried on by millions of association neurons. The development of integrative functions at the head end of the organism is the outstanding factor associated with neural evolution. In the following discussion we shall turn our attention to the evolution of the brain, indicating the chief changes which have appeared from the earliest brains to those of man. The significance of these changes for the evolution of intelligent behavior will be our prime concern.

Evolution of the brain

The precursor of the vertebrate brain is the ganglion which appears at the head end of many of the higher invertebrates. Some idea of the nature of this ganglion, as presented in the earthworm, may be gathered

from Figure 41. The ganglion at each segment (see Figure 25) exerts some control over
that segment, but the large ganglion at the
head serves to integrate movements of the
worm as a whole. Herrick [53] has pointed out
that the nervous system of worms offers a
rough pattern of that to be found in vertebrates.

There is a tendency for the gross weight
of the brain to increase as we go from lower
to higher animals, but there are exceptions
to this general trend. The whale and the
elephant, for example, have brains which are
much larger than ours. It is thus not possible to gauge the evolution of intelligence
in terms of brain weight *per se*. An extremely
large animal like the whale *must* have a large
brain if for no other reason than that a tremendous body surface must find representation in the brain, and this organ must activate
and integrate the responses of many ponder-
ous effector mechanisms. What is more important as an indicator of possible intelligence
at various levels is the relation of brain weight
to body weight. But this is not too reliable
an index either. We find such brain-weight/
body-weight ratios as: whale 1/10,000; elephant, 1/500; gorilla, 1/250; cat, 1/110; and

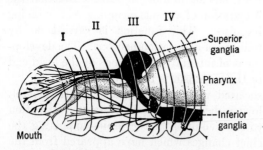

**Figure 41. The Brain and Anterior
Nerves of the Earthworm**

The brain of the earthworm comprises the two ganglia
and the ring which connects them. This end of the
worm plays a dominant role in the development of
other structures during ontogeny and in the integration of the movements of the mature organism. (By
permission of The Macmillan Co., modified from Ship-
ley and McBride's *Zoology* by C. J. Herrick, *Neurological Foundations of Animal Behavior*, Holt, 1924,
p. 129.)

monkey, 1/50.[54] But gorillas are certainly
more intelligent than cats and probably more
intelligent than monkeys. Moreover, man,
who is certainly more intelligent than a monkey, by whatever criterion one applies, also
has a brain-weight/body-weight ratio, of 1/50.

What is perhaps the most important morphological index which we can apply is the
ratio of brain weight to spinal-cord weight.[55]
This would place man at the top, since, in
proportion to the size of his brain, he has a
very small spinal cord. The ratio for apes is
15/1 and in man 55/1. This implies that, in
man, the routine functions of cutaneous sensitivity and reflex activity, with which the
spinal cord is almost entirely concerned, require relatively little brain tissue. In the
frog, where these functions predominate,
the weight of the spinal cord is even greater
than that of the brain. This point will be
clarified further when we look at the human
brain itself and see how relatively little of it is
set aside for purely sensory and motor functions.

From the lowest vertebrates to man there
has been increasing elaboration of the forebrain, or cerebrum. The grosser aspects of
this evolution are apparent in Figures 42 and
43. There is, at first, merely a relative increase in the size of the cerebrum. This is due
largely to increased representation of sensory
and motor mechanisms like those just considered. The increase is at first quite small
in proportion to the size of the older brain
mechanisms, which are concerned to a large
extent with olfactory sensitivity and reflex
activity. A dogfish, for example, has no cerebrum at all and a pigeon has very little.
During the development of sensory representation, however, there is a relative reduction in the size of the area given over to olfaction and a relative increase in the amount
of tissue set aside for visual and auditory
functions. In the higher mammals there also
occurs a gradual increase in the amount of
tissue not dominated by sensory and motor
structures. Such tissue, which goes to make
up the bulk of the cerebral cortex (outer layer

of the cerebrum), consists almost entirely of association neurons. These serve to integrate sensorimotor functions as well as to retain and integrate the effects of past activities. The large increase in association fibers is evidenced by an increase in the size of the cerebrum, but more particularly by changes in its surface structure. In higher mammals the exterior surface of the cerebrum folds inwards to form many creases and furrows. These infoldings, known as invaginations, become increasingly evident as the human level of evolution is approached. The significance of invagination is that it makes possible an increased number of association neurons within a restricted space.

The relative space allotted to association, sensory, and motor areas in the brains of three different mammals is suggested by Figure 43. The areas without designated functions are largely associational. Destruction of the specialized sensory and motor areas leads to various disturbances of the functions indicated, as well as to disturbance of associational processes. Destruction of tissues in the association areas is followed by a more general disturbance of behavior than follows destruction of tissues in the sensory and motor areas. In order to gain an idea of the significance of these parts of the brain in various animals below man we shall summarize some of the findings of recent research on the role of cerebral mechanisms in processes of adjustment.

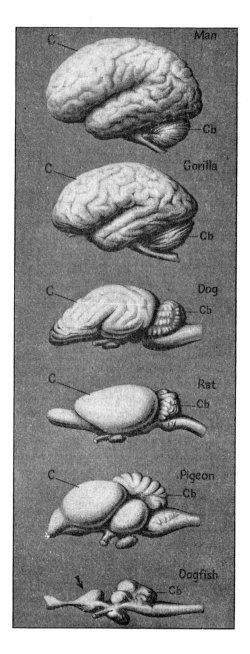

Figure 42. The Brain from Fish to Man

These brains are drawn to the same length so that the smaller ones will show adequate detail. Their relative size may be gathered from the following approximate weights, given in grams: man, 1500; gorilla, 400; dog, 130; rat, 2; pigeon, 2.2.; and dogfish, 3. The cerebrum (C) not only gets larger but it also gets larger in proportion to body weight. In the dogfish there is no cerebrum, but comparable structures are indicated by the arrow. The gorilla is much heavier than man, but his brain-weight is only one-fourth of man's. Note, also, the invaginations shown in the dog's brain. These are more pronounced in the gorilla and human brains. The smell brain, so prominent at the left of the three lower brains, undergoes a recession in higher brains. Cb is the cerebellum. Note its prominence in the pigeon, which of course exhibits behavior notable for its complex coordinations. (From N. L. Munn, *Psychology*, 2d ed., Boston: Houghton Mifflin, 1951, p. 49.)

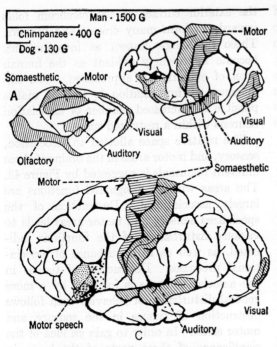

Figure 43. The Left Hemispheres of Three Mammalian Brains Drawn to Scale to Show the Relative Lengths

A more accurate measure of the size relations of these three brains is given by the graphs at the top which indicate the relative weights of entire brains weighed fresh. *A*, the brain of a large adult dog. *B*, the brain of a young adult chimpanzee. *C*, from a human brain somewhat below the average size. The position of certain primary sensory centers is indicated. In the primate brain the small olfactory centers do not show in this view. The greater part of the visual area is on the inner side of the hemisphere so that it does not appear here. The region which corresponds to the human motor speech area in the chimpanzee is indicated by small dots. It is quite uniform in structure as compared to the structurally complex motor speech area of man. (After Campbell, from S. W. Bartelmez, "Man from the Point of View of His Development and Structure," in *The Nature of the World and of Man*, University of Chicago Press.)

Functions of the brain in adjustment

Disturbances following cerebral injury become progressively greater as one goes from the lower to the higher vertebrates. Marquis [56] has pointed out that this increased dependence upon the cortex as the higher vertebrates are approached is most clearly indicated for visual functions. In fishes and amphibians there are practically no visual projection fibers in the forebrain, and this may be removed completely without disturbance of visual functions. Layman's [57] experiments on the function of the visual cortex in the chicken's discrimination of visual patterns show, for example, that subcortical centers are quite adequate for this discrimination. In the lower mammals, there is a clearly defined projection of retinal fibers upon the cerebrum. The visual fibers go to the area striata and, as Lashley [58] has shown for the rat, entire destruction of this area permanently destroys all ability to discriminate the finer details of visual objects. However, the visually decorticated rat is still capable of discriminating gross brightness differences.[59] It is also able to avoid objects. The dog, on the other hand, appears to be totally blind following removal of the visual cortex. Marquis [60] demonstrated that, following such an operation, the dog bumps into walls and into objects placed in its path, fails to respond to food placed before its eyes, and makes no response to threatening gestures. He says: "It moved about very cautiously and slowly, with its head lowered to the floor, refusing to jump from the edge of a stool or to descend stairs unless it could explore the next step with its nose or forepaw. It appeared as fully incapacitated as a dog which had been blinded by the destruction of the retinas." Despite this apparent blindness, however, the dog was trained to discriminate brightness differences. Its ability in this regard was but slightly inferior to that of normal dogs. Also, conditioned responses to light were developed as readily in the visually decorticated dog as in normal animals. Essentially similar results were obtained for monkeys. The operated animals were apparently blind, but they were conditioned to respond to a flash of light. In human beings, on the other hand, there is total and permanent blindness following destruction of the visual projection areas of the cortex. Only the pupillary reaction to light is retained. In summarizing his discussion of the above data Marquis [61] says:

It is apparent that in the evolutionary development from the fish to man a complete reorganization of the central visual system has taken place. In the lower vertebrates the visual functions are carried out entirely by mesencephalic centers, while in man the cortex has taken over all the optic functions with the exception of the pupillary reflex to light. This reorganization has not appeared suddenly but can be traced by gradual stages in the intermediate animals. In reptiles and birds there is a small optic projection tract to the forebrain, but these animals do not possess a true striate cortex. Within the mammalian series, from the rodents to the primates and man, there is a progressive shifting of visual functions from the superior colliculus to the striate cortex. Analysis of these functions has shown that the discriminative and spatial functions are first assumed by the cortex.

In the case of motor responses there is, from the lower vertebrates to man, a gradual evolution in the direction of cerebral localization. The cerebellum serves for reflex coordination and there is, in lower vertebrates, no disturbance of motor functions as long as this is intact. In mammals, however, destruction of the motor areas of the cortex leads to paralysis. Although there is frequently recovery of motor functions after destruction of the motor areas, such recovery becomes less evident, as well as slower, as the higher mammals are approached. In monkeys and man stimulation of the motor cortex leads to definite movements, and destruction of that part of the motor cortex which leads to, say, movements of the arm, paralyzes this member. In some instances, by proper training the function is recovered. According to Franz [62] other parts of the brain serve, in such instances, a vicarious motor function.

Injury to sensory or motor areas is followed by more than mere sensory or motor disturbance. Lashley's [63] investigations have shown that the disturbances of behavior which follow cortical destruction in the sensory areas are much greater than those which follow interference with the sensory functions alone. For example, normal rats learned a maze and, when their eyes were removed, made an average of only five errors in relearning the problem to the former degree of accuracy. When *blind* rats (with eyes removed) learned the maze and the visual cortex was destroyed (of course without interfering with vision as such), they made an average of 353 errors in relearning. Similar results were obtained in experiments upon other sensory areas. Injury to the motor cortex likewise yielded evidence that more than a mere motor function was affected. Cortical destruction, then, does more than destroy sensory and motor abilities.

Thus, in addition to its sensory and motor functions, for which there is, in higher forms, a rather definite localization, the cerebrum performs an associative or integrative function. Lashley [64] has shown that, as far as this function is concerned, the effect of brain lesions is proportional to the *size* of the lesion and not to its locus. His results show, also, that the more complex the task confronting the animal, the greater the decrease of learning ability for cerebral destruction of a given amount.

Cerebral functions are especially important for the so-called higher learning processes, which involve use of symbols. Symbols are modifications of the organism which represent past experience and which may be combined in novel ways to solve new problems, as in reasoning. The most widely used tests of symbolic response in animals are variations of the delayed-reaction technique, first used by Hunter. These methods are discussed in the next chapter (pp. 138–144) but their essential nature may be summarized here as follows: The animal is confronted with a situation in which two or more responses are possible. The cue for correct response has been given, but is no longer present. Will the animal remember? If it has seen food placed in one of three boxes, for example, will it remember which box contains the food? The controls are such that the only basis for consistent correct response is recall of the earlier situation. The interval between the giving of the cue and the test of recall may be increased until an animal fails the test. The various reasoning tests require a response in terms of combinations of past experiences (symbolic representations) or a generalization or principle.

A large amount of research with rats, which has been summarized elsewhere,[65] demonstrates quite clearly that their performance of delayed-reaction and reasoning tests is greatly impaired by cerebral lesions. There is also a strong suggestion that bilateral lesions in the prefrontal areas produce greater impairment than lesions elsewhere, a finding which is of course different from that found by Lashley for maze learning.

The research on delayed reaction in prefrontally operated monkeys has been highly controversial. The earlier studies by Jacobsen[66] implied that monkeys bilaterally deprived of the prefrontal areas are no longer able to perform delayed reactions. Several later investigators, however, did not find a total loss of delayed-reaction ability in similarly operated monkeys. There was impairment, but this was in some instances alleviated by conditions calculated to remove distractions, to make the monkey more attentive, or to improve motivation.[67] The situation has also been complicated by the fact that different investigators have used different delayed-reaction tests. Moreover, very few animals, sometimes only two, have been involved. A recent study by Harlow and others[68] summarizes the earlier controversial literature and presents a further research on 12 monkeys, four normal, four prefrontally lobectomized, and four with posterior lesions. In 12 daily sessions of 36 trials each, the percentage of error on a five-minute delay problem was, respectively, 0.4, 36.5, and 5.8. The prefrontally lobectomized monkeys were thus greatly handicapped, as compared with the others. They

did, however, exhibit a better-than-chance performance, thus justifying the conclusion that recall memory was not completely lost. In other experiments with conditions calculated to facilitate delayed response, the results for the monkeys with prefrontal lesions were sometimes better and sometimes poorer than those cited. In every experiment, however, the performance of monkeys with prefrontal lesions was significantly poorer than that of normal and posterior-operated animals. Because of the comprehensiveness of this experiment and its direct bearing on various controversial aspects of earlier research, the following conclusions[69] are worth quoting:

The data support the original contention of Jacobsen that the deficit in delayed response is characteristic of prefrontal ablations.... The striking findings of these investigations are the severity of deficit on delayed-response performance that is produced by prefrontal lesions, the persistence of this deficit over a long period of time, and the failure to obtain any indication of improvement in delayed-response performance by the frontal monkeys as a function of intensive training.

Visual discrimination learning was not impaired by frontal operations although it was impaired by those involving the posterior cortex.

Pribram and others,[70] in an experiment on delayed reaction in baboons, found greater disturbances of delayed reactions than of other discriminations following prefrontal operations. They suggest that a restricted area of the frontal cortex may be essential for successful delayed reactions. Jacobsen and others[71] found that their two chimpanzee subjects were greatly handicapped in delayed reaction when subjected to bilateral prefrontal lobectomy, but Blum[72] has found conflicting results. Two similarly operated chimpanzees studied by him responded correctly after delays of respectively one and four minutes. Hebb[73] suggests that this discrepancy could be accounted for if Blum's animals had less postoperative scar tissue than Jacobsen's.*

Prefrontal operations on human patients have had variable results which are difficult to interpret. Sometimes a patient's mental test performances are as good after as before the operation and sometimes there is a marked deficit. Hebb,[74] who has had an opportunity to study such cases, has this to say:

> In the clinical field, the frontal lobe and the frequency with which lobotomized patients are available for study continue to tempt the unwary student of cerebral localization to draw hasty conclusions, positive or negative. It is reasonably certain that damage to man's frontal lobe inevitably produces intellectual and emotional changes. But it is a long step, from the kind of evidence available, to demonstrate that some particular function is "localized" in the frontal lobes.

In Jacobsen's report on his two chimpanzee subjects, he emphasized the emotional change which took place following bilateral removal of frontal tissues, and this observation is said to have suggested to Moniz the so-called psychosurgery operation, modifications of which are now widely used to relieve psychotics of their morbid anxieties and melancholia. These operations, to which Hebb referred in the statement just quoted, have drawn attention to the possibility that, in addition to their contributions to intelligent behavior, the frontal lobes play an important role in personality.

The relevance of the preceding discussions to the topic of this chapter is the light which such studies may throw upon the evolution of intelligent behavior. It is certain that this evolution is greatly dependent upon that of the cerebral cortex, and it may well be that the evolution of the prefrontal cortex is especially related to the appearance of the higher

* This suggestion comes from the fact that there is a certain degree of unpredictable damage following a brain operation. Even though equivalent operations are performed on different animals, the end result may be different. One brain may heal with less scar tissue than another, hence with less brain damage added to that produced by the operation as such.

learning processes which, in animals, are to some extent revealed by tests of delayed reaction and reasoning. There is also the possibility that aspects of personality are related to frontal lobe evolution. It is clearly apparent, however, that much more comparative research is necessary before any such relationships can be established.

Summary and Conclusions

We have observed that intelligence is a capacity inferred from differences in non-stereotyped adaptation. As the term has been used above, intelligence refers to the capacity for making flexible adjustments. Basic factors in intelligence thus defined are sensory, motor, and neural structures and functions. Of particular significance are central neural mechanisms which make memory and reasoning possible.

The evolution of sensory processes was approached from the standpoint of structure and of discriminatory behavior. An increasing specialization of peripheral as well as of central sensory structures is observed to be characteristic of evolution in animals. This specialization is especially noticeable in the cases of vision and audition, the chief distance senses. The data from discrimination and conditioned-response experiments indicate that there is an increasing ability to differentiate the finer details of the environment as the higher organisms are approached.

The evolution of locomotor and manipulatory dexterity was traced. Of especial significance, in this evolution, are (1) assumption of the upright posture, (2) freedom of the mouth, throat, and related musculature from manipulatory functions and their increasing specialization for vocalization, and (3) the increasing specialization of the hands for fine finger and thumb prehension. Man's heritage of language and implements has been rendered possible by these motor accomplishments and the correlated superiority of his central neural mechanisms.

Our consideration of the evolution of central nervous mechanisms brought to attention the fact that, from the lowest organisms to man, there has been a trend in the direction of increasing cortical elaboration. This has involved integration of lower sensory and motor functions by specialized neural mechanisms in the cortex. It is apparent that, as the higher animals have evolved, their sensory and motor functions have become increasingly dependent upon the integrity of these neural mechanisms. Data concerning effects of brain injury on learning and retention clearly indicate that in addition to its specific sensory and motor functions, the cerebral cortex performs associative functions.

Man's superior learning ability and his acquisition and use of symbols have been made possible by the elaboration of his cortical neurons. His cerebrum has large associa-

tion areas in each of the lobes; larger, in proportion to sensorimotor areas, than in any other animal. It has been claimed that the prefrontal areas of the cerebrum are especially involved in the higher learning processes like recall memory and reasoning. Delayed reactions, which indicate the presence of ability to recall, may occur after prefrontal operations, but their level of accuracy is usually impaired. Operations outside of the frontal lobes do not impair ability to do delayed reactions. There is thus evidence that the frontal lobes are of especial importance for recall memory and the processes which depend upon it. This is not to say that symbolic processes are localized in the frontal lobes, but only that prefrontal involvement seems of great importance for the efficient acquisition and use of these processes.

REFERENCES

1. Edwards, A. S., "Intelligence as Capacity for Variability or Versatility of Response," *Psych. Rev.*, 1928, *35*, 198–210.
2. Nissen, H. W., "Phylogenetic Comparison," Chapter 11 in S. S. Stevens (ed.), *Handbook of Experimental Psychology*. New York: Wiley, 1951. See especially pp. 350–352.
3. See J. Huxley, "Genetics, Evolution and Human Destiny," Chapter 26 in L. C. Dunn (ed.), *Genetics in the 20th Century*. New York: Macmillan, 1951.
4. Yerkes, R. M., *The Dancing Mouse*. New York: Macmillan, 1907.
5. See the discussion of the research of Fields, Lashley, and others, in N. L. Munn, *A Handbook of Psychological Research on the Rat*. Boston: Houghton Mifflin, 1950, pp. 146–148.
6. Munn, N. L., "An Apparatus for Testing Visual Discrimination in Animals," *J. Genet. Psychol.*, 1931, *39*, 342–358.
7. Brown, C. W., and E. E. Ghiselli, "A Multiple-Unit Apparatus for Measuring the Rat's Ability to Discriminate Visual Patterns," *J. Comp. Psychol.*, 1934, *18*, 451–454.
8. See N. L. Munn and B. R. Steining, "The

Relative Efficacy of Form and Background in a Child's Discrimination of Visual Patterns," *J. Genet. Psychol.*, 1931, *39*, 73–90; L. W. Gellerman, "Form Discrimination in Chimpanzees and Two-Year-Old Children," *J. Genet. Psychol.*, 1933, *42*, 1–50; and K. U. Smith, "Visual Discrimination in the Cat," *J. Genet. Psychol.*, 1934, *44*, 301–320.
9. Verrier, M. L., "Le sens Visuel chez les Vertebrés," *J. de Psychol.*, 1929, *26*, 74–100.
10. See N. L. Munn, *A Handbook of Psychological Research on the Rat*. Boston: Houghton Mifflin, 1950, pp. 134–143.
11. Frisch, H. von, *Bees: Their Vision, Chemical Senses, and Language*. Ithaca: Cornell University Press, 1950, Chapter 1.
12. Walls, G. L., *The Vertebrate Eye*. Bloomfield Hills, Michigan: Cranbrook Institute of Science, 1942, pp. 472–490.
13. Lashley, K. S., "Color Vision of Birds," *Anim. Behav.*, 1916, *6*, 1–26.
14. Hamilton, W. F., and T. B. Coleman, "Trichromatic Vision in the Pigeon as Illustrated by the Spectral Hue Discrimination Curve," *J. Comp. Psychol.*, 1933, *15*, 183–191.
15. Pumphrey, R. J., "The Sense Organs of

Birds," *Annual Report of Smithsonian Institution*, 1948, pp. 305–330.

16. Munn, N. L., *Handbook of Psychological Research on the Rat*. Boston: Houghton Mifflin, 1950, pp. 134–142.

17. Fox, H. M., *The Personality of Animals* (rev. ed.). London: Penguin Books, 1952, p. 48.

18. Grether, W. F., "Color Vision and Color Blindness in Monkeys," *Comp. Psychol. Monogs.*, 1939, *15*, 4; "Chimpanzee Color Vision," I–III, *J. Comp. Psychol.*, 1940, *29*, 167–192; "A Comparison of Human and Chimpanzee Spectral Hue Discrimination Curves," *J. Exper. Psychol.*, 1940, *26*, 394–402; R. B. Malmo, and W. F. Grether, "Further Evidence of Red-Blindness (Protanopia) in Cebus Monkeys," *J. Comp. Psychol.*, 1947, *40*, 143–147.

19. Much of this research has been reviewed in M. F. Washburn, *The Animal Mind* (4th ed.). New York: Macmillan, 1936, pp. 229–330.

20. See von Frisch, *op. cit.*, pp. 21–24.

21. Meesters, A., "Über die Organisation des Gesichtfeldes der Fische," *Zeit. f. Tierpsychologie*, 1940, *4*, 84–149.

22. Casteel, D. B., "Discriminative Ability of the Painted Turtle," *J. Animal Behav.*, 1911, *1*, 1–28.

23. Bingham, H. C., "Visual Perception of the Chick," *Behav. Monogs.*, 1922, *4*, No. 4; H. M. Johnson, "Visual Pattern Discrimination in Vertebrates," *J. Anim. Behav.*, 1914, *4*, 319–361; *ibid.*, 1916, *6*, 169–221; N. L. Munn, "The Relative Efficacy of Form and Background in the Chick's Discrimination of Visual Patterns," *J. Comp. Psychol.*, 1931, *12*, 41–75; R. H. Gundlach, "The Visual Acuity of Homing Pigeons," *J. Comp. Psychol.*, 1933, *16*, 327–342; and W. F. Hamilton and J. L. Goldstein, "Visual Acuity and Accommodation in the Pigeon," *J. Comp. Psychol.*, 1933, *15*, 193–197.

24. For a review of this literature, see the summary in Munn's *Handbook*, pp. 146–151.

25. Smith, K. U., "Visual Discrimination in the Cat. I. The Capacity of the Cat for Visual Figure Discrimination," *J. Genet. Psychol.*, 1934, *44*, 301–320.

26. Fields, P. E., "Studies in Concept Formation. IV. A Comparison of White Rats and Raccoons with Respect to Their Visual Discrimination of Certain Geometrical Figures," *J. Comp. Psychol.*, 1936, *21*, 341–355.

27. Karn, H. W., and N. L. Munn, "Visual Pattern Discrimination in the Dog," *J. Genet. Psychol*, 1932, *40*, 363–374.

28. See C. C. Neet, "Visual Pattern Discrimination in the Macacus Rhesus Monkey," *J. Genet. Psychol.*, 1933, *43*, 163–196; L. W. Gellermann, "Form Discrimination in Chimpanzees and Two-Year-Old Children," *J. Genet. Psychol.*, 1933, *42*, 1–50.

29. Spence, K. W., "Visual Acuity and its Relation to Brightness in Chimpanzee and Man," *J. Comp. Psychol.*, 1934, *18*, 333–361.

30. Wever, E. G., and C. W. Bray, "Auditory Sensitivity of Katydids and Crickets," *Psych. Bull.*, 1933, *30*, 548.

31. Frisch, K. v., and H. Stetter, "Untersuchungen über den Sitz des Gehörsinnes bei der Elritze," *Zsch. fur verg. Physiol.*, 1932, *17*, 686–801.

32. Pumphrey, R. J., "Hearing," in *Physiological Mechanisms in Animal Behaviour*. New York: Academic Press, 1950.

33. Wever, E. G., *Theory of Hearing*. New York: Wiley, 1949.

34. Munn, N. L., *Psychology* (2d ed.). Boston: Houghton Mifflin, 1951, pp. 460–463.

35. Stetter, H., "Untersuchungen über den Gehörsinn der Fische, besonders von *Phoxinus laevis* L. und *Ameiurus nebulosus* Raf," *Zsch. fur verg. Physiol.*, 1929, *9*, 339–477.

36. Kurodo, R., "Experimental Researches on the Sense of Hearing in Lower Vertebrates, including Reptiles, Amphibians, and Fishes," *Comp. Psychol. Monog.*, 1926, *3*, No. 16.

37. Wever, E. G., and C. W. Bray, "Hearing in the Pigeon, as Studied by the Electrical Responses of the Inner Ear," *J. Comp. Psychol.*, 1936, *22*, 353–364.

38. See Munn's *Handbook*, pp. 158–168.

39. Upton, M., "Auditory Sensitivity of Guinea Pigs," *Am. J. Psychol.*, 1929, *41*, 412–421; G. P. Horton, "A Quantitative Study of Hearing in the Guinea Pig," *J. Comp. Psychol.*, 1933, *15*, 59–73.

40. Herrington, G. B., and R. H. Gundlach, "How Well Can Guinea Pigs and Cats Hear Tones?" *J. Comp. Psychol.*, 1933, *16*, 287–303; S. Dworkin, J. Katzman, G. A. Hutchinson, and J. R. McCabe, "Hearing Acuity of Animals as Measured by Conditioning Methods," *J. Exper. Psychol.*, 1949, *26*, 281–298; W. D. Neff, "The Effects of Partial Section of the Auditory Nerve," *J. Comp. & Physiol. Psychol.*, 1947, *40*, 203–215.

41. Andreyev, L. A., "Extreme Limits of Pitch Discrimination with Higher Tones," *J. Comp. Psychol.*, 1934, *18*, 315–332.

42. Galambos, R., and D. R. Griffin, "Obstacle Avoidance by Bats: The Cries of Bats," *J. Exper. Zool.*, 1942, *89*, 475–490. See also Boring, Langfeld, and Weld's *Foundations of Psychology.* New York: Wiley, 1948, pp. 386–389 (written by Griffin and based upon above reference).

43. Katz, D., *Animals and Men.* New York: Longman's, 1937, Chapter V.

44. Wendt, G. R., "Auditory Acuity of Monkeys," *Comp. Psychol. Monog.*, 1934, *10*, No. 51.

45. Elder, J. H., "Auditory Acuity of the Chimpanzee," *J. Comp. Psychol.*, 1934, *17*, 157–183; "The Upper Limit of Hearing in Chimpanzees," *Am. J. Psychol.*, 1935, *112*, 109–115.

46. Yerkes, R. M., *Chimpanzees.* New Haven: Yale University Press, 1943, pp. 96–98.

47. See Munn's *Handbook*, pp. 176–179.

48. Yoakum, C. S., "Some Experiments on the Behavior of Squirrels," *J. Comp. Neur. & Psychol.*, 1909, *19*, 541–568.

49. Kinder, E. F., "A Study of Nest-Building Activity in the Albino Rat," *J. Exper. Zool.*, 1927, pp. 117–161.

50. Parker, G. H., and R. E. Sheldon. "The Sense of Smell in Fishes," *Bull. Bureau of Fisheries*, 1912, *32*, 35.

51. Pfaffman, C., "Gustatory Afferent Impulses," *J. Cell. & Comp. Physiol.*, 1941, *17*, 243–258.

52. Köhler, W., *The Mentality of Apes.* New York: Harcourt, Brace, 1925. A moving-picture demonstration occurs in Huxley and Zuckerman's "Monkey Into Man" produced by Strand Films.

53. Herrick, C. J., *Neurological Foundations of Animal Behavior.* New York: Holt, 1924.

54. Various brain weights and brain-weight/body-weight ratios are tabulated by R. H. Wheeler, *The Science of Psychology* (2d ed.). New York: Crowell, 1940, p. 373.

55. See A. J. Carlson and N. Johnson, *The Machinery of the Body* (rev. ed.). Chicago: University of Chicago Press, 1948, p. 438.

56. Marquis, D. G., "Phylogenetic Interpretation of the Functions of the Visual Cortex," *Arch. Neur. & Psychiat.*, 1935, *33*, 807–815.

57. Layman, J. D., "The Avian Visual System: I," *Comp. Psychol. Monog.*, 1936, *12*, No. 3.

58. Lashley, K. S., and M. Frank, "The Mechanism of Vision. X." *J. Comp. Psychol.*, 1934, *17*, 355–391.

59. Lashley's earlier report on this point raised much controversy, but subsequent research (see Munn's *Handbook*, pp. 128–130) has supported his position.

60. Marquis, D. G., "Effects of Removal of the Visual Cortex in Mammals, with Observations on the Retention of Light Discrimination in Dogs," *Proc. Assoc. Res. Nerv. Ment. Dis.*, 1934, *13*, 558–592.

61. Marquis (citation 56), p. 812.

62. Franz, S. I. "The Evolution of an Idea: How the Brain Works." Lecture published 1929 by the University of California at Los Angeles.

63. Lashley, K. S., *Brain Mechanisms and Intelligence.* Chicago: University of Chicago Press, 1929. This report was followed by a large amount of relevant research by Lashley and others. This is summarized in Munn's *Handbook*, pp. 329–341.

64. See citation 63.

65. See Munn's *Handbook*, pp. 339–341.

66. Jacobsen, C. F., "A Study of Cerebral Function in Learning. The Frontal Lobes," *J. Comp. Neur.*, 1931, *52*, 271–340; "Functions of the Frontal Association Area in Primates," *Arch. Neur. & Psychiat.*, 1935, *33*, 558–569; "Studies of Cerebral Function in Primates," *Comp. Psychol. Monog.*, 1936, *13*, No. 3.

67. See especially J. L. Finan, "Delayed Response with Pre-Delay Reinforcement in Monkeys After the Removal of Frontal Lobes," *Am. J. Psychol.*, 1942, *55*, 202–214; R. B. Malmo, "Interference Factors in Delayed Response in Monkeys After Removal of the Frontal Lobes," *J. Neurophysiol.*, 1942, *5*, 295–308

68. Harlow, H. F., R. T. Davis, P. H. Settlage, and D. R. Meyer, "Analysis of Frontal and Posterior Association Syndromes in Brain-Damaged Monkeys," *J. Comp. & Physiol. Psychol.*, 1952, *45*, 419–429.

69. *Ibid.*, pp. 427–428. Permission to quote granted by American Psychological Association.

70. Pribram, K., N. Mishkin, H. E. Rosvold, and S. J. Kaplan, "Effects on Delayed-Response Performance of Lesions of Dorsolateral and Ventromedial Frontal Cortex of Baboons," *J. Comp. & Physiol. Psychol*, 1952, *45*, 565–575.

71. Jacobsen, C. F., J. B. Wolfe, and T. A. Jack-

son, "An Experimental Analysis of the Functions of the Frontal Association Areas in Primates," *J. Nerv. & Ment. Dis.*, 1935, 1–14.

72. Blum, R. A., "The Effects of Bilateral Removal of the Prefrontal Granular Cortex on Delayed Response Performance and Emotion-

ality in Chimpanzee," *American Psychologist*, 1948, *3*, 237–238.

73. Hebb, D. O., "Animal and Physiological Psychology," in *Annual Review of Psychology*, 1950, p. 189.

74. *Ibid.*, p. 179.

SUGGESTIONS FOR FURTHER READING

Beach, F. A., "The Snark Was a Boojum." *American Psychologist*, 1950, *5*, 115–124.

Fox, H. M., *The Personality of Animals* (rev. ed.). London: Penguin Books, 1952, Chapters I and II–V.

Frisch, K. v., *Bees*. Ithaca: Cornell University Press, 1950, Chapters I and II.

Katz, D., *Animals and Men*. New York: Longmans, Green, 1937. Chapters 2 and 3. Also published 1953 as a Penguin Book.

Maier, N. R. F., and T. C. Schneirla, *Principles of Animal Psychology*. New York: McGraw-Hill, 1935. Part I and Chapter XIV.

Marquis, D. G., "The Neurology of Learning," Chapter 9 in C. P. Stone (ed.), *Comparative Psychology* (3d ed.). New York: Prentice-Hall, 1951.

Morgan, C. T., "The Psychophysiology of Learning," in S. S. Stevens (ed.), *Handbook of Experimental Psychology*. New York: Wiley, 1951.

Morgan, C. T., and E. Stellar, *Physiological Psychology* (2d ed.). New York: McGraw-Hill, 1950, pp. 51–57, 134–136, 172–190, and 266–273.

Munn, N. L., *Handbook of Psychological Research on the Rat*. Boston: Houghton, Mifflin, 1950, Chapter 5 and pp. 329–341.

Pauli, W. F., *The World of Life*. Boston: Houghton Mifflin, 1949. See Parts V and VI, espe-

cially, for a profusion of illustrations of animal forms from unicellar organisms to man.

Pumphrey, R. J., "Hearing," in *Physiological Mechanisms in Animal Behavior*. New York: Academic Press, 1950.

Smith, K. U., "Discriminative Behavior in Animals," Chapter 10 in C. P. Stone (ed.), *Comparative Psychology* (3d ed.). New York: Prentice-Hall, 1951.

Strausbaugh, P. D., and B. R. Weimer, *General Biology* (3d ed.). New York: Wiley, 1952, Chapters 11, 12, and 32.

Tansley, K., "Vision," in *Physiological Mechanisms in Animal Behavior*. New York: Academic Press, 1950.

Walls, G. L., *The Vertebrate Eye*. Bloomfield Hills, Mich.: Cranbrook Institute of Science, 1942.

Walter, W. G., *The Living Brain*. New York: Norton, 1953, Chapter 10.

Warden, C. J., T. W. Jenkins, and L. H. Warner, *Comparative Psychology*. Volume III. Vertebrates. New York: Ronald, 1936. See the discussion of receptive processes in each of the chapters — pisces, amphibia, reptilia, aves, mammalia, and primates.

Yerkes, R. M., *Chimpanzees*. New Haven: Yale University Press, 1943, Chapter VI.

5

Evolution of Intelligent Behavior:
Learning and Higher Processes

This chapter continues our discussion of intelligent behavior. We have already seen that the evolution of sensory processes broadens an organism's environment, making possible a more adequate adjustment to changing circumstances, and also that the evolution of effector processes increases its ability to move around in and manipulate the environment. The utilization of these sensory and motor abilities in adjustment is tested with learning problems of various kinds.

The most widely used tests of animal intelligence involve mazes of complexity varying from a single T-unit to patterns with many blind alleys; discrimination learning tests which, at the upper levels of complexity, call for such higher processes as abstraction, generalization, and concept formation; problem situations which require manipulation of bolts, latches, strings, and instruments of various kinds; detour tests requiring a roundabout approach when the direct route is blocked; delayed-reaction tests designed to ascertain an animal's ability to recall objects or events from the past; and a large variety of situations which can be solved only by reasoning.

It would be convenient indeed if our animal tests were carefully standardized, were combined into batteries adequate for testing all important aspects of intelligence, and were applicable to all animals from the lowest to the highest. But this sort of program, so common at the human level, is not at all possible with animals. Even among human beings there are seemingly insuperable difficulties involved in comparisons of racial intelligence. Such difficulties are magnified many times when we turn to animal intelligence. This is because there are large differences, from one phylum or species to another, in such factors as motivation, docility, size, and dexterity.

We may use hunger to motivate a mammal, but it is not so easy to motivate a paramecium, or even an ant. Monkeys and higher primates, on the other hand, may be motivated as much by curiosity as by hunger, which is in itself perhaps an indication of their high level of intelligence.

The docility of the cat, dog, monkey, and chimpanzee is such that we are able to get good "cooperation" in the test situation, but how about the lion, tiger, or fully grown gorilla? A gorilla may be much more intelligent than a monkey, but how can we know this when he will not submit to the same tests under comparable conditions? And how can we discover the intelligence of a gibbon when his volatile temperament makes it practically impossible to work with him?

Size is of course a factor to be considered in laboratory testing. Investigators of porpoise intelligence [1] bewail the fact that their research budget and limitations of space will not permit them to test the animal on detour problems comparable with those used to test intelligence in other animals. All large animals, and especially the aquatic ones, are difficult to test. How is one ever going to discover the level of intelligence of the whale?

Dexterity is still another factor. Many animals cannot open a puzzle box, although for all we know they may have the requisite brain capacity to do it. They might also utilize implements if finger-thumb opposition were present.

Another difficulty is that, when you remove the animal from his native habitat and put him in a cage, or confine him in a laboratory or a home, he may in many respects be a different animal. An animal motivated by natural motivators in its native environment may exhibit a much higher level of performance than the same animal tested in laboratory situations. One can, of course, rarely test intelligence in the field, although he may be fortunate enough to see what appears to be an expression of it.

Tinbergen's [2] studies suggest certain other difficulties which the tester of animal intelligence may encounter. Some animals apparently possess "localized dispositions to learn." That is to say, certain of their responses are more readily modified than others. The "disposed" responses would be different in different species, and hence lower the comparability of any intelligence test which utilized them. The concept of "imprinting" which Lorenz [3] and Tinbergen have both emphasized in their discussions of learning in birds is also relevant here. This is the concept that certain responses are much more readily learned at certain stages of individual development than at others. Such critical stages, if universal, would differ for different species and thus would reduce the comparability of learning tests. Only future study can show the significance, or lack of significance, of these interesting concepts for the problem that concerns us in this chapter.

We have suggested only a few of the difficulties encountered by investigators of comparative intelligence in animals. Enough has been said, however, to put the reader on his guard against expecting a definitive statement about the relative intelligence of animals.

Phylogenetic comparisons of intelligence have, in the past, been based largely upon morphology, and particularly the development of brain structures. But as Zuckerman [4] has pointed out, with reference to monkeys and apes, we need behavioral data to supplement the morphological. It is by no means certain, for example, that the anthropoid apes (chimpanzee, gorilla, orangutan, and gibbon) are more intelligent than monkeys, despite their larger and more elaborate brains. Adequately comparative tests of intelligence, with a representative sampling of the respective groups can alone provide an answer to the question: Which is more intelligent?

Utilizing the information at present available, this chapter can do little more than indicate the nature of the apparatus and procedures most widely used to test animal intelligence at various phyletic levels, the sorts of processes which the tests purport to reveal, and outcomes of the applications of such tests, including what they suggest about the order of intelligence of the various animals studied.

Basically, the criterion of intelligent behavior is flexibility, in the sense of modifying reactions to adjust to changed circumstances. But behavior is not modified unless a more favorable or desirable state is thereby achieved. All tests of animal intelligence must take cognizance of this fact. The animal must have an incentive for learning. To provide adequate motivation, the animal is frequently deprived of food, water, sexual partners, or something else associated with optimal physiological conditions. It is then given the opportunity, by overcoming certain obstacles placed in its path, to obtain that of which it has been deprived. Sometimes, rather than subjecting the animal to deprivation, we place it in a situation to which the natural response is avoidance. Such situations involve electric shock, immersion in water, or confinement. Escape is rendered difficult, again by the use of obstacles. One determines whether or not, and if so with what degree of facility, the animal learns to escape. In studying lower organisms we sometimes use novel forms of motivation, since the above motivators, while useful with the higher forms of life, are in many instances ineffective with the lower. This will be apparent in the following discussion of learning in invertebrates.

We shall see that the earliest appearance of learning is somewhat problematical. Modifiability is discerned, but is it true learning? Sensory and physico-chemical processes may undergo modification, as in adaptation and fatigue, but we do not regard this as learning. Modification of this sort adds no new response and is temporary. Unless the modification adds to the organism's behavioral repertoire, unless it is clearly due to stimulation and response rather than to growth processes (as in maturation), and unless it is retained after a rest period, we do not consider that learning has occurred.

Learning in Invertebrates

Where does learning ability begin? Is it a function of relatively simple protoplasm or does it require a nervous system? Questions like these have led several investigators to undertake the difficult task of looking for evidence of modifiability in microorganisms like *Stentor* and *Paramecium*.

Jennings [5] observed that *Stentor*, the trumpet-shaped animalcule shown in Figure 44, makes adaptive responses to such noxious stimulation as that produced by carmine

Figure 44. Stentor Being Tested With Carmine

(After H. S. Jennings, *Behavior of Lower Organisms*, Columbia University Press, 1906.)

powder introduced near the mouth. While there is a steady stream of carmine powder, the organism makes apparent attempts to avoid it. First it bends on its stalk away from the substance. Then when this reaction fails to get rid of the carmine particles, the animal's cilia, situated around the mouth region, reverse their beat, thus sending currents away from, rather than into, its mouth. If the noxious stimuli persist, the stentor folds into its tube. When this reaction fails to get rid of carmine, the animal detaches itself from the substratum and moves to a different locality. Such an adjustment is not long retained, however. A few minutes later when it is again subjected to carmine powder, the stentor reacts as it did at first rather than as it did upon the last test. As Maier and Schneirla [6] have pointed out, it is likely that the summation of physico-chemical processes within the organism, in relation to an excitation-conduction gradient between the funnel end and the attached end, can account for this modification and that it is therefore not an instance of learning.

Several investigators [7] have produced in paramecia a modification of behavior which has many of the characteristics of learning. In these experiments a paramecium was drawn into a fine glass capillary tube as illustrated in Figure 45. The diameter of the tube was too narrow for normal turning movements to occur. Doubling of the body, as shown in the illustration, was the only possible means of reversing the direction of movement. The animal moved toward the end of the tube, and upon making contact with the surface film, apparently "attempted" to turn around. Finally the reaction shown in the figure, one which does not occur in a normal environment, was exhibited. In successive contacts with the surface film this reaction was accomplished with increasing facility. Day and Bentley [8] present "learning" curves for eight paramecia. These show a decreased number of inadequate responses as a function of the number of contacts with the film and associated "attempts" to turn. Paramecium D, for example, made in successive reversals the following number of unsuccessful "attempts": 25, 29, 8, 4, 3, 1, 10, 3, 1, 1, 2, 1, 2, 1, 1. Time for reversals showed a similar decrease. Buytendijk,[9] as a result of his own investigations, believes that the modification shown in these experiments does not represent true learning. When he rendered the body of a paramecium more flexible by immersion in chloroform, the animal made the doubling reaction upon its first contact with the film. Buytendijk assumes that activity in the capillary tube produces physicochemical changes in the animal's body and that these changes, in a cumulative fashion, render the body wall more flexible. The paramecium's behavior thus gives the appearance of learning. However, Day and Bentley's subjects retained some effects of the previous activity for periods ranging from 10 to 20 minutes. When replaced in the tube after a period of activity in an open watch glass, they made the turning response much more readily than they did when first tested in the tube. Thus, whatever its ultimate basis, such modification and retention is akin to what we call learning when it is found in higher forms of animal life.

What appears to be still clearer evidence of learning in paramecia has come from two other investigations which involve different approaches from that just described. French [10] sucked a paramecium into a glass tube which, unlike that illustrated, was wide enough for free swimming. The animal could escape by swimming out of the lower end of the tube. This it did more and more quickly as the situation was repeated. The median escape time for 20 animals was reduced, in 30 trials, from around 30 seconds to 10 seconds. There was great variability from one animal to another, some showing no evidence of improvement and others improving steadily so that a more or less typical learning curve could be plotted for them. The improved performance was not due to an increase in general activity, as shown by observations made before and after each test. As further evidence that learning was present, the author describes some instances of individual behavior. In the initial trials an animal would move back and forth across the tube and up and down a short distance before escaping from the bottom. Later it would move back and forth briefly then take a long dive through the bottom of the tube.

Gelber [11] says that paramecia which are not fed will tend to go to the bottom of a tube anyway, and she appears to think that

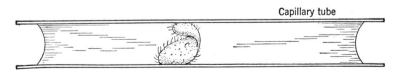

Figure 45. Paramecium Turning Around in a Capillary Tube

(From S. Smith, "The Limits of Educability in Paramecium," *J. Comp. Neur. and Psychol.*, 1908, *18*, 506.)

French has not produced valid evidence of learning. But her own experiment, which involves an entirely different method and type of motivation, also favors the view that paramecia are capable of learning. When a sterile platinum wire is lowered into a culture of about 128 paramecia and left there for a few minutes, two or three animals will adhere to it. The evidence for learning comes from the fact that, when the wire has been wiped with a culture of bacteria on which paramecia feed, there is a gradual increase, from test to test, in the number of paramecia adhering to the wire.

Two cultures were compared, one reinforced by the presence of bacteria on the wire and the other presented only with a sterile wire. During 40 trials the number of experimental animals adhering to the wire increased from 23 to 46, whereas the number of matched control animals adhering to the wire remained approximately constant. Both the experimental and control groups were later tested with a sterile wire. This test yielded a statistically significant difference in favor of the reinforced animals. Training without reinforcement had no detectable effect on approaches to the wire. The investigator therefore feels that she has demonstrated learning in paramecia.

All the investigations so far reported have produced evidence of what appears to be learning in paramecia. If comparable results were obtained in high organisms, there would be no hesitancy at all in saying that learning had been demonstrated.

One of the best experiments with lower multicellular organisms is that of Fleure and Walton.[12] A sea anemone, when it was first given pieces of filter paper, carried them to its mouth by means of the tentacles to which they were presented. In successive daily trials the filter paper was ingested with decreasing frequency and finally it was rejected by the tentacles. This negative reaction was retained for from six to ten days. Ven[13] obtained what, on the surface, appears to be clear evidence of learning in the star-

fish. The animal was restrained by means of pins placed at the angles of the rays. In addition, collars were slipped over the two rays most frequently used. At first these rays were used in fruitless efforts to escape. After a time the other rays came increasingly to be used and there was a consequent reduction in the time required for escape. Ven presents three curves similar to those found for learning in higher animals. Jennings[14] established in a starfish a righting reaction which involved rays not predominantly used under normal circumstances. The animal was prevented from using the normally dominant rays. This reaction was retained for five days. Maier and Schneirla[15] regard the results of Ven and Jennings as evidencing local changes in the restrained rays, the changes being due to irritation. Such localized irritation might lead to a shift of dominance. They doubt whether modification of the organism as a whole is present in such experiments.

Worms learned the habit of turning to the right in the maze shown in Figure 46. In Yerkes's[16] experiment with the earthworm, one animal made 10 consecutive errorless trials after its first 20 trials. Several hundred

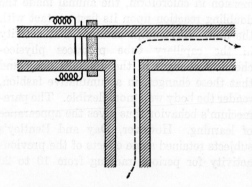

Figure 46. A Simple T-Maze Adapted for Investigating the Learning Ability of Worms

The arrow indicates the path followed by a worm in reaching a dark chamber which appeared to the right. A left turn was followed by an electric shock. A strip of sandpaper appeared just before the grid. The path is that followed on the animal's thirtieth trial. (After Yerkes.)

further trials were given, and then the five anterior segments of the worm were removed. Removal of these segments, including the brain, did not interfere with performance of the habit. There was some retention over a period of three weeks. Heck [17] repeated this experiment with essentially the same results. The average errors for 11 worms were, in successive groups of 40 trials: 17.4, 14.0, 13.0, 9.0, 4.0, and 4.0. When the positions of the dark chamber and electrode were reversed, the new turn was learned with greater facility than was the original one. Nobody has questioned the right of this behavior to be called learning, although there has been, as indicated above, much hesitation in attributing learning ability to animals lower than worms. The clear-cut evidence of modifiability of the whole organism in these animals probably is due to the fact that here, for the first time, there is a true synaptic nervous system together with marked centralization. (See Figure 25.) There is also bilateral rather than radial symmetry. This change in symmetry brings greater facility and integration in sensory and motor activities.

In the mollusks there is a further advance in neural development and integration, although the general features of the nervous system are very much like those of the worms. Several investigations have been made with snails. These right themselves with increasing facility when they are turned on their backs. They also, as Piéron [18] has shown, learn not to withdraw their tentacles (an unlearned response) when a shadow, which leads to no harmful result, is thrown on them. However, the best-known and most thorough learning experiments on snails are those of Thompson [19] and Garth and Mitchell.[20] Thompson developed a conditioned reaction in *Physa*, a fresh-water snail. When food touches its oral region, the snail opens its mouth. Pressure on the foot leads to no such reaction. After simultaneous presentation of food to mouth and pressure to foot for approximately 250 trials, the pressure alone was sufficient to elicit mouth movements. Stimulation of the foot alone elicited these movements for eight successive trials. Twelve non-reinforced trials (that is, trials without food) led to the apparent loss of this conditioned response. The animal could be reconditioned, however, in fewer trials than were required for the original conditioning. The snails failed to learn a simple maze. In Garth and Mitchell's experiment, however, the land snail *Rumania* was trained, in a T-maze somewhat like that shown in Figure 46, to turn to the right, toward a dark alley, and thus avoid a shock associated with a left turn. A heated wire, activated whenever the snail became motionless, was used to keep the animal moving. One trial was given twice daily. The one snail that completely survived the experiment made 32 correct turns in succession after it had received 70 trials.

The octopus, a much more highly evolved mollusk than the snail, has been the subject of several learning experiments which are summarized by Schiller,[21] whose own experiment will alone be considered here. Schiller's learning situation is illustrated in Figure 47. It involves a detour designed to obtain evidence of delayed reaction. Four octopuses were used. After an octopus had responded to an inaccessible crab placed to the right or the left of the entrance door, this door was opened and, upon emerging from the other end of the opaque central corridor, the animal could proceed to the right or left feeding chamber. It was credited with a correct response if it went to the side on which the crab had been responded to some seconds earlier. In critical trials a dummy instead of a live crab was used as bait. This was to remove the possibility of continuing vibratory or chemical cues. The bait was alternated from right to left in a chance order. When the central corridor was about the stretch of the animal's body (20 inches), the accuracy of response reached a high level, sometimes with as many as ten consecutive correct responses. When a longer detour was involved (40 inches), the animals stopped at the usual

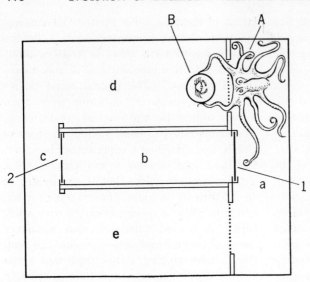

Figure 47. Ground Plan of Detour Device Used to Study Learning in the Octopus

a, starting compartment; *b*, passageway; *c*, choice compartment; *d*, *e*, feeding chambers. The entrance is at 1 and the exit at 2, showing hole through which the octopus squeezed during tests to eliminate postural cues. The octopus (*A*) makes its initial response to the crab (*B*) before reaching it via the central passageway. (From P. H. Schiller, "Delayed Detour Response in the Octopus," *J. Comp. Psychol.*, 1949, *42*, 222).

turning distance, showing retention of the earlier turning habit, but they soon overcame this tendency. Response with the longer delay reached an accuracy of 75 to 80 per cent. Analysis in terms of the actual time spent in the central passageway showed that when this time was under 40 seconds the octopus practically never made an error. Although learning was clearly present in this experiment, there is, as the author points out, no evidence of the use of higher processes (central representative factors) such as are involved in delayed reaction tests of recall memory (see pp. 137–143). During the delays involved in the present experiment, the octopus kept contact with the wall on the side on which the bait had been observed, and its beak and the majority of the suction cups were continually turned toward the bait. When controls were instituted to interfere with bodily orientation during locomotion, accuracy was no better than chance.

The most highly evolved invertebrates are the arthropods, which include such diverse creatures as crabs, lobsters, and the various insects, of which bees and ants have been most widely studied by psychologists. Hermit crabs were conditioned so that a withdrawal response to touching with a wire was elicited by light alone and they learned not to

respond to shells sealed with corks.[22] The crayfish studied by Yerkes and Huggins [23] learned a right-turning maze habit in from 50 to 100 trials and partially retained it after a period of two weeks.

That insects learn was clearly shown by Lubbock,[24] who did pioneer work (see p. 3) with these organisms. We have already mentioned (p. 93) that bees acquire discrimination habits. On learning in ants, the most extensive and reliable information comes from Schneirla's [25] maze studies. Ants, when suitably motivated, learn quite complicated mazes. In Figure 48 is represented a maze which Formica ants learned in approximately 35 trials. A learning curve for one ant is also shown. In many respects this compares favorably with curves found for maze learning in vertebrates. Evans [26] used a simpler maze than those of Schneirla and obtained even more rapid learning in ants.

Cockroaches can be conditioned to avoid darkness, thus reversing their negative phototropism. The reversal is obtained by administering an electric shock every time the animal runs into a darkened chamber. After from 16 to 18 trials, ten cockroaches in Szymanski's [27] experiment avoided the dark entirely. The negative response to darkness was relearned, after from one to nine days, in

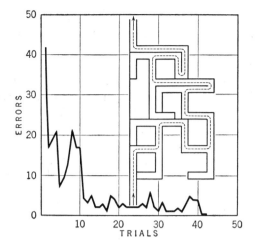

Figure 48. Maze Pattern and Curve for
Learning of Same by Ants

(From T. C. Schneirla, "Motivation and Efficiency in
Ant Learning," *J. Comp. Psychol.*, 1933, *15*, 245, 250.)

from 7 to 17 trials. Somewhat similar results
were obtained by Turner[28] and Hunter.[29] In
another experiment by Turner[30] cockroaches
learned an elevated maze having four blind
alleys. Trials were given at half-hourly intervals. The cockroaches required between
20 and 24 trials before they learned to avoid
blind alleys.

Learning in Inframammalian Vertebrates

So far as learning of simple discrimination
and maze problems is concerned, vertebrates
do not exhibit significantly greater ability
than some higher invertebrates. All the inframammalian vertebrates learn discrimination problems when the stimuli to be discriminated fall within their sensory capacities.
Several of the discrimination experiments
with these organisms were discussed earlier
(pp. 93–94). Conditioned responses have
also been developed in all the vertebrates so
far tested.

Fishes

Fishes are readily conditioned. Haralson
and Bitterman[31] describe an apparatus in

which African "mouth breeders" were conditioned to depress a lever with the snout,
their reward being a worm. Kellogg and
Spanovick[32] discuss much of the earlier research, and also report an experiment of their
own in which striped mullet were conditioned
either to a light or to a bell. The unconditioned stimulus, an electric shock, produced
violent escape reactions, but a light or bell
elicited only slight partial responses. Within
70 trials or less, the paired stimulation produced clear-cut conditioned reactions. These
were different from the original responses to
either the conditioned or unconditioned
stimuli, constituting a slow withdrawal from
the location of the positive electrodes of the
aquarium. There was also conditioning of
respiration, as indicated by mouth and gill
movements, which increased during conditioning and decreased during extinction
trials, allegedly indicating the building up,
and alleviation, of an "anxiety state." Several investigators, beginning with Churchill,[33]
have taught goldfish to find their way through
simple mazes. Much of the earlier research is
reviewed by French,[34] whose own study is
concerned primarily with the effect of temperature on retention of a four-blind linear
maze habit. The learning ability of minnows
has been subjected to extensive study by
Zunini,[35] whose series of researches deal
primarily with absolute and relational discrimination of visual stimuli. The minnow
is apparently capable of learning on either
basis. It also learns to enter a bottle to obtain food, a response initially not present
because, apparently, of fear.

Schiller[36] found that minnows will, under
certain circumstances, give up a direct approach to food which is accessible only via a
detour and take the roundabout route. One
of the most difficult detours to learn was that
involving a T-shaped glass partition with the
food on one side of the stem of the T and the
fish on the other. In order to reach the food
it was necessary to detour around the top of
the T, but the usual response was to persist
in a direct approach. The detour was more

readily learned if the stem of the T was partially opaque so that once leaving the position opposite the food, a fish could not again see the food until it got to the other side. There was no evidence of sudden solutions like those which, in higher animals, are said to be indicative of insight.

In another experiment with minnows, Schiller [37] found what he believed to be delayed reactions of the kind previously reported only in mammals and thought to be impossible in animals as low in the scale as fishes. His experiment, however, leaves much to be desired from the standpoint of adequate control of secondary cues, and it should certainly be repeated, with these controls instituted, before the results are accepted as indicating the presence of symbolic processes in fishes. The apparatus was somewhat like that used in Schiller's experiment with the octopus (Figure 47). The animal was shown food on a hook through a glass partition, which was to the right or left of a central detour alley. After the fish had given evidence that it responded to the bait, a door was opened admitting it to the central alley, traversing of which took about five seconds. After reaching the T-shaped end of the alley, a fish could turn right or left and, if the turn were correct, proceed to the food. If it took the wrong turn, the fish came up against a glass door. One should mention here that the side on which the bait appeared was determined by the animal's previous response. The bait was always placed on the side opposite that on which a correct response had previously occurred. It remained on the same side, in other words, until a correct response occurred. As the responses became increasingly correct, the placement of the bait would thus closely approximate a right-left alternation. It is conceivable, therefore, that an alternation rather than a delayed reaction of the sort claimed was being learned. As far as one can tell from the description of the experimental controls, this alternation of the lure was maintained even in the final critical

tests, in which a hook, but no food, was present at the time of response (to prevent chemical diffusion which might give a clue to the location of bait) and in which partitions at the detour end, which had been closed during the experiment, were open (to eliminate possible cues from water currents). The fish did not, like the octopus, maintain any apparent bodily orientation toward the stimulus, so there was no need to control this. In the final 48 critical trials, all but one of the six fish actually improved its performance. Four fish achieved a level of 24 successive correct performances. A comparable apparatus was built for rats, and these learned the problem much more readily than did the minnows.

In another delayed-response experiment with minnows, reported in the same paper, Schiller followed a more conventional procedure. Food on a hook was shown at one of two windows and then moved aside where it could not be seen. After a delay of four or five seconds, both windows were opened and the fish could respond by entering either opening. In this experiment there was a more or less random positioning of the bait, but even during final tests the food was always in the water at the time of response. It is quite likely, although the author discounts this possibility, that the fish were responding to the chemically diffused stimulus rather than to an absent stimulus as in a well-controlled experiment on delayed reaction. This problem proved more difficult than the earlier one, but four minnows, given over 400 trials each, finally achieved a very high accuracy of response, one of them making no mistakes in 48 successive trials.

There is ample evidence that fish of various kinds are capable of learning a wide variety of problems. In this respect they are apparently more versatile than invertebrates. Their successful delayed reactions, even though learned with difficulty and involving only a few seconds between perception of the stimulus and the delayed response, suggest the presence of processes not hitherto suspected at this level of animal life.* For this reason it is very important that we attempt to verify Schiller's findings on delayed reactions under conditions where representative processes provide the only possible basis of correct response.

Amphibians and reptiles

The amphibians have largely been neglected by psychologists, although several have shown that frogs and toads are capable of developing conditioned responses and of acquiring simple maze habits. Experiments summarized by Warden, Jenkins, and Warner [39] show that toads and frogs learn to cease snapping at inedible or distasteful substances. Yerkes [40] trained frogs to take the correct turn in a T-shaped maze, although 100 trials were required. Using a simplified version of this maze, Burnett's [41] frogs developed the habit in 20 trials. Even tadpoles, as shown by the writer, [42] are capable of learning simple mazes involving from one to three blind alleys, but 200 or more trials, with electric shock for errors, are required and the habits are poorly retained.

Seidman [43] studied the learning and reversing of a simple T-maze habit in newts (lizard-like amphibians) and terrapins (fresh-water turtles, hence reptiles). As soon as an animal learned to escape (to darkness and water) by

making a right turn at the end of the T, it was required to reverse the habit, that is, to escape by making a left turn. There were nine such reversals following acquisition of the initial habit. Six newts and six terrapins learned the problem and the successive reversals. Comparisons based upon trials, time, and errors during various stages of the experiment favor the terrapins, which are apparently "one step ahead" of the newt in behavioral plasticity, a superiority attributed to appearance of a true non-olfactory cortex (neopallium).

Turtles, as we have already pointed out, learn discrimination problems involving visual cues. They are also conditioned quite readily to respond to a variety of stimuli, including the location of the feeding place. [44] Yerkes [45] and Tinklepaugh [46] trained turtles to escape from mazes varying in complexity from a simple T to a pathway having as many as five blind alleys. Snakes also learn simple mazes, as demonstrated in an experiment by Kellogg and Pomeroy. [47]

Too little of a truly comparative nature has been done on learning in fishes, amphibians, and reptiles to allow an adequate comparison of the level of ability achieved in each of these vertebrates. On the basis of what has been done so far, it would be rash indeed to conclude that their order of intelligence is in the order of their appearance in the evolutionary scale. It might even be argued that the fishes are superior to the other two forms, but this impression would be biased by the fact that fishes have been more widely studied. There is certainly room for truly comparative research in which the three classes are tested on comparable problems under comparable conditions as in Seidman's experiment with newts and terrapins, which, for this type of problem at least, suggests the superiority of the reptiles.

Birds

Pigeons are readily conditioned, especially by the operant-conditioning procedures de-

---

* It is possible that we may have to revise our concept of delayed reaction as a measure of higher processes or else attribute these processes even to wasps and fishes. Referring to some experimental observations made by Baerends on digger wasps, Tinbergen [38] claims that these animals are capable of delayed responses over periods of as long as 15 hours. He says, "Apart from the amazing length of the delay, this fact demonstrates the importance of carefully selecting that part of normal behaviour in which a delayed reaction normally plays a part. It is highly probable that a delayed-reaction test carried out in the conventional way, for example with a foraging wasp, would not have the slightest result. Thanks to the preparatory survey of the whole behaviour pattern of the species, Baerends was able to find out where a delayed reaction played a part. This particular 'localization' of higher processes to certain phases of behaviour is by no means rare." (p. 10) See also our discussion of difficulties involved in phylogenetic comparisons (pp. 112–113).

veloped by Skinner.[48] With this procedure the animal obtains a reward whenever it operates a lever or, in the case of a bird, pecks a specified object. Pigeons and hens also learn discrimination problems of various kinds, as described earlier (pp. 93–94). These and other birds have discriminated between different numbers of objects, such as bits of grain, but without demonstrating evidence that they are capable of counting in the human sense.[49]

There have been many maze-learning studies, in all of which the birds tested have shown slow but sure habit formation. The most complicated mazes were used in three studies with, respectively, pigeons, hens, and canaries. In Hunter's[50] investigation, pigeons learned a six-blind maze slowly but retained the habit almost perfectly after one month. Warden and Reiss[51] trained chickens on a series of linear mazes ranging in length from two to ten units. From 10 to 20 trials were required to reach the criterion of 9 out of 10 successive correct runs, but there was no clear relation between the difficulty of the maze and its length. Zerga's[52] was a very different type of maze problem from those conventionally used with animals, and it is especially adapted to birds. This maze is vertical rather than horizontal and it comprises a pattern of 85 perches through which the canary hops from the entrance at the bottom to the goal cage at the top. The correct path is in some cases vertical and in others diagonal. For either path, the minimum number of hops is 13. In the best learning record, a canary decreased the number of hops from 125 in the first trial to 13 in the third, and the time from 345 to 12 seconds.

Birds are the lowest organisms with which puzzle boxes requiring manipulation have been used. Porter[53] found that sparrows, cowbirds, and pigeons learned to open puzzle boxes by manipulating strings and other devices. They used the beak and the feet. There was very good retention of these problems over periods ranging from 30 to 140 days. Rouse[54] found essentially similar results for pigeons, although learning was slower than in the sparrows.

Birds have also solved multiple-choice problems. A multiple-choice apparatus similar in principle to that used with birds is shown in Figure 49. The nature of the problem is described in the legend to this figure. In Coburn and Yerkes's[55] experiment with the crow, there was mastery of the *door-at-the-right* and *door-at-the-left* problems, but failure to master the problem requiring response to the *second-door-at-the-left*. In an adaptation of the apparatus, which more

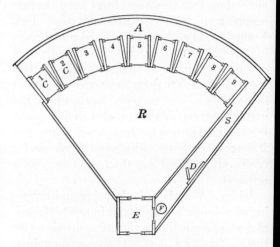

Figure 49. Yerkes's Multiple-Choice Problem

Scale: 1:10. *E*, entrance box; *R*, reaction chamber; *C*, reaction mechanisms; *A*, back alley; *S*, side alley; *D*, sliding door; *F*, food dish. The doors, except *D*, move vertically and are operated by weighted cords. The animal is required to respond to some constant relation between the open doors. Doors 1, 2, and 3 may be open, for example, and the animal is required to enter the door at the right, 3. In the next trial, doors 7, 8, and 9 may be open. A correct response will now be that of entering 9. In the next trial, doors 2, 3, 4, 5, and 6 may be open. Entrance into 6 would constitute a correct response. The problem may require the animal to enter the *middle door* of a variable number, the *second door from the left*, the *second door from the left on one trial and the second door from the right on the next*, etc. If the animal enters the wrong door it is confined or punished in some other way. If it enters the correct door the animal receives food. (From H. E. Burtt, "A Study of the Behavior of the White Rat by the Multiple-Choice Method," *J. Anim. Behav.*, 1916, *6*, 224.)

closely approximated natural conditions, von Haartman [56] trained several species of small European birds to solve problems like those failed by Coburn and Yerkes's crow. Among these were such problems as *second-nest-from-the-left* and *third-nest-from-the-top*. The middle-door problem was learned by Sadovnikova's [57] European siskin.

Birds are the only inframammalian vertebrates tested for "concept" formation. Bingham [58] trained chickens to discriminate a triangle on its base from a circle of equal area and brightness. After the chicks were discriminating the triangle with a high degree of accuracy, it was inverted. The *form* (triangularity) was identical with the one involved in training, but the *shape* (retinal distribution of light) was now different. The chicks failed to discriminate under the changed conditions. Washburn [59] attributes this failure to lack of ability to form the *concept of triangularity*. Munn [60] confirmed Bingham's conclusion that chicks do not respond to form *per se*. The response is purely sensory, depending upon a given retinal distribution of light. We shall see that even the lower mammals show a much higher type of response than this, although their vision is poorer than that of chicks. The optic thalamus of birds is large, but there is not much cerebrum. Response to form *per se* apparently requires more cerebrum than the chicken has at its disposal.

Birds sometimes exhibit an interesting form of learned social behavior not observed in lower vertebrates. Schjelderup-Ebbe [61] observed that after a group of chickens had been together for some time, a social pecking hierarchy was established. The chick at the top of the hierarchy pecked all those below it, but was pecked by none in return; the next chick pecked all those below it and was pecked by only one, that above it; and so down to the chick at the bottom of the social hierarchy, which was pecked by all and pecked none in return. In Murchison's [62] study, 36 weeks were required before such a hierarchy became firmly established. The dominant chick was superior in all measured traits such as weight, speed, aggressiveness, and so on. Katz and Toll [63] found that the dominant member of a group of chickens tended, as measured by learning ability, to be the most intelligent.

It is apparent that the other chickens learn to avoid the dominant member of the group, whereas it learns that it can, with impunity, peck all. The chick lowest in the hierarchy, usually the smallest and least intelligent, learns to avoid all the others. The various stimuli associated with a given chick (odor, color, size, etc.) apparently become signs (as in the conditioning and discrimination experiments) for certain consequences. They assume such significance during the weeks of conflict which precede the appearance of the hierarchy.

Learning In Mammals

Except at lower phyletic levels, puzzle boxes, discrimination problems used as tests of learning, and mazes fail to differentiate the various animal forms. Birds and all the mammals so far tested exhibit good ability in opening puzzle boxes, provided that the mechanisms fall within their manipulative capacities. The primates can, of course, learn more complicated puzzle boxes than the lower forms. All the mammals so far tested have shown ability to learn complicated maze pathways. It is doubtful, however, whether they have greater ability in this respect than do ants and birds when these are suitably motivated. Nor do the higher mammals, including man, show significantly greater facility than lower mammals in learning discrimination problems. In a comparison by Gardner and Nissen [64] of simple discrimination learning in human aments, chimpanzees, cows, horses, and sheep, such small differences were found (in favor of the domestic animals) that the learning of such problems as a basis of phylogenetic comparison was discredited. One might expect that human beings would far outdistance the white rat in mastering complicated maze pathways. In the light of the phyletic distance separating these two mammals, however, the difference in their maze-learning scores is insignificant. In studies by Husband and Lathan and Fields,[65] university students were compared with white rats in the learning of a complicated maze. Rats ran the maze while students traced it. In Husband's experiment the students learned the maze in slightly fewer trials than the rats. But in their more recent comparison of maze learning in rats and college students, Lathan and Fields found that the rats were superior to students in learning, while the students were superior to the rats in retention after an interval of 30 days.

Lashley,[66] in his consideration of learning in mammals, makes the following pertinent comments:

There is little evidence that the rate of formation of simple mechanical habits changes in the mammalian series. . . . Considering the far greater novelty of the entire training situation for the rats than for the human subjects, the results do not indicate any significantly greater learning ability in the latter.

Such data are not conclusive, but do suggest that the rate of formation of simple habits has increased little, if at all, through the evolution of the cerebral cortex. Other facts bear out this opinion. Simple habits are acquired by the feeble-minded about as readily as by normals. Extensive cerebral lesions markedly retard the formation of complex habits, yet produce little effect upon the rate with which simpler ones are formed.

Lashley goes on to suggest that, while the *rate* of formation of simple habits has not changed significantly in the course of vertebrate evolution, the *limits of training* have changed considerably. In other words, the higher an organism is in the phyletic series, the more complex are the problems which it may be trained to perform. This suggestion is supported by investigations on complex manipulatory habits, use of instruments, imitation, cooperative problem solving, complex discriminations, concept formation, complex multiple choice, delayed reactions, and double alternation. We shall now consider

the limits of ability in mammals ranging from rats to man.

Complex Manipulatory Habits

Warden's students [67] at Columbia University, using the triple-plate problem apparatus shown in Figure 50, found that a more complex sequence of manipulatory movements was learned by higher than by lower mammals. Guinea pigs, rats, kittens, rhesus monkeys, and cebus monkeys were used in these studies. The animals were first required to step on plate 1 of the problem box in order to receive food. After this response was mastered, they were required to step on plate 1 and then plate 2. The next task, undertaken after this one was mastered, called for a response to plates 1, 2, and 3 in that order. The fourth problem involved stepping on plates 1, 2, 3, and then 2 (see Figure 50 and legend). Problem 5 required response to 1, 2, 3, and then a reversal to 2 and 1 in that order. Thus the complexity of the

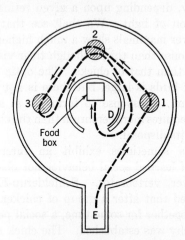

Figure 50. Floor Plan of Jenkins's Triple-Plate Problem Box

The door *D* opens when the animal steps upon the plates in the appropriate order. In the present instance the animal must step upon plates 1, 2, 3 and then reverse to 2 in order to open the door and receive a reward. (From H. A. Fjeld, "The Limits of Learning Ability in Rhesus Monkeys," *Genet. Psychol. Monog.*, 1934, *15*, 403.)

problem was gradually increased, the animal going to a more difficult sequence after learning the simpler one. It is significant that the same type of manipulatory response (that is, stepping on a plate) was required of each animal; thus, as far as this aspect is concerned, the problem was comparable for all. The motivating, punishing, and rewarding factors were also alike for all the subjects. A given step was regarded as solved whenever the animal correctly performed it in nine out of ten successive trials. If the animal, after 1000 trials, failed to reach this criterion, its limit of learning on the triple-plate problem was assumed to have been reached. The limits for the various animals are indicated in Table 2. These results suggest an increase in the limits of achievement as the higher mammals are approached. The difference between the performances of the two types of monkeys is statistically unreliable.

There is, as far as comparison of different animal forms is concerned, an apparently insurmountable inadequacy in this method of determining limits of learning ability. In the first place, although the motivating conditions, procedure, and the like are similar for all animals concerned, one can never be sure that the same stimuli are arousing comparable processes in all animals. The rat, for example, may be responding on the basis of a simple position habit, the kitten on the basis of a more complex position habit, and the monkey on the basis of some symbolic process comparable with counting. For all we know, the monkey may be utilizing a combination of position habits and symbolic processes. Thus, the *nature* of the problem may not be comparable for all animals even though the external conditions are similar.

Instrumentation

Situations in which animals are called upon to use instruments as a means of getting food are also lacking in comparability, partly because they usually require manipulations not possible even to many of the mammals. They are designed in most instances for use with primates.

In Köhler's [68] well-known experiments with chimpanzees, some of these animals, among other things, stacked boxes to reach food suspended over their heads, used sticks of appropriate length to reach food situated outside of their cages, and fitted two sticks together to pull in food too far distant to be reached by either stick alone. Some typical examples of these forms of behavior, which Köhler regards as manifestations of *insight*, are given below. Köhler defines *insight* in terms of ability to perceive relationships between a need, the food inaccessible directly, and the implements the manipulation of which will bring the food within reach. Describing the behavior of Sultan in stacking boxes to reach food suspended above his head, the boxes having been scattered in the vicinity, Köhler [69] says:

The objective hangs still higher up; Sultan has fasted all the afternoon and, therefore, goes at his task with great zeal. He lays the heavy box flat

Table 2. Limits Reached by Various Mammals Tested on Jenkins's Triple-Plate Problem Apparatus

	No. of animals	Range of steps	Median	Average
Guinea pigs (Riess).......	16	0– 1	1.0	0.5
Rats (Riess).............	24	0– 2	1.0	0.9
Kittens (Shuey)	62	3– 7	3.0	3.6
Rhesus monkeys (Fjeld) ..	17	2–22	5.0	7.4
Cebus monkeys (Koch)...	6	5–15	9.5	9.8

underneath the objective, puts the second one upright upon it, and, standing on the top, tries to seize the objective. As he does not reach it, he looks down and around about, and his glance is caught by the third box, which may have seemed useless to him at first, because of its smallness. He climbs down very carefully, seizes the box, climbs up with it, and completes the construction.

Other chimpanzees exhibited similar behavior, some of them stacking four boxes. One more quotation from Köhler will be given, this time that relating to Sultan's fitting together of two sticks. The animal had, after first receiving the sticks, been using them in numerous inappropriate ways.

Sultan, as before pushes one stick with the other toward the objective, and as this pseudo-solution does not satisfy him any longer, he abandons his efforts altogether, and does not even pick up the sticks when they are both again thrown through the bars to him. The experiment has lasted over an hour, and is stopped for the present, as it seems hopeless, carried out like this. As we intend to take it up again after a while, Sultan is left in possession of his sticks; the keeper is left there to watch him. Keeper's report: "Sultan first of all squats indifferently on the box, which has been left standing a little back from the railings; then he gets up, picks up the two sticks, sits down again on the box, and plays carelessly with them. While doing this, it happens that he finds himself holding one rod in either hand in such a way that they lie in a straight line; he pushes the thinner one a little way into the opening of the thicker, jumps up and is already on the run toward the railings, to which he has up to now half turned his back, and begins to draw a banana toward him with the double stick."

When called to the scene, Köhler verified this behavior, for it was repeated on various occasions.

It is only when the solution of a problem occurs suddenly, as in the case of Sultan, that insight is inferred. But unless the relevant past experience of the animal is known, one cannot be sure that the observed instance is the first, and that it is anything but the culmination of earlier attempts at solution. It is unlikely that Sultan had ever before handled sticks which could be fitted together,

so there is a strong presumption in favor of sudden learning. In other observations, where the animals swung outward on ropes to reach a lure, there might well have been previous experience with vines prior to capture.

Following Köhler's report on chimpanzees, several other investigators studied the solution of problems requiring instrumentation and, in these and other situations, sought evidence of insight in animals. Some infra-primates, like rats,[70] squirrels,[71] and cats,[72] have learned simple instrumentation problems, and some instances of apparent insight in these animals have been reported. But most of the research involving instrumentation has, for obvious reasons, been concentrated on primates. Monkeys learn to reach otherwise inaccessible food by stacking boxes, by using a single stick, by using sticks to haul in successively longer sticks until they bring to hand a sufficiently long instrument to reach the lure, by upending and climbing sticks to reach a suspended lure, by using rakes, by fitting sticks together, and by using a stick to push the reward out of a pipe or elongated box.[73] They learn such problems gradually, by a process suggestive of trial and error, and rarely do they show evidence of insightful solution. Even among the higher apes, who do not always learn these problems any more readily than monkeys, the sort of solution exhibited by Sultan is rare. When instances of sudden solution have occurred, they have been preceded by much previous experience with the instruments and with the type of situation requiring solution.

Schiller[74] tested 25 chimpanzees on a series of problems which required use of one or more sticks. The learning of all animals, including the older ones, was characterized as "gradual learning" by "specific experience." Bingham[75] repeated Köhler's box-stacking experiments, but used chimpanzees known to have had no previous experience with boxes or comparable objects. The animals learned to upend and to stack as many as four boxes, but insight, where it was apparent, involved "a new focus of response units" rather than something essentially novel. Birch [76] came to a similar conclusion after studying the use of sticks by six chimpanzees.

Yerkes [77] found a young female gorilla to be less apt than chimpanzees in learning to obtain food by pushing it out of a long box with a stick. She marched about the box, danced on it, beat her chest in irritation, but used the stick only as a plaything until given much tuition in its use in relation to the problem. One chimpanzee, on the other hand, achieved a sudden solution reminiscent of that achieved by Sultan in the stick-joining test, but only after a large amount of previous relevant experience. Similar problems have been used to test children. These studies are considered in Chapter 7, but we can say here that young children, like monkeys and apes, require relevant experience before they give evidence of insightful solution.

It is not possible to conclude, on the basis of instrumentation studies, whether one type of monkey is brighter than another or even whether chimpanzees are brighter than monkeys. One reason is that the test situations have not been comparable. Another is that "personality" differences play an important role in solution of such tests. Yerkes mentions the "businesslike" way a chimpanzee went about a given test while the gorilla was "unattentive," "willful," and "uncooperative." There are even greater differences between monkeys and apes which may render the instrumentation tests far from comparable. It is quite evident, however, that monkeys and apes exhibit a level of complexity in the performance of instrumentation problems which cannot be approached by the mammals below them. This is of course partly due to their better vision and manual dexterity but it is undoubtedly also dependent upon their superior associative processes.

Detour behavior

Köhler [78] called attention to the fact that a good test of animal intelligence is the readiness with which an animal will give up an in-effective direct approach to the goal in favor of an effective roundabout approach. We have already (p. 119) discussed detour behavior in fishes, but these animals had to learn the detour by what was apparently a trial-and-error procedure. What we have reference to here is the *sudden* giving up of the direct in favor of the indirect approach, a form of behavior considered to be evidence of insight.

When chickens, dogs, and monkeys are confronted by food seen through a fence, but not within reach directly, they all try a direct attack. If there is a hole in the fence a short distance to the right or left of the food, and the animals have been familiarized with its existence, they will at first still try the direct approach. The chickens tend to persist in this approach, getting to the food, if at all, by accidentally entering the opening during their back-and-forth activity before the food. A dog, on the other hand, soon takes the detour. Monkeys and chimpanzees will sometimes take it immediately after perceiving the inaccessibility of the food by a direct approach.*

In Köhler's experiments, as well as in later researches by Guillaume and Meyerson [79] and Jackson,[80] chimpanzees were given the opportunity of using a stick to circumvent the barrier. In one such situation, Köhler placed food beyond reach outside of the cage. Nearby was a short stick, one too short to enable the animal to reach the food. Some distance away, beyond the bars, was an adequately longer stick. The detour involved using the short stick to bring in the longer one, then using that to reach the goal. Initially all the animals tried the short stick. Some of them then perceived the long stick, pulled it in, and got the food. In the other researches mentioned above, the animal sometimes was required to push the food away, and around a barrier, in order finally

---

* This description is based upon behavior illustrated in the film "Can Animals Think," distributed by Institutional Cinema Service, Inc., 1560 Broadway, New York 36, N.Y.

to bring it closer. This was an especially difficult problem.

Detour tests of various kinds have been administered to chimpanzees with Bingham's [81] channel transportation apparatus shown in Figure 51. Some chimpanzees exhibited such a high level of performance on such tests that Bingham inferred the presence of ideas. A banana hung below the knob B, as illustrated. By moving the knob along appropriate channels intersecting at X the banana could be brought within reaching distance of a small opening in the cage (O_1, O_2, O_3, or O_4). With the food in a certain position the animal might have to move the knob to the left and then toward right or left, and so on. Ideational processes were inferred from the fact that the animals inhibited or subordinated the final move until requisite preceding ones had been made, and from the fact that they abandoned the readiest apparent

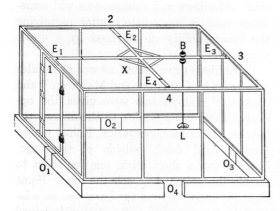

Figure 51. Bingham's Channel Transportation Apparatus

B, knob by means of which the banana could be moved to any location along the channels intersecting at X. O_1, O_2, O_3, O_4, openings through which the banana could be reached. In a given problem all but one of these were blocked. The rest of the cage was covered with wire mesh. A simple problem is as follows: O_1, O_2, and O_3 are closed, O_4 open. The banana is suspended from the knob at E_3. In order to obtain the banana, the animal must move the knob to E_4, where it can be reached through O_4. (From H. C. Bingham, "Selective Transportation by Chimpanzees," *Comp. Psychol. Monog.*, 1929, *5*, 6.)

way of securing the food, which was blocked, and pursued a roundabout course.

Patterned string tests

A wide variety of mammals may be taught to pull in a baited string, either with the mouth or with the forepaws. Only the primates, however, have been tested with patterned-string problems where the baited string may be confused with one or more others having no bait.

Harlow and Settlage [82] used 31 monkeys of a variety of species. In Figure 52 a monkey is shown solving one of the patterns. One string is baited with a piece of apple. If the animal attempts to pull any string other than the baited one, he receives no food. On this particular test the per cent of errors (2450 trials) for 31 monkeys was only 16. Some settings were more difficult than the one illustrated; others were much simpler. After reviewing results obtained with somewhat comparable tests on other animals and human children, the authors say that "monkeys are markedly superior in these tests to all mammals not included in the primate order. Monkeys appear to solve these tests with about the same facility as three-year-old children."

Finch [83] duplicated the Harlow-Settlage patterned-string tests and administered them to six young chimpanzees. The same tests were later given by Riesen and others [84] to three young gorillas in Chicago's Lincoln Park Zoo. There were eleven tests. Comparisons between monkeys and apes were in favor of the latter, except in a few tests where there was apparently no difference in performance. The performance of the two species of apes was judged to be approximately equal, with possibly a slight superiority of the gorillas.

Imitation

Can animals learn skills like the instrumentation and patterned-string problems merely by observing a skilled performance?

Figure 52. Monkey Solving Patterned String Test

The animal is required to pull the string on which the bait (apple) appears. It is prevented from seeing the strings arranged and the food placed. During experimentation its cage is shielded from other cages. This is one of the 20 different patterns used. (From H. F. Harlow and P. H. Settlage, "Comparative Behavior of Primates: VII. Capacity of Monkeys to Solve Patterned String Tests," *J. Comp. Psychol.*, 1934, *18*, 425.)

Sudden solution of problems on this basis has been considered a sign that higher processes are operative. But the results of a long list of researches on animals ranging from birds to chimpanzees have, for the most part, been either negative or equivocal.[85] It is only in monkeys and apes that anything clearly approximating such observational learning can be demonstrated and even at this level the problems solved by imitation are relatively simple.

Warden and Jackson[86] report that some rhesus monkeys learned simple manipulations observationally. Two identical cages were placed side by side, the inside of each being observable from the other. A puzzle box was placed in a comparable position in each cage. New puzzle devices could be inserted in the boxes for different tests. For a given test

both boxes had identical puzzle devices. One monkey, the imitatee, was trained until he manipulated a given puzzle device with facility. Such devices included a chain to be pulled, a knob to be turned, a simple latch to be operated, or a double latch to be manipulated. In the test of imitation, the untrained animal (imitator) watched the imitatee open the puzzle box. He was then given 60 seconds in which to copy the behavior by manipulating the same kind of puzzle device in his own cage. Fifteen monkeys imitated, the best of them doing so 23 times in 24 tests. In a later study,[87] cebus as well as rhesus monkeys learned such problems observationally.

Crawford and Spence[88] found that only one of their nine chimpanzees clearly learned a discrimination problem by observing a trained animal. In a recent report on Viki, their home-raised female chimpanzee, however, Hayes and Hayes [89] describe several instances of spontaneous imitation like the following: applying cosmetics to face and lips before the mirror, operating a spray gun, prying the lids off cans with a screwdriver, and inserting a pencil in a sharpener, then turning the handle. These activities were learned by observation without training or reward of any kind. Indeed, Viki has probably demonstrated a higher level of imitating ability than any other infrahuman animal so far studied.

In an imitation test series, where Viki was given the command "do this" and then given a demonstration, many items were reproduced immediately after the demonstration. Experiments designed to test for imitational problem solving also yielded clear evidence of imitation. Viki did about as well in these experiments as two- to three-year-old children and much better than a caged chimpanzee. Two of the problems are illustrated in Figure 53. In each case the solution was demonstrated, then the experimenter allowed Viki two minutes to attempt a solution. Viki solved the stick-and-string problem immediately after a single demonstration, although she displaced the string upwards whereas the experimenter had pressed down. Three children also solved the problem after a single demonstration. The caged chimpanzee failed it after six demonstrations. Viki's "fascination" with the candle flame appeared to interfere with her solution of the string-and-candle problem, although she solved it after the fourth demonstration. The three children solved it after a single demonstration. It was not given to the caged animal. A problem involving the operation of three levers in a particular sequence was given to Viki and the children. Viki operated the levers after a single demonstration, but in the wrong sequence. It took 32 trials to teach her the correct sequence, although the children learned it after from one to four demonstrations and reversed it after one demonstration. On the other problems, Viki and the children did about equally well, but the caged chimpanzee showed a lower type of performance.

There is thus evidence that imitational learning occurs in monkeys and chimpanzees as well as in human children, but the solutions

Figure 53. Two Imitation Problems Being Solved by Viki

In the stick-and-string test (A), the lure is put in the box, which will open only when the string is displaced. The subject was not allowed near the string, but had to get at it from a distance, which was possible only with the stick. The string-and-candle problem (B) also involved a lure in a box, but in this case the string was to be severed by burning it with the candle flame. (From K. J. Hayes and C. Hayes, "Imitation in a Home-Raised Chimpanzee," *J. Comp. & Physiol. Psychol.*, 1952, *45*, 455.)

imitated must be relatively simple. Even then it is only rarely that an animal not already familiar with the instruments involved gives any evidence of ability to learn by observation alone.

Learning to imitate is, by contrast with spontaneous imitation, relatively easy. Animals from rats up can be taught to copy simple performances, like a right or left turn in the maze, by rewarding them for doing what the other animal does. This is a very different sort of thing from the immediate imitation which we have been discussing.[90]

Cooperative Problem Solving

Cooperative behavior, although of a low order, has been demonstrated in rats, where two animals learn to take turns at sitting on a platform so that each may eat without receiving a shock.[91] The clearest instances of cooperative problem solving in animals are to be found in Crawford's [92] work with chimpanzees. Similar experiments with monkeys [93] have failed to elicit cooperative behavior.

Crawford trained chimpanzees to pull in, by means of a rope, a box containing food. After each chimpanzee had learned individually to draw the box to the bars of his cage, the box was made too heavy for an animal to draw it in alone. Two ropes were attached and the chimpanzees were paired. The animals were then taught to pull together and thus to bring the box within reach. At first their pulling was uncoordinated. By helping and by giving the command "pull" at appropriate moments, the investigator eventually got the animals to pull together. After such tuition, the chimpanzees began to watch each other and to coordinate their pulling without help or commands from the experimenter. Finally, one animal actively solicited the cooperation of another who was failing to pull. Some of the types of solicitation are illustrated in Figure 54. Vocalizations as well as manual gestures were involved in solicitation. Soliciting in this experiment

was similar to that observed by Nissen and Crawford [94] in their study of food-sharing behavior. Regarding the solicitation as communication, Crawford [95] says:

It appears . . . that the solicitation observed in this experiment was not different in its essential patterning from social responses already well known in chimpanzees. It is difficult to show in what ways, if any, the pattern was specifically adapted to the pulling-in situation, beyond its obvious orientation in space. We may venture the opinion that such gestures, whenever they occur, have essentially the same meaning. Support for this opinion may be found in the observation that the solicitation in this experiment was usually responded to with activity, although not always with the same behavior. The response might be negative or positive; it might consist in withdrawal or approach, of offers to march in tandem with the solicitor, or of attempts to groom him, and, in rare instances, the solicitor might be presented with some bit of material in the possession of the solicitee. In short, it appeared that the solicitee was stimulated to some activity, oriented with respect to the solicitor, but not immediately with rope-pulling. Often only after persistent solicitation did the partner take his rope and begin to pull.

It is suggested that these gestures and associated behavior make up a unit of chimpanzee communication, if we choose to call it such, which always has the same meaning. For such a unit of communication students of linguistics have used the term *recurrent same*. The meaning of the gestures seems to be generalized; it might be phrased, if it could be spoken by the solicitor, as "Do something for me."

Crawford also points out that soliciting behavior is limited to a *signaling* function. It does not involve a *predicative* function. In other words, the response does not tell the other animal *precisely* what to do and it does not *describe* the objects. The gestures have no directive meaning beyond their spatial orientation in a given situation.

In a later experiment, Crawford [96] again observed cooperative behavior, including solicitation like that already described. His subjects were first trained to operate four devices in a proper sequence indicated by color

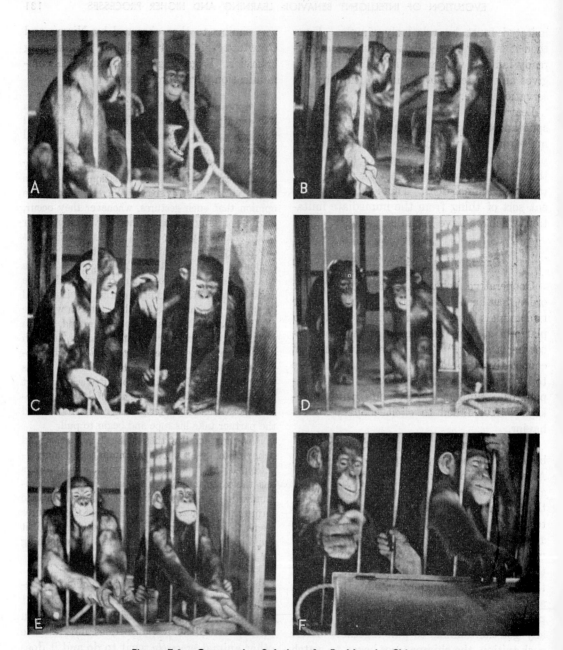

Figure 54.   Cooperative Solution of a Problem by Chimpanzees

A. Bula beckons Bimba forward to the grille.   *B.* Bula touches Kambi near the mouth and turns Kambi's head toward the grille.   *C.* Bula's hand is on top of Kambi's pushing it down toward a rope.   *D.* Bimba urges Bula forward with her hand on Bula's neck.   *E.* Bula and Bimba pull together.   *F.* Bula and Kambi have drawn the box within reach and are taking the food.   Enlargements from 16 mm. cinema film.   (From M. P. Crawford, "The Cooperative Solving of Problems by Young Chimpanzees," *Comp. Psychol. Monog.*, 1937, *14*, 59.)

tabs, but varying spatially. Thus they had to push the yellow, green, red, and blue devices in that order. Food would then come from a vendor. Finally the subjects were separated by means of a grille with two devices on one side and two on the other. Each side had its food vendor. The proper sequence could now be achieved only when the pushing of one chimpanzee complemented that of the other. If yellow and red were on one side and green and blue on the other, chimpanzee A would have to push yellow, wait for B to push green, then push red and wait for B to push blue, whereupon the food would appear. Four of the animals watched their partner and responded appropriately and two of these solicited when their partner did not make the proper response. They did this by reaching through the bars and turning him in the right direction or pushing him. No pointing occurred nor, according to Crawford, has it ever been reported in chimpanzees. The linguistic significance of soliciting behavior such as that described will be considered in a later chapter when we discuss the evolution of language. It clearly falls within the category of symbolic behavior.

Multiple-Choice Tests

The only mammals tested in multiple-choice situations (see pp. 122–123) have been rats, pigs, monkeys, an orangutan, chimpanzees, and man. In the infrahuman mammals there has been slight evidence of an increasing ability on this type of test as higher forms are approached. For example, Burtt [97] found that rats could solve the problem requiring response to the *door-on-the-right* but not the problem requiring response to the *second-door-from-the-left*. In their experiment with pigs, Yerkes and Coburn [98] obtained solution of the problems requiring respectively, a response to the *door-on-the-right*, response to the *second-door-from-the-left*, and response to *alternately-the-extreme-right-and-left-doors*. The *middle-door* problem was failed by the pig as by the rat. Yerkes [99]

obtained response to the *door-on-the-left* in monkeys and in a young orangutan. In the case of the orangutan, the solution was extremely sudden, and Yerkes believes that this indicates the presence of ideas. The problem requiring a response to the *second-door-from-the-right* was solved by monkeys but not by the orangutan. One monkey solved the *alternate-right-and-left-door* problem and the *middle-door* problem. In his later investigation, involving four chimpanzees, Yerkes [100] obtained, in some of his subjects, solution of all of the above problems except that requiring a response to the *middle-door*. He says: "The chimpanzee subjects exhibited an order of ability to respond to controlled settings significantly different from that of mammals, other than anthropoid apes and man, for which comparable observations are available." Human subjects respond on a much higher level than any of the other animals tested on multiple-choice problems. They have readily solved all of the above-mentioned problems and many greatly complicated ones besides.

As in the case of the Jenkins's triple-plate problems discussed in a preceding section (pp. 124–125), the multiple-choice tests may call for the use of different processes as they increase in complexity. The *door-at-the-right* problem, for example, can perhaps be solved on the basis of relatively simple position habits, whereas the difficult *middle-door* problem may require higher processes.

Complex Discriminations

Discrimination learning in its simplest form is more a measure of sensory capacity than of learning ability. In *spatial* discrimination learning, the correct stimulus is that on the right or left, or that above or below. The position is what counts. In *non-spatial* discrimination learning, which is somewhat more difficult than the spatial, an animal is required to respond to an object, or to some stimulus characteristic such as color or form, regardless of its spatial position. Tests of non-spatial discrimination usually involve the chance right-left positioning discussed when we considered methods of studying sensory processes. The animal masters such problems only after it learns to ignore the spatial characteristics of the situation. Providing an animal has the necessary sensory equipment, is well motivated, and is tested under conditions where the significant stimuli will, so to speak, be forced upon its attention, such problems are readily learned, even by inframammals like bees, fish, and birds. One may, however, proceed stepwise to increasingly difficult discrimination problems. These require response to a variety of stimuli in terms of abstracted similarities and differences, or in terms of multiple relationships such as: If the stimuli differ in color, the larger is correct; if they differ in shape, the smaller is correct; if they differ in size and color the red one is correct; and so on. Problems of this complexity are solved only by primates. First we consider some problems involving concepts. Our attention will then turn to complicated conditional reactions which only primates have learned.

Tests of concept formation

No animals below the mammalian level have demonstrated any ability to develop concepts. Fields,[101] however, trained white rats to respond to a wide variety of different triangles when these forms were presented with a circle of equal area and brightness. Control tests showed that the rats were not merely making a negative response to the circle. Apparently they were responding to the different triangles in terms of some property common to all, such as three-sidedness or triangularity. Fields believes that the animals developed a *concept* of triangularity during the course of training. He obtained similar results with raccoons, which, although they have poorer vision than rats, are far superior in developing the concept of triangularity.[102] In an investigation reported by Smith,[103] cats responded to a triangle in terms perhaps comparable with the above.

The animals were trained to discriminate a triangle from a circle of equal area and brightness. They learned to make a positive response to the triangle. When a square was substituted for the circle, some of the animals failed to discriminate. Apparently they were responding negatively to the circle rather than to the triangle as such. Some of the cats, however, continued to discriminate when the square was substituted for the circle. This indicates that they were discriminating the triangle rather than merely avoiding the circle. When the triangle was inverted, thus changing the retinal distribution of light, these animals continued to discriminate the triangle in some terms other than its particular shape or retinal distribution of light.

In Neet's [104] investigation, one monkey responded appropriately after inversion of a triangle to which it had been trained to go. Andrew and Harlow [105] used a somewhat different technique to investigate the same problem. Their apparatus is illustrated in Figure 55, which shows a monkey confronted by a triangle and circle. There is a food well under each stimulus object, but only that below the triangle contains a raisin or comparable reward.

After the monkeys had learned to select the triangle with a high level of consistency, regardless of position, they were presented with a series of generalization tests in which other stimuli than those involved in training were used, but in each pair of which, the element of triangularity was present in one member. Their performance on this test was only slightly better than would be expected from chance. No abstraction of triangularity had occurred in the previous training. Subsequently the animals were given training with a large variety of triangles, as in the research by Fields on rats and raccoons. Tested with these and new figures, the animals showed unmistakable evidence of reacting to triangularity as such, even to the extent of selecting the more triangular of two figures having elements of triangularity. Chimpanzees have not been subjected to comparable tests, but there is little doubt of their ability to respond on a similar basis.[106] Human children, as we shall see later, shift very readily, responding at first to a particular triangle and then to triangularity.

Matching-from-sample and related tests

The pioneer work on matching-from-sample, which is now widely used in clinical psychology as well as in experimental research with monkeys, chimpanzees and children, was reported thirty years ago by Nadie Kohts,[107] a Russian psychologist, whose subject was a pet chimpanzee. Basically the procedure is as follows: The subject is handed a sample object (such as a patch of color or a particular shape) and is then required to select one like it from two or more test objects. Using this technique with monkeys, investigators at the University of Wisconsin have carried out an impressive series of researches in which they have proceeded from simple matching to tests of abstraction, generalization, and concept formation like those used in psychological clinics with human beings. The apparatus used in these studies is a modification of that already described. Basically the only change is in the test tray, which may accommodate a sample and several other objects instead of the two illustrated in Figure 55.

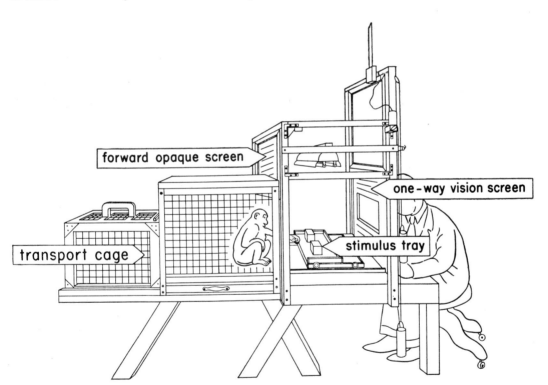

Figure 55.   The Wisconsin Test Apparatus Used with Monkeys

While the stimuli are arranged and the well under one is baited, the opaque screen is lowered. The test tray is then moved toward the animal and the screen is raised. A one-way-vision screen eliminates cues which the monkey might get from watching the experimenter. When it pushes the correct form aside, the monkey can obtain food from the well beneath it. In some such tests, the animal is not allowed to respond to the other stimulus after a mistake. The tray is withdrawn or the screen is lowered. This test situation is used to investigate a variety of discrimination problems, as well as matching and delayed reactions. Some of these are considered in the following pages. (After Harlow.)

In Weinstein's [108] color-categorizing experiments, a monkey was carried in stages from simple matching, where the response was to the stimulus as such, to matching in which the response had to be based upon a conceptual interpretation of the stimulus. Two monkeys were first trained, with a food reward for correct responses, to select an object like the sample from two objects on the test tray. When this was learned, the number and variety of the test objects was gradually increased. Matching on the basis of color, regardless of differences in size, shape, or position was then mastered. The samples were a red triangle and a blue ellipse. Each test tray contained red and blue objects having a variety of shapes and sizes. Following presentation of a red sample, the animal was to move all the red objects. A blue sample meant that all blue objects were to be moved. Matching at this stage was in terms of color identity; such associated features as shape, size, and position had to be disregarded. One monkey proceeded by stages to matching in terms of categories rather than of identical aspects. In these tests a triangle without color meant that all the red objects were to be moved and the blue objects untouched. An ellipse served similarly as a symbol for displacement of all blue objects. Sometimes no test object fell within the category symbolized by the sample. Thus an uncolored ellipse might be presented when all objects on the test tray were wholly or in part red and there were no blue objects. In this case, the monkey learned to refrain from touching any object. Weinstein points out that the behavior of this monkey became decreasingly stimulus-bound and increasingly conceptual as it was carried from basic matching to matching (and non-matching) in terms of samples which were not identical with, nor even like, the objects to be selected. The samples had become representative of things other than themselves. They had become symbols in the same sense that words are symbolic of things to which they bear no resemblance at all. This is somewhat comparable with the transition from picture writing to use of symbols which occurs in the evolution of written language.

Harlow and his collaborators have carried out a long series of researches somewhat similar to the above. These studies have been summarized recently by Harlow; [109] here we shall do no more than indicate a few of the problems studied and their general outcomes. Several experiments, all with monkeys, have dealt with the *oddity* and *non-oddity* principle in matching. As illustrated in Figure 56, three objects are presented, two of which are alike. The subject is rewarded for selecting the odd object — that which, although it differs in color, shape, size, and position from trial to trial, is always presented singly. The mastery of this problem sometimes requires as many as 1500 trials, although some animals learn it in 400 trials. In a *non-oddity* test, the animal is of course required to respond to the two like objects and to disregard the one presented singly. Monkeys are reported by Harlow to require about 2000 trials to learn this problem. Two chimpanzees studied by Nissen and McCulloch [110] required less than 100 trials to learn to respond to the odd form or color presented with 11 other stimuli, all of which were alike, such as one triangle among 11 circles. The chimpanzees had received earlier training on similar problems, and the test situation was different from that used by Harlow. Thus the more rapid learning by the chimpanzees cannot be taken as an index of superior intelligence.

Adaptations of the Weigl matching test, used clinically as an index of abstraction, have been learned by monkeys and chimpanzees. In one adaptation described by Harlow,[111] a sample object was presented which might or might not have a reward under it. The presence or absence of a reward gave the cue for response to the test objects. The test tray might, for example, have three objects as follows: red triangle, red square, and cream square. In terms of color, the cream square was odd, but in terms of shape, the triangle was odd. What the

Figure 56. Two Oddity Tests Solved by Monkeys

Shown above is one form of the oddity test, where the monkey must move the odd object, regardless of its color, shape, position, and the nature of associated objects. In the lower illustration is shown a form of the Weigl principle oddity test. On a cream-colored tray (left) the odd form is correct, whereas on an orange-colored tray, the odd color is correct. (Photos courtesy Dr. Harry Harlow.) (From H. F. Harlow, "Primate Learning," in C. P. Stone, *Comparative Psychology*, 3d ed., New York: Prentice-Hall, 1951, pp. 189 and 195.)

animal was required to do was this: If the sample had a reward under it, the odd color was correct (that is, the cream square); otherwise the odd shape was correct (that is, the red triangle). During the tests, different samples and test objects were used, but the same principle was always involved. Another variety of this test is illustrated in the lower half of Figure 56. Monkeys learn to respond in terms of such principles, although

as many as 6000 trials are sometimes required. Nissen and his collaborators [112] have taught similar principles to chimpanzees, but they do not learn them as readily as monkeys. This may be due to differences in technique and in person-to-animal relationships. Harlow attributes it to personality differences.

Sets in discrimination learning

Another indication of higher processes in

discrimination learning comes from experiments in which animals are required to learn successive reversals of a discrimination (such as learning to choose black instead of white where white was previously correct) or to shift from one basis of response (such as oddity) to another basis (such as non-oddity, or color, or shape). An index of behavioral plasticity is the readiness with which the animal shifts from one basis of discrimination to another. As we have already seen (p. 121), even the newt and the terrapin learn to reverse discriminations more readily in successive problems, although the terrapin shows somewhat greater plasticity than the newt in doing so.

Monkeys are especially adept at learning to shift from one discrimination problem to another. Harlow,[113] who uses the terms "learning sets" and "learning how to learn" to characterize this phenomenon, has reported that some monkeys achieve a level where they shift, after a single trial, from one basis of discrimination to another. One trial is of course necessary, since it must provide the clue as to what is required. Finding the odd object rewarded, for example, the animal then responds to oddity; finding the red object rewarded, it shifts to red; and so on. Chimpanzees have also demonstrated ability to shift sets, but the tests were different from those used with monkeys; hence there is no basis for comparing the relative plasticity of the two with respect to this behavior.[114]

Delayed-Reaction Tests

Delayed-reaction techniques, with which we are already somewhat familiar (see pp. 105–107), have been used widely to test the ability of animals and human children to recall previous stimulation.

In the original Carr-Hunter technique, which was used by Hunter[115] to investigate recall memory in rats, dogs, raccoons, and children, what the subject was required to remember was the *location* of the stimulus. Certain details of this procedure are described in the legend of Figure 57. After the subject had learned to associate a light with food, the light was turned off some seconds or minutes before the response could be made. Now the problem was to remember *in which compartment the light had been.* In some respects, this is like a spatial discrimination problem where the subject learns to respond always to the right, left, or middle position. But it is more complicated than such a problem because, instead of remaining spatially constant, the proper position shifts in a random order from trial to trial. The animal is not called upon to respond to a fixed position in space, but to the position in which the light previously appeared. This can be any of the possible positions.

In some modifications of the Carr-Hunter technique, non-spatial stimuli have been used to signify the correct location. In one such experiment Yerkes[116] confronted a gorilla with a series of colored tins, all of the same shape and size. These appeared around the outer edge of a turntable. As the gorilla watched, a piece of food was placed in, let us say, the red can. The turntable was then spun around to change the location of the correct can. Later, when the gorilla was returned to the scene, it turned the table until the red tin was at hand, then got the food. On each trial another color would be used. Here, instead of remembering where the food had been located (a spatial delayed reaction), the animal had to remember the *color of the can in which it had previously seen the food placed.* This is somewhat like a non-spatial discrimination problem, but one important difference is that, whereas the latter always associates the reward with a particular stimulus (food always with red, for example), the delayed-response problem involves a different stimulus at each setting. It is relatively easy for the animal to learn that red *always* signifies food, but much more difficult to remember, with a different color at each test, which one just previously, or even a long time earlier, was associated with food.

We have discussed discrimination experi-

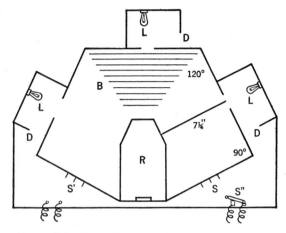

Figure 57. Hunter's Delayed Reaction Apparatus

This particular form of the apparatus was used with rats. The animal, in the glass release box R, could be stimulated by the lights L. It was required to associate a light, appearing in any one of the three doors in a chance order, with the presence of food. An electric shock (grids were in front of each door) was administered whenever the animal attempted to enter an unlighted chamber. Food was obtained at the front of the apparatus whenever the correct chamber had been entered. In the training series the release box R was raised while the light was still present. After the association between a lighted compartment and food had been thoroughly established, the light was turned off before release. The animal was now required to remember in which compartment the light had appeared. If it continued to go to the previously illuminated compartment, a longer delay between the turning off of the light and the raising of the release cage was instituted. The time of delay was gradually increased until the animal could no longer remember which compartment had been illuminated. D, doors through which the animal made its exit from the light box; S, switch connected with grids; S', light switches. (From W. S. Hunter, "The Delayed Reaction in Animals and Children," *Behav. Monog.*, 1913, *2*, 24.)

ments with monkeys and chimpanzees, where they learn to shift *set* from trial to trial. Here the difference between the delayed-reaction and discrimination procedures is of course minimal. In the discrimination test, however, the animal responds and is rewarded immediately whereas, in the delayed-response test, it must wait some seconds, minutes, or hours before responding, and hence before getting the reward.

Thus, even where discrimination and delayed-reaction techniques are similar, the latter always involves a delay, both in the response itself and in the reward. The problem becomes increasingly difficult, in comparison with mere discrimination, as the delay increases from a few seconds to minutes, or even to hours. In human children,

as we shall see, the delay followed by correct response is sometimes as long as a month or more.

In order to be sure that the delayed response is in terms of absent cues (having seen the food put in a certain place or having seen it associated with a certain color or shape), and not to present cues (such as odors or kinesthetic stimulation derived from keeping a bodily orientation), various controls must be instituted. It is easy to eliminate odor as a differential cue by placing it in all possible locations or by smearing the various possible containers with it. In the experiment with the gorilla, for example, all cans were smeared with banana although the actual banana was in only one of them. One of the minnow experiments (p. 119) failed to eliminate the possibility that a chemical cue guided the animals to the bait. Bodily orientation is still another problem. An animal may turn its head, or its whole body, in the direction of the baited compartment (or container), then go straight to it when released. In the experiment with the octopus, which was described earlier (p. 117), orientation of the beak and tentacles in the direction of the bait was eliminated by making the animal squeeze through a small opening during the delayed detour. It could then no longer "remember" the side on which the bait had been placed. Hunter's rats and dogs also failed when, during the delay, he turned them around in such a manner as to disturb bodily orientation. Under similar circumstances, raccoons could still respond correctly, even after a delay of 25 seconds.

Delayed reactions elicited under conditions where there is neither external guidance nor guidance from present kinesthetic cues, such as in bodily orientation, must be mediated by symbolic processes. That is to say, by internal processes which, during the delay and at the time of response, substitute for (or represent) the absent situation. Such processes are involved when we recall where we put something, or saw it placed, and when we recall absent things, persons, or events.

Delayed reaction in infraprimate mammals

In Hunter's experiment with rats, dogs, and raccoons, the latter were, as we have seen, the only animals which responded successfully without maintaining bodily orientation. Hunter thus concluded that they alone evidenced symbolic response. But several later investigations, which have been summarized elsewhere,[117] gave unmistakable evidence of symbolically mediated delayed reactions in rats. In a study by McCord,[118] whose apparatus and technique are described in Figure 58, rats delayed successfully for periods as long as six minutes. They did this without maintenance of bodily orientation and without external guidance. In a situation like Hunter's, Walton[119] demonstrated delayed

reaction in dogs. This bridged an interval of five minutes and did not require bodily orientation. In experiments by Cowan[120] and Adams,[121] cats delayed successfully, without bodily orientation, for periods up to 16 hours. These experiments thus demonstrate that infraprimate mammals are capable of recall memory, although the various delays reported are far from comparable. This is due to the different procedures and the small number of subjects used. It would thus be unwise to conclude, for example, that the recall memory of cats is necessarily superior to that of dogs.

Delayed reaction in primates

Although all the primates so far tested have demonstrated ability to do delayed reactions under conditions indicating the use of symbols, the delays reported, like those discussed above, differ a great deal from one study to another. Monkeys have been credited with delays of from two minutes in some studies to 20 hours in others.[122] The data for chimpanzees and gorillas are similar, although a maximal delay of 48 hours has been reported for each of these animals.[123] An orangutan had a maximal delay of only five minutes. Such discrepancies are probably attributable to the varied techniques used, the small number of subjects, and variations in the rapport existing between the experimenter and his subject. They do not warrant the conclusion that, for example, orangutans have a poorer memory than chimpanzees or gorillas. In any event, a single orangutan or gorilla might not represent the level of ability of his species.

In primates the complexity of the process exhibited is more impressive than the length of successful delay. Monkeys not only remember where some object was hidden, or with what color or shape it was associated, but also the nature of the object itself. They remember the correct location or the proper sign even when several possibilities, rather than only two or three, are involved. And they also learn to make a series of delayed reactions involving as many as 16 pairs of con-

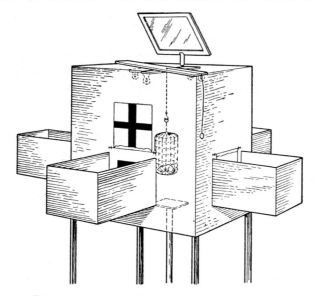

Figure 58. Apparatus for Testing Delayed Reaction in Rats

The rat is held in a restraint cage while the response cue is given and during the delay. A rat is shown being lowered to the platform after the delay. When the cage reaches the jumping platform, it is disengaged from the bottom and raised, thus allowing the rat freedom to jump. The training cue is the thrusting of a hand holding a food dish through a particular door. This door changes from one test to the next, in a random order. Although each of the four doors contains a different figure (the cross illustrated, a diagonal, a vertical, or a horizontal bar), the remembered cue may actually be spatial rather than non-spatial. The animal could perhaps be forced to respond to the figures if, after a cue has been given, the figure associated with it were shifted. Then, in order to get its reward, the animal would need to disregard the position in which the food had appeared and respond to the figure with which it had appeared. The mirror is for the investigator to observe the rat without himself being observed. (From F. McCord, "The Delayed Reaction and Memory in Rats. I. Length of Delay," *J. Comp. Psychol.*, 1939, *27*, plate I.)

tainers. In some of these experiments there have been adaptations of discrimination tests like those used to study response to multiple signs.

Most research with primates has utilized the direct method of testing delayed reaction, a method first used by Hunter [124] with children and so designated because it requires no preliminary training like that involved in Hunter's original research and in the research of later investigators (like McCord) on infra-primate mammals. The direct method, as used by Tinklepaugh [125] to test for delayed reaction in monkeys, is illustrated in Figure 59. A spatial response is required.

After a monkey had seen a piece of banana placed under one of the two cups, it was taken away from the situation and later returned, whereupon it responded by lifting a cup. In some tests, after the piece of banana had been placed under one of the containers, a piece of lettuce was secretly exchanged for it. Now when the monkeys turned over the correct cup, and found the lettuce instead of the banana, they usually dropped the lettuce and acted as though they were searching for the banana. They examined the vicinity and then walked off, leaving the lettuce. Although this test was of the spatial variety, there was certainly a non-spatial type of reaction. When children were subjected to the same kind of substitution test, they responded

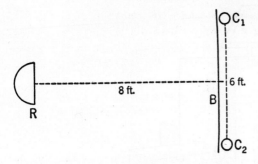

Figure 59. Direct Method of Studying Delayed Reaction

R, restraining cage; *B*, board screen used to hide food cups C_1 and C_2 after the animal has seen food placed in one of them. The animal was first trained to sit in the restraining cage *R*, and to remain there until given a signal to get down. While the monkey was looking, the experimenter placed food under cup C_1 or C_2. The actual cup (right or left) varied in a chance order from trial to trial. The board *B* was raised so that the animal could no longer see the cups. When, after a certain period of delay, the signal to get the food was given, the animal was required to select one of the cups. If the wrong cup was lifted, no food could be obtained until the next trial. Control of cues from the experimenter, of odor cues, and of postural or kinesthetic cues were introduced so that the only possible basis of a high percentage of correct reactions was use of symbolic processes. (After Tinklepaugh.)

in a similar fashion, but they also made comments.

Delayed-reaction tests of greater complexity than the above have been carried out by Harlow [126] and Tinklepaugh [127] on a number of primates. In Harlow's test, as in Tinklepaugh's, food was placed in one of two cups within view of the animal. The cups were then hidden by a screen during the period of delay. The response was regarded as correct if the animal, upon removal of the screen, immediately lifted the correct cup. Harlow complicated the test in the following ways: The animal was disoriented and distracted during the period of delay by being fed at the opposite end of the cage; it was forced to solve two delayed-reaction problems at the same time; and the positions of the containers were shifted during the period of delay so that

their relative and absolute positions were altered. Delays ranging from 15 to 300 seconds were used with each animal. Lemurs made the greatest number of errors, but the Old-World (Catarrhine) monkeys responded with a high degree of accuracy to all the above complications of the problem. A gibbon exhibited a lower level of ability than baboons and macaques. Baboons exhibited the most accurate performances.

Tinklepaugh's complicated delayed-reaction study was made with three monkeys, two chimpanzees, four children, and five adults. Each situation involved a pair of similar cups under the right or left member of which the subject had observed food being placed. (See Figure 59.) In some of the experiments the receptacles were presented, one pair each, in a series of rooms ranging, in different tests, from one to ten in number. After observing the food placed in each room the animal was taken back to the first room and required to walk through the rooms, lifting the correct cup in each. In a ten-room situation, the chimpanzees were correct in 88 and 92 tests, respectively, out of 100. Reversing the order of rooms (last to first) failed to influence the accuracy of response. With only five pairs of containers in five rooms, the monkeys made many more mistakes than the chimpanzees made on tests involving ten rooms. Eighty per cent was the highest accuracy reached by the monkeys in this simpler test. These subjects were very distractible. In other tests, pairs of containers ranging in number from three to sixteen were arranged in a large circle within one room, each pair being distinguishable from other pairs in terms of size and color. The subject sat in the center of the circle and observed food being placed under one receptacle of each pair. He was then required to find the food. The results for the chimpanzees and monkeys are represented in Table 3, which indicates the percentage of correct responses for different numbers of containers. A chance performance would, of course, yield accuracies of only 50 per cent. In the sixteen-pair test, adult human sub-

Table 3. **Responses of Chimpanzees and Monkeys in Multiple Delayed-Reaction Tests**

	3 pairs	4 pairs	6 pairs	8 pairs	12 pairs	16 pairs
Monkeys............	73 77	64 84	50 78	56 66		
Chimpanzees........				85 90	81 79	78 89

jects performed with no greater accuracy than did the chimpanzees. Children from seven to nine years old were inferior to the apes in the same problem. Chimpanzees responded correctly to a situation involving three pairs of containers after a week's delay. The author says that chimpanzees showed "surprise and disappointment" when an undesirable object had been secretly substituted for a desirable one which the animal had observed being placed under the receptacle.

Another delayed-reaction test which has been used with monkeys is illustrated in Figure 60. Here the subject is required to recognize which of several test objects was presented some time earlier as a sample. It must match the sample, so to speak, by displacing the same object on the test tray. This is non-spatial delayed reaction because the object itself must be remembered and its position disregarded. In situations comparable with that illustrated, Weinstein's [128] monkeys responded with a high level of accuracy after intervals ranging up to 60 seconds. Finch [129] used a somewhat different matching procedure with chimpanzees. The longest successful delay reported to him is 40 seconds. When we compare these delays of a minute or less with those of from minutes to hours found for spatial delays in a two-place situation, we realize how difficult even the simplest delayed-matching test must be.

Figure 60. Delayed Matching-from-Sample

The object at the left (a different object from trial to trial) is first shown by itself. By displacing it, the animal gets a small reward, such as a raisin or grape. After this a screen falls and a delay occurs. Then the screen rises and a tray with four objects, including one like the sample, is presented. Now, in order to obtain its reward, the monkey must displace the object seen earlier. The test may be complicated in various ways as described in the text. (Photos courtesy H. F. Harlow.)

This type of delayed-reaction test is also extremely difficult for young children, as we shall see later.

The delayed-matching test may be complicated in many ways, as were the discrimination tests already discussed. In one such complication, two "samples" are presented, but only one can be displaced, and hence supply a reward. In the test, which follows some seconds later, both of the "samples" are presented, either alone or with other objects. The animal is required to displace the object previously rewarded and to refrain from touching the other, or any of the associated objects, if such are also used. Monkeys tested by Weinstein [130] have succeeded in performing such tests with significantly better than chance accuracy after a delay of one minute.

A more complicated test of delayed matching-after-sample was given to monkeys by Simpson and Harlow.[131] This involves the Weigl principle considered earlier. The sample is given, but it is sometimes associated with a reward and sometimes not. If the monkey finds a reward after displacing it, the animal is to displace the object of the same color when tested later. But if no reward is found with the sample, the test calls for displacement of the object having the same shape. This is an extremely difficult problem. The maximum successful delay, after 3500 trials, is reported to be around 12 seconds.

The Double-Alternation Test

Double alternation in the temporal maze is one of the best available comparative tests of reasoning in animals.* It can be used in

essentially the same form with animals from the lowest to the highest. Actually, however, no animals below the rat have been given this test. The white rat does so poorly on double alternation that is doubtful whether giving the test to lower forms would be worth the time and effort involved.

Double alternation in the temporal maze calls for a response in terms of temporal relations under conditions where there are no differential sensory cues. The apparatus is called a temporal maze because the sequence of turns is determined temporally rather than spatially. In mazes of the spatial variety, (see Figures 46 and 48), the animal is confronted by new stimuli in every unit of the path. These serve as signs for initiation of turns, for approach, or for avoidance. In the temporal maze, as indicated in the legend to Figure 61, the animal is to make, say, two turns to the right, followed by two turns to the left, after emerging from the central alley. The same central alley, *with identical stimuli from one moment to the next*, must bring forth a right turn at one moment and a left turn at the other, the particular turn depending upon a temporal relation to previous turns. There are no differential stimuli such that one could be associated with right turns and another with left turns, as in discrimination and maze problems. Hunter [133] has pointed out, furthermore, that kinesthetic processes cannot give differential cues which would enable the animal to solve the *rrll* sequence. A sequence like *rlrlrl* . . . could be solved readily on a kinesthetic basis. The right turn might leave a residue of kinesthetic effects which would become associated with a left turn at the next emergence from the central alley, and so on. In other words, having-just-gone-to-the-right might, in a *rlrl* sequence, serve as a cue for going to the left on the next turn, and having-just-gone-to-the-left might serve to initiate a turn to the right. In the *rrll* sequence, however, such kinesthetic cues cannot control the response any more than external cues can control it. Having-just-gone-to-the-right would have to serve as a stimulus

* Maier's [132] test of reasoning has been used only with rats and human children. The subject first learns two separate habits. He is then confronted with a problem situation whose solution requires that he combine elements of the earlier habits, neither of which is now adequate in itself. Since they can "put two and two together" in this way, rats are credited by Maier with reasoning ability. Children do much better than rats, and in both rats and children performance improves with age.

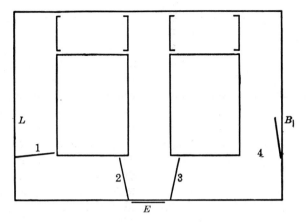

Figure 61. Hunter's Double Alternation Problem

1, 2, 3, and 4, doors which serve to block the progress of the animal following an incorrect response. *E*, entrance and food box. The brackets indicate the extent and position of the electric grids. The animal is placed in the apparatus at *E*, and is allowed to advance up the central alley as far as the top of the T-shaped pattern. If the series is to be *rrll*, the animal must turn to the right at this point. If he turns to the right the animal crosses the grid and the doors 4 and 3 are quietly opened, allowing him access to food at *E*. Without removal from the apparatus the animal is now required to repeat the performance. If he should turn to the left when a right turn is required, for example, a shock is administered and the door 1 prevents entrance into the food box. The animal is then required to traverse the correct pathway. After two turns to the right, the subject is required, on the basis of the same spatial stimuli (central alley), to make two turns to the left. After the problem has been learned, the animal is run through the apparatus without use of the doors to see whether these have contributed any cues. (From W. S. Hunter, "The Behavior of Raccoons in a Double Alternation Temporal Maze," *J. Genet. Psychol.*, 1928, *35*, 379.)

for a turn to the right on the next trial and, on the third trial, as a stimulus for a turn to the left. According to Hunter, if the response is to be learned there must be a physiological residue from the preceding units which serves to initiate the correct turns, or there must be a symbolic representation of the temporal order of the turns. The latter would be similar to saying "Twice to the right followed by twice to the left" or "Right, right, left, left." Hunter claims that since sensory residues from previous units of the temporal maze cannot serve at one moment to initiate a turn to the right and at another time to initiate a turn to the left, the problem must be solved, if at all, by the use of symbols. Some implicit process, in other words, must enable the animal to respond on the basis of a *temporally* arranged rather than a spatially arranged order.

The animal is required, then, to turn twice to the right and twice to the left (or vice versa). While making these turns, it is not aided by any differential sensory cues. It runs down the same central alley before making each turn, and the same stimuli are present whether the turn is to be a right one or a left one. In order to make the *rrll* response in the absence of differential sensory (spatial and kinesthetic) cues the animal must use an implicit process similar, in essential respects, to that involved in complex delayed-reaction tests. In experimenting with human subjects one at first observes trial-and-error behavior like that of any other mammal. Suddenly, however, the subjects exclaim, implicitly or overtly, "Right, right, left, left," "Why, you go twice to the right and twice to the left," and so on. Human subjects have no difficulty, once they have formulated the problem symbolically, in repeating the response or in extending it from the initial *rrll* series to *rrllrrllrrllrrll*. . . . The infrahuman animal which solves the double-alternation problem must, according to Hunter, use a process somewhat comparable to that exhibited by human subjects.

The results obtained with animals so far tested on the double alternation problem in the temporal maze may be summarized briefly. In Hunter's [134] tests on white rats there was complete failure to learn the *rrll* response, although over 1000 trials were given. Hunter and Nagge,[135] however, found that some rats could be trained to make the *rrll* response in the temporal maze if each of the turns was first learned in a separate apparatus, probably providing differential sensory cues. A rat learned to turn to the right in box 1, to the right in box 2, to the left in box 3, and to the left in box 4. It was then trained to turn twice to the right in box 1 and twice to the left in box 2. Finally, when placed in a single box (temporal maze) it made the *rrll* series of turns. The series could not be extended beyond the four turns. A few of Hunter and Hall's [136] rats learned double alternation in a spatial maze under conditions where differential sensory guidance was eliminated (blind rats, rotated maze units, maze rotation).

In his experiment on raccoons, Hunter [137] obtained the *rrll* response in the temporal maze, and at the same time found in some subjects an extension of the response to *rrllrr*. Karn [138] taught two cats the *rrll* response in a temporal maze like Hunter's, but neither animal extended the response. Human subjects, as we shall see, not only learned this problem far more rapidly than monkeys, but they also more effectively extended the sequence.[139]

Although few infraprimates have learned the double-alternation problem under the above-mentioned conditions, it is apparent that cats and raccoons perform at a much higher level than rats and that monkeys are far superior to these lower mammals.

Summary and Conclusions

Intelligence, which may be defined as flexibility or versatility in adjustment, is a function of sensory and motor processes, but more specifically of ability to learn. We have seen that simple modifiability is present to some degree in certain unicellular organisms. It is perhaps an inherent property of protoplasm.

The paramecium makes simple escape reactions with increasing facility, and it becomes increasingly prone to attach itself to a source of food. Whether or not such modification exemplifies learning is a controversial issue, especially since the paramecium has no nervous system. The retention of modifications, even though of brief duration, favors the view that this is learning.

Learning of a simple sort is indisputably present in such invertebrates as worms, snails, cockroaches, and ants. Some of these learn simple conditioned reactions as well as avoidance of noxious stimuli. Worms and cockroaches learn simple mazes. Ants are particularly adept at learning to find their way through mazes with several blind alleys. Insects such as bees and wasps learn discrimination problems. The octopus, another invertebrate whose learning has been studied by psychologists, learns to find food by traversing a detour, but there is no evidence of insight, recall memory, or other higher processes.

Inframammalian vertebrates, of which fishes, frogs, terrapins, snakes, and birds have been most extensively tested, demonstrate no significantly greater susceptibility to conditioning than the higher invertebrates. In learning simple discrimination and maze problems they are not clearly superior to arthropods like the ant. It is apparent that the *rate* with which such problems are learned (time, trials, errors) is not a good basis of phylogenetic comparison. This is also true when we compare the inframammals with the mammals and the lower mammals with the primates. Human beings, for example, learn sensorimotor maze habits no more readily than rats. In some respects the rats are actually ahead.

The birds are superior to the lower vertebrates in their learning of problem boxes, but this is probably more an advance in motor dexterity than in learning ability as such. Some birds learn simple multiple-choice problems. Lower vertebrates, however, have not been subjected to such tests. It has been claimed that minnows are capable of recall memory, as indicated by simple delayed detour tests. Since birds have not been given comparable tests, there is no basis for comparing fish and birds in this respect. Birds have failed in tests of concept formation, but so also have several mammals until given additional training not involved in the bird experiments. It is apparent that much more comparative research, using the same sorts of tests, is required before we can gauge the level of intelligence of birds as compared with lower vertebrates.

All mammals so far tested have shown good susceptibility to conditioning and good ability to learn discrimination problems, mazes, and problem boxes. The rate with which they learn such things is, however, not significantly greater than in the lower vertebrates. We must therefore seek other tests with which to gauge mammalian intelligence. These tests emphasize the *complexity* of what can be learned and not so much the rate of learning.

The rat, which is one of the lowest mammals, has been the most extensively tested infraprimate. What can it do that the infra-mammals cannot do? It learns to open rather complicated problem boxes which, at lower levels, only the birds have accomplished. From the learning of simple discrimination it can be trained to the point where it is responding on the basis of a concept, such as of tri-angularity. Whether birds are capable of making this transition from simple to conceptual discrimination remains to be seen. In detour problems the rat sometimes takes short cuts, a behavior which suggests the presence of insight. In delayed-reaction tests it demonstrates ability to recall past stimulation and can thus be credited with the acquisition and use of symbolic processes. In double alternation and other reasoning tests it has demonstrated the ability to solve problems by reasoning, by "putting two and two together." It is the lowest animal which has ever unmistakably demonstrated insight, recall memory, and reasoning ability.

From rat to man there are of course many animal forms, but few have been tested on such a basis as to provide very adequate phylogenetic comparisons. Every higher mammal, tested in a comparable way, could undoubtedly perform at as high a level as the rat. But what have the higher mammals done that rats have not done? Tests of complex manipulatory habits (where the animal had to move from one of three platforms to another in certain sequences) show that the limit of complexity attained is higher in cats than in rats and guinea pigs and much higher in monkeys than in cats. Rats use implements, such as single strings, but only the primates have solved *complex* instrumentation problems, requiring the use of sticks, boxes, or strings. Chimpanzees are the only infrahumans to join two sticks in such a manner as to achieve a goal inaccessible by either alone. The sudden solution of such problems is taken as an indication of insight, which itself is apparently dependent upon relevant past experience. Insight is also inferred from the sudden taking of detours when a goal is otherwise inaccessible. Dogs are far ahead of rats in such tests, but monkeys and apes show such behavior to the highest degree among infrahumans. The superiority of the primates over infraprimates is especially shown in complications of discrimination tests, complex delayed-reaction tests, and double-alternation tests.

Both monkeys and chimpanzees learn to match samples, and from simple matching-from-sample they may, by steps, be led to the point where they are matching on the basis of complex relationships and categories rather than in terms of the samples as such. In other words, the samples become representative signs or symbols. In learning a succession of such problems, both monkeys and chimpanzees demonstrate to a much higher degree than infraprimates the phenomenon known as "learning sets" and "learning how to learn." Given the cue, they readily shift from one basis of response to another. A further complication of discrimination tests is delayed matching-from-sample in which, after the sample is given, the animal must wait a certain period before the opportunity to match is provided. This becomes especially difficult when, instead of matching one object (say a red cross) with another like it, the animal must match on the basis of shape under certain conditions, of redness under others, and perhaps of blueness under still others.

In the spatial type of delayed reaction test, there is an increase in the duration of the optimal delay as one goes from rats to primates. Under comparable conditions, the maximal delays involve seconds in rats and from minutes to hours in monkeys and apes. Non-spatial delayed-reaction tests (where the animal must remember a color, shape, or object independent of its location) have not been given to animals below the primates, presumably because such responses are believed to be far beyond their capacities. The delayed matching-from-sample test is of this kind, although the use of more than two items on the test tray is an added complication. Still more complicated are spatial delayed-reaction tests in which the animal must remember under which member of each of several pairs of objects the food has been hidden. Only primates have passed tests at this level of complexity. Monkeys have demonstrated that they recall not only *where* something was hidden previously, but *what* was hidden.

In the double-alternation tests in the temporal maze (where the animal must make the correct sequence of turns without guidance

from sensory cues) rats do very poorly. They learn the problem, but only after much help from cues which are later gradually withdrawn. Cats, raccoons, and monkeys learn this problem without such aid. Both raccoons and monkeys, once having learned an *rrll* sequence, continue to a longer sequence, showing that they are capable of applying their symbolic representation of the problem to a sequence longer than that on which they were trained.

Because of the difficulties mentioned at the beginning of this chapter it is not possible to make a definitive ranking of animals in terms of intelligence. Here, however, are some very tentative suggestions.

The impression one gets from psychological data so far available is that the level of intelligence of fishes, amphibians, and reptiles is clearly above that of any of the invertebrates, even including the highly evolved arthropods, like the bees and ants. Among the fishes, amphibians, and reptiles it is difficult to say which is psychologically superior. The fishes have certainly demonstrated more versatility than the others, but they alone have been very extensively tested. Birds are apparently higher in intelligence than the lower vertebrates. Their excellent vision and motility, their vocalizations, and their reactions in multiple-choice and other learning tests add to this impression. As compared with even the lowest mammals, however, their learning ability seems, on the whole, to be very poor. This may be due in part to the great role which instinctive behavior plays in bird adjustment.

Among the infraprimate mammals there is much uncertainty as to the relative standing of different orders. This is partly because adequate comparative tests have not been administered to a sufficient number of animal forms. Rats certainly have lower intelligence than cats and dogs, and there is good evidence for placing the intelligence of dogs above that of cats. But how about domestic mammals like the goat, the cow, the horse, and the sheep? How about the lion, the tiger, and the elephant, and the many other kinds of mammals which are to be found in any large zoo? And how about aquatic mammals like seals, porpoises, and whales? We know so little of a reliable nature about the learning ability of these and the many other mammals that it is not even possible to make a good guess as to their relative level of intelligence. We do know quite definitely, however, that the infrahuman primates are far superior to infraprimates in intelligence. No lower mammal could conceivably learn the complex discriminations, requiring generalizations and concepts, which monkeys and chimpanzees learn; and no lower mammal could conceivably show such versatility as is demonstrated in the monkey's change of set from one discrimination problem to another. The delayed-reaction and double-alternation tests also place primates very definitely above the mammals below them.

It is not possible, with any high degree of confidence, to rank the infrahuman primates in order of intelligence. In all but the com-plex delayed-reaction and instrumentation tests, monkeys have done better than chimpanzees and gorillas. This may, however, reflect a difference in personality more than in intelligence. Monkeys often seem quite "businesslike" and "intense" in their approach to problem solving whereas chimpanzees are "easy-going" and highly distractible. Gardner and Nissen [140] remark that "chimpanzees are extremely sensitive to the slightest changes in an otherwise familiar situation; a new pair of shoes worn by the regular caretaker may temporarily transform the animal's attitude from friendly, confident approach to one of wary avoidance. The enormous effect of displacing the stimulus an inch or two from its original position in a discrimination problem has been demonstrated experimentally." All of which only adds to the impression that these "almost human" animals may be the geniuses of the infrahuman world. Just where the other great apes stand is problematical because they have not been sufficiently tested.

REFERENCES

1. McBride, A. F., and D. O. Hebb, "Behavior of the Captive Bottle-Nose Dolphin, *Tursiops truncatus*," *J. Comp. & Physiol. Psychol.*, 1948, *41*, 111–123.
2. Tinbergen, N., *The Study of Instinct*. London: Oxford University Press, 1951, pp. 145–150.
3. *Ibid.*, p. 150.
4. Zuckerman, S., *Functional Affinities of Man, Monkeys and Apes*. New York: Harcourt, Brace, 1933.
5. Jennings, H. S., *The Behavior of Lower Organisms*. New York: Columbia University Press, 1906.
6. Maier, N. R. F., and T. C. Schneirla, *Principles of Animal Psychology*. New York: McGraw-Hill, 1935.
7. Smith, S., "The Limits of Educability in Paramecium," *J. Comp. Neur. & Psychol.*, 1908, *18*, 499–510; and references below.
8. Day, L., and M. Bentley, "A Note on Learning in Paramecium," *J. Anim. Behav.*, 1911, *1*, 67–73.
9. Buytendijk, F. J., "Acquistion d'Habitudes par des Êtres Unicellulaires," *Arch. Néerl. Physiol.*, 1919, *3*, 455–468.
10. French, J. W., "Trial and Error Learning in Paramecium," *J. Exper. Psychol.*, 1940, *26*, 609–613.
11. Gelber, B., "Investigations of the Behavior of *Paramecium aurelia*: I. Modification of Behavior after Training with Reinforcement," *J. Comp. & Physiol. Psychol.*, 1952, *45*, 58–65.
12. Fleure, H., and C. Walton, "Notes on the Habits of Some Sea-Anemones," *Zoöl. Anz.*, 1907, *31*, 212–220.
13. Ven, C. D., "Sur la Formation d'Habitudes, chez les Asteries," *Arch. Néerl. Physiol.*, 1921, *6*, 163–178.
14. Jennings, H. S., "Behavior of the Starfish," *Univ. Calif. Publ. Zoöl.*, 1907, *4*, 53–185.
15. Maier, N. R. F., and T C. Schneirla, *op. cit.*
16. Yerkes, R. M., "The Intelligence of Earthworms," *J. Anim. Behav.*, 1912, *2*, 332–352.
17. Heck, L., "Über die Bildung einer Assoziation

beim Regenwurm auf Grund von Dressur-versuchen," *Lotos. Naturwiss. Zsch.*, 1920, *68*, 168–189.

18. Piéron, H., "La Loi de l'Oublie chez la Limnée," *Arch. Psychol.*, 1909, *9*, 39–50.

19. Thompson, E., "An Analysis of the Learning Process in the Snail, *Physa gyrina*, Say.," *Behav. Monog.*, 1917, *3*, No. 14.

20. Garth, T. R., and M. P. Mitchell, "The Learning Curve of a Land Snail," *J. Comp. Psychol.*, 1926, *6*, 103–114.

21. Schiller, P. H. "Delayed Detour Response in the Octopus," *J. Comp. & Physiol. Psychol.*, 1949, *42*, 220–225. See also, the interestingly illustrated report of avoidance-learning in an octopus which appears in J. Z. Young, *Doubt and Certainty in Science.* London: Oxford University Press, 1951, pp. 28–37.

22. See the summary by C. J. Warden, T. N. Jenkins, and L. H. Warner, *Comparative Psychology: Plants and Invertebrates.* New York: Ronald, 1940, pp. 795–796.

23. Yerkes, R. M., and A. Huggins, "Habit Formation in the Crawfish (Cambarus Affinis)," *Psych. Rev. Monog. Suppl.*, 1903, *1*, 565–577.

24. Lubbock, J., *On the Senses, Instincts, and Intelligence of Animals, with Special Reference to Insects.* New York: Appleton, 1883.

25. Schneirla, T. C., "Learning and Orientation in Ants," *Comp. Psychol. Monog.*, 6, 1929, p. 143; "Motivation and Efficiency in Ant Learning," *J. Comp. Psychol.*, 1933, *15*, 243–266; "The Process and Mechanism of Ant Learning: The Combination Problem and the Successive Presentation Problem," *J. Comp. Psychol.*, *17*, 303–328.

26. Evans, S., "An Experiment in Maze Learning with Ants," *J. Comp. Psychol.*, 1932, *14*, 183–189.

27. Szymanski, J. S., "Modification of the Innate Behavior of Cockroaches," *J. Anim. Behav.*, 1912, *2*, 81–90.

28. Turner, C. H., "An Experimental Investigation of an Apparent Reversal of the Light Responses of the Roach," *Biol. Bull.*, 1912, *23*, 371.

29. Hunter, W. S., "The Effect of Inactivity Produced by Cold upon Learning and Retention in the Cockroach, *Blatella germanica*," *J. Genet. Psychol.*, 1932, *41*, 253–266.

30. Turner, C. H., "Behavior of the Common Roach in an Open Maze," *Biol. Bull.*, 1913, *25*, 348–365.

31. Haralson, J. V., and M. E. Bitterman, "Lever-Depression Apparatus for the Study of Learning in Fish," *Amer. J. Psychol.*, 1950, *63*, 250–256.

32. Kellogg, W. N., and P. Spanovick, "Respiratory Changes During the Conditioning of Fish," *J. Comp. & Physiol. Psychol.*, 1953, *46*, 124–128.

33. Churchill, E., "The Learning of a Maze by Goldfish," *J. Anim. Behav.*, 1916, *46*, 124–128.

34. French, J. W., "The Effect of Temperature on the Retention of a Maze Habit in Fish," *Exper. Psychol.*, 1942, *31*, 79–87.

35. Zunini, G., *Animali e Uomo*, Milan: Catholic University, 1947.

36. Schiller, P. H., "Analysis of Detour Behavior. I. Learning of Roundabout Pathways in Fish," *J. Comp. & Physiol. Psychol.*, 1949, *42*, 463–475.

37. Schiller, P. H., "Delayed Response in the Minnow," *J. Comp. & Physiol. Psychol.*, 1948, *41*, 233–238.

38. Tinbergen, N., *op. cit.*, pp. 9–10.

39. Warden, C. J., T. N. Jenkins, and L. H. Warner, *Comparative Psychology: Vertebrates.* New York: Ronald, 1936.

40. Yerkes, R. M., "The Instincts, Habits, and Reactions of the Frog. I. Associative Processes in the Green Frog," *Psych. Rev. Monog. Suppl.*, 1903, No. 1, 579–597.

41. Burnett, T. C., "Some Observations on Decerebrate Frogs with Special Reference to the Formation of Associations," *Am. J. Psychol.*, 1912, *30*, 80–87.

42. Munn, N. L., "Learning Experiments with Larval Frogs," *J. Comp. Psychol.*, 1940, *29*, 97–108.

43. Seidman, E., "Relative Ability of the Newt and the Terrapin to Reverse a Direction Habit," *J. Comp. & Physiol. Psychol.*, 1949, *42*, 320–327.

44. See N. R. F. Maier, and T. C. Schneirla, *op. cit.*, pp. 223–228.

45. Yerkes, R. M., "The Formation of Habits in the Turtle," *Pop. Sci. Mo.*, 1901, *58*, 519–525.

46. Tinklepaugh, O. L., "Maze Learning of a Turtle," *J. Comp. Psychol.*, 1932, *13*, 201–206.

47. Kellogg, W. N., and W. B. Pomeroy, "Maze Learning in Water Snakes," *J. Comp. Psychol.*, 1936, *21*, 275–295.

48. Skinner, B. F., *Science and Human Behavior.* New York: Macmillan, 1953. See pigeon experiments listed in his index.

49. A summary of these experiments is given in D. Katz, *Animals and Men.* New York: Longmans, Green, 1937, pp. 89–93. Also issued as Penguin Book, 1953.

50. Hunter, W. S., "Some Labyrinth Habits of the Domestic Pigeon," *J. Anim. Behav.*, 1911, *1*, 278–304.

51. Warden, C. J., and B. F. Riess, "The Relative Difficulty of Mazes of Different Lengths for the Chick," *J. Psychol.*, 1941, *11*, 411–419.

52. Zerga, J. E., "An Introductory Investigation of Learning Behavior in Birds," *J. Comp. Psychol.*, 1940, *30*, 337–346.

53. Porter, J. P., "A Preliminary Study of the Psychology of the English Sparrow," *Amer. J. Psychol.*, 1904, *15*, 313–346; "Further Study of the English Sparrow and Other Birds," *Am. J. Psychol.*, 1900, *17*, 248–271; "Intelligence and Imitation in Birds, a Criterion of Instinct," *Am. J. Psychol.*, 1910, *21*, 1–71.

54. Rouse, J. E., "The Mental Life of the Domestic Pigeon," *Harvard Psych. Stud.*, 1906, *2*, 581–613.

55. Coburn, C. A., and R. M. Yerkes, "A Study of the Behavior of the Crow by the Multiple Choice Method," *J. Anim. Behav.*, 1915, *5*, 75–114.

56. von Haartman, L., "Eine Methode zum Verzleichenden Studium der optischen Wahrnehmungsfahigkeit höherer Tiere," *Behavior*, 1947, *1*, 35–55.

57. Sadovnikova, M. P., "A Study of the Behavior of Birds by the Multiple-Choice Method," *J. Comp. Psychol.*, 1923, *3*, 249–282.

58. Bingham, H. C., "Size and Form Perception in *Gallus Domesticus*," *J. Anim. Behav.*, 1913, *3*, 260–273; "A Definition of Form," *J. Anim. Behav.*, 1914, *4*, 136–141; "Visual Perception of the Chick," *Behav. Monog.*, 1922, *4*, No. 4.

59. Washburn, M. F., *The Animal Mind* (3d ed.). New York: Macmillan, 1926. (4th ed., 1936.)

60. Munn, N. L., "The Relative Efficacy of Form and Background in the Chick's Discrimination of Visual Patterns," *J. Comp. Psychol.*, 1931, *12*, 41–75.

61. Schjelderup-Ebbe, T., "Beiträge zur Sozialpsychologie des Haushuhns," *Zsch. f. Psychol.*, 1922, *88*, 225–252; "Social Behavior of Birds," in C. Murchison (ed.), *A Handbook of Social Psychology*, Worcester: Clark University Press, 1935.

62. Murchison, C., "The Experimental Measurement of a Social Hierarchy in *Gallus Domesticus*. I. The Direct Measurement of Social Reflex No. 1 and Social Reflex No. 2," *J. Gen. Psychol.*, 1935, *12*, 3–39.

63. Katz, D., and A. Toll, "Die Messung von Charakter und Begabungsunterscheiden bei Tieren. (Versuch mit Hühnern)," *Zsch. f. Psychol.*, 1923, *93*, 287–311.

64. Gardner, L. P., and H. W. Nissen, "Simple Discrimination Behavior of Young Chimpanzees: Comparisons with Human Aments and Domestic Animals," *J. Genet. Psychol.*, 1948, *72*, 145–164.

65. Husband, R. W., "A Comparison of Human Adults and White Rats in Maze Learning." *J. Comp. Psychol.*, 1929, *9*, 361–377; C. Lathan, and P. E. Fields, "A Report on the Test-Retest Performance of 38 College Students and 27 White Rats on the Identical 25–Choice Elevated Maze," *J. Genet. Psychol.*, 1936, *49*, 283–296.

66. Lashley, K. S., "Nervous Mechanisms and Learning," in C. Murchison (ed.), *Handbook of General Experimental Psychology.* Worcester: Clark University Press, 1934, p. 467.

67. See A. M. Shuey, "The Limits of Learning Ability in Kittens," *Genet. Psychol. Monog.*, 1931, *10*, 287–378; H. A. Fjeld, "The Limits of Learning Ability in Rhesus Monkeys," *Genet. Psychol. Monog.*, 1934, *15*, 369–535; B. F. Riess, "The Limits of Learning Ability in the White Rat and Guinea Pig," *Genet. Psychol. Monog.*, 1935, *17*, 163–234.

68. Köhler, W., *The Mentality of Apes.* New York: Harcourt, Brace, 1925.

69. *Op. cit.;* first quotation, p. 142; second, pp. 132–133.

70. See especially B. F. Skinner, *The Behavior of Organisms.* New York: Appleton-Century, 1938, pp. 339–340. Pictures of the rat's performance appeared in *Life*, and some are reproduced in Munn's *Psychology* (2d ed.), Boston: Houghton Mifflin, 1951, p. 189.

71. Instrumentation in a squirrel is illustrated in a film by L. F. Beck entitled "Squeak the Squirrel" and distributed by Psychological Cinema Register, State College, Penna.

72. Adams, D. K. "Experimental Studies of

Adaptive Behavior in Cats," *Comp. Psychol. Monog.*, 1929, *6*, No. 1.

73. Warden, C. J., A. M. Koch, and H. A. Fjeld, "Instrumentation in Cebus and Rhesus Monkeys," *J. Genet. Psychol.*, 1940, *56*, 297–310; and H. F. Harlow, "Primate Learning," in C. P. Stone (ed.), *Comparative Psychology* (3d ed.), New York: Prentice-Hall, 1951, pp. 216–222.

74. From correspondence reported by Harlow, reference No. 73 above, p. 218.

75. Bingham, H. C., "Chimpanzee Translocation by Means of Boxes," *Comp. Psychol. Monog.*, 1929, *5*, No. 3.

76. Birch, H. G., "The Relation of Previous Experience to Insightful Problem-solving," *J. Comp. Psychol.*, 1945, *38*, 367–383.

77. Yerkes, R. M., *Chimpanzees*. New Haven: Yale University Press, 1943, pp. 137–138.

78. Köhler, W., *op. cit.*, pp. 179–191.

79. Guillaume, P., and I. Meyerson, "Recherches sur l'usage de l'instrument chez les signes," *J. de Psychol.*, 1930, *27*, 177–236.

80. See the film by T. A. Jackson, entitled "The Use of Tools by the Chimpanzee in Problem Solving," New York: Films Inc., 1934; also the article "Use of the Stick as a Tool by Young Chimpanzees," *J. Comp. Psychol.*, 1942, *34*, 223–235.

81. Bingham, H. C., "Selective Transportation by Chimpanzees," *Comp. Psychol. Monog.*, 1920, *5*, No. 4.

82. Harlow, H. F., and P. H. Settlage, "Comparative Behavior of Primates. VII — Capacity of Monkeys to Solve Patterned String Tests," *J. Comp. Psychol.*, 1934, *18*, 423–435.

83. Finch, G., "The Solution of Patterned String Problems by Chimpanzees," *J. Comp. Psychol.*, 1941, *32*, 93–90.

84. Riesen, A. H., B. Greenberg, A. S. Granston, and R. L. Fantz, "Solutions of Patterned String Problems by Young Gorillas," *J. Comp. & Physiol. Psychol.*, 1953, *46*, 19–22.

85. See the review by M. P. Crawford, "The Social Psychology of the Vertebrates," *Psych. Bull.*, 1939, *36*, 407–446.

86. Warden, C. J., and T. A. Jackson. "Imitative Behavior in the Rhesus Monkey," *J. Genet. Psychol.*, 1935, *46*, 103–125.

87. Warden, C. J., H. A. Fjeld, and A. M. Koch, "Imitative Behavior in Cebus and Rhesus Monkeys," *J. Genet. Psychol.*, 1940, *56*, 311–322.

88. Crawford, M. P., and K. W. Spence, "Observational Learning of Discrimination Problems by Chimpanzees," *J. Comp. Psychol.* 1939, *27*, 133–147.

89. Hayes, K. J., and C. Hayes, "Imitation in a Home-Raised Chimpanzee," *J. Comp. & Physiol. Psychol.*, 1952, *45*, 450–459.

90. For a discussion of learning to imitate in rats, see N. L. Munn, *Handbook of Psychological Research on the Rat*. Boston: Houghton Mifflin, 1950, pp. 457–468.

91. Daniel, W. J., "Cooperative Problem Solving in Rats," *J. Comp. Psychol.*, 1942, *34*, 361–368; "Higher-order Cooperative Problem Solving in Rats," *J. Comp. Psychol.*, 1943, *35*, 297–305.

92. Crawford, M. P., "The Cooperative Solving of Problems by Young Chimpanzees," *Comp. Psychol. Monog.*, 1937, *14*, No. 2.

93. Warden, C. J., and W. Galt, "A Study of Cooperation, Dominance, Grooming and Other Social Factors in Monkeys, *J. Genet. Psychol.*, 1943, *63*, 213–233.

94. Nissen, H. W., and M. P. Crawford, "A Preliminary Study of Food-Sharing Behavior in Young Chimpanzees," *J. Comp. Psychol.*, 1936, *22*, 383–419.

95. Crawford, M. P., citation 92, pp. 67–68.

96. Crawford, M. P., "Cooperative Solution by Chimpanzees of a Problem Requiring Serial Responses to Color Cues," *J. Soc. Psychol.*, 1941, *13*, 259–280.

97. Burtt, H. E., "A Study of the Behavior of the White Rat by the Multiple-Choice Method," *J. Anim. Behav.*, 1916, *6*, 222–246.

98. Yerkes, R. M., and C. A. Coburn, "A Study of the Behavior of the Pig (*Sus Scrofa*) by the Multiple-Choice Method," *J. Anim. Behav.*, 1915, *5*, 185–255.

99. Yerkes, R. M., "The Mental Life of Monkeys and Apes," *Behav. Monog.*, 1916, *3*, No. 1.

100. Yerkes, R. M., "Modes of Behavioral Adaptation in Chimpanzee to Multiple Choice Problems," *Comp. Psychol. Monog.*, 1934, *10*, No. 1.

101. Fields, P. E., "Studies in Concept Formation. I. Development of the Concept of Triangularity by the Rat," *Comp. Psychol. Monog.*, 1932, *9*, No. 2.

102. Fields, P. E., "Studies in Concept Formation. IV. A Comparison of White Rats and Raccoons with Respect to their Visual Discrimination of Certain Geometrical Fig-

ures," *J. Comp. Psychol.*, 1936, *21*, 341–355.

103. Smith, K. V., "Visual Discrimination in the Cat. II. A Further Study of the Capacity of the Cat for Visual Figure Discrimination," *J. Genet. Psychol.*, 1934, *46*, 336–357.

104. Neet, C. C., "Visual Pattern Discrimination in the Macacus Rhesus Monkey," *J. Genet. Psychol.*, 1933, *43*, 163–196.

105. Andrew, G., and H. F. Harlow, "Performance of Macaque Monkeys on a Test of the Concept of Generalized Triangularity," *Comp. Psychol. Monog.*, 1948, *19*, No. 3.

106. In Gellermann's experiment with chimpanzees his two subjects failed to react to an inverted triangle as they had to the upright, but he did not, as in the experiments cited, continue training with varied triangles. See L. W. Gellermann, "Form Discrimination in Chimpanzees and Two-Year-Old Children," *J. Genet. Psychol.*, 1933, *42*, 1–50.

107. Kohts, N., *Infant Ape and Human Child* (English Summary). Moscow: Darwinian Museum, 1935. The original studies were published in 1921 and 1923.

108. Weinstein, B., "The Evolution of Intelligent Behavior in Rhesus Monkeys," *Genet. Psychol. Monog.*, 1945, *31*, 3–48.

109. Harlow, H. F., "Primate Learning," in C. P. Stone (ed.), *Comparative Psychology* (3d ed.). New York: Prentice-Hall, 1951.

110. Nissen, H. W., and T. L. McCulloch, Equated and Non-Equated Stimulus Situations in Discrimination Learning by Chimpanzees. III. Prepotency of Response to Oddity through Training," *J. Comp. Psychol.*, 1937, *23*, 377–381.

111. Harlow, H. F., *op. cit.*, 194–196.

112. Nissen, H. W., "Analysis of Complex Conditional Reaction in Chimpanzees," *J. Comp. & Physiol. Psychol.*, 1951, *44*, 9–16. See this reference for earlier similar studies by Nissen and J. S. and R. Blum.

113. Harlow, H. F., *op. cit.*, pp. 200–208.

114. Nissen, H. W., A. H. Riesen, and V. Nowlis, "Delayed Response and Discrimination Learning by Chimpanzees," *J. Comp. Psychol.*, 1938, *26*, 361–386.

115. Hunter, W. S., "The Delayed Reaction in Animals and Children," *Behav. Monog.*, 1913, *2*, No. 1.

116. Yerkes, R. M., "The Mind of a Gorilla," *Genet. Psychol. Monog.*, 1927, *2*, 1–193.

117. See Munn's *Handbook*, pp. 272–278.

118. McCord, F., "The Delayed Reaction and Memory in Rats," *J. Comp. Psychol.*, 1939, *27*, 1–37, 175–210.

119. Walton, A. C., "The Influence of Diverting Stimuli During Delayed Reaction in Dogs," *J. Anim. Behav.*, 1915, *5*, 259–291.

120. Cowan, E. A., "An Experiment Testing the Ability of the Cat to Make Delayed Response to a Varying Stimulus," *J. Comp. Psychol.*, 1923, *3*, 1–9.

121. Adams, D. K., "Experimental Studies of Adaptive Behavior in Cats," *Comp. Psychol. Monog.*, 1929, *6*, No. 1.

122. Tinklepaugh, O. L., "An Experimental Study of Representative Factors in Monkeys," *J. Comp. Psychol.*, 1928, *8*, 197–236. Delays of up to 20 hours are reported in this study. Shorter delays, with different methods, are reported by H. F. Harlow, H. Uehling, and A. H. Maslow, "Comparative Behavior of Primates. I. Delayed Reaction Tests on Primates from the Lemur to the Orang-Utan," *J. Comp. Psychol.*, 1932, *13*, 313–344; and by F. J. Buytendijk, "Considérations de Psychologie Comparée à propos d'Expériences Faites avec le Singe (*Cercopithecus*)," *Arch. Néerl. de Physiol.*, 1921, *5*, 42–48.

123. Köhler, W., *op. cit.;* R. M. Yerkes and D. N. Yerkes, "Concerning Memory in the Chimpanzee," *J. Comp. Psychol.*, 1928, *8*, 237–271; Harlow, Uehling, and Maslow, *op. cit.;* and R. M. Yerkes, "The Mind of a Gorilla," *Genet. Psychol. Monog.*, 1927, *2*, 1–193.

124. Hunter, W. S., "The Delayed Reaction in a Child," *Psych. Rev.*, 1917, *24*, 75–87.

125. Tinklepaugh, O. L., *op. cit.*

126. Harlow, H. F., "Comparative Behavior of Primates. III. Complicated Delayed Reaction Tests on Primates," *J. Comp. Psychol.*, 1932, *14*, 241–252.

127. Tinklepaugh, O. L., "Multiple Delayed Reaction with Chimpanzees and Monkeys," *J. Comp. Psychol.*, 1932, *13*, 207–243.

128. Weinstein, B., "Delayed Matching from Sample in Monkeys." A film distributed by the University of Wisconsin. See also Weinstein's "Discriminative Delayed Matching from Sample," in R. H. Seashore (ed.), *Fields of Psychology*. New York: Holt, 1942.

129. Finch, G., "Delayed Matching-from-Sample

and Non-Spatial Delayed Response in Chimpanzees," *J. Comp. Psychol.*, 1942, *34*, 315–319.

130. Reported by H. F. Harlow, "Primate Learning," in C. P. Stone (ed.), *Comparative Psychology* (3d ed.). New York: Prentice-Hall, 1951, pp. 226–227.

131. Simpson, M. M., and H. F. Harlow, "Solution by Rhesus Monkeys of a Non-Spatial Delayed Response to the Color or Form Attribute of a Single Stimulus (Weigl Principle Delayed Reaction)," *J. Comp. Psychol.*, 1944, *37*, 211–220.

132. See Munn's *Handbook*, pp. 279–282, for a discussion of Maier's tests and a bibliography of his numerous studies with this test.

133. Hunter, W. S., "The Behavior of Raccoons in a Double Alternation Temporal Maze," *J. Genet. Psychol.*, 1928, *35*, 374–388.

134. Hunter, W. S., "The Temporal Maze and Kinaesthetic Sensory Processes in the Rat," *Psychobiol.*, 1920, *2*, 1–18; "Sensory Control of the Maze Habit in the Rat," *J. Genet. Psychol.*, 1929, *36*, 505–537.

135. Hunter, W. S., and J. W. Nagge, "The White Rat and the Double Alternation Temporal Maze," *J. Genet. Psychol.*, 1931, *39*, 303–319.

136. Hunter, W. S., and B. E. Hall, "Double Alternation Behavior of the White Rat in a Spatial Maze," *J. Comp. Psychol.*, 1941, *32*, 253–266.

137. Hunter, W. S., "The Behavior of Raccoons in a Double Alternation Temporal Maze," *J. Genet. Psychol.*, 1928, *35*, 374–388.

138. Karn, H. W., "The Behavior of Cats on the Double Alternation Problem in the Temporal Maze," *J. Comp. Psychol.*, 1938, *26*, 201–208.

139. Gellermann, L. W., "The Double Alternation Problem. I. The Behavior of Monkeys on a Double Alternation Temporal Maze," *J. Genet. Psychol.*, 1931, *39*, 50–72; "III. The Behavior of Monkeys on a Double Alternation Box-Apparatus," *J. Genet. Psychol.*, 1931, *39*, 359–392.

140. Gardner, L. P., and H. W. Nissen, *op. cit.*, p. 161.

SUGGESTIONS FOR FURTHER READING

Guillaume, P., *La Psychologie Animale*. Paris: Colin, 1940, Chapter V.

Harlow, H. F., "Primate Learning," Chapter 7 in C. P. Stone (ed.), *Comparative Psychology* (3d ed.). New York: Prentice-Hall, 1951.

Hobhouse, L. T., *Mind in Evolution* (3d ed.). New York: Macmillan, 1926.

Heron, W. T., "Learning," Chapter 6 in C. P. Stone (ed.), *Comparative Psychology* (3d ed.). New York: Prentice-Hall, 1951.

Katz, D., *Animals and Men*. New York: Longmans, 1937. Also issued in Penguin Books, 1953.

Köhler, W., *The Mentality of Apes*. New York: Harcourt, Brace, 1925.

Moore, J. V., "Human and Animal Intelligence," in H. S. Jennings, *et al.*, *Scientific Aspects of the Race Problem*. New York: Longmans, 1941.

Maier, N. R. F., and T. C. Schneirla, *Principles of Animal Psychology*. New York: McGraw-Hill, 1935, Chapters I–XI and XX.

Munn, N. L., *Handbook of Psychological Research on the Rat*. Boston: Houghton Mifflin, 1950, Chapter 7.

Nissen, H. W., "Phylogenetic Comparison," Chapter 11 in S. S. Stevens (ed.), *Handbook of Experimental Psychology*. New York: Wiley, 1951.

Russell, E. S., *The Behavior of Animals* (2d ed.). London: Arnold, 1938.

Warden, C. J., T. N. Jenkins, and L. H. Warner, *Introduction to Comparative Psychology*. New York: Ronald, 1934. Sections dealing with modifiable behavior at the ends of Chapters VIII–XX. The following reference is more detailed.

Warden, C. J., T. N. Jenkins, and L. H. Warner, *Comparative Psychology*. New York: Ronald. Vol. 1, 1935; Vol. 3, 1936; Vol. 2, 1940.

Washburn, M. F., *The Animal Mind* (4th ed.). New York: Macmillan, 1936.

Yerkes, R. M., *Chimpanzees*. New Haven: Yale University Press, 1943.

6

Prenatal Behavior

In discussing the development of prenatal behavior we leave the field of phylogeny as such and begin our review of ontogenetic psychology. As was said earlier, the ontogenetic psychologist studies behavioral development in individuals of any phylogenetic level in which he may be interested. Numerous animals, at various phylogenetic levels, have been studied from this standpoint. Among the mammals thus studied are rats, guinea pigs, cats, sheep, and human beings. In our discussion, however, chief attention is centered upon individual human development. We consider developmental studies with infrahuman forms only when these throw light upon unsolved problems of human development or aid us in evaluating various controversial generalizations about the way in which behavior develops.

Discussions of human behavioral development logically begin with conception; hence the present chapter traces the development of behavior and correlated structures from the time of conception until birth. Ensuing chapters deal with the development of certain significant behavioral processes from the time of birth until maturity, as well as certain changes with old age.

Some of the questions considered in this chapter are: What is the role of inheritance in controlling prenatal development? What is the role of the prenatal environment? What

fundamental structures and processes precede the appearance of behavior? At what age does behavior first appear? How may such behavior be characterized? At what ages do other responses occur? What generalizations apply to the prenatal development of behavior? Is the unborn human being sensitive to aspects of its environment? Is it susceptible to conditioning; is it able to learn? What behavioral repertoire is characteristic of the newborn human child?

We begin by reviewing the chief facts and principles of embryology and by indicating the role played by inherent and environmental factors in the cellular growth and differentiation associated with the appearance of those structures which underlie behavior. We shall find that congenital behavior, that which exists at or from the time of birth, and upon which many later acquisitions are based, has a developmental history which begins at around two months after conception. Gradually the behavioral repertoire unfolds and responses already present develop increasing adaptiveness, as if to prepare the individual for his independent postnatal existence. Maturation is of especial importance at this early stage of life. It represents the interrelated influence of both heredity and environment, but with heredity largely responsible for the repertoire and its sequential development.

Embryology and Genetics

Every mammal begins its individual existence when a mature ovum is penetrated and fertilized by a spermatozoon. Fertilization usually occurs while the ovum is on its way from the ovary to the uterus. Unfertilized ova reach the uterus and are absorbed or expelled from it at the time of menstruation. Normally the fertilized ovum reaches the uterus and continues its development there.

Growth during the prenatal period

After fertilization has occurred, the ovum undergoes a progressive change. The sequence of development is as follows: The nuclei of the ovum and the sperm unite; the chromosomes are duplicated and two cells are formed; these cells divide to form a total of four; these to form a total of eight; and so on until many cells, each having the same chromosome constitution as the fertilized ovum, are packed together in a ball-like mass. As multiplication continues, some cells are forced to the top of the mass and it becomes a hollow sphere such as appears in Figure 62. The upper mass of cells gives rise to the embryonic organism. Some cells grow more rapidly than others and there is an infolding (invagination) and outfolding (evagination) which produces three layers. The outer layer, known as the *ectoderm*, is the primary origin of such later structures as the sense organs and nervous system. The *mesoderm*, or intermediate layer, is the principal point of

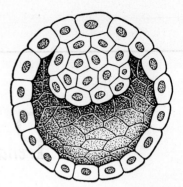

Figure 62.   A Typical Mammalian Blastula

It is from the upper mass of cells that the organism develops.

origin of the skeletal, muscular, and circulatory systems. The *entoderm*, or inner layer of embryonic cells, gives rise to several vital organs including some of the glands of internal secretion. Many structures are derived partly from one layer and partly from another. These layers are illustrated in Figure 63.

Until the second week after fertilization, the human ovum is unattached. During this period the cell layers have developed and undergone considerable differentiation. In addition to what is to become the embryo, these cell layers give rise to the fetal membranes. During the second week of life the new organism becomes attached to the uterus. From this time until about the end of the second month it is known as an *embryo*. The organism is referred to as a *fetus* from the be-

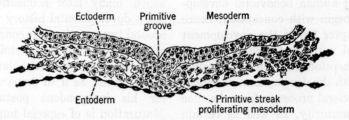

Figure 63.   Transverse Section Through an Extremely Early Human Embryo

This cross-section shows the primitive groove, where the spinal cord will develop, as well as the three cell layers mentioned in the text. (After Streeter. From L. B. Arey, *Developmental Anatomy*, 5th ed., Philadelphia: Saunders, 1946, p. 73.)

ginning of the third month until birth. As embryo and fetus, it obtains its food from the mother. Respiration and excretion of waste products are performed likewise. There is, however, no actual connection of the maternal and fetal circulations. The maternal blood is separated from the fetal blood by membranes. Through these membranes, however, food and oxygen pass from the mother to the fetal circulatory system. Carbon dioxide and other waste products pass in the opposite direction and are eliminated by the maternal circulatory system. Certain details of this relation between fetal and maternal organisms are illustrated in Figure 64.

The chief bases of structural growth and differentiation

We have already considered the inherent and environmental factors which influence prenatal development (pp.13–45). Here the chief points of the previous discussion are summarized and related more specifically to the problem of human prenatal development.

There is considerable structural differentiation of the ovum prior to fertilization. This is apparently produced by the maternal genes alone. Upon entry of the sperm nucleus, the full complement of chromosomes and genes is present in the ovum. These appear to be completely duplicated in every body cell derived from the original fertilized ovum. The two nuclei merge and the ovum divides to form two cells, these divide to form four cells, and so on, as indicated previously. During the first few divisions of the ovum there is believed to be duplication of its cytoplasmic differentiation in each cell. In later divisions, however, the cytoplasmic constitution of the cells varies. Thus, the same genes now are subject to different *intracellular* conditions. We have suggested how these cytoplasmic variations lead to organisms with different structures. As soon as two or more cells are present, the *intercellular* condition arises. It has been pointed out in this connection that certain regions of the organism grow more rapidly than others and exert a mechanical or

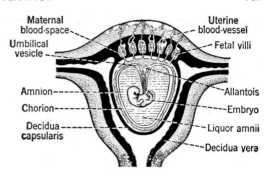

Figure 64. Diagram Showing the Relationship Between the Uterus, the Membranes, and the Embryo During Early Pregnancy

The embryo is suspended in the amnionic sac, which is filled with a liquid. This, the amnionic fluid, which has a specific gravity somewhat greater than water, supports the embryo and prevents adhesions. It also serves to prevent the embryo from receiving mechanical jars. The amnion is surrounded by another sac, the chorion, with its villi. The allantois, which in lower mammals serves nutritive, respiratory, and excretory functions, is rudimentary in man. The umbilical vesicle connects the embryo to the mother through the placenta, the part of the chorion attached to the uterus by means of the fetal villi. The decidua vera and decidua capsularis are linings of the uterus, but differing in position. At birth the membranes surrounding the fetus rupture. Shortly after the child is born, the membranes are torn away from the uterus and expelled. These constitute the afterbirth. (From L. Carmichael, "The Origin and Prenatal Growth of Behavior," in C. Murchison, ed., *A Handbook of Child Psychology*, Clark University Press, 1933, p. 50.)

electrochemical dominance over neighboring cells. The development of cell layers is an example of differentiation produced largely by mechanical pressure of cell on cell. Growth of the nervous system involves both mechanical and electrochemical factors. In the human embryo the most rapidly differentiating cells are those along the axis from head to tail. The cells in the head end of this axis show the greatest activity. There is, as Child [1] pointed out, a physiological gradient of such a nature that the head end asserts its greatest dominance over development of immediately adjacent cells, a slightly weaker dominance over cells a little farther away, and so forth. Likewise, the part of the body axis which becomes the spinal cord exerts a decreasing dominance over cells farther and farther toward the periphery of the body.

Another important intercellular condition of development is the glandular one. The endocrine glands (thyroid, thymus, parathyroid, pituitary, adrenal, islands of Langerhans of the pancreas, pineal, and gonads) are developed early in prenatal life under the influence of the genes, the cytoplasm, and the interaction of cells. As soon as the glands make their appearance and begin to pour out their hormones, the nature and the rate of development of certain regions of the organism are markedly affected.

The *external* environment of the prenatal organism is also significant for normal growth. Rate of cleavage in the ovum is a function of the temperature of the surrounding medium. In the case of the human individual this temperature, being that of the mother, is normally maintained at approximate constancy. Chemical changes immediately external to the organism may affect growth in significant ways. The amnionic fluid is normally maintained at approximate constancy. Chemical changes immediately external to the organism may affect growth in significant ways. The amnionic fluid is normally of constant chemical constitution and specific gravity; however, any significant change in its characteristics might effect marked alterations of the organism. That maternal hormones influence the development of offspring is now well known. Toxic conditions of the mother may also influence the development of the individual. Nutritional factors are likewise important. These influences, glandular, toxic, and nutritional, are, as already indicated, brought to the embryo through the placenta. The cell membranes of the placenta present a barrier which is, however, highly selective in regard to the substances that may pass from the maternal to the fetal blood stream, and vice versa. Abnormal position of the individual *in utero* is another external environmental condition which may affect development. Unusual constriction of one part of the organism by another part (such as cutting off of circulation in an organ around which the umbilical cord has twisted) leads to marked abnormality of development. Insufficient oxygen also produces anomalies, as recent experiments have shown.[2] As soon as the fetus becomes active, there are further changes in the external conditions of development. The fetus may stimulate itself in many ways.

The genes

Before discussing the development of the structures primarily involved in the appearance of behavior, it will be of interest to observe what is believed to be the role of the genes in the cellular differentiation which produces the characteristic structures of the developing organism. We have already pointed out that appropriate functioning of genes depends upon the presence of a normal intracellular, intercellular, and external environment. How the interaction of the genes and the environmental conditions is achieved is not definitely known. It is generally believed, however, that the genes are enzymes and that their function, like that of other catalysts, is to accelerate chemical processes in and around the cell without themselves undergoing differentiation. Pointing out that biologists are divided in their opinions concerning the relative significance of the genes and the cytoplasm, Davenport [3] says:

This controversy seems unnecessary. The genes can do nothing without the cytoplasmic contents to activate. The cytoplasmic chemical processes would be relatively inert without activation by the enzymes. The division of opinion here is as futile as that concerning the relative importance of heredity and of environment. Of course, the organism is absolutely dependent on the environment for its survival; also what the environment does depends upon the nature of the stuff upon which it acts.

It appears that the full complement of the enzymes is brought into the egg at the moment of fertilization. The enzymes are distributed to all the cells of the developing body by doubling of the chromosomes and their genes at every cell division.

Very early ... the cells of the developing embryo begin to undergo *differentiation*. How can the same full equipment of genes in each cell function so differently? To this question Weismann gave his answer: The different cells do not contain the same active genes. There must be a regularly proceeding segregation of the genes in ever smaller groups until finally there remains in each cell only one kind of gene, namely, that which controls or determines the character of that cell. It is highly improbable, Weismann says, that all genes are carried into all stages of ontogenesis.

On the other hand, a careful comparison of the cells of different tissues of the adult body leads to the conclusion that, in general, these cells have the same chromosomes as the fertilized egg from which they were all derived. However, similarity of chromosomes does not imply identity of their constituent genes; for genes may change without altering the form of the chromosomes.

It is urged that widespread capacity of regeneration of lost parts in various vertebrate species ... proves that somatic cells must contain a full equipment of genes. Indeed, a piece of the leaf of certain plants is able to function like an egg. But this is not adequate proof that all somatic cells contain the same genes, for in all parts of the body there are two kinds of cells, which have long been recognized: first, the relatively unspecialized cells, which probably have a more or less complete set of genes, and which are inactive until called forth by injury; secondly, the active cells, which are specialized (or differentiated). It is probable that such specialized cells cannot regenerate the whole organism or any part of it.

If, then, somatic cells in general possess the same chromosomal complex, what is probably the nature of the change in the chromosomes that is responsible for differentiation?

This problem appears less difficult if we consider again how the enzymes work. The work that the enzymes do depends upon the nature of the substrate. Now, under the influence of the enzymes of the genes that substrate is constantly changing. Hence the same genes can do the same work in different part of the body or even in the same part of the body at different times.

We must recall that the action of any particular enzyme is highly specific. Thus, *zymase* (an enzyme from yeast) ferments d-glucose, and is quite inactive with l-glucose. The two glucoses have the same structure except for a different position in the molecule of certain atom-groups. Consequently, for long periods during development a particular enzyme may have no work to do, because the nature of the substrate is such that that particular enzyme has before it no chemical reaction which it is able to accelerate.

To make this clearer, we may consider a series of changes in the cell induced by enzymes splitting up. We may assume that at a certain stage enzyme Ea will cause the hydrolysis of the substrate molecule Sa; and this molecule splits up, into Sb and Sc. Enzyme Ea cannot split (hydrolize) molecules Sb and Sc, but some other enzymes, Eb and Ec, are able to do so and thus produce new cell products. So in successive generations.

If, following cell division, the cytoplasm of two daughter cells is unlike (as often occurs), then although the genes be the same in both daughter cells, the reactions occurring in the cells under the influence of these enzymes will be quite different — and cell differentiation will show itself. Such a differentiation once started will tend to become exaggerated in later cell generations, and in time the various parts of the developing organism will become very different. Thus, each moment of development sets the stage for the next phase, and the time and place of action of the genes are automatically determined. . . .

Structural Bases of Behavioral Growth

Behavior does not appear until certain structural mechanisms have emerged within the growing organism. Receptors and effectors must develop and certain elements of the neural architecture must be laid down and connect them before the previously inert organism is capable of responding to stimulation. The nervous system makes its appearance, in elementary form, before there are any receptor and effector mechanisms to connect. And it continues its growth, making increasingly intricate interconnections, long after the receptors and effectors are functional. In human beings this growth occurs over a period of somewhere between fifteen and twenty years.

Growth of nervous processes

The appearance of the nervous system is

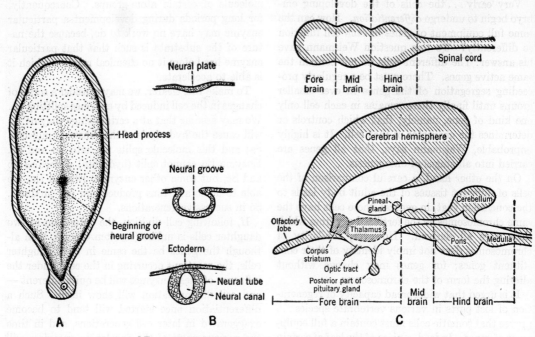

Figure 65.   **Stages in the Early Growth of Neural Mechanisms**

A. A nineteen-day human embryo (after Ingalls).   *B.* Development of the neural tube
C. Formation of the three brain vesicles and their derivatives (after Lickley).

foreshadowed by the primitive groove, which becomes the axis of the developing nervous system.   A neural groove is quite evident in the nineteen-day human fetus, as seen in Figure 65 *A.*   What is at first a neural groove becomes a hollow tube.   (Figure 65 *B.*)   The forward end of this tube (the upper end in primates) then forms three vesicles (Figure 65 *C*) which eventually produce the various brain structures.   The remainder of the tube becomes the spinal cord.

An early stage in the development of the reflex-arc system is illustrated in Figure 66. From primitive motor cells within the developing cord, fibers grow out to the periphery of the body, finding their ultimate endings in the muscles and glands.   Primitive sensory cells, with their origin on the outside of the neural tube, send fibers outward to the receptors and inward to the growing spinal cord. Certain cells within the tube give rise to fibers which grow toward the brain, and cells within

the brain send fibers downward and in various other directions to interconnect with ascending tracts and association fibers.   Cells outside of the neural groove also give rise to the

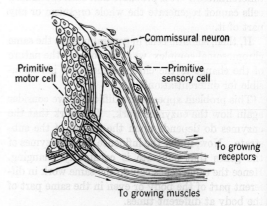

Figure 66.   **Diagram to Illustrate Early Growth of the Reflex-Arc System**

Arrows show the direction followed by growing nerve fibers.   Fibers connect both sides of the spinal cord, but only the right side is shown.   (After Arey.)

sympathetic nervous system which, together with certain fibers from the brain stem, connects with the visceral and other vital organs.

Mechanics of neural growth

How is this intricate architecture of the nervous system laid down? How do the billions of embryonic nerve fibers reach their appropriate destinations in muscles, glands, receptors, and central nervous nuclei and projections? They do this with precise developmental timing, in a manner characteristic of the species, and independent of activity. Indeed, until they find their destinations, no activity of the parts of the organism to which they go can normally occur.* Embryologists, experimenting with amphibians and other animals, are seeking the answer to this apparent mystery. Their experiments have shown that damaged nerve fibers regenerate and grow to their proper locations, and that muscles and receptors deprived of their neural connections, and even transplanted to new locations, attract to themselves those fibers which enable them to carry out the functions for which they are normally fitted. All of this suggests that something within the developing organism must guide growing nerve fibers in such a way as to guarantee that organs will get the specialized central connections which they need in order to function. Several theories have been presented in an attempt to account for this finding by nerve fibers of their proper destinations. These theories have been discussed by Sperry,[4] who believes that the guidance involved is to a large extent biochemical. According to him, there is a chemical affinity between particular nerve fibers and particular terminal structures such that, when a fiber having this sort of affinity approaches the structure which "needs" it, the proper connection occurs. With reference to connections between optic fibers and the visual projection area of the cortex, Sperry[5] says:

* Some muscles (see p. 172) respond to direct stimulation if this is sufficiently intense.

As the optic fibers invade the optic lobes, they have opportunity to make many connections among the dense population of nerve cell bodies, dendrites, axons, blood capillaries, glial cells, and other optic fibers that have preceded them into the area. Of these many contacts only a few result in the formation of synaptic endings. The fiber tips grow around and past glial cells, capillaries, axons and the majority of dendrites and nerve cell bodies they happen to encounter. But, when they reach the appropriate part of the optic lobe, they meet neurons whose physiochemical nature is right for the formation of synaptic end feet. It is likely that a single optic axon terminates on a large number of secondary neurons whose dendrites may spread over a considerable portion of the optic tectum but whose cell bodies occupy only a small area. The cells in the center of such an area would receive the greatest number of terminals from that particular axon. . . .

For us the mechanics of neural growth is only a background problem. The fact is that fibers *do* find their proper terminals in receptors and effectors and in the nuclei and other specialized loci of the central nervous system.

Growth of the brain

The external characteristics of the brain soon undergo marked change. The foremost vesicle (forebrain), which is at first relatively inconspicuous, becomes the predominant brain structure, as illustrated in Figure 67. From it develop the cerebral hemispheres, the thalamus and the hypothalamus. The other vesicles give rise to various structures of the brain stem, including the cerebellum. These changes are associated with the multiplication and differentiation of nerve cells and their fibers.

During the fetal period there is a rapid increase in the size of the cerebrum, which remains smooth until between the sixth and seventh months. It then begins to show invaginations, as pictured in Figure 68. These become increasingly complex until, at birth, they have a marked similarity to those of the adult cerebrum. During this period, as il-

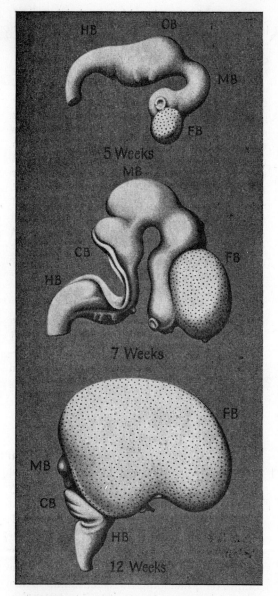

Figure 67. Growth of the Brain During the Early Weeks of Prenatal Life

FB, forebrain; *MB*, midbrain; *HB*, hindbrain; *CB*, cerebellum. The stippled region is the developing cerebrum. (From Munn's *Psychology*, after an illustration in the *Scientific American*.)

lustrated, the cerebellum also undergoes rapid growth.

The entire brain is at birth only one-fourth of its eventual size, yet it has all the nerve cells

of the adult brain. Its growth during early postnatal life comes from an increase in the size and in the interconnections of the original cells. During this early growth, some parts of the cerebrum have become specialized for the handling of impulses originating in receptors. Other regions have developed motor functions, so that they can send impulses, conveyed to them from the sensory areas of the brain, to muscles and glands. Still other parts of the cerebrum have developed into an intricate network of association fibers whose primary function is integration of incoming and outgoing impulses. The cerebellum is of especial significance in relation to development of motor coordinations.

The functioning of the heart, which begins at approximately three weeks after insemination, does not depend upon nervous control. When Hooker [6] removed the entire nervous system of frog embryos before fibers could reach the heart, this organ began to function at the same time as in normal frogs. Muscles will sometimes respond when stimulated electrically or when cut, but their normal functioning in response to tactual stimuli depends upon sensorimotor nervous connections. In the human organism there is no sign of behavior (other than the heartbeat and the responses of muscles to direct excitation) until the peripheral nervous connections are made. These connections are laid down gradually as the embryo develops, and as suggested above, they are outgrowths from the spinal cord and brain.

What neural developments immediately precede the appearance of responses to tactual stimuli by human embryos? This question has stimulated a large amount of research on embryos of about eight weeks menstrual age, the approximate age at which behavior can first be elicited.* Hogg [8] found an un-

---

* Since the exact age of a human embryo (i.e., the time since fertilization) is seldom known, the ages given are always approximations based upon various criteria. Carmichael [7] (pp. 114–119) presents a summary of the methods of calculating the age and size of human embryos. Menstrual age refers to the age since the preceding menstruation, which is usually not

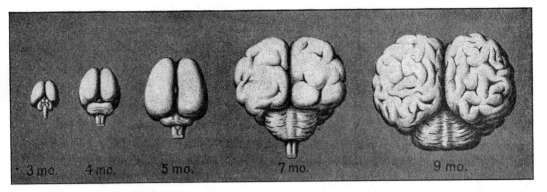

Figure 68. Growth of the Human Brain During Fetal Life

The brain is viewed from above and behind. Observe the increase in size and the presence of invaginations by the seventh month. (After Retzius and Broman, from Gilbert's *Biography of the Unborn*, Baltimore: Williams and Wilkins, 1939.)

developed state of sensory and association neurons in the dorsal funiculus of an eight-weeks embryo which failed to respond to stimulation. Windle and Fitzgerald [9] observed spinal reflex arcs in an embryo of eight weeks. The most extensive information, however, has come from a series of studies by Humphrey [10] on the embryos investigated at the University of Pittsburgh. As we shall report in more detail later, the earliest observed responses have occurred at what is calculated to be about $8\frac{1}{2}$ weeks menstrual age, and they have been responses involving contralateral neck and upper trunk reflexes. The pathway whose growth apparently makes this response possible is illustrated in Figure 69. Stimulation of the head or neck sends impulses over the fifth cranial nerve and from the pons down into the cervical cord on the same side, thence across the cord to the contralateral ventral side, where connections are made with motor fibers running to the dorsal longitudinal muscles of the left side.

It has often been observed that there is a lag in appearance of neurally mediated responses even after the gross anatomical connections are evident. This may, as Coghill [11]

very accurately determined. Roughly speaking, embryos of $8\frac{1}{2}$ weeks menstrual age would be about 8 weeks from insemination.

has suggested, be due to the fact that nerve fibers reach their destinations before the receptors and effectors are themselves ready to function. It was once thought that the nerve fibers had to be myelinated (or encased with a fatty sheath) before impulses could be transmitted. But, although the myelin sheath may play some part in fully developed neural functioning, it is not necessary for the appearance of reflex activities. Angulo y Gonzalez,[12] working with fetal rats, has shown that reflex activity clearly precedes myelination. Other theories which attempt to explain this lag in neural functioning after gross connections are laid down tend to stress subtle changes in synapses or chemical alterations in the neurons and end plates of muscle fibers.[13]

It is thus apparent that the appearance of fetal behavior awaits the development of functional nervous connections between receptors and effectors, as well as the functional development of these organs. Whatever the necessary antecedents of neural functioning may be (once the gross connections are laid down), myelination is not one of them. The minute histological and physicochemical details of nervous development prior to functional maturity are yet to be disclosed, although several suggestions have been provided by recent research like that mentioned.

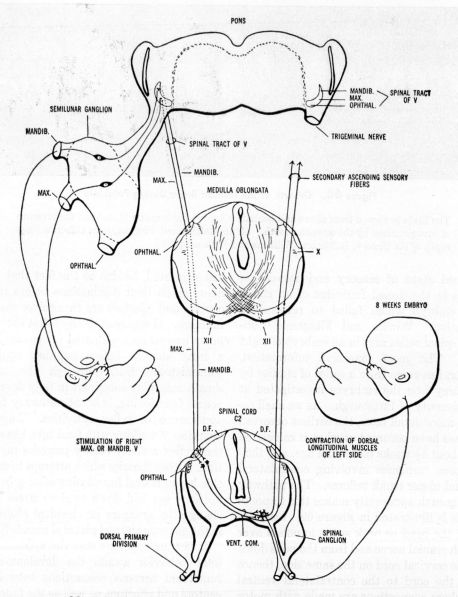

Figure 69. Diagram of the Reflex Pathway Involved in the Earliest Tactually Aroused Human Responses

This diagram is based upon histological examination of three human embryos around the age of eight weeks, but certain details are filled out from knowledge of the similar distribution of the corresponding nerve fibers in adults. (From T. Humphrey, "The Spinal Tract of the Trigeminal Nerve in Human Embryos between $7\frac{1}{2}$ and $8\frac{1}{2}$ Weeks of Menstrual Age and Its Relation to Fetal Behavior," *J. Comp. Neur.*, 1952, 97, 180.)

Sensory Processes

Evidence concerning sensory development in human fetuses has come from two general sources: (1) studies of the growth of the receptors in prenatal life, and (2) investigation of sensory functions in prematurely delivered fetuses. The evidence from these sources may be summarized briefly. The structural data are considered first and the functional second.

The sensory mechanisms, like the central nervous structures with which they are intimately connected, develop primarily from the ectodermal layer of embryonic cells. Some of them have certain parts which originate in the mesodermal layer. To a large extent, the olfactory, visual, and auditory receptors are differentiations of the embryonic brain. Their external auxiliary structures are clearly evident early in the second month of prenatal life, as shown in Figure 70.

Olfactory processes

The olfactory structures are present quite early in fetal life. They make their initial appearance as invaginations of the ectoderm. Two pits are formed, and after these have undergone further differentiation, the olfactory nerves grow from them into the brain. Until the time of birth the nasal cavities are filled with liquid. It is doubtful whether liquid substances can serve as olfactory stimuli; hence olfactory sensitivity is in all probability absent prior to birth. Another factor which would suggest absence of responses to olfactory stimuli prior to birth is the relative chemical constancy of the amnionic fluid. The odor of this fluid would very likely be constant, and change is one of the prime requirements for sensory stimulation. Studies with fetuses delivered prematurely suggest response to olfactory stimulation. However, the stimuli eliciting responses have been acetic acid, ammonia, and other such irritants. Thus the observed responses may have been to tactile irritation rather than to odor as such.

Gustatory processes

Taste buds are present by the third month of fetal life. It is doubtful, however, whether adequate stimulation of these is possible before birth. The only "taste," if any, would be that of the amnionic fluid, which, as mentioned above, is relatively constant in chemical composition.

Visual processes

The eye develops from an evagination of a portion of the forebrain, as illustrated in Figure 71. The evagination is evident as early as approximately the third week following fertilization. A vesicle is formed at the side of the brain and this grows outward, leaving a stalk which connects it to the point of origin. This stalk becomes the optic nerve. The vesicle at the end of the stalk becomes differentiated to form the layers of the retina.

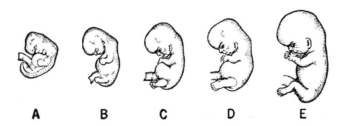

A   B   C   D   E

Figure 70. Summary of Later Developmental Stages of the Human Embryo

The figures are approximately life size. *A*, 31–34 days; *B*, 39–40 days (15.5 mm.); *C*, 47–51 days; *D*, 52–54 days; *E*, 60 days. (After His. Redrawn from F. R. Bailey and A. M. Miller, *Textbook of Embryology*, William Wood & Co., 1929, pp. 115–116.)

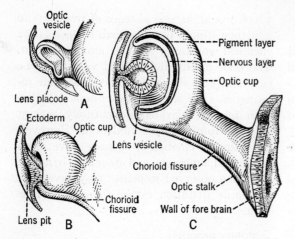

Figure 71. Three Early Stages in Development of the Human Eye

The lens is, in each case, cut through or near the middle. In *A* and *C* the wall of the optic cup has been partly cut away. *A* is from a human embryo 4.5 mm. long, *B* from an embryo 5.5 mm., *C*, 7.5 mm. (After drawings in Mann's *Development of the Human Eye* and Davenport's *How We Came by Our Bodies*. By permission of the *British Journal of Ophthalmology* and Henry Holt.)

The skin in the region of the optic vesicle thickens and then invaginates. Finally the edges join, forming a rounded mass of cells, the lens vesicle. These cells develop transparency and become the lens. From other tissues in and around the eye cup, the cornea, eyelids, lachrymal glands, and eye muscles develop. The rods and cones, which differentiate out of the nervous layer of cells, are developed before birth. One will observe in Figure 72 that even at three months rods and cones have begun to develop.

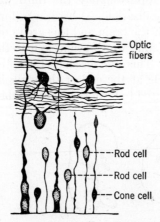

Figure 72. Section of the Nervous Layer of the Retina from a Fetus of Three Months

Compare this with Figure 35, p. 91, which is a diagram of the mature human retina and which indicates the direction of light and of nerve impulses. (After Prentiss.)

Eye movements occur in fetal life, but these are associated with static rather than with visual processes. Because of the nature of the prenatal environment, adequate visual stimulation is impossible prior to birth. However, there is some evidence, from studies of prematurely delivered fetuses, that differentiation between light and dark is possible at seven months after fertilization. Pupillary responses to light are also present in late fetuses. Peiper [14] obtained data which led him to conclude that late fetuses respond to color. (See Chapter 8 for a discussion of this work.)

Auditory processes

The inner ear, which consists of the cochlear duct, the saccule, the utricle, and the semicircular canals, results from the differentiation of a primitive auditory vesicle which, beginning as an invagination of the ectoderm, finally moves toward the brain. The auditory nerve grows out to connect with the vesicle. Branches of this nerve go to different regions of the inner ear. One main branch (the vestibular) goes to the semicircular canals and vestibule, where it mediates static sensitivity. The other main branch (the cochlear) goes to the hair cells in the basilar part of the cochlea. Here it mediates auditory processes. The middle ear is seen in Figure 73. It comprises the auditory tube, the tympanic cavity, and

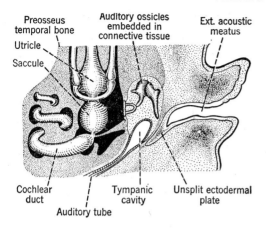

Figure **73.** Schematic Diagram of Section of the Human Ear in a Fetus of Three Months

(From L. B. Arey, *Developmental Anatomy*, 5th ed., Philadelphia: Saunders, 1946, p. 503.)

three small bones (auditory ossicles.) The external ear and the tympanic membrane which separates it from the middle ear result from differentiations of the primitive gill slits. Prior to birth, the external ear is closed and the middle ear is filled with a gelatinous substance. Hence it has been thought that the fetus must be deaf until after birth. Several studies have shown, however, that late fetuses *in utero* do respond to auditory stimuli.

Peiper [15] found that fetuses situated in a normal manner within the mother move in response to loud noises. The movements were recorded through the mother's abdomen, and there is evidence that they were not produced by the mother herself. Forbes and Forbes [16] also observed fetal movements in response to loud sounds. Thirty-one days before a baby was born, its mother was lying in a bathtub full of warm water. A child accidentally struck the side of the tub, producing a loud noise. Instantly the mother felt what appeared to be a sudden "jump" of the fetus. The experience was reported to be quite different from that aroused when the fetus kicked or made other limb movements. Five days later an experimenter made a loud noise under similar conditions, watching the woman's abdomen for movements. A fraction of a

second after the noise was made, there was clearly visible a "single quick rise of the anterior abdominal wall." The woman reported feeling the fetus jump as before. She was not herself startled by the sound and her muscles were relaxed during the stimulation. Experiments were made which show that the tactile vibration associated with the sound was not perceptible to the woman; hence, supposedly, the fetus must have responded to the sound waves rather than to tactile vibration. Nineteen days later the woman was seated on the floor when a piece of wood fell beside her with a clatter. The fetus was felt to give the same kind of movement as before. Ray [17] also found that fetuses respond to sounds while *in utero*. A loud sound was made and the mother pressed on a key whenever fetal movements were felt. Simultaneously the fetal movements were recorded from the mother's abdomen by means of tambours. There was a high degree of correspondence between the fetal movements as reported by the mother, as recorded by the tambour, and as seen by observation of the abdomen. Control data are reported to indicate that the mother did not herself make the movements. Spelt has conditioned this fetal response so that it is aroused by vibration of the mother's abdomen (see p. 180). Changes of the fetal heart rate in response to changes in auditory stimuli have been reported by Bernard and Sontag.[18] In addition to these data there are observations of the responses of premature and newborn infants to loud noises. There is no information concerning the ability of fetuses and newborn infants to respond to tones.

Static processes

The semicircular canals and vestibular structures are well differentiated by the end of the second month after fertilization. When they begin to function in the human fetus is, however, not known. Carmichael [19] summarizes the results of several investigations on infrahuman fetuses. Righting reactions and eye movements appear and seem to be controlled by mechanisms of the non-auditory labyrinth. The only data on statically controlled behavior in human fetuses are those of Minkowski.[20] He reports that responses controlled by the semicircular canals and the structures of the vestibule appear in early fetuses (see p. 176). However, it is difficult to differentiate between static and proprioceptive functions; and there is, as Carmichael suggests, a possibility that the responses attributed to functioning of the non-auditory labyrinth are actually controlled by proprioceptors.

Proprioceptive processes

The receptors for proprioceptive or kinesthetic sensitivity are located in the muscles, tendons, and joints. They emerge as finer differentiations of these structures. Proprioceptors are stimulated by flexion and extension of the muscles and by deep pressure. According to Hooker,[21] proprioceptive processes are probably functional in the fetus at the time when motility first appears; that is, shortly after the eighth week. The earliest responses of human and infrahuman fetuses are apparently generalized in nature, involving the whole organism. Carmichael[22] suggests in this connection that "Much of the 'movement of the organism as a whole,' which so many writers refer to, seems to be the result of rather specific proprioceptive stimulation. Such stimulation often leads to the 'spread' of what are really quite delicately timed families of specific responses which can easily be mistaken for 'vague' or 'diffuse' behavior."

Cutaneous processes

Little is known about the time of appearance of the cutaneous receptors (end bulbs of Krause, Pacinian corpuscles, Meissner's corpuscles, Ruffini's corpuscles, and free nerve endings), and there is some doubt as to the correlation between these differentiations of the skin and specific cutaneous processes.

In most of the studies of fetal behavior, tactile stimulation has been used. The human fetus of a little over two months responds to light contact with a hair, and the sensitivity of the skin to such stimulation probably increases with age. Sensitivity is usually found to be greater in regions of the body in close proximity to the head than in regions farther removed. There is also, as the fetus gets older, indication of increasing ability to make responses appropriate to the location of the tactile stimulus. Pressure with a needle, a heavy hair, or the like also elicits responses. It is possible that such responses are mediated by proprioceptors rather than by tactile and pressure receptors. Hooker[23] suggests that some of the "specific" responses elicited in early fetuses by such stimulation may be reactions of the muscles to direct stimulation rather than to tactile stimulation as such.

Since the fetus resides in an environment of relatively constant temperature, there could be no opportunity for differential temperature stimulation to occur prior to delivery. However, the requisite receptors are probably developed long before birth. Carmichael and Lehner[24] have demonstrated, in the case of the guinea pig, that responses to temperature stimulation are present from about the middle of the fetal period, that is, approximately 28 to 38 days. From this time until about 39 to 49 days there is an increase in the frequency of responses elicited by temperature stimulation. Responses to temperature stimulation have also been observed in human fetuses delivered prematurely. At the normal time of birth there is good evidence of differential sensitivity to temperature changes. (See Chapter 8.)

Responses to stimuli which normally elicit pain are often absent in the fetal period and at birth. Injury to the skin, except that which elicits direct muscular response, often fails to produce a reaction. Several studies, which will be discussed in more detail later, indicate that newborn babies often make no avoidance response to needle-pricks.

Organic sensory processes

Organic sensory processes are those associated primarily with functioning of organs situated within the body cavity. It is well known that hunger is associated with a lowering of blood sugar and contractions of the stomach musculature. Absence of nourishment is the immediate stimulating condition. Thirst is associated with drying of the skin and particularly of the mucous lining of the throat. Although the mechanisms which mediate such processes are present in the fetus long before birth, there is little likelihood that they are normally called upon to function in a manner comparable with that of postnatal life. The fetus obtains all of its nourishment and its liquid from the mother through the placenta (see Figure 64), and the "need" for these things may never arise. Other organic processes of a sensory nature are perhaps present before birth. Carmichael [25] says:

> ... The rate of fetal heart beat can be modified by external stimulation, thus possibly leading to vascular stimuli of the sort often considered to fall under the heading of "organic experience." The possibility of respiratory experiences, or "feelings of suffocation," is certainly present, so far as may be judged from a knowledge of stimulation and response. But there is, of course, no evidence that any introspective state actually follows such stimulation. ...

Before closing this discussion of sensory processes it should be mentioned that much self-stimulation may appear before birth. The movements of the fetus act as proprioceptive stimuli for further movement. Movement in a liquid medium also offers possibilities for tactual stimulation. Carmichael [26] observed a guinea-pig fetus "stimulate its head and face by appropriately cupped 'hands,' not once but over and over again, until it would seem that the surface must be irritated by the friction."

Motor Processes

The chief motor processes are the movable parts of the skeleton, the muscles, and the glands both of external and internal secretion.

Skeletal development

The skeleton first makes its appearance in the form of cartilage. It gradually ossifies as the individual becomes older. Associated with its development is that of the muscles. These are of two kinds, striped and smooth. The striped muscles are those of the external body, the functioning of which is most obvious in overt behavior. Smooth muscles are found especially in the body cavity, where they are associated with activity of the stomach, intestines, and other internal organs. The skeleton, the striped muscles, and the smooth muscles arise primarily from differentiations of the mesodermal layer of cells.

The limbs first appear as budlike appendages, as shown in Figure 74. These are evident in the thirty-day embryo (see Figure 70). They gradually lengthen and their extremities differentiate to form the fingers and toes. Some of the more important muscle groups are well developed by the end of the second month. The parts which are to form the fingers and toes are also quite evident. The kinesthetic receptors develop in and with the muscles, tendons, and joints. As indicated in a previous discussion, the nerve fibers must grow out to and make functional connection with the muscles before sensorimotor activities can occur.

Development of the glands

The glands of external secretion develop along with the parts of the body with which they are associated. The sweat glands, for example, develop with the cells which form the skin. The lachrymal glands develop from cells in the region of the developing eye cup. Although the activities of the glands of external secretion are important in connection with emotional expression, psychologists are more interested in the glands of internal secretion.

The glands of internal secretion, known as endocrines, are distinguished from those of external secretion by the fact that they produce chemical products (hormones) which are discharged directly into the blood stream.

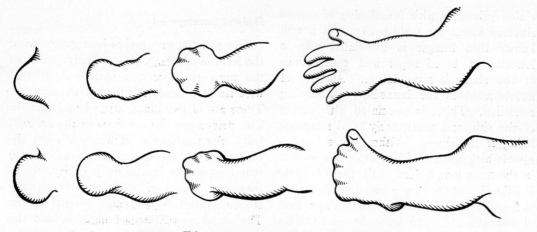

Figure 74. Development of the Human Limbs

The development here depicted covers the period from the fifth to the eighth week of prenatal life. Observe that the development of the hand at the eighth week is in advance of
that evidenced by the foot. (After Arey.)

The hormones are carried in the blood to every part of the body and exert a marked influence upon structural and behavioral development. The influence of the hormones upon prenatal development is often not so apparent as their influence upon the development and normal functioning of children and adults. This is perhaps due, in part, to the fact that the fetus normally obtains adequate hormone supplies from the mother. Furthermore, it is not until the glands become diseased (which seldom occurs before birth) that we realize the extent to which normal structural and behavioral development depends upon them. (See Chapter 16 for a discussion of glandular influences in the growth of personality.)

The endocrine glands develop primarily from the endodermal layer of cells and, as already indicated, serve as important aspects of the intercellular environment of the developing organism. Most of them are clearly apparent during the end of the second month after fertilization. The general locations of the chief endocrine glands in the child and adult are shown in Figure 75.

Having completed our review of the chief features of prenatal structural development and related functions, we now consider the more general reactions apparent during the various stages of prenatal life.

The Prenatal Growth of Behavior

Knowledge of prenatal behavior has come from four general sources. (1) *Reports of mothers concerning fetal movements.* Such reports are obviously limited in their scientific value. Movements may occur long before they are perceptible to the mother. Activity in the alimentary canal may be confused with

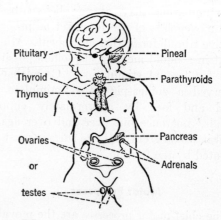

**Figure 75.   A Sketch Showing the General Loca-
tions of the Principal Endocrine Glands**

fetal movements. In any case, the movements can be reported only in a very general manner, no knowledge of their differential nature and the stimuli which arouse them being clearly apparent. (2) *Instrumental observations by physicians of movements apparent through the body wall of the mother.* Such movements as heartbeat, contractions of the thorax, and changes in position of body and limbs may be observed by the use of stethoscope, X-ray, and other instruments. Here again, the observations yield behavior data of limited scope. (3) *Observations of the prematurely born.* Systematic scientific studies of such individuals are usually out of the question so long as life is present and there is a possibility of its continuance. (4) Practically all of our accurate systematic information about the development of human prenatal behavior has come from *studies of embryos and fetuses delivered by Caesarian section* because allowing them to develop further would endanger the life of the mother. When these are less than six months of age there is no possibility that they can be saved. It is customary, therefore, to lay them aside until death ensues, which is usually a few minutes after delivery. Systematic studies of such material have been made by several investigators. These have taken the organism as soon as it was removed from the mother, have placed it in a physiological solution maintained at blood temperature, and have observed its "spontaneous" movements and reactions to stimulation. In some of the earlier studies the responses were recorded stenographically, but in recent investigations cinematographic recording was used. One value of cinematographic recording is that the data are available for study at any time. Many responses which are too rapid to be analyzed at the time of their appearance may be studied later at normal speed, and in addition may be subjected to minute analysis by observation of successive frames of the film.

In a systematic genetic investigation of prenatal behavior it is necessary to obtain organisms at representative stages of development. Furthermore, one should observe large numbers at each developmental age; otherwise there is a possibility that individual differences in rate of development will lead to false impressions concerning the most typical responses present at each age. In experiments upon infrahuman animals one may obtain as many cases of a given age as he desires. Investigators of human prenatal development, however, have been required to confine their observations to cases provided by circumstances over which they had no control. Thus the available human data are quite limited in scope. Less than 250 human fetuses have been studied carefully from the standpoint of behavior. Minkowski studied a total of 75; Bolaffio and Artom 12, and an unknown number beyond; Hooker 131; and Windle and Fitzgerald 17.

The systematic study of prenatal behavior in any mammal is rendered difficult by the fact that the anesthetic used on the mother to alleviate the pain of the operation may anesthetize the embryo or fetus being observed. Another difficulty is that, while being observed, the organism is slowly succumbing to anoxia. Hooker [27] has discussed the effect of different drugs, administered to the mother, upon the condition of the embryo at the time of delivery. Most of his later cases have been derived from hysterotomies where local or spinal novocaine, which does not affect the embryo, was used. Since the embryo cannot get oxygen except through the maternal placenta, the separation which takes place during hysterotomy produces oxygen deficiency. The organism slowly asphyxiates. In two instances reported by Fitzgerald and Windle,[28] however, the fetuses were examined briefly *in utero* while still attached to the maternal placenta. As we shall see later (p. 183) the presence of fetal anoxia has complicated certain theoretical considerations with respect to the sequence of prenatal development.

The general procedure after an embryo has been placed in a physiological solution is to record any apparently spontaneous * movements which may occur. It is then subjected to electrical or tactile stimulation. After it has died the organism is frequently examined histologically in order that the neural (see Figure 69) and other correlates of the observed behavior may be ascertained.

The following brief discussion of the development of human prenatal activity is based upon Minkowski's pioneer studies, Bolaffio and Artom's work, the studies of Windle and Fitzgerald, and the recent comprehensive researches of Hooker which, because he used a relatively large number of cases and a cinematographic technique, offer the most accurate descriptions of human prenatal behavior available in the literature. Carmichael [29] has summarized the above studies as well as the numerous incidental observations reported from time to time.

Initial appearance of behavior

Nothing which would be designated behavior in the usual sense is present until the end of the embryonic or beginning of the fetal stage — that is to say, until about eight weeks. Although the embryonic heart becomes active during the third week, no other response occurs. Attempts to activate muscles by pressing upon them or by stimulating them directly with electrical currents have failed to produce results until near the end of the sixth week, when electrical stimulation elicits reactions of the muscles stimulated. Yanase [30] reports movement of an arm in an embryo estimated to be $7\frac{1}{2}$ weeks old, but there is evidence suggesting that this movement was produced by rigor mortis. On the basis of his own observations, Hooker [31] says that "Until the middle of the seventh week of menstrual age, the human embryo appears to be incapable of any type of reflex activity. There is certainly no area of integument sensitive to

* It is doubtful whether any behavior results without stimulation of some kind, internal or external. When investigators report that movements are spontaneous, they merely indicate that no external stimulation has been applied experimentally.

exteroceptive stimulation before this time."

In embryos of about eight weeks menstrual age there is clear evidence of response to tactual stimulation and, as we have seen, the histological data show that reflex pathways from the fifth cranial nerve are established at around this time. Hooker and Fitzgerald and Windle [32] have observed behavior in embryos estimated to be around eight weeks old. Hooker's [33] description of his observations on two unanesthetized embryos is as follows:

From approximately the middle of the seventh to just before the eighth week, when the embryo is between 20 and 23 mm. CR,* stimulation by lightly stroking the upper or lower lip or the alae of the nose with a hair exerting a minimum bending pressure of 10 to 20 mg. causes typically a contralateral flexion of the neck and uppermost trunk, with little or no participation of the upper extremities and none of any other portion of the body.

Fitzgerald and Windle's embryos were 18–26 mm. CR and assumed to be between seven and eight weeks from insemination. They were still attached to the maternal placenta when first observed and they were not anesthetized. Tapping lightly on the amnion in one case produced a quick response of the legs and lower trunk. A heavier tap elicited movements of all appendages. No head movements were observed. After detachment from the uterus, strong stimulation of these fetuses produced what the authors describe as "mass movements" of the neck, trunk, arms, and legs.

The third month

Five unanesthetized fetuses of about $8\frac{1}{2}$ weeks menstrual age were found by Hooker [34] to be responsive to light stroking of the mouth region with a hair. The response of one such fetus is illustrated in Figure 76. These responses were repeatedly aroused and in a stereotyped pattern. Typically the response, as described by Hooker, whose statement is paraphrased, consisted of the following elements: contralateral flexion of the neck and

* CR refers to length from crown to rump.

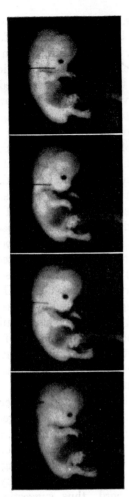

Figure 76. **Response to Light Tactual Stimulation of the Face in a Human Fetus of Approximately 8½ Weeks**

Note especially the downward and return movement of the arms. (Copyrighted by Davenport Hooker.)

trunk; backward movement of the arms at the shoulder, with no participation of the elbow, wrist, or fingers, which were moved only passively; rotation of the rump toward the contralateral side, with apparently only passive movement of the legs. The neck-trunk and arm movements were simultaneous, but in some fetuses the rump movement was slightly delayed. After this response, the arms returned to their original position, followed by the neck, rump, and trunk. During

this time the fetus was of course slowly asphyxiating. After a few such responses to light tactual stimulation were aroused, stronger stimulation was necessary to produce their repetition. Two of Hooker's 8½ week fetuses, when stimulated as above, exhibited side-to-side repetitions of the response, which suggests the presence of spontaneous movement. Fetuses of about one week later exhibited reactions without any stimulation by the observer. Such movements are of course more clearly spontaneous than those of the 8½ week fetus.

At 9½ weeks menstrual age, the only area responsive to light tactual stimulation is still the face. Hooker [35] reports that "rump rotation becomes still more marked and tends to become separated from the usually contralateral trunk flexion and bilateral arm extension at the shoulder as a distinct phase of the response." He also reports that "the vigor of movements of the caudal end of the trunk has increased over that seen at 8½ weeks." What appears to be a "body-righting reflex" was elicited in 9½ week fetuses when Hooker rotated the body by twisting the umbilical attachment of the fetal membranes. He believes that this response may have a vestibular origin. Typical stretch responses, apparently kinesthetic in nature, were sometimes obtained by the experimenter's extension of the fingers. This caused flexion of the wrist, elbow and shoulder. Up to about this time, only strong stimulation produced isolated responses. The most typical responses, elicited by light stimulation with a hair, and only when such stimulation was applied to the face, were the widespread responses involving head, trunk, rump, and limbs which we have already described. The constituent responses did not occur separately. This tendency of the earliest exteroceptively aroused responses (those initiated by touch or light pressure) to be generalized rather than specific is the subject of controversy which will be considered later.

Toward the end of the third month of prenatal life, specific responses to exteroceptive as well as proprioceptive stimuli (see p. 168) begin to appear. Hooker [36] observed that at about 10½ weeks there is no change in the response to light facial stimulation, but that responses confined to the palm of the hand can now be elicited. Light strokes from a hair bring partial closure of the fingers, but without participation of the thumb. In fetuses a few days older, "stimulation of the volar or lateral surfaces of the upper arm may cause independent arm extension at the shoulder; of the upper eyelid, contraction of the orbicularis oculi muscle; and of the sole of the foot, plantar flexion of the toes."[*] This of course not only shows the beginning of particularized (as well as generalized) responses to light tactual stimulation, but it also indicates that the area of the skin which is sensitive to such stimulation is becoming more extensive. Hooker finds that the facial region is still the only one which arouses generalized responses. Stimulation of other sensitive areas elicits specific reactions.

From the 11th to the 12th week the generalized response begins to show evidence of internal modification. Hooker [37] says that, at about 11 weeks, this response "becomes modified by the appearance of an element of trunk extension, either alternating with or partially combined with the lateral flexion. Arm extension, which has hitherto accompanied the trunk flexion, is giving way to medial rotation of the brachia, which will reach its full development in another few days. There is also some slight rotation of the thighs in the total pattern response." Movements of the forearm as well as finger closure and plantar and eye reflexes are also elicited by local stimulation. By about 11½ weeks the area sensitive to stimulation has shown further extension. The upper chest is now showing evidence of exteroceptive sensitivity. Many new activities, as well as modifications of older ones, begin to appear. Arm and trunk movements are extended. The fingers are sometimes brought together during these

movements. Particularized responses of the arm, including flexion of the forearm and wrist, may be seen. Stimulation of the sole produces flexions resulting in a kick.

Many of the responses described by Hooker were observed earlier by Minkowski,[38] who, however, not having the advantage of motion picture photography, could not provide descriptions of equal detail. Minkowski found evidence of tendon reflexes for the first time in fetuses near the end of the third month. The patella reflex (knee jerk) was elicited in two fetuses estimated to be 11 weeks old. Bolaffio and Artom [39] failed to observe tendon reflexes at this age, possibly because their fetuses were deeply anesthetized. Carmichael [40] has raised a question as to whether these are true tendon reflexes. He points out that the response elicited by striking a tendon could result from cutaneous stimulation, from direct muscle stimulation, or from a true tendon-stretch muscle stimulation. It is difficult, in early fetuses, to distinguish between these possible causes.

Both Minkowski and Hooker have observed lip movements by this age, suggesting the beginnings, although remote, of the sucking reflex. Minkowski [41] reported seeing flexions of the fingers, simulating a grasping response. This was abolished by sectioning the spinal cord, thus suggesting a neural basis rather than direct muscular stimulation. Bolaffio and Artom [42] found that removing the cerebrum of fetuses near the end of the third month intensified activity in response to stimulation. This suggests that the cerebrum may, at this age, already be assuming inhibitory functions.

Our survey of prenatal behavior up to the end of the third month has brought out the following significant points: (1) Responses to light tactual stimulation are at first aroused only by stimuli applied to the face, in the region of the mouth; (2) these responses are for the most part stereotyped and generalized, involving the neck, trunk, rump, and limbs in combination rather than separately; (3) the sensitive zones become more extensive, so

[*] This means a bending of the toes toward the sole of the foot.

that stimuli applied to the hands or feet may elicit reactions; (4) these reactions, which develop increasing specificity, become more frequent as the end of this period approaches; (5) the widespread response aroused by facial stimulation also exhibits changes, its elements becoming less passive and more articulated within themselves. (6) At any time after behavior begins, strong stimulation applied to particular regions may elicit something simulating particularized reflex reactions, but there is some question as to the basis of such responses. As we shall observe again in a later discussion, there is the possibility that they are produced by direct stimulation of the muscles or tendons involved, or perhaps by proprioceptive instead of cutaneous stimulation.

The fourth month

During this month many clear-cut reflexes are elicited by light tactual stimulation. In fetuses of $12\frac{1}{2}$ weeks, Hooker [43] observed that facial stimulation produces "marked extension of the neck and trunk accompanied by a wide variety of movements at many of the joints in the upper extremities. The responses are still quite mechanical in their execution and the fetuses continue to be very active, but there is somewhat greater variety in the exact components of the responses, one differing from another in the accompanying movements." Specific responses which appear at this age include eyelid reflexes, lip closure, and fanning of the toes. The generalized pattern of activity begins to disappear, to be replaced by a wide variety of reflexes. Such reflexes may be aroused by stimulating any part of the body except the back and top of the head, which are insensitive. Soon the total pattern of response, which has so far been predominantly evident, disappears except when aroused by strong stimulation or by the nearness of asphyxia.

Hooker regards the 13th to 14th week as an important period in the development of fetal activity because the total pattern is at this time replaced by many reflexes of the newborn. These "are not all in the final form they will assume, but, with the addition of a number not yet present, they lay the framework for gradual development into the reflexes of postnatal life." [44] The reflexes elicited in this period involve the head, face, trunk, and extremities. Foot withdrawal, as illustrated in Figure 77, is quite specific at $14\frac{1}{2}$ weeks. At 15 weeks finger closure is maintained, instead of fleeting. But it is not yet sufficiently strong to hold an object. Abdominal reflexes and lip reflexes, involving lip closure, are also elicited at this age level, as are all the reflexes observed earlier.

Minkowski [45] presents direct evidence that the responses of fetuses in the fourth month are actually reflexes. Sectioning the spinal cord at various levels abolishes activity in the neurologically related structures. Removal of the whole spinal cord eliminates all activity except that which can be aroused by direct stimulation of muscle tissues. The cerebrum apparently has no influence over fetal responses up to this time except that, as mentioned earlier, its removal leads to a greater intensity of response. It does not influence the repertoire of responses. Transection of the midbrain does not eliminate responses, but it seems to weaken them.

In general, it appears that the most characteristic advance in development during the fourth month of prenatal life is the appearance of numerous reflexes and the breaking up, as it were, of the generalized pattern which has hitherto dominated. Toward the close of this period, many reflexes, like those of the fingers, approximate more closely to those evident in the newborn baby. Almost all of the body surface is now responsive to light tactual stimulation which at an earlier age aroused responses only when applied to narrowly prescribed regions. The responses aroused are mediated exclusively by subcortical mechanisms, and especially by those of the spinal cord.

The fifth month

During this month the reflex responses apparent earlier are more readily elicited and

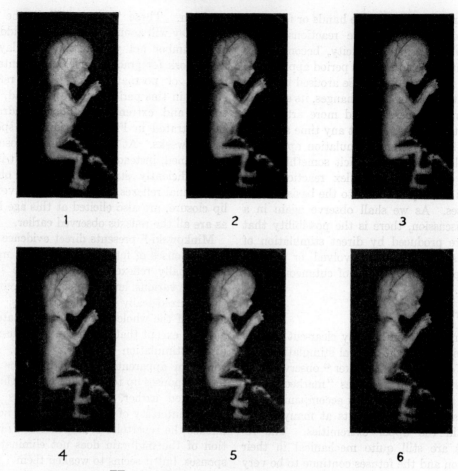

Figure 77. Response to Tactual Stimulation of the Right Foot
in a Fetus Aged about 14 Weeks

Note that the foot is withdrawn, but without participation of the rest of the body such as
occurs in the generalized reactions of earlier fetal life, when the facial region is alone responsive to light tactual stimulation. (Copyrighted by Davenport Hooker.)

are more clear-cut. Hooker [46] observed
"weakly effective grasping" at 18½ weeks.
A thin glass rod was held, but the thumb was
not always involved. At 22 weeks the lip
movements more closely approached those
used later in sucking. Tendon reflexes were
now clearly elicited.

Minkowski [47] found that movements of the
head in space aroused equilibratory responses
of the limbs. Passive movement of the fetus
elicited responses effecting a return to the
position of departure. The movements were
rhythmical and repetitive. Percussion of the

abdominal wall aroused abdominal reflexes.
Minkowski [48] observed that at this age stimulation of one foot may elicit flexion of the
corresponding leg and extension of the contralateral one. Stimulation of the foot may
also arouse a diagonal reflex, that is, a response
of the opposite hand. Minkowski suggests
that this is a "trot" reflex. It is assumed to
underlie postnatal locomotor activities such
as crawling and walking. Minkowski [49] also
reported that he had seen Ahlfeld's breathing
movements in a fetus of approximately the
19th week. These movements were slow

rhythmical ones which simulate those of respiration. Hooker [50] saw similar responses in fetuses of about this age. Effective respiration, however, was not observed until $23\frac{1}{2}$ weeks. This was accompanied by a high-pitched cry. The general activity of the fetus *in utero* increases so markedly during the fifth month that the mother is clearly aware of it. According to Kellogg's data,[51] based upon abdominal recording and reports of the mother, there is increasing activity, with some fluctuations, from this time until birth.

Bolaffio and Artom [52] made a study of cerebral control in fetuses of the latter part of the fifth month and the beginning of the sixth. Direct stimulation of the cortex elicited no response. Various movements of the chest, shoulders, diaphragm, and head and neck resulted from direct stimulation of the medulla. Electrical exploration of the cerebrum yielded no response. When the internal capsule and peduncles were exposed and stimulated electrically there was likewise no effect. Stimulation of the pons led to movements of muscles served by the facial nerve. Respiratory movements appeared when the medulla was stimulated. Stimulation of the spinal cord aroused various movements of the trunk and extremities.

The evidence concerning activity in the fifth month indicates, therefore, that while a few new responses appear, and greater complexity of reflex action, such as the "trot reflex" is elicited, the fetus is still largely a spinal organism. The cerebrum, while quite complex, as yet has no specific control over behavior.

From the sixth month until birth

Late in the fifth month, as already suggested, "respiratory" movements begin to appear. These movements of the mechanisms later involved in respiration soon become more pronounced, and by about the 27th week of menstrual age (about 25 weeks actual age) some fetuses are viable. That is to say, some may live if given adequate care. This would of course not be possible until respiration had been established. Hooker [53] says that

The change in activity following respiration is startling, although except for the possibility of eliciting tendon reflexes, no new activities appear. Indeed little new appears during the next two or three weeks. It is almost as though the fetus were developing its respiratory capacity at the expense of the appearance of new responses. This may, at least in part, be the result of the explosive appearance of "spontaneous activity" which renders the eliciting of reflexes difficult of evaluation. As a rule, it is almost impossible to determine whether a movement following stimulation was caused thereby or would have occurred without it.

Fetuses of about 27 weeks were found by Hooker to have a grasp sufficiently strong to all but sustain body weight. Thumb participation was feeble. By 29 weeks there was an audible sucking response. A startle response had appeared by this time. Blinking was also elicited. According to Bolaffio and Artom,[54] stimulation of the cerebral cortex was without effect at this age level, although stimulation of lower brain centers produced changes in respiration and in limb movements.

From the seventh month on, fetuses frequently survive if carefully nurtured in incubators. Gesell [55] has reported systematic observations of the behavior of such "fetal infants." A few of the earlier age levels are also represented in the studies which we have been quoting. The fetal infant of about 28 to 32 weeks is portrayed by Gesell as a skinny, senile-appearing, loosely articulated creature weighing somewhere around two pounds and easily held on the palm of one hand. It breathes poorly and its sucking and swallowing are so inadequate that it must be fed by tube or by some instrument, such as a nasal spoon, which runs the liquid into a nostril. There are brief periods of activity, but torpor predominates. When activity does occur, it involves the face, eyes, head, and limbs. Sometimes an arm moves, but its movement is arrested and it remains in a fixed (catatonic) pose until relaxed. Stretching occurs. This is sometimes of one leg and sometimes of both, in which case a scissor-like attitude is assumed. There is an apparent aversion to light. At about the end of this period several investigators have observed a pupillary response.

Gesell reports that the fetal infant of 21 to 36 weeks looks more like a baby, is much more robust, and acts more vigorously than infants of the earlier period. It has sometimes doubled its body weight during the preceding month. Drowsiness prevails, but there is apparently the beginning of true wakefulness.

The average age of birth is around 40 weeks, so that infants between the 36th and 40th week are referred to as "circumnatal" rather than fetal. In these infants all the reflexes of the newborn (see pp. 179–181) may be aroused. Gesell presents evidence that the infant is beginning to perceive its surroundings. Its eyes may follow a dangling ring; they seem at times to fixate it. The infant responds to caresses with what Gesell characterizes as "rapt enjoyment."

There is very good evidence that the cerebrum still exerts very little, if any, influence over the repertoire of activity. Infants born without a cerebrum (acephalic infants) have the usual repertoire of reflex activities. Brain injuries incident to birth do not affect behavior until months later. Even during the early months of postnatal life, as Lindsley[56] has shown, there are only occasional and irregular electroencephalograms. Behavior during the prenatal period, and possibly for some time after birth, thus appears to be controlled subcortically.

Gesell[57] compares mature fetal infants with infants of the same age but born at the normal time. In general, their behavioral repertoire is the same. This suggests that maturation rather than stimulus-response is responsible for the sequence of prenatal development. Although the repertoire of behavior is alike in both groups, there are differences. The fetal infant has already made

adaptations to the extrauterine environment. It has partially adjusted to such aspects of the postnatal environment as light and dark, temperature changes, feeding, and people. Respiration and sucking are more efficient and there is less regurgitation. The fetal infant also appears to pay more attention to the human face. Its behavior is more predictable. It shows some conditioned responses to sounds and other stimuli. Part of this difference in favor of the fetal infant (and perhaps all of it) is attributable to extrauterine experience. It must be remembered, however, that the mature newborn is possibly suffering from the birth trauma. The fetal infant, because of its size, has escaped the sort of trauma through which the full-term infant has gone, unless, of course, the latter has been delivered by Caesarian section. If it had any such trauma, it would have had time to recover. In many instances, the normally born infant suffers head molding, if not injuries. Gesell says that within a month it is not possible to distinguish infants born in the fetal period from those born at term. It is interesting to note, in this connection, that birth is sometimes delayed a month or more beyond the normal end of term.

Prenatal Conditioning

We have already pointed out that the cerebral cortex appears to have no specific influence over the repertoire of prenatal behavior. This fact, as well as certain theoretical considerations, aroused interest in the possibility of conditioning the responses of fetuses *in utero*. Pavlov[58] had suggested that the cerebral cortex is necessary for conditioning. If this were true, fetuses probably could not be conditioned. Since that time, however, several investigators[59] have shown that decorticate animals, and possibly even those with only their spinal cord involved, are susceptible to conditioning. Theoretically, therefore, it should be possible to condition fetuses, although their relative inaccessibility introduces technical difficulties. Holt[60] and others have suggested on theoretical grounds that some of the responses of the fetus and the newborn may be conditioned reactions rather than outcomes of maturational processes alone.

That fetuses respond to loud sounds during the last month *in utero* has already been noted. This fact suggested to Ray and Sontag and Wallace [61] that the response to sound might be conditioned to some other stimulus. It seemed that the best stimulus for this purpose would be vibration of the mother's abdomen. If sufficiently intense, this would presumably reach the fetus. But these investigators failed to get clear-cut evidence of fetal conditioning.

Spelt [62] tried again, using a more adequate technique, and succeeded in conditioning fetuses estimated to be within a month or more of term. The arrangement of his apparatus is shown in Figure 78 A. The unconditioned stimulus, as in earlier studies, was a loud clapper sounded near the mother's abdomen. This elicited a "startle response" which could be recorded, as illustrated in Figure 78 B. Tactile vibration of the mother's abdomen initially aroused no fetal reaction. But after as few as fifteen paired presentations of the vibration followed by the noise, some fetuses began to respond to the vibration alone. From five to eleven successive conditioned responses were elicited. One fetus, the only one subjected to prolonged study, retained the conditioned response over a period of at least eighteen days. Experimental extinction and spontaneous recovery were also obtained. Controls, involving the application of vibration at various age levels, but without the noise, showed that the development of a response to vibration does not result from maturation alone. To discover whether the response might be simulated by the mother herself, the same procedure was applied to non-pregnant women, but without anything resembling conditioned responses. Neither the pregnant nor non-pregnant women knew the nature of the experiment in which they participated.

There is thus clear evidence that late fetuses are susceptible to conditioning, a fact which supports the research on conditioning in decorticate organisms, against the views of Pavlov, and which also suggests the possibility, although perhaps not the probability, of prenatal conditioning under non-experimental uterine conditions. Later we shall have more to say about this issue.

The Human Behavioral Repertoire at Birth

The following classification of the responses of the newborn gives a good idea of the variety and complexity of behavior which has developed during the seven months beyond the non-motile stage of fetal life. This classification is that of Dennis [63] based upon his review of the literature pertaining to newborn human behavior. It is greatly abridged here. The original references will be found in Dennis's article.

RESPONSES OF THE NEWBORN

Eyelid
Two reflexes. Opening, closing.

Pupillary
Contraction and expansion. Consensual (contraction or dilation of one when the other is stimulated).

Ocular
Pursuit movements.
Saccadic movements (similar to those later used in reading).
Nystagmus (combination of saccadic and pursuit such as appears after rotation of the body).
Coordinate compensatory eye-movements (jerking head in one direction leads to eye-movement in opposite direction).
Position of eyes in sleep most frequently up and sideways.
Coordination of eyes sometimes appears at one day.
Convergence (rare).

Tear secretion
During crying and nasal irritation.

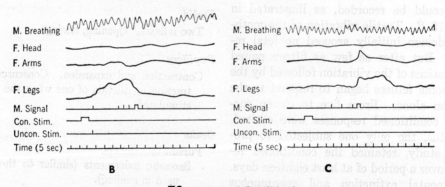

Figure 78. Prenatal Conditioning

A. The apparatus and general arrangement of the stimulating and recording equipment. B. The type of record obtained initially. The fetus responded to the noise (uncon. stim.) but not to the vibratory stimulus (con. stim.). C. Here, after the vibration had been followed by a noise for a number of trials, the fetus responded to the vibration alone. Its response was, however, somewhat delayed as compared with when the noise was used. Maternal breathing was recorded to see whether it contributed to the recorded activity. The tambours were placed so as to give separate records for head, arms and legs. The mother signaled, by pressing a button, when she felt movements of the fetus. (From D. Spelt, "The Conditioning of the Human Fetus in Utero," *J. Exper. Psychol.*, 1948, 38, 339.)

Facial and mouth

Opening and closing mouth.

Upper and lower lip responses to touch. Also turning to stimuli at side.

Sucking.

Grimace, wry face, twisting mouth.

Rejection of substances from mouth.

Yawning.

Licking or mouthing.

Compression of lips in response to touching.

Pursing lips.

Frowning.

Wrinkling of forehead.

Pulling down corners of mouth.

Smiling (sometimes first day).

Smacking lips.

Turning lower lip when full.

Throat responses

Crying. (There is a question concerning differences in cries, i.e., for hunger, colic, rage. Crying is often accompanied by activity of arms and legs.)

Cooing.

Sobbing after excessive crying.

Sneezing (sometimes precedes birth cry).

Coughing.

Gagging.

Swallowing.

Holding breath.

Hiccoughing.

Vomiting.

Head movements

Upward and downward moving of head.

Turning face to side, especially at nose-cleaning.

Head shudder to bitter tastes.

Balancing head (appears at two days).

Hand and arm responses

Radius reflex.

Scapulo-humeral reflex.

Closing hand.

Arm flexion (withdrawal to flip of finger against hand or to pricking).

Rubbing of face.

Slashing movements.

Arm play (random?).

Startle response (arms thrown outward with associated tremor).

Trunk reactions

Arching back (produced by pinching nose).

Twisting (head rotated, shoulders and pelvis twist opposite from direction of head).

Abdominal reflex (drawing in of stomach).

Sexual responses

Cremasteric reflex (raising of testes to stimulation of inner thigh).

Penis erection.

Foot and leg responses

Knee jerk.

Achilles tendon reflex.

Flexion of leg (always accompanied by plantar flexion of foot).

Extension of leg (accompanied by dorsal flexion of foot).

Kicking (alternate and together).

Stepping movements (when child is held upright with feet touching surface).

Toe phenomena (plantar and Babinski, or toe-spreading, reflexes).

Coordinate response of many body parts

Resting and sleeping position (legs flexed, fists closed, upper arms out straight from shoulder and forearms flexed at right angles so that they lie parallel to head).

Opisthetonic position (strong dorsal flexion from head to heels, often in crying).

Backbone reflex (concave bending of side that is stimulated).

Lifting head and rear quarters in unison.

"Fencing" position. (If one rotates the head, the arm towards which the head is rotated extends, the other flexes.)

"Springing position." (If infant is held upright and then inclined slightly forward, the arms extend forward and the legs are brought up.)

Stretching.

Startle response. (Arms go apart, fingers spread, legs extend, and head is thrown backward. Response elicited by loud noises, falling: start like that of adults dropping off to sleep.)

Mass activity involving crying and general unrest.

Creeping. (Rare — baby in prone position draws arm and legs under body, lifts head; if feet are given traction they push and arms also become active.)

Shivering and trembling.

Extremities extended to side (rotation around vertical axis, arms and legs extended in direction of rotation).

Bodily jerk. (Arms and legs flex and jerk upwards in response to loud noise.)

Supporting weight by grasping.

Sneezing.

Nursing posture. (If infant is hungry and given a nipple it begins to nurse, and at the same time the arms flex so that the fists are pulled against the body in the neighborhood of the chin, while the legs and toes are extended and raised somewhat. As satiation approaches, this posture gradually relaxes.)

Posture of defecation. (With each abdominal contraction the legs and toes are extended and raised and the forearms are held to the upper chest. Grunting and reddening of the face often accompany this response.)

Generalizations on the Prenatal Course of Behavioral Development

Many students of behavioral development have tacitly assumed that the earliest responses to appear in ontogeny are reflexes, and that complex activities result from learned or unlearned integrations of these. This assumption has been subjected to criticism from Gestalt psychologists as well as from a group of experimental anatomists and neurologists. These investigators offer, in its stead, the generalization that perfectly integrated behavior involving the whole organism exists before reflexes make their appearance. According to this view, the reflex, rather than being elementary, is derived from the pre-existing pattern through a process of differentiation or individuation.

Coghill's research

The research of Coghill [64] on behavioral development in embryos of the salamander, *Amblystoma*, has given strong support to the latter generalization. The embryos were observed from the time at which the first movement appeared until the customary behavioral repertoire was present. One aspect of the research was observation of the correlation between the growth of neuromuscular mechanisms and the development of behavior.

Coghill stimulated the embryos with a human hair. His purpose in using so light a stimulus was to prevent direct excitation of muscles. He was interested in tactually elicited behavior, and as we shall observe later, his generalization may not apply to behavior elicited by stimulation sufficiently intense to arouse proprioceptive responses.

Until a certain level of development had been attained the amblystoma embryos made no response to tactile stimulation. The earliest movement to such stimulation was "a bending of the head to one side." In older embryos the contraction extended farther down the trunk until it culminated in a coil such as that illustrated in Figure 79 *A*. The next reaction, which appeared at a slightly greater age, was that shown in Figure 79 *B*. A flexion started toward the tail end of the animal, giving the impression that a coil was to appear. Before the flexion reached the tail, however, it was reversed. This so-called "S" reaction is the fundamental movement in swimming. When it is repeated in rapid succession the animal rises from the substratum and swims away. So far each reaction has involved every part of the organism capable of functioning at the time of stimulation. When the limbs appear some time later they are at first passively moved with the trunk and are pressed toward the body by water currents. The further development of behavior is described by Coghill [65] as follows:

A day or two ordinarily elapses between the time when the arm begins to move with the action of the

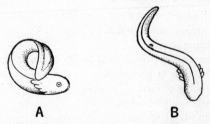

A   **B**

Figure 79. Two Early Responses of Amblystoma Embryos

A, the coil or "C" reaction. *B*, the "S" reaction involved in swimming. (After Coghill.)

trunk before it acquires the ability to respond to a local stimulus without the perceptible action of the trunk. Such independence of limb action appears to be acquired by a gradual reduction in the action of the trunk. At any rate, movement of the limb has been frequently observed to occur with slight movement of the head just before limb movement without perceptible trunk movement made its appearance. It is obvious, therefore, that the first limb movement is an integral part of the total reaction of the animal, and that it is only later that the limb acquires an individuality of its own in behaviour. The local reflex of the arm is not a primary or elementary behaviour pattern of the limb. It is secondary, and derived from the total pattern by a process of individuation.

In the further development of the behaviour pattern of the arm the same principle is observed: the first elbow flexion occurs with action of the arm as a whole, and the forearm only later acquires the independence of a local reflex. So also is it with the movements of the hand and the digits.

Coghill's work on amblystoma embryos has precipitated a large amount of research on various organisms, including chickens, rats, guinea pigs, and cats. It has also stirred up a minor controversy concerning the universal applicability of the generalization that reflexes arise by differentiation from a preexisting perfectly integrated behavior pattern.

Coghill's generalization applied to human fetuses. Coghill [66] analyzed the data of Minkowski and reached the view that it is consonant, by and large, with the generalization derived from his work on amblystomas. Hooker,[67] on the basis of his own investigations and those of previous workers with human fetuses, has reached a similar conclusion. The chief critics of this conclusion are Windle and his co-workers. Fitzgerald and Windle,[68] as we have already noted, were able to observe reacting human fetuses *in utero*. When the amnion was tapped, one of these responded with quick movements of the limbs and lower trunk which were interpreted by the observers as spinal reflexes. They claim that, so long as a fetus of eight weeks is "adequately supplied with oxygen, is unnarcotized,

unanesthetized, and otherwise undamaged, the excitability of its nervous system is high" and "various local reflexes can be elicited . . . before the fetuses become asphyxiated."

The role of anoxia

The implication of the preceding statement is that Minkowski's and Hooker's fetuses were not acting normally, principally because anoxia was setting in while they were being observed. Windle implies that the generalized response is the response of an organism undergoing anoxia. Hooker [69] has answered this criticism at length. His stimulation was exteroceptive, as we have seen. Moreover, he knew not only the receptors involved, but also the neural pathway. The fibers of this circuit "are of the smallest caliber" and evidence of various kinds shows that these are "resistant to asphyxia." The pathway itself is primarily spinal and, "in view of the fact that the spinal cord has the lowest oxygen requirement of any region of the central nervous system, exteroceptive reflexes which are dependent on the cord for their synaptic transmission, as are those over the trigeminal nerve (Figure 69) should be the last to succumb to anoxia." Moreover, anoxia and asphyxia do not change the nature of responses actually aroused. "Not only are reflexes ultimately abolished by these conditions, but initially they are also facilitated by them." With reference to the series of responses observed by him, Hooker [70] says that "All responses in the series are normal steps in the development of behavior, whether or not they are somewhat facilitated by anoxia, or whether or not the earliest occur *in utero*."

Exteroceptive and more intense stimulation

In an earlier discussion we pointed out that sufficiently strong stimulation sometimes arouses a response in the organ stimulated even though light tactual (exteroceptive) stimulation arouses a generalized response of the whole organism, or of all of it which is capable of responding at the time. This is another crucial factor in the controversy between followers of Coghill on the one hand and followers of Windle on the other.

As Angulo y Gonzalez [71] has observed, there are perhaps three stages in the development of responsiveness to external stimulation, namely: (1) *myogenic*, in which movement is aroused by stimulation of a muscle directly; (2) *neurogenic*, in which it is aroused by direct stimulation of motor neurons; and (3) *sensorimotor*, in which movement is neurally mediated from a distance, as where stimulation of the face elicits reactions in various body parts not directly stimulated. Strong stimulation applied locally may cause reflex-like movements which are not reflexes at all, but reactions of myogenic or neurogenic origin. Such stimulation may also activate receptors within the muscles, and thus involve proprioception.

The issue of which comes first, the generalized pattern or the reflex, is present in much of the research on infrahuman fetuses. A great deal of this research, which we shall now consider briefly, has been undertaken in an effort to resolve the above-mentioned conflict and also to test the universality of any generalization reached with respect to human prenatal behavior.

Research on infrahuman organisms

We have seen that the research which touched off the controversy concerning the priority of generalized patterns or reflexes was done with amphibians. Later research has dealt primarily with chickens, rats, guinea pigs, cats, and sheep.

The development of behavior in chickens, from the time when activity first appears until the time of hatching, has been studied by Kuo [72] and Orr and Windle.[73] Both studies deal with normal development within the egg,* but the latter investigators also

stimulated chicks removed from the egg. In both studies, behavior at first appeared to be generalized along the lines of what Coghill had observed in Amblystoma, but Orr and Windle also elicited certain "reflexes" of wings and legs before these were involved in overall response. The strong stimulation used, such as tapping a leg or flipping a wing, raises the question as to whether these "reflexes" were actually so or merely myogenic or neurogenic.

The data on rats are similarly equivocal. Angulo y Gonzalez [75] and Rose [76] find a Coghillian sequence in development of behavior, whereas Windle and his collaborators,[77] again using strong stimulation, find the prior existence of "reflexes." The research on cats suggests that both generalized patterns and reflexes may exist from the start. Windle and others [78] find some evidences of a "massive and generalized" early pattern, but also the appearance, at the same time, of what they interpret as reflexes. Coronios [79] comes to similar conclusions, although his fetal cats were stimulated with a small brush instead of a probe such as Windle has customarily used. Barcroft [80] and his collaborators, working with fetal sheep, at first favored Windle's viewpoint, but more recently Barcroft and Barron [81] have said that "local mechanisms do appear to become segregated out from a total response in the sense implied by Coghill in his account of the development of behavior in *Amblystoma*."

The most thorough investigation of fetal behavior in infrahuman organisms is un-

---

* By means of a technique as ingenious as it is simple, Kuo observed the development of the chicken without interfering with its normal prenatal environment. The shell at the blunt end of the egg was removed without disturbing the inner membrane. This membrane was coated with a thin layer of vaseline which, at the temperature of the incubator, remained liquid. The inner membrane was by this method transformed into a window through which Kuo could observe the movements of the chicken. The egg was placed in an incubator with a window through which the chicken could, with appropriate instruments, be observed. Orr and Windle, not being able to obtain the degree of transparency reported by Kuo, were forced to remove the inner membrane of the egg. Despite the difference in technique, however, the results of Kuo and Orr and Windle are in most respects quite similar. Kuo and Carmichael [74] have obtained moving pictures of the behavior of chick embryos through the type of window described by Kuo.

doubtedly that of Carmichael [82] on guinea pigs. Before his investigation began, Carmichael prepared a map showing certain areas to be stimulated in fetuses representing every day of development from the 25th (prior to the appearance of motility) to the 60th (the normal time of birth). There was an attempt to present comparable stimulation from fetal stage to fetal stage. The stimulation was chiefly with a coarse hair, although some spots were at times stimulated with a needle, electric shock, or temperature cylinder. The total number of fetuses observed was 178. The earliest response elicited by external experimental stimulation appeared in a 31-day fetus. Carmichael says that when he touched this fetus on the face "no definite response could be elicited, but when the aesthesiometer was applied to the region which would later form the fully developed concha of the ear, definite fore-leg movements were elicited which were accompanied by a flexion of the neck which led to a bowing of the head." Examination of Carmichael's protocols shows that the initial responses are often as specific as this. Sometimes the entire trunk is involved and sometimes not. Specific reflexes frequently appear before and without any definite relation to the total pattern of behavior. In summarizing his investigation of fetal development in guinea pigs, Carmichael [83] says:

Facts which, as far as the author knows, are presented in this study for the first time . . . seem to demonstrate clearly that in this typical fetal mammal the development of response, *in relation to specific receptor* stimulation at successive growth stages, is far too specialized to be summarized with validity by an existing general theory of the development of behavior.

In a later study by Bridgman and Carmichael,[84] it was shown that active behavior begins as early as the last hours of the 25th day after insemination. In the period immediately following this earliest response, 146 fetuses from 47 litters were studied. As a result, Bridgman and Carmichael conclude that the earliest responses can best be char-

acterized as "specific" *and* "generalized." In a still more recent study, Carmichael [85] has used a graded series of aesthesiometers and shown that, at all typical fetal stages, more general patterns of behavior are elicited by intense stimulation than by mere supraliminal stimuli.

We thus see that neither the view that patterns of behavior are derived from integrations of reflexes nor the view that reflexes are derived from pre-established patterns of response is consonant with all the observed facts. Some studies support this former generalization and some the latter. Some suggest the failure of either generalization to embrace all the findings. Nor is it a case of some species developing in one sort of sequence and others in another. The differences appear to result from: (1) different sorts of stimulation from one study to another, (2) different interpretations of the same facts by investigators favoring Coghill's or Windle's viewpoint, and (3) the possibility that both reflexes and generalized patterns are coexistent in early prenatal development. It may be, as Hooker has suggested, that the Coghillian sequence holds for responses elicited by light (exteroceptive) stimulation, but this generalization certainly does not hold for behavior elicited by stimuli such as those used by Windle and his collaborators and by Carmichael and workers in his laboratory. The writer agrees with Carmichael [86] that:

Too much emphasis cannot be placed upon the fact that easy generalizations, such as the assertion that all behavioral development occurs from a generalized total pattern of the organism to the specific responses of adult life, must be taken with great caution. While this description may be true in many respects, particularly if the word "pattern" is given an unambiguous meaning, it seems certain on the basis of the specific responses considered above that it cannot be indiscriminately applied. Before generalizations can be made with assurance, there must be a large amount of accurate measurement and the determination of a series of statistical norms in regard to the development of each of the specific developmental stages in each form considered. Typical cross-sections in development in every form and in all responses from significant receptor surfaces must be considered before such a generalization can be made. Certainly the late fetus has an elaborately organized and in some respects quite specific response mechanism. To some stimuli the relatively early fetus makes quite definite responses. . . . It seems hard to believe that anyone who knows anything of the structure and function of the tracts and centers of the central nervous system can read the report of fetal activity at various developmental levels . . . and still feel that there is much to be gained by saying that before birth the organism reacts as a whole, as certain psychologists, possibly under the influence of a mistaken view of the *Gestalttheorie*, have suggested. Much of the nervous system may, in some sense, be involved in any partial activity of that system, but this does not mean that the system is not in many respects sharply differentiated.

What Carmichael says concerning the generalization that mass activity precedes specific activity of a reflex nature may also be said of several other generalizations which have grown out of the work on fetal development.

Other generalizations concerning prenatal development

One generalization is that the development of behavior proceeds in a cephalocaudal direction, that is, from head to tail. Another is that the development of behavior is proximodistal in direction, that is, from the center of the body to the periphery. Both of these generalizations are based upon data similar to those already discussed above. In several of the investigations of fetal behavior,[87] the cephalocaudal and proximodistal directions of development have been given specific notice. In a very general sense, the development of behavior does take a cephalocaudal and proximodistal course. However, responses which do not seem to fit this sequence often appear.

The generalization that ontogeny recapitulates phylogeny has been applied to the development of fetal structural characteristics more than to the development of fetal behavior. However, some have seen in the "swimming" and "grasping" responses of the fetus vestiges of our animal ancestry. Since there is no way of proving or disproving such a generalization, it is of little if any scientific value.

Another generalization which has been made with respect to the prenatal development of behavior is that *it results from the unfolding of potentialities resident within the genes* and is thus inherited. The term "maturation" has often been used to designate such an unfolding process. As we have used this term, however, it designates the growth processes resulting from an integral relation of genes and their constantly changing surroundings. We have shown (pp. 35–43) that the structures and structural integrations of the individual result from interaction of genes and the intracellular, intercellular, and external (prenatal and postnatal) conditions of development. Development cannot, in the light of the great amount of work on experimental embryology, be regarded as potential within the genes alone. Nor can it be regarded as essentially determined by environmental factors. It is a product of these two sets of conditions. Only under artificial laboratory conditions is one able, as it were, to segregate the separate factors.

Although inherent and environmental factors are at all times involved in the development of the structures and structural integrations which underlie behavior, it can be demonstrated that *exercise* is not a prerequisite for the development of these. As one example of this fact we have already (pp. 57–58) cited Carmichael's ingenious experiment on the swimming responses of amblystoma and frog embryos. It will be recalled that even though a drug made the animals immobile, their sensory, neural, and motor structures continued to grow and integrate so that, when given an opportunity to do so, they were able to swim as adequately as animals which had received the usual opportunities for exercise. The structures of the eye continue to develop in mammalian fetuses even though stimulation with light is absent. Many other examples of the phenomenon of growth without exercise could be cited. It is obvious, moreover, that the structures and structural integrations which precede the earliest responses of normally developing fetuses cannot result from *exercise*, although environmental factors of a relatively non-specific nature are of course involved in their growth. Before exercise can occur, the structures must have attained a certain degree of functional maturity. After a certain degree of functional maturity has been attained, however, exercise conceivably may determine part, at least, of further developments.

Woodworth and Marquis [88] cite an experiment by Morpurgo [89] which suggests, on the other hand, that the type of growth resulting from exercise may differ from that produced by maturation. The phenomenon which characterizes maturation is the production of new structures. In Morpurgo's experiment it was clearly demonstrated that exercise of a muscle merely increased the size of muscle fibers already present. The number of fibers was not increased. A factor which limits the conclusions to be derived from this experiment, however, is that the exercise was of muscles already in a state of maturity. It would be interesting to carry out an experiment in which the partially developed structures of a group of animals were given forced exercise for a given period of time and the histological structure (neural and motor) then compared with that of a comparable group given no unusual exercise. The results of such an experiment would enable one more adequately to determine the validity of Kuo's [90] claim that the structural and behavioral growth of fetuses may be determined in part by the exercise forced upon them as the result of changing dynamic situations within the prenatal environment. Using the method discussed above (p. 184), Kuo observed chick embryos from the time at which the earliest movements appeared until the animals emerged from the egg. He noted that beating of the heart produced "passive vibrating movements of the head and the body," and that passive movements of the chick also resulted from contractions of the amnion and movements of the yolk sac. Such passive motion, he believes, may act as stimulation for the development of the characteristic activities of the embryonic and mature chicken. Kuo also reports that changes in the size of various parts of the embryo cause it to change its position in the egg, and that such changes in position bring, not only new forms of stimulation, but restriction of previously established responses.

Some students of behavioral development have stressed in this connection the theory of Kappers [91] concerning growth of nerve fibers. This theory, known as that of neurobiotaxis, assumes that excitation of nerves gives rise to differences in electrical potential in neighboring regions. Such differences in potential produce bioelectric currents to which immature nerve cells are positively tropistic. These immature cells, according to the theory, send out fibers to the region of activity and new neural pathways and integrations are formed. In discussing this view, Lashley [92] mentions that Carmichael's work on swimming in salamanders and frogs exemplifies development without, at least, external stimulation produced by exercise. He says,

The doctrine that the reflex paths are established as a result of sensory stimulation begs the question . . . for in assuming that electrical currents from the point of stimulation determine the direction of growth, it presupposes the existence of those paths of high conductivity between sensory and motor zones whose origin it seeks to explain.

No one can doubt that such factors as Kuo has stressed must play a part in behavioral development. On the other hand, we have, as already suggested, considerable evidence of development without such stimulation and exercise. If the responses of the amblystoma, for example, were dependent upon stimulation and exercise for their development, it is hard to see how they could appear in their customary form in animals deprived of such conditions. The universality of the reflex responses of fetuses of a given species and the tendency of these responses to make their appearance in something approximating a sequence are probably presumptive evidence for the generalization that early fetal behavior, at least, is dependent primarily upon maturation of sensory, neural, and motor structures. After the organism attains a certain degree of motility it is, of course, able to stimulate itself. Movements of the trunk and limbs not only cause movements of the amniotic fluid and consequent tactile stimulation, but lead to proprioceptive stimulation of neighboring regions. There are possibilities, also, of direct tactile stimulation of parts of the body by the hands and feet. Granting the possibility of such stimulation, however, one still finds it difficult to see how the development of the various responses present in late fetuses and in the newborn could be achieved thereby. To the writer it appears almost inconceivable that the development of fetal behavior should take such a steady course and the large number of reflexes (including those of the tendons) be achieved by the time of birth unless some maturational process (as defined above) is primarily responsible. There is too much variability in the forms of "exercise" elicited from one fetal organism to another to suppose that this "exercise" could account for universal and sequentially developing responses. Furthermore, it is seemingly impossible for the fetal organism to receive general stimulation and exercise capable of forwarding the development of all specific reflex responses. The pupillary reflex, for example, appears at the time of birth when light is presented for the first time. How could such a reflex be accounted for except by supposing that it results from maturation? Many other reflexes could serve similarly to illustrate the point. Hence, while Kuo's work has brought to attention the wide possibilities for external stimulation and exercise during prenatal development, it does not force us to the conclusion that all fetal behavior is learned. Kuo

himself does not make such a claim. He merely stresses the fact that the opposite generalization — namely, that all fetal behavior is a result of the unfolding of inherent potentialities — is, in the light of his evidence, questionable. He, like Carmichael, is of the opinion that no clear-cut distinction between heredity and environment and between maturation and learning can be made on the basis of evidence at present available.

Summary and Conclusions

After describing the grosser anatomical developments of human prenatal life, we cited data concerning the chief bases of structural growth and differentiation. We were forced to the conclusion that prenatal growth is a function of the integrated action of the genes and the intracellular, intercellular, and external conditions of the organism. In discussing the ontogeny of the nervous mechanisms, the fact was emphasized that, until the time at which functional neural connections between receptors and effectors are present, no responses to external stimulation can occur. Some of the antecedents of neural functioning, including the growth of nerve fibers to their proper terminations, were indicated. It was observed that the sensory mechanisms develop gradually and are quite in evidence, even in embryos. They are apparently functional before the time of birth, although adequate stimulation of some (the gustatory, olfactory, and visual) is not present in the prenatal environment. Our discussion of motor mechanisms, in addition to indicating the origin of the skeleton, muscles, and glands of external secretion, drew attention to the prenatal growth of the endocrine glands.

Sources of information concerning prenatal activity were discussed. We then traced the development of human behavior from the first month until the time of birth. Behavior, other than heart activity and responses of muscles to direct excitation, fails to appear until the late embryonic or early fetal period. Around the eighth week, responses to tactile stimulation of the face may be elicited. These responses tend to be of a rather gross nature, involving the head, trunk, and extremities. So-called "spontaneous" movements are present during the middle of the third month, and are similar in nature to those aroused by light tactile stimulation in the region of the nose and upper lip. Reflexes of a rather precise nature are clearly apparent during the fourth month. At this time, stimulation may arouse a specific response of the stimulated organ, whereas it formerly aroused a rather generalized response of the organism. In the ensuing months, although generalized reactions still appear, there is increasing evidence of specific reflex responses. At birth, as shown by the classification presented, the individual has a wide variety of reflex reactions.

Evidence on the functions of the central nervous system during fetal life indicates that the behavior of the fetus, until approximately the end of the fifth or the beginning of the sixth month, is controlled by spinal mechanisms. At a slightly greater developmental age there is evidence that the medulla and lower brain centers participate in the control of specific reflex activities. There is no evidence that the cerebral cortex exerts any specific influence upon behavior until some time after birth. Adequate integration of higher and lower central nervous mechanisms, therefore, is not achieved during the prenatal period.

Fetuses within one month of term may be conditioned to respond to previously noneffective stimulation. In the experiment described, the conditioned stimulus was a loud noise, to which the fetus responded with something resembling startle. The conditioned stimulus was vibration applied to the mother's abdomen. Paired stimulation, with vibration followed by sound, soon elicited response to the vibration alone. This was shown to be an actual conditioned response and not one resulting from maturation or maternal movements.

The generalization that specific responses are individuated from a pre-established total pattern is premature, if not incorrect, in the light of the fact that specific responses may be elicited before total patterns appear. There is a possibility, however, that the generalization may hold for responses elicited by tactile although not by other forms of stimulation, such as the proprioceptive. Generalizations concerning the cephalocaudal and proximodistal directions of development receive support from the data on fetal development, but here again some exceptions are at times noted. Presumptive evidence for such a principle perhaps resides in the cephalocaudal and proximodistal directions taken by the developing nervous system. There is little evidence either to deny or to affirm the generalization that fetal behavioral development recapitulates the behavioral history of the race. Such a generalization would in any case be of restricted scope, for only the apparent "swimming" and "grasping" responses are claimed to have any specific relation to phylogenetic behavioral developments. The generalization that prenatal behavior is inherited is not supported by the facts. Development is at all times a product of both inherent and environmental factors. However, there is good evidence that maturation (conceived as growth resulting from the interaction of the genes and their surrounding conditions rather than growth by exercise) accounts for at least some of the responses of the fetus and the newborn.

REFERENCES

1. Child, C. M., *Physiological Foundations of Behavior*. New York: Holt, 1924.
2. Becker, R. F., and W. Donnell, "Learning Behavior in Guinea Pigs Subjected to Asphyxia at Birth," *J. Comp. & Physiol. Psychol.*, 1952, *45*, 153–162.
3. Davenport, C. B., "Child Development from the Standpoint of Genetics," *Scientific Monthly*, 1934, *39*, 104.
4. Sperry, R. W., "Mechanisms of Neural Maturation," Chapter 7 in S. S. Stevens, *Handbook of Experimental Psychology*. New York: Wiley, 1951.
5. Sperry, R. W., *op. cit.*, p. 248.
6. Hooker, D., "The Development and Function of Voluntary and Cardiac Muscle in Embryos without Nerves," *J. Exper. Zoöl.*, 1911, *11*, 159–186.
7. Carmichael, L., "The Onset and Early Development of Behavior," Chapter 2 in L. Carmichael (ed.), *Manual of Child Psychology* (2d ed.). New York: Wiley, 1954, pp. 114–119.
8. Hogg, I., "The State of Development of the Central Nervous System of a 16 mm Human Embryo," *Anat. Rec.*, 1933, *55*, 19–20.
9. Windle, W. F., and J. E. Fitzgerald, "Development of the Spinal Reflex Mechanism in Human Embryos," *J. Comp. Neur.*, 1937, *67*, 493–509.
10. Humphrey, T., "The Spinal Tract of the Trigeminal Nerve in Human Embryos between 7½ and 8½ Weeks of Menstrual Age and in Relation to Fetal Behavior," *J. Comp. Neur.*, 1952, *97*, 143–209.
11. Coghill, G. E., *Anatomy and the Problem of Behavior*. Cambridge: Cambridge University Press, 1929.
12. Angulo y Gonzalez, A. W., "Is Myelinogeny an Absolute Index of Behavioral Capacity?" *J. Comp. Neur.*, 1929, *48*, 461.
13. See especially J. F. Fulton, in *Howell's Textbook of Physiology* (15th ed.). Philadelphia: Saunders, 1946, pp. 125–134.
14. Peiper, A., "Ueber die Helligkeits und Farbenemfindungen der Fruhgeburten," *Arch. f. Kindernhk.*, 1926, *80*, 1–20.
15. Peiper, A., "Sinnesempfindungen des Kindes vor seiner Geburt," *Monatsschr. f. Kinderhk.*, 1924, *29*, 236–241.

16. Forbes, H. S., and H. B. Forbes, "Fetal Sense Reactions: Hearing," *J. Comp. Psychol.*, 1927, *7*, 353–355.
17. Ray, W. S., "A Preliminary Report on a Study of Fetal Conditioning," *Child Development*, 1932, *3*, 175–177.
18. Bernard, J., and L. W. Sontag, "Fetal Reactivity to Tonal Stimulation: A Preliminary Report," *J. Genet. Psychol.*, 1947, *70*, 205–210.
19. Carmichael, L., *op. cit.*, pp. 146–148.
20. Minkowski, M., "Uber Fruhzeitige Bewegungen, Reflexe und Muskuläre Reaktionen beim Menschlichen Fötus und ihre Beziehungen zur Fötalen Nerven und Muskelsystem," *Schweiz. med. Woch.*, 1922, *52*, 721–724, 751–755.
21. Hooker, D., "Early Fetal Activity in Mammals," *Yale J. Biol. and Med.*, 1936, *8*, 579–602.
22. Carmichael, L., *op. cit.*, p. 146.
23. Hooker, D., *op. cit.*, p. 586.
24. Carmichael, L., and G. F. J. Lehner, "The Development of Temperature Sensitivity During the Fetal Period," *J. Genet. Psychol.*, 1931, *50*, 217–227.
25. Carmichael, L., citation 7, p. 149.
26. *Ibid.*, pp. 140–141.
27. Hooker, D., *The Prenatal Origin of Behavior*. Lawrence: University of Kansas Press, 1952, pp. 58–59.
28. Fitzgerald, J. E., and W. F. Windle, "Some Observations on Early Human Fetal Activity," *J. Comp. Neur.*, 1942, *76*, 159–167.
29. See citation 7.
30. Yanase, J., "Beiträge zur Physiologie der Peristaltischen Bewegungen des Embryonalen Darmes. II. Mittelung. Beobachtungen au Menschlichen Föten," *Pflug. Arch. f. d. ges Physiol.*, 1907, *119*, 451–564.
31. Hooker, D., *The Prenatal Origin of Behavior*, pp. 62–63.
32. See citations 27 and 28.
33. Hooker, D., citation 27, p. 63.
34. *Ibid.*, p. 64.
35. *Ibid.*, p. 65.
36. *Ibid.*, p. 68.
37. *Ibid.*
38. See citation 20.
39. Bolaffio, M., and G. Artom, "Ricerche Sulla

Fisiologia del Sistema Nervosa del Feto Umano," *Arch. di. sci. biol.*, 1924, 457–487.

40. See citation 7, p. 130.

41. See citation 20.

42. Bolaffio and Artom, *op. cit.*

43. Hooker, D., citation 27, p. 70.

44. *Ibid.*, p. 73.

45. See citation 20.

46. Hooker, citation 27, p. 75.

47. Minkowski, M., "Uber Bewegungen und Reflexe des Menschlichen Foetus wahrend der Erstern Halfte Seiner Entwicklung," *Schweiz. Arch. f. Neur. u. Psychiat.*, 1921, *8*, 148–151.

48. Minkowski, M., "Zum Gegenwartigen Stand der Lehre von der Reflexen in Entwicklungsgeschichtlicher und der Anatomisch-physiologischer Beziehung," *Schweiz. Arch. f. Neur. u. Psychiat.*, 1924–1925, *15*, 239–259; *16*, 122–152.

49. See citation 20.

50. Hooker, D., citation 27, p. 75.

51. Kellogg, W. N., "A Method for Recording the Activity of the Human Fetus *in Utero*, with Specimen Results," *J. Genet. Psychol.*, 1941, *58*, 307–326.

52. See citation 39.

53. Hooker, D., citation 27, p. 76.

54. See citation 39.

55. Gesell, A., *The Embryology of Behavior*. New York: Harper, 1945.

56. Lindsley, D. B., "Brain Potentials in Children and Adults," *Science* 1936, *84*, 354; "Electrical Potentials of the Brain in Children and Adults," *J. Gen. Psychol.*, 1938, 285–306.

57. Gesell, A., *op. cit.*, pp. 140–143.

58. Pavlov, I. P., *Conditioned Reflexes*. London: Oxford University Press, 1927.

59. See R. G. Bromiley, "Conditioned Responses in a Dog after Removal of Neocortex," *J. Comp. & Physiol. Psychol.*, 1948, *41*, 102–110. This reference also reviews the earlier studies on cats and dogs.

60. Holt, E. B., *Animal Drive and the Learning Process*. New York: Holt, 1931.

61. Ray, W. S., "A Preliminary Report on a Study of Fetal Conditioning," *Child Development*, 1932, *3*, 175–177; L. W. Sontag and R. F. Wallace, "Study of Fetal Activity: Preliminary Report of the Fels Fund," *Am. J. Dis. Child.*, 1934, *48*, 1050–1057.

62. Spelt, D. K., "The Conditioning of the Human Fetus in Utero," *J. Exper. Psychol.*, 1948, *38*, 338–346.

63. Dennis, W., "A Description and Classification of the Responses of the Newborn Infant," *Psych. Bull.*, 1934, *31*, 5–22.

64. Coghill, G. E., *Anatomy and the Problem of Behavior*. Cambridge University Press, 1929.

65. *Ibid.*, pp. 18–20.

66. See citation 64.

67. Hooker, D., "Early Fetal Behavior in Mammals," *Yale J. Biol. and Med.*, 1936, *8*, 579–602; *The Origin of Overt Behavior*, Ann Arbor: University of Michigan, 1944; and citation 27.

68. Fitzgerald and Windle, see citation 28.

69. Hooker, citation 27, pp. 104–110.

70. Citation 27, p. 110.

71. Angulo y Gonzalez, A. W., "Development of Somatic Action in Albino Rat Fetuses," *Proc. Soc. Exp. Biol. and Med.*, 1933, *31*, 111–112.

72. Kuo, Z. Y., "Ontogeny of Embryonic Behavior in Aves," I, *J. Exper. Zool.*, 1932, *61*, 395–430; II, *ibid.*, 1932, *62*, 453–489; III, *J. Comp. Psychol.*, 1932, *13*, 245–271; IV, *ibid.*, 1932, *14*, 109–122; V, *Psych. Rev.*, 1932, *39*, 499–515.

73. Orr, D. W., and W. F. Windle, "The Development of Behavior in Chick Embryos: The Appearance of Somatic Movements," *J. Comp. Neur.*, 1934, *60*, 271–283.

74. Kuo, Z. Y., and L. Carmichael, "A Technique for Motion-Picture Recording of the Development of Behavior in the Chick Embryo," *J. Psychol.*, 1937, *4*, 343–348.

75. Angulo y Gonzalez, A. W., "The Prenatal Development of Behavior in the Albino Rat," *J. Comp. Neur.*, 1932, *55*, 395–442.

76. Rose, D. "Comparisons of Fetal Development in Normal and Hyperthyroid Rats," *J. Comp. & Physiol. Psychol.*, 1949, *40*, 87–104.

77. Windle, W. F., and E. B. Baxter, "Development of Reflex Mechanisms in the Spinal Cord of Albino Rat Embryos. Correlations between Structure and Function and Comparisons with Cat and Chick," *J. Comp. Neur.*, 1936, *63*, 189–210; and W. F. Windle, W. L. Minear, M. F. Austin, and D. W. Orr, "The Origin and Development of Somatic Behavior in the Albino Rat," *Physiol. Zool.*, 1935, *8*, 156–185.

78. See especially W. F. Windle, *Physiology of the Fetus*. Philadelphia: Saunders, 1941, Chapter XII and the references cited there.

79. Coronios, J. D., "Development of Behavior in

the Fetal Cat," *Genet. Psychol. Monog.*, 1933, *14*, 283–386.

80. Barcroft, J., *Researches in Pre-Natal Life.* Springfield, Ill.: C. C. Thomas, 1947.

81. Barcroft, J., and D. H. Barron, "The Development of Behavior in Foetal Sheep," *J. Comp. Neur.*, 1939, *70*, 500.

82. Carmichael, L., "An Experimental Study in the Prenatal Guinea-Pig of the Origin and Development of Reflexes and Patterns of Behavior in Relation to the Stimulation of Specific Receptor Areas During the Period of Active Fetal Life," *Genet. Psychol. Monog.*, 1934, *16*, 339–491.

83. *Ibid.*, p. 478.

84. Bridgman, C. S., and L. Carmichael, "An Experimental Study of the Onset of Behavior in the Fetal Guinea Pig," *J. Genet. Psychol.*, 1935, *47*, 247–267.

85. Carmichael, L., "Pressure Stimulation and the Specificity versus Generality of Response in Fetal Life," *Psych. Bull.*, 1937, *34*, 710.

86. See citation 7, p. 138.

87. See especially the citations indicated: Coghill (64), Kuo (72), Angulo y Gonzalez (75), and Coronios (79).

88. Woodworth, R. S., and D. G. Marquis, *Psychology* (5th ed.). New York: Holt, 1947, pp. 283–284.

89. Morpurgo, B., "Ueber Activitats-Hypertrophie der willkurlichen Muskeln," *Arch. Path. Anat.*, 1897, *150*, 522–554.

90. Kuo, Z. Y. See citation 72.

91. Kappers, C. U. A., "Further Contributions on Neurobiotaxis. IX. An Attempt to Compare the Phenomena of Neurobiotaxis with Other Phenomena of Taxis and Tropism. The Dynamic Polarization of the Neurone," *J. Comp. Neur.*, 1917, *27*, 261–298.

92. Lashley, K. S., "Nervous Mechanisms in Learning," in C. Murchison (ed.), *A Handbook of General Experimental Psychology.* Worcester: Clark University Press, 1934, pp. 459–460.

SUGGESTIONS FOR FURTHER READING

Carmichael, L., "The Experimental Embryology of Mind," *Psych. Bull.*, 1941, *38*, 1–28.

Carmichael, L., "The Onset and Early Development of Behavior," Chapter 2 in L. Carmichael (ed.), *Manual of Child Psychology* (rev. ed.). New York: Wiley, 1954.

Coghill, G. E., *Anatomy and the Problem of Behavior.* Cambridge University Press, 1929.

Corner, G. W., *Ourselves Unborn.* New Haven: Yale University Press, 1945.

Gesell, A., *The Embryology of Behavior.* New York: Harper, 1945.

Gilbert, M. S., *Biography of the Unborn.* Baltimore: Williams and Wilkins, 1939.

Hooker, D., *The Prenatal Origin of Behavior.* Lawrence, Kansas: University of Kansas Press, 1952.

Sperry, R. W., "Mechanisms of Neural Maturation," Chapter 7 in S. S. Stevens (ed.), *Handbook of Experimental Psychology.* New York: Wiley, 1951.

Weiss, P., *Principles of Development.* New York: Holt, 1939.

Windle, W. F., *The Physiology of the Fetus.* Philadelphia: Saunders, 1941, Chapters X–XIII.

7

Basic Factors in the Behavioral Development of Children

THE chief significance of birth, from the developmental point of view, is that it introduces the organism to environmental conditions not previously encountered. The postnatal environment is more complex than the prenatal. In the first place, it provides adequate stimulation for all the receptors, whereas only a few of them were stimulated adequately before birth. In the second place, patterns of stimulation are more complex after than before birth. Such patterns of stimulation include the various social influences to which the infant is subjected.

Not only is the postnatal environment more complex than the prenatal, but it is of extremely greater variability. The postnatal environment differs greatly from individual to individual, and for the same individual from time to time.

Another factor associated with birth, but which is probably of greater physiological than psychological significance, is the assumption of relative organic independence. The fetus, as we have seen, receives its nourishment and oxygen and carries on excretory functions through the maternal organism. Continued survival after birth, however, is dependent upon adequate functioning of the individual's own alimentary and respiratory mechanisms and upon its own mechanism of temperature control.

Despite this transition to a more complex and variable environment than was present before birth, and despite this gain in relative organic independence, birth introduces no essentially different principles of development than were apparent earlier. The genes, cytoplasm, and cells continue their interaction, producing further structural growth and differentiation. Exercise of structures, present long before birth, is only less restricted after the individual is born. There is, as we have seen, the possibility that some conditioned responses are developed before birth. Postnatal development of behavior is dependent upon conditioning and habit formation to an increasing degree as the infant becomes older.

In the present chapter consideration will be given to investigations of the factors of maturation and exercise, conditioned responses, and learning as they apply to the development of behavior in infancy * and early childhood.

*There is little consistency in the use of the term "infancy." In recent psychological literature, however, there is a tendency to designate the first two

In this connection we shall take special cognizance of the relationship existing between these factors. We shall also consider their significance for the development of certain sensorimotor activities.

Maturation and Exercise in Early Development

Maturation has already been defined as growth resulting from an integral relationship of genes and their constantly changing surroundings, thus setting it off from growth as a result of exercise of sensorimotor structures. Exercise is a general term which covers any functioning of sensorimotor structures, whether this functioning be so-called "spontaneous" movement, response to known internal or external stimuli, or practice of some response to be learned. The reader will recall that Spalding, Cruze, Stone, and others have observed, in infrahuman organisms, the development of behavior under conditions of greatly restricted activity. It will be recalled, also, that the salamander and frog embryos studied by Carmichael developed adequate swimming responses under conditions where exercise was prevented entirely.

Much, if not all, prenatal development is, as we have seen, also independent of exercise. The earliest responses are obviously due to maturation alone. Reflexes for which stimulation is absent during the prenatal period must also result from maturation. The pupillary response is one of the clearest examples of such reflexes. As the time of birth approaches and the fetus becomes more active, there are large opportunities for exercise of certain structures, and the repertoire of reactions at birth may include many items which have developed, partly at least, as a result of exercise.

After birth it is possible to arrange experiments to determine the relative influence of maturation and exercise in the further development of the individual. Theoretically, we could isolate the infant as chickens, rats, and other animals have been isolated. Theoretically, also, we could restrict its activities as Spalding restricted the movement of birds. Practically, however, it is not possible to subject human infants to such rigid experimental procedures.

The experiments to be described here approximate, as closely as is possible with human beings, the experiments on maturation and exercise in which animals participated. They involve certain restrictions of normal activity and normal social stimulation.

Restricted activity and social stimulation

Dennis [1] subjected fraternal female twins to conditions involving restriction of social intercourse as well as of bodily activity of certain kinds. When the twins * were a month old they were placed in a special experimental room. They remained in this room until nine months of age. The infants were kept on their backs in their cribs and thus had no opportunity to practice sitting or standing. Even while being bathed, they were kept in the horizontal position as much as possible. Opportunity to reach for objects was prevented by allowing the infants no toys or other objects (except clothes, bedclothes, and crib), by placing their hands under a tightly held bib or napkin while they were eating, by tucking the bedclothes so tightly that the hands could not be withdrawn, and by failing to offer anything to them in a manner which might encourage attempts at reaching. The aim was not to prevent all activity, but, as far as possible, to remove all opportunity for practicing such specific activities as reaching for seen objects, sitting, and standing. Incidentally, of course, there was some restriction of activities other than these. In addition to such restrictions, the early months

---

years as the period of infancy. The term "neonate" is most generally applied to the child who is between the age of birth and two weeks.

* The fact that these infants were twins is of no significance for the experiment. Two non-related infants of approximately the same age could just as conveniently have been used. The mother of the twins loaned them to the experimenters for the duration of the experiment.

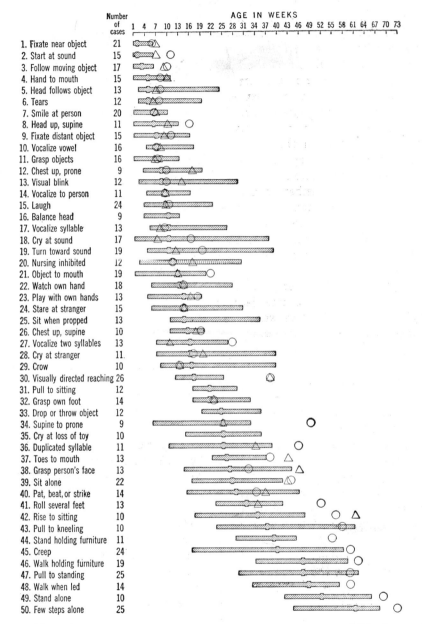

Figure 80. The Median Age and Age Range for the Appearance of Fifty Items of Infant Behavior Recorded in Forty Biographical Investigations and the Age at Which These Behavior Items Appeared in Infants Reared under Experimental Conditions of Restricted Activity and Social Stimulation (Courtesy Wayne Dennis)

of the experiment were further marked by the fact that the experimenters (and visitors) kept a straight face before the infants. For several months no smiling, frowning, or speaking occurred in their presence. The infants were not played with in any way. There was no fondling or other stimulation of the kind usually given by adults. At no time were the infants encouraged to exhibit any response. No training of any kind was given. The infants could not see each other until relatively late in the experiment when they stood in their cribs. There were no opportunities for imitation. The general purpose of the experiment was to determine whether or not development of behavior in infancy will follow its normal course if certain restrictions are placed on specific activities and if the actions of the surrounding adults are reduced to an approximate minimum.

The results of this experiment are illustrated in Figure 80. This represents data derived from forty baby-biographies [2] as well as results obtained in the above experiment. A similar comparison was made with Shirley's [3] data on motor development in twenty-five infants reared under normal conditions. Both comparisons yielded essentially similar results.

Horizontal bars indicate the normal age range for initial appearance of the activities. The median age at which each of the activities appeared is shown by the small vertical bar. The age at which the restricted infants first exhibited a response is indicated by a triangle for Del and a circle for Rey. For example, biographers of babies have reported the earliest fixation of a near object in the first week. The latest appearance of this response reported by them is at about six weeks. The median age is about two weeks. Del, one of the restricted infants, first gave this response at the seventh week. Rey, the other infant, exhibited it during the sixth week. The rest of the data are to be interpreted in a similar manner.

It is apparent from these results that there was little if any retardation of behavior during the first nine months. The infants reared under conditions of restricted activity and social stimulation exhibited the usual behavior items within, or very close to, the normal range for non-experimental infants. After nine months, however, the effects of restriction became noticeable. This was particularly true with respect to the prehensile and locomotor responses which had been especially restricted.

Despite the retarded appearance of visually directed reaching (Figure 80, item 30) the infants soon developed the response when given an opportunity to do so. A dangling ring was presented above the crib once per day for 40 days, beginning with the 245th day. Neither child reached for the ring when it was first presented, although analysis of the data in Figure 80 shows that reaching for an object should, under normal conditions, have appeared some time before the 200th day. Neither of the experimental infants reached for the ring until the 13th daily presentation, although they fixated it upon each presentation. *Their reaching was acquired as a result of self-initiated activity; no training or encouragement was given.* The infants were allowed their first opportunity to sit when they were 262 and 263 days old, respectively. Neither one was able to support itself in the sitting position. The degree of retardation for this activity is shown in Figure 80. Del sat alone by the 298th day, Rey not until the 326th day. Again, there was no special training of the infants, self-initiated activity being sufficient to develop the responses. Supporting the body weight while standing with help, a response present by at least the 270th day under normal conditions of development, did not appear in these infants when they were given their first test at 364 days. Within three days, however, both infants supported their own weight for a period of two minutes or more. Walking alone was not greatly, if at all, retarded in Rey. She walked by the 17th month. Del, however, did not walk until the 26th month.*

* In personal correspondence with the writer, Dennis has pointed out that Del, although she showed no

Motor activities which develop during the first year are thus not greatly, if at all, retarded by such social restrictions and restrictions of activity as were involved in this experiment. The normal sequence of behavioral development results partially from growth processes (maturation) and partially from the child's self-initiated activities. Dennis [4] concludes that "the infant's responses are in the main *autogenous*, meaning that he develops them of himself, not only through growth but also through his own activities."

Restrictions on motor activity somewhat like those involved in the above study are sometimes characteristic of a culture. Some groups of Hopi Indians, for example, follow the practice of binding their infants to a cradle board almost continuously for the first three months and then increasingly freeing them from the board as they grow older. An infant on the cradle board is unable to raise his body, turn around, or release his hands, which are bound to his sides. He is unwrapped only once or twice daily, to have a bath or to have soiled clothes removed. Certain groups of Hopis have, on the other hand, been influenced by white practices to give up the cradle board. Their children are as unrestricted as our own.

This disparity in the practice of different Hopi groups suggested to Dennis and Dennis [5] that it might be a good idea to compare the motor development of the restricted and unrestricted children. Their comparison was based upon various activities, but particularly walking. It showed no significant effect of the restriction incident to cradling. The babies of both groups carried objects to their mouths, reached for their toes, put their toes

in their mouths, sat, crept, and walked at about the same age. Both groups walked without assistance at approximately 15 months. This is later than the average age of walking in white children (see Chapter 10), but the retardation was alike for unrestricted as well as restricted infants. The reason for such retardation of Hopi children was not apparent.

Even when restriction is followed by retardation, as in failing to reach, sit, or stand when first tested, the infants in whom such activities have been delayed acquire an unusually rapid mastery of these responses. It will also be recalled, in this connection, that chicks prevented from pecking for several days (pp. 53–57) exhibit a faster rate of improvement than non-delayed chicks.

Thus the influence of maturation may be such as either to provide a response at the first opportunity for its occurrence or, in the event that the response is not immediately exhibited, to facilitate its acquisition.

So far we have emphasized the influence of restriction upon motor development. But what would be the effect of introducing a greater than normal amount of activity? If motor development were thereby speeded up, one could argue that activity *does* facilitate such development. Failure of the extra activity to influence development would argue for the importance of maturation.

How do different degrees of activity influence motor development?

It was in an attempt to answer this question that McGraw [6] undertook her experiment with the twins, Johnny and Jimmy. The ideal experiment would be one in which the hereditary factor were held constant. This could be accomplished by using identical twins, as in the co-twin control experiments to be considered later.* Johnny and Jimmy

___

evidence of it during the earlier part of the experiment, had apparently suffered a cortical birth injury. This may have retarded her walking. It was apparent a few years later that she had a partial paralysis of the left side (partial hemiplegia) and that her Stanford-Binet I.Q. was only 70 as compared with Rey's 107. The failure of cortical injury to have early effects in this child accords with what was said in the previous chapter about the failure of the cortex to exert much, if any, control over fetal and early infant behavior.

* The basic assumption underlying the method of co-twin control, first used by Gesell, is that where individuals are identical in inheritance and reared in a similar environment, it is probable that they will mature at a like rate. The influence of specific exercise versus absence of specific exercise, or the effect of dif-

were at first thought to be identical, especially since they appeared to have a single placenta. After the experiment was well under way, however, it became apparent that the twins were not identical. This, of course, raised questions as to whether the observed differences resulted from different heredity or from different experimental conditions. Despite this ambiguity of interpretation, McGraw's study did have some valuable outcomes.

The twins were studied from the age of twenty days until they were six years old. Throughout the earlier part of the experiment both infants were brought to the clinic seven hours daily for five days of each week. During this time Johnny, who was selected as the experimental subject, was given exercise at two-hour intervals in the performance of the various activities normal for a child of his chronological age. When he was older, training in various skills like swimming and skating was added to the program. Jimmy, acting as a control, lay in his crib behind a screen while Johnny was being exercised. Later, he was left to play with a few toys while Johnny was swimming, climbing, and skating. Jimmy was tested at certain intervals and his performance on the various activities compared with that of Johnny in order to discover the effects, if any, of the exercise or training. Moving pictures were taken during the comparisons and analyzed later with a view to discovering any differences in performance between the two infants. The behavior of Johnny and Jimmy was compared, at significant stages, with that of a group of 68 infants developing in the usual surroundings and with the average degree of "spontaneous" exercise.

There was, in general, no significant influence of exercise upon *phylogenetic* activities; that is to say, upon activities which were alike in all human infants. Such activities

ferent degrees of specific exercise, may thus be investigated in individuals of comparable ability who are developing at a comparable rate.

included the typical reflexes, grasping with body suspension, crawling, creeping, and walking. The time at which these appeared and the general patterns of movement involved were greatly similar for Johnny, Jimmy, and the large group of infants. In interpreting these results, McGraw [7] says,

The major aspects of these phyletic activities have become determined during phylogeny to such an extent as to be resistant to alteration through external influences during the development of an individual. Minor details, however, are subject to modification through exercise and use of the performance. While use of the activity will not alter the general method of progression, exercise may influence the grace with which he steps, his speed, and his mien of progression.

The results for *ontogenetic* activities (habits which the normal infant may or may not acquire) were quite different. Exercise had a considerable influence upon the development of such activities as swimming, skating, riding a tricycle, climbing, and stacking boxes. One of the most significant factors underlying differences in the ontogenetic activities of Johnny and Jimmy was Johnny's attitude toward the problems and toward the general experimental situation. Special experimental exercise apparently gave him a more cooperative attitude and greater confidence than was shown by his brother. Such attitudes transferred to the various tasks required of him. A follow-up study at six years [8] demonstrated that some of the skills acquired in the laboratory had deteriorated during the period of no practice, while others showed little if any change. There was no clear evidence that the excessive earlier exercise of Johnny as compared with Jimmy, had led to permanent attitudinal or personality differences.

McGraw points out that many activities are at first controlled by subcortical mechanisms and that there is, as the infant grows older, a gradual shift of control from lower to higher cerebral mechanisms. Exercise, she believes, has little influence upon activities until they are well represented at the higher levels. Such a view would, of course, imply that maturation is involved in the elaboration of lower cerebral functions to a greater relative degree than in the elaboration of higher ones.

Maturation in the Young of Different Species

Human beings are the slowest of all organisms to reach maximum maturity, but the level finally attained is far in excess of that exhibited by any other organisms, even including such close relatives as the higher apes. This differential maturation, and its influence upon the learning process in the same physical surroundings, is interestingly illustrated by Kellogg and Kellogg,[9] who reared a female chimpanzee infant (Gua) and their own male infant (Donald) under comparable conditions.

Their chief aim was to discover whether the chimpanzee would, as a result of its human environment, come to exhibit any essentially human characteristics. Gua was brought into the home of the investigators at the age of $7\frac{1}{2}$ months. She was two months younger than Donald. Both infants were given comparable treatment in every way, even to the point of kissing and other endearments. They were fed, dressed, punished, and spoken to in a similar manner. Both slept in similar beds and had similar playthings. During the course of the experiment, which covered a period of nine months, both infants became very much attached to each other. The ape developed many peculiarly human forms of behavior, including upright locomotion (Figure 81). Of special interest to us, in this connection, is the fact that in acquiring such

Figure 81. Gua and Donald

(From W. N. Kellogg and L. A. Kellogg, *The Ape and the Child*, New York: McGraw-Hill, 1933, facing p. 275.)

responses as skipping, cooperation, obedience, kissing for forgiveness, opening of doors, anticipation of bladder and bowel reactions, eating with a spoon, and drinking from a glass, Gua, although chronologically younger, was far superior to Donald. She was also superior in strength, localization of sounds, memory, and response to verbal stimulation such as "kiss-kiss," "come here," "shake hands," and "bad girl." At the age of twelve months she responded appropriately to twenty such verbalizations, whereas Donald, at the same age, responded to only three. The authors point out that a factor of great importance in explaining their success at "humanizing" the chimpanzee faster than her playmate was her superior learning ability. They [10] say that "What enabled the chimpanzee to eat with a spoon, drink from a glass, skip, and announce her bladder and bowel needs better than the average child of her own age was unquestionably the fact that she *learned* this behavior more rapidly. It should be clear, therefore, that, as far as Gua is concerned, an increased rate of maturation parallels to a considerable extent an increased rate of learning."

Gua at first matured much faster than Donald. Toward the end of the experimental period, however, the child's development advanced more rapidly than that of the chimpanzee. Had the experiment continued much longer, there is no doubt that Donald would have far surpassed Gua in all responses other than those dependent upon sheer strength. Even at earlier ages, despite the handicap of relative immaturity, he surpassed his companion in many activities.

Although it does not involve a chimpanzee-child comparison, the study of the female chimpanzee Viki (Figure 53) by Hayes and Hayes [11] does verify the finding that a chimpanzee reared in a human environment acquires many characteristically human responses.* Viki not only imitated many

* The attempt to humanize Viki came to a sad conclusion when, in the spring of 1954, she died of what was apparently a virus infection.

human responses (see pp. 129–130) but she also learned, through a process of training, to speak three words. This aspect of the study is considered in Chapter 12, on development of language.

The above experiments on maturation and exercise suggest that: (1) maturation is a factor which must be considered in any adequate envisagement of behavioral development in infants; (2) for the initial appearance of very specific sensorimotor activities, such as visually directed reaching, sitting alone, and standing, a certain amount of exercise is required; (3) many responses are exhibited without adult training or encouragement, seeming to depend upon self-initiated activities of the infant; (4) special training has little if any effect upon the rate of formation and nature of simple racially derived (phylogenetic) responses; (5) special training in infancy has a marked influence upon the formation and nature of individually derived (ontogenetic) responses, including attitudes of cooperation, confidence, and the like; (6) special training is effective in changing the rate of development and nature of responses only when they are controlled at higher cortical levels; and (7) the efficacy of exercise or of special training is directly proportional to the degree of maturation of the underlying mechanisms.

The Definition of Learning

We now turn our attention to the learning process, giving special consideration to conditioned responses, development of sensorimotor skills, and problem solving.

In discussing the evolution of intelligent behavior we assumed that learning involves individually acquired adaptive modifications, especially modifications which are retained. We did not draw fine distinctions. Now, as we approach the role of learning in individual development, it is necessary to examine this process more closely.

Learning is so intimately bound up with and similar to maturational and other physiological processes which play a part in individual behavior that a simple and direct definition is impossible. If one should define learning as *a trend in the direction of better adaptation,* he would be confronted immediately with the fact that maturational processes, although they develop more slowly, usually exhibit such a trend. The accuracy of chicks in striking small grains shows improvement as a function of age, or degree of maturation. We have also observed that certain aspects of fetal and infant development have a similar basis. This trend is present despite absence of opportunities to practice responses. Learning, however, is a trend in the direction of *improved adaptation as a function of specific exercise or practice.* While more accurate than the definition given above, even this is inadequate. Fatigue is a function of exercise and may even be regarded as an adaptive trend, yet it would be quite incorrect to consider it an instance of learning. The trend in fatigue is decremental and temporary. Sense organs, muscles, and glands also undergo progressive changes as a result of repeated stimulation. We say that "adaptation" occurs. But this sort of adaptation, especially since it involves restricted parts of the organism and, like fatigue, is temporary, should be excluded by a definition of learning. With these features of learning in mind, we may define the process as *a more or less permanent incremental modification of behavior which results from activity, special training, or observation.* A given learned performance, whether motor or verbal, is often referred to as a *habit.*

Conditioned Responses

Conditioned responses play an important role in the development of individual behavior, especially during infancy and early childhood. The ontogeny of many sensori-motor activities, of emotional behavior, of language, and of attitudes is explicable, at least partly, in terms of conditioned responses. We have already had occasion to discuss conditioned responses. The use of conditioned-response techniques to investigate the sensory abilities of animals was considered in earlier discussions. Some consideration was also given to the conditioning of human fetuses. We did not, however, give an adequate characterization of the conditioned response, as such, and of the phenomena associated with it. Such a characterization seems appropriate at this point, especially since much work has been done on the conditioning of infants, and since further discussions of behavioral development necessarily will involve consideration of the process of conditioning.

The procedure used in a conditioning experiment is, in general, as follows: (1) Some response is selected for conditioning — salivation, withdrawal of the hand or leg, contraction of the pupil, or the like. (2) The usual (*unconditioned*) stimulus for the response is determined. (3) A stimulus (*conditioned*) which fails to elicit the response in question is selected. (4) The conditioned and unconditioned stimuli are presented either simultaneously or close together in temporal sequence, usually with the conditioned stimulus preceding the unconditioned. One observes whether the conditioned stimulus comes to elicit the response which was formerly associated only with the unconditioned stimulus (or some modification of this response) and also whether it elicits any other responses (e.g. anticipatory) which were absent prior to conditioning. When the child consistently responds to the conditioned stimulus, we say that conditioning has occurred. The following conditioned-response experiments with children have been selected from the literature in order to illustrate typical procedures and at the same time give a rather concrete idea of the general characteristics of conditioning.

Krasnogorski [12] and Mateer [13] adapted Pavlov's method of conditioning to investigations with children. Pavlov conditioned the salivary response of dogs to such stimuli as a bell, tactile irritation, and light. The salivary reaction is normally aroused only in association with food. Pavlov collected the saliva through a fistula to the parotid gland. Krasnogorski's method with children was to observe the swallowing reactions, using these as an index of the amount of saliva secreted. Upon being offered food, the child would rid his mouth of excess saliva by swallowing. An unusual number of swallowing movements was not, at first, present to the sound of a bell. After successive presentation of bell and food for several periods, a greatly increased number of swallowing reactions appeared to the bell alone. In some of his later experiments, Krasnogorski placed a tambour over the thyroid cartilage, thus obtaining a graphic record of swallowing reactions. Krasnogorski and several other investigators also used saliometers to collect saliva. These are small cups with tubes attached. The cup fits over the salivary gland and collects the secretion. This is transmitted to the recording apparatus through a tube. Mateer's method was quite similar, in essential respects, to that of Krasnogorski. She used the swallowing reaction and anticipatory mouth-opening as the responses to be conditioned. When a bandage was pulled over the child's eyes he did not have an unusual number of swallowing reactions; nor did he open his mouth. Training consisted of placing food in the mouth as soon as the bandage was pulled over the eyes. After a while, conditioned swallowing and mouth opening, as in anticipation of the food, began to appear to the movement of the bandage alone.

Marinesco and Kreindler [14] have performed one of the most clear-cut experiments on conditioning in children. Withdrawal of the foot to a weak electric shock served as the unconditioned response. One electrode was attached to the child's abdomen and another to its foot, the arrangement being such that shock was received on the foot. A thread attached to the subject's foot and to the marker on a smoked drum served to record movements of the limb. The time in seconds, the onset and duration of a metronome (conditioned stimulus), and the onset and duration of the shock (unconditioned stimulus) were also recorded on the drum. The beating of the metronome was continuously present for 50 seconds prior to the onset of the shock, which lasted 20 seconds. Part of the record obtained in the conditioning of a child of 26 months is shown in Figure 82. Eleven successive presentations of metronome and shock were required before conditioning occurred. It will be noted that there was no response to

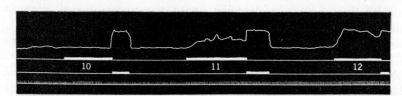

Figure 82.   Development of a Conditioned Withdrawal Response in an Infant of Twenty-Six Months

The lowest line indicates time in seconds. Above this is a line which shows the onset and duration of the electric current. The next line indicates the onset and duration of the metronome. The infant's withdrawal of its foot is represented in the uppermost line. Note that the metronome began to sound approximately 50 seconds before the onset of the shock and that it continued to sound until the shock was given. Until the 11th presentation of the metronome there was no foot withdrawal. At the 11th presentation, however, there was an anticipatory reaction, a partial reaction as though in anticipation of the shock to follow. A response similar to that which had previously appeared only to the shock was elicited by the metronome on the 12th presentation. (From G. Marinesco and A. Kreindler, "Des réflexes conditionnels: I. L'organisation des réflexes conditionnels chez l'enfant," *J. de Psychol.*, 1933, *30*, 873.)

the metronome on the tenth trial. The first response to this stimulus was exhibited on the next trial. This was an *anticipatory* movement rather than the customary reaction to the shock. Such responses frequently occur and are sometimes the only evidence of conditioning. A response like that previously elicited by the shock alone was obtained upon the twelfth presentation of the metronome. Twenty-five infants ranging in age from 25 days to $3\frac{1}{2}$ years were conditioned in this way. Some of the infants retained the responses when tested months later.

Marinesco and Kreindler's experiment, like those of Krasnogorski, was undertaken to determine whether the phenomena reported by Pavlov as characteristic of the conditioned response in dogs could be verified for human infants. Most of these phenomena were clearly verified. One such phenomenon, which is of special interest in connection with the development of many responses of infancy and early childhood, is that of *conditioned differentiation of movements*. The responses of the infants to the shock and to the metronome were at first quite diffuse, quite generalized. All four limbs moved, although shock was applied only to one. As conditioning proceeded, however, differentiation occurred and there was withdrawal of only one limb; that to which the electrode was connected. Part of a record showing this result is reproduced in Figure 83. Shock was applied to one hand.

At first there developed a generalized anticipatory response to the onset of the metronome. The illustration shows that the response of a leg gradually decreased while the response of the arm to which the electrode was attached retained its amplitude. The last presentation of the metronome elicited an anticipatory arm movement but no leg movement.

After an infant has been conditioned to some stimulus, other stimuli may also elicit the response. For example, the infant conditioned to respond to a metronome may make the same response when a buzzer is sounded or a bell rung. It may also respond to other stimuli which are in any way similar to the conditioned stimulus. We say that the various stimuli which elicit a similar response are, as far as that response is concerned, equivalent. All but one of these stimuli may be made non-effective, however, by differential conditioning. The procedure is, in general, as follows: All the stimuli which elicit the response are presented, but in a random sequence. For example, the order may be: bell, metronome, buzzer, buzzer, bell, metronome, buzzer, metronome, metronome, bell, bell, etc. The unconditioned stimulus (shock, for example) is presented *with the metronome alone*. As conditioning proceeds, the infant makes fewer and fewer responses to the stimuli not associated with the shock. Instead of a conditioned response to a group

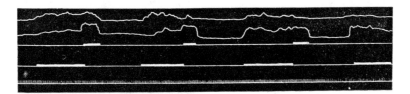

Figure 83.   A Conditioned Differential Reaction in an Infant

From bottom to top the lines represent, respectively, time in seconds, onset and duration of the sound of the metronome, onset and duration of the shock, movement of the forearm, movement of the foot. The electric shock was applied to the arm. Anticipatory responses to the metronome include movements of arms and legs, until the last presentation shown, in which case the response of the foot is almost negligible and that of the arm as pronounced as before. The infant was 21 months of age. (From G. Marinesco and A. Kreindler, "Des réflexes conditionnels: I. L'organisation des réflexes conditionnels chez l'enfant," *J. de Psychol.*, 1933, *30*, 873.)

of stimuli, we now get the reaction to the metronome alone. Let us take another example from experiments with dogs and human adults. If a given point on the skin is stimulated just prior to presentation of the unconditioned stimulus, a conditioned response to tactile stimulation will develop. Stimulation of neighboring points will, however, elicit the same response. Several tactile stimulations are, in other words, equivalent with the conditioned one. By associating the unconditioned stimulus with stimulation of a given point and not with stimulation of other points, a specific response to the conditioned point will appear. According to Pavlov such phenomena are due to *irradiation* of the effects of stimulation. Stimulation of a given point affects, to some extent, parts of the nervous system other than those directly connected with that point. Naturally, then, stimulation of any portion of the affected area may elicit a somewhat equivalent response. It is only after the generalized area has been made non-effective by conditioning of a differential nature that the specificity of a given stimulus and response is developed. Differentiation between two stimuli, such as two colors, two tones, or two intensities of light, is developed in the manner described above. One stimulus is associated with the unconditioned stimulus while the other is not. If the response comes to be elicited by only one of the stimuli, we say that the infant can differentiate between them.

Disappearance or *extinction* of a conditioned response is effected by use of the same general method as that producing non-effectiveness of stimuli in differentiation. The conditioned stimulus is presented without reinforcement from the unconditioned stimulus. With successive presentations of a metronome without shock, for example, the conditioned response becomes progressively less evident and finally disappears. This process has been designated by Pavlov as *experimental extinction*. It effects a more rapid loss of the response than will naturally occur. Very frequently, however, a response will reappear after it has been

made to disappear as a result of experimental extinction. This phenomenon, known as *spontaneous recovery*, has been observed by Marinesco and Kreindler in infants. They say that the experimentally extinguished response will frequently reappear after the infant has been allowed to rest for a few minutes.

These are only a few of the conditioning phenomena observed in Marinesco and Kreindler's study. Among others are: *external inhibition* (failure of the conditioned response to appear when an extraneous stimulus accompanies the conditioned stimulus); *trace responses* (delay in appearance of the conditioned response, after the conditioned stimulus is presented, the delay being equivalent to the lapse of time between presentation of the conditioned stimulus and the unconditioned stimulus during the conditioning trials); and *higher-order conditioning* (use of the conditioned stimulus, in place of the unconditioned stimulus, to condition the response to other stimuli).

The experiments so far cited have served to delineate the chief phenomena of conditioning and to show the similarity between conditioning in animals and in children. Other experiments carried on with newborn infants and older children have dealt with questions like the following: Are newborn infants susceptible to conditioning, and if so, what responses may be conditioned, and to what stimuli? How is susceptibility to conditioning related to age? What is the later significance of childhood conditioning?

Are newborn infants susceptible to conditioning?

Since certain fetal responses can apparently be conditioned, one might expect conditioning to be even more apparent in newborn infants. Most of the research supports this expectation. Among the responses conditioned during the first two weeks of life are sucking movements in response to a buzzer which has preceded the feeding period [15]; blinking in response to vibration of the foot, although this has previously been elicited only by a flash of light [16]; foot-withdrawal and respiratory changes to such stimuli as a tone or light after these responses have previously been elicited only by electrical stimulation [17]; and changes in general bodily activity in relation to the feeding schedule. One of these investigations, that of Wickens and Wickens,[18] warrants further consideration because of its bearing on earlier studies and because it brings out some of the difficulties involved in conditioning experiments with infants.

Wickens and Wickens used three groups, one experimental and two control. There were 12 infants aged 10 days or under in each group. The unconditioned stimulus was a shock administered to the foot in such a way as to produce withdrawal. Since the infant was in a sound-proof room with the shocking mechanism outside, there was no buzz associated with the shock. This is important because the conditioned stimulus was the muffled sound of a buzzer. No subjects withdrew to the buzzer when it was first presented. The experimental group received 12 buzz-shock stimulations per day for three days. They were then given presentations of the buzzer alone. Out of the 12 subjects in this group, 9 withdrew to the sound of the buzzer, the total number of withdrawals prior to extinction being 23. Spontaneous recovery was observed one day later, when a total of 48 responses occurred to the buzzer.

The control groups were to test two possibilities: (1) that the infants might be withdrawing to the buzzer on the test days because they were older (the response might have matured) and not as a result of conditioning; or (2) that shock alone, without pairing with the buzzer, might so modify the infant as to produce later response to the buzzer alone. The latter would be an example of what has been called "pseudoconditioning." The group used to test the maturation possibility was given stimulation with the buzzer alone on one day and then again two days later. But only one infant out of the 12 made a withdrawal reaction to the buzzer alone. Thus maturation could

not account for the withdrawals of the experimental group. The group used to test for pseudoconditioning did, however, respond very much like the experimental group. After 36 presentations of the shock alone, distributed over three days, as in the experimental group, 11 of the control infants responded to the buzzer. The total number of responses prior to extinction was 25, and 37 further responses occurred during tests of spontaneous recovery given the next day. The most likely explanation of this result is that, while being stimulated with the shock alone, these infants were learning to respond to *any sudden stimulus* or to *a change in the situation*. Although they had not previously been stimulated with the buzzer, this was like shock in being sudden. It also represented a change in the preceding conditions of relative quiet. If other stimuli than the buzzer had been used, these might also have elicited withdrawal responses. Should the above interpretation be correct, this was true conditioning, of a generalized nature, despite its failure to fit the usual conditioning paradigm.

Marquis [19] claims that, regardless of the questions raised by Wickens and Wickens concerning earlier conditioning studies, adaptation to a feeding schedule, which occurs during the first few days, is clear evidence for conditioning in neonates. A group of infants shifted from a three-hour to a four-hour feeding schedule showed a significant increase in general bodily activity as a result, especially during the last hour before the new feeding time. Marquis points out that this sort of adaptation to feeding schedules is the earliest form of acculturation: that is, the earliest "civilizing" process which the child undergoes.

Most of the conditioned reactions observed in infants are anticipatory, as in the experiment just cited. It is as if the conditioned stimulus arouses the expectation that the related condition will follow. The anticipatory nature of such reactions is still quite evident at later age levels, as in Kantrow's [20] experiment on 16 children aged from 44 to 117 days. At

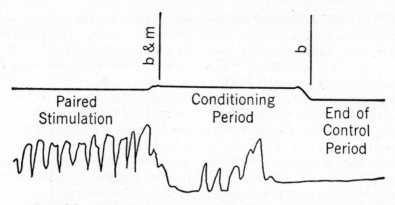

Figure 84. Polygraph Record of Conditioned Sucking in an Infant

Read from right to left. After a control period (*b*), a buzzer was presented for 5 seconds (*b* to *b* & *m*) then continued for 15 more seconds with the bottle. Anticipatory sucking during the conditioning period is the evidence for conditioning   (From R. W. Kantrow, "An Investigation of Conditioned Feeding Responses and Concomitant Adaptive Behavior in Young Infants," *University of Iowa Studies in Child Welfare*, 1937, *13*, 11.)

the end of a control period, a buzzer was sounded for 20 seconds. After five seconds of such stimulation, a nipple was placed in the baby's mouth, then both buzzer and milk continued for 15 more seconds. The sucking activity was recorded pneumatically via a chin harness attached to a polygraph. A typical record of such a conditioned reaction appears in Figure 84. It shows that, after 54 paired stimulations with buzzer and nipple, the child sucks when the buzzer comes on and before the nipple appears. The child of course continues to suck, and more vigorously and persistently, when milk is also present. From 16 to 72 paired stimulations were required before stable anticipatory sucking occurred. Successive stimulations with the buzzer alone produced experimental extinction.

Although newborn infants are susceptible to conditioning, the stability of conditioned responses increases with age. This is apparent when Kantrow's results on conditioned sucking are compared with similar experiments on the newborn.

Instrumental conditioning in children

All the researches on conditioning during infancy have dealt with what has come to be called "classical conditioning." This is con-

ditioning where, as in the classical studies of Pavlov and Bechterev, the unconditioned stimulus follows the conditioned stimulus whether or not a conditioned reaction occurs. Marinesco and Kreindler's children received a shock on the foot whether or not they withdrew it in response to the metronome (see Figure 82). Had anticipatory withdrawal allowed them to escape the shock, we would have had an instance of so-called "instrumental conditioning." This is called "instrumental" because the response is instrumental in escaping punishment, or, in certain other situations, in producing a reward.

The studies on instrumental conditioning in children have involved a food reward. Ivanov-Smolensky [21] used the apparatus illustrated in Figure 85 to condition a grasping reaction in children aged from 4 to 15 years. If the child learned to time the squeezing of the bulb in proper relation to the sounding of the bell, it obtained a small piece of chocolate. Eventually it squeezed the bulb in response to the bell even though no chocolate was released. Stable conditioning occurred in from 2 to 88 paired presentations of bell and chocolate. Light was also used as a conditioned stimulus.

Warren and Brown's [22] experiment illus-

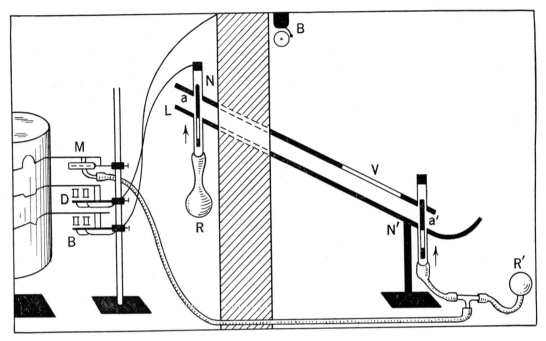

Figure 85.   Ivanov-Smolensky's Conditioning Technique

The child sits with the bulb R' in its hand. It is instructed to squeeze this bulb whenever it sees a piece of chocolate slide past the window V. If the squeeze is properly timed, the float at a' goes up so as to admit the piece of chocolate to the curved platform. The child then takes possession of it. The experimenter, in an adjoining room, releases the chocolate by squeezing the bulb R. As this bulb is squeezed, a mark is made on the revolving drum. The subject's squeezing of his bulb is also registered. A bell (or a light) is presented a few seconds before the chocolate falls. This is the conditioned stimulus. When conditioning has occurred, the response is made before the chocolate is released. (After A. G. Ivanov-Smolensky, "On the Methods of Examining the Conditioned Food Reflexes in Children and in Mental Disorders," *Brain,* 1927, *50,* 139.)

trates not only instrumental conditioning, but also what Skinner [23] has called "operant conditioning." * Their experiment is a repetition, with children, of Skinner's well-known lever-pressing experiments with rats. When an external stimulus elicits a conditioned response, as did the bell in the above experiment, Skinner speaks of "respondent" be-

* Instrumental and operant conditioning are alike in that the individual's response is instrumental in obtaining a reward or in escaping punishment. In operant conditioning, however, there is no external unconditioned stimulus, like food in the mouth or an electric shock. The behavior conditioned is "spontaneous" in the sense that it is emitted by the organism and not, as in other forms of instrumental conditioning, by some external stimulus introduced by the experimenter.

havior. In his experiments with rats, however, there was no external conditioned stimulus such as is used in the usual conditioning procedure. The behavior of pressing the lever was "emitted" by the animal, first as an aspect of exploratory activity and then, presumably, in response to internal stimuli associated with hunger. Its emission brought a small pellet of food. The food is said to "reinforce" the emitted response and, through such reinforcement, increase its rate of occurrence. The comparable experiment with children involved nine subjects between the ages of 2 and 5 years. Their playroom had a lever which delivered pellets of candy when pressed. Conditioning was evident when, upon finding his responses reinforced, the child pressed at a faster rate. In one case, for example, the child did not press the lever for several minutes. He then pressed it and received a candy pellet. After about 8 minutes he was pressing at the rate of 20 times per minute. This rate increased and then declined as the experiment continued. The child finally settled down to a rate of about 8 times per minute. The results for other children were somewhat less consistent. In this experiment, as in that involving bulb-pressing, various phenomena which occur in "classical" conditioning, such as experimental extinction and spontaneous recovery, were observed.

Conditioning as a function of age

Three investigations, using different procedures and together covering the ages from one to 19 years, suggest that susceptibility to conditioning increases during the early years, then declines. Mateer [24] used subjects ranging from one to $7\frac{1}{2}$ years. Conditioning involved anticipatory mouth-opening and swallowing such as we have already described (p. 202). The correlation between chronological age and the number of trials required for conditioning was .57. However, children between 5 and $7\frac{1}{2}$ years showed an increase in the number of requisite trials. In other words, the number of trials declined between one and 5 years, then increased. Osipova [25] conditioned the withdrawal response to shock so that it was elicited by the sound of a bell. His youngest subjects were 7 years old. Despite the differences in procedure, these children required about the same number of trials as Mateer's seven-year-olds. From 7 to 19 years there was a rather steady increase in the number of trials required to produce stable conditioning. The same was also true in an experiment by Dernowa-Yarmolenko [26] on 1000 Russian pupils ranging in age from 8 to 19 years. The subjects were asked to raise their hand when the teacher did so. Two seconds before she raised her hand, however, the teacher tapped with a pencil. Soon the subjects were exhibiting anticipatory hand-raising in response to the tap. The percentage of such responses within 10 trials was around 90 at age 8. This percentage declined with age. At the upper age level there were few such conditioned reactions.

Razran,[27] who has summarized these and other data on susceptibility to conditioning with age, attributes the reversal of susceptibility to conditioning at around age five to the appearance of processes which make the subject less willing to submit to the usual laboratory conditioning techniques. He says that *"the decrease in the speed of conditioning in older children is due not to a reversal and deceleration of an old factor but to the emergence and acceleration of a new factor, . . . the children do not become less 'able' but more 'unwilling' to be conditioned."* This "new factor" is attitudinal or central, perhaps symbolic. Razran says that *"there is no evidence for central or attitudinal control of conditioning . . . in the first year of human life, this control making its first appearance at the age of 3–5, probably coeval with the child's instrumental mastery of his verbal and conscious processes."* This does not imply, according to Razran, that the significance of conditioned processes for the development of behavior ceases in early childhood. From his point of view, symbolic and attitudinal processes are themselves derived from conditioning.

Significance of conditioning in child development

In his *Brave New World*, Aldous Huxley has the infants conditioned, by methods such as we have discussed, so that they will like those things which the leaders of the state want them to like, and dislike those things which, according to the leaders, they should for the good of the state avoid. This is of course a fictional envisagement of the view that, if you have control over the conditioning of their responses during early childhood, you can mold individuals to suit your purposes. While it is true that the likes and dislikes of children may be conditioned to particular situations, nobody acquainted with the research on conditioning would suppose that personality in general can be so molded. The experiments on conditioning of emotional reactions have been largely responsible for the view that aspects of personality are products of conditioning.

In Watson and Raynor's [28] study of conditioned fear reactions, a child was shown a rat, a rabbit, and other furry animals. Although he was nine months old, the subject had never before seen these objects. They aroused reaching and similarly positive reactions. A loud noise, however, elicited a decidedly negative reaction, a reaction clearly indicative of fear. By associating the loud noise with a white rat, Watson developed a conditioned fear, not only of the white rat, but of many other furry and otherwise similar objects (see Figure 86). The child soon cried and tried to avoid the rat, the rabbit, and other objects to which the fear had generalized. Jones [29] conditioned the galvanic skin reflex (often regarded as an index of emotional reaction) to previously neutral stimuli. His subjects were infants and preschool children. There is no doubt, even from general observation, that association of previously neutral stimuli with situations which elicit emotional reactions may give these stimuli potency to arouse the same or similar emotional reactions, as in the experiments of Watson and Jones. Conditioned-response techniques have also been used to render situations pleasant rather than fear-provoking. Such aspects of emotional development are given further consideration in Chapter 14.

The conditioning process is also a factor in the early stages of language development, which is considered in greater detail in Chapter 12. Watson [30] called attention to the fact that the association of sounds with objects is developed as a conditioned response. When a child was babbling da-da, Watson placed the nipple of a milk bottle in its mouth.

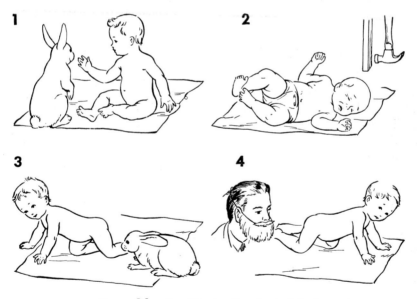

Figure 86. Conditioning Fear in an Infant

Before conditioning (1) the child makes positive (approach) reactions to the rabbit. A loud noise (2) produces startle and apparently fear. Paired association of a white rat and noise produced an avoidance response not only to the rat but also (3) to the rabbit. Finally (4) furry objects of various kinds, which were ineffective earlier, also elicit avoidance reactions. (After Watson, from G. G. Thompson, *Child Psychology*, Boston: Houghton Mifflin, 1952, p. 144.)

After a few such associations of the milk bottle with this response, the child used *da-da* as a name for the bottle and, later, in the absence of the bottle, said "*da-da*" as a means of obtaining it. As we shall observe while discussing language, the child acquires much of his early vocabulary in this way.

Whether they involve emotion, language, or other acts, conditioned responses are simple habits. This is recognized by all psychologists. There is, however, much difference of opinion concerning the claim, first made by Pavlov,[31] that *all* habits are conditioned responses. Pavlov and early Behaviorists like Watson regarded even complex habits (e.g. motor skills) as chains of conditioned responses, each response in the series providing the conditioned stimulus for the next. Recent theories of learning have been greatly influenced by such concepts, as we shall see later in this chapter. Some of them stress a much more detailed envisagement of the role of conditioning than that held by Pavlov and Watson. Others hold that while conditioning accounts for certain aspects of the learning process, or for certain kinds of learning, it does not account for all of them.

Regardless of their theoretical significance, as indicated in the above references to emotion, language, and the learning process in general, conditioned-response procedures have certain practical applications. We are already acquainted with the fact that these procedures are useful in discovering the sensory capacities of animals. They are similarly useful in research on the sensitivity of infants. Sometimes a conditioned response is the only evidence that a baby is responsive to particular forms of stimulation. In one clinical case [32] an infant made no response to sounds and was thought to be deaf. Pricking its foot produced a withdrawal reaction. After a sound had preceded the prick a few times, the sound alone produced withdrawal, thus showing that hearing was present despite failure to react to sound in other ways. By conditioned-response methods it is also possible to discover how small a difference, as

between brightnesses or tones, the infant is capable of differentiating. This application is considered in Chapter 8.

Another practical application of conditioning procedures is in the elimination of enuresis (bed-wetting). Such procedures are used here to sensitize the child to stimuli which, while they were present, were not previously effective. The stimuli in question are those associated with bladder tension. Failure to respond to these stimuli causes the child to sleep on and, in time, to void without getting up and going to the bathroom. Mowrer [33] and later users of this technique have had the child sleep on a mat wired electrically so as to short-circuit and ring a bell when voiding occurs, but without giving the child a shock. The child is told at the beginning that if the bell rings he is to turn it off and go to the bathroom to finish voiding. After a variable number of nights, depending upon the individual, waking occurs before the bell rings, and the child goes to the bathroom. It is apparent that associating the bell with bladder tensions has caused the latter to wake the child. The former response to the bell alone is now elicited by the previously ineffective bladder tensions.

We have mentioned enough theoretical and practical applications of conditioning concepts and procedures to suggest their significance for students of child development. Now, before considering theoretical aspects of the learning process, we turn our attention to investigations of learning and problem solving which, on the surface at least, are of far greater complexity than the conditioned reactions to restricted stimuli which we have so far considered.

Acquisition of Sensorimotor Skills

Many studies of sensorimotor learning in children have adopted methods comparable with those used to investigate animal intelligence. Mazes have been much in evidence. Other studies have used typically human skills like getting quoits over a peg and hitting a target. The developmental aspects of these studies concern such questions as: How does learning of sensorimotor skills in children compare with the learning of comparable skills by animals and adults? How is acquisition of skill influenced by age, by level of maturation? And is acquisition influenced by intelligence and sex?

Animals, children, and adults

Certain similarities and differences in the maze learning of rats, children, and adults were brought out in an experiment by Hicks and Carr.[34] The children and adults walked through a large maze of the same pattern as the smaller one through which the rats ran. The rats were motivated by hunger and the human subjects by such rewards as praise, blame, and pride of accomplishment. All suitably motivated subjects, when first placed in the maze, exhibited a great deal of apparently random activity characterized as trial-and-error. This involved repeated entrances into blind alleys, retracing, and other excess movements. Such ineffective activities decreased with practice, as illustrated in Figure 87. This decrease was quite similar for the three groups. Actually, however, as shown by their reports, the human subjects were utilizing symbolic processes such as counting

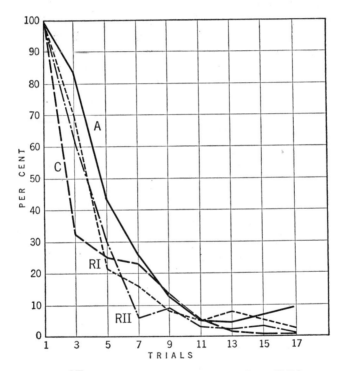

Figure 87. Curves for Maze Learning in Rats, Children, and Human Adults

The maze was a large one through which the individuals walked. Rats learned a maze which was different from, yet somewhat comparable with, that used for human subjects. *A*, adults. *C*, children. *RI* and *RII*, two groups of white rats. The curves are based upon error elimination, reduction in time, and reduction in distance traveled, these three factors being combined. Furthermore, improvement is shown as the percentage reduction of the scores manifested on the first trial. Each point in the curve, except for the first, comprises the average of two trials. (From V. C. Hicks and H. A. Carr, "Human Reactions in a Maze," *J. Anim. Behav.*, 1912, *2*, 109.)

turns, attempting to visualize the pattern, and in general trying to figure out the nature of the task before them. Such processes would probably be more elaborate in adults than in children. As the learning curves show, however, such "higher" processes had little if any effect on the efficiency of learning this task. Children did somewhat better than rats, and rats better than adults. In another comparison of children and adults, Gould and Perrin [35] found the maze learning of adults slightly superior to that of children, but this small difference might have been unreliable.

We have already (pp. 123–124) pointed out that acquisition of sensorimotor habits does not provide an adequate test of intelligence in animals ranging from rats to men. On problems requiring complex manipulations and use of symbolic processes, however, human subjects have a marked advantage over animals, and, usually, adults have an advantage over children. The adult advantage, where it exists, might result in part from maturity, but it might also be due to such factors as better motivation, better attention to the task at hand, or application of relevant previous learning.

Acquisition of sensorimotor skills in children as a function of age

Earlier discussions dealing with animals and children have shown that maturation brings increasing facility in acquisition of simple activities. Maturation underlies accuracy in pecking at grains, the swimming response in salamanders, and, with self-induced activity, the reaching, sitting, and other early motor adjustments of infants. Phylogenetic activities thus develop without specific training.

Activities peculiar to the individual *do* require practice. If they are complex, they require special training. These activities, previously referred to as ontogenetic, are our prime concern in the present discussion. We wish to know how age, or maturation, influences their acquisition.

At the early age levels it is very difficult to differentiate the respective contributions of learning and maturation to acquisition of sensorimotor skills. One must compare acquisition in trained and untrained co-twin controls or in carefully matched control and experimental groups. Only in this way can we observe whether improvement is a function of maturation, or training, or both.

It is generally recognized among child psychologists that the infant must have reached a certain level of maturation before training can become effective at all. McGraw, in her experiment with the fraternal twins Johnny and Jimmy, sometimes found that her early attempts to train Johnny in certain skills were of no avail. At a later age, however, he acquired the skills with ease. Although tricycling was introduced to Johnny at 11 months, it was not until 19 months that the long and hitherto futile practice periods began to have effect. Jimmy was not put on a tricycle until he was 22 months old, but he learned quite readily.

Co-twin control studies. McGraw,[36] using the co-twin control method, found that toilet training during the early months of infancy is futile. She used two sets of identical twins. One twin of a pair was given toilet training from an early age while the other was given no training. When the trained twin had attained a high level of success in restricting his micturation to the toilet situation, his brother was introduced to toilet training. The results, for both sets of twins, are shown in Figure 88. One will observe that, without previous toilet training, success is almost as great as with months of earlier training. This is apparent despite the differences between one set of twins and the other. McGraw feels that the rapid improvement which began in Peter Dalton at around one year and in Hugh Putney at 530 days marks the inception of cortical participation in control of micturation. At this time the children began to attend to the act, and to the result. McGraw believes that training should be postponed until there is evidence of such participation, which of course occurs

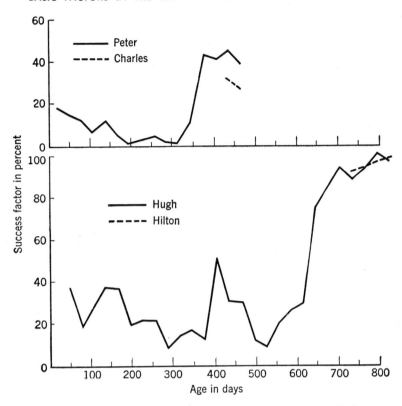

Figure 88.   Achievement Curves Indicating the Effect of Early Toilet Training

The success factor is the ratio between toilet urination and the total number of urinations during seven hours of each day. It is plotted, in per cent, against the chronological age in days. (From M. B. McGraw, "Neural Maturation as Exemplified by the Achievement of Bladder Control," *J. Pediatrics*, 1940, *16*, 84.)

at different ages, depending upon the individual child.

In Gesell and Thompson's [37] experiment on learning and maturation in identical female twins, one twin (T) was given specific daily practice in stair climbing for 6 weeks, beginning at the age of 46 weeks. The other twin (C) was used as a control. She was allowed no contact with stairs until the age of 53 weeks. Twin T did not climb the stairs when first tested at the age of 46 weeks. Her reactions to training were passive and she required assistance on each of the five steps. At the age of 50 weeks, however, she had progressed to the point where the staircase was climbed with avidity and without assistance

of any kind. At 52 weeks she was climbing the staircase in 26 seconds. When twin C was tested at the beginning of the 53d week, however, she climbed the stairs unaided, even though no practice had been given. She required 45 seconds to complete the performance. In order to see what training would do at this developmental age for the infant which had received no previous training, two weeks of practice in climbing the stairs were given. At the end of this practice period (the 55th week) Twin C climbed the stairs in 10 seconds. Gesell and Thompson report that "The climbing performance of Twin C at 55 weeks was far superior to the climbing performance of Twin T at 52 weeks, even though Twin T had been trained 7 weeks earlier and three times longer. The maturity advantage of 3 weeks of age must account for the superiority." The same twins were subjected to a similar experiment in manipulating cubes. After a period of 6 weeks during which Twin T was given specific training in cube manipulation and Twin C was given no such training, there was no significant difference in the cube-manipulating behavior of the two infants. The failure of Twin T to profit from specific training on cube manipulation is believed to be due to maturational limitations. Gesell [38] emphasized, in this connection, the point that "Training does not transcend maturation." Hilgard,[39] in a study of the same twins at a later age, found evidence that, for some of the activities studied, delayed practice resulted in greater gains than early practice.

There have also been investigations of the effectiveness of training on acquisition of sensorimotor skills at higher age levels than those already considered. In these studies matched groups have been used.

Matched groups. Hilgard [40] found that older children learn to climb up and down a ladder much faster than do younger ones. Two groups, each consisting of 8 two-year-old children, were matched in mental age, sex, and initial climbing performance. One group was then given intensive training for a period of 12 weeks. The other group received no training. The trained group, at the end of the 12 weeks, exhibited a performance much better than that of the untrained group. Only one week of training, however, equalized the performances of the two groups. These results are shown graphically in Figure 89. Cutting and buttoning activities were also tested and here again, the rate of improvement was greater for the older (control) than for the younger (experimental) group. The control group, however, did not within a week of practice reach the level of the experimental group. Maturation thus appears to be a more potent factor in certain activities than in others.

Mattson's [41] investigation of sensorimotor skill in children deals with maze learning, a skill much more complicated than those already considered. It shows, among other things, that when skills are complicated, the

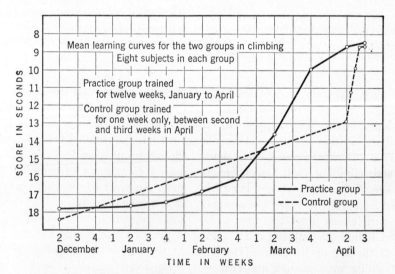

Figure 89. Effect of Maturation and Specific Training on Climbing Activity of Preschool Children

(From J. R. Hilgard, "Learning and Maturation in Preschool Children," *J. Genet. Psychol.*, 1932, *41*, 50.)

relative influence of learning, as compared with maturation, is greatly increased. Three patterns were used. In each case the child was to manipulate the maze itself so as to make a marble move between rows of pins which constituted the units of the correct path. The simplest pattern had no blinds; the intermediate, three blinds; and the complex, six blinds. Practice and control groups ranging in age from 58 to 72 months were matched for age, sex, intelligence, and initial maze performances. After four days of initial practice, the practice group continued for 26 days while the controls had no further contact with the maze.

Then a test involving 8 days of practice was given. For all three mazes, the practice groups were superior to the controls. This held for time and error scores at the end of the training period and also for retention tests 60 days later. However, the differences in favor of the practice group became larger and more reliable the more complex the maze pattern. This is shown in Table 4.

While this study was concerned primarily with the respective influence of training and maturation, over a period of 26 days, on performance of skills at different levels of complexity, other investigations have dealt with the age factor more directly. The most extensive of these, which also utilized maze learning, was that of McGinnis.[42] There were 10 boys and 10 girls in each of three age groups averaging, respectively, three, four, and five years. The problem was to take a shoe to a boy by moving the shoe-topped stylus along a grooved channel until the figure of the boy was reached. Each group received five trials five days per week for two weeks. Learning curves for time and errors are reproduced in Figure 90. These show that the older the group, the better the initial performance. The final levels of performance did not differ greatly for the three age groups. Differences which did exist were small and, in most instances, statistically unreliable. One of the most interesting outcomes of this study was the finding that 50 trials of practice produced greater *absolute* gains in the younger than in the older groups. That is, the younger children, with poorer initial performance than the older ones, showed the greater improvement in time and error scores. The younger children thus learned more than the older. But this does not mean that their learning ability was superior to that of the older children. Their greater gain resulted from the fact that the older children, being initially closer to perfection in this skill, had less to gain before achieving mastery. It is the same sort of thing which exists in sports, where the person already near the record (near the physiological limit) has less chance of gaining from practice than the person who is far below the record.

Elsewhere the writer[43] has summarized data from several other researches on age effects in children's learning. These show that acquisition of sensorimotor skills improves with age during infancy and early childhood, probably to a large extent because of increasing maturation. This, as we have seen, is also true for susceptibility to conditioning. At later age levels, as in the experiment of McGinnis, the child's acquisition of sensorimotor skills does not seem to improve with age. The older child usually starts at a higher level, which may reflect greater

Table 4. Differences in Time and Error Scores for Practice and Control Groups on Mazes of Three Degrees of Complexity (After Mattson)

Maze	Average Time	Average Errors
Simple............	2.71 ± 0.40 CR 6.73	$.19 \pm 0.07$ CR 2.65
Intermediate......	15.00 ± 1.17 CR 12.80	4.80 ± 0.584 CR 8.21
Complex.........	32.94 ± 0.30 CR 14.34	10.21 ± 1.008 CR 10.13

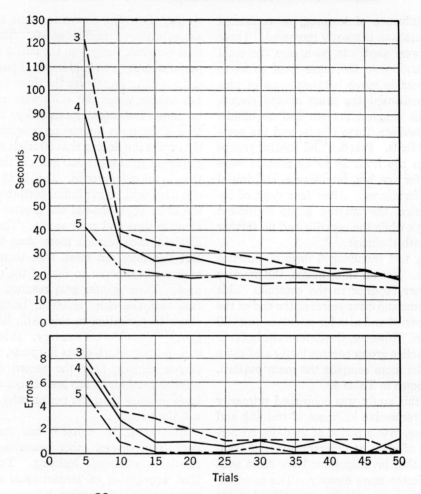

Figure 90. Curves for Maze Learning in Three Age Groups

The figures, 3, 4, and 5 refer to the average age of the groups. (From E. McGinnis, "The Acquisition and Interference of Motor-Habits in Young Children," *Genet. Psychol. Monog.*, 1929, *6*, 241, 244.)

maturity or more extensive earlier experience than the younger child, but he does not show a greater rate of improvement for equal amounts of practice than does the younger child. Experiments on learning in animals have yielded similar results. They show that there is a clear relation between age and ability to acquire motor skills, but only at early age levels. A maximum ability to acquire such skills is apparently reached early in life and then maintained until later maturity. It is interesting in this connection to note that there is no relation between

mental age and the acquisition of such skills.[44] When acquisition and use of symbolic skills is involved in the task to be learned, the story is very different. Here, as we shall see in later discussions of symbolic processes, there is a decided correlation between rate of learning and age and intelligence.

In a sense the absence of a relation between age and acquisition of sensorimotor skills parallels the phylogenetic data considered in earlier discussions. These demonstrated that the rate of acquisition of such skills does not increase as we ascend the evolutionary scale from lower to higher mammals, whereas there is at the same time a marked evolution in the facility with which symbolic processes are acquired and utilized in adjustment.

Are there sex differences in rate of acquiring sensorimotor skills?

In the maze-learning experiments of Mattson and McGinnis which we have already discussed, there were comparable groups of boys and girls. The data from these experiments have been analyzed in the attempt to discover possible sex differences in rate of acquisition. Mattson found the acquisition curves for boys and girls to be almost identical. This was true for both time and error scores. In the experiment by McGinnis, the boys were initially ahead of the girls, who soon equaled their skill. The girls thus showed greater absolute gains than the boys. As in the case of age comparisons, however, this may mean that the boys, being initially nearer to the limit of skill, had less chance than the girls to make a large gain. In a study by Batalla,[45] in which 58 boys and 50 girls averaging 12 years of age learned to walk through a foot maze, the boys gave a better performance than the girls. This was true both initially and at the end. Here, however, there was a clear motivational difference. The boys are reported to have been much more interested in the task than were the girls. These studies, and their outcomes, are representative of several others reviewed elsewhere.[46] They show no clear evidence of a superiority of either sex in the learning of such motor skills as traversing a maze, throwing balls at a target, and mirror drawing.

Sensorimotor learning and problem solving

Sensorimotor learning in children, as well as in animals and adults, is characterized by elimination of errors and fixation of correct responses, by restriction of excess movement, by reduction in the amount of energy expended, by decreasing expenditure of time per trial, and by increasingly greater integration of correct responses. As the learning curves which we have reproduced will show, this is a more or less gradual process. It appears that the skill is built up step by step. It does not suddenly emerge. All of this suggests that activity which is initially random is gradually channelized. This has often been characterized as trial-and-error learning to distinguish it from learning where sudden solutions occur.

It has been claimed by Köhler[47] and others, that the trial-and-error nature of the learning behavior described above is an artifact; in other words, that it is forced upon the individual because of the nature of the learning situation. It is claimed that, if all significant aspects of the situation to be learned are simultaneously present in the field of perception, the individual may perceive relations between important aspects and use *insight* rather than random, or trial-and-error, behavior in achieving a solution. We have already, it will be recalled, discussed this point as it relates to animal learning (see pp. 125–127). Situations similar to those used by Köhler with apes have been presented to children with a view to determining whether sudden learning, or *insight*, is exhibited by them. These situations are very different, in certain respects, from those involved where skills like buttoning a dress, hitting a target, climbing a ladder, skating, or swimming are acquired. In the case of such sensorimotor skills, observation of all of the significant aspects, observation of a skilled performance, and even intensive thought could hardly be expected to produce skill. Significant aspects might become apparent in these ways, and one might, as a result, reduce the randomness of his approach, but practice could alone produce skilled performance. In the case of problems to be considered now, where such a process as insight can conceivably effect a solution, what the individual learns is not so much a skill as perception of a relationship or a principle, application of which brings solution. It often happens that the only immediate goal of human learning is discovery of some such principle.

Problem Solving in Early Childhood

Problem solving in infants was studied by Richardson,[48] who required her subjects to obtain a lure by pulling on the appropriate string of two to three arranged in a pattern, or by turning the short arm of a lever the proper number of degrees. The subjects of these experiments were 10 boys and 6 girls between the ages of 28 and 52 weeks. They were tested at monthly intervals; thus any improvement with increasing age could be attributed to maturation and also to previous experience with the strings and levers. As the children became older, they responded more directly to a string or a lever as a means of achieving the goal. The degree of *perceptive attitude* or *insight* was therefore said to improve as a function of age.

Some of the experiments on problem solving in children involve situations like those used by Köhler with chimpanzees. These are instrumentation problems where, in order to reach a lure, the child must make effective use of sticks or other potential implements. The most comprehensive of these studies is that of Alpert[49] on 44 nursery-school children. These were confronted with problem situations like the following: An object was suspended from the ceiling. This could be obtained by placing a nearby block underneath and standing upon it. An attractive toy was placed too far from bars of the pen to be reached with the hand. A stick was lying within the pen. Solution was achieved by poking the stick through the bars and pulling in the toy. In another situation, the toy was placed at a greater distance from the bars and two halves of a fishing rod were lying within the pen. If the two halves were fitted together in an appropriate manner, the joined stick would be of sufficient length to bridge the gap between child and toy.

The data of such experiments do not very readily lend themselves to quantitative treatment because, after a period of what appears to be trial-and-error activity, there is seemingly a sudden solution. On succeeding trials there is no further improvement. If learning curves were derived for the quantitative aspects of the behavior, there would be indicated a large time and error score for the initial trial, but succeeding trials would require a minimum of time and would involve no errors. The characteristics of learning in situations such as the above are indicated in a description of the subject's behavior. Alpert gives the following description of the attempts of a girl 38 months old to solve the two-stick problem described above:

First exposure — Subject examined one of the sticks and tried to reach objective with it over the top of pen; examined the other stick and used it in the same way, repeating, "I can't" over and over; tried out the stick between the bars, over the top of the pen, finally striking it viciously against the floor; complained bitterly, and tried again to reach as before, stretching and straining; tried to climb out and whined, "I can't." Experimenter terminated exposure to avoid fatigue.

Second exposure — Subject reached for objective as above and in 10 seconds said, "Look, I can't," but continued her efforts; fitted sticks up against bars of pen, banged them together, etc. Subject tried to reach objective with her hand through the spaces, to force her way out, to shake the pen, etc.; said, "Dolly does not want me to get him."

Third exposure — As above, complaining intermittently and finally giving up.

Fourth exposure — Subject stretched for objective over top of pen, striking out angrily with stick, complaining and asking Experimenter to move object closer. Subject said, "Let's try big stick on little one," picked up the other stick, examined ends carefully and succeeded in fitting them, with a shout of "Bang!" Subject angled for objective, reached it exultantly, and repeated stunt several times.

If success marks the termination of each trial, as in maze, puzzle box, and similar problems, then all of the above description refers to the first trial. There is usually no further failure, the child putting the sticks together and then pulling in the doll immediately. Alpert characterizes the behavior which precedes solution of the problem as *exploration and elimination*. True *random* responses are, she believes, present only under conditions where the child is emotionally upset, owing to failure in reaching the objective. *Chance* is believed to be a factor involved in the getting of *insight* only when it throws the various elements of a situation into constellations of such a nature as to make *insight* easier of attainment.

Next to Alpert's, the most extensive investigation of instrumentation in children is that of Matheson,[50] which involved 28 subjects between the ages of two and $4\frac{1}{2}$ years. Some of the problems were quite different from those already discussed. One of these was to get a lure by lowering a basket. This could be lowered only by unhooking a ring. Another was to stack boxes in order to reach an otherwise inaccessible lure. Still another involved crossed strings, only one of which was attached to the lure. Solution of these problems was far from easy for the children. It was only rarely that a child achieved a solution by merely looking the situation over. A common response was manipulating the instrument and pointing or reaching toward the lure. This was characterized by Matheson as trial-and-error activity. The most interesting outcome of her study is perhaps the evidence which it gives of a correlation between solution of such problems and age and intelligence; something which, it will be recalled, was not evident in acquisition of sensorimotor skills. Two-year-olds solved none of the problems. They were solved by 62 per cent of the four-year-olds. The correlation between solution and age was .46 ± .10; that between solution and mental age, .422 ± .107. Although these correlations are not high, they are at least suggestive of a relationship in problem solving which does not exist in sensorimotor learning.

A positive relationship between age and learning is also clearly apparent in problems where the child, in order to reach a solution, must combine separate earlier experiences. Maier[51] used a swastika-shaped apparatus through which the child walked. There were four possible goal booths, one at the end of each pathway, and any one of them could be reached from the others. The child's *first experience* involved exploration, which enabled him to observe how the booths were connected. He made his exit through one of the booths. His *second experience* comprised entrance into another booth from outside the apparatus. Here he found a toy house which, when a penny was dropped into it, played a tune. Then he was taken to a third booth, different from the other two. He was told to go to the booth where the tune had been played. If he did so without error he would have to utilize what he had learned about the general layout and about the position of the goal booth. He would, as Maier says, have to put "two and two together." The test was repeatedly given, but with a different entrance and goal booth from test to test. Since there were three alternatives at each test, only one of which was correct, chance accuracy would approximate 33 per cent. The age range of Maier's subjects was from 42 to 112 months. In five successive age groups, involving from four to twelve children each, the accuracy scores in per cent were approximately 32, 44, 59, 73, and 83. The lowest age group had an average age of four years. All children of this group failed to reach the criterion of learning. The next age group, averaging about five years, did not do much better than one would expect from chance. It was not until an average age of about six years was reached, that accuracy far exceeded chance expectancy. Maier concluded that the ability to combine experiences as required by his test is not achieved by the average child until the age of six. Scores increased with mental age, but better than chance accuracy was not achieved by children with a mental age below six years.

Harter's [52] experiment on problem solving with and without overt trial and error is of especial interest here because it provides a comparison of the performances of 75 children and 40 adults and also because it again shows a decided relationship between level of performance and age and intelligence. The apparatus, illustrated in Figure 91, comprises a grooved path along which the red peg R is to be moved to the red hole in the center. In moving it there, the subject must somehow circumvent the yellow and green pegs (Y and G), which block the path. He may do this by moving the obstructing pegs into the side grooves (say 2 and 3) or by placing R in a side groove until he moves them out of the way. By studying the situation beforehand, the subject may achieve an errorless solution. An overt trial-and-error solution involves trying to lift the pegs, which cannot be removed, and sliding them in ways which are inadequate or which involve manipulation in excess of that required.

Errorless solutions of problems like that described did not occur in children below the age of five years, but, from three to six years, successively fewer inadequate moves were made. The correlation between chronological age and the fewest number of moves

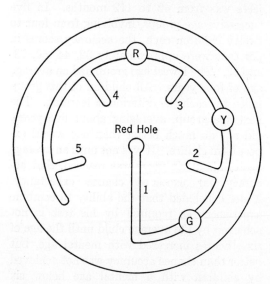

Figure 91. Obstacle Peg Test Used to Study Problem Solving in Children and Adults

The peg R is to be slid around to *Red Hole* with as few moves as possible. One solution is to move Y into 3 and G into 2 before moving R. (From G. L. Harter, "Overt Trial and Error in the Problem Solving of Pre-School Children," *J. Genet. Psychol.*, 1930, *38*, 362.)

required in solving such problems ranged from .54 ± .08 to .73 ± .06. The comparable correlations for mental age ranged from .49 ± .09 to .57 ± .08. Adults not only had many more errorless solutions than children, but also took much less time.

The double-alternation problem, with which we are already familiar (pp. 144–146), has also been used to compare learning at various age levels from infancy to adulthood. One will recall that the subject is required to make turns in the order *right, right, left, left,* or the reverse, after emerging from the central alley of a temporal maze (Figure 61, p. 145). There are no differential sensory cues to aid in solution. In order to solve this problem the individual must observe that, after making two right turns, the appropriate further response is to make two left turns. Gellermann's [53] subjects were 38 children, ranging in age from 3 to 13 years, and 25 college students. A large temporal maze with alleys sufficiently large for an adult to walk through them was built. No information was given concerning the nature of the problem. Unless they guessed it, the subjects even did not know that they were to solve a problem. Each subject was invited to enter the apparatus and to keep moving while in it. Whenever an incorrect response was made, a door blocked further progress. The subject was thus forced to go back and make the correct turn. As soon as he had made the correct moves and reached the exit the individual was greeted with "all right," "out." No other words were spoken. No questions were answered until solution had been achieved. The subject was readmitted to the apparatus after completion of each trial. This was continued until three correct trials in succession had been completed. For children the sequence of turns was *rrll* while for adults it was *rrllrrll*. After the criterion of learning had been attained, each individual, without any warning, was required to give a series of *rrll* turns which was twice the length of that involved in training. In conclusion, the subject was asked: "What did you think of it [the problem]?" "How did you learn that [the solution]?"

Adults mastered the problem in an average of 6.2 trials, while the children required an average of 15.4 trials. The range of trials required for learning was one to 16 for adults and 4 to 37 for children. The average number of errors per subject was 16 for adults and 30 for children. Average errors per trial showed a similar difference for the two groups. The correlation (ρ) between chronological age and trials to learn was .02 ± .14 for adults and .28 ± .11 for children. For the entire group of subjects it was .35 ± .08. Two children (3 and 4 years old) failed to master the problem. Beyond the age of 4 years there was at successive age levels a gradual decrease in the number of trials required for learning. For adults there was a correlation of .58 between intelligence score and trials to learn. The correlation between accuracy and intelligence was similarly high. No correlations between intelligence and learning were calculated for children.

Two five-year-olds failed to extend the series by the tenth and twelfth extended trials, respectively. The three six-year-old children exhibited perfect extension of the series on the third trial. All subjects above 7 years of age were successful on the second extended trial.

The verbal responses of subjects who solved the problem indicate that they eventually achieved a generalization comparable with "twice to the right and twice to the left." An idea of the type of verbalization during and after learning is given in the following samples of children's responses.

Ten-year-old requiring fourteen trials to learn: "First I thought all the walls would close in, and you were going to test my nerve or something like that. Then I found the doors were open, and I kept on walking. I thought there was something to it, because sometimes the doors were closed. After awhile I found you must go around each place twice."

Twelve-year-old requiring twenty-two trials to learn: *During learning:* "What's this?" "Can you watch me through that?" "Boy! I was scared when that first door closed behind me. I tried to go back through that door, but it didn't work." "Is this what I am supposed to do? Am I supposed to walk around in here?" *After learning:* "It's a lot of walking. First I didn't know what to do. I thought the doors opened by electricity in a certain way — twice around to the right of it, and twice around to the left of it. Then the last time you made me do it double." In response to the question, "How did you learn it?" he said, "When I finally decided to get the knack of it I took four or five trials, and told by which doors were closed which way I should go."

The responses of the children and adults in this experiment were quite superior to those of infrahuman animals.

Another method of investigating double alternation is to use a double-box apparatus in which the reward is found, for example, two times in the right box, two times in the left, two times in the right, then two more times in the left. This sort of apparatus was used by Hunter and Bartlett [54] to study learning in 31 children aged from 2 to over 6 years. Children below the third year did not solve the problem of opening the boxes in a *rrllrrll* sequence. Out of eight three-year-olds, only two learned the sequence. An average of 20 trials was required. All of the eleven four-year-olds achieved the solution. The average number of trials was 16.9. Five-year-olds averaged 11 and six-year-olds 6.5 trials. Every child who learned the problem could continue the series beyond the original eight responses. A five-year-old was the youngest child to verbalize the problem, that is, to make some such statement as "two times and two times." The correlation (ρ) between chronological age and trials to learn was .86 ± .32. Between mental age and trials to learn, the correlation was .81 ± .04. One will observe that these correlations are much higher than those obtained by Gellermann with the temporal maze.

Our discussion of learning in children has carried us by stages from conditioning, to sensorimotor learning at different levels of complexity, and finally to problem solving where insight and, at the higher levels, putting-two-and-two together and generalizing a principle, have been involved. We have gone, in other words, to the level of complexity where solution tends to be implicit and to involve increasingly complex symbolic processes, sometimes with verbal formulation of a principle. At this level we have entered the area of thought processes, including the reasoning process.

Tests of reasoning at higher age levels are predominantly verbal. These are discussed in the chapter on symbolic processes, which also deals with such related processes as recall, imagination, generalization, and concept formation. Some of these topics recur in later discussions of language and intelligence.

Some Basic Factors in Learning

Without launching upon a detailed discussion of learning theories, which are at present concerned primarily with the simpler learning processes observed in animals like the rat, we shall here consider certain principles that are directly relevant to habit formation in children. These principles are important in human as well as in animal learning, and they have an important place in modern theoretical concepts, but their application in human learning often has peculiarly human aspects. Take, for example, the principle that learning requires motivation. This is as true for rats as for children, but whereas the rat can be motivated only by such physiological drives as hunger, thirst, and sex, children are especially motivated by such things as intrinsic interests and desire for recognition. The chief theoretical concepts to be considered here are those involving motivation, reinforcement, and repetition.

Motivation

There is no more firmly established principle than that which, although variously stated in different theories, gives emphasis to the importance of motivation. Even those who, like Tolman,[55] argue for *latent learning* and a difference between *learning* and *performance*, have failed to produce convincing evidence that motivation is unimportant.

The concept of latent learning is based upon the observation that rats placed in a maze without hunger, or with hunger but without a food reward, and who show no reduction of time and errors under such conditions, later learn the maze quickly and in relatively few trials. It appears that they were learning something even though they did not show it when unrewarded. Perhaps they were acquiring information, although this was not evident (utilized) in early performance.* This issue is raised here for two reasons: (1) to emphasize the point that a seemingly unrewarded learning could be rewarded by factors not manipulated by the experimenter, and (2) to introduce discussion of a somewhat comparable study done with children.

Those who refuse to accept the view that a non-hungry or non-food-rewarded rat is unmotivated, stress such possibilities as the following: it may be satisfying an activity drive or an exploratory drive, or it may be rewarded by getting out of the maze eventually and being returned to its cage. Non-manipulated motivations may be extremely significant in seemingly unmotivated human learning. The child may be competing with himself, trying to better his earlier performance. He may be competing with others, with or without recognizing that he is doing so. He may enjoy what he is doing, such as trying to solve a puzzle or an arithmetical problem, even though no other incentive conditions such as praise, blame, or grades are involved. Because of the possibility of such hidden motives, nobody has yet been able to prove conclusively that any learning is completely unmotivated. On the other hand, many researches on animals, children, and adults show a positive relation between motivating conditions and the efficiency of learning. These researches range all the way from

* For a critical review of this literature see Munn.[56]

conditioned responses, through sensorimotor skills, to symbolic learning.

An experiment with children which was patterned after the latent learning experiments with rats is that of Abel [57] in which she used boys between the ages of 9 and 10 years. These learned a finger relief maze (1) without any but intrinsic rewards, (2) with verbal rewards (praise), or (3) with material rewards (money). In one of these studies Abel utilized no reward (other than the sort designated as intrinsic) until relatively late in training. This was to parallel Tolman's no-reward-reward group, which was given no reward at first, then later rewarded. As might have been predicted, the monetary and verbal rewards were more effective than intrinsic rewards alone. In the final stages of learning, the monetary reward was significantly more effective than the verbal reward. The most effective of all rewards was the promise of twenty-five cents to be received at mastery. This was quite effective even though some children failed to master the maze and hence received nothing.

The latent learning study with children failed to disclose anything like that found for rats. There was a rather steady improvement without the manipulated rewards, then a somewhat faster rate of improvement after other rewards were introduced, but the improvement was not marked and it was not maintained. The error curve rose again so that, near the end of training, there were no consistent differences between the performances of those rewarded throughout and those rewarded later. Failure to obtain anything resembling the results with rats suggests that good intrinsic movitation was there throughout the experiment. Finishing the task could mean that a child would get out and play sooner, that he would please the experimenter, that he would enhance his self-regard, or that he would receive recognition.

Jones [58] studied the effect upon sensorimotor learning of signaling cues having different preference values for his subjects. It was thought that the subject's preference for a particular signal (such as a light or tone) might facilitate mastery of a punch-board maze pattern. There was no such facilitation, hence the suggestion that "sugar coating" does not necessarily facilitate learning. Using a similar task, Grace [59] found that the personality of the child was a more significant variable than the type of approval associated with correct performance.

Other researches on the role of motivation in learning by children have been done in classrooms with school subjects like arithmetic. [60] In general, these demonstrate the positive effect of such incentives as praise versus reproof, rivalry, knowledge of results, and recognition in the form of having one's name put on the board and having a star or some other citation for good performance.

The social-recognition type of motivation is cultural in origin and it grows with age and experience. Where studies like the above show only small advantages of the motivation manipulated by the investigator, as they often do, this may be because there are already strong incentives at work in the classroom, such as curiosity, self-rivalry, and desire to please parents or teachers.

Reinforcement

All organisms have needs. Some of these are inborn and physiological, like the need for food and the need to escape injury. Others are acquired. Acquired needs are especially prevalent in human beings. Among these are the need for affection, and, especially in our culture, the need for social recognition. There are also needs peculiar to the individual, as the need to add to one's collection or to further one's education. It is well known that organisms activated by needs tend to continue those activities which satisfy their needs and to discontinue those which prove ineffective or frustrating. This observation underlies the various theories of *effect* [61] with which psychologists have attempted to explain, at least in part, how learning occurs. The concept of *reinforcement*, which provides the core of Hull's [62] learning theory, is a modern version of the principle of effect.

Instead of stressing the pleasant or unpleasant effects of an activity, or its agreeableness or annoyingness, as earlier psychologists did, Hull stresses its effectiveness in reducing a need, or in reducing or terminating tensions associated with presence of the need. A hungry organism, for example, can be assumed to have tensions which only food will reduce, or alleviate. The child who seeks recognition has tensions which can be reduced only when it gets attention from others. When motivated by such needs, or the associated tensions, an organism usually does something. It becomes increasingly active, it may explore, or it may, at the human level, do things calculated to satisfy its needs. The school child craving affection, for example, may bring flowers, cake, or some other gift to the teacher. What we have to keep in mind, then, are *needs*, the *acts motivated by them*, and the *consequences of these acts;* that is, their effectiveness in alleviating, or as Hull would say, reducing needs. Reinforcement, as Hull conceives of it, is not need-reduction itself but the strengthening of stimulus-response associations which results from need-reduction.

Primary reinforcement. Primary need-reduction (and primary reinforcement) results when some need is reduced by what might be regarded as its natural alleviator. Hunger, for example, is directly alleviated by food. A need for affection is most directly and naturally alleviated by fondling, hugging, or kissing. Responses associated with such needs are presumably more or less random at first. Hull [63] says that "In case one of these random responses, or a sequence of them, results in the reduction of a need dominant at the time, there follows as an indirect effect, what is known as reinforcement." This is Hull's concept of primary reinforcement. It is said to increase the tendency for stimulating conditions which produce need-reducing behavior to elicit such behavior in the future. Thus the hungry child presses a lever or squeezes a bulb (see pp. 206–207) and, as a result, gets food. Since this behavior is instrumental in getting food, and thus reducing the need, there is an increment to the tendency for the child to press the lever or squeeze the bulb under similar circumstances in the future.

Secondary reinforcement. Secondary reinforcement is assumed to operate in the same way as primary reinforcement, even though the need-reducers are different. Hull [64] says that

Careful observation and experiment reveal, particularly with the higher organisms, large numbers of situations in which learning occurs with no associated primary need reduction. When these cases are carefully studied it is found that the reinforcing agent is a situation or event involving a stimulus aggregate or compound which has been closely and consistently associated with the need reduction. Such a situation is called a secondary reinforcing agent, and the strengthening of the receptor-effector connections is known as secondary reinforcement. This principle is of immense importance in the behavior of the higher species.

The well-known token-reward experiment [65] on chimpanzees may be taken as one illustration of secondary need-reduction. The chimpanzees at first operated the "chimp-o-mat" for food rewards. Later they were given poker chips in association with food rewards — a white chip with one grape, a blue chip with two grapes, and so on. Finally animals worked for poker chips alone. These could later be exchanged for food. The investigator concluded that the poker chips, through their association with food, had become "secondary or surrogate rewards." In conditioning experiments with rats [66] it was demonstrated that a click associated with lever-pressing, and with a pellet of food, later acquired reinforcing properties of its own. It could, to a certain extent, be used as a substitute for food. When the child who craves affection comes to get satisfaction out of kind words, now unaccompanied by fondling or the like, we have a somewhat comparable example of secondary need-reduction.

Although there are theories of learning

which discount the role of reinforcement, attributing apparent reinforcement to other factors, these theories are not widely accepted and there is little experimental evidence to support them. On the other hand, many researches on motivation in learning and on the effects of delaying reinforcement, which retards learning, lend strong support to reinforcement theories.

Repetition

Although motivation and reinforcement are significant factors in learning, it is usually necessary to arouse and reinforce a response repeatedly. This is true except in those instances where learning occurs in one trial. Such learning is usually simple, like learning not to put one's finger on a hot object, or like learning to fear dogs after being barked at loudly and frighteningly. Some have pointed out that intensity of motivation and great vividness in the stimulating circumstances are conducive to such rapid learning.

The role of repetition in learning is stressed in the so-called "law of exercise." As expressed by Thorndike [67] this law says that "Any response to a situation will, other things being equal, be more strongly connected with the situation in proportion to the number of times it has been connected with that situation and to the average vigor and duration of the connections." By "the average vigor" of the connections, Thorndike is implying that the associations between stimulus and response must be reinforced. At least it is apparent, from many researches on the role of repetition, that repetition as such is of little or no consequence. What is important is that the stimulating situation, the response elicited by it, and the associated reinforcement be repeated in close temporal contiguity. Under these conditions reinforced responses become more firmly fixed; unreinforced responses are gradually eliminated. This is especially true in so-called trial-and-error learning where skills like the maze habit are gradually developed.

The response reinforced from one trial to the next does not, however, need to be identical with the preceding one. Sometimes there is a sequence in which successive responses are increasingly adaptive. Take, for example, Skinner's [68] experiments on pigeons. A hungry pigeon pecks at various objects around it. When it pecks one of these objects, say a stick, food becomes accessible. Very soon the pigeon pecks at the stick and nowhere else. Each time it pecks at this object a food drawer opens and grains of corn are available. From this point on, the habit may be narrowed so that, as in the following classroom experiment by Hilgard,[69] the pigeon pecks only at a white spot on a black card.

The hungry pigeon is in the cage with the spotted cardboard at the back. The stick the pigeon previously learned to peck is not in the cage. The experimenter feeds the pigeon briefly. Now the pigeon becomes very active, moving about the cage restlessly. When the pigeon is facing toward the card, the reward is introduced. Now the pigeon tends to return near to the place where it was rewarded. The experimenter waits until it turns toward the card and perhaps takes a step toward it. Then he presents the reward again. The rewarding of all approach responses leads the pigeon before long to stand before the card.

The pigeon is active, occasionally looking over toward the source of food. Now near the card, it may peck at the lower right-hand corner. This pecking is rewarded, and the pigeon returns again, perhaps pecking the same place. This time the pecking is not rewarded. Presently the pigeon begins to peck at different places on the card. Such varied pecking is rewarded. Finally the pigeon pecks the white spot. From this time on, only the pecking of the spot is rewarded. The pigeon soon regularly pecks the spot, and only the spot. The whole learning process has taken less than five minutes.

We see that repetition here is not of exactly the same stimulus-response association. What is reinforced is always a peck, but in a narrowing context until it is oriented toward the desired stimulus.

In some of Skinner's experiments a click, once associated with food, could be used in place of food. All that was then necessary was to present this secondary reinforcement every time the animal's behavior approximated that desired by the experimenter. This produced an even closer association of a response and reinforcement than could occur when the subject had to stop to eat. When such secondary rewards are used, their effectiveness eventually decreases unless primary reinforcement is occasionally associated with them. Secondary reinforcement is relevant to what we have elsewhere called higher-order conditioning (p. 204.)

The role of repeated reinforcement is especially evident in conditioned-response and trial-and-error learning. In problem solving, where the solution is often symbolic and may appear suddenly, it is difficult to assess the role played by reinforcement. Motivation is important in such learning, and so presumably is reinforcement, but the latter is by no means apparent. In many instances one would have to assume that it is implicit — such as satisfaction with recognized symbolic progress toward a solution. Repetition is sometimes of obvious importance in such learning and at other times not evident at all. Acquiring information, as from books or teachers, is even more difficult to envisage in terms which serve to account for conditioning and trial-and-error learning.

Some theorists assume that when we have a thorough understanding of the simpler forms of learning, we shall be able to extend the principles which apply there so as to embrace learning at higher levels of complexity, including the symbolic.[70] Others assume that there are different kinds of learning and that the principles which account for one kind will not necessarily account for other kinds.[71]

It is too early to predict the eventual outcome of learning theory. Only future research will determine whether all learning is reducible to such principles as we have mentioned or whether these are applicable only to conditioning and to trial-and-error learning, where they are certainly of very great importance.

Summary and Conclusions

Basic factors in the behavioral development of infants have been discussed. We have shown that, while maturation and exercise are integrally related in the early development of behavior, it is possible to arrange experiments which show their separate contributions. The influence of maturation as such is apparently greatest for early activities, especially those of phylogenetic origin. But even activities of individual origin cannot be developed until a certain degree of functional maturity has been attained. Specific exercise has little influence upon the development of many relatively simple phylogenetically derived activities, while it is, of course, essential for the development of all activities of ontogenetic derivation. The ability of a child to profit from special training is limited by its level of maturity.

Our discussion of the learning process dealt with conditioned responses, sensorimotor skills, and problem solving. Learning was defined as a more or less permanent incremental modification of behavior which results from activity, special training, or observation. Conditioned responses are readily developed in infants, and their characteristics are like those observed in animals. There is some indication that, with increasing age, the susceptibility to laboratory conditioning is weakened. It has been suggested that attitudes and symbolic processes of various kinds, themselves the result of conditioning, are responsible for this. They apparently decrease the willingness of the individual to submit to laboratory techniques. In the everyday conditions of life, on the other hand, these factors may actually facilitate the conditioning process. This process is especially important in development of emotional attitudes and early language responses.

Sensorimotor learning is seemingly a trial-and-error process in which inadequate responses are eliminated and adequate ones fixated. Development of simple sensorimotor skills in early childhood is greatly influenced by maturation. Some of these skills develop without special training. Maturation and self-initiated activity are alone necessary. At higher age levels, and especially with skills of greater complexity, training becomes relatively more important than further maturation, although the level of maturation is always a limiting influence upon what can be achieved by training. Beyond the early age levels, where increasing maturation is so important, there is a negligible correlation between rate of learning and chronological age. Older children tend to have higher initial sensorimotor skill than younger ones, perhaps due to maturation and earlier relevant experience, but they do not show a faster rate of acquisition. This may be due to the fact that they are closer to the physiological limit and thus have less to gain from further training. There is no clear evidence of sex differences in learning of sensorimotor skills.

Infants and preschool children have solved various instrumentation problems like those used with monkeys and chimpanzees. Insight is rare at the lower age levels, but it becomes more evident as a function of age, possibly because of the accumulation of relevant past experience. In solution of problems requiring discernment and use of a principle, children below the age of three years are usually unsuccessful. The frequency of successful solutions increases with age. There is also a fairly high positive correlation between success in problem solving and mental age. Verbal formulation of a principle, such as the *right, right, left, left,* principle of the double-alternation problem, also becomes increasingly prevalent as a function of age.

Without launching into a detailed discussion of learning theory, we have emphasized the importance of motivation, reinforcement, and repetition, especially in conditioning and in the acquisition of sensorimotor skills. It is doubtful whether learning ever occurs without some form of motivation. Human motivation is often intrinsic, like the desire to improve one's performance, to please others, or to obtain social recognition.

Reinforcement is the strengthening of stimulus-response associations which results from need-reduction. Primary reinforcement comes from reduction of a need by directly relevant, or natural, reducers. Thus primary reinforcement in the case of hunger motivation comes from food. Secondary reinforcement comes from substitute rewards, from those which, because they were associated with primary reinforcement, have acquired reinforcing properties of their own. Thus a click associated with food may be used, within limits, as a substitute for a food reward. Similarly, children motivated by the desire for affection may be rewarded by kind words which were once associated with primary reinforcement in the form of fondling and other pleasurable stimulation of the body. Repetition is important in learning only when it involves reinforcement. It is repeated reinforcement which brings about an increase in the strength of conditioning and which develops sensorimotor skill. The role of motivation, reinforcement, and repetition in problem solving and related symbolic activities is not clearly discernible. Whether the reinforcement principle can be extended to embrace them, or whether some other principle of explanation is required, remains for further research to disclose.

REFERENCES

1. Dennis, W., and M. G. Dennis, "The Effect of Restricted Practice upon the Reaching, Sitting, and Standing of Two Infants," *J. Genet. Psychol.*, 1935, *47*, 17–32.
2. Dennis, W., "A Bibliography of Baby Biographies," *Child Development*, 1936, *7*, 71–73.
3. Shirley, M. M., *The First Two Years:* Vol. I *Postural and Locomotor Development.* Minneapolis: University of Minnesota Press, 1931.
4. Dennis, W., personal correspondence.

5. Dennis, W., "The Effect of Cradling Practices upon the Onset of Walking in Hopi Children," *J. Genet. Psychol.*, 1940, *56*, 77–86.

6. McGraw, M. B., *Growth: A Study of Johnny and Jimmy.* New York: Appleton-Century, 1935.

7. *Ibid.*, p. 119.

8. McGraw, M. B., "Later Development of Children Specially Trained during Infancy," *Child Development*, 1939, *10*, 1–19.

9. Kellogg, W. N., and L. A. Kellogg, *The Ape and the Child.* New York: McGraw-Hill, 1933.

10. *Ibid.*, p. 319.

11. Hayes, K. J., and C. Hayes, "Imitation in a Home-Raised Chimpanzee," *J. Comp. Psychol.*, 1952, *45*, 450–459. Also see C. Hayes, *The Ape in our House.* New York: Harper, 1951.

12. Krasnogorski, N., "Ueber die Bedingungsreflexe im Kindesalter," *Jahrh. fur Kinderhk.*, 1909, *19*, 1–24.

13. Mateer, F., *Child Behavior.* Boston: Badger, 1918.

14. Marinesco, G., and A. Kreindler, "Des réflexes conditionnels: I. L'organisation des réflexes conditionnels chez l'enfant," *J. de Psychol.*, 1933, *30*, 855–886.

15. Marquis, D. P., "Can Conditioned Responses be Established in the Newborn Infant?" *J. Genet. Psychol.*, 1931, *39*, 479–492.

16. Wenger, M. A., "An Investigation of Conditioned Responses in Human Infants," *Univ. Iowa Stud. Child Welfare*, 1936, *12*, No. 1, 7–90.

17. *Ibid.*

18. Wickens, D. D., and C. Wickens, "A Study of Conditioning in the Neonate," *J. Exper. Psychol.*, 1940, *25*, 94–102.

19. Marquis, D. P., "Learning in the Neonate: the Modification of Behavior under the Feeding Schedules," *J. Exper. Psychol.*, 1941, *29*, 263–282.

20. Kantrow, R. W., "An Investigation of Conditioned Feeding Responses and Concomitant Adaptive Behavior," *Univ. Iowa Stud. Child Welfare*, 1937, *13*, No. 3.

21. Ivanov-Smolensky, A. G., "On the Methods of Examining the Conditioned Food Reflexes in Children and in Mental Disorder," *Brain*, 1927, *50*, 138–141.

22. Warren, A. B., and R. H. Brown, "Conditioned Operant Response Phenomena in Children," *J. Gen. Psychol.*, 1943, *28*, 181–207.

23. Skinner, B. F., *The Behavior of Organisms.* New York: D. Appleton-Century, 1938.

24. Mateer, F., *Child Behavior.* Boston: Badger, 1918.

25. Osipova, V. N., "The Speed of Formation of Association Reflexes in Children of School Age," *Nov. Refl. Fiziol. Nerv. Sist.*, 1926, *2*, 218–234. (See G. H. S. Razran, "Conditioned Responses in Children," *Arch. Psychol.*, New York, 1933, 148.

26. Dernowa-Yarmolenko, A. A., "The Fundamentals of a Method of Investigating the Function of the Nervous System as Revealed in Overt Behavior," *J. Genet. Psychol.*, 1933, *42*, 319–338.

27. Razran, G. H. S., "Conditioned Responses: An Experimental Study and a Theoretical Analysis," *Arch. Psychol.*, New York, 1935, 191; quotation from pp. 117–118.

28. Watson, J. B., and R. Raynor, "Conditioned Emotional Reactions," *J. Exper. Psychol.*, 1920, *3*, 1–4. Also see J. Watson, *Psychological Care of Infant and Child.* New York, Norton, 1928.

29. Jones, H. E., "The Retention of Conditioned Emotional Reactions in Infancy." *J. Genet. Psychol.*, 1930, *37*, 485–498.

30. Watson, J. B., *Behaviorism.* New York: Norton, 1930.

31. Pavlov, I. P., *Conditioned Reflexes.* London: Oxford University Press, 1927, p. 395.

32. Aldrich, C. A., "A New Test for Hearing in the Newborn, the Conditioned Reflex," *Am. J. Dis. Children*, 1928, *35*, 36–37.

33. Mowrer, O. H., and W. M. Mowrer, "Enuresis — A Method for its Study and Treatment," *Am. J. Orthopsychiat.*, 1938, *8*, 436–459. See also S. Smith, *The Psychological Origin and Treatment of Enuresis.* Washington: University of Washington, 1948.

34. Hicks, V. C., and H. A. Carr, "Human Reactions in a Maze," *J. Anim. Behav.*, 1912, *2*, 98–125.

35. Gould, M. C., and F. A. C. Perrin, "A Comparison of Factors Involved in the Maze Learning of Human Adults and Children," *J. Exper. Psychol.*, 1916, *1*, 122–154.

36. McGraw, M. B., "Neural Maturation as Exemplified by the Achievement of Bladder Control," *J. Pediatrics.*, 1940, *16*, 580–590.

37. Gesell, A., and H. Thompson, "Learning and Growth in Identical Infant Twins: An Experi-

mental Study by the Method of Co-Twin Control," *Genet. Psychol. Monog.*, 1929, *6*, 1–124.

38. Gesell, A., *An Atlas of Infant Behavior.* New Haven: Yale University Press, 1934.

39. Hilgard, J. R., "The Effect of Early and Delayed Practice on Memory and Motor Performances Studied by the Method of Co-Twin Control," *Genet. Psychol. Monog.*, 1933, *14*, 493–567.

40. Hilgard, J. R., "Learning and Maturation in Preschool Children," *J. Genet. Psychol.*, 1932, *41*, 36–56.

41. Mattson, M. L., "The Relation Between the Complexity of the Habit to be Acquired and the Form of the Learning Curve in Young Children," *Genet. Psychol. Monog.*, 1933, *13*, 299–398.

42. McGinnis, E., "The Acquisition and Interference of Motor-Habits in Young Children," *Genet. Psychol. Monog.*, 1929, *6*, 209–311.

43. Munn, N. L., "Learning in Children," chapter 7 in L. Carmichael (ed.), *Manual of Child Psychology* (2d ed.). New York: Wiley, 1954.

44. See the studies by Mattson (citation 41) and McGinnis (citation 42). These data are also summarized in Munn (citation 43).

45. Batalla, M. B., "The Maze Behavior of Children as an Example of Summative Learning," *J. Genet. Psychol.*, 1943, *63*, 199–211.

46. See Munn, *op. cit.*, pp. 395–397.

47. Köhler, W., *The Mentality of Apes.* New York: Harcourt, Brace, 1925.

48. Richardson, H. M., "The Growth of Adaptive Behavior in Infants: An Experimental Study of Seven Age Levels," *Genet. Psychol. Monog.*, 1932, *12*, 195–359; "The Adaptive Behavior of Infants in the Utilization of the Lever as a Tool: A Developmental and Experimental Study," *J. Genet. Psychol.*, 1934, *44*, 352–377.

49. Alpert, A., "The Solving of Problem-Situations by Pre-School Children: An Analysis," *Teach. Coll. Contrib. Educ.*, 1928, No. 323.

50. Matheson, E., "A Study of Problem Solving Behavior in Preschool Children," *Child Development*, 1931, *2*, 242–262.

51. Maier, N. R. F., "Reasoning in Children," *J. Comp. Psychol.*, 1936, *21*, 357–366.

52. Harter, G. L., "Overt Trial and Error in the Problem Solving of Pre-School Children," *J. Genet. Psychol.*, 1930, *38*, 361–372.

53. Gellermann, L. W., "The Double Alternation Problem. II. The Behavior of Children and Human Adults in a Double Alternation Temporal Maze," *J. Genet. Psychol.*, 1931, *39*, 197–226. Quotation from page 207.

54. Hunter, W. S., and S. C. Bartlett, "Double Alternation Behavior in Young Children," *J. Exper. Psychol.*, 1948, *38*, 558–567.

55. Tolman, E. C., *Purposive Behavior in Animals and Men.* New York: D. Appleton-Century, 1932.

56. Munn, N. L., *Handbook of Psychological Research on the Rat.* Boston: Houghton Mifflin, 1950, pp. 316–319, 401–407.

57. Abel, L. B., "The Effects of Shift in Motivation upon the Learning of a Sensori-Motor Task," *Arch. Psychol.*, 1936, *29*, No. 205.

58. Jones, H. E., "The Laws of Emphasis and Effect in Children's Learning," *Psych. Bull.*, 1934, *31*, 597–598; "Trial and Error Learning with Differential Cues," *J. Exper. Psychol.*, 1945, *35*, 31–44.

59. Grace, G. L., "The Relation of Personality Characteristics and Response to Verbal-Approval in a Learning Task," *Genet. Psychol. Monog.*, 1948, *37*, 73–103.

60. See especially E. B. Hurlock, "The Value of Praise and Reproof as Incentives for Children," *Arch. Psychol.*, 1924, *11*, No. 71; "The Evaluation of Certain Incentives Used in School Work," *J. Educ. Psychol.*, 1925, *16*, 145–149. These and other studies are considered in N. L. Munn, "The Psychology of Learning and Its Classroom Application," *Peabody J. Educ.*, 1942, *19*, 257–265.

61. See especially E. L. Thorndike's *Animal Intelligence.* New York: Macmillan, 1911, p. 244; and his *Human Learning*, New York: D. Appleton-Century, 1931, p. 46.

62. Hull, C. L., *Principles of Behavior.* New York: Appleton-Century-Crofts, 1943.

63. *Ibid.*, p. 386.

64. *Ibid.*, p. 387.

65. Wolfe, J. B., "The Effectiveness of Token-Rewards for Chimpanzees," *Comp. Psychol. Monog.*, 1936, *12*, No. 5.

66. Skinner, B. F., *The Behavior of Organisms.* New York: D. Appleton-Century, 1938. See especially pp. 81–83.

67. Thorndike, E. L., *Animal Intelligence.* New York: Macmillan, 1911, p. 244.

68. Skinner, B. F., *Science and Human Behavior.* New York: Macmillan, 1953.

69. Hilgard, E. R., *Introduction to Psychology.* New York: Harcourt, Brace, 1953, p. 223.
70. See especially C. L. Hull, *op. cit.;* and his *A Behavior System,* New Haven: Yale University Press, 1952.
71. Tolman, E. C., "There Is More Than One Kind of Learning," *Psych. Rev.,* 1949, *56,* 144–155; and G. K. Yacorzynski, "The Postulation of Two Different but Functionally Related Mechanisms in Adaptive Behavior," *J. Gen. Psychol.,* 1949, *41,* 111–123.

SUGGESTIONS FOR FURTHER READING

Barker, R. G., J. S. Kounin, and H. F. Wright, *Child Behavior and Development.* New York: McGraw-Hill, 1943, Chapters V (Wenger) and XIII (Gesell and Thompson).

Dennis, W., *Readings in Child Psychology.* New York: Prentice-Hall, 1951, Chapter I, readings 5 (Wickens and Wickens), 6 (Dennis); Chapter III, reading 1 (Dennis and Dennis); Chapter IV, readings 1 (Hilgard), 2 (McGraw), and 4 (McGraw).

Hilgard, E. R., *Theories of Learning.* New York: Appleton-Century-Crofts, 1948.

Hilgard, E. R., and D. G. Marquis, *Conditioning and Learning.* New York: D. Appleton-Century, 1940.

Hull, C. L., *Principles of Behavior.* New York: Appleton-Century-Crofts, 1943. See especially Chapters VI and VII.

Hull, C. L., *A Behavior System.* New Haven: Yale University Press, 1952. See the discussions of reinforcement.

Kuhlen, R. G., and G. G. Thompson, *Psychological Studies of Human Development.* New York: Appleton-Century-Crofts, 1952, readings 2 (Gesell and Thompson) and 11 (Maier).

McGraw, M. B., *The Neuromuscular Maturation of the Human Infant.* New York: Columbia University Press, 1943.

Munn, N. L., *Handbook of Psychological Research on the Rat.* Boston: Houghton Mifflin, 1950, Chapter 9.

Munn, N. L., "Learning in Children," Chapter 7 in L. Carmichael (ed.), *Manual of Child Psychology* (2d ed.). New York: Wiley, 1954.

Osgood, C. E., *Method and Theory in Experimental Psychology.* New York: Oxford University Press, 1953, Chapter 9.

Skinner, B. F., *Science and Human Behavior.* New York: Macmillan, 1953, Chapters IV and V.

Smith, F. V., *The Explanation of Human Behavior.* London: Constable, 1951, Part III.

Tolman, E. C., *Purposive Behavior in Animals and Men.* New York: D. Appleton-Century, 1932.

Tolman, E. C., "There Is More Than One Kind of Learning," *Psychol. Rev.,* 1949, *56,* 144–155.

8

Development of Sensory Processes

THE postnatal development of sensorimotor functions has been subjected to a large amount of research which, for purposes of convenience in discussion, we can consider under three major headings: sensory processes, spatially coordinated behavior, and motor functions. Our aim in this and the following two chapters is to present and integrate the results of this research in such a manner as to reveal significant trends. There is no attempt to mention every research. Emphasis is given to those researches which, taking cognizance of the weaknesses of earlier studies, have presented the most comprehensive and reliable data.

Sensory, perceptual, and motor processes are at all times interrelated and interdependent to a high degree. It should be more or less obvious, on the basis of previous discussions, that our only information about sensory development in early life is mediated by motor processes. Until the infant exhibits overt responses of a differential nature, there is no way of knowing the status of its sensory abilities. Also, adequate development of motor processes depends upon sensory functions. In responding to and in manipulating objects, the infant acquires information about them. He learns of their spatial characteristics. Any discussion of sensory and motor processes which failed to take cognizance of

their interrelated and interdependent development would therefore entail much artificiality. As indicated in the introductory chapter of this book, it is impossible, except theoretically, to consider at the same moment every interrelated aspect of behavioral development, desirable as this type of consideration undoubtedly is. In the present instance we shall be forced to concentrate on sensory development at one moment, and on motor development at another. We shall not, however, fail to observe interrelationships wherever such are apparent.

In the present chapter we trace the development of sensory processes, as such, from the point at which we left them in the late fetus. It will be recalled that sensory mechanisms develop gradually during the embryonic and fetal stages and that all of them are presumably ready to function to some extent by the time of birth. Reactions to tactual stimulation applied to the face are present by the late embryonic or early fetal period. The reflexogenous zone spreads from the facial region, and by the fourth or fifth month has reached to the extremities. During the late fetal period there are responses to loud sounds, and as we have seen, these have been conditioned to tactual vibration of the mother's abdomen. It is also possible that the static sense is activated before birth, by the movements of the mother and by those of the fetus itself. It is doubtful, however, whether any of the other senses are adequately stimulated prior to birth. There is of course no light to stimulate the eyes. But responses to light are possible in the late fetal period, as shown by the reactions of fetal (prematurely delivered) infants to visual stimuli. Since the temperature of the amnionic fluid is constant, there could hardly be any temperature sensitivity before birth. There is, by the same token, little if any possibility that the gustatory, olfactory, and organic senses could be activated during the prenatal period.

Methods of Studying Sensitivity in Infants

Since the infant can tell us nothing of what it experiences, if anything, our approach to

the investigation of its sensitivity must be like that used with animals. But the infant's helplessness imposes still another handicap. Unlike the animal, which can be trained to respond to stimuli in discrimination boxes, the infant lies helpless in its crib. At the early stages it can neither sit up nor reach. This means that we must to a great extent rely upon direct observation. We must present and vary stimuli, observing what the infant does. Differential activity in response to differences in stimulation is what we look for.

The stabilimeter-polygraph, illustrated in Figure 92, has been widely used to record differential activity levels in response to differences in stimulation of various kinds. Differences in the frequency and pattern of sucking may reveal taste and temperature sensitivity. Eye movements in response to visual stimuli may tell us something about the in-

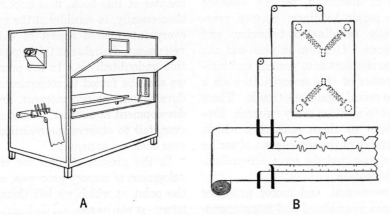

Figure 92.   The Stabilimeter-Polygraph and Experimental Observation Cabinet

The experimental cabinet, A, isolates the infant from the rest of the room and renders possible a careful control of stimulation. Temperature is regulated by means of a thermostat. The *stabilimeter* is a platform, shown within the cabinet, which rests upon ball bearings and "wobbles" whenever the infant moves. The movements of the stabilimeter are recorded automatically upon a roll of paper moving at a constant speed. The recording apparatus shown outside of the cabinet and in B is a Renshaw-Weiss *polygraph*. As indicated in B, movements of the stabilimeter platform are transmitted, by means of string-and-pulley mechanisms, to two pens of the polygraph. A marker records time via another pen. The remaining pen is operated by the experimenter to indicate presentation of stimulating conditions. Fluctuations of the polygraph pens indicate the magnitude and temporal relations of stabilimeter movements. They do not, however, indicate the precise nature of an infant's responses. (Drawing from J. F. Dashiell, *Fundamentals of General Psychology*, 3d ed., Boston: Houghton Mifflin Company, 1949, p. 68. It is based upon descriptions by Weiss and Pratt, Nelson, and Sun.)

fant's visual sensitivity. If, for example, he fixates one color significantly longer than he fixates another, and does so regardless of their position, we know that color differentiation is present. In some instances the investigator has looked for physiological signs of differentiation. Differences in respiration, and even in the pulsations of the fontanelle (which is the membranous space at the junction of the cranial bones) have been taken as indicative of differential sensitivity. As the infant becomes older, we may discern a great deal from manual responses, such as reaching and pointing. Several studies of visual sensitivity have utilized such responses.

Although direct methods such as we have mentioned are widely used to study infant sensitivity, conditioned-response procedures are also used. These can show whether the child is sensitive to particular stimuli, they can reveal thresholds of sensitivity, and they can provide evidence of differential sensitivity, such, for example, as discrimination of two tones.

With older children it is possible to use various discrimination techniques. Their verbal reports may also be taken as evidence of sensitivity. But the latter are often ambiguous. It is not always possible to tell whether the apparent improvement in sensitivity is real or whether it comes from an improved vocabulary. This is especially true when color naming is taken as an index of color sensitivity.

Olfactory and Gustatory Processes

Olfaction

Although there have been several researches on olfaction in infants, very little is known concerning the status of this process at birth or concerning its further development. The most extensive studies have been those of Pratt, Nelson, and Sun and of Disher. Pratt, Nelson, and Sun [1] observed responses of newborn infants to valerian, acetic acid, oil of cloves, and ammonia. A puff of air served

as a control stimulus. Either the air or a vaporized odor was pumped into the infant's nostrils. Movements of a stabilimeter (Figure 92) containing the infant were recorded, and the activity before presentation of the stimuli was compared with the activity after presentation. Movements of the extremities as well as sucking reactions were also noted. The age of the forty-eight subjects ranged from birth to twenty-one days. In all, 378 tests were given. Only 48 per cent of the total stimulations elicited activity. Of the general activity to the various stimuli, 59 per cent was to ammonia, 32 per cent to acetic acid, 5 per cent to valerian, 3 per cent to oil of cloves, and one per cent to air. It will be noted that those odors which possess a marked tactile-irritating quality were the only ones which elicited a high incidence of activity. It is thus doubtful whether olfactory sensitivity was responsible for the reactions. There was no significant change in the incidence of activity as a function of age. Pratt, Nelson, and Sun point out that, to adults, ammonia appeared stronger than acetic acid, yet the *intensity* of an infant's reactions was about equal for the two stimuli. They thus conclude that "the newborn infant does not react to stimuli in the same way as do adults."

Disher [2] used seven olfactory stimuli — violet, asafoetida, sassafras, citronella, turpentine, pyradine, and lemon. These stimuli were presented and responses to them recorded in a manner comparable with that of Pratt, Nelson, and Sun. Puffs of air served as controls. Ninety-one infants aged from three hours to ten days were used. All odors elicited a greater percentage of activity than did puffs of air. There was, however, no clear change in the percentage of activity to the odors as the infants became older. Differential activity to odor intensity was noted. The greater the intensity of an odor, the higher the percentage of activity elicited by it.

There have been several incidental observations of the reactions of infants to gustatory stimulation. However, Canestrini [3] conducted the first carefully controlled experimental study. He observed differential pulsations of the fontanelle and differential abdominal respiratory movements to various gustatory stimuli. Sucking movements were also systematically observed. Thirty-five infants from one to fourteen days of age were subjected to stimulation with sweet, sour, salt, and bitter substances as well as with cow's and mother's milk. Each solution was warmed to body temperature before application to an infant's mouth. All solutions elicited changes in fontanelle and abdominal responses. Sweet appeared to have a calming influence. Restlessness and cessation of sucking were elicited by salt. Responses to sour and bitter could be distinguished from those to sweet and salt. Mother's and cow's milk elicited similar responses. Age differences in gustatory sensitivity are not reported by Canestrini.

The investigations of Pratt, Nelson, and Sun and of Jensen offer the most clear-cut evidence of differential taste sensitivity in early infancy. Using the stabilimeter-polygraph technique, Pratt, Nelson, and Sun [4] recorded general activity elicited by sugar, salt, quinine, citric acid, and distilled water, all at room temperature. Sucking, facial movements, and other specific reactions were also noted. The method of stimulation was that of inserting into the infant's mouth an applicator which had been dipped into a solution. The applicator was inserted after a light touch at a corner of the infant's lips had caused it to open its mouth. Twenty-eight infants ranging in age from birth to fifteen days were used. Eighty-five per cent of the presentations were followed by activity changes. General bodily movement comprised a relatively small proportion of all of the activity noted. The most frequent response to sugar was sucking. This response increased in frequency from birth until the time at which the child left the hospital. The most frequent response to salt was likewise sucking. There was an increase in the percentage of such sucking reactions from the time of birth until the fifth to the seventh

day, after which there was a decrease. To quinine the infants responded 29 per cent of the time by various facial grimaces and 22 per cent of the time by sucking. The facial responses increased with age, while the sucking responses decreased. Citric acid elicited a very low per cent of sucking reactions. Mouth movements other than sucking followed 32 per cent of the stimulations. The frequency of grimaces increased with age, while mouth movements decreased. Of the responses aroused by water, 32 per cent were sucking, 26 per cent grimaces, and 16 per cent reactions of the whole body. Sucking and other mouth responses to water were most prevalent during the first day and decreased with age, whereas grimaces had their lowest frequency in the first day and their highest at the age of eleven to twenty-five days. When the percentage of specific responses to water is subtracted from the percentage of specific responses to other substances, one finds little evidence of differential taste sensitivity. The authors of the experiment say that,

If the taste reaction is the product of two stimuli, liquid plus a taste, then the component due to taste alone may be calculated by subtracting the percentage of the specific movements to water, 15 per cent, from the percentage of specific movements to the taste stimuli. This gives citric acid 10 per cent, quinine 9 per cent, sugar 4 per cent, and salt 2 per cent. This would support the conclusion that taste is not well developed at birth for the strength of stimuli used in these experiments.

It is obvious from the results of this experiment, however, that, whatever the sensory basis may be, there is an increasingly positive response to sugar and an increasingly negative response to quinine and citric acid as the infant becomes older. Pratt, Nelson, and Sun indicate that for taste, as for smell, the reactions of infants and adults differ. A citric acid solution which appeared weak to adults elicited a strong infant response, and a quinine solution to which adults reacted strongly called forth a relatively weak response from infants.

Sucking is ordinarily a poor index of taste sensitivity in infants for the reason that it may be elicited by any stimulation of the mouth region. Jensen,[5] however, has developed a technique for obtaining objective records of differential sucking activity to gustatory and thermal differences. A specially constructed feeding bottle attached pneumatically to the pen of a polygraph was used to measure the nature of sucking activity in response to solutions containing glucose, acid, salt, milk, and combinations of these substances. An example of the differential response obtained with this method is presented in Figure 93. Differential sucking activity was obtained for milk and salt solution, salt and acid-milk solutions, milk and salt-and-glucose solutions, and solutions having different percentages of salt. These differential responses were obtained with solutions at the same temperature. Of course, it is possible that *tactual* rather than gustatory factors formed the basis of differentiation. There were no differential responses to milk and acid milk, which would probably have similar tactile qualities. However, differential responses were not elicited by milk versus glucose and milk versus sterile water, combinations with markedly different tactual qualities. Differential responses were made to salt solutions differing by only .025 per cent. If a tactual difference existed here, it must have been extremely small. The author does not give any information concerning changes in differential responses to the gustatory stimuli as a function of age.

It should be apparent, from the data discussed above, that we have little evidence concerning the growth of olfactory and gustatory sensitivity in infants. Much more research will need to be done before definite statements can be made.

Vision

Because of its extreme importance for human adjustment, the development of vision has been extensively studied. Some investigations, like those of Gesell, Ilg, and Bullis [6] on the development of vision in infant and child, fall more appropriately into a chapter on visual space perception than into one concerned with elementary sensory processes. This is because the emphasis in these investigations is upon visual fixation, eye movements, and bodily attitudes in response to stationary or moving objects. Other investigations, like those of Senden [7] on the responses of congenitally blind people who have recovered their sight, and of Riesen [8] on chimpanzees reared in darkness and then tested for visual response, are also more appropriately considered from the standpoint of visual perception than of vision *per se*. They are concerned more with the ontogenesis of visual meanings than with elementary sensitivity. Certain aspects of these studies are, however, relevant to what we shall say about pattern vision and size constancy later in the present chapter. Other aspects have especial relevance to localizing behavior, which is considered in the following chapter.

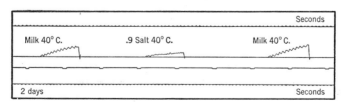

Figure 93. Differential Sucking Reactions of a Two-Day-Old Infant to a .900 Salt Solution and to Milk of the Same Temperature

The bottom and top lines indicate time in seconds. The line just below the sucking record represents time in 10-second intervals. (From K. Jensen, "Differential Reactions to Taste and Temperature Stimuli in Newborn Infants," *Genet. Psychol. Monog.*, 1932, *12*, 423.)

A general question raised by these studies is whether vision is present from birth or whether it develops later, on the basis of maturation or learning, or both. There is general agreement that some vision is present from birth and that older individuals who have been deprived of visual experience do not have to learn to see. The chimpanzees of Riesen's study all made reflex responses to light from the start, and the verbal reports of the previously blind patients showed that they were able to see. What was lacking, however, was a proper interpretation and utilization of what was seen.

We begin our discussion of the elementary aspects of vision by considering researches on responses to intensity and wave-length differences in light.

Responses to light intensity

The newborn child responds to light in several ways. There is the pupillary reflex which, as Guernsey [9] has shown, becomes more rapid to a given intensity of light as the infant becomes older. Sherman and Sherman [10] demonstrated that, between the time of birth and 360 hours, weaker intensities of light are sufficient to elicit this reflex. The sudden onset of a light of sufficient intensity also elicits something resembling a "startle response." This has been called an "eye-neck" reflex. Changes in respiration and in circulatory responses are also produced by stimulation with light.[11]

The most extensive investigations of infant responses to intensities of illumination have utilized some form of the stabilimeter-polygraph technique. Weiss [12] demonstrated differences in motility to minimal, dim, and moderate illumination. In general, the babies became less active as the intensity of illumination increased from minimal to moderate. Redfield [13] verified the observation that light has an inhibitory influence over infant activity. His subjects ranged in age from birth to nine days. These infants, through their differential reactions to the same intensity of light after different periods in the dark, dem-

onstrated the presence of dark adaptation. Using much stronger light than previous investigators, Irwin [14] again found a reduction in bodily activity as a function of increased illumination. His subjects were infants under ten days of age.

These studies of general motility show that newborn infants are sensitive to light. They also demonstrate that newborn babies differentiate intensities of illumination and that they dark-adapt. None of the studies has disclosed how small a difference in intensity is discriminable at this age level.

Responses to wave length

Color vision in early infancy has interested many students of child development. They have asked whether the newborn infant possesses color vision or whether ability to distinguish between colored and colorless objects or between objects of different color develops as the infant grows older.

It is of course important, in this connection, to recognize the fact that stimuli may differ in wave length (the physical correlate of color) and in intensity (the physical correlate of brightness). As we have already shown (p. 92), color-blind organisms exhibit differential responses to colored lights upon the basis of brightness differences. When the colors are equated in brightness for the eye of the color-blind organism, all differential responses cease. In work with animals and human infants, investigators have usually equated the brightness of the color for the adult human eye. This may not be an adequate control of brightness, the reason being that the brightness value of a color may differ for the human and the infrahuman eye and the adult and infant eye.

The brightness value of colored lights. Peiper [15] claims that the relative brightness values of spectral colors are alike for human infants and adults. His subjects were four premature infants. When stimulated with light the infants threw back their heads. This (eye-neck) reflex was shown to depend upon the intensity of light; thus Peiper conceived the idea of using it as an indication of the brightness value of lights of different hue. Blue light, for example, was flashed on and the response noted. The intensity of blue light was then gradually decreased until the reflex no longer appeared. The same procedure was followed with green, yellow, and red light. Peiper found that when the infants were light-adapted, the yellow light had the greatest brightness value. This result was found for all four infants. Peiper reported that when the infants were dark-adapted the yellow light decreased in brightness value, while the blue light increased (Purkinje phenomenon). All of his results indicated that the yellow *did* show a marked drop in brightness value under conditions of dark adaptation. However, the results for blue were not clearly in accordance with his claims. Only two of Peiper's infants were subjected to both light and dark adaptation. One of these subjects showed a slight, but probably insignificant, increase in sensitivity to blue under conditions of dark adaptation. The other infant exhibited no change in sensitivity to blue. Both infants, when subjected to dark adaptation, exhibited increased sensitivity to red. The increase was, however, small and probably insignificant. The shift in brightness value of yellow was the only clear-cut change produced in Peiper's infants by dark as compared with light adaptation. This change occurs in adults. However, the increase in brightness value of blue under conditions of dark adaptation is also present in adults. As indicated above, only one of Peiper's subjects showed such a change in sensitivity to blue, and this change was very small. Peiper, on the basis of these somewhat equivocal results, claimed that he had demonstrated the Purkinje phenomenon in newborn infants. This phenomenon is not present in color-blind individuals and is regarded as evidence that both rods and cones are functioning. Hence Peiper concluded that the brightness value of colors is alike for infants and adults.

Smith's [16] conclusions do not agree with those of Peiper. She failed to obtain evidence of the Purkinje phenomenon, and she claims that newborn boys are totally color blind and newborn girls are partially color blind. However, her conclusions are not justified by her data. She used twenty infants — ten boys and ten girls — ranging in age from seven to nine days. Her method of testing for the brightness value of blue, green, and red (she did not use yellow) was briefly as follows: The infant was subjected to dark adaptation for five minutes. A colored light was then presented for a period of five minutes, during which time the infant's general activity and crying were measured. It had been shown by previous investigators that light tends to inhibit the general activity and crying of newborn infants, since activities decrease with an increase in the intensity of light. Thus the relative brightness value of different colors was inferred from their inhibiting effect upon activity. The colors were equated in physical energy. Taken at their face value, the data obtained in this way show the colors to possess inhibiting (brightness) value in the following order: For boys blue, green, and red, the red being equivalent with darkness. For girls, blue, red, and green. However, these differences are of doubtful reliability. This is true of sex differences and the differences in brightness value for the different colors. One has, upon the basis of these data, no clear evidence to support the claims made by Smith.

As Smith has clearly indicated, Peiper's data are inadequate to demonstrate *equivalent* brightness value of colors for infants and adults. On the basis of these results one must conclude that the relative brightness value of different hues for the eye of the infant has not yet been determined. This is an important point, for investigators of color differentiation in infants have accepted Peiper's work at its face value and have equated the brightness of colors for the adult human eye. If the brightness value of hues is alike for infant and adult, the results of these experiments indicate color differentiation in very young infants. If the brightness value of the various hues is not the same for infant and adult, most of the data on color vision in infants are equivocal.

Differentiation of colors. Canestrini [17] is the only investigator who has failed to find at least some evidence of color discrimination in infants. He regards his results as inconclusive. Pratt, Nelson, and Sun [18] question the presence of color vision, but they admit that their results are equivocal. Eleven other investigators, most of whom equated their colors in brightness for the adult eye, have obtained what, in their opinion, is clear evidence of color discrimination in young infants. Only two of these investigators, Staples and Chase, have investigated the problem systematically with large numbers of infants. The following discussion of color vision in infants will be confined to their work. Chase's study, since it involves infants younger than those of Staples, will be considered first.

Chase [19] used a method suggested by Beasley. Beasley [20] pointed out that when a spot of light moves across the infant's field of vision, pursuit movements may be elicited. He suggested, therefore, that if a spot of colored light should be moved across a colorless field of equivalent brightness, following of the spot by the infant's eyes would constitute proof of color vision. Chase moved one colored area within another, the two colors being equated in brightness for the adult eye.* If

* Chase cites Peiper's work as justification for assuming that the different hues are of equivalent brightness value for infants and adults. The colored lights were equated in brightness by means of a Westinghouse light meter which embodies the Westinghouse Photox cell. Chase says that "The color response of the Photox cell for all wave lengths of visible light compares very closely to the sensitivity of the average human eye." As Chase indicates, a totally color-blind child might be able to discriminate, in terms of brightness differences, colors equated in brightness for the average adult eye. He argues, however, that the possibility that all of his subjects were totally color blind is extremely remote. He assumes, of course, that the luminosity curve is alike for normal adults and normal infants. This only brings to attention the fact already stressed, namely, that equation of colors in brightness for the normal adult eye will, unless Peiper's claims can be substantiated, lead to equivocal data in work with infants.

the infant followed the moving area with its eyes, it was assumed to be discriminating between the two colors. Twenty-four infants ranging in age from fifteen to seventy days were used in the investigation. The subject lay on its back with its head held in a fixed position. Its eyes were directly below a screen on which the colored areas were projected. The color combinations (large and small area) were red and yellow-green, red and green, red and blue-green, yellow-green and green, yellow-green and blue-green and green and blue-green. Ocular pursuit was observed in all subjects and in from 90 to 100 per cent of the total presentations. Failure of an infant to pursue a given area was usually due to sleepiness and other extraneous conditions. When a red area was moved within a red area (to determine whether the fused outline of the two areas was an effective stimulus) there was no evidence of pursuit. When a colored area of different brightness was moved in the field of the same color, there were likewise no pursuit movements. Negative results were also obtained when a colorless area was moved across a colored area of different brightness. In each control the moving area was 24 to 25 per cent darker than its background. These controls suggest that differential brightness was not a factor underlying pursuit movements. However, such controls are not completely adequate unless the brightness values of the colors for the infant's eyes are known. Brightness differences between the colors might, for example, be greater than 25 per cent. Chase concludes that the infants were responding to differences in wave length and not to extraneous factors. No age differences were apparent, nor was there evidence that one color combination could be discriminated any more readily than another.

Staples [21] used a preference method of testing for color discrimination. (Figure 94.) She assumed that if an infant responds to one stimulus more than to another, the difference in response being significantly greater than could occur by chance, the infant *prefers* the stim-

 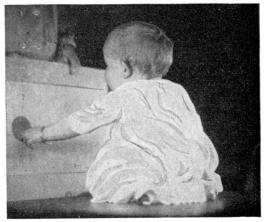

Figure 94. Staples' Methods for Studying the Responses of Infants to Color

A. The fixation method. By looking through a narrow slit between the two disks, the experimenter observed the time involved in the fixation of each disk. The time of fixation for each disk was measured by means of a stop watch, one for each disk held in each hand. Each test lasted for two minutes, starting with the infant's fixation of the cardboard containing the disks. The colors, red, yellow, blue, and green were each presented with gray, the gray disk appearing as many times to the infant's right as to his left in separate tests. This method was used with infants ranging in age from 60 to 143 days.

B. The reaching method. This method, used with infants ranging in age from $5\frac{1}{2}$ to 24 months, is similar to that of *A* except that a larger cardboard was used and reaching instead of fixation was timed. If the infant failed to respond, he was urged to "get the ball," or to "show me the ball." (Courtesy of University of Minnesota Institute of Child Welfare. From F. L. Goodenough, *Developmental Psychology*, New York: Appleton-Century, 1934, p. 226.)

ulus which elicits the greater response. In this experiment the response was fixation of a stimulus or reaching for it. If the infant indicated a preference for one of the two stimuli he was assumed to be discriminating between them.

The infants were confronted by two disks pasted six inches apart upon a piece of cardboard. The disks were of equal area, were equidistant from an infant's eyes, and were of equal brightness to the adult human eye.* For an adult, the only difference between the disks was their color. In some experiments a gray and a colored disk of equal brightness

* The "Atlas" colors of the Munsell Color System were used. These are designated in the Munsell System as Red 5/10, yellow 5/7, green 5/7, blue 5/6, and neutral (gray) 5. The 5 refers to brightness value for the adult human eye. The other numbers refer to saturation.

were presented, while in other experiments two colors of equal brightness were used. The gray cardboard on which the disks appeared was equivalent to them in brightness. A given disk appeared as many times to the infant's right as to his left.

Staples carried out an experiment to check the possibility that brightnesses, although equated for the adult eye, were not equated for the infant eye. In this control experiment the disks were made to vary in brightness as well as in color. Presumably, if the infant had been responding to a brightness rather than to a color difference, this control would elicit a shift in preferences. If, for example, blue were originally brighter than gray and a control involved the same blue but a lighter gray, an infant which had selected blue on the basis of brightness would now select gray.

Table 5. Responses to Colors When Compared with Gray
Infants 5½–24 Months. N. 124

Colors compared	Type of response	Age Group					Totals
		I (6–8 mos.)	II (9–11 mos.)	III (12–14 mos.)	IV (15–18 mos.)	V (19–24 mos.)	
		N 28 per cent	N 27 per cent	N 22 per cent	N 22 per cent	N 25 per cent	N 124 per cent
Red	Reaching for color.....	68.8	80.3	86.8	94.8	93.0	83.7
Gray	Other responses........	31.2	19.7	13.2	5.2	7.0	16.3
Yellow	Reaching for color.....	59.3	81.8	84.0	92.6	100.0	81.7
Gray	Other responses........	40.7	18.2	16.0	7.4		18.3
Green	Reaching for color.....	45.9	60.7	76.8	88.1	90.1	70.9
Gray	Other responses........	54.1	39.3	23.2	11.9	8.9	29.1
Blue	Reaching for color.....	49.5	70.1	75.4	94.7	92.2	74.9
Gray	Other responses........	50.5	29.9	24.6	5.3	7.8	25.1

Reaching for color represents pointing and reaching toward color. *Other responses* include pointing or in other ways responding to gray disk, response to center of card, failure to notice disk, etc.

It should be pointed out, however, that what appears to be a brighter (or darker) gray to the adult human eye may not (unless Peiper's results present a true picture of infant color vision) be a brighter gray to the infant's eye. Unless there is a reversal of brightness relationships *for the infant's eye*, such a control as the above may be quite inadequate.

The specific procedures used in Staples' experiment are indicated in Figure 94 and the attached legend. The investigation was divided into three parts. Part I involved twenty-three infants aged from 60 to 143 days and concerned differential responses to gray as compared with red, yellow, green, and blue. In every comparison, the total number of seconds involved in fixation was higher for the colored than for the gray disk. Yellow was the only single color which elicited a statistically significant longer response than gray. However, responses to gray had a total duration of 1301.1 seconds and those to all of the colors combined had a total duration of

2443.3 seconds. As the difference of the averages was more than five times its standard error, it could not be attributed to chance. The author concluded, therefore, that infants within the age range tested in this study can differentiate colored from colorless light.

Part II of the investigation dealt with 124 infants ranging in age from 5½ to 24 months. The general problem and procedure was similar to that already discussed, except that reaching movements rather than eye fixations were involved. The data are reported for five age groups, as indicated in Table 5. They show (1) a significantly greater total response to each color than to the gray disk with which it was paired, (2) a tendency toward an increasingly greater response to color as a function of age, and (3) a greater tendency to select red and yellow than green and blue. Controls involving a gray brighter than the background and the color (as judged by the adult eye) led to no change in the nature of the responses to color. Variations in the dis-

**Table 6. Percentage of Positive Responses to Paired Colors
Infants 6–24 Months. N. 121**

Colors compared	Age Group					All cases N 121
	I	II	III	IV	V	
	6–8 mos. N 26	9–11 mos. N 26	12–14 mos. N 23	15–18 mos. N 23	19–24 mos. N 23	
	Per cent of responses	Per cent of responses	Per cent of responses	Per cent of responses	Per cent of responses	Per cent of responses
Red.............	64.0	73.1	65.2	52.2	52.2	61.7
Yellow...........	36.0	26.9	34.8	47.8	47.8	38.3
Red.............	83.3	65.4	60.9	59.1	43.5	62.7
Green...........	16.7	34.6	39.1	40.9	56.5	37.3
Red.............	72.0	69.2	68.2	59.1	73.9	68.6
Blue............	28.0	30.8	31.8	40.9	26.1	31.4
Yellow..........	60.0	46.2	50.0	59.1	47.8	52.5
Green...........	40.0	53.8	50.0	40.9	52.2	47.5
Yellow...........	54.2	65.4	63.6	57.1	43.5	56.9
Blue............	45.8	34.6	36.4	42.9	56.5	43.1
Green...........	45.8	46.1	34.8	36.4	34.8	39.8
Blue............	54.2	53.9	65.2	63.6	65.2	60.2

tance between the gray disk and the infant were likewise without effect.

Part III was an investigation of the paired comparison of colors of equivalent brightness. One hundred and twenty-one infants ranging in age from 6 to 24 months were used. These infants were different from those used in Parts I and II. The paired disks were red-yellow, red-green, red-blue, yellow-green, yellow-blue, and green-blue. Table 6 indicates the percentage of pointing and reaching responses to each of the paired disks, five age groups being represented. One will notice that red elicits from approximately two to five times as many responses as any of the other colors paired with it. This difference in favor of red cannot be attributed to chance, for it is from 3.7 to 6.3 times its standard error. Blue elicits a higher percentage of re-

sponses than does the green with which it is paired. This difference is statistically reliable, being 3.2 times the standard error of the difference. Yellow receives a higher response than blue and green, but the differences are not reliable statistically. With the exception of blue, the tendency is for color preferences to become less marked as a function of age. According to Staples,[22] the results of her study

... suggest that color may be perceived, at least to a certain degree, by the age of three months. Further, color becomes an increasingly effective stimulus until the end of the fourteenth month. Probably by twelve and at least by fifteen months, saturated red, yellow, blue, and green are seen clearly. Between the ages of six and fifteen months, the different colors vary in their effectiveness in bringing about a response from the infants, the order being red, yellow, blue, and green. This order is consistent throughout the experiment, appearing when the colors are paired with gray, in the paired comparison of colors, in the maintenance of the interest of the subjects, and in the sex difference.

A supplementary experiment to discover possible changes in color preferences beyond the age of two years was also carried out by Staples. She found that the order of preference for preschool children is red, green, blue, and yellow; for grade-school children, blue, red, green, and yellow; and for adults, blue green, red, and yellow. The low preference for yellow is attributed to the fact that it was of poor saturation, closer to a tan than to a real yellow. This did not have as marked an effect on infant preferences as it did on preferences of school children and adults.

Cook [23] studied the development, in children between 2½ and 6 years, of ability to match and to name colors. In this study Munsell colors equated in brightness and saturation were used. Some parts of the experiment required the children to match colors which varied in saturation or in brightness, the aim being to ascertain the influence of brightness and of saturation. The colors were red, green, blue, and yellow. The children comprised 45 girls and 65 boys. Each child was shown the colors one at a time and told to match a color with one of the four standard colors. Sometimes the color differed from these in brightness, sometimes in saturation, but it was always like one of them in hue. The two-year-olds were able to match colors with an accuracy of 45 per cent. By the age of six years, however, the accuracy of matching had increased to 97 per cent. Accuracy of naming increased from 25 per cent at two years to 62 per cent at six years. Children of every age matched more accurately on the basis of hue than on the basis of brightness or saturation. Red, yellow, blue, and green were matched with equal ease.

Whether this improvement in color matching and color naming in older children is to be attributed to increased sensitivity to differences in hue as a function of age, or whether it is to be attributed to increase in ability to understand instructions or to pay attention to the stimuli, one cannot say upon the basis of the present evidence. Cook avoided the last two factors as much as was possible by giving the children extensive preliminary training, by making them correct their errors, and by praising them for initially correct responses.

Color matching and color naming are involved in several tests of intelligence for the preschool child. The tests of Baldwin and Stecher [24] and Stutsman [25] give special attention to color discrimination, but the evident improvement as the child becomes older may be accounted for on the basis of increased ability to comprehend instructions, and the like. There is no indication that it represents increased color sensitivity. In general, the results of these studies agree with those of Cook.

Experiments with tests of color blindness have also shown improved scores as a function of age. Smith,[26] whose youngest subjects were six years old, used color-matching tests. Scores improved rapidly with increasing age, but the author attributes this improvement to "attitudinal factors" rather than to "receptor physiology." Synolds and Pronko [27] and Pronko and others [28] used the Dvorine Color Perception Test, requiring children to name or to trace the figures. At three years there was complete failure on these tests. By the eighth year, however, correct responses approximated 80 per cent. The latter study was made with children from kindergarten through the third grade. Color naming was very poor in the kindergarten group, at about the 70 per cent level of accuracy in the first graders, and almost perfect in the second and third graders. There were no sex differences. Perception of the digits of the Dvorine charts also improved with age and again there were no sex differences.

The improvement shown in these experiments might have the same explanation as that demonstrated by Cook. All that can be said with assurance is that, as they become older, children improve in color naming and in their discrimination of the figures in pseudo-isochromatic charts like those in the Ishihara and Dvorine tests. It is interesting to note, in this connection, that sexual differences in color sensitivity do not show up in young children as they do in adults, where more males than females are color blind.

The literature on color vision in children includes several investigations in which the subjects were given an opportunity to match objects on the basis of color or form.[29] It is generally agreed that children tend to match on the basis of color until about the sixth year, after which they match predominately on the basis of form. In Brian and Good-enough's [30] experiment, which is quite similar to the others, the child was confronted with two objects that differed from a third one in either color or form. For example, he might be confronted with a blue ball and a red cube. The third object, which was to be placed with the one "just like it," was perhaps a blue cube. Would the child place it with the red cube (matching on the basis of form) or with the blue ball (matching on the basis of color)? Until about the sixth year, the matching tends to be blue ball with blue cube. After this age, the predominant response is to place the blue cube with the red cube. Again, it is doubtful whether this change in matching as a function of age depends upon actual changes in visual sensitivity. It is probably due to increased attention, better knowledge of instructions, or use of symbolic processes which give added meaning to color and form.

Responses to other aspects of visual stimuli

In addition to the investigations of brightness and color vision which we have just considered there have been others on visual acuity, pattern vision, size discrimination, and perception of the third dimension. Acuity and pattern and size discrimination will be considered here, but the discussion of depth perception will be left for the following chapter, which deals more specifically with certain localizing aspects of space perception.

Visual acuity. This is measured in terms of ability to differentiate visual details, such as a minimal separation of lines, or letters like E and F when observed from such a distance as to make their discrimination difficult. The Snellen Tests, which are widely used by oculists to determine levels of acuity, were given to children by Peckham.[31] His subjects ranged from 21 to 62 months. Tests with the younger children required them to pick up a cut-out which matched the letter or figure seen at a distance. This procedure was adequate for children over 28 months. From this age level, acuity was as good in children as in adults.

Pattern discrimination. The ability of infants to discriminate objects in terms of shape is present by at least the sixth month. Ling [32] studied such discrimination in 50 infants between the ages of six and fifteen months. At each trial the infant was confronted with two bright yellow blocks which differed in shape (triangle versus square, circle versus triangle, ellipse versus circle, and so on). The correct block was sweetened and could be picked up and carried to the mouth. Its partner was fixed to the tray so that it could not be moved. Even the youngest subjects learned this problem and were not confused when the triangle, for instance, was inverted. They thus gave evidence of response in terms of the form (triangularity) of an object. The problem of response to form *per se* was considered earlier in our discussion of conceptual response in animals (p. 134) and it will be considered further when symbolic behavior in children is discussed (Chapter 11).

Results essentially similar to those of Ling have been obtained in older children by several investigators. The age range in these studies was from 15 to 46 months. Munn and Steining [33] trained a child of 15 months to discriminate by opening a small door containing the correct form, and thus obtaining a piece of chocolate. The door with the incorrect form was locked. Position and other extraneous cues were controlled. In one experiment the correct shape was a cross versus a square and in the other a triangle versus a circle. Inversion of the triangle did not disturb discrimination. Gellermann [34] repeated this experiment with two-year-old children and chimpanzees. His results with children were similar to those of the previous investigators. The children, probably because they named the figures, showed more evidence of conceptual response than did the chimpanzees. Weinstein's [35] experiment, in which the procedure used was matching-from-sample, also suggests better generalizing of form in children than in monkeys.

A relevant experiment by Skeels [36] closely approximates form-board tests of intelligence. His subjects were 41 children between the ages of fifteen and forty-six months. Form discrimination boards were used. The child was trained to lift a block of a given shape in order to obtain the reward, a cooky. For example, blocks in the form of a lozenge, a maltese cross, a square, and a circle were presented simultaneously before the child. Each block fitted into a recess in the form discrimination board. The position of a given block was changed from trial to trial. The child was taught, for instance, that the reward was situated under the circle. Eight or more correct responses (lifting the circle) out of ten consecutive trials was regarded as evidence that the circle was discriminated from the other figures. Other problems involved discrimination of blocks representing animate and inanimate objects. Discrimination was present at all ages, and there was no indication of greater rapidity of learning or of better discrimination as a function of age. Preschool children, although they discriminated the forms, failed to fit them into the appropriate holes of a regulation form board. This suggests that the child is capable of discriminating in terms of shape before he can pass regulation form-board tests. Improved ability in form-board manipulation as the child becomes older, like improved matching and naming of colors, is apparently dependent upon other factors than improved visual sensitivity, such as better attention and understanding of instructions.

Size-constancy and size discrimination. Older children and adults respond to objects in a manner which does not vary in accordance with variations in the size of the retinal area of stimulation. This phenomenon, designated as size-constancy, is exemplified when objects of the same size, but presented at different distances from the eye (so that their retinal areas of stimulation differ), arouse equivalent responses. In other words, size-constancy is present when an individual responds to objects in terms of their *actual*, rather than their retinal, size. Likewise, objects of unequal size, but at distances such that their retinal areas of stimulation are equal, do not arouse equivalent responses. Again, the individual responds in terms of *actual* rather than retinal size.

Cruikshank [37] investigated this problem in a large group of infants ranging in age from ten to fifty months. The test involving the most crucial evidence of size constancy was one in which the babies were presented with rattles which differed in size and distance from the eye (Figure 95) but which produced a retinal image of the same magnitude. If size-constancy were absent, the baby should not distinguish between the two rattles. It should react in terms of the identity of their

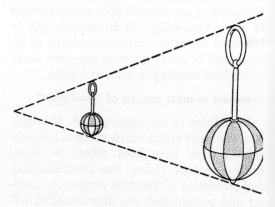

Figure 95. Rattles Like Those Used in the Experiment on Size Constancy

(After R. M. Cruikshank, "The Development of Visual Size Constancy in Early Infancy," *J. Genet. Psychol.*, 1941, *58*, 335.)

retinal images. The eye movements in response to a rattle, as well as arm movements and incipient grasping responses, did not differ consistently for the two rattles until around the age of six months. From this age on, responses to the small nearby rattle were clearly different from those to the large and more distant one. Among other things, the fingers closed as if to grasp the near rattle but did not close in this way for the distant one. Although such results suggest that size-constancy is present by this age, they do not throw light on its origin. One might argue that, since it was not evident in the younger infants, it is learned rather than innate. It might be maintained, on the other hand, that size-constancy is innate, but that it fails to mature until around the sixth month. The data do not allow us to choose between these alternatives. It could be that both innate and acquired functions are involved. The tendency to perceive in terms of constancy increases between the ages of two and ten years, as shown in a study by Beyrl which is described by Werner.[38]

Investigations of size discrimination in children have been reported by several investigators. Although size differentiation is placed at the fourth year in the Stanford-Binet test, it is sometimes evident as early as two years. Goodenough[39] found that children of two years are sometimes able to select the longer of two lines and that 92 per cent of four-year-olds are successful on this test. Long[40] used a discrimination procedure which required children between four and seven years to differentiate between pairs of circles, squares, and rectangles of different size. A candy reward was given for correct responses. The initial size discrimination required from 5 to 437 trials, but once it was mastered there was almost complete transfer to further size discrimination problems. Thus a child who learned that he could obtain candy by reaching into the compartment with the large square, but not by reaching into that with the small square, subsequently responded with a high degree of accuracy on such pairs as large versus small circles and even a large rectangle versus a small circle. Tests of this nature lead us to symbolic response and generalizing, discussed in Chapter 11.

Summary of visual processes

We have seen that brightness and color vision may be present at or soon after birth. The data of Chase and Staples, which are the most satisfactory available, show that infants differentiate between colored and colorless light and between different colors of equivalent brightness to the adult human eye. Ability to match and to name colors, as well as to respond accurately on standard tests of color blindness, increases with age, but this improvement may be a function of nonvisual factors such as better attention, better ability to follow instructions, and the like. Visual acuity is apparently as well developed in two-year-old children as in adults. Differentiation of figures is present as early as six months, the youngest age tested. Infants of this age have responded to *form* as such, indicating the presence of form concepts. Size-constancy begins to appear at around the sixth month. Ability to differentiate visual stimuli upon the basis of magnitude is evident in some children by the second year.

Hearing

The fact that fetuses respond to loud sounds, and that these responses can be conditioned, would warrant the assumption that newborn babies can hear; yet there has been much doubt concerning the status of hearing in the newborn. Some investigators have claimed that the neonate is deaf for hours, or even for days. This belief has received support from the observation that the middle ear is filled with amnionic fluid for some time after birth. However, the apparent deafness of neonates is not absolute. It is due to their poor acuity, which makes them unresponsive to the normal sounds of their environment. Loud, sharp, and sudden sounds do arouse responses, even from birth. This has been demonstrated in several investigations. Pratt, Nelson, and Sun [41] observed 59 newborn infants ranging in age from birth to twenty-one days and their observations indicate that sensitivity to sound is present even in the youngest infants. They used the stabilimeter-polygraph technique. In addition to measures of general activity, however, records of pacifying reactions and specific movements were kept. The sounds were produced by striking a tin can, snapping a device like a mouse trap, ringing an electric bell, hitting a Chinese wooden bell, and activating a 350-cycle tuning fork. Considering all the sounds as a group, the lowest frequency of reaction occurred in subjects from birth to one day old. General activity in response to sound was also lowest for this age group. The number of specific movements, however, was as great at this age as at later ages, except eight to ten days. Pacifying reactions had a low frequency at every age grouping. After from two to four days, there was no further increase in reaction frequency or in the number of specific movements. General activity, however, increased slightly at each successive age group. Considering the separate stimuli, irrespective of the age at which they were used, the measurable activity was 47 per cent to the tin can, 21 per cent to the electric bell, 16 per cent to the snapper, 9 per cent to the wooden bell, and 7 per cent to the tuning fork. This was not the order of the intensities of the respective stimuli. Reactions to sound, according to Pratt, Nelson, and Sun, are thus only partially associated with loudness, as measured by adult hearing. The wooden bell, which gave a sharp and shrill sound of approximately 1500 to 2000 cycles and of short duration, was next to the tin can in loudness to the adult ear. Yet the total amount of measurable activity in response to this stimulus was practically as low as that for the tuning fork, which had the lowest loudness to the adult ear.

The bell and the tuning fork were almost pure *tones* as compared with *noise* of the other stimuli. This raises a question as to the ability of young infants to respond to tone. On the basis of Pratt, Nelson, and Sun's data, as well as those of others, there is no doubt that response to a loud noise is present at birth. The data do not, however, give clear evidence of response to tone. One might say that, since the infants exhibited a different amount of activity for noise than for tonal stimuli, they were differentiating the two types of stimulation. However, activity to the wooden bell and tuning fork was practically negligible. Hence the results actually suggest that there was response to noise and absence of response to tone.

These findings are supported by others obtained more recently in a study by Froeschels and Beebe [42] on the responses of 33 newborn infants to whistles and tuning forks. The infants ranged from about twelve hours of age to nine days. No blinking, grimaces, or other bodily responses were elicited by tuning forks. Loud whistle sounds, however, did arouse such responses, and especially blinking. The authors are convinced that the majority of their newborn subjects were hearing the whistles. Since whistles have a marked noise component, this result cannot be interpreted as response to tone.

There have been several studies of tonal discrimination in infants, but the results have not been especially convincing. Stubbs [43] found that tones ranging in frequency from 128 to 4096 cycles per second did not arouse differential respiratory and bodily activities in 75 infants between the ages of one and ten days. Although there were no differential reactions elicited by differences in pitch, increases in the duration and loudness of a given tone produced an increase in activity. Haller's [44] study with infants of three to five weeks suggests that high frequencies at a high level of loudness have the greatest "discomforting" effect.

Kasatkin and Levikova [45] investigated tonal differentiation with the conditioned-response method. Sucking was the response conditioned and feeding with the milk bottle the unconditioned stimulus. Three infants were used. At the beginning of the experiment, these were from 11 to 30 days old. Differential sucking reactions were conditioned to a difference of almost two octaves ($11\frac{1}{2}$ tones) between the ages of $2\frac{1}{2}$ to $3\frac{1}{2}$ months. It was not until 4 months and 4 days that differential sucking to a difference of $5\frac{1}{2}$ tones could be conditioned. Attempts to obtain differential conditioning with differences of $2\frac{1}{2}$ and $3\frac{1}{2}$ tones were unsuccessful.

From the data presented above, it is obvious that we know very little of a definite nature concerning the tonal sensitivity of infants. Nothing, except the work of Kasatkin and Levikova, has been reported on changes in tonal sensitivity as the infant becomes older. Even here, only three subjects were used.

Studies on acuity changes as a function of age have also been reported. Williams's [46] results suggest that acuity increases with age. The subjects ranged in age from three to seven years. A recorded human voice repeating numbers heard by the child through a telephone receiver served as the stimulus. Thresholds were determined by gradually decreasing intensity until the child could no longer report the number being repeated. Weinberg and Fischgold [47] report a similar experiment. School children, 387 in number, were tested with a Western Electric audiometer. These ranged in age from six to thirteen years. The results show an increase in auditory acuity from the sixth to the tenth year. Whether such studies indicate an actual change in acuity, or whether they demonstrate improved ability to follow instructions, pay attention, and the like as the child becomes older, is not known.

Other Sensory Processes

There is no doubt concerning the ability of the newborn infant to respond to cutaneous, kinesthetic, and static stimulation. Investigations of cutaneous sensitivity in infants have been concerned with differential responses to temperature and with changes in response to noxious stimulation.

Pratt, Nelson, and Sun,[48] using techniques similar to those involved in their studies of the other senses, found that infants as young as a few hours after birth reacted less strongly to temperatures higher than the body temperature than to those lower than this temperature. More recent work by Jensen and Crudden has not verified this result.

Jensen's [49] investigation of temperature sensitivity involved the method already described for taste (see p. 235). Typical records of differential sucking activity to milk varying in temperature are shown in Figure 96. The control temperature was 40° C. Ability of infants to differentiate, from this, temperatures above and below it was investigated. Seventeen infants ranging in age from two to sixteen days were used in the study. For 12 of these infants, differential reactions above 50° C. were identical with those to temperatures below 23° C. Differential thresholds ranged from 8° to 13°. The data do not enable one to ascertain whether the differential threshold changed as a function of age.

To produce differential temperature stimulation, Crudden [50] used a capsule attached to the infant's leg. Stimulation was constant in area (23 mm.), in position, and in pressure. The only differences in stimulation were those produced by passing water of various temperatures through the cylinder. Variations of temperature were from a neutral point (33°–34° C.) up to 45° C. and from the neutral point down to 16° C. Responses to temperature changes were recorded cinematographically and in writing. These records were later analyzed to determine the nature of activity changes. The subjects were nine sleeping infants ranging in age from 41 to 1045 hours. A total of thirty-six tests were involved in the study. In every test changes in temperature elicited activity. Two infants responded to a change as small as 5° C. Four responded to a change of 6° C. Except for changes from neutral to 40° C. and from 40° C. to neutral, the total number and magnitude of responses tended to be greater for changes from neutral to some

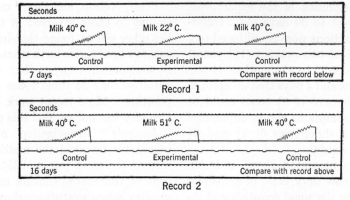

Figure 96. Temperature Discrimination in Young Infants

The top record is for a seven-day infant. It shows a differential response to milk at 22° and 40° C. The smallest *difference* below 40° C. which the infant could discriminate was 18° C. as shown. It failed to make differential sucking reactions to a 23° C., a difference of 17°. At 20° and 19° C., increasingly greater differential reactions were obtained. The lower record, for an infant of 16 days, shows differential sucking to temperatures of 40° and 51° C. Increasingly greater differential responses were present for temperatures of 52°, 53°, and 55° C. The differential threshold above the standard was thus 11° C. (From K. Jensen, "Differential Reactions to Taste and Temperature Stimuli in Newborn Infants," *Genet. Psychol. Monog.*, 1932, *12*, 431.)

other point than from some other point to neutral. In 33.8 per cent of the responses there was apparent localization of the stimulus. In some instances the infant's opposite foot came to the stimulated point and pushed at the capsule. One infant repeatedly pushed the capsule off. Adaptation to the changed temperature was rapid.

Newborn infants apparently have a low degree of sensitivity to pain, and there has been some doubt as to their ability to sense it at all. In most of the experimental studies of response to noxious stimuli in infants, the stimuli used have been needle-pricks. Crying, withdrawal of the stimulated limb, and general activity following stimulation have been taken as evidence of pain sensitivity. In general, these studies have been concerned with three problems: (1) whether or not sensitivity is present at birth, (2) how the different body areas differ in sensitivity, and (3) how sensitivity changes with age.

At birth there is no clear evidence of pain sensitivity. McGraw[51] found no response to a light pinprick in newborn babies, although

heavy pressure brought various postural responses. Within a week or ten days, even a light prick elicited reactions. Sherman and Sherman[52] and Sherman, Sherman, and Florey[53] obtained withdrawal of a limb when pricks were repeatedly given, so as to produce a summative effect. Electric shocks also produced withdrawal reactions. One cannot, on the basis of these results, say whether or not pain sensitivity is present at birth. Referring to the failure of neonates to respond to a pinprick, McGraw[54] says, "It is impossible to know whether such absence of response should be attributed to an undeveloped sensory mechanism or to lack of connections between sensory and somatic centers, or between receptor centers and those mechanisms governing crying."

Which region of the body is most sensitive to noxious stimulation? The Sherman studies as well as McGraw's agree that the facial region, mediated by the trigeminal nerve, is most sensitive. The first responses aroused by noxious stimuli are diffuse, involving any parts of the body, often accompanied by crying. Localizing clearly develops with age. Mc-Graw [55] and Dockeray and Rice [56] observed that the child eventually turns his head away, or withdraws the stimulated limb. This aspect of response to cutaneous stimulation is treated more extensively in the following chapter.

There is no doubt an increase in responsiveness to noxious stimulation as the infant gets older. McGraw says that, although there is little or no response to a pinprick at birth, there is usually a marked response within a week to ten days. The Sherman studies demonstrate that fewer pinpricks are required to elicit responses in older than in younger infants. McGraw claims that this growth in responsiveness to noxious stimuli is a function of neuromuscular maturation. There is no evidence that it represents an increase in pain sensitivity as such.

Summary and Conclusions

There is no completely satisfactory information on the olfactory and gustatory sensitivity of infants. Although available researches suggest that such sensitivity is present at or soon after birth, the tactual aspects of stimulation have not been sufficiently controlled.

Newborn infants exhibit differential activity in response to differences in the intensity of light. Higher intensities of illumination have an inhibiting influence. Researches on the brightness value of light of different wave lengths for the eye of the infant are unsatisfactory. Peiper claims that the brightness value of red, blue, yellow, and green is the same for infants and adults, while Smith claims exactly the opposite. Neither investigation has yielded conclusive results. When stimuli are equated in brightness value for the adult eye, infants as young as fifteen days exhibit clear-cut differentiation of colored from colorless light and of various colors such as red versus green and green versus blue. Differential responses to color become more evident as the infant grows older. Ability to match colors and to differentiate the

figures in tests of color blindness increases during the early years of childhood, reaching its fullest development by approximately the sixth year. This improvement may not indicate an increase in color sensitivity as such. Studies of the visual acuity of children indicate that by the end of the second year detail vision is equal to that of adults. Visual discrimination of patterns and figures has been observed in infants as young as six months. Size-constancy appears in infants six months of age. Some two-year-olds differentiate objects in terms of their size.

Before and at birth, only very loud noises elicit auditory responses. Auditory acuity increases markedly in the first few days of infancy. Tests of auditory acuity in children suggest that improvement may continue until approximately the tenth year. There is a possibility, however, that increased attention and ability to follow instructions, rather than more highly developed acuity as such, accounts for this improvement. There is no evidence that the newborn infant responds to tone. The earliest differential responses to tone have been obtained by the conditioned-response method in infants of $2\frac{1}{2}$ to $3\frac{1}{2}$ months.

Newborn infants respond to temperature differences. Development of temperature sensitivity as a function of age has not been studied. There is evidence of tactile, static kinesthetic, and organic sensitivity prior to birth. Such sensitivity is present at birth, but its development beyond this age has not yet been investigated systematically. Sensitivity to noxious stimuli is apparently weak or absent at birth. Responsiveness to noxious stimulation increases rapidly during the first days of infancy. The facial region appears more sensitive than other parts of the body. Localizing responses improve with age.

Ingenious objective methods have been devised to test for the presence and growth of sensory functions, and many suggestions have been given concerning ways in which these methods may be applied to solve genetic problems, but much more research must be done before developmental trends are clearly disclosed.

REFERENCES

1. Pratt, K. C., A. K. Nelson, and K. H. Sun, *The Behavior of the Newborn Infant.* Columbus: Ohio State University Press, 1930.

2. Disher, D. R., "The Reactions of Newborn Infants to Chemical Stimuli Administered Nasally," *Ohio State Univ. Stud., Contrib. Educ.*, 1934, *12*, 1–52.

3. Canestrini, S., *Über das Sinnesleben des Neugeborenen.* Berlin: Springer, 1913.

4. *Op. cit.* The quotation is from page 122.

5. Jensen, K., "Differential Reactions to Taste and Temperature Stimuli in Newborn Infants," *Genet. Psychol. Monog.*, 1932, *12*, Nos. 5–6.

6. Gesell, A., F. L. Ilg, and G. E. Bullis, *Vision: Its Development in Infant and Child.* New York: Hoeber, 1950.

7. Senden, M. V., *Raum-und Gestaltauffassung bei Opierten Blindgeborenen vor und nach der Operation.* Leipzig: Barth, 1932.

8. Riesen, A. H., "The Development of Visual Perception in Man and Chimpanzee," *Science*, 1947, *1*, 107–108; and "Post-Partum Development of Behavior," *Chicago Med. School Quar.*, 1951, *13*, 17–24.

9. Guernsey, M., "A Quantitative Study of Eye Reflexes in Infants," *Psych. Bull.*, *26*, 160–161.

10. Sherman, M. C., and I. C. Sherman, "Sensorimotor Responses in Infants," *J. Comp. Psychol.*, 1925, *5*, 53–68.

11. See Canestrini, *op. cit.*

12. Weiss, L. A., "Differential Variations in the Amount of Activity of Newborn Infants under Continuous Light and Sound Stimulation," *Univ. Iowa Stud.: Stud. in Child Welfare*, 1934, *9*, No. 4.

13. Redfield, J., "The Light Sense in Newborn Infants," *Univ. Iowa Stud.: Stud. in Child Welfare*, 1939, *16*, No. 2, 105–145.

14. Irwin, O. C., "Effect of Strong Light on the Bodily Activity of Newborns," *J. Comp. Psychol.*, 1941, *32*, 233–236.

15. Peiper, A. "Ueber die Helligkeits und Farbenemfindungen der Fruhgeburten," *Arch. f. Kinderhk.*, 1926, *80*, 1–20.

16. Smith, J. M., "The Relative Brightness Value of Three Hues for Newborn Infants," *Univ. Iowa Stud.: Stud. in Child Welfare*, 1936, *12*, 91–140.

17. Canestrini, *op. cit.*

18. Pratt, Nelson and Sun, *op. cit.*

19. Chase, W. P., "Color Vision in Infants," *J. Exper. Psychol.*, 1937, *20*, 203–222.

20. Beasley, W. C., "An Investigation of Related Problems in the Vision of Newborn Infants," *Psych. Bull.*, 1933, *30*, 626.

21. Staples, R., "The Responses of Infants to Color," *J. Exper. Psychol.*, 1932, *15*, 119–141.

22. *Ibid.*, p. 137.

23. Cook, W. M., "Ability of Children in Color Discrimination," *Child Development*, 1931, *2*, 303–320.

24. Baldwin, B. T., and L. L. Stecher, *The Psychology of the Pre-School Child.* New York: Appleton, 1924.

25. Stutsman, R., "Performance Tests for Children of Pre-School Age," *Genet. Psychol. Monog.*, 1936, *1*, No. 1.

26. Smith, H. C., "Age Differences in Color Discrimination," *J. Gen. Psychol.*, 1943, *29*, 191–226.

27. Synolds, D. L., and N. H. Pronko, "Exploratory Study of Color Discrimination in Children," *J. Genet. Psychol.*, 1949, *74*, 17–21.

28. Pronko, N. H., J. W. Bowles, Jr., F. W. Snyder, and D. L. Synolds, "An Experiment in Pursuit of Color Blindness," *J. Genet. Psychol.*, 1949, *74*, 125–142.

29. Déscoedres, A., "Couleur, Forme, ou Nombre," *Arch. de Psychol.*, 1914, *14*, 305–341; M. Eljasch, "Neue Abstraktionsversuche bei Vorschulflichtingen Kindern," *Zsch. f. Psychol.*, 1927, *105*, 1–42; H. D. Tobie, "Die Entwicklung der Teilinhaltlichen Beachtung von Farbe und Form in Vorschulpflichtigen Kindesalter," *Zsch. f. angew. Psychol.*, 1927, 12, 38, 103; and C. R. Brian, and F. L. Goodenough, "The Relative Potency of Color and Form Perception at Different Ages," *J. Exper. Psychol.*, 1929, *12*, 197–213.

30. Brian and Goodenough, *op. cit.*

31. Peckham, R. H., "Visual Discrimination in Pre-School Children," *Child Development*, 1933, *4*, 292–297.

32. Ling, B-C., "Form Discrimination as a Learning Cue in Infants," *Comp. Psychol. Monog.*, 1941, *17*, No. 2.

33. Munn, N. L., and B. R. Steining, "The Rela-

tive Efficacy of Form and Background in a Child's Discrimination of Visual Patterns," *J. Genet. Psychol.*, 1931, *39*, 73–90.

34. Gellermann, L. W., "Form Discrimination in Chimpanzees and Two-Year-Old Children. I. Discrimination of form *per se;* II. Form Versus Background," *J. Genet. Psychol.*, 1933, *42*, 1–50.

35. Weinstein, B., "Matching-from-Sample by Rhesus Monkeys and by Children," *J. Comp. Psychol.*, 1941, *31*, 195–213.

36. Skeels, H. M., "A Study of Some Factors in Form Board Accomplishments of Pre-School Children," *Univ. Iowa Stud.: Stud. in Child Welfare*, 1933, *7*, No. 2.

37. Cruikshank, R. M., "The Development of Visual Size Constancy in Early Infancy," *J. Genet. Psychol.*, 1941, *58*, 327–351.

38. Beyrl, F., "Die Grössenauffassung bei Kindern," *Zsch. f. Psychol.*, 1926, *100*, 344–371. See H. Werner, *Comparative Psychology of Mental Development.* New York: Harper, 1940, pp. 132–134.

39. Goodenough, F. L., *The Kuhlmann-Binet Tests for Children of Pre-School Age.* Minneapolis: University of Minnesota Press, 1928.

40. Long, L., "Size Discrimination in Children," *Child Development*, 1941, *12*, 247–254.

41. Pratt, Nelson, and Sun, *op. cit.*

42. Froeschels, E., and H. Beebe, "Testing the Hearing of Newborn Infants," *Arch. Otolaryng.*, 1946, *44*, 710–714.

43. Stubbs, E. M., "The Effect of Factors of Duration, Intensity, and Pitch of Sound Stimuli on the Responses of Newborn Infants," *Univ. Iowa Stud.: Stud. in Child Welfare*, 1934, *9*, No. 4.

44. Haller, M. W., "The Reactions of Infants to Changes in the Intensity and Pitch of Pure Tone," *J. Genet. Psychol.*, 1932, *40*, 162–180.

45. Kasatkin, N. I., and A. M. Levikova, "On the Development of Early Conditioned Reflexes and Differentiation of Auditory Stimuli in Infants," *J. Exper. Psychol.*, 1935, *18*, 1–19.

46. Williams, H. M., "An Audiometric Test for Young Children," *Child Development* 1932, *2*, 237–241.

47. Weinberg, D., and F. Fischgold, "Recherches sur l'Acuité Auditive chez les Ecoliers," *Année Psychol.*, 1932, *33*, 120–145.

48. Pratt, Nelson, and Sun, *op. cit.*

49. Jensen, *op. cit.*

50. Crudden, C. H., "Reactions of Newborn Infants to Thermal Stimuli Under Constant Tactual Conditions," *J. Exper. Psychol.*, 1937, *20*, 350–370.

51. McGraw, M. B., "Neural Maturation as Exemplified in the Changing Reactions of the Infant to Pin Prick," *Child Development*, 1941, *12*, 31–41.

52. Sherman, M. C., and I. C. Sherman, "Sensori-Motor Responses in Infants," *J. Comp. Psychol.*, 1925, *5*, 53–68.

53. Sherman, M. C., I. C. Sherman, and C. D. Flory, "Infant Behavior," *Comp. Psychol. Monog.*, 1936, *12*, No. 4.

54. McGraw, M. B., *The Neuromuscular Maturation of the Human Infant.* New York: Columbia University Press, 1943, p. 102.

55. McGraw, M. B. See reference 51.

56. Dockeray, F. C., and C. Rice, "Responses of Newborn Infants to Pain Stimulation," *Ohio State University Stud., Contrib. Psychol.*, 1934, *12*, 82–93.

SUGGESTIONS FOR FURTHER READING

Dewey, E., *Behavior Development in Infants.* New York: Columbia University Press, 1935, pp. 77–102; 220–242.

Gesell, A., F. L. Ilg, and G. E. Bullis, *Vision: Its Development in Infant and Child.* New York: Hoeber, 1950.

McGraw, M. B., *The Neuromuscular Maturation of the Human Infant.* New York: Columbia University Press, 1943, Chapter IV.

Pratt, K. C., "The Neonate," Chapter 4 in L. Carmichael, (ed.), *Manual of Child Psychology* (2nd ed.). New York: Wiley, 1954.

Pronko, N. H., and J. W. Bowles, *Empirical Foundations of Psychology.* New York: Rinehart, 1951, Chapter 4, readings IV and VI.

Thompson, G. G., *Child Psychology.* Boston: Houghton Mifflin, 1952, pp. 67–78.

Werner, H., *Comparative Psychology of Mental Development.* New York: Harper, 1940, Chapter III.

9

Development of Spatially Coordinated Behavior

ALTHOUGH we have evidence that infants respond to visual, auditory, and other stimuli, and also that they respond differentially to stimulus differences, we know nothing at all about the experiences, if any, which these stimuli and stimulus differences arouse. When we turn from sensitivity, as such, to perception, we are confronted by the same experiential impasse. Responses to the locations and interrelationships of stimuli are clearly evident, but we have no information at all on the interesting question of whether there are correlated experiences, and if so, what these are, or what they "mean" to the infant.

If an infant could provide us with verbal reports, or if we could remember what, if anything, we experienced during the earliest days of life, at least some information would be available to us. But infants cannot tell us what they experience and our own early life is, experientially, a complete blank. These facts have not, however, prevented philosophers and psychologists from imagining what the infant's "sensations" and "perceptions" might be like.

Most of the speculations about perception have dealt primarily with vision, although similar issues are involved in auditory and tactual perception. Basic questions are: Why does the world look as it does? Why, since the retinal image is only two-dimensional, do we perceive (or react in terms of) solidity, distance, and depth? Why, since the retinal image is inverted, do we see things right-side up instead of upside down? These and other such questions have usually brought forth two basically different interpretations.

Some imagine that the infant at first has meaningless "bits of experience," or what are otherwise called "sensations" of light, color, sound, and so forth. This is the view expressed by the so-called "empiricists." Others claim that there is some organization, or some meaning, from the first moment of stimulation. These are the "nativists." They assume that the brain imposes its own organization upon whatever comes to it through the senses. Something akin to this view is expressed by Gestalt psychologists, who find support for it in experiments on visual perception, and especially apparent motion. There is evidence, for example, that certain visual illusions, including the phi-phenomenon,* are present in animals as well as in human beings and that these perceptions are

* The phi-phenomenon is apparent motion such as underlies the principle of the motion picture, where a succession of still pictures gives the impression that movement is present. It can be simply demonstrated, as in "moving signs," by flashing on a light now here and now there. If spacing, timing, and so on are just right, the light is seen to move from one position to the other.

independent of previous experience.[1] All these theorists suppose that the data which underlie our perception of the visual world are discrete stimuli emanating from aspects of the environment and impinging upon the retina. Empiricists say that we learn the meaning of such stimuli, whereas nativists say that, at least to some extent, the brain organizes the resulting impulses in such a manner as to produce meanings (such as solidity and depth) from the start.

A somewhat different concept, which takes issue with aspects of both of these views, has recently been expressed by Gibson.[2] Certain features of Gibson's concept are considered later, but his basic idea is relevant to the present discussion. This is that the stimuli for vision are not points, but patterns. These patterns comprise gradients of texture, slope, and shape. The retinal pattern is assumed to be a correlated but not necessarily a pictorial representation of these features of the external world, sometimes even an ordinal rather than an anatomically fixed pattern. An ordinal pattern is one which, as in the moving letter of a sign on Times Square, maintains its shape as it moves along even though different bulbs (in the eye, different receptors) carry the pattern. All of this is of course very complicated, and Gibson devotes a whole book to its elaboration in relation to problems of spatial perception and spatially coordinated behavior. It implies that some patterning, given by the environment and the correlated visual representation, is present from the start. This is to some degree a form of nativism. If true, it accounts for some order prior to learning. This concept implies that visually perceived solidity, depth, and distance are, so to speak, generated by the effect of the stimulus pattern on the eye and not by some subsequent intellectual process based upon past experience. But past experience is assumed to play a role in determining some of the meaning of our visual world. Assume that a congenitally blind man, who recovers his sight, has had tactual experience with a ball, but no visual experience of it. Let us suppose, now, that he is confronted with the same ball visually. According to Gibson's concept, the retinal representation of the ball will cause the person to perceive and react to it as different from other non-circular, or possibly non-spherical, objects. This is the nativistic aspect of perception. But the man will not recognize it as a ball, or the object previously felt, until he has had both tactual and visual experiences with it. Nor can he name it. It is in these respects that learning is assumed to be important.

Much of the research considered in this chapter is oriented with respect to the empiricist-nativist controversy. Some investigations trace the development in infants of localizing responses to tactual, auditory, and visual stimuli. Others involve research on adults and animals under conditions designed to disclose innate and acquired aspects of perceptual response.

Rats and chimpanzees, for example, have been reared in darkness until later stages of maturity and then tested for accuracy of visual localization and depth discrimination. A high initial accuracy under these circumstances would of course support the nativistic viewpoint, whereas failure to show evidence of space perception would lend support to the empiricist position. The experiments with adults also have genetic significance. Some of these involve tests given to congenitally blind people whose sight has been gained through removal of cataracts. Here, as in the case of the animal experiments, the presence of space perception immediately after the first visual stimulation would support the nativistic position. Absence of such perception would strengthen the position of the empiricists.

Certain experiments with adults have changed accustomed relations to their environment, as by turning the visual image right-side up (and thus the seen world upside down). The relevance of such experiments to the genetic problem is twofold. They may suggest what (if any) congenitally organized relation exists between certain kinds of stimulation and certain aspects of space perception. In the second place, where disruption of the accustomed relationships disrupts spatially oriented behavior, one may study the process of regaining orientation.

As we discuss the data on children, and integrate with this information the relevant findings of research on animals and human adults, it will soon become apparent that the contributions of nature and nurture * are usually inseparable and that specific spatially coordinated responses are often dependent upon contributions from several senses and from motor processes as well. There are apparently some innately organized perceptual responses. But conditioned sensorimotor activities also play an important role in the development of spatially coordinated reactions.

Tactual-Kinesthetic Localization

Tactual-kinesthetic localization is touching or making any other response appropriate to the location of a tactile stimulus. Raney and Carmichael [3] demonstrated that rat fetuses, as they grow older, exhibit increasingly specific reactions to the location of tactile stimuli. Similar data have been reported (see p. 176) for human fetuses. Specificity of reaction to the location of tactile stimuli shows a definite increase after birth, although even in newborn infants responses are often quite specific. In their investigation of newborn infants, Sherman, Sherman, and Flory [4] found that the most frequent response to a needle-prick on the face was movement of the opposite hand to the point stimulated. The most frequent response to a needle-prick or electric shock administered to the foot was withdrawal of the stimulated member. Further evidence for tactual-kinesthetic localization in young infants comes from Sherman, Sherman, and Flory's [5] study of coordinated defense reac-

* By *nature* we of course mean what is inborn, or dependent upon heredity. *Nurture* refers to influences brought to bear upon the individual after he is born. In a sense it is synonymous with environment and with opportunities to learn.

tions to pressure applied on the chin. A coordinated defense movement is defined as pushing with both hands against a stimulating instrument in such a manner as to remove it. Figure 97 shows that the percentage of coordinated defense movements increases rather steadily with age, the age range in this study being from shortly after birth until the 13th day. Reactions to the pressure stimulus were "strikingly accurate, the hands locating the stimulus at its very application to the skin." Although McGraw [6] observed "local reflex withdrawal of the stimulated member" in newborn babies pricked with a pin, a diffuse nonlocalized response was more often elicited. A general localization gradually developed. Finally the child could carry his hand to the precise point of stimulation. Crudden,[7] it will be recalled, found (p. 247) that 38 per cent of the responses of newborn infants to a thermal stimulus indicated localization of the stimulus.

There have been several studies of tactual-kinesthetic localization in children and adults.[8] The method of investigation in each instance was as follows: The individual was required, without the use of vision, to touch a stimulated point on the skin. More specifically, the

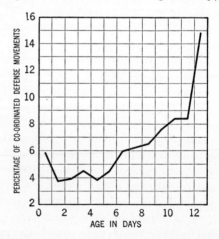

Figure 97. Percentage of Coordinated Defense Movements of the Arms, in Response to Pressure, as a Function of Age

(From M. Sherman, I. Sherman, and C. D. Flory, "Infant Behavior," *Comp. Psychol. Monog.*, 1936, *12*, 44.)

blindfolded subject held a stylus in his hand. His problem was to place the point of the stylus on the stimulated part of the skin as quickly as possible without exploratory movements.

All investigators agree that this sort of localizing becomes increasingly accurate as a function of practice. This is true whether the subjects are children or adults. An investigation by the writer,[9] using adults as subjects, suggests that some of the improvement resulting from such studies is due to increasing knowledge of the sensory topography of the skin (that is, of "local signs"). Some improvement also results from increasing accuracy of localizing movements as such.

Dunford[10] investigated the initial accuracy and improvement of tactual-kinesthetic localization in ten children at each of the following age levels: three, five, seven, nine, eleven, and fifteen years. Each child was given 50 trials every other day until a total of 250 trials was reached. Every group exhibited improvement in the accuracy and localization. Children of five, seven, and nine years exhibited greater initial and final accuracy than did children of eleven and fifteen years. The fifteen-year group was less accurate, on the whole, than was the three-year group. There is a possibility that the small number of subjects in each age group accounts for the absence of increased accuracy at the later age levels. However, Renshaw[11] found that his adults made larger initial localizing errors than children and also improved more slowly. He felt that the greater inaccuracy of adults might be attributed to a shift, sometime during the later part of childhood, from a tactual-kinesthetic to a visual form of localization; a shift which would place adults at a relatively greater disadvantage than children when called upon to localize with the eyes closed. In order to test this hypothesis, Renshaw compared the localizing of two children and two adults, making use of a visual rather than a tactual-kinesthetic method of localizing. The subjects had their eyes closed while being stimulated, but as soon as the stimulus was removed they

opened their eyes and placed the point of the stylus as nearly as possible on the point believed to have been stimulated. This test showed the adults to be superior to the children, thus offering some evidence for Renshaw's view. In a further investigation by Renshaw, Wherry, and Newlin,[12] congenitally blind children and adults were tested. The results offered further substantiation of the view that there is a shift from tactual-kinesthetic to visual localization in seeing individuals. The blind adults were significantly more accurate than were the blind children. Thus, without the possibility of a shift from tactual-kinesthetic to visual localization, there is improvement in localizing ability from childhood to adulthood.

Renshaw and Wherry,[13] in order to obtain a further check on the possibility of a shift from tactual-kinesthetic to visual localization as adulthood is approached, tested fifty-five boys ranging in age from six to sixteen years. There were five children at each age level. Each subject made fifty tactual-kinesthetic localizations. Tactual-kinesthetic localizations were more accurate than visual for all of the groups below thirteen years. From thirteen to sixteen, visual localizations had the greater accuracy. Accuracy in both forms of tactual localization improved as a function of age. Only the *relative* accuracy of kinesthetic and visual localization exhibited a reversal at thirteen years.

Auditory Localization

It is a well-known fact that a source of sound presented in the midline of the body, where it is equidistant from the ears, cannot be localized correctly, even by adults. If the source of sound is moved to the right or to the left of the midline, however, it is closer to one ear than to the other. With a source of sound in such positions, each ear is stimulated differently and localization may be present. Providing there is a sufficiently great difference in the distance of the sound source from each ear, the closer ear will be *stimulated somewhat ear-*

lier than the other. There is a decrease in the *complexity* of sounds as a function of their distance from the ear, hence the ear closer to the source of sound will receive a stimulus of greater complexity than the one farther away. Furthermore, a difference in the distance of a sound source from the two ears may result in *phase differences.* When the source of sound is equidistant from the ears, the waves produced by the vibrating body stimulate both ears while in exactly the same phase. Both ears will be stimulated, for example, by troughs or crests of the sound wave. With a difference in the distance of the ears, however, one ear may be stimulated by a trough, the other by a crest of the wave. The factors which we have just mentioned are regarded as the bases of our discrimination of the distance of sound sources and of their position relative to our own bodies.

Presumably, the infant must learn the significance of these factors before he can localize a source of sound. No extensive ontogenetic studies have been carried out, but there is, nevertheless, some incidental information concerning the ability of infants of different ages to localize auditory stimuli. In Pratt, Nelson, and Sun's [14] investigation of infant behavior it was observed that movement of the head in response to auditory stimulation increased during the first eleven days. The frequency of head movements was, for the various age groups, as follows: Birth to one day, 1; two to four days, 3; five to seven days, 4; eight to ten days, 11; and eleven days and older, 31. The total number of infants was 59, hence these numbers indicate a very infrequent head movement to auditory stimuli. The authors do not report the *direction* of movement with respect to the sound source. Thirty-four per cent of the movements in response to an auditory stimulus were of the eyes (blinking and movements of eyeballs). The frequency of eye movements did not, however, show a definite increase with age. For the above-mentioned groups the frequency of eye movements was, respectively, 85, 227, 185, 181, and 103. The authors say,

"The high value for eye movements probably indicates that the sensorimotor mechanism for the visual localization of sound stimuli begins to function even at these early ages." There is no information in this study which would enable one to ascertain the development of *localizing accuracy* of the eyes in response to an auditory stimulus as a function of age.

Visual localization of auditory stimuli has been observed by Blanton [15] as early as the thirteenth day. Gesell [16] finds that infants of five months turn their heads in such a manner as to localize a bell rung six inches laterally from the ear. Infants younger than five months fail this test. Discrimination and conditioned-response techniques, if applied to this problem, might serve to fill out the extensive gaps in our knowledge of the ontogenesis of auditory localization.

Visual Localization

The chief types of localizing responses to visual stimuli are eye movements and fixations, head movements, and reaching movements.* In their book on the development of vision in infant and child, Gesell, Ilg, and Bullis [17] attempt to trace the growth of vision almost entirely through development of such spatially coordinated visual responses. Their data are derived from examination of film records obtained with children ranging from birth to school age. The newborn is pictured as primarily a sleeper who, when he does open one or both eyes, seems to stare off into space. With increasing age, however, the infant comes to fixate nearby objects, often at first with only one eye, then with two. Sometimes one eye moves while the other is fixating. According to Sherman, Sherman, and Flory,[18] who have studied these aspects intensively, coordinated movements predominate from the start. The highest incidence of ocular incoordination in the newborn is reported by them to be only 14 per cent.

---

* We have already (p. 167) suggested that eye movements are related to posture. Here our concern is with those elicited by visual stimuli.

Several investigators [19] have reported that newborn babies exhibit a tendency to follow a moving light with their eyes (ocular pursuit), but that such movements are not sustained, the eyes "losing" the object and showing inability to reverse when the light moves in the opposite direction. It is two weeks or later before the eyes follow a moving light with any consistency.

McGinnis,[20] who used oscillating black and white stripes and recorded the eye movements cinematographically, says that

During the first two weeks, and even during the first hours after birth, movements of the visual field have a definite effect upon the eye-movements of the infant. However, during the first two weeks this effect is not an ocular pursuit, but only a tendency toward pursuit. The pursuit is not well sustained, but is broken by movements in the opposite direction interspersed between correctly directed pursuit movements . . . With increasing age there is a gradual increase in the number of eye-movements corresponding in direction with the movements of the stimulating object, and a gradual decrease in the number of movements in the opposite direction. . . .

Consistent ocular pursuit was observed during the third and fourth weeks. Jones,[21] who used a slowly moving diffused light, found that ocular pursuit of horizontal movement was first consistently present at about one month, but there were large individual differences. The median age for such pursuit was 58 days. Pursuit in the vertical direction did not appear until 51 days. The median age was 65 days. Pursuit of circular movement appeared in some infants of 51 days, but the median age was 78 days. These differences in the ages at which the three kinds of pursuit occur show close agreement with results reported by Shirley [22] for pursuit of a moving steel tape. The results reported from Gesell's [23] laboratory, where a dangling ring was used to elicit visual pursuit, are also in general agreement with those already discussed. All investigators agree that, rather than being fully developed at birth, the ability to follow moving objects with the eyes develops more or less gradually. This development could result from maturation, from learning, or from a combination of these influences. The latter is the most likely possibility, as we shall now see.

If children could be reared in complete darkness for the first few months of life, and then tested visually, we might be able to discover to what degree their visual responses are dependent upon experience. This sort of experimentation with human beings would never be sanctioned. Some children, however, are born with cataracts and have them removed in later childhood. Prior to cataract removal, these children are not completely blind. They perceive moving lights and bright objects, such as windows. Nevertheless, as the data summarized by Dennis [24] show, a long period of postoperative learning is necessary before normal visual organization and meaning are acquired.*

Although its subjects were chimpanzees instead of human children, Riesen's [26] experiment is relevant to the issue before us. He reared two chimpanzees in darkness for the first 16 months and then tested them for visual response. These visually deprived chimpanzees, like human babies tested at birth, had good pupillary responses to changes in illumination and they responded with "startle" to sudden changes in illumination. They also turned head and eyes toward a source of light, pursued a moving light with the eyes when tested with it in darkness, and made optokinetic responses to moving black and white stripes. This not only shows that such responses were congenitally organized, but it also demonstrates that they did not deteriorate during months of visual deprivation beyond the time of birth. In other respects, however, the chimpanzees acted as though they were blind.

. . . For a long time there was no eye blink when an object was brought rapidly toward the eyes.

* In a widely quoted book, von Senden also reviews data on the after-effects of cataract operation. Michael Wertheimer has recently questioned the reliability of this information as well as the interpretation given to it by Hebb.[25]

An object brought slowly toward the face produced no response until contact was made, when the animal reacted with a quick jerk in the typical startle pattern. . . . Many repetitions of experience with objects presented visually were necessary before any recognition of such objects appeared in either subject. The feeding bottle, for example, was thoroughly familiar tactually and kinesthetically. If the bottle or nipple touched the hand, arm, or face, either animal promptly seized the nipple in its mouth. First signs of *visual* recognition occurred in the female when she protruded her lips toward the bottle on the 33rd meal. . . .

In a later experiment, Riesen [27] reared three chimpanzees under different conditions of deprivation. One was reared in complete darkness for seven months. One was given $1\frac{1}{2}$ hours of light daily but this light was admitted through a white plexiglas mask. It was thus diffused, somewhat like that received through cataracts. The other animal was reared with $1\frac{1}{2}$ hours of normal light which enabled him to respond to his crib, moving persons, sight of the bottle, and other patterned aspects of his immediate environment.

The latter animal, when removed to normal daylight surroundings, exhibited visual performances which were indistinguishable from those of chimpanzees normally reared. Both of the other chimpanzees showed retardation somewhat like that observed in the two animals of the original experiment. It required 13 days for one animal (diffused light) and 30 days for the other (no light) to "acquire the ability to pursue a moving person with the eyes, and they did this by a series of refixations instead of following smoothly as normal animals of comparable age do." Another chimpanzee reared in darkness until she was only three months old, also showed retardation and was slower to adjust than were the older animals, possibly because of her relative immaturity.

According to Riesen,[28] these experiments demonstrate that use of the eyes in response to visual stimulation is necessary for normal visual development, but, he says,

they also indicate that during the first few months of an infant's life visual development is advanced by growth factors which are entirely independent of practice. Normally reared animals, for example, do not blink in response to the movement of visual objects across the visual field until they have reached the age of two months; the older darkroom animals, despite previous lack of experience, began to show this response within two weeks after they were transferred to daylight surroundings.

This is somewhat comparable with the finding (pp. 55–57) that older chicks reared in darkness acquire pecking accuracy at a faster rate, when placed in the light, than younger chicks developing normally.

Saccadic movements such as are used in reading are to some extent present at birth. These movements comprise changes in fixation from one part of the visual field to another. McGinnis,[29] in his investigation of nystagmus, observed large saccadic eye movements (the quick phase of nystagmus) and a succession of short saccadic movements (the slow phase of nystagmus) in newborn infants.* Changing of fixation from one part of the environment to another occurs in some infants soon after birth. By the fourth week, according to Gesell and Thompson,[30] the infant exhibits a frequently changing fixation of objects in its surroundings. It fixates upon a dangling ring, shifts regard to the observer, to the observer's hand, to its own hand, and so on.

Although eye movements in response to visual stimuli are the first visual localizing responses to appear, there are also head movements, followed later by reaching movements. Eye movements are much more frequent than head movements. Pratt, Nelson, and Sun [31] observed 407 eye movements and only 41 head movements in their tests of visual localization administered to infants between the ages of birth and eleven days. Visually directed reaching movements do not, according to Dennis,[32] occur until around the tenth week. The median age is given as four-

---

* Nystagmus has reference to the eye movements which follow rotation.

teen weeks. The development of visually directed prehension is discussed in the following chapter.

Upright Vision

It is a well-known fact that refractive media of the eye invert light rays before they reach the retina. The lower retina receives stimulation from the upper part of an object and the upper retina receives stimulation from the lower part. Likewise the right-left relationships between object and retinal stimulation are reversed. This fact raises questions like the following: Why do we see right-side up when the retinal image is upside down? Is upright vision innately associated with an inverted retinal image? Or, on the other hand, does the infant at first see things upside down and gradually learn to see them right-side up?

Obviously, there is no direct way of getting an answer to these questions. The infant is unable to tell us what it sees. We do not remember our initial visual experiences. For the whole of our lives, as far back as we can recall, objects have been localized where seen. Objects seen in the upper field of vision have been localized there by the eyes, the head, and the hands. Furthermore, we have felt and heard them in the same position as those in which we have seen them. Tactual, kinesthetic, and auditory cues agree with the visual.

There have been several indirect approaches to this problem. The chief of these are as follows:

(1) *Observation of the localizing responses of infants.* Is there an initial "confusion" concerning the position of objects? As an object moves to the right do the eyes of an infant at first move to the left, responding to the inverted visual cues? If an object is above, does the infant first reach for it in the lower visual field? In localizing responses of infants there is no clear evidence of such inversion. The only suggestion of it resides in the fact that infants sometimes move their eyes in the direction opposite to that of a moving object.

Movement in the same direction as the moving object is, however, the most prevalent response, even in the newborn.

(2) *Observation of the initial visual localization of the congenitally blind in whom cataracts have been removed.* Von Senden[33] and Dennis[34] have summarized the results of many such cases reported in the literature. There is no evidence that these individuals, blind from birth, see upside down when first stimulated visually. They tend, however, to be greatly confused when the bandages are removed. Seen objects are interpreted in terms of previous tactual, kinesthetic, and auditory experience. One patient, whose case is reported in detail by Latta,[35] identified the face of the house surgeon by *feeling his own face.* He was also aided by hearing the house surgeon speak. What he saw was thus interpreted in terms of what he already knew on the basis of non-visual processes.

(3) *Observation of writing and drawing responses in children.* Some children write mirror script. Others are not greatly hindered in reading material that is inverted or in interpreting objects which are upside down. Upside-down drawing is often reported. Some psychologists have assumed that these and similar phenomena show that infants at first see upside down, but gradually learn to see right-side up. The children who write mirror script, invert their drawings, and the like, are regarded, in accordance with this view, as having failed the problem of learning to see right-side up. Carr[36] claims, however, that the child who writes mirror script should, according to this view, also write upside down, draw upside down, read inverted print, and the like. No cases in which all of these phenomena occur in the same person have been reported. Carr points out, moreover, that the child who sees upside down must draw right-side up so that *to him* the drawing is inverted. In other words, his drawings would not differ from those of children with normal vision. Thus inverted drawing, mirror writing, and similar phenomena do not support the view that infants have inverted vision.

(4) *Experiments in which the retinal image has been reinverted*. The assumption underlying such experiments is that, if a readjustment of visual and other sensory and motor processes is achieved, and upright vision results, the normal relationship between the position of the retinal image and space localization could have been acquired during infancy and early childhood. There is also the possibility, of course, that such an unlearned relationship could be altered as a result of training. Negative results from such an experiment might mean (1) that the normal relationship between the position of the retinal image and space localization is innate, or (2) that the experiment has not been carried out sufficiently long to overcome the interference of relationships acquired early in life. As we shall observe shortly, however, the results of experiments on inverted vision indicate that learned and unlearned coordinations are both involved in normal visual localization, and that the question of upright vision reduces itself to a problem of intersensory and motor coordination.

Stratton [37] performed the pioneer experiment on visual inversion. In order to determine whether an inverted image is requisite to normal upright vision, Stratton placed a tube containing a system of double convex lenses over his right eye. The tube was held in place by a plaster cast. No light could enter the eye except through the lenses. The left eye was blindfolded. The system of lenses inverted light rays before they reached the eye. Reinversion by the eye produced an upright image upon the retina. Under these conditions Stratton saw all objects upside down and transposed right to left as in a mirror. Visually perceived objects of course maintained their same *relative* positions. The result was similar to that observed in a photograph which has been rotated through 180 degrees. Disruption of the normal relations between vision and hearing, vision and touch, and vision and kinesthesis was present. A feeling of helplessness resulted. Stratton saw an object on his left and heard it on his right, where it actually was situated. He saw an object below the level of his eyes, yet heard it above him. An object moving to the right was seen as moving to the left. It was heard at the right. Stratton's feet were seen as pointing toward him, yet he felt them pointing away. When he tapped upon his knee with a pencil he felt the pencil at one place and saw it at another. When he reached for an object seen to the left Stratton failed to grasp it, for it was actually to his right. Thus the effect of visual inversion was to disrupt the normal harmonious relation between vision and the other senses. If the subject closed his eyes and reacted solely on the basis of auditory, tactual, and kinesthetic cues, his localization was correct. It was also correct for points in the exact center of the field of vision, since the rays of light from this region are not inverted.

Stratton at first wore the lenses for a period of $21\frac{1}{2}$ hours, distributed over three days. In his later experiment they were worn for 87 hours, distributed over eight days. Even after three days Stratton's initial helplessness had largely vanished and he was able to locate objects with greatly increased accuracy. Reporting on the results of his longer experiment, Stratton [38] says that by the fourth day "actions appropriate to the new visual perception frequently occurred without any conflict or apparent tendency to react by a misinterpretation of visual positions. My hands, in washing, often moved to the soap or to the proper position of the basin, without premeditation or any need of correcting movement." This tendency became more pronounced as the experiment proceeded. The correct localization of many objects became so automatic toward the end of the experiment that Stratton at times *felt* the visual scene to be right-side up once more. He nowhere specifically says that he *saw* it right-side up, as some have supposed. In several places Stratton does report, however, that he came to see certain objects where he felt and heard them. For example,

I felt that my legs were where I saw them, or

where they were vividly represented, if they were out of sight. If I tapped my knee in plain sight, the contact was localized only where sight reported it to be. . . .

He also says that

Localization of sounds varied, being different when the source of sound was in sight from what it was when this was out of sight, and also in the latter case differing with different directions of attention, or with different suggestions as to the direction from which the sound came. The fire, for instance, sputtered where I saw it. The tapping of my pencil on the arm of my chair seemed without question to issue from the visible pencil.

In the theoretical discussion of his results, Stratton [39] claims that continued localizing responses to an object seen in one place and felt in another will eventually lead to a "new visual translation" of the tactual cues. It is thus assumed that the actual position of a retinal image has no *a priori* relation to upright vision and the cooperation of the senses in localization. He says:

We are now enabled to see what the harmony between touch and sight really is. The experiment clearly shows that an object need not appear in any particular position in the visual field in order to admit a union or identification of the tactual and visual perceptions of the object. The visual position which any tactual experience suggests — the visual place in which we "feel" that an object is — is determined, not by some fundamental and immutable relation of tactual and visual "spaces," but by the mere fact that we have constantly seen the object there when we have had that particular touch-experience. . . . This harmony does not require that the visual manifestation of a tactual object should be just here and not there, or in this direction and not in that.

The inverted position of the retinal image is . . . not essential to "upright vision," for it is not essential to a harmony between touch and sight, which, in the final analysis, is the real meaning of upright vision. For some visual objects may be inverted with respect to other visual objects, but the *whole system* of visual objects can never by itself be either inverted or upright. It could be inverted or upright only with respect to certain non-visual experiences with which I might compare my visual system — in other words, with respect to my tactual or motor perceptions.

In terms of our present problem, which is that of ascertaining why the individual visually localizes objects in their actual positions even though the retinal image in relation to these objects is inverted, Stratton's view could be interpreted as follows: For the newborn infant *visual objects* have no spatial significance, that is, they are neither upright nor inverted, neither to the right nor to the left. They can have these spatial characteristics only after the data of other senses are compared with the visual. In responding to objects, the infant is stimulated tactually and kinesthetically. Tactual and kinesthetic stimulation corresponds with the *actual* position of the objects. The visual stimuli, which at first have no spatial significance, now receive such significance in terms of touch and kinesthesis. They gradually come to be *seen* and *felt* in the same position. Auditory stimuli are, according to this view, also brought into harmony with vision. Such a view is empirical, opposing the concept of upright vision as due to some *innate* or *unlearned* sensory organization. Carr [40] accepts this viewpoint. He claims that, were Stratton's lenses worn from the time of birth, vision would be normal as it is with an inverted retinal image:

Let us assume that such a system of lenses had been worn continuously from birth. The problem of reinversion would never have arisen. Vision and contact would have become adjusted in respect to their spatial significance just as readily as in normal vision, and undoubtedly such a hypothetical subject would have developed an *appropriate* concept of up and down. Stratton's conclusion that optical inversion is not essential to seeing objects right side up in respect to either the tactual or conceptual standard is undoubtedly correct.

This concept of visual localization receives support from Stratton's alleged observation that, under conditions of lenticular inversion, eventually *the visual field turned right-side up* and that objects *were eventually seen where they were felt* and otherwise located. Ewert [41] however, failed to verify these observations, despite the fact that his lenses were worn over both eyes (Figure 98) and that his experiment was carried out over a period twice as long as Stratton's. Stratton was both subject and experimenter. He wrote his reports some time after the experiences occurred. His study was introspective rather than objective. He reports no systematic experimental data. Ewert wore the lenses himself and then repeated the experiment using two other subjects, Walter S. Hunter and the writer. Each subject was accompanied by a person who recorded his verbal reports as they were given. Errors of recall were thus avoided. Moreover, each individual was subjected to an intensive

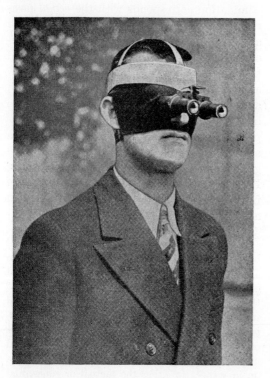

Figure 98. The Inversion Lenses Worn by Ewert and His Subjects

This apparatus was removed only for shaving, when the individual kept his eyes tightly closed, and for sleep, during which time a bandage covered the eyes. (From P. H. Ewert, "A Study of the Effects of Inverted Retinal Stimulation upon Spatially Coordinated Behavior," *Genet. Psychol. Monog.*, 1930, 7.

experimental program. The accuracy of his visual, tactual, kinesthetic, and auditory localizations was tested daily before, during, and after the period of inversion. In addition, many hours daily were involved in all kinds of non-experimental activity. The subjects went for walks and engaged, so far as was possible, in their customary daily activities. One of the subjects attended the theater several times, went to the amusement park, where he engaged in the usual activities prevalent at such places, rode the street cars, rode in elevators, took a boat ride, and so on. The subjects tried to depend upon visual cues at all times rather than to ignore them.

Ewert and his two subjects had the same *initial* experiences as those reported by Stratton. Furthermore, like Stratton, they rapidly learned to make appropriate *motor adjustments* to the objects in their surroundings. At no time, however, did any of the subjects see the visual field or any object in it right-side up. The visual field was as inverted at the end of the experiment (after fourteen days of continuous wearing of the lenses) as at the beginning. The subjects reported no reinversion of the visual field, and careful laboratory tests failed to disclose any evidence of it. Localizing reactions became so automatic at times that a "feeling of normalcy" was present. This is probably the feeling reported by Stratton and interpreted by some as "seeing right-side up." The feeling was not due to a reinversion of the visual field but to an increasing tendency to disregard the visual distraction, despite an effort to regard and adjust to it. In another paper on this problem Ewert [42] claims that

the "feeling of normalcy" in the visual field following a period of continuous inversion, is merely an illusion resulting from a lapse of attention to the experience of inversion. The illusion is further attributable to the fact that the pattern of a seen object is not altered by the inverting lenses.

Another possible interpretation is that the individual at times responds "absent-mindedly" to the situation before him, just as in typing, one who habitually looks at the letters on the keys before he strikes them, sometimes, after the habit has become more or less automatic, hits the correct keys without looking at or thinking about them. In the same way an individual who has worn the inverting glasses for several days may localize correctly without noticing that objects are visually inverted and without thinking about the adjustments to be made.

Not only did Ewert's subjects fail to observe a reinversion of the visual field, but they also failed to see objects where they felt them. Ewert's [43] conclusion concerning this point is based on several objective tactual localization experiments as well as on the reports of his subjects:

Inverted vision was found to be a forceful distraction to normal touch localization. The interference is perhaps due to the incompatibility of the new visual cues with the old localizing habits. There was rapid adjustment to the distracting visual interference until at the end of fourteen days of practice the problem was practically mastered. The comparatively great improvement shows that the subject again learns to point accurately to the visual area where a spot was touched. There is no evidence that a given tactual area would ever shift to the disoriented visual spot . . . the disrupted retinal-motor habits become organized again so as to conform to the "old" touch and the "new" vision.

Experiments on visual-auditory localization showed that sound localization as such had "no tendency to swing into line with visual localization." After the lenses had been removed, there was an immediate return to the former (non-experimental) accuracy of localization. Dizziness and slightly exaggerated eye and head movements were the only after-effects of a fourteen-day period of inverted vision.

The late Joseph Peterson * wore the lenses

* Peterson died before his results were prepared for publication, but the information given here was conveyed to Ewert through correspondence. See P. H. Ewert, "Factors in Space Localization During Inverted Vision. I. Intra-Sensory and Inter-Sensory-Motor Antagonism," *Psych. Rev.*, 1936, *43*, 522–546.

of the above experiment for a period of three weeks under conditions as nearly as possible comparable to those of Stratton. He confirmed Ewert's results. There was no reinversion of the field of vision and no realignment of vision with the other senses as reported by Stratton and stressed by Carr in his interpretation of upright vision. In the recent experiment reported by Snyder and Pronko [44] a somewhat comparable system of lenses was worn by one subject for thirty days. Although most of the tasks were different from those involved in Ewert's experiment, the results were essentially like his. The initial wearing of the lens system seriously disrupted previously developed habits of card sorting, mirror drawing, pegboard manipulation, and walking a visual maze pattern; but continued practice, over a period of thirty days, gradually restored the pre-inversion skill, and in some instances even improved upon it. Removal of the lenses was in some instances slightly disturbing, but the preceding skill was almost immediately restored.* Like Stratton and Carr, these investigators feel that space perception "does not exist at birth" but "comes into being only as the result of a series of 'contacts' between the organism and features of its surroundings."

Such conclusions are not substantiated by Sperry's [46] experiments on frogs. In these experiments, the eye itself was inverted. Sperry turned the eyeball through 180 degrees while leaving the optic nerve intact. The eyeballs healed in this position. Then the frogs reacted to the position and movements of objects much as human beings with inverted lenses had reacted. Objects above were reacted to as below, and vice versa.

* Foley's [45] inverted-vision experiment on a monkey yielded behavioral results like those found in human subjects. Upon introduction of the lens system, there was a marked interference with every aspect of visually controlled behavior. During a period of seven days, however, the effects of inversion were overcome, so that spatially coordinated behavior approximated normality. When the lenses were removed, there was a temporary slight disturbance, as in the human subjects.

Moreover, when an object moved in one direction, the head moved in the opposite direction. Sperry found that these responses persisted indefinitely without correction. He says that "This refractoriness to re-education suggests, in itself, that the structure mediating these reactions is not organized by the learning process." One could not, by the same token, however, say that because human subjects *do* learn to readjust to an inverted image, they must have learned to locate objects in space. The frog is notoriously a poor learner (see p. 121), and in any event no special training was introduced, such as punishing it for incorrect localizing responses. Another difference resides in the fact that human beings react symbolically to their predicament. They "figure out" how to react appropriately to the new situation. Still another difference, although of problematical significance, is surgical inversion in the frog as against lenticular inversion in human subjects.

The experiments on inverted vision have been dealt with at such length because they bring to a focus many significant factors involved in spatially coordinated behavior. Although vision is most directly implicated, other senses, as well as efferent processes, are responsible for appropriately coordinated reactions to the uprightness of our objective visual world.

In the first place, we are confronted with the fact that, although the eye is in some respects a camera-like mechanism, and projects an inverted image onto the retina, the image is not fixed there, as in a camera, and we do not react to it as an image. There is no "inner man" to look at the image and be confused by its inversion. As Gibson [47] points out, moreover, the overlap between adjacent nerve fibers in the retina, through lateral connections, and also within the optic tracts, is such that the "image" on the brain, if there were such a thing, would be very blurred. "In all probability, it should not be thought of as an image, and even less, as a literal picture. It is an event composed not of light but of nerve-cell discharges, and if a surgeon exposed the brain to view, there would be nothing to see." One might say, therefore, that since there is no retinal "photo" for us to observe, there is no inversion and thus no problem of "why we see right-side up when the image is upside down." It might be argued, as Stratton and Carr argued, that we *learn* to see things where they are, as indicated by our other senses. But this does not completely remove the problem. The external world *does* produce retinal effects. If these do not constitute an image to which we respond as such, they are at least correlated with external stimuli, in some such manner as Gibson has supposed. We might say that they are "inversely correlated," since rays of light coming from above stimulate the lower part of the retina, and rays coming from the left stimulate the right of the retina. Moreover, the retinal pattern is represented cortically without reinversion.[48] The problem which still remains, therefore, is why all of this does not confuse us.

Ewert [49] was of the opinion that a purely empirical theory of spatial localization is unsatisfactory. None of the subjects of the experiments on inverted vision learned to see anything right-side up while they wore the lenses. So these experiments provide no evidence to support an empirical theory. Ewert pointed out, in this connection, that reinversion of any *part* of the perceived world would be impossible. If anything at all became reinverted visually, everything would have to be reinverted. Moreover, head, eye, and general body movements are also affected by lenticular inversion, and in a manner which, according to Ewert, makes their *complete* reharmonization highly improbable. Movements of the head and body induce unlearned and automatic compensatory eye movements. These movements are of vestibular origin. They mediate static processes, those which, without visual cues, indicate the position of the body in space. Such eye movements are not affected by inverted vision. In addition to such non-visual eye movements, there are the visually elicited eye movements involved in ocular fixation and pursuit. Since early infancy these visually elicited movements have been in operational harmony with those of vestibular origin and those involved in perception of motion. When moving in one direction, for example, we have been accustomed to seeing the environment move, as it were, in the opposite direction. Under conditions of inverted vision this relationship is disrupted. These eye reflexes (which are elicited by body movements) remain unchanged by inversion. On the other hand, fixational eye movements (those elicited by visual stimuli) are *reversed*. Under such conditions, visually perceived objects are seen to be moving in a direction which is the opposite of that in which they are actually moving. One now sees objects moving in the same direction as that in which his body is felt to be moving. Under such circumstances one feels that he is traveling in the *opposite* direction from that in which he is actually moving. While going up in an open elevator, for example, the person wearing inversion lenses sees the floors going up, rather than down; hence he feels that he is going down. No matter how much he tries to overcome it, the feeling persists. The same is just as true of horizontal movement, where objects are seen as going in a direction opposite to what is normal. Ewert [50] doubted whether this "experimentally induced antagonism could be completely eliminated. Such antagonism would probably persist as in reversal of handedness, i.e., as when a manual shift is made from the preferred to the non-preferred hand." Inversion of visual stimulation by means of lenses also produces a disruption between other physiological functions and visual stimulation. The distance relationship of objects is reversed. Depth is reversed so that an awning, for example, looks like an upturned receptacle. Such effects were not overcome. Ewert [51] said that:

Perception of locality, distance, and depth are largely dependent upon convergence, accommodation, retinal disparity, and other physiological and

psychological factors. During lenticular inversion a number of these factors are reversed. Having attained a given structural inter-relationship in the course of evolution, with reference to gravity and the upright position of man, these processes would undoubtedly resist a complete ontogenetic adaptation. This view, however, does not necessarily rule out such types of adaptation as may occur in the inter-sensory-motor and conceptual processes. Nor does it rule out the normal types of intra-sensory adaptation. . . . Hence, we are not forced, by virtue of this interpretation, to accept an unqualified nativistic theory of space perception.

Ewert [52] stressed the fact that innate and acquired factors are both involved in space localization and that any theory which stresses one factor to the exclusion of the other must be unsatisfactory. The problem of upright vision is reduced to one of intersensory and motor cooperation. The real problem is how visual and non-visual processes achieve the cooperation which we find in normal space localization. This cooperation, according to our best evidence, is partly innate and partly acquired.

In consideration of the visual perception of depth, the problem of intersensory and motor cooperation, together with the question of innate and acquired aspects, is still with us.

Responses to Depth

Children and adults respond to the relative distance of objects and discern whether the objects are spherical, cubic, and the like.* These responses to the distance, depth, and solidity of visually presented aspects of our world have raised the issue of how, since the retinal image is flat, we are able to see, and respond in terms of, tridimensionality.** The

There is no adequate means of differentiating, in any fundamental way, between depth vision and distance vision. Warren's *Dictionary of Psychology* (Boston: Houghton Mifflin, 1934) defines depth perception as "direct appreciation of the distance of a given object or objects from the observer, or of the relative distance from front to back in the perception of solid objects, bas-reliefs, and intaglios." Investigators tend to use the two terms interchangeably.

** The entire retina is, of course, cup-shaped. It thus possesses tridimensionality. The retinal image

image observable on the back of a freshly excised eye is bidimensional, like a photograph or plane drawing. What we respond to, however, is not a pictorial representation of the world in front of our eye. We respond to patterns of neural excitation carried from the retina to the brain. According to Gibson's concept, which we have already considered briefly, the retinal stimulation, although lacking tridimensionality in a stereoscopic sense, does contain a representation of tridimensionality. The following quotation from Gibson [53] amplifies this point and some of its implications.

The qualities of solidity and depth ... do not have any replica in the two-dimensional retinal image but they may very well prove to have correlates there. An assumption will be borrowed from geometry which states that when a three-dimensional physical world is projected optically, the slant and shape of its surfaces undergo a mathematical transformation in the projection but that they do not on this account vanish or disappear.

There is a naïve theory of perception to the effect that the outer world somehow gets into the eye. Almost the first principle the beginning student learns is that nothing gets into the eye but light. This ... assumption can be sharpened by saying that, in a special sense, the outer world *does* get into the eye. It implies that at least the surfaces, slopes, and edges of the world have correlates in the retinal image specifically related to their objective counterparts by a lawful transformation. If this is correct, the problem of the restoration of the lost third dimension in perception is a false problem.

There is another naïve theory of the visual process to the effect that a retinal *picture* is transmitted to the brain by the optic nerve. ... there is no need for a picture-theory of psychophysical correspondence since perception may be a correlate, not a copy of the image. If the image is neither a replica of the world nor a picture for the perception, but a complex of variations, it may prove easier to trace its specific correspondence to both.

conforms to the contour of the retina, but if the stimulated area is small, as is often the case, little curvature is involved. In any event, actual tridimensionality cannot exist in the image itself, even though it does fall upon a concave surface.

Although the retinal image is without depth, and even though it may possess correlates of depth in the sense stressed by Gibson, there are several physiological and psychological phenomena which have long been recognized as possible depth cues. It has generally been assumed that perceptions based upon physiological cues are innate and that those based upon psychological cues are learned. Conceivably, however, we may have to learn to interpret even the physiological cues.

Two of the possible physiological cues are actually of little if any significance in depth perception. One of these is the curvature of the lens, which varies in fixation of near and far objects. The other is convergence of the eyes, which is of course greater in fixating near than more distant objects. The assumption has been that kinesthetic impulses associated with such muscular activity lead to "unconscious inferences" concerning the distance of objects. But Woodworth [54] presents evidence that these cues would be of no importance if objects were farther away from the eyes than six to twelve inches. Another physiological cue is of great significance for tridimensional vision. It is utilized in the stereoscope and in so-called "3D" motion pictures. This is retinal disparity. It is a binocular cue, since the disparity referred to is a difference in the images on the two retinae. If one is looking at a chair, for instance, the left eye is stimulated somewhat differently from the right eye. When a drawing or photograph is representative of the right-eye view, and another of the left-eye view, and these representations are viewed binocularly through a stereoscope or through special glasses, as in so-called "3D" motion pictures, the tridimensionality of objects and situations is clearly apparent. Experiments on stereoscopic vision in children are discussed later. It should be mentioned at this point, however, that retinal disparity as a depth cue is of lesser importance for distant than for nearby objects and situations.

The so-called psychological cues are present

in an ordinary photograph viewed monocularly. One such cue is the relative size of objects at different distances. Other things being equal, a smaller image of a known object, like an airplane, would indicate that the plane is more distant than when its image is larger. When one object obviously overlaps another, like a tree with a house behind it, the object which obstructs our view is perceived as nearer. This is the interpositional cue. Shadows give an impression of depth and one may sometimes reverse the depth effect by reversing the shadows. Thus a crater may become a mound when the picture is inverted. Linear perspective is another cue. The road seems to narrow as it stretches off in the distance. Aerial perspective, which involves perception of distance in terms of the clarity of objects, is included among psychological cues. The same object, seen through a fog, appears farther away than when viewed under clear conditions. Relative movement is still another possible cue. If the observer is stationary and objects are moving, the object seeming to move fastest is judged to be nearest. If the observer is moving and objects are stationary, those nearby seem to move in the opposite direction while those in the distance appear motionless or to move with the observer.

The above-mentioned cues are regarded by Gibson [55] as "variables" or "gradients of the retinal image," and he discusses each of them in these terms. Whereas most psychologists regard depth perception as, in large measure, dependent upon learned reactions to such cues, Gibson looks upon it as more or less immediately given by "the gradual change of size and density in the image as the objects and elements recede from the observer." He is saying that we do not have to learn to interpret something which is at first meaningless, with respect to space, for the retinal image contains spatial meaning from the start. Perhaps few would doubt that the retinal image, pictorially or in terms of correlates (see p. 266), does represent the gradients of texture so much stressed by Gibson. But the problem of whether or not we have to learn to interpret what is in the image is as much an unsolved problem as before. The most widely accepted view probably approximates that expressed by Goodenough [56] with reference to retinal disparity and response to depth. She says:

. . . our two eyes, being placed a little distance from each other, give us slightly different views. The left eye sees a little further around one side, the right eye around the other side. In looking at distant objects or at near-by flat objects, the image formed by the lens on the sensitive retina at the back of the eye is essentially the same for both eyes; that is, corresponding parts of the two retinas are affected. The action currents coming in to the brain from the two eyes may be said to have the same spatial pattern, and when this occurs the object is perceived as one. Now when the two images are only slightly different, as is the case when we look at a near-by solid object, the incoming nerve impulses still give the sensation of a single object, but the sensation is not the same as that produced by nerve impulses from exactly corresponding parts of the two retinas. Very early in life and without being aware that we are doing so we learn to interpret this difference in visual sensation in terms of the tactual and muscular sensations we get from handling objects that give us visual sensations of this kind. When we say that the tree-trunk *looks* rounded we mean only that the visual sensation has the qualities that from infancy on we have learned to associate with objects that *feel* rounded. The infant at first lacks this experience, and so, even though his visual sensation may be exactly the same as ours, it does not have the same meaning for him that it has for us.

Like the problem of upright vision, that of depth perception is not open to direct attack. This is because the infant cannot tell us about its experiences and because we cannot remember if we have been without ability to discriminate depth.

Observations on depth discrimination in children

In their book on the development of vision in infant and child, Gesell and others [57] find no evidence of response to the depth aspect of objects until the age of 36 weeks, and even then their evidence is not especially compelling. They say that the child of this age

is better oriented in space. He looks into distant space in a more penetrating manner. . . . He peers into the cavity of an empty cup. We are not sure that he sees the bottom, but he is entering the domain of a third dimension. He even thrusts his hand part way into the cup. . . . Optically speaking, his depth perception is still so meager that he has only a dim apprehension of container and contained.

As the infant nears the age of one year,

the tridimensional world consists of minute distances, as well as of far reaches. And it is the minutiae of this world of intimate near vision with which the infant is pre-eminently concerned during the closing months of the first year. With his inquisitive index finger he punctures and penetrates the third dimension.

Gesell looks upon this development as largely maturational.

Biographical data on depth discrimination in infants are summarized by Updegraff,[58] but all the studies reported have used reaching as an index of response to distance. This is found to be quite inaccurate at first. Such results are hard to evaluate. They may merely indicate that the requisite muscular coordination has not yet developed.

In her own investigation of distance discrimination, Updegraff tested the ability of ten four-year-old children (previously tested for their understanding of "nearer" and "farther") and six adults to indicate the nearer of two lighted areas presented horizontally before them in a room which was otherwise dark. One area was at a constant distance of 505 centimeters. The other was moved away from the subject or toward him. The distance between this area and the standard was decreased until the threshold had been determined. Distance discrimination was exhibited by the children, but their acuity was inferior to that of adults. The distance of the stimuli (505 centimeters) was greater than the range of accommodation and of convergence. Hence these factors could not have mediated the discrimination. Since the

room was otherwise dark, the various monocular pattern factors were eliminated. The two areas were sufficiently separated to eliminate overlapping. The only other factors which might have been significant bases of distance discrimination were binocular disparity and the size and intensity of the retinal image. Tests showed that the binocular factor was not involved. A further series of tests in which the size factor was varied indicated that both children and adults judged the larger area to be the nearer and the smaller area to be the farther. A test of the effect of linear perspective showed that six of the children and two of the adults reacted to diverging stimuli as nearer than converging ones.

Distance discrimination at 195 meters was tested out-of-doors. Fifteen four-year-old children evidenced good distance vision. It was difficult or impossible under these circumstances to respond to a differential distance of three meters. Monocular cues such as size, intensity, linear perspective, and clearness were the only ones available.

In another experiment with nineteen children ranging in age from $2\frac{1}{2}$ to four years Updegraff determined ability to discriminate whether a ball dropped in front of or behind a partially open screen at a standard distance of one meter. The child was required to get the ball and the experimenter noted to which compartment it responded. Distances in both directions were varied. All the children discriminated a difference of 5 centimeters, but only five were successful at 3.5 centimeters. No errors were exhibited by sixteen adults tested under the same conditions.

Carr[59] reports a previously unpublished study on stereoscopic vision in children ranging in age from two years and five months to five years. Stereograms of three objects were drawn. The children, none of whom had previously seen a stereoscope, were given a period of training in its use. They were then shown the stereograms by means of the stereoscope. The response tested was that of identifying an object and its stereoscopic representation. The youngest group (four children of two years and five months to two years and eight months) made only 26 correct identifications out of 72, the average accuracy being 36.1 per cent. Since there were three objects presented an equal number of times, a chance accuracy would have been 33.3 per cent. Repetition of the test after three days of special training, involving identification of the objects by the experimenter, led to an average accuracy of only 38.8 per cent. Correction of errors after each of 72 further tests led to 30.5 per cent correct identification in a child who had previously exhibited an accuracy of 44.4 per cent. Groups of children ranging in age from three years and one month to five years showed a high percentage of correct identifications. The accuracy ranged from 79 per cent in the youngest of these groups to 99 per cent in the oldest. Carr is of the opinion that, with respect to the "innate or empirical origin of the stereoscopic mechanism," these results are ambiguous in import. This is because ability to focus the stereoscope properly may itself improve with age, thus contributing to the better scores of older children without the necessary implication that stereopsis itself has improved. This criticism also applies to the data of Gesell, Ilg, and Bullis,[60] who have tested stereoscopic vision from the age of five. In one of their tests the child views pictures of a bird and a nest through a regulation stereoscope. Some five-year-olds respond binocularly, that is, say they see the bird in the nest, but this response is more consistent at the six-year level and it improves further with age.

The criticism applicable to tests involving the stereoscope does not apply to those carried out by Johnson and Beck [61] with the apparatus shown in Figure 99. Even one-year-olds exhibit tridimensional vision when tested in this way. The task is as simple as that undertaken by anybody who looks at "3D" movies through polaroid lenses. In this instance the test is so arranged that, if tridimensional vision is present, a doll is seen to be between the child and the screen. Children from one year of age reach for the doll where it is seen by adults who view the picture through polaroid lenses. The published study does not include children younger than two years but Beck has informed the writer that one-year-olds have since been tested and that they also react as if the doll were between them and the screen.

We can conclude, therefore, that tridimensional vision is present in one-year-olds. But we do not know whether it exists at birth or whether it develops during the first year, either through maturational processes, or learning, or a combination of these processes.

The fact that children do not at first draw with perspective has led some to suppose that they are defective in depth discrimination. But children's drawings provide no evidence of response, or absence of response, to tridimensionality. Stern's [62] daughter could identify simple drawings in perspective at the age of one year and ten months, but she could not draw the objects with perspective until years later. Most of us, even as adults, require special training before we draw in perspective. Primitive peoples, who doubtless perceive depth, are noted for the fact that their drawings lack perspective.

Depth vision after removal of cataracts

There is general agreement concerning inaccuracy of distance vision following removal of cataracts from the congenitally blind. The summary by Dennis [63] shows that patients, blind before removal of their cataracts, are unable successfully to reach for objects placed before them. Latta [64] found absence of stereoscopic vision in his subject. The test was given a month after the operation. Carr [65] reports that operated cataract patients respond to all objects as flat and that they fail to see the vista effect in landscapes. The inaccuracy of distance vision in such individuals is often quite ludicrous. One patient reported that objects touched his eyes. Another looked out of a window and tried to touch the pavement below with his walking stick. One man said that if he kept his eyes open while walking he raised his feet so high that people laughed at him. Since a cataract operation

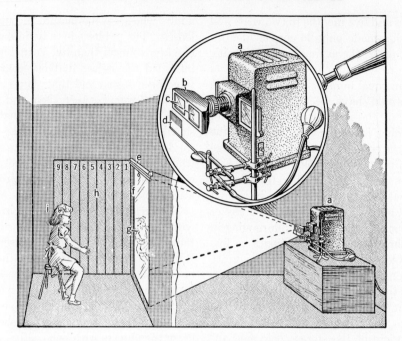

Figure 99. A Device for Demonstrating Depth Perception Based upon Retinal Disparity

a, Leitz projector for showing 2″ × 2″ slides.
b, Steroly attachment which splits light from projector into two beams.
c, Polaroid screens that polarize the two beams, one vertically, the other horizontally.
d, Pneumatically operated blind.
e, Window shade.
f, Ground glass screen.
g, Polarized images thrown by projector.
h, Ruled cardboard indicating distances from screen.
i, Child viewing the polarized images through polarized spectacles. The phenomenal position of the doll is revealed by the reaching responses of the child.
(After B. Johnson and L. F. Beck, "The Development of Space Perception: Stereoscopic Vision in Preschool Children," *Journal of Genetic Psychology*, 1941, *58*, 250.)

destroys the lens, accommodatory cues are eliminated. Moreover, excitement following removal of the bandages makes accurate quantitative data difficult to obtain. Thus the results are equivocal. On the basis of the data from cataract patients, one could argue that depth vision is innate (depending upon the destroyed accommodatory mechanisms) or that it is of empirical origin.

Animal experiments on distance discrimination

As suggested in an earlier discussion, animal experiments sometimes allow us to use controls which we could not use with children.

Riesen's [66] experiment in which chimpanzees were reared in total darkness is a case in point. But the visually deprived chimpanzees exhibited no manual responses to visually presented objects, and, except for certain optic reflexes, they were apparently blind. This experiment therefore tells us nothing about possible depth or distance discrimination.

Another experiment on chimpanzees is relevant, but also inadequate from the standpoint of providing crucial data on the genesis of visual depth perception. This is the experiment in which Nissen, Chow, and Semmes [67] restricted the tactual, kinesthetic, and manipulatory experience of a chimpanzee by encasing its limbs in cardboard cylinders. The responses of the restricted animal were compared with those of chimpanzees normally reared. Restriction began at the end of the first month of life and extended, except for test periods, until the 31st month. Tests of visual depth and distance discrimination given at the ages of 14 and 31 months yielded results which suggest that the animal's inability to use its hands and feet in manipulating objects did not retard its responses to visual depth. Only its tactual discrimination was seriously retarded. The investigators themselves point out, however, that their experiment is a far from conclusive check on the idea (p. 267) that visual stimuli get their tridimensional meanings in terms of related tactual and kinesthetic experiences. This is because the chimpanzee was always able to manipulate objects with its mouth and to move around in its environment, thus possibly getting kinesthetic cues as to the distance of visually presented objects.

Russell [68] did an experiment on rats which suggested the presence of visual distance discrimination, and Lashley and Russell [69] later used the same technique to test for the presence of such discrimination in rats reared for the first 100 days of life in darkness. It was found that rats, in jumping to a food platform, use more force as the platform is more distant. This, as well as the accuracy of jumps to different distances, was used as a criterion of visual distance discrimination. The visually deprived rats, after preliminary training with the food platform at a constant distance, also regulated the force of their jump in accordance with the distance of the food platform. This observation led Lashley and Russell to conclude that "the visual perception of distance and gradation of force in jumping to compensate for distance are not acquired by learning, but are the product of some innately organized neural mechanism." Recently, however, Greenhut and Young [70] repeated Russell's original experiment, with certain modifications, and obtained results not in

agreement with his. These investigators observed a gradation of force with distance only when the distances were held constant for several trials, or when they were sequentially increased. When the distances were randomized from trial to trial, there was no evidence of distance discrimination. When the distance was shortened for the next trial, the rat tended to overjump. When it was increased, the rat tended to underjump. The high correlation between distance and force which the earlier investigators had reported was also absent. Greenhut and Young therefore concluded that "rats cannot perceive distance through their visual apparatus alone to any marked extent, but require learning and kinesthetic cues."

These investigators used shock to force the rat to jump from the platform, and Russell and Lashley did not. There is thus the possibility that the discrepancy in the results of the two experiments is due to the excitement produced by shock. Greenhut and Young admit this possibility, but their analysis of the results for shock and no-shock jumps does not indicate a significant effect of shock. Another possible source of the discrepancy is that Lashley and Russell failed to randomize their distances as Greenhut and Young did in their experiment.

Thus the issue of whether rats have visual distance discrimination, and, if so, whether it is innate or learned, is still without an unequivocal answer. The animal experiments which held out so much promise of settling a fundamental issue which could not be solved with human subjects directly have proved disappointing. It is true, of course, that rats may not be the best subjects for such experiments. The bird that swoops from a height and catches fish and the squirrel that jumps from limb to limb are exhibiting distance discrimination. With such animals one might obtain results much more conclusive than those with rats.

Conclusions concerning responses to depth

In general, the data on development of depth discrimination suggest that both learned and unlearned factors are operative. It would not be surprising if response to retinal disparity should turn out to depend more upon maturation of optic coordination than upon tactual and kinesthetic experience with objects. But there might be some basis for claiming that optic coordination is itself learned. There is also the possibility, as Gibson has suggested, that even the so-called psychological cues produce some depth perception prior to learning, this perception being a direct response to aspects of the retinal image. But until there is some proof for this assertion, most psychologists will probably persist in the view that we have to learn to interpret such cues. These questions, as we have seen, are very difficult to resolve. So far there is not a single experiment which provides crucial evidence in support of either a nativist or an empiricist theory of depth perception. We are probably on safe ground, however, in assuming that innate organization and learning are both important in the development of depth discrimination, as well as in the development of all other aspects of space perception. The influence of learning seems especially evident when spatially coordinated behavior requires an integration of contributions from more than one sense, as in integrating the visual impression of a ball with its tactual qualities, or the visual height of an object with kinesthetic impulses aroused in reaching for it.

Summary and Conclusions

Research on spatially coordinated behavior has to a large extent been animated by a desire to resolve issues aroused by the nativistic and the empiristic concepts of the origins of space perception. As often happens in the case of theoretical controversies, the research stimulated by the controversy has greatly enlarged our factual information but failed to resolve the theoretical issues at stake. With respect to spatially coordinated behavior we have achieved no clear disentanglement of the innate and acquired contribu-

tions, both of which seem clearly to be present, but we do have a great deal of information on development of tactual, auditory, and visual localization. We also know much more than was formerly known about development of depth or distance discrimination.

Spatially coordinated behavior of various kinds is apparent at or soon after birth. Localizing movements in response to tactile stimulation are present before birth. Such responses are more evident at birth than earlier, and they increase in frequency and in accuracy as a function of age. Experimental studies of tactual-kinesthetic localization in seeing children and adults have shown that accuracy increases until about the thirteenth year and then shows a decline. The decline does not appear in blind subjects. Seeing adults localize better by the visual than by the tactual-kinesthetic method. Hence, the decline is attributable to transfer from a tactual-kinesthetic to a visual method of localizing in seeing subjects as adulthood is approached. In localizing a tactile stimulus, children improve faster than adults.

Auditory localization in infants is evidenced by such responses as turning the eyes or the head in the direction of the source of sound. Such responses are very infrequent during the early weeks of infancy. They increase in frequency and in accuracy as a function of age. Before the age of six months, such responses may be quite accurate.

Visual localization is to some degree present in newborn infants, as evidenced by movements of the eyes. In these localizing responses there is rapid improvement during early infancy. Horizontal ocular pursuit of a moving light is almost perfect in some infants at six weeks. Head movements in response to visual stimuli are present in the newborn, but they are much less frequent than eye movements. Vertical and circular pursuit are relatively late in developing. Reaching in response to visual stimuli is not present at first, but it normally appears by the tenth week.

Experiments in which chimpanzees were reared in darkness suggest that simple reflex responses of the eyes, including visual pursuit, are innately organized and that their growth during early life is dependent on maturation rather than on learning. These experiments show, on the other hand, that reaching and other "meaningful" responses to visual objects do not appear from the start but are dependent on repeated visual stimulation. In some respects, the visually deprived chimpanzees were like the congenitally blind who were stimulated following removal of cataracts. From the standpoint of responding to the meaning of objects, the chimpanzees and human patients had to "learn to see." With respect to such aspects of perception, human babies probably go through a similar learning process, but at a lower level of maturity.

It is not known whether the visual world looks upright from the start, despite an inverted retinal image, or whether we have to learn to see upright. It should be remembered in this connection, however, that we do not see the image on our eye but respond only to a pattern of neural excitation in the brain. Human beings subjected to experiments on inverted vision do not learn to see right-side up, but they do learn to readjust so that their manual responses are adapted to visual inversion. In other words, they learn to reach for things where these really are rather than where they see them. We do not know what monkeys see, when subjected to comparable inversion, but we do know that they make a similar sensorimotor readjustment. Some effects of lenticular inversion (and inversion of the eyeball, as in frogs) fail to readjust. This has been taken as evidence that these aspects of upright vision are innately organized. Among such aspects are visual pursuit movements and perceptions of movement and depth.

Children give evidence of depth discrimination by the end of the first year. Experiments on distance discrimination show improvement with age. The data do not, however, enable us to resolve the nativist-empiricist controversy. From the moment a child is able to coordinate its eyes, retinal disparity could conceivably produce perception of depth, prior to contact with objects involved. But we do not know whether this is so, or whether depth perception is based upon a learned association of visual with tactual and kinesthetic stimulation, as some have claimed. Nor do we have evidence to prove or disprove the claim that the characteristics of the retinal image produce some depth perception prior to learning. According to the opposing view, we have to learn to interpret the so-called psychological cues. Here, as in the case of upright vision, innate organization and learning are possibly both involved. Animal research may yet resolve some of these issues.

REFERENCES

1. For an elementary presentation of such data, see N. L. Munn, *Psychology* (2d ed.). Boston: Houghton Mifflin, 1951, pp. 403–409.
2. Gibson, J. J., *The Perception of the Visual World*. Boston: Houghton Mifflin, 1950.
3. Raney, E. T., and L. Carmichael, "Localizing Responses to Tactual Stimuli in the Fetal Rat in Relation to the Psychological Problem of Space Perception," *J. Genet. Psychol.*, 1934, *45*, 3–21.
4. Sherman, M. C., I. C. Sherman, and C. D. Flory, "Infant Behavior," *Comp. Psychol. Monog.*, 1936, *12*, No. 4.

5. *Ibid.*, p. 46.
6. McGraw, M. B., *The Neuromuscular Maturation of the Human Infant*. New York: Columbia University Press, 1943, pp. 101–110.
7. Crudden, C. H., "Reactions of Newborn Infants to Thermal Stimuli Under Constant Tactual Conditions," *J. Exper. Psychol.*, 1937, *20*, 350–370.
8. Motivation for these studies has come from Lotze's doctrine of local signs (*Outlines of Psychology*, Boston: Ginn, 1886, p. 63) and Peterson's concept of local signs as orientation tendencies (*Psych. Rev.*, 1926, *33*, 218–236).

9. Munn, N. L., "Tactual Localization Without Overt Localizing Movements and Its Relation to the Concept of Local Signs as Orientation Tendencies," *J. Exper. Psychol.*, 1937, *20*, 581–588.

10. Dunford, R. E., "The Genetic Development of Cutaneous Localization," *J. Genet. Psychol.*, 1930, *37*, 499–513.

11. Renshaw, S., "The Errors of Cutaneous Localization and the Effect of Practice on the Localizing Movement in Children and Adults," *J. Genet. Psychol.*, 1930, *38*, 223–238.

12. Renshaw, S., R. J. Wherry, and J. C. Newlin, "Cutaneous Localization in Congenitally Blind versus Seeing Children and Adults," *J. Genet. Psychol.*, 1930, *38*, 239–248.

13. Renshaw, S., and R. J. Wherry, "The Age of Onset of Ocular Dominance," *J. Genet. Psychol.*, 1931, *39*, 493–496.

14. Pratt, K. C., A. K. Nelson, and K. H. Sun, *The Behavior of the Newborn Infant.* Columbus: Ohio State University Press, 1930.

15. Blanton, M. G., "The Behavior of the Human Infant During the First Thirty Days of Life," *Psych. Rev.*, 1927, *24*, 456–483.

16. Gesell, A., *The Mental Growth of the Pre-School Child.* New York: Macmillan, 1925.

17. Gesell, A., F. L. Ilg, and G. E. Bullis, *Vision: Its Development in Infant and Child.* New York: Hoeber, 1950.

18. See citation 4.

19. Sherman, M. C., and I. C. Sherman, "Sensori-Motor Responses in Infants," *J. Comp. Psychol.*, 1925, *5*, 53–68; see also citation 4, and the four following references.

20. McGinnis, J. M., "Eye-Movements and Optic Nystagmus in Early Infancy," *Genet. Psychol. Monog.*, 1930, *8*, 321–430. Quotations are from pp. 403–404 and 417.

21. Jones, M. C., "The Development of Early Behavior Patterns in Young Children," *J. Genet. Psychol.*, 1926, *33*, 537–585.

22. Shirley, M. M., *The First Two Years:* Vol. I. *Postural and Locomotor Development.* Minneapolis: University of Minnesota Press, 1931.

23. Gesell, A., and H. Thompson, *Infant Behavior: Its Genesis and Growth.* New York: McGraw-Hill, 1934. Also see citation 17.

24. Dennis, W., "Congenital Cataract and Unlearned Behavior," *J. Genet. Psychol.*, 1934, *44*, 340–351.

25. Senden, M. von, *Raum-und Gestaltauffasung bei operierten Blindgeborenen vor und nach der Operation,* Leipzig: Barth, 1932; D. O. Hebb, *The Organization of Behavior,* New York: Wiley, 1949; M. Wertheimer, "Hebb and Senden on the Role of Learning in Perception," *Am. J. Psychol.*, 1951, *64*, 133–137.

26. Riesen, A. H., "The Development of Visual Perception in Man and Chimpanzee," *Science,* 1947, *106*, 107. Also see following references.

27. Riesen, A. H., "Arrested Vision," *Scientific American,* 1950, *183*, 16–19; and "Post-Partum Development of Behavior," *Chicago Med. School Quar.*, 1951, *13*, 17–24.

28. Riesen, A. H., "Arrested Vision," *Scientific American,* 1950, *183*, 19.

29. See citation 20.

30. See citation 23.

31. See citation 14.

32. Dennis, W., "The Effect of Restricted Practice upon the Reaching, Sitting and Standing of Two Infants," *J. Genet. Psychol.*, 1935, *47*, 17–32.

33. See citation 25.

34. See citation 24.

35. Latta, R., "Notes on a Case of Successful Operation for Congenital Cataract," *Brit. J. Psychol.*, 1904, *1*, 135–150.

36. Carr, H. A., *An Introduction to Space Perception.* New York: Longmans, 1935.

37. Stratton, G. M., "Some Preliminary Experiments in Vision without Inversion of the Retinal Image," *Psych. Rev.*, 1896, *3*, 611–617; "Vision without Inversion of the Retinal Image," *ibid.*, *41*, 341–360; 463–481.

38. *Ibid.*, pp. 352–467.

39. *Ibid.*, pp. 475–476.

40. Carr, H. A., *op. cit.*, pp. 90–91.

41. Ewert, P. H., "A Study of the Effects of Inverted Retinal Stimulation upon Spatially Coordinated Behavior," *Genet. Psychol Monog.*, 1930, *7*, 177–363.

42. Ewert, P. H., "Factors in Space Localization during Inverted Vision," I, *Psych. Rev.* 1936, *43*, 526.

43. Citation 42, p. 236.

44. Snyder, F. W., and N. H. Pronko. *Vision with Spatial Inversion.* Wichita, Kansas: University of Wichita Press, 1952.

45. Foley, J. P., "An Experimental Investigation of the Effect of Prolonged Inversion of the Visual Field in the Rhesus Monkey (Macaca Mulatta)," *J. Genet. Psychol.*, 1940, *56*, 21–51.

46. Sperry, R. W., "Mechanisms of Neural Matur-ation," in S. S. Stevens (ed.), *Handbook of Experimental Psychology*. New York: Wiley, 1951. See especially pp. 242–248. The quota-tion is from p. 235.

47. See citation 2.

48. See R. W. Sperry, *op. cit.*, p. 252, for references on this point.

49. Ewert, P. H., "Factors in Space Localization During Inverted Vision," I, *Psych. Rev.*, 1936, *43*, 522–546; II, *ibid.*, 1937, *44*, 105–116.

50. Ewert, P. H., "Factors in Space Localization during Inverted Vision," I, *Psych. Rev.*, 1936, *43*, 528.

51. *Ibid.*, pp. 529–530.

52. Ewert, P. H., "Factors in Space Localization during Inverted Vision: II. An Explanation of Interference and Adaptation." *Psych. Rev.*, 1937, *44*, 105–116.

53. Gibson, J. J., *op. cit.*, pp. 8–9.

54. Woodworth, R. S., *Experimental Psychology*. New York: Holt, 1938. See especially p. 674.

55. Gibson, J. J., *op. cit.*, p. 78.

56. Goodenough, F. L., *Developmental Psychology*. New York: D. Appleton-Century, 1934, pp. 138–139.

57. Gesell, A., F. L. Ilg, and G. E. Bullis, *Vision: Its Development in Infant and Child*. New York: Hoeber, 1950, quotations from pp. 96–97.

58. Updegraff, R., "The Visual Perception of Dis-tance in Young Children and Adults. A Com-parative Study," *Univ. Iowa Stud.: Stud. in Child Welfare*, 1930, *4*, No. 4.

59. See citation 36.

60. See citation 57.

61. Johnson, B., and L. Beck, "The Development of Space Perception: Stereoscopic Vision in Pre-School Children," *J. Genet. Psychol.*, 1941, *58*, 247–254.

62. Stern, W., *Psychology of Early Childhood*. New York: Holt, 1924.

63. See citation 24.

64. See citation 35.

65. See citation 36.

66. See citations 26–28.

67. Nissen, H. W., K. L. Chow, and J. Semmes, "Effects of Restricted Opportunity for Tactual Kinesthetic, and Manipulative Experience on the Behavior of a Chimpanzee," *Am. J. Psy-chol.*, 1951, *64*, 485–507.

68. Russell, J. T., "Depth Discrimination in the Rat," *J. Genet. Psychol.*, 1932, *40*, 136–159.

69. Lashley, K. S., and J. T. Russell, "The Mech-anism of Vision: XI. A Preliminary Test of Innate Organization," *J. Genet. Psychol.*, 1934, *45*, 136–144.

70. Greenhut, A., and F. A. Young, "Visual Depth Perception in the Rat," *J. Genet. Psychol.*, 1953, *82*, 155–182.

SUGGESTIONS FOR FURTHER READING

Carr, H., *Introduction to Space Perception*. New York: Longmans, 1935.

Curti, M. W., *Child Psychology*. New York: Long-mans, 1930, pp. 221–238.

Dennis, W., "Congenital Cataract and Unlearned Behavior," *J. Genet. Psychol.*, 1934, *44*, 340–351.

Ewert, P. H., "The Effect of Inverted Retinal Stimulation on Spatially Coordinated Behavior," *Genet. Psychol. Monog.*, 1930, *7*, 177–363.

Gibson, J. J., *The Perception of the Visual World*. Boston: Houghton Mifflin, 1950.

Hebb, D. O., *Organization of Behavior: A Neuro-psychological Theory*. New York: Wiley, 1949, Chapters 1–5. While this discussion deals pri-marily with visual perception of figures and patterns, it has much material relevant to our discussion of spatially coordinated behavior.

Hilgard, E. R., "The Role of Learning in Percep-tion," in R. R. Blake and G. V. Ramsey, *Per-ception: An Approach to Personality*. New York: Ronald, 1951.

Latta, R., "Notes on a Case of Successful Opera-tion for Congenital Cataract in an Adult," *Brit. J. Psychol.*, 1904, *1*, 135–150.

Osgood, C. E., *Method and Theory in Experimental Psychology*. New York: Oxford University Press, 1953, pp. 225–228.

Riesen, A. H., "Arrested Vision," *Scientific Ameri-can*, 1950, *183*, No. 1, 16–19.

Snyder, F. W., and N. H. Pronko, *Vision with Spatial Inversion*. Wichita, Kansas: University of Wichita Press, 1952.

Woodworth, R. S., and H. Schlosberg, *Experi-mental Psychology* (rev. ed.). New York: Holt, 1954, pp. 523–527.

10

Motor Development

THE earliest source of information on motor development in children was the baby-biography. What such biographies disclosed concerning the motor repertoire in early childhood, the median age at which each response appears, and the range of individual differences has been indicated by Dennis,[1] whose findings were summarized in Figure 80, p. 195. The baby-biographies finally gave way to questionnaire studies. Parents were asked to indicate when, for example, their child first stood without help, when he took his first steps alone, and so on. The difficulty with questionnaires, as with the biographies, is that parents are not trained observers. Moreover, the information is often put down some time after the event, and hence is subject to errors of memory. Students of motor development have now come to rely upon systematic experimentally controlled observations on relatively large numbers of children. The data are collected by trained observers. Quite often a movie record is taken so that the behavior can be analyzed at leisure and in greater detail than would be possible when ordinary observation is used. Speaking generally, there are two approaches here, the cross-sectional and the longitudinal. In a typical *cross-sectional* study, sample groups of infants at different age levels are observed and the trend from one level to the other is thus discerned. In a typical *longitudinal* study, on the other hand, each child is followed from early to later stages of development.

Systematic studies of motor development fall into two general classifications. Many of them are *normative*. That is to say, they involve determination of the average or median age at which a given motor item appears. Other studies are *analytical*. Their chief purpose is to discover the precise nature and mechanics of particular motor developments. Many studies are both normative and analytical. The trend today is away from normative studies, since the norms have been pretty well established, and toward an analysis of each motor activity from the standpoint of its mechanics, its dependence upon heredity and environment, its neural correlates, and its significance in relation to other aspects of development.

Maturation and learning both contribute to the motor development of infants, as shown in our earlier discussion (pp. 194–200). In the case of those responses (phylogenetic) which characterize the race, it is evident that heredity is a prime determiner and that they are therefore more dependent upon maturation than upon opportunities to learn. It is in this connection that self-initiated (autogenous) activity plays an important role. In the case of responses (ontogenetic) which

276

develop in some individuals and not in others, learning is of prime importance, although the aptitude shown in acquiring them is itself a function of maturation. That is to say, the more mature the child, the faster he learns motor skills. He also learns skills of greater complexity than those within the scope of the less mature individual. Thus, even in the case of ontogenetic motor skills, maturation is also a factor to be considered. This is especially true during early childhood. It is related to sensorimotor development and the growth of the brain.

In the present chapter we are concerned more with motor activities which characterize the human race, and which normally develop in every child, than we are with individual skill, acquisition of which was considered in Chapter 7. This does not mean, however, that every response discussed here results from maturation alone. Maturation and learning are both involved. In some instances, such as using a cup, spoon, or knife, the particular response, although common to all children, is of cultural rather than racial origin. When the child of our society is sufficiently mature, and is given the proper stimulation, he learns these responses. Without such a cultural background and such stimulation, he would not learn them. Such relatively individualistic responses as skating, riding a bicycle, and playing basketball are not considered here.

Our discussion is confined largely to five questions: (1) What is the nature of motor activity in the newborn? (2) What motor developments are normal at particular age levels? (3) How does locomotion develop, from both the standpoint of the sequence involved and the mechanics of antigravity reactions? (4) What is the sequence involved in development of reaching and grasping, and particularly the finger-thumb opposition which is so important for human culture and individual development? (5) What is the origin of handedness?

Activity In the Newborn

In our discussion of fetal development we considered in detail the generalization that specific responses are individuated from an original undifferentiated total behavior pattern. We indicated that neither this generalization nor the opposite one, namely, that behavior patterns are compounded out of separate reflexes, is consonant with all the facts. The same issue has been raised in relation to behavior in the newborn. This issue, as it relates to postnatal behavior, was precipitated largely by Irwin's [2] investigation.

Irwin used the stabilimeter-polygraph technique which we have already described (pp. 232–233). Its use was supplemented by non-instrumental observation. In this way the activity of human infants was observed during the first ten days of life. It was observed continuously during this period. The four infants used in Irwin's investigation were kept under conditions of relatively constant external stimulation. Even without external variations in stimulation, the infants were quite active. Irwin points out that internal stimuli (probably from the alimentary canal) undoubtedly elicited this activity. The behavior of the newborn falls, according to him, into two descriptive categories: *specific movements* and *mass activity*. By specific movement he means "a movement of a part or segment of the infant organism." By mass activity, on the other hand, he means "those movements that involve the entire organism."

According to Irwin, mass activity is not the only behavior of the newborn, but it is the most obvious and the most characteristic behavior under conditions of constant external stimulation. In a series of critical reviews and theoretical discussions,[3] he presents the view that specific infant responses are gradually individuated from a primitive matrix of mass activity. In one place, Irwin [4] suggests that mass activity exists prior to birth and that much individuation has already appeared when the child is born. His view is that mass activity is at its maximum during the early fetal months, but that it is still present at birth, enabling one to differentiate behavior of the newborn into specific activities and mass activity.

Dennis [5] and Gilmer [6] do not agree with Irwin. They do not believe that a newborn infant's behavior can adequately be classified in this manner. Gilmer obtained motion-picture records of the "spontaneous" behavior of newborn infants and found, when he analyzed them frame by frame and at various speeds, that Irwin's so-called "mass activity" comprised several identifiable response patterns, each of which possessed a characteristic combination of essential "elements." Gilmer [7] says that his study "supports Dennis's claim that mass activity is not the only total bodily response of infants, but that, on the contrary, there are many total bodily responses." These are included under the heading "coordinate responses of many body parts" in Dennis's classification of responses of the newborn (see p. 179). Mass activity is there cited as one of several "spontaneous" coordinated responses. Many other generalized and specific responses in the classification are elicited by known external stimuli.

The newborn infant thus exhibits specific reflexes, some of them in response to internal and some in response to external stimuli. It also exhibits several responses involving coordination of many body parts. Whether these reflexes and patterns of response are individuated from a matrix of mass activity or whether they result from an integration of simpler response units, one cannot at present say. The available data suggest, however, that some responses originate in one way and others in another. McGraw [8] presents the situation very well when, at the end of her study of Johnny and Jimmy, she says:

The apparent controversy over individuation versus integration is clarified if the different stages of development of particular action-patterns are taken into account. . . . It is easily seen that at one stage of development the process of growth is predominantly a matter of eliminating waste motion, development being from an undifferentiated state

to a more specific one, or a process of individuation. But once a pattern, or an aspect of a pattern, has attained an appropriate degree of specificity, further development is indicated by an integration of two or more action-patterns, or aspects of an action-pattern, into another of greater complexity. It is not, therefore, a question of one theory being correct and the other wrong. The two processes are by no means mutually exclusive. Actually, both processes can be observed in the actions of the same individual at the same time, but the processes represent different stages of maturation in the growth cycle.

Although the issue involved here concerns the responses which normally occur in all infants during early life and which depend to a great extent upon maturation of the sensorimotor system, including the cerebral cortex and cerebellum, something which resembles a general to specific sequence is found in learning of sensorimotor skills, even at later age levels. In its initial response to learning situations the child shows much excess movement. This is gradually reduced, during the learning process, so that only the necessary responses

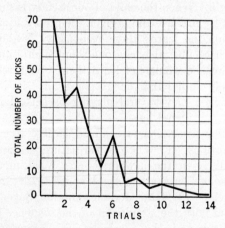

Figure 100. Curve Showing the Progress of an Infant in Learning to Grasp a Rattle Held Before It

Each trial consisted of a presentation of the rattle for exactly one minute. The curve shows the decrease in diffuse (kicking) activity involved in attempts to grasp the rattle. The infant was 129 days old at the beginning of the experiment. (From M. W. Curti, *Child Psychology*, New York: Longmans, Green, 1930, p. 170.)

are made. Curti,[9] for example, observed the number of kicking movements made by a child of four to five months while it was learning to grasp a rattle. As Figure 100 shows, the number of kicks (and probably the incidence of other diffuse activity) gradually decreased as a function of practice, until the rattle was grasped without movement of the feet. This is like the learned specificity considered elsewhere (p. 203) in relation to the conditioning process. Even in locomotion, which is perhaps primarily unlearned, the same picture is presented. There is much activity which, while it may help the child to balance, is unnecessary in walking. Gradually, as in the case of the kicking responses of Curti's experiment, these excess movements are extinguished. This point is considered further in our discussion of upright locomotion.

Motor Development as a Function of Age

Although individual biographical studies provide an unreliable indication of motor development, a summary of these studies such as Dennis [10] has made shows a *sequence* of development not unlike that obtained in researches involving groups of infants observed under uniform conditions by trained observers. The *initial appearance* and the *median age* of appearance of the items tend, however, to be earlier in the biographical than in the more extensive studies. This is probably because those infants whose parents are sufficiently interested to keep detailed biographies, and to publish them, are themselves somewhat advanced in development. It is also likely that items are noticed earlier by biographers, who are with the infants almost

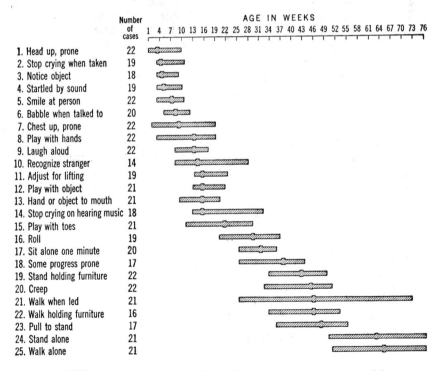

Figure 101. The Median Age and Age Range for the Appearance of Aspects of Infant Behavior as Revealed by Shirley's Study of Twenty-Five Infants

Compare these findings with those of the biographical studies represented in Figure 80, p. 195. Based upon a figure in W. Dennis, "Infant Development under Conditions of Restricted Practice and of Minimum Social Stimulation," *J. Genet. Psychol.*, 1938, *53*, 154.

continually and not merely at stated intervals, as is usually the case in more extensive studies. For an indication of the growth of motor activities, as revealed by biographical studies, examine the motor items in Figure 80, p. 195. Compare these data with those of Shirley [11] (Figure 101), which were obtained in a study of twenty-five infants during the first two years of life. Shirley observed these infants at intervals of one day until they were one week old; at intervals of two days until they were two weeks old; at intervals of one week until they were a year old; and then at intervals of two weeks until the end of the second year was reached. The parents of the infants reported on their progress during the intervals, using specially prepared forms to do so.

Additional information on the development of motor skills has come from several normative studies, including those of Gesell,[12] Bayley,[13] and Bühler and Hetzer.[14] These and other workers have prepared so-called tests of motor development. The norms differ somewhat from one test to another, but in sum they are probably more representative of the general population than norms based upon biographical data.

Table 7 is an abridgment of a tabulation published by Stoddard and Wellman.[15] It combines the data from several normative studies, including those carried out by workers at the Iowa Child Welfare Research Station. The tabulation also takes cognizance of Shirley's findings. When an activity is reported at different ages by different investigators, it is indicated at the earliest reported age. Verbal activities are of course both motor and symbolic, hence they are included along with predominantly motor activities.

Table 7. Characteristic Motor Activities Observed at Various Age Levels of Infancy

One month
   Lifts head from shoulder
   Crawling movements when prone
   Stares at large objects
   Retains hold of large ring placed in hand
   Holds chin up while lying on stomach

Two months
   Lifts head when suspended dorsally
   Assists, on being lifted
   Kicks feet in bath
   Carries object to mouth
   Turns head and eyes toward moving object
   Winks when object threatens eyes
   Follows light horizontally
   Follows light vertically
   Follows light circularly (two and one-half months)
   Holds chest up while on stomach
   Eyes follow moving person

Four months
   Holds head steady when carried
   Hands frequently opened
   Closes in with both hands on dangling ring when on back
   Splashes hand in bath
   Sits momentarily unsupported on mother's lap
   Takes cup off toy
   Accepts a second cube
   Locates sudden sound a foot from ear
   Examines toy (five months)
   Knees straighten, when child is held erect
   Opposes thumb
   Laughs aloud
   Responds vocally

Six months
   Sits momentarily
   Retains block in each hand momentarily
   Bangs spoon on table
   Reaches for object on sight
   Turns head toward sharp sound
   Rings bell
   Pokes at pellet in other person's hand
   On stomach, pushes with knees
   On back, rolls over
   Plays with toes
   Transfers object from hand to hand
   Drinks from cup
   Uses several syllables

Nine months
   Sits alone
   Opposes thumb on seizing cube
   Raises self by chair
   Picks up pellet from other person's hand
   Walks with help (ten months)
   Moves forward (and backward) when on stomach
   Creeps (ten months)

Walks when led (ten and one-half months)
Says "da-da" or its equivalent
Waves bye-bye

One year
Lowers self from standing to sitting position
Unwraps paper from cube
Holds cup to drink
Sits alone two minutes
Stands alone momentarily
Puts cork in bottle
Puts penny in bank
Accepts third cube
Says two words
Combines two or three syllables
Imitates movements

Fifteen months
Walks alone
Builds tower of two blocks
Uses spoon
Places five round pegs in board
Puts sand in jar with spoon
Throws ball to familiar person
Marks with pencil
Places lid on (and off) round box
Takes object out of round box
Says four words
Cooperates in dressing

Eighteen months
Throws ball into box
Scribbles vigorously
Accepts four cubes
Turns pages of book
Climbs stairs
Drinks from glass
Uses spoon or fork
Spits out distasteful solids
Points to nose, eyes, or hair
Says a few words

Two years
Runs
Piles six blocks
Imitates vertical and horizontal strokes
Tries to make a circle
Nests four boxes
Places blocks in row
Points to objects on card
Creases paper in imitation
Unwraps paper from candy
Uses words in combination

Tables like this are useful for parents and others who wish to know whether a child's motor development is normal. It should be recognized, however, that there are wide individual differences in the age at which particular items appear. The item "walks alone" occurs before the end of the first year for some children and not until eighteen months or later for others. Moreover, as we have already said, the median performance differs from one study to another. Although Shirley's study of 25 infants gives the item "walks alone" at fifteen months, Bayley's, which involved 61 infants, gives it at a little under thirteen months. For these reasons, parents should not be alarmed if their child deviates from the above norms in certain respects.

Gesell [16] and others once thought that the rate of motor development was indicative of later mental growth. It was assumed that the child of average motor accomplishment has average intelligence, that the child who is retarded in motor development has lower than average intelligence, and that the child who is precocious in motor development has higher than average intelligence. We now know that motor development, although positively correlated with later mental development, as measured by intelligence tests, is correlated only to a very low degree.[17] The newer "baby tests," while they have many motor items, also include a great deal of verbal and other symbolic material. These, as we shall see in Chapter 13, correlate more highly than purely motor tests with tests like the Stanford-Binet, which is primarily a measure of the development of symbolic processes.

Normative studies show the age at which various motor accomplishments are to be expected, but they do not, as such, tell us anything about the development of a particular activity from its initial to its final stages. The two sequences of motor development which genetic psychologists have studied most intensively from this standpoint are those culminating in upright locomotion and in prehensile use of the thumb opposed to the forefinger.

Development of Locomotion

For purposes of convenience, we may consider the development of locomotion under three headings: prone progression, assumption of an erect posture, and erect locomotion.

Prone progression

The newborn baby, when placed in the prone position, assumes a posture in which the legs and arms are flexed and the face rests on the surface, as illustrated in Figure 102 *A*. The head is sometimes lifted momentarily and there is often a great deal of activity in the lower extremities, but no progression is normally present. In McGraw's [18] observations on 82 infants, this phase of development gradually gave way, within the first 100 days, to that shown in Figure 102 *B*, which was most evident at 100 days. This phase, according to McGraw, suggests the beginnings of cortical control over movement and posture. Instead of merely bobbing his head up and down, as in the earlier phase, the baby can now hold it off the surface for a while. The arms are less flexed than formerly and there is random rather than rhythmically organized activity of the legs. The next phase (Figure 102 *C*), which overlaps the two preceding ones but which has its greatest frequency at about 150 days, is characterized by sustained raising of the head and chest, use of the elbow or palm to provide support, and generalized activity directed toward a desired object. The child may "pat the surface with his hands or, resting on his abdomen, kick his legs and wave his arms in a random fashion, but he shows no distinct evidence either in shoulder or pelvic regions of an urge to move his body forward." [19] Phases *D*, *E*, and *F* overlap a great deal in time with the preceding stage and with each other. They are most evident at around 200 days. Phase *D* differs from *C* in only one important respect, the presence of an impulse to progress, which is not successful, although pivoting and even backward movement may occur. In phase *E*, as illustrated in Figure 102, there are propulsive movements in the hip region and pushing with the feet as well as reaching out with the hands. These movements are usually not sufficiently synchronized to produce actual propulsion. Phase *F* is characterized by assumption of a creeping posture, but also, "in most infants a pause or recession in the manifestation of a propulsive urge." [20] The child may raise his abdomen from the surface by flexing his legs and lifting his head and shoulders (as in the first part of Figure 102 *F*) or he may do this with straightened legs (as in the second picture). In phase *G*, which has a wide age range, but which is most evident in babies between the ages of 200 and 300 days, there is apparently deliberate but unorganized progression. The knees may be brought forward in a sort of hopping movement or the child may move forward with the abdomen sliding on the surface. According to McGraw's description, there are many other activities at this stage, all related to the job of trying to move toward the desired object, yet without effective organization. Phases *H* and *I*, which begin in some infants at around 200 days, are characterized, respectively, by organized progression (which is somewhat staccato) and progression with improved integration (which is relatively smooth). McGraw believes that these successive phases in prone progression reflect an increasing control of bodily movements by the developing cerebral cortex.

As might be expected, other descriptions of the development of prone progression differ somewhat from that of McGraw and from each other. For purposes of comparison, therefore, the fourteen stages differentiated by Ames [21] in her analysis of moving-picture records obtained with twenty babies are shown in Figure 103. The median ages at which the successive stages were reached are indicated in the legend. In a motion picture study by Burnside,[22] which involved nine infants, three stages are especially noted. These are: *crawling*, or locomotion with the abdomen on the surface (Figure 102 *G*; Figure 103 *F*); *hitching* (Figure 102 *H*); and *creeping* (Figure 102 *H–I*; Figure 103 *G*, *K*, *L–N*).

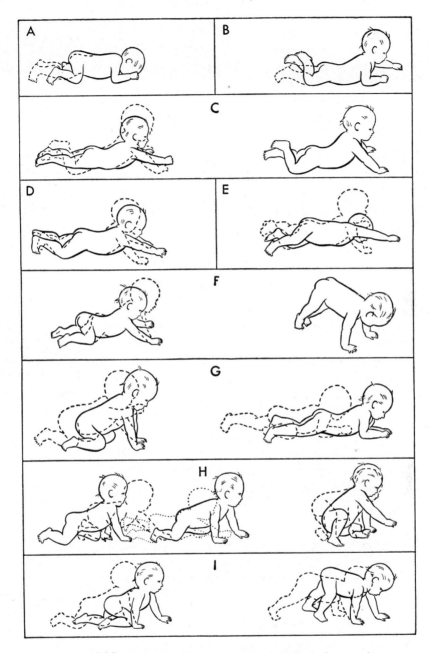

Figure 102. Phases in the Development of Prone Progression

According to McGraw, these nine phases are clearly distinguishable and represent gradual assumption of control by the maturing cerebal cortex. For descriptions of these phases and an indication of the age levels at which they appear, see the discussion in the text. (From M. B. McGraw, *The Neuromuscular Maturation of the Human Infant*, New York: Columbia University Press, 1943, p. 51.)

Although these various descriptions, and attempts to differentiate phases or stages of prone locomotion, are not in complete agreement, all investigators stress the sequential nature of development and they all attribute it to neuromuscular maturation. We shall consider this point again when other aspects of locomotion have been discussed.

Assumption of upright postures

Antigravity reactions like sitting upright and standing, with or without help, have been subjected to intensive study, especially by

McGraw in her observations of 82 infants. Children of course sit up before they stand without help, but they often walk alone (after pulling up on furniture or being helped into the erect position by others) before they can get to the erect position by their unaided efforts. Nevertheless, we shall discuss assumption of erect postures before walking is itself considered.

McGraw's analysis of the development of a sitting posture notes several phases, as in the case of prone locomotion, but these need not concern us here. Mature sitting, which be-

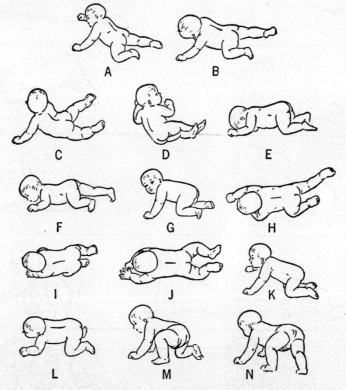

Figure 103.   Fourteen Developmental Stages in Prone Progression

The median ages of attainment of each stage by 20 infants are given in parentheses. *A.* One knee and thigh forward beside the body (28 weeks). *B.* Knee and thigh forward, inner side of foot contacting the floor (28 weeks). *C.* Pivoting (29 weeks). *D.* Inferior low creep position (30 weeks). *E.* Low creep position (32 weeks). *F.* Crawling (34 weeks). *G.* High creep position (36 weeks). *H.* Retrogression (36 weeks). *I.* Rocking (36 weeks). *J.* Creep-crawling (36 weeks). *K.* Creeping on hands and knees (40 weeks). *L.* Creeping, near step with one foot (42 weeks). *M.* Creeping, step with one foot (45 weeks). *N.* Quadrupedal progression: creeping on hands and feet (49 weeks). (From L. B. Ames, "The Sequential Patterning of Prone Progression in the Human Infant," *Genet. Psychol. Monog.*, 1937, *19*, 436.)

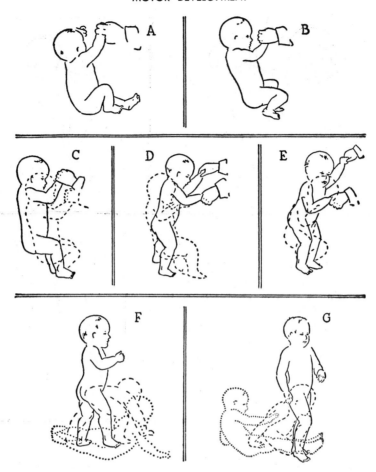

Figure 104. Some Stages in the Development of Ability to Assume an Erect Posture

At early stages, the upright position is achieved only by holding onto furniture or other objects or by being helped by others. (From M. B. McGraw, *The Neuromuscular Maturation of the Human Infant*, New York: Columbia University Press, 1943, p. 87.)

comes especially evident between the ages of 200 and 300 days, is defined by McGraw [23] as "that stage in which the infant can maintain an erect sitting position on a flat surface, usually with one of the lower extremities flexed and abducted, while the other is extended in front of the body. The arms are free to engage in other movements."

After standing by pulling up to furniture, standing with help, and continuing to stand with help withdrawn, the infant reaches the stage where he assumes the upright posture unaided. This began to appear in McGraw's infants by the age of around 400 days, after some children, helped to an upright posture, were maintaining it and taking a few steps. McGraw's analysis disclosed several phases, some involving help from others. The ability to roll from a supine to a prone position and the assumption of a sitting position were found to be necessary antecedents. Some phases of this series of developments are illustrated in Figure 104. McGraw points out that, in addition to cortical participation, and maturation of other neural centers, these developments may be influenced by anatomical

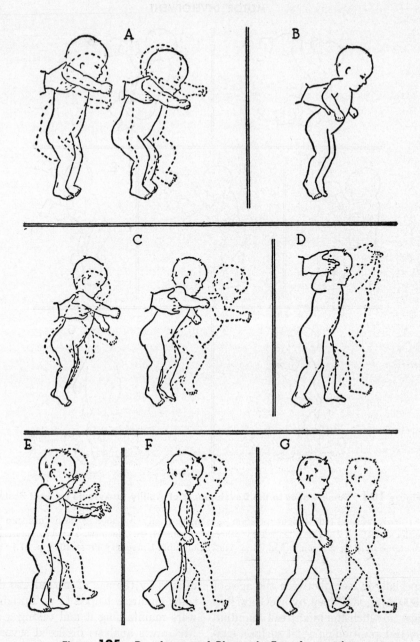

Figure 105. Developmental Phases in Erect Locomotion

A. Newborn posture with reflex stepping movements which become somewhat more prevalent during the first three weeks. *B.* Inhibition, or static phase. This is characterized especially by better head control, as well as suppression of reflex stepping reactions. *C.* Transition stage, noted for up-and-down movements of the body and stepping motions which are noticeably different from those of the newborn. *D.* Deliberate stepping while supported. *E.* Independent stepping. *F.* Heel-toe progression. *G.* More mature, well integrated, locomotion. (From M. B. McGraw, *The Neuromuscular Maturation of the Human Infant,* New York: Columbia University Press, 1943, p. 77.)

changes, such as changes in the ratio between leg length and body length.[24]

Erect locomotion

More attention has been centered upon walking than upon any other purely motor activity. This is quite understandable in view of the fact that man is one of the few animals who characteristically walk erect. Our great interest in this accomplishment also stems from the fact that it marks an important stage in the child's transition from dependence to independence.

One will recall from an earlier discussion (p. 176) that something akin to walking motions may be observed during late fetal development. Some newborn babies, when supported under the armpits so that the feet are in contact with a surface, will exhibit reflex stepping movements. According to McGraw,[25] these reflex stepping movements are more evident at around the third week than immediately after birth. At a later stage (phase *B* in Figure 105), reflex stepping motions are apparently suppressed and head posture is more adequately related to general body posture. In phase *C*, as illustrated, the infant tends to move his body up and down, while holding the feet in position; to stamp; and to make stepping movements which, however, differ from the reflex stepping movements of the newborn. McGraw[26] says that "it appears as if those mechanisms which activate movement are being interwoven with those governing antigravity and static postural control." From this stage on, there are self-initiated stepping movements, at first with body support and then without it. Subsequent stages are marked by a narrowing of activity to necessary motions alone, to changes in the contacts made by the feet, and to improved coordination. Some of these aspects will be considered in our discussion of the mechanics of locomotion.

The sequential nature of locomotor development

Although different children reach a certain phase of locomotor development at different ages, there is a marked tendency for the developmental sequence to be maintained from one child to another. Shirley[27] used this as an argument for the unlearnedness of these early aspects of motor development. In her investigations of motor development in twenty-five infants, she found that only 15 per cent of the activities which appeared within six weeks of each other in the sequence had their order of appearance reversed. When the median age for the appearance of each of forty-two items was correlated with each infant's sequential order, for the given items, the correlations ranged from .93 to .98. Thus the individual sequence was quite similar to that which was apparent from the median age at which an item appeared. Such a sequence is also clearly present in the biographical studies (p. 195) and in those by McGraw and others which we have just been considering.

The definiteness of this locomotor sequence is, as Shirley[28] pointed out, a strong argument in favor of the view that locomotor development is a function of maturation rather than, or at least to a greater extent than, of learning. If such a clear-cut sequence were attributed entirely, or predominantly, to learning, one would have to suppose that all children are subjected to comparable external stimulation at successive periods of early life. The fact is, however, that there are wide differences in the sorts of stimulation and encouragement to which different children are subjected. Ames[29] and McGraw[30] join Shirley, not only in stressing the sequential nature of early motor development, but also in stressing the role of maturation. McGraw, as we have seen, amplifies her emphasis upon maturation by relating her sequential findings to neuromuscular developments, including assumption of control by the growing cerebral cortex. Other investigators,[31] especially with respect to equilibratory aspects, have also stressed the rapid growth of the cerebellum (see Figure 42) during the period when locomotion is reaching maturity. Its weight increases by about 300 per cent during the first year.

The sequentiality of locomotor development is not the only basis for assuming that it results from maturation. McGraw's results with Johnny and Jimmy (see pp. 197–198) demonstrated that special exercise has little influence upon the nature and time of appearance of the various items in the locomotor sequence. The study of Hopi children (p. 197) also failed to show that restriction of activity during early life had any influence upon the age of sitting upright, reaching, walking, and other aspects of early motor development. The twins whose early activities were restricted by Dennis (pp. 194–196) also showed the normal sequence of development, although sometimes with some retardation. Dennis recognizes the influence of maturation, but also stresses the autogenous activity engaged in by the infants as soon as restrictions are removed.

Shirley [32] believed that development of activities in the locomotor sequence is saltatory*— in other words, that there are more or less sudden emergences, as against a gradual transition from one phase to another. She presented saltatoriness as further evidence for a maturational basis of locomotor development, her grounds being that a learned response would be more likely to undergo gradual development than would one dependent upon maturation. Actually, however, both learned responses and those due to maturation may develop slowly or suddenly, depending upon the circumstances.

McGraw [33] takes issue with Shirley on the question of saltatory versus gradual development of locomotion. She finds reason to emphasize the "gradual and continuous" nature of such development, saying that the infant never passes "completely and irretrievably from one stage into another. There is always a merging of patterns and parts of patterns both in the degree of perfection of the action and in the frequency of occurrence. There are often regressions to the less mature response."

The discrepancy between these two studies, with respect to the saltatoriness or gradual-

* The word comes from *saltation*, which means a leap or an abrupt change.

ness of development, perhaps hinges upon the fact that Shirley observed her infants at intervals (see p. 280) whereas McGraw observed hers almost continually for five days per week. Research on fetal development and on other motor development in infants tends to support the view that development is gradual rather than saltatory. This need not, however, prejudice the case for maturation.

In the light of the evidence so far available it is clear that locomotor development involves a sequence of activities and that this sequence is very similar for most infants. Whether all patterns of behavior involved in the sequence emerge suddenly or gradually is not clearly established, although the weight of the evidence suggests gradual emergence with a large amount of overlapping. For the most part, investigators agree that the typical human form of locomotion is a function primarily of maturation, although self-initiated activity plays a role in perfecting it. Places at which activity may improve locomotion are particularly evident when we consider the mechanics involved.

The mechanics of locomotion

The mechanical aspects of locomotion have been especially investigated by Burnside,[34] Shirley,[35] and McGraw.[36] Burnside took moving pictures (slow motion and normal) of locomotion in nine infants. She then analyzed the film records in order to discover the way in which the various activities are coordinated. Footprint records were also made, the aim being to determine length of step, width of step, and type of contact with the floor. Burnside observed that, before any locomotion takes place, the infant makes many apparently incoordinated movements in an effort to reach a goal. Locomotion appears when these movements are appropriately coordinated. There is at first an excess of movements. This gradually decreases. Appropriate coordination of the arms appears before that of the legs. According to Burnside, the precocious development of arm movements may be attributed to the greater degree of freedom of the shoulder joints as compared with those of the hips, thus allowing for greater diversity of movement.

In the initial stages of progression, the abdomen remains in contact with the floor (see Figure 102). Apparently the muscles of the trunk and extremities are as yet neither sufficiently strong nor sufficiently coordinated to maintain the body weight. This stage is usually designated as crawling. Creeping, progression with the abdomen off the floor, involves new problems of coordination. Equilibrium is frequently unstable and progression is effected by movement of one limb at a time, or by movements of the arms and legs to produce hopping movements. Great individual differences are often apparent. Eventually there develops a cooperation of the limbs such that the flexion and extension of an arm and of the contralateral leg tends to be synchronous with the opposite phase of the other limbs. After creeping begins, one aspect of progress is the gradual increase in speed.

Not all children perfect this creeping form of progression before attempting upright locomotion. Moreover, a regression to creeping is present whenever the infant who has begun to walk finds himself in difficulty.

As Hřdlicka [37] pointed out, children frequently run on all fours. This type of locomotion may reappear long after upright locomotion has been perfected. Hřdlicka believed, as already indicated (p. 5), that such behavior is to be explained on the basis of recapitulation. However, running on all fours could easily develop as a result of chance variations in creeping. Moreover, infants conceivably could copy it from the patterns set for them by adults (in play) or by animals. Hřdlicka claimed that such locomotion tends to retard the time of walking, but Dennis [38] demonstrated, from Hřdlicka's own data, that children who run on all fours walk at the normal time.

Burnside's analysis of upright locomotion shows some of the mechanical problems involved. As soon as the upright posture is assumed, there are only two points of contact with the surface. These are so small, the center of gravity so high, and the weight of the body so slight that unstable equilibrium results. Restoration of equilibrium requires a high degree of muscular coordination; hence any slight imbalance causes the infant to fall. Burnside points out that wide placing of the feet increases the basal area of support, that flexion of the hip and knee lowers the center of gravity, and that raising the arms provides further help in the problem of balancing. As the child's ease in walking increases, these aspects of locomotion undergo a marked change. One especially noticeable change is the lowering of the arms, with an eventual easy suspension of the sides.

Shirley's data, as well as those of McGraw, support the above description of locomotor mechanics. Note the wide base in D of Figure 105 (p. 286), the bending at hips and knees in E, where the baby is first taking steps without assistance, also the raising of the arms in E, and the change in these aspects which are to be observed in G. The wide base, as well as the change from digital, to plantigrade, and finally to heel-toe progression are evident in Figure 106, which shows footprints recorded by McGraw.

From the footprints of her subjects, Shirley [39] measured changes in length of step as a function of the time before and after walking. She found that the median length of the step increases as a function of age and also as a function of the number of weeks that the child has been walking alone. The distance traversed by the infant in one minute of walking was also recorded and it was found that, with increases in age and in walking experience, the speed of progression increases. This is true until approximately the twenty-sixth week of walking. Then there is a slight decrease in speed, which may mean that walking has ceased to be a problem and that the child is engaged in other pursuits which detract from speed of progression.

Although we have stressed the motor aspects of locomotion, it should be remembered that sensory coordination is also of very great

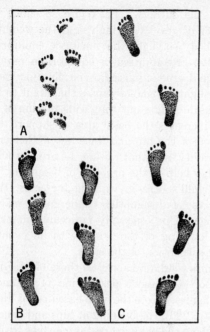

Figure 106. **Footprints Illustrating Changes in Surface Contacts as Upright Locomotion Develops**

A. Digital progression, narrow base. *B.* Plantigrade progression, wide base. *C.* Heel-toe progression, normal base. (From M. B. McGraw, *Growth: A Study of Johnny and Jimmy,* New York: Appleton-Century, 1935, p. 85.)

significance. In the development of walking, especially, the infant must make appropriate responses to tactual cues received from the feet; to kinesthetic cues associated with movements of the muscles, tendons, and joints; and to directive visual cues of various kinds. Walking thus involves inter-sensory-motor coordination to a high degree.

Factors conducive to delay in walking

In a very interesting paper based upon data derived from various biographical and experimental sources, Dennis [40] shows that several conditions, singly or in combination, may retard the onset of walking. Among these conditions are sensory handicaps and low intelligence.

The several studies summarized by Dennis agree in showing that blind children stand alone and walk unaided at a much later age than seeing children. Children who are both blind and deaf prior to the onset of walking are apparently even more retarded and require special assistance in learning to walk. This retardation of blind and blind-deaf children may, as Dennis points out, have several possible sources. It may result from the absence of normal visual stimulation, including the sight of others walking; from excessive fear and timidity, related to inability to see; from inhibition induced by injuries sustained in early attempts to stand and walk; from the fact that blind children are kept in bed more than usual and may be muscularly weak; or perhaps from a combination of these factors.

The data summarized by Dennis also show that mental defectives are retarded in locomotor development, the retardation being most marked with respect to walking, where it may amount to a year or more. Mongolian defectives are especially retarded. Their average age of walking is approximately three years, as compared with fifteen months or earlier for normal children. Although one might suppose that deficient intelligence retards walking because of a related deficiency in learning ability, there is no evidence to support this conclusion. Both the low intelligence and motor retardation are perhaps reflections of a more general deficiency, not only in the cortex, but in subcortical centers as well as in general neuromuscular maturation. If intelligence as such were the important factor here, we would expect high intelligence to be positively correlated with the age at which walking occurs. Such a correlation, according to the data summarized by Dennis, has not been established.

Restrictions such as Dennis imposed upon the twins discussed earlier (pp. 194–197) may have retarded the onset of walking, but there is no clear indication that they did. The twins were behind the biographical norms but well within the range reported by Shirley. We have seen, moreover, that restrictions such as some Hopi Indians impose on their children (p. 197) do not delay the age of walking. We also know, from the results of McGraw (pp. 197–199), that special activity does not speed the onset of walking. This is probably because, although learning undoubtedly plays a role in perfected upright locomotion, training is ineffective until the necessary neuromuscular maturation has been achieved.

It should be apparent from the preceding discussions that, although neuromuscular maturation sets the pace, and probably the basic patterns of locomotor activity, stimulation as well as exercise of the emerging patterns are requisite for expert performance. Actually it is not possible to draw the line between maturation and learning. We do not know, for example, how much upright locomotion is dependent upon seeing others walk or, in the case of the blind, being encouraged by others to assume the upright posture. But we do know, from experiments on lower animals (p. 57), that the typical forms of locomotion in these are not dependent upon such stimulation.

Chimpanzees may be induced to walk upright through human contacts and encouragements (pp. 199–200).* But we also know that chimpanzees are better built for all-fours locomotion and men for upright locomotion and that either is handicapped when attempting to walk like the other. Until such time as an otherwise normal child is reared without seeing human locomotion, without having objects around on which it can pull up to a stand, and without stimulation conducive to upright posture and locomotion, we shall not know for certain whether characteristically human locomotion, while we are built better for this than for any other, and while it devel-

* If they could be substantiated, the reports on feral or wild children, those reared by animals, would provide interesting human analogies.[41] In these alleged instances, the children have walked on all fours. Assuming the observations to be authentic, there are of course other possible interpretations besides the view that our typical mode of locomotion is based upon observation of others. The infants may have been physically and mentally retarded; their living quarters, such as caves, would not be conducive to upright locomotion; and for these or other reasons, they may have fixated at the creeping, or the walking-on-all-fours, stage of development.

ops sequentially without sequentially arranged environment aids, can to any extent develop in the absence of learning.

Development of Prehensile Behavior

Prehensile behavior is distinguished from the grasping reflex, which is present in fetuses and is strong in infants during the first months of life, in that it may be elicited by visual as well as tactual stimuli.[42] The grasping reflex as such disappears during the second half year, but prehensile grasping remains and develops with age. It is eventually under voluntary control.

Reaching and grasping

Prehensile behavior has been studied from various angles by several investigators, most of whom have used motion picture techniques which allowed detailed analysis after the event.

In McGraw's [43] study, the emphasis is on reaching-prehensile behavior as a function of neuromuscular maturation. She differentiates several overlapping phases and attempts to correlate them with changes occurring in the infant's visual projection mechanisms as well as in his neuromusculature. A passive phase, in which there is no evidence of object vision, is followed by the object-vision phase in which the chief evidences for object vision are the convergence and accommodation elicited by an object. At this stage there are no associated hand movements. These come in the "visual motor" stage. The arm and digit movements at this stage appear to be reflexly aroused by visual stimulation. Following this phase, and becoming especially evident after the 200th day, are deliberate, or less compulsive, manipulative movements. The child may reach toward the object, withdraw his hand, and reach out again. While this is going on, the object is continually fixated. Later in the so-called "visual release" phase the child may look at the object and start reaching movements which continue even though his eyes have turned elsewhere. The final phase is marked by a reduction of visual and muscular activities to the minimum required for reaching and grasping the object.

Investigators in Gesell's laboratory have been especially interested in prehensile behavior for what it reveals concerning the development of vision.[44] Certain aspects of these studies have already been considered in relation to visual perception (pp. 267–268). Other investigations by Gesell and his associates have focused upon approach movements made in reaching for an object and upon ways in which various objects are grasped once the infant's hand has reached them. In this connection the investigators have been especially interested in development of thumb and finger opposition, which, as we have seen (pp. 100–101), has great phylogenetic as well as ontogenetic significance.

In the studies from Gesell's laboratory, groups of infants were tested under standard conditions at various age levels from soon after birth until 60 weeks. Each infant was placed at a table, the top of which was marked off with lines which facilitated analysis of the extent and direction of movement. After attracting the infant's attention, the experimenter placed an object on the table before it. The object was placed in a position midway between the hands and then moved toward the infant in a uniform manner.

In such situations an infant may fixate the object, move the hands toward it, and grasp it. Until about the age of 20 weeks, fixation is the only response elicited by a distant object. Some infants of 20 weeks make arm movements in the general direction of the object. In successively older groups, these movements become more direct. Contact with the object is at first inadequate for prehension. At successive age levels, however, the object is prehended with increasing success and with decreasing waste motion.

Halverson,[45] who used cubes and other objects, and Castner,[46] who used small pellets, agree that approach movements are, in general, of three kinds. The *backhand approach* is the earliest to appear. In this approach the hand sweeps outward and forward toward

the cube in a curvilinear manner, as illustrated in *A* of Figure 107. The next approach (*B*), which is present in some infants of 24 weeks, is designated as the *circuitous approach*. This approach becomes more direct (*C*) until, at around 36 weeks, the *straight approach* (*D*) is most prevalent. The *vertical approach* likewise varies with age.

Halverson also distinguishes between a *loop approach*, a *planing approach*, and a *slide approach*. In the first-mentioned approach, the hand comes relatively close to the object and then descends upon it. In the planing approach, the hand begins to descend some time before the object is close to the hand. The slide approach is one in which the hand moves along the table top until the object is reached. There is some overlapping of these approaches, but they tend to develop in the order designated. In an intensive study of

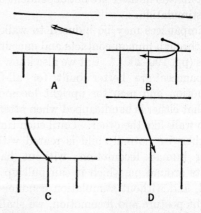

Figure 107. Forms of Approach Used by Infants in Attempting to Reach an Object

These are drawings based upon the individual frames of a film. They show the route followed by the forefinger of the infant in attempting to reach a cube placed at the edge of the lines of the table top. *A* represents the approach of a 20-weeks infant. The hand moves laterally across the table top, cutting short of the cube. *B* shows the circuitous approach of a 28-weeks infant. The hand sweeps around the cube from a lateral direction. *C*, the more direct approach of a 26-weeks infant. *D*, the direct approach of a 52-weeks infant. (From H. M. Halverson, "An Experimental Study of Prehension in Infants by Means of Systematic Cinema Records," *Genet. Psychol. Monog.*, 1931, *10*, 175.)

reaching, Halverson [47] verified the fact that approach is increasingly direct as the infant grows older. At 60 weeks the characteristic approach is a smooth, direct movement toward the object, which is contacted with little spatial error.

Halverson [48] found that grasping of objects, like a cube, cup, string, ball, or pellet, becomes increasingly effective until the age of 60 weeks, at which time it closely approximates that used by adults. In cube prehension a sequence divisible into ten more or less distinct stages is exhibited. Infants tend to pass through successive stages in this sequence. Grasping and its developmental sequence differ for various objects, as shown in Figure 108. The most characteristic type of grasp used in prehending a given object at each of six successive age levels is indicated. Figure 109 shows the position of an object held in the infant's palm at different age levels. It also illustrates aspects of hand development. In Gesell and Halverson's [49] study of thumb opposition, special attention is given to the changing functions of various muscle groups as opposition appears. Halverson,[50] who looks upon his results as evidencing a proximodistal direction of prehensile development, points out that both maturation and learning are involved. He says:

The development of reaching and grasping affords excellent examples of the progress of maturation from the coarser to the finer muscles. The early approach patterns consist largely of crude shoulder and elbow movements in which slow and somewhat angular action predominates, while the later approach patterns employ better directed shoulder and elbow action, in addition to wrist movements and hand-rotation, under the dominating influence of the forefinger and thumb. The early approach reveals a crudely functioning hand at the end of a poorly directed arm, while the later approach reveals a well coordinated arm under the directing influence of a pretty well developed prehensile organ. In grasping we find at first a clawing type of closure in which the thumb is practically inactive and no digits predominate, succeeded by a nipping, pressing type of closure the dominating factors of which are the thumb and forefinger, i.e., a crude palming movement giving way to a refined forefinger-tip grasp which includes precise placement of the digits upon the cube.

The increase in the number of higher types of

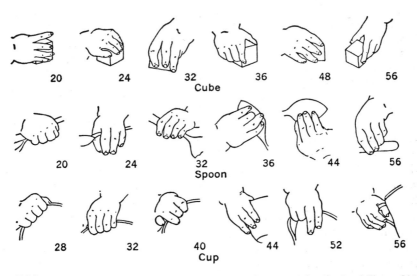

Figure 108. A Series of Grasps in Developmental Sequence for Each of Three Objects

The numbers below each drawing indicate the age (in weeks) at which that grasp characteristically occurs. (From H. M. Halverson, "A Further Study of Grasping," *J. Gen. Psychol.*, 1932, 7, 41.)

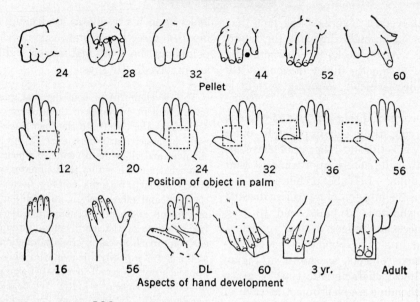

24   28   32   44   52   60

Pellet

12   20   24   32   36   56

Position of object in palm

16   56   DL   60   3 yr.   Adult

Aspects of hand development

Figure 109.   A Series of Grasps in Developmental Sequence

This figure also shows the six successive positions on the palm against which the fingers press objects, such as cubes. Above the caption, *Aspects of hand development*, appear, in order: the forearm of a 16-weeks infant, the forearm of a 56-weeks infant; the developmental line (note broken line) of opposition in grasping; and digital grasping by a 60-weeks infant; by a 3-year-old child, and by an adult, respectively. (From H. M. Halverson, "A Further Study of Grasping," *J. Gen. Psychol.*, 1932, 7, 44.)

grasp and the increase in the amount and variety of digital manipulation of the cube in infants from sixteen to fifty-two weeks of age are due in part to anatomical growth of the digits of the hand, in part to maturation of its neuromusculature, in part to training, and in part, perhaps, to increase in cutaneous sensibility of the fingertips.

Handedness

What is meant by "handedness" is of course the predominant use of one hand in such activities as eating with a spoon or fork, cutting, writing, and hammering. In activities like those mentioned, we tend to use one hand exclusively. With respect to these activities we are said to be "unimanual." There are, however, many activities in which both hands are used, but with one playing the dominant and the other the subordinate role. Among such "bimanual" activities are using the fork in the left hand to hold food which we cut with the knife in the right hand and

holding a nail with the left hand while we hit it with the hammer in the right. According to the studies summarized by Hildreth,[51] about 95 per cent of children in our society eventually use the right hand for those unimanual activities in which it is customarily used. Among the 5 per cent who are not predominantly right-handed are the left-handed and the ambidextrous, those who use right and left hands with about equal facility.

How did such predominance of right-handedness come about? It is not a trait which we can trace from our animal ancestry, for even our close relatives, the chimpanzees, fail to show hand preference. In tests especially designed to disclose such preference, Finch[52] found that chimpanzees are about equally divided with respect to right-handedness, left-handedness and ambidexterity. Hildreth[53] points out that archaeologists have found prehistoric implements designed both for right- and left-handed users. In the Stone

Age, if we may accept these accounts, the right- and left-hand weapons were about equally prevalent. Two-thirds of later prehistoric implements are said to have been designed for right-handed and one-third for left-handed users. This sort of evidence, including Biblical references to rare left-handers, suggests that human right-handedness may have had a cultural origin.

There are obvious advantages for uniform handedness, especially in military activities. But why should right-handedness have been adopted? Watson,[54] who was a strong advocate of the view that right-handedness is a trait of cultural origin, thought that it might have had utility in protecting the heart. The heart, being toward the left side, was covered with a shield held in the left hand. The right hand was then used for wielding weapons. If right-handedness had some such origin, and subsequently became a culture trait, how did it spread to primitive peoples out of contact with those who adopted it? Since even the most primitive human beings are predominantly right-handed, one would have to suppose either that there was originally diffusion of this cultural acquisition or that it was independently hit upon in all societies. The theory of cultural origin is thus highly speculative. But so, also, are opposing theories, which stress either dominance of the left cerebral hemisphere (which controls the right side of the body) or other human asymmetries which might make for greater dexterity in the right than in the left hand. Although much research has been done in an effort to obtain decisive evidence for or against the brain-dominance and similar biological theories, no unequivocal evidence one way or the other has been revealed. All of this research has been on animals, which are not predominantly right-handed anyway; hence it may not have much relevance to human handedness.[55]

Turning, now, to the human infant, we do have certain facts upon which all investigators agree. They agree that there is no hand preference during the early months of life. In a study by Lippman,[56] which verifies the earlier data of Watson, infants younger than four months used the left hand as much as the right in reaching for objects. By the end of the first year, 70 per cent of Lippman's infants were showing a right-hand preference. Hildreth has summarized the results of many such studies of handedness in children, and her summary reveals a rapid increase in right-handedness during the preschool years.

We also have general agreement, among those who have studied it, that before dominance becomes fixed there is much fluctuation. Gesell and Ames[57] have described the change from bilateral to unilateral response and have emphasized the "developmental flux" which characterizes the process. Ames[58] says that, at the earliest age levels, the two hands "work very closely together as though they had not separated off from each other functionally." From about the ninth to the twelfth month, although the two hands work together, "a separation and differentiation into an active and passive hand seems to be working itself out." From about the eighteenth month on, the hands still move together, but "now in a voluntary simultaneous bilateral grasp" in which they "are nevertheless capable of working quite independently." Beginning at around two years, according to Ames, "the passive hand seems to become more passive and to take on more the subordinate role in unilateral behavior, — but in bilateral behavior the two hands are becoming more equal to each other." She says, moreover, that, although "the two hands may work together at the same time, they tend to manipulate objects differently." Both Gesell and Ames attribute such fluctuations to developing inner forces, that is, to maturation. Others, including Hildreth, say that it represents a phase in cultural conditioning.

Actually, when handedness is established, it is only relative. Heinlein[59] and later observers have noted that, even from the fourth year on, the right hand is not consistently used. In Heinlein's study, involving a variety of activities, only 25 per cent of her four- to twelve-year-olds were consistently right handed. Consistent right-handedness usually occurred only in those activities, like eating and writing, where social pressures dictate the hand to be used.*

Throughout her publications on development of handedness, Hildreth [60] stresses the fact that efficient performance of many every-day activities requires that either one hand or the other have dominance. If this were not so, there would be a continual conflict and division of attention between the two hands. Moreover, many devices of modern civilization are designed for right-handed rather than left-handed or ambidextrous people. Hildreth describes how, in nursery school and home situations, teachers and parents foster predominant use of the right hand even without thinking of the fact that they are doing so. The arrangement of eating utensils, the way a spoon is handed to the child, and so on, are conducive to development of right-handedness. In our home and school environments there are thus strong inducements to become right-handed, and these begin their influence long before a tendency toward left-handedness is noted and attempts are made to change it. Under these circumstances, some regard the persistent left-hander as a hardy individualist — one who has more or less successfully resisted the social pressures which would make him right-handed.

It is not as yet possible to decide between the innate and acquired theories of handedness. The fact that handedness develops gradually might be attributed to maturation or to learning, depending upon the theory favored. There may even be an innate tendency which makes it easier to learn right-handedness than left-handedness. However,

hand preference shows cultural differences, it develops gradually, it fluctuates a great deal before becoming established, it differs with the task at hand, and it is markedly susceptible to training; all of which are points favoring the view that it is learned.

Practical questions relating to handedness, such as whether or not and, if so, how to change hand preference in a child who seems headed toward left-handedness, need not concern us here. A very thorough discussion of handedness, including related educational problems, will be found in the series of papers by Hildreth.[61] These are based upon her own researches and a very extensive literature.* Thompson [62] gives a briefer discussion of handedness which also deals with many educational aspects.

Other Aspects of Motor Development in Childhood

A great deal has been written and a large amount of research has been done on general motor development in children. In some studies [63] there has been an attempt to relate aspects of physical growth with development of various motor skills, including those involved in play. In the following discussion we confine our attention to speed of reaction as an aspect of motor development and to certain tests designed to gauge development of motor skills as a function of age.

Speed of reaction

All investigations, whether dealing with simple reaction time or with time required to perform complex coordinations, have found decreasing time as a function of age.

Goodenough [64] measured the reaction time to sound in 240 children between the ages of $2\frac{1}{2}$ to $5\frac{1}{2}$ years. Her results show faster reactions and less variability as a function of age. Philip [65] studied speed of reaction to light and sound stimuli, with and without a ready sig-

* It is interesting, in this connection, to compare the eating habits of the English and Americans. The former hold their fork in the left hand while steadying food being cut with the knife in the right hand, just as we do. But they bring food to the mouth with their *left hand* while we change the fork over and use the *right hand* for this purpose. Arabs use the right hand exclusively for eating, and the left for sanitary activities in which we customarily use the right. So there is inconsistency from one culture to another, as well as in the handedness of individuals.

* Even the 258 references listed by Hildreth are but a small fraction of the complete literature on handedness.

nal, in 165 girls and 146 boys between the ages of nine and sixteen years. At these later ages there was still improvement as a function of age. Boys were slightly quicker than girls, a finding which Philip attributes to greater experience, among the boys, in activities calling for fast reactions. Moore's [66] study, dealing with speed of complex reactions in 602 children ranging from six to sixteen years, also shows increasing speed as a function of age. The task comprised placing marbles in small holes, one marble to a hole. There were 32 holes in rows of 8, and an individual's score was the total time on three trials (a total of 96 marble placements). The task was an interesting one and well within the range of ability of all subjects tested. There is thus reason for supposing that a sheer speed factor was tested. The correlation between total time and chronological age was $-.82\pm.009$. Other studies, involving such activities as simple and complicated tapping, buttoning, and ball play have likewise shown an increase in speed of performance as a function of age.[67] The upper limit of speed is usually reached in later childhood. Of possible relevance in this connection is Hazard's [68] finding of an increase in neural conduction rate as a function of age. Conduction rate, obtained in terms of the rapidity of the patellar reflex and the length of the reflex arc involved, increases steadily during the first decade, then shows little if any further improvement.

Motor skills

Studies of motor skills in children show, in general, that initial ability on all tasks increases with age (see pp. 215–216). Skills tested have included dart throwing, tossing quoits, skipping, buttoning, balancing, skating, drawing, dressing, and writing. Several books and monographs [69] provide extensive accounts of such activities. The play activities of children have also been studied by various investigators, sometimes from the standpoint of what such activity reveals about motor development and sometimes from the standpoint of what it reveals about social

development.[70] We have already (pp. 5–6) considered G. Stanley Hall's cultural recapitulation theory of play. There are several other theories, including Spencer's, which claims that play represents a release of excess nervous energy. These and other aspects of the psychology of children's play would lead us too far afield if we discussed them here. The reader is referred to Gilliland's [71] discussion.

Tests of motor skill

Several tests of motor skill as a function of age have been developed. Cunningham [72] devised such a test for children from twelve to thirty-six months. At the later age levels it involves such activities as climbing, throwing objects into holes, walking along beams, and jumping. The median scores on this test increase gradually as a function of age. Bayley's [73] tests, which overlap the upper levels of the above test, also include various jumping and hopping activities. The age levels from four through sixteen years are covered in Oseretzky's [74] test, which is arranged in year levels somewhat like individual mental tests (Chapter 13). There is in this test a stress upon motor speed and coordination in the performance of specified tasks. Brace's [75] test, which has been used extensively to gauge motor development in the age range from eight years to adulthood, takes cognizance of such skills as putting the head to the floor, kicking as high as the shoulders, jumping into the air and making a full body turn, and balancing while maintaining complex postures. A study involving 775 subjects showed yearly age increments in the number of items passed. Scores ranged from around 8 at eight years to 15 at eighteen years. Correlations between the Brace scores and chronological age were, however, quite low. They ranged from .18 to .21. Correlations between test scores and athletic skill, on the other hand, were between .70 and .80. This test, like the others which go into the upper age levels, is doubtless to a large degree measuring acquired skill as well as sheer motor maturity. It is, as a matter of fact, almost impossible to measure motor ability of older children and adults in such a manner as to reveal maturational factors as such.

Summary and Conclusions

Studies of activity in the newborn human infant reveal a large number of reflexes, most of them developed prior to birth, and several extensive behavior patterns including what, for want of a better name, has been called "mass activity." As in the case of prenatal behavior, the activity of newborn babies is involved in controversy. There are those who look upon specific reflex activities as differentiating out of a pre-existing pattern of generalized or mass activity. Others hold to the view that so-called "mass activities" are patterns of specific responses. Still others, represented by McGraw, say that neither extreme view is correct, and that both mass and specific activities can be observed in the same individual at the same time. It is rather generally true that development of motor skills is characterized, in its early stages, by excess activity which is minimized as a function of practice.

Biographical and large-scale normative studies, while differing somewhat in their age norms for particular items of motor development, are largely in agreement concerning the sequential order of appearance of major items like sitting, creeping, standing, and walking. It has been claimed that such a sequential order of appearance of motor items argues for their dependence on maturation rather than on social stimulation and learning. Studies have been reviewed which attempt to correlate the locomotor sequence with physical growth factors, including the growth of the cerebellum and the growth and increasing dominance of the cerebral cortex. The question whether items in the sequence emerge suddenly or gradually, and what this might mean in terms of the maturation concept, has not received a definitive answer. It seems clear, however, that later stages in the coordination of motor activities like creeping,

standing, and walking are dependent to a great extent upon the learning process. This view is supported by studies focused upon the mechanics of such activities. When the child stands unsupported and attempts to walk, he is confronted by such mechanical problems as a high center of gravity, small contact with the surface, and incoordination of arm and leg movements. He overcomes these problems by learning to coordinate not only his motor activities, but these activities in relation to tactual, kinesthetic, static, and visual stimuli. Maturation no doubt provides the requisite mechanisms, but learning is also necessary. The great importance of sensory stimulation is shown when we consider that blind and blind-deaf children are greatly retarded in locomotor development. The feebleminded are similarly retarded, but this may be a reflection of general neuromuscular immaturity rather than, or in addition to, poor learning ability. In locomotor development there is evidence of a cephalocaudal sequence, with activities of the head, shoulders, and arms appearing in advance of activities of the lower parts of the body.

Prehensile development begins with ocular activities and generalized arm movements and culminates in prehension, with thumb and forefinger, of such small objects as a pill or pellet. It is to be distinguished from reflex grasping, which is elicited only by contact with the palm and which gradually disappears as the child grows older. Detailed cinematographic studies of prehensile development have shown that three types of approach, developing sequentially, are involved in visually directed reaching. A backhand approach gives way to a circuitous approach and this to a direct approach. Considered vertically, there are also three approaches: the loop, planing, and slide approaches. Once the infant is able to reach out and grasp an object, various types of grasp are noted. More adequate grasping activities develop as the infant becomes older. By the end of the first year, the essential characteristics of adult grasping, with finger and thumb opposition, have developed. Development of prehension appears to involve a proximodistal growth sequence.

Hand preference is not present at birth, but develops gradually during infancy and early childhood. Whether handedness is to any degree innate, being associated with differential development of the cerebral hemispheres, or with other sorts of bodily asymmetry, is not definitely known. Much of the available evidence suggests that it may be determined by social pressure which has its remote origin in habits developed by our primitive ancestors. Some psychologists, however, feel that this evidence is equivocal

and favor the view that handedness is to a considerable degree innate. The view held appears to depend more on one's partiality for environmental or for hereditary explanations than upon factual data. The evidence at present available certainly cannot settle this issue.

Speed of reaction increases with age. This is true of simple reactions and also of complex coordinations. The number and complexity of motor skills increases during childhood, but how much of the increase is attributable to motor maturation as such, and how much to learning, is not known.

REFERENCES

1. Dennis, W., "Infant Development under Conditions of Restricted Practice and of Minimum Social Stimulation: A Preliminary Report," *J. Genet. Psychol.*, 1938, *53*, 149–158.
2. Irwin, O. C., "The Amount and Nature of Activities of Newborn Infants under Constant External Stimulating Conditions During the First Ten Days of Life," *Genet. Psychol. Monog.*, 1930, *8*, No. 1.
3. Irwin, O. C., "The Organismic Hypothesis and Differentiation of Behavior: I. The Cell Theory and the Neurone Doctrine," *Psych. Rev.*, 1932, *39*, 128–146; "The Organismic Hypothesis and Differentiation of Behavior. II. The Reflex Arc Concept," *Psych. Rev.*, 1932, *39*, 189–202; "The Organismic Hypothesis and Differentiation of Behavior. III. The Differentiation of Human Behavior," *Psych. Rev.*, 1932, *39*, 387–393; "Dennis on Mass Activity: A Reply," *Psych. Rev.*, 1933, *40*, 215–219; with A. P. Weiss, "A Note on Mass Activity in Infants," *J. Genet. Psychol.*, 1930, *38*, 20–28.
4. *Op. cit.*, III, 1932.
5. Dennis, W., "The Role of Mass Activity in the Development of Infant Behavior," *Psych. Rev.*, 1932, *39*, 593–595.
6. Gilmer, B. v. H., "An Analysis of Spontaneous Responses of the Newborn Infant," *J. Genet. Psychol.*, 1933, *42*, 392–405.
7. *Ibid.*, p. 403.
8. McGraw, M. B., *Growth: A Study of Johnny*

and Jimmy. New York: Appleton-Century, 1935, p. 311.
9. Curti, M. W., *Child Psychology.* New York: Longmans, Green, 1930.
10. See citation 1.
11. Shirley, M. M., *The First Two Years: Postural and Locomotor Development.* Minneapolis: University of Minnesota Press, 1931.
12. Gesell, A., *Infancy and Human Growth*, New York: Macmillan, 1928; *An Atlas of Infant Behavior*, New Haven: Yale University Press, 1934; and with C. S. Amatruda, *Development Diagnosis*, New York: Hoeber, 1941; and others including (with Ilg) *Child Development*, New York: Harper, 1949.
13. Bayley, N., "Mental Growth During the First Three Years: A Developmental Study of Sixty-one Children by Repeated Tests," *Genet. Psychol. Monog.*, 1933, *14*, No. 1; *The California First Year Mental Scale*, Berkeley: University of California Press, 1933.
14. Bühler, C., and H. Hetzer, *Testing Children's Development from Birth to School Age.* New York: Farrar and Rinehart, 1935.
15. Stoddard, G. D.., and B. L. Wellman, *Child Psychology.* New York: Macmillan, 1934.
16. Gesell, A., "The Early Diagnosis of Mental Defect," *Arch. Neur. and Psychiat.*, 1929, *22*, 522–529.
17. Goodenough, F. L., *Mental Testing.* New York: Rinehart, 1949. See pp. 310–311.
18. McGraw, M. B., *The Neuromuscular Matura-*

tion of the Human Infant. New York: Columbis University Press, 1943. This monograph summarizes the findings reported in several lengthier studies, the references to which are there cited.

19. *Ibid.*, p. 54.
20. *Ibid.*, p. 56.
21. Ames, L. B., "The Sequential Patterning of Prone Progression in the Human Infant," *Genet. Psychol. Monog.*, 1937, *19*, 409–460.
22. Burnside, L. H., "Coordination in the Locomotion of Infants," *Genet. Psychol. Monog.*, 1927, *2*, 284–372.
23. See citation 18, p. 70.
24. Citation 18, p. 92.
25. Citation 18, p. 76.
26. Citation 18, p. 79.
27. Shirley, M. M., "The Sequential Method for the Study of Maturing Behavior Patterns," *Psych. Rev.*, 1931, *38*, 507–528.
28. Shirley, M. M., "A Motor Sequence Favors the Maturation Theory," *Psych. Bull.*, 1931, *28*, 203–204.
29. Citation 21.
30. Citation 18.
31. See especially K. Koffka, *The Growth of the Mind,* New York: Harcourt, Brace, 1924; and M. M. Shirley, "Locomotor and Visual-Manual Functions," in C. Murchison (ed.), *A Handbook of Child Psychology* (2d ed.), Worcester: Clark University Press, 1933.
32. Shirley, M. M., "Is Development Saltatory as well as Continuous?" *Psych. Bull.*, 1931, *28*, 664–665.
33. McGraw, M. B., *Growth: A Study of Johnny and Jimmy.* New York: Appleton-Century Co., 1935, p. 69.
34. See citation 22.
35. See citation 11.
36. See citation 33.
37. Hrdlicka, A., *Children Who Run on All Fours.* New York: McGraw-Hill, 1931.
38. Dennis, W., "The Age of Walking of Children Who Run on All Fours," *Child Development,* 1934, *5*, 92–93.
39. See citation 11.
40. Dennis, W., "On the Possibility of Advancing and Retarding the Motor Development of Infants," *Psych. Rev.*, 1943, *50*, 203–218.
41. See A. Gesell, *Wolf Child and Human Child,* New York: Harper, 1941; W. Dennis, "The Significance of Feral Man," *Am. J. Psychol.*,

1941, *54*, 425–432; and R. M. Zingg, "A Reply to Professor Dennis," *Am. J. Psychol.*, 1941, *54*, 432–435. Clarence Leuba's *The Natural Man* is the most recent consideration of this subject. It was published in 1954 by Doubleday.
42. Halverson, H. M., "Studies of the Grasping Responses of Early Infancy," *J. Genet. Psychol.*, 1937, *51*, 371–449; and M. B. McGraw, "Suspension Grasp Behavior of the Human Infant," *Am. J. Diseases of Children,* 1940, *60*, 799–811.
43. See citation 18.
44. Gesell, A., F. L. Ilg, and G. E. Bullis, *Vision: Its Development in Infant and Child.* New York: Hoeber, 1949.
45. Halverson, H. M., "An Experimental Study of Prehension in Infants by Means of Systematic Cinema Records," *Genet. Psychol. Monog.*, 1931, *10*, 107–286; "A Further Study of Grasping," *J. Gen. Psychol.*, 1932, *7*, 34–64.
46. Castner, B. M., "The Development of Fine Prehension in Infancy," *Genet. Psychol. Monog.*, 1932, *12*, 105–193.
47. Halverson, H. M., "The Acquisition of Skill in Infancy." *J. Genet Psychol.*, 1933, *43*, 3–48.
48. See citation 45.
49. Gesell, A., and H. M. Halverson, "The Development of Thumb Opposition in the Human Infant," *J. Genet. Psychol.*, 1936, *48*, 339–361.
50. Halverson, H. M., "An Experimental Study of Prehension in Infants by Means of Systematic Cinema Records," *Genet. Psychol. Monog.*, 1931, *10*, 279–280.
51. Hildreth, G., "The Development and Training of Hand Dominance: II. Developmental Tendencies in Handedness," *J. Genet. Psychol.*, 1949, *75*, 221–254.
52. Finch, G., "Chimpanzee Handedness," *Science*, 1941, *94*, 117–118.
53. Hildreth, G., "The Development and Training of Hand Dominance: I. Characteristics of Handedness," *J. Genet. Psychol.*, 1949, *75*, 197–220.
54. Watson, J. B., *Behaviorism.* New York: Norton, 1930.
55. For references to the research on handedness in rats, see N. L. Munn, *Handbook of Psychological Research on the Rat,* Boston: Houghton Mifflin, 1950, p. 332. The footnote (p. 332) on the work of Peterson and Kirk needs modification in that both Peterson and Kirk found

localization of handedness in the contralateral hemisphere. The hemispheres were found by Kirk to be equipotential only with respect to the visual function and intelligent behavior. The results on handedness in rats do not necessarily favor the concept that human right-handedness results from dominance of the left cerebral hemisphere. On this point see S. A. Kirk, "Hemispheric Cerebral Dominance and Hemisphere Equipotentiality," *Comp. Psychol. Monog.*, 1935, No. 55, pp. 24–25, 34–35. Nor is there any evidence that rats (or human beings) inherit handedness. On this point see G. M. Peterson, "The Rat in Animal Psychology," in P. L. Harriman, *Encyclopedia of Psychology*, New York: Philosophical Library, 1946, p. 777.

56. Lippman, H. S., "Certain Behavior Responses in Early Infancy," *J. Genet. Psychol.*, 1927, *34*, 424–440.
57. Gesell, A., and L. B. Ames, "The Development of Handedness," *J. Genet. Psychol.*, 1947, *70*, 155–175.
58. Ames, L. B., "Bilaterality," *J. Genet. Psychol.*, 1949, *75*, 45–50. Quotations are from p. 50.
59. Heinlein, J. H., "A Study of Dextrality in Children," *J. Genet. Psychol.*, 1929, *36*, 91–119.
60. Hildreth, G., "Manual Dominance in Nursery School Children," *J. Genet. Psychol.*, 1948, *72*, 29–45. See especially p. 44.
61. Hildreth, G., "The Development and Training of Hand Dominance: II. Developmental Tendencies in Handedness," *J. Genet. Psychol.*, 1949, *75*, 221–254; "III. Origins of Handedness and Lateral Dominance," *ibid.*, 1949, *75*, 255–275; "IV. Developmental Problems Associated with Handedness," *ibid.*, 1950, *76*, 39–100; "V. Training of Handedness," *ibid.*, 1950, *76*, 101–144.
62. Thompson, G. G., *Child Psychology*. Boston: Houghton Mifflin, 1952, pp. 259–268.
63. For a summary of such studies, see W. C. Olson, *Child Development*. Boston: Heath, 1949, Chapters III and IV.
64. Goodenough, F. L., "The Development of the Reactive Process from Early Childhood to Maturity," *J. Exper. Psychol.*, 1935, *18*, 431–450.
65. Philip, B. R., "Reaction Times of Children," *Am. J. Psychol.*, 1934, *46*, 379–396.
66. Moore, J. E., "A Test-of-Eye-Hand Coordination," *J. Appl. Psychol.*, 1937, *21*, 668–672.
67. See F. L. Goodenough, "A Further Study of Speed of Tapping in Early Childhood," *J. Appl. Psychol.*, 1935, *19*, 309–319; W. H. Pyle, *The Examination of School Children*, New York: Macmillan, 1913; B. T. Baldwin and L. I. Stecher, "*The Psychology of the Pre-School Child*, New York: Appleton, 1924; R. Stutsman, "Performance Tests for Children of Pre-School Age," *Genet. Psychol. Monog.*, 1936, *1*, No. 1.
68. Hazard, C., "The Relation of Reflex Conduction Rate in the Patellar Reflex to Age in Human Beings," *Univ. Iowa, Stud. Child Welfare*, 1936, *12*, 183–197.
69. See M. Gutteridge, "A Study of Motor Achievements of Young Children," *Archives of Psychology*, 1939, No. 244; A. Espenschade, "An Experiment in Testing the Motor Ability of Preschool and Kindergarten Children," Wellesley: Bulletin, Mary Heminway Alumnae Association, 1932–1933; A. T. Jersild, *Child Psychology* (4th ed.). New York: Prentice-Hall, 1954, pp. 155 ff.
70. See E. B. Hurlock, *Child Development*, New York: McGraw-Hill, 1942, Chapter X; W. C. Olson, *Child Development*, Boston: Heath, 1949, Chapter IV.
71. Gilliland, A. R., *Genetic Psychology*. New York: Ronald, 1933, Chapter 10.
72. Cunningham, B. W., "An Experiment in Measuring Gross Motor Development of Infants and Young Children," *J. Educ. Psychol.*, 1927, *18*, 458–464.
73. Bayley, N., "Mental Growth During the First Three Years: A Developmental Study of Sixty-one Children by Repeated Tests," *Genet. Psychol. Monog.*, 1933, *14*, No. 1.
74. See E. A. Doll, "The Oseretzky Tests of Motor Proficiency." Minneapolis: Educational Test Bureau, 1946.
75. Brace, D. C., *Measuring Motor Ability*. New York: Barnes, 1927.

SUGGESTIONS FOR FURTHER READING

Barker, R. G., J. S. Kounin, and H. F. Wright, *Child Behavior and Development.* New York: McGraw-Hill, 1943, Chapters III and IV.

Carmichael, L. (ed.), *Manual of Child Psychology* (2d ed.). New York: Wiley, 1954, Chapter 6 (by Gesell).

Dennis, W., *Readings in Child Psychology.* New York: Prentice-Hall, 1951, Chapter II, readings 2 and 4; Chapter III, readings 1–5.

Gesell, A., and F. L. Ilg, *Child Development.* New York: Harper, 1949. Use the index to trace discussions of motor behavior from birth to the tenth year.

McGraw, M. B., *The Neuromuscular Maturation of the Human Infant.* New York: Columbia University Press, 1943, Chapter III.

Olson, W. C., *Child Development.* Boston: Heath, 1949, Chapters III and IV.

Shirley, M. M., *The First Two Years: A Study of Twenty-Five Babies.* Vol. I. Minneapolis: University of Minnesota Press, 1931.

Thompson, G. G., *Child Psychology.* Boston: Houghton Mifflin, 1952. See especially pp. 259–282 for a more complete discussion of handedness and motor abilities of later childhood than is given in this chapter.

11

Symbolic Processes in Children

SOME of the more general characteristics of symbolic processes were considered in Chapter 5. Our discussion of their evolution disclosed that these are first clearly shown in lower mammals and that they become increasingly apparent as the human level is approached. In the present chapter we consider the development of typical symbolic processes in children.

Characteristic symbolic processes are customarily designated by such terms as *memory, imagery, imagination, ideation, conception, generalization, abstraction, thinking,* and *reasoning.* Memory, as exhibited in delayed-reaction tests, is perhaps the simplest of these. The most complex is reasoning.

All the symbolic processes represented by the above terms possess certain characteristics in common. One characteristic is that they are primarily *implicit*; in other words, they are inner activities of the organism. Since they are beyond direct observation by individuals other than those in whom they appear, such activities are difficult to investigate objectively. Their presence is inferred from overt behavior. Prior to the development of language one finds evidence of symbolic activity in behavior of the delayed-reaction type. As soon as language is acquired, the investigation of symbolic processes of various kinds is greatly facilitated. Another

characteristic common to all symbolic processes is their *representative* function. As already indicated (p. 105), the basic factor is some modification of the organism which acts as a representative of, or substitute for, past stimulation. Because of this modification and its use as a symbol, we are able to make appropriate responses to stimuli in their absence. For example, the child looks for a ball that has disappeared or recalls where he placed his toys.

Symbolic activities such as imagination involve manipulation of symbols rather than of the objects and situations which these represent. When such manipulation takes a definite direction, as in the solution of a problem, the process is designated as reasoning. The development of these and other symbolic activities in early childhood is considered in the following pages.

Our attention at first turns to the development of mnemonic processes, and especially *recall* memory. Biographical, clinical, and experimental evidences of such memory at different age levels are considered. Emphasis is, however, given to experimental research on delayed reaction, which provides an objective measure of recall memory functioning below the level of verbalization. The discussion takes in certain normative data on delayed reaction, correlations between test results and age and intelligence, and information on the question of whether recall is in terms of spatial or nonspatial cues. Attention is also given to the development of memory span, of ability to recall narratives, and of ability to recall events. The latter has to do with the Aussage or testimony test.

In presenting the genetically significant data on imagery, a great deal of attention has been given to the especially vivid variety (eidetic) which is found in many young children. Tests of imagination are considered briefly. Many of these are projective in nature (see Chapter 16) but scored in terms of what they indicate with respect to imaginative versatility rather than in terms of what they may indicate about more general personality characteristics.

There is an extensive literature on concept formation in children, but our discussion has focused on representative studies dealing with such concepts as: triangularity, roundness, middleness, number, time, and life. Piaget's research on the concept of what it means to be alive has stimulated a large amount of research and discussion on the so-called "animistic" concepts of children. This question is considered here in some detail.

There is a transition from simpler aspects of learning, through problem solving, to the higher levels of reasoning. Problem solving at or below the level where verbalization begins to play a part was considered in the earlier discussion of learning. The discussion of reasoning in this chapter is concerned primarily with higher levels, where verbalization plays an important role, and where the problem is usually one of developing adequate generalizations and applying them. The break between this and the earlier discussion of problem solving is an artificial one, to be sure, but it seemed wise to delay the discussion of the material presented here until some consideration had been given to elementary symbolic processes (like recall memory) and to the development of concepts.

Memory

Symbolic memory is evidenced by ability to perform delayed reactions and to recall and verbally reproduce past experiences.* Investigations of symbolic memory in animals and in human infants not yet possessed of verbal responses must be confined to the delayed reaction phenomenon. After acquisition of verbal responses has occurred, one is able to investigate memory span, verbal reproduction of past experiences, and the like. We shall first confine our attention to the delayed reaction.

The delayed reaction

Information concerning delayed reaction in children comes from three sources: biographical, clinical, and experimental. Biographical studies offer incidental observations concerning responses to objects which have disappeared from the child's view. Clinical tests contain standardized items aimed at measuring the development of ability to make such responses. Experimental researches, beginning with those of Hunter [1] have tested the ability of children to perform delayed reactions under rigid conditions of controlled stimulation. As we shall see, these researches have been more analytical than normative.

The only data on delayed reactions during the first year are primarily biographical and clinical. We shall discuss and critically evaluate these before undertaking consideration of experimental studies with older children.

Biographical data. Hurlock and Schwartz [2] have summarized the memory data reported in thirty-six infant biographies. Many observations deal with behavior of the delayed-reaction type. Examples are cited of infants who, during the first year of life, exhibited responses judged to be attempts at locating objects which had just previously disap-

---

* Retention which can be evidenced only in relearning (increased efficiency of relearning as compared with original learning) is the most primitive type of memory. It is present to some degree in most animals (see Chapter 5). This form of memory is not, however, necessarily symbolic.

peared. Preyer, for example, reports that an infant of three months cried and looked about the room, vainly seeking his nurse, who had been gone "only a day." Shinn reports such behavior in an infant of four months. Numerous similar observations are recorded by other biographers. The biographical data suggest an increasing ability in such performances as a function of age. However, one cannot place much reliance upon such information. Fact and interpretation are often hopelessly interwoven, and the precise conditions under which the behavior appeared are not known. In many instances the response may be a chance one which is interpreted by the observer as having higher behavioral significance. There is no doubt, however, that even very young infants evidence some memory of the delayed-reaction type.

Clinical data. Clinical studies carried out on large numbers of babies under standardized test conditions suggest that responses like those reported by biographers are quite prevalent in early infancy. These studies lack the careful control of stimulation and the objective recording which characterize experimental investigations. There is often the possibility that an infant is responding to unintentional cues provided by the tester. Furthermore, judgments concerning the significance of an infant's reaction are impressionistic, as will be observed in the examples which follow. On the other hand, these tests are less artificial than those of most experiments. They are carried out in the infant's normal environment under conditions as natural as those involved in everyday play activities.

Characteristic clinical tests of the delayed reaction have been described by Charlotte Bühler[3] and her collaborators, Hetzer, Wolf, and Köller. The earliest test of the delayed reaction is devised for infants of three months. After the face of the experimenter suddenly disappears, the child of this age, according to Bühler, characteristically "looks for several seconds after the human face or shows some form of negative expression — such as crying,

wrinkling the brow, screwing the mouth." The next test, passed by most five-months infants, is that of looking for a toy which has just been removed. Bühler says that the infant of this age characteristically "turns his head in the direction in which the toy disappeared and looks about searchingly." More complicated tests of this nature are described for successive age levels. During the second year such tests as the following are used: A ball is squeezed and a chicken comes out. (Figure 110) The infant plays with the ball, making the chicken appear and disappear, for a period of one minute. The experimenter then removes the ball and encourages other activities for a period of three minutes. At the end of this time the baby is given a ball like the first one, but without a chicken. The test is passed if the child, upon squeezing the ball, shows "distinct astonishment" at absence of the chicken, or if he looks "questioningly" at the experimenter, or examines the hole in the ball with his fingers. Children of 15 to 17 months characteristically perform this test after a delay of eight minutes. The same test, but with a delay of 17 minutes, is used at the age level of 21 to 24 months. Hetzer and Wislitzky[4] report that a one-minute interval is the maximum possible for

Figure 110. Materials for a Delayed-Reaction Test

The child is shown that the chicken pops out. Later, when a ball without the chicken is presented, recall is indicated by reactions suggesting surprise or curiosity as to the whereabouts of the chicken. (After C. Bühler, and H. Hetzer, *Testing Children's Development from Birth to School Age*, New York: Rinehart, 1935, p. 142.)

children from 10 to 11 months of age. Children of 19 to 20 months respond in the usual way after a period of 15 minutes. Over 400 infants were used in the standardization of the above tests.

Delayed-reaction experiments. The number of infants involved in delayed-reaction experiments has been quite small in comparison with those used in clinical studies. On the other hand, the detailed analysis of delayed-reaction behavior derived from experimental studies is not forthcoming from the usual clinical investigation. Furthermore, an ideal experimental study controls conditions of stimulation with such rigidity that one is sure that memory and not some other function is being tested. Experiments on the delayed reaction have, for the most part, dealt with older children than are included in biographical and clinical studies.

It will be recalled that Hunter,[5] in his pioneer investigation of the delayed reaction, compared the performances of rats, dogs, raccoons, and children. The animal subjects (see p. 139) were confronted by three compartments. They had already learned that a reward was to be obtained by going to the lighted one. The problem which faced them was that of going to the compartment in which the light had just previously appeared. The children, instead of going to the previously lighted compartment, pressed a button which sounded a buzzer. Unless they maintained a fixed bodily orientation, assumed while the light was on, rats and dogs were unable to respond correctly. This indicated, according to Hunter, that they could not react on the basis of the absent stimulus. Bodily orientation served as a continuing kinesthetic stimulus for correct response. The raccoons and children, on the other hand, did not need to maintain any given type of orientation with respect to the previously lighted compartment. Hunter assumed, therefore, that they were responding on the basis of some internal (intra-organic) cue representative of the absent light.

The five children used in this investigation ranged from $2\frac{1}{2}$ to eight years. The youngest girl could respond with a high degree of accuracy after the light had been out for 50 seconds. Longer delays led to a significant drop in the percentage of correct responses. The other children, three of whom were six years old, responded correctly after delays of 25 to 38 minutes. In a later experiment Hunter[6] used the direct method (see p. 141) to test for delayed reaction in a girl of 13 months. The infant was confronted with three boxes having hinged covers. A toy was given to her, taken away, and then hidden in one of the boxes. After she had observed that the toy was in a given box, the lid was closed and the child was prevented from opening it until after a definite period had elapsed. Hunter disoriented the infant in various ways during the period of delay. On delays ranging from eight to twelve seconds she was successful in locating the toy 72 per cent of the time. A chance score would be 33 per cent, hence she was responding with significantly higher than chance accuracy. At 16 months she could locate the toy after a period of delay amounting to 24 seconds. Rugh, in an unpublished investigation mentioned by Skalet,[7] obtained delayed reactions after a period of $8\frac{1}{2}$ minutes in an infant 18 months old. Her method apparently was similar to that of Hunter. It involved hiding an object under one of three pans placed before the infant. One does not know whether orientation was prevented during delay or whether cues from the experimenter were eliminated adequately. Because of the small number of subjects, these experiments fail to indicate developmental trends.

Allen's[8] experiment with 50 boys and 50 girls of about one year old was similar in some respects to those of Hunter and Rugh. While sitting on its mother's lap, the child was confronted with three identical boxes arranged as in Figure 111, so that they were each at the same distance from him. The mother kept her eyes closed so that she would not know the correct box and could therefore not give the child any clue as to its location. While the

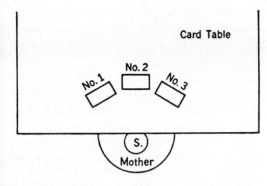

Figure 111. A Delayed-Reaction Situation for Testing Infants

While the infant watched, a toy was placed in one box. The table was then pulled out of reach. When the table was pushed back again, the infant, if he recalled where it was hidden, could get the toy. The position of the correct box was varied in a random manner from one test to the other. (From C. N. Allen, "Individual Differences in Delayed Reaction of Infants," *Archives of Psychology*, 1931, no. 127, p. 14.)

child was looking, a toy was tapped on a box, then dropped in out of sight. The table was pulled away during the delay period. When it was again pushed within reach, the child had a chance to get the toy. The position of the correct box was of course shifted in random order from one trial to the next.

Chance accuracy would approximate 33 per cent, but, after a ten-second delay, there was an accuracy of 61 per cent for boys and 66 per cent for girls. After a delay of twenty seconds, the respective percentages were 65 and 57. A thirty-second delay brought the respective percentages down to 50 and 48. Longer delays produced chance percentages. There was no evidence of significant sex differences.

Miller [9] was particularly interested in the cues used by children. Since the child no longer sees the object, but must remember having seen it placed, and where, his response is of course symbolically controlled. But does he remember the *position* of the box containing the lure, with respect either to his own position or to the position of other boxes; does he remember the *characteristics* of the box,

such as size, color, or shape; or does he remember some combination of such cues?

Miller's experiment, carried out with 98 children between $11\frac{1}{2}$ and 162 months of age, involved a delay of 10 seconds. There were always two boxes in one of which a toy was hidden. After a child had made two correct responses in succession, changes were introduced to bring out the nature of the remembered cues. For example, if the original setting involved a red and a yellow box in a particular position with respect to each other, this relationship was changed in critical trials. After the toy was hidden, a screen was interposed so that the child could no longer see the boxes. A duplicate toy was placed in the "wrong" box, so that the child would get the toy in any case. Then the boxes were shifted. If, say, the red box had been on the right, and the toy had been placed in it during the test, the child might now respond to the right-hand box (now the yellow one) or to the red box (now on the left). The absolute position of the boxes (relative to the child) might also be changed (with or without reversing color positions).

The chief outcomes of this experiment were as follows: Children under two years (of which there were only four) all responded in terms of position relative to the other box. Children between two and three years (eleven in number) responded 80 per cent of the time to such spatial cues and 20 per cent of the time in terms of color. Color became an increasingly important basis of response in successively older groups. Other bases of response were infrequent at all age levels, although placing the boxes a greater distance apart tended to increase the frequency of responses in terms of position relative to the subject himself.

Skalet's [10] investigation, in which 60 children of from 2 to $5\frac{1}{2}$ years were used, offers data concerning ability in delayed reaction as a function of age. Two types of tests were used. The first was quite similar to Hunter's direct method. While the child was looking, an animal cracker was hidden under one of three plates. The child then left the room and engaged in the usual activities until again confronted with the plates. He was then required to find the hidden object. If the child did this without error, he was allowed to eat the cracker. The plate under which the cracker was placed varied from trial to trial in a predetermined chance order. The experimenter was out of view while a response was being made; hence the child could receive no cues from her while making the reaction. Periods of delay ranged from one to thirty-four days. The average accuracy decreased from 64.8 per cent at delays of one to three days to 46.2 per cent for delays of twenty-one to twenty-nine days. For delays of greater duration than this, accuracy was no better than could be accounted for by chance. The correlation between maximum correct delay and age was .478 ± .077. This suggests an increase in the maximum correct delay as a function of the child's age.

In her second type of delayed-reaction experiment, Skalet required the children to indicate, from samples scattered before them, a figure exposed some time previously.* Three tests were used. One involved objects such as a cat, a camel, or a boy. Another made use of familiar geometrical figures such as a triangle or a circle. The third test required the child to indicate, by pointing to a card, which of six unfamiliar figures had been exposed previously. These tests were too difficult for most children. The first one was used with the former intervals of delay. Seventy per cent of the total number of responses were incor-

* This test is similar, in many respects, to the delayed matching-from-sample tests used with animals (see pp. 143–144) and administered to two children by Weinstein.[11] One three-year-old child achieved 80 per cent accuracy in selecting, from a group of items, the one previously handled. Accuracy did not vary with the interval of delay, which involved 5, 10, or 15 seconds. The other child, who was slightly younger, refused to respond when the interval was increased from 5 seconds, where she had 18 correct responses out of 25, to 10 or 15 seconds. As in Skalet's experiment, it was necessary to recall (or recognize) the sample object. Spatial cues were rendered ineffective. This may account for the great difficulty of such tests when applied to children who are in the stage of responding spatially (see the discussion of Miller's experiment, p. 307).

rect. The most familiar objects were remembered best. The correlation between maximum correct delay and age was .669 ± .093. Delays ranging from a few minutes to five days were used in the test involving geometrical figures. There was no definite evidence that the length of delay influenced the accuracy of response in this test. Nor was there a significant correlation with age. Similar results were obtained with the test which made use of unfamiliar figures.

Skalet suggests that verbal responses may have played a large role in enabling children to make correct reactions after delay. As an example of the verbal and other behavior exhibited in the three-plate experiment, the following protocol [12] is reproduced:

Child 37

This child responded correctly after the longest delays of any of the children tested; in none of the trials was an incorrect response or even a questionable correct one made. She was given two trials in 1929; having made a correct response on the first trial after one hour, she made an immediate correct response on the second trial after an absence of sixty-four days. She went directly to the plate where the cookie had been hidden the time before, and when asked, "Are there any cookies under the other plates?" she answered, "No." Since this delay was three times as great as that obtained for any other child, it was not counted as a maximum delay. In 1930, she responded correctly after a delay of thirty-four days, which was also longer than any delay obtained for any of the other children. Her chronological age at this time was fifty months, and her mental age sixty-five months. At the time the cookie was hidden for the last trial, she gave some evidence of the method she used in remembering, and gave adequate justification for assuming the delayed response after thirty-four days to be a result of correct memory. She pointed to each of the plates, saying as she did so, "I look at them and say 'One, two,' and then I look under three (stimulus in this case) and get the animal cookie." By reinforcing the stimulus in this way, she was enabled to make a correct response after a much longer period of time than she would have if she had not used these memory devices. Her responses in the other experiments were about the average for her age.

At the age of thirty-eight months, this child came up to the experimenter and said, "See my new watch." About twenty minutes later she said, "See my new watch. Oh, I showed you before, didn't I?" About fifteen minutes later she said, "I showed you my watch before, didn't I?" This incident is illustrative of her general behavior.

Emerson [13] investigated the effect of changes in bodily orientation upon delayed reaction in 32 children ranging in age from 29 to 59 months. The test was one of memory for position of objects, but the essential principle involved is that of the delayed-reaction experiment. Hunter, it will be recalled, found that disorientation during delay markedly influenced the accuracy of his rats and dogs. His raccoon and human subjects, however, could respond correctly after considerable disorientation. Emerson's aim was to test whether, in a complex delayed-reaction situation, young children would be disturbed by various changes in bodily orientation during delay. The children were confronted by an easel containing 42 pegs distributed uniformly over its surface. There were seven rows, each containing six pegs. A child watched the experimenter place a small ring over a given peg, which differed from trial to trial in a predetermined chance order. The child then attempted to reproduce the experimenter's performance on the same easel or on another placed in various positions which required different degrees of bodily orientation. About five seconds elapsed between the placing of a ring by the experimenter and reproduction of the performance by the child. Nine degrees of change in orientation were used. The simplest situations were those in which (1) the same easel (2) two easels side by side, and (3) easels one behind and a little to the right of the other were used. Other situations were as follows: (4) easels at right angles requiring a quarter turn to the left, (5) easels at right angles requiring a quarter turn to the right, (6) easels at right angles requiring a three-quarter turn to the left, (7) easels at right angles requiring a three-quarter turn to the right, (8) easels facing each other, and (9) one easel requiring movement to the opposite side for reproductions of the observed performance.

The average number of correct placements for each of these changes in orientation was, respectively, as follows: 17.82, 6.45, 6.86, 5.55, 4.96, 5.43, 4.64, 3.71, and 1.81. The data thus indicate that bodily disorientation during delay greatly decreases accuracy. Considering tests for all positions, the three-year-old children exhibited an average of 43.75 correct placements. Four-year-old children made an average of 56 correct responses. The average score for five-year-olds was 59.24. The correlation between average number of correct placements and age was .77 ± .05, while with mental age it was .758 ± .05. There was no significant sex difference.

We see from these experiments on delayed reaction in children that recall memory is present to some degree even in early infancy and that it becomes increasingly evident as the child grows older. Once delayed reactions are apparent, further growth is indicated by ability to make longer delays, and to make them under conditions of increasing complexity. Language greatly facilitates ability to bridge the gap between an event and recall of it. Recall on the basis of spatial cues antedates recall on the basis of color. While there is no apparent sex difference in ability to perform tests of delayed reaction, there is clearly a positive correlation between such ability and level of intelligence. Several tests of infant intelligence now include items involving delayed reaction. The two-year-old tests of the 1937 revision of the Stanford-Binet include an item based upon Hunter's (p. 306) study of delayed reaction in a child.

Memory span

An individual's memory span is the number of items which he can recall after they have been given a single brief presentation. Presentation may be auditory or visual and recall oral or written. The most commonly used items are groups of digits, words, or objects. Obviously, the memory span varies for different kinds of materials and for different methods of presentation and reproduction. We shall summarize, very briefly, some of the findings which seem to possess developmental significance.

Recall of digits presented verbally is the most common test of memory span. Starr [14] measured the auditory-vocal memory span for digits in two thousand subjects from four to fifteen years of age. The average span was 4 digits at the fourth and fifth years; 5 digits at the sixth, seventh, and eighth years; 6 digits at the ninth, tenth, eleventh, and twelfth years; and 7 digits beyond this age. The Terman-Merrill Revision of the Stanford-Binet Test of Intelligence gives the normal memory span for digits as 2 at two and a half years, 3 at three years, 4 at four and a half years, 5 at seven years, and 6 at ten years. The span for superior adults is given as from 8 to 9 digits. These norms are, in general, substantiated by Starr's results and by numerous other individual investigations summarized by Hurlock and Newmark. [15]

Tests of the memory span for words have shown a similar increase with age, beginning with the eighteenth month. Stutsman [16] finds that this is the earliest age at which such tests can be used extensively. In an investigation by Lumley and Calhoun [17] the average memory span for words was shown to be 2.1 for third-grade children. Children in the twelfth grade had a memory span of 4.7 words. The average adult memory span is approximately six words.

Memory span for objects is measured with the Ellis Memory Test described by Bronner and others. [18] Ten objects are presented, one at a time in a definite order. The child names the objects as they are presented, receiving help if necessary. All the objects are then removed and the child is required to name them in the order in which they were originally presented. As the child names each object, it is placed on the table before him. Thirty seconds are allowed for each response. McElwee [19], using this test on 360 subjects, found that the memory span increased gradu-

ally from 5.1 at five years to 7.7 at thirteen years. Girls were slightly ahead of boys. Essentially similar results are reported by Dewey, Child, and Ruml [20] for 500 Jewish children of nine to thirteen years of age.

Several investigations have focused upon the relation between memory span and I.Q. In each instance a positive correlation has been found. This ranges, for different kinds of material, from .40 to .76. The memory span increases as materials become more meaningful. [21]

Some investigators have found a sex difference (usually in favor of girls) but others have not. [22] One can therefore draw no definite conclusions about sex differences in memory span.

Recall of narratives

Foster [23] has investigated the accuracy with which children of various ages reproduce stories that have been read to them. Her subjects were 31 nursery-school children (15 boys and 16 girls) ranging in age from two years and seven months to four years and nine months. On its first presentation a story was read without pauses. On the next presentation, however, pauses were introduced at definite intervals and the child was encouraged to continue with the story as far as possible. Correct reproductions were rewarded with a "good" from the experimenter. Incorrect responses were corrected. This procedure was continued until each child had heard ten readings of the story, one reading per day. The child was then read another story. Eight stories of approximately the same length were used. Each word reproduced by the subject was recorded. A child's score consisted of the total number of words reproduced per story. Older children recalled more than younger ones. The average number of words recalled by two older groups (average ages three years and eight months and four years and three months) increased markedly during nine repetitions of the story. There is no evidence that the limit had been reached by the ninth repetition. Learning curves of two younger groups (average ages two years and eleven months and three years and four months) indicate that the limit of ability to recall had been reached by the eighth repetition. There was a correlation of .74 between the total score on all stories and chronological age. Although the group of subjects is small, this suggests that chronological age is a significant factor in enabling children to reproduce verbal material of the above nature. It is quite possible, of course, that the larger vocabulary of older children and their better grasp of the meaning of the stories were responsible for the high correlation between reproduction scores and chronological age. The correlation with mental age was .65. Boys tended to make higher scores than girls. Because of the smallness of the groups, however, this sex difference is, as the author suggests, somewhat questionable.

Accuracy of testimony

The Aussage * test, which was first used extensively by Stern,[24] measured the accuracy with which an individual describes a situation, or relates the details of an event, previously witnessed. This test obviously measures more than recall memory. An individual's ability to relate what he has witnessed will depend upon the accuracy of his original observation, upon his vocabulary, and upon his proneness to fantasy, as well as upon his ability to remember. However, when a simple situation is presented, when all the items fall within the individual's vocabulary, and when incorrect responses are ignored, the number of items reported is primarily a measure of recall memory.

Winch [25] gave Stern's test to children ranging in age from three to twelve years. His aim was to measure accuracy of perception. The picture was a simple one, and the included items fell within the experience of all of the children, regardless of age. The vocabulary required was that for such items as boy,

* *Aussage* is a German term comparable to *testimony*.

woman, bread, knife, table, and the like. Children were scored in terms of the number of items correctly mentioned and the number of questions correctly answered. The subject was told that a picture would be shown and that he would later be called upon to tell what it was about. After the picture had been exhibited for one minute, the child was asked to tell what he had seen. He was then given a list of fifty questions concerning the picture. Some of the questions were framed in such a manner as to suggest the existence of items not actually present. One week later, without his having seen the picture in the meantime, each child was asked to give a second report.

Over two hundred children were tested in this manner. Fifty of the subjects, ten at each age from three to seven, came from a school district of low socio-economic status. Other children were located in a district of better socio-economic status. At each age group there was an attempt to select an equal number of bright, average, and dull subjects. The children from three to seven years were tested individually, while all but a control group of the older ones were tested in groups. The children from three to seven gave an oral report, the others a written one. The subjects and the methodology are thus not comparable throughout the whole age range. However, the groups from four to seven years consisted of an equal number of children from each type of district. For these and the three-year-olds the methods of presentation and recall were alike.

The results for ages three to seven are shown in Table 8. It will be observed that all the scores (number of items recalled and correct answers) improve with age. This improvement is at first rapid and then relatively slow. Older children than those represented here did not show any further improvement. Control tests indicated that this failure to improve was not due to the fact that a written recall was required. It is doubtful, furthermore, whether the group method of presentation accounts for this failure. Winch believes that ability to recall material of the type used

Table 8. Recall Scores as a Function of Age*

Age level	No. of subjects	Av. no. of items reported, 1st test	Correct answers	Av. no. of items reported, 2d test
3–4	10	8.3	13.2	10.9
4–5	20	16.1	22.5	21.3
5–6	20	26.5	27.7	34.5
6–7	20	30.0	31.7	43.2
7–8	20	35.6	34.3	45.1

* Based upon two of Winch's tables.

in this test reaches its limit at about seven or eight years.

From Table 8 it will be observed that scores on the second recall, given one week after the picture was last seen, are larger than those on the first, given immediately after removal of the picture. Discussion among the children, implicit rehearsal, and the questioning which followed the first report may account for this improvement. Improved recall after lapse of time, however, has been observed in other investigations of memory. Ballard [26] found, for example, that the average accuracy with which *incompletely* learned poems were recalled by children of six years exhibited an increment some time after practice had ceased. The improvement was evident for from one to six days after original learning. Ballard called this phenomenon *reminiscence*. His research gave impetus to many further researches on reminiscence.[27]

Winch's claim that accuracy of report fails to improve after the seventh year is not supported by McGeoch's data. McGeoch [28] used large groups of subjects (50 to 162) at each of the yearly age levels between nine and fourteen. The children came from four schools of the same general class. All the tests at a given school were administered on the same day. Three types of material were used: (1) a card containing various objects such as a penny, a stamp, and so on; (2) a picture entitled "The Disputed Case"; and (3) an event carefully rehearsed and then acted before the subjects. The tests were given to a class at a time. Reports were written. They consisted of a description of the object or event and answers to 50 questions. With each of the types of material used the total number of items correctly reported and the total number of correct answers increased with age. The percentage of correct responses also increased. The increases at successive age levels between nine and fourteen years were small and statistically insignificant. Differences between these two extreme age levels were rather small, but statistically significant. The event yielded the greatest age difference while the object-card yielded the smallest.

Imagery and Imagination

Our only evidence for the existence of imagery is derived from verbal or other behavior which is descriptive of situations that have ceased to be present. The most easily identified images are those which follow removal of some intense stimulus, such, for example, as a bright red light. After the light has been turned out, the subject may report that he sees red or that he sees its complementary color, green. He responds as though stimulated by red or by green; or he describes the stimulus or its complement. In the first instance we say that he has a positive after-image and, in the second, that his after-image is negative. Such images are probably not central, but peripheral; that is, they can be reported only while specific activity is taking place in the eye. They are often designated as "after-sensations" rather than as images. In all cases of imagery some underlying modification of the organism persists after the stimuli which produced it have disappeared. Except possibly in the case of so-called after-images, this modification is believed to be primarily central; that is, in the central nervous system.

Ontogenetic investigations of most forms of imagery are rare. This is probably because of the subjectivity of these phenomena and the difficulties of investigating them in children. Unless children report imagery spontaneously, as was the case with Helson's [29] child, the investigator must ask them questions. These questions may suggest the phenomena about which information is desired. However, if the questions are worded in such a manner as to avoid suggesting the answer, and if the child is asked to give various objective representations of what he "sees" after a stimulus has been removed, reliable data on imagery may be gathered from very young children.

Eidetic imagery

The only elaborate genetic investigations of imagery in children have dealt with eidetic phenomena. Owing to the studies of Jaensch [30] and numerous later workers, eidetic imagery appears to possess marked genetic significance. Jaensch found that some children report images of unusual vividness and having extreme clarity of detail. Such images are of "hallucinatory clearness," yet the individual realizes that the stimuli which served as their basis are no longer present. Eidetic images may be experienced with eyes closed or open. When the eyes are open, the child often moves his eyes from one part of the screen to another as though looking at a picture projected upon it.

One test of eidetic imagery is to present some picture containing many details, such as the one in Figure 112. After the picture has been removed, the child is required to give a detailed description. Eidetic children can describe the picture and answer questions about its details just as though it were still before them. The inaccuracy present in the usual Aussage test (see p. 311) is not exhibited

Figure 112.   A Picture Used to Study Eidetic Imagery

This picture was used by Allport in a research on eidetic imagery. The picture was withdrawn after 35 seconds, then the child gave its description. (Used by G. W. Allport in "Eidetic Imagery," *Brit. J. Psychol.*, 1924, *15*, 99–120.)

by a child with good eidetic imagery. The long unfamiliar foreign word in the picture provides another test. After removal of this word the child is asked to spell it. When they perform this feat, eidetic children act as though the word were still before them and they were naming, in order, the letters seen. Acoustic as well as visual eidetic images are reported. A child with acoustic eidetic imagery can usually repeat long lists of digits after hearing them once. Imagery of this type is believed by Jaensch [31] to be only one-tenth as prevalent as the visual. Eidetic imagery in other sensory fields has also been reported.

Most of the investigations of eidetic phenomena have been with individuals of school age or older. These investigations have disclosed that very few adults and probably less than 50 per cent of children have vivid eidetic imagery. Investigators differ as to the age of childhood at which eidetic phenomena are most prevalent and as to the age at which the images are most vivid. Peck and Walling,[32] in an investigation with twenty children ranging in age from 24 to 64 months, found that ten of their subjects indicated the presence of eidetic images. On a second test, the same subjects were the only ones who reported such images. Correlation of the results for richness of detail reported on the first and second test was .75, which indicates rather high reliability. The following is a sample of the type of report given by a good eidetic subject. The subject was a girl of 58 months. A picture had been exposed and then removed.

"Yes, I can see it. It's black and white. Two little boys and one man, a tree and a girl, and some leaves and grass. (Color of boys?) Black. (Where is the old man?) He's on the steps. He has his hat on. (Still see a bird?) Yes, he's sitting on the tree right there (pointing). (Leaves?) One here and one here and one here (pointing). (How does the children's hair look?) It's straight, with one little curl on each one's head, right here (pointing).

The image, according to the child's report, lasted seven minutes and eleven seconds.

First-grade children were also given the test for eidetic imagery. Approximately 42 per cent (average age 80 months) reported eidetic imagery. The average duration of their images was only twenty-six seconds, as compared with fifty-three seconds for the preschool children. The average number of details reported was approximately the same for both groups. The authors say that the imagery of their preschool children was apparently more vivid than that of the older group.

One of the most recent discussions of eidetic imagery in young children is that of Peck,[33] which gives a number of interesting case studies and points out certain educational implications.

The influence of age upon eidetic imagery is not definitely known. Klüver,[34] who has himself done extensive research in this field, says that

While there seems to be agreement that EI disappear, as a rule, during or after puberty, the period of the "acme" of eidetic imagery, the age at which EI are most frequently found, and found in the highest "degree," is not yet agreed upon. Most often the age of twelve years has been suggested; but, after Roessler's investigation, six years or below promises to be more correct.

Imagination

Several investigations of the development of imagination in children of various ages have appeared in the literature. Markey[35] has summarized the methods and results of many such investigations.

Imagination has been defined in various ways. All definitions stress reaction based upon stimuli not present at the time of response. Whipple[36] claimed that imagery is imaging or, especially, manipulation of images in such a manner as to produce new patterns. In her investigation of imaginative behavior in preschool children, Markey defines this behavior in terms of language or other overt behavior which deals with objects, materials, activities, and situations as though they had properties or attributes other than those which they apparently or actually seem to possess. In other words, imaginative behavior is response in terms of absent aspects of stimulus situations. Imagination, as already indicated, involves implicit *manipulation* of symbols, but manipulation not so highly directive as in reasoning.

Typical tests of imagination are as follows: The individual may be shown ink blots and the fertility of his imagination measured in terms of how many different objects an inkblot may suggest. He may be confronted with the silhouette produced by a horizontal strip of material moving in clockwise direction (Miles's[37] kinephantoscope). As far as the subject knows, many kinds of movement may be present. To an individual with good imagination, according to Miles, the silhouette will seem to move in a counterclockwise direction, will seem to expand and contract like a rubber band, and so on. The more types of motion reported, the more fertile is the imagination of the subject assumed to be. The individual may be presented with a number of words arranged in chance order. His imaginative ability is measured in terms of the number of different sentences he can produce with these words. Drawings which possess varying degrees of completeness (the Heilbronner Test, described by Franz [38]) may be presented, the subject being required to name the object pictured. According to this test, the most imaginative person will require very little detail before recognizing the object. Street's [39] Gestalt Completion Test is of a somewhat similar nature. Children's drawings, modelings, and other types of construction are often regarded as indicative of the level of imaginative behavior. Eng [40] and Johnson [41] give good examples of these. Fantasy, expressing itself in stories, poems, and the like, is also indicative of imaginative ability. Musical creations are of a similar character. The less an individual's creations have a counterpart in reality, the more imaginative he is said to be.*

The most extensive experimental investigations of imaginative behavior in preschool children are those of Andrews and Markey. Andrews [42] used a tachistoscope to expose various objects, parts of objects, combinations of lines, and so on, in the window of a small house. The children were asked to tell what they saw after the stimulus had been exposed one second and then removed. Over one hundred subjects ranging in age from two to six years were used. The lowest type of response, in terms of imagination, was assumed to be verbal reproduction of the stimulus. Such responses increased with age, leading the author to assume that imagination decreases with age. Responses were scored in terms of their frequency (the least frequent responses were given the highest imagination scores) and in terms of complexity of response (reports of greatest complexity were given the highest scores). Scores based upon these criteria of imagination increased with age up to about four years, and then decreased. As Markey suggests, older children could perhaps

observe the stimuli more accurately than younger ones. This might explain why older children tended to report what was actually presented, thus obtaining low scores for imagination.

Markey [43] kept a diary record of frequency of imaginative response, ideas expressed in imaginative games, leadership, proneness to participate in imaginative games, and other aspects of imaginative behavior exhibited in the free play of preschool children. She also tested the children in a block-building and in a housekeeping situation. In the block-building experiment, scoring was in terms of the number and originality of the objects constructed and named. The housekeeping experiment involved observation of the responses of children to a small set of kitchen furniture and three small dolls. The children were required to do as many things as possible with these materials. Each child's score was based upon the originality of overt behavior (including language) elicited during play with the kitchen furniture and dolls. From 50 to 89 children were observed under each of the above conditions. There was a high correlation between the ratings given the children by different observers; hence the author regards her scoring as reliable. Correlations between imagination score and chronological age ranged from .34 to .62, while those between imagination scores and mental age ranged from .37 to .63. The author concludes that total imaginative behavior increases with age during the preschool period. She also points out the difficulty of obtaining comparable tests of imaginative behavior for different age levels.

Data on the development of imagination beyond the preschool level show no consistent trend. This is perhaps due to the complexity and varied nature of imaginative phenomena, as well as to the fact that comparable tests for various age levels have not been developed.

Children's Concepts and Their Origins

We have already (p. 134) considered concept formation in infrahuman animals. The

* The various projective tests (Rorschach, T. A. T., etc.; see Chapter 16) may of course also be regarded as tests of imagination.

existence of concepts, it will be recalled, is inferred from equivalence of responses to diverse objects or situations. For example, the rats of Fields's investigation learned to make a positive response to triangles which differed widely in shape (isosceles or equilateral), in position (apex up or down), in size, in brightness, and in their backgrounds. Since an equivalent response was made to all of these different triangles, Fields assumed that the rats had developed a *concept of triangularity*. It will be recalled (p. 243) that Ling's [44] infants of six months and older learned to respond to a triangular block in an equivalent manner regardless of its position. Munn and Steining [45] and Gellermann (pp. 243–244) [46] obtained similar results in older children (fifteen months to two years) by utilizing methods adapted from those used with animals. The child was given food whenever it opened a door containing a triangle and was given no food when it opened a door containing some other figure. After the discrimination had been learned, a rotated triangle was responded to as equivalent with that used in training. It was assumed, therefore, that the subjects were responding in terms of the common property of the different triangles, that is, triangularity. Both the rats and the children may have observed, for example, that every configuration associated with food possessed three sides or three corners. Differentiation of such common properties from objects and situations is designated as *abstracting*. When the common properties have come to have a given meaning, such as food, regardless of their immediate setting, it is said that the organism has evolved a *concept*.

Concepts are symbolic in that they depend upon properties of absent objects and situations as well as upon the properties of objects and situations present at the time of response. The present stimulating situation must be compared with and related to situations experienced in the past. Concepts are not necessarily conscious, however; nor are they always verbalized. The fact that infrahuman organisms may learn to respond upon a conceptual

basis is proof that verbalization is unnecessary. Further proof that individuals may respond upon a conceptual basis without having achieved a verbal generalization has been obtained by Ray [47] in children, and by Smoke [48] and Heidbreder [49] in adults. In each of these experiments, some subjects responded in an equivalent manner to the common properties of otherwise diverse situations, yet they could not report the principle or generalization which underlay their responses.

Although Hull's [50] investigation of concept formation was confined to adults, we mention it here because it offers an excellent illustration of certain basic factors in the development of concepts. Hull's view was that *common elements* in diverse objects or situations serve to unite these objects or situations under a common term or concept. He prefaced his experimental work with the following suggestions as to how a child may evolve the concept "dog."

A young child finds himself in a certain situation, reacts to it by approach say, and hears it called "Dog." After an indeterminate intervening period he finds himself in a somewhat different situation and hears that called "dog." Later he finds himself in a somewhat different situation still, and hears that called "dog" also. Thus the process continues. The "dog" experiences appear at irregular intervals. The appearances are thus unanticipated. They appear with no obvious label as to their essential nature. This precipitates at each new appearance a more or less acute *problem* as to the proper reaction . . .; the intervals between the "dog" experiences are filled with all sorts of other absorbing experiences which are contributing to the formation of other concepts. At length the time arrives when the child has a "meaning" for the word dog. Upon examination this "meaning" is found to be actually a characteristic more or less common to all dogs and not common to cats, dolls and "teddy-bears." But to the child the process of arriving at this meaning or concept has been largely unconscious. He has never said to himself, "Lo! I shall proceed to discover the characteristics common to all dogs but not enjoyed by cats and 'teddy-bears.'" The formation of the concept has never been an end deliberately sought for itself. It has always been a means to an end. . . . Such in brief is our standard or normal type of concept evolution.

The characteristics common to all (or to most) of the dogs encountered by the child may have been that they barked or that they jumped upon him. Cats, dolls, and "teddy-bears," since they never responded in this way, would be placed in a different category from "dog."

The subjects of Hull's experiment were presented with Chinese characters, exposed one at a time in the window of a memory apparatus. The characters were arranged in series. Each member of a given series, while markedly different from every other member, contained an element common to all. Thus the characters 派, 汜, 汞, 汏, and 洎 possessed 氵 as their common element; the characters 橣, 樅, and 槊 contained 木. In their presentation to the subject, the characters of various series were arranged in a mixed-up order. The subject's problem was to learn that a given term applied to all characters having a given common element. All members of the first set of characters mentioned fell into the *oo* category; the second into the *fid* category, and so on.

As Smoke [51] pointed out, Hull's experiment deals more with the process of abstracting precise common elements than with concept formation as it most frequently exists in everyday life. Situations encountered by the child in the normal course of his development usually do not contain such obvious common properties as did the Chinese characters of Hull's experiment. Smoke claims that the common properties of objects and situations are not *elements*; that they involve relationships, dynamic pattern aspects, and so on. The definition of concept formation which he believes to be most acceptable is as follows: "By 'concept formation,' 'generalization,' or 'concept learning' we refer to the process whereby an organism develops a symbolic process (usually, but not necessarily linguistic) which is made to the members of a class of stimulus patterns but not to other stimuli." Smoke's change of emphasis from Hull's *common element* idea to his *dynamic whole* is demonstrated by the nature of his experiment. The subjects, all adults, were confronted with geometrical figures which differed in color, shape, size, and the like. However, a given series of figures possessed some common internal relationship. All the figures which fell under the concept, or term, *dax* consisted of a circle with two dots, one dot being outside of the circle and one dot within; all those which fell within the *zif* classification consisted of three dots, the distance between the two farthest ones being twice the distance between the two nearest ones; and so on. Figures in which these common properties were closely approximated were presented from time to time. Thus a circle with two dots inside might be confused with the *dax* figures until the subject noted that one dot had to be inside and the other outside. The problem was one of noting the common properties of certain of the configurations and then gathering all possessing these properties under the appropriate symbol, *dax*, *zif*, and so on.

Studies of concept formation

One method of studying concept formation in children is that already considered (pp. 134–135) in relation to form discrimination. It will be recalled that both animals and children may respond in an equivalent manner to forms which, while they differ in certain details, have some feature in common. The subject may be trained, for example, to discriminate between a triangle and a circle. Let us say that the triangle, responses to which are reinforced, is on its base. After the child learns to select the triangle without regard to position, or other extraneous cues, some other figure is substituted for the circle. If the triangle is still selected, we know that the child is responding positively to it and not negatively to the circle. Then the triangle is inverted. If, under these circumstances, the child makes a response to the inverted triangle which is equivalent to that elicited by the triangle on its base, we assume that it is responding to *triangularity* and not merely to a particular distribution of light. When other, quite dissimilar, triangles are also reacted to in an equivalent manner, there is further evidence that triangularity has been abstracted and that a conceptual response is being made. The data summarized in our discussion of form discrimination indicated that some infants are capable of such responses as, also, are some animals.

The concept of roundness. In an experiment by Long,[52] children were first trained to discriminate between a ball and a block. In each instance the child pressed on a glass through which the object was seen. If it pressed the correct glass, a piece of candy was automatically made accessible. After mastery of the initial discrimination, in which response to the ball was rewarded, new items were introduced. When these were discriminated with a high level of accuracy, still another pair was presented. This continued until it was clear that the child had abstracted *roundness* as the correct cue. Among the stimulus-pairs were such items as: red ball, cream-colored wooden triangle; small ball, small cube; marble, rectangle; orange, flattened paper drinking cup; circular glass bottle, rectangular glass bottle; and so on. Thirteen children ranging in age from three years to six years and three months served as subjects. There was clear evidence that the concept "roundness" was learned. All children transferred from the initial situations to later ones involving spherical objects. A change to cylindrical objects, to two-dimensional round objects, or to two objects one of which was more round than the other, led to an initial drop in accuracy. Nevertheless, eleven of the thirteen children learned to respond to the roundness aspect of such divergent objects as spheres, cylinders, and plane figures. Some of the children verbalized, like the six-year-old who said "Everything got to be round to get candy out."

Concepts of magnitude. Discrimination of size by children has already been considered (p. 244). What we are concerned with here is the concept of size as represented by such terms as big, little, or intermediate. We desire answers to such questions as: At what age are children capable of acquiring this concept? How may it be developed? How is it related to language development?

Several investigators have studied size concepts in a variety of ways. One of the most extensive of these studies is that of Hicks and Stewart.[53] They required children to point to the middle-sized cube of three which differed in absolute size and in right, left, and middle location from one trial to another. The correct cube always had a toy hidden beneath it. Only one out of ten two-year-old children was successful in indicating the cube of middle size. From the third to the fifth year, as shown by the responses of ten children at each yearly age level, there was a gradual decrease in error and in the number of trials required to attain a criterion of fifteen correct responses in succession. Most of the three- to five-year-olds learned the meaning of "middle size" early in the experiment and then applied it to all successive situations with little or no error.

Thrum's[54] investigation also involved two- to five-year-olds. It dealt with the concepts "large," "small," and "middle size." Three objects (large, intermediate, and small) were placed before the child. Toy automobiles and various forms were used. These objects were varied in relative position from time to time. The general instructions were: "Look at these (pointing to objects) very carefully and give me the one I ask for." The child was asked for the "big," "little," or "middle" automobile, square, or circle. The subjects were not informed concerning the accuracy of their choices, and only one choice was given for each arrangement of sizes. Twenty-five children served as subjects.

Accuracy was 88 per cent for "big," 68 per cent for "little," and only 48 per cent for "middle." Four of the subjects made errors on "big," thirteen on "little," and eighteen on "middle." Age was not shown to have a significant effect, since younger and older children made similar errors. In a further experiment of the same type as that described, the children were tested with circles, squares, and triangles and then given a retest after six months. The initial test yielded accuracies of 88, 91, and 48 per cent for "big," "little," and "middle," respectively. Retest accuracy was 100, 92.2, and 67 per cent. Again, age was not influential. In a third experiment of the same type, the forms varied in color from trial to trial. Thrum's aim was to ascertain whether color and size would be confused. Color was not confused with size. The percentage of accuracy was 96 for "big," 95 for "little," and 62 for "middle." No significant age differences were apparent.

With respect to the above experiments, one might ask whether the difficulty of the middle-ness concept is due to inadequate vocabulary or to inability to discriminate middleness. This question seems especially pertinent in view of the fact that animals have been trained to discriminate middleness.[55] However, Welch [56] studied this concept in children under conditions where, as in animal experiments, no language was involved. Only three out of eleven children trained on the problem were successful in achieving the middleness concept. These children were two years or older. Welch regards his results as similar, essentially, to those reported by the earlier investigators who used language.

Even at the age of seven, the development of a "middle-sized" concept is difficult. This was brought out in an experiment by Graham and others.[57] The aim of the experiment was to develop the concept of *middle size*, then see whether this would transfer to middleness in general, such as the medium density of stimuli of the same or different size. A discrimination procedure involving three doors was used. If the child selected the door containing the correct stimulus, he found a piece of candy. No understanding of language was necessary. The subjects were 75 children ranging in age from seven to nine years. Only 9 out of 25 seven-year-olds learned the middle-sized concept. It was learned by 16 out of 25 eight-year-olds and all 25 of the nine-year-olds. Transfer to problems calling for a response to

middle density or to middle density-area was poor in the first age group, but improved with age. Thus only 2 seven-year-olds, 6 eight-year-olds, and 11 nine-year-olds were completely successful. Although no verbalization was required, some children did verbalize their concepts. They used such terms as "middle-sized square," "medium one," "next to the biggest," and "the middle number of dots."

Development of number concepts. The Stanford-Binet test (p. 368) involves the counting of four objects at year five. At year six the child is asked to give the tester the requested number of objects. Some children can of course pass such items at earlier age levels.

In an experiment by Long and Welch,[58] children between the ages of two and one-half and seven years were required to discriminate and to match numbers. One hundred and thirty-five children took part in the experiment. In the discrimination experiment, a child was told that he would always find a toy under the box with the *most* marbles. At first there were 10 marbles versus one marble. After 10 trials, during which the position of the correct box and the patterns made by the marbles were varied in a random fashion, 10 marbles were presented with 5. If the child mastered this discrimination within a set period, one more marble was added to the smaller group, so that there were now 10 versus 6 marbles. If the child failed at 10 versus 5, he was confronted with 10 versus 4. The final score was the number of marbles discriminated from 10.

Average scores on this test improved with age, beginning with an average of .80 in the 30–35 month group and ending with an average of 7.87 in the 78–83 month group.

In one of two matching tests, the child was required to make a pile of marbles to match a group placed before him by the experimenter. At first there were two marbles, which he was to match from the 10 to 15 marbles handed to him. When this was accomplished, three marbles were given to be matched. This continued until the child failed to match the set number of marbles. The score assigned was the number of marbles correctly matched.

This problem proved to be somewhat more difficult than the preceding one. The lowest age group had an average score of .60. This was increased, somewhat irregularly, with age. From 60 to 83 months the average score approximated 7.

A group matching test was also given. Here the child was confronted with four groups of marbles: two groups of two each, and two groups of three each. He was required to point to the groups containing the *most* marbles; then to the groups containing the *smallest number* of marbles. As one problem was passed, the groups became larger, until there were finally two groups of 9 and two of 10 marbles. The point where the child could no longer point out the larger (or smaller) groups gave him his score. Again the average scores increased with age, ranging from .40 at the lowest age level to about 6 at the upper level.

All three curves tended to flatten off at the six- to seven-year level, suggesting that ability on such tests has undergone most of its development by this age level. That there is a certain degree of communality between the three tests is suggested by inter-test correlations of around .40. According to the authors, there is no significant correlation between test scores and I.Q.

Although the first of these tests merely involved discrimination of a larger from a smaller group of objects, there was not necessarily any concept of number. In the other tests, however, it was necessary for the child to respond in terms of such verbalized concepts as *most* or *smallest number*. It is in such terms that number concepts are involved in intelligence tests as well as in aspects of our everyday life.

In the concepts which we shall now consider, language plays an exceptionally important role. Such concepts include time, and life, or animism.

The concept of time. Two methods were

used by Ames [59] in her study of time concepts in children. One was to observe spontaneous verbalizations involving or implying time expressions. This method was used in a nursery school while the children were at play. The second method was to ask questions dealing with various aspects of the time concept. The children questioned ranged from eighteen months to eight years of age. Among the questions were: What day is today? What time do you come to school? Is this morning or afternoon? What does *time* mean? There were marked individual differences at each age level, but Ames discerned a developmental sequence. She says that

Words indicating the present come in first, then words indicating the future, and finally those indicating the past. Thus "today" (24 months) precedes "tomorrow" (30 months), which in turn precedes "yesterday" (36 months). This trend is evident both in spontaneous verbalization, in answers to questions, and in sheer volume of verbalization. There is a suggestion that time in relation to ends of things is understood before time in relation to beginnings.

Fifty per cent or more of the four-year-olds knew whether it was morning or afternoon; of the five-year-olds, what day it was; of the seven-year-olds, what season; and of the eight-year-olds, what year and what day of the month. Ames says that "superior" eight-year-olds, in their answers to the question "What does *time* mean?" gave evidence of understanding "the more generalized concept of time." She does not, however, reproduce answers regarded by her as revealing such a generalized concept. Even adults asked the same question often have difficulty in answering it in a generalized manner.

The concept of life. Piaget [60] investigated children's concepts with a question-and-answer method. Among the concepts studied was that of "life." Many answers indicated the presence of animistic concepts, that is, the attribution of life to inanimate objects like the sun, stones, and chairs.

In studying the concept of life, Piaget asked

the child a question such as "Do you know what it is to be alive?" When the child replied, it was questioned further. The following is an example of the method and the kind of results obtained:

Vel (8½): "Is the sun alive? — *Yes.* — Why? — *It gives light. It is alive when it is giving light, but it isn't alive when it is not giving light.* — Is a bicycle alive? — *No, when it doesn't go it isn't alive. When it goes it is alive.* — Is a mountain alive? — *No.* — Why not? — *Because it doesn't do anything* (!) — Is a tree alive? — *No; when it has fruit it's alive. When it hasn't any it isn't alive.* — Is a watch alive? — *Yes.* — Why? — *Because it goes.* — Is a bench alive? — *No, it's only for sitting on.* — Is an oven alive? — *Yes, it cooks the dinner and the tea and the supper.* — Is a gun alive? — *Yes, it shoots.* — Is the play-bell alive? — *Yes, it rings.*" Vel even goes so far as to say that poison is alive — "*because it can kill us.*"

At this stage of development, according to Piaget, the child attributes life to *activity in general.* A later stage is characterized by attribution of life solely to *things which move.* For example:

Zimm (8:1): "Is a stone alive? — *Yes.* — Why? — *It moves* (*il marche*). — When does it move? — *Some days, sometimes.* — How does it move? — *By rolling.* — Is the table alive? — *No, it can't move.* . . ."

A third stage in the development of the concept "life" comes, according to Piaget, when the child restricts his concept to those *things which move spontaneously.* An example follows:

Sart (12½): "You know what it means to be alive? — *Yes.* — Is a fly alive? — *Yes.* — Why? — *Because if it wasn't alive it couldn't fly.* — Is a bicycle alive? — *No.* — Why not? — *Because it is we who make it go.* — Is a horse alive? — *Yes.* — Why? — *He helps man.* — Are clouds alive? — *Yes.* — Why? — *No, they're not* — Why not? — *Clouds aren't alive. If they were alive they could come and go as they wanted* (*Ils seraient en voyage*). — *It's the wind that drives the clouds.* — Are streams alive? — *Yes, because the water is flowing all the time.* — Is a motor? — *No, it's the engine that makes it go.* — Is the engine alive? — *No, it's man who makes the engine go.* — Is the sun alive? — *Yes, it makes the sunshine and gives light during the day.* — Is the lake alive? — *No, because the lake is all alone and it can't ever move by itself* (*il bouge jamais*)."

The fourth, and final, stage indicated by Piaget is that in which the concept "life" is confined to *plants and animals.* In a given child, the answers to some questions suggested one concept of "life" and the answers to others a quite different concept. In general, however, the concepts acceptable to educated adults were more consistently and closely approximated as the children became older.

Piaget's research on this and other concepts aroused various criticisms and at the same time gave the impetus to considerable further research. One of the most serious criticisms pointed to the absence of a standardized procedure which would allow quantitative analysis of his data. A related criticism was that Piaget, by the nature of his questioning, may at times have suggested answers to the children. When he asked, for example, "Who put the snow there?" he was suggesting some personal agency. He should, of course, have asked "How did the snow get there?" Another criticism was that the stages in the development of animism which Piaget claimed to have found might have been imposed on the data by Piaget himself, that is, might have been products of his subjective interpretation of the facts. The question asked was whether impartial observers going over the same data would also discern these stages. Still another criticism was that although the child said something was alive, this word might not have the same meaning to the child as to the adult, who placed his own interpretation upon it. This criticism was leveled by Huang,[61] not only at Piaget's research on animistic concepts, but also at the later research which we are about to discuss. Huang and Lee [62] have shown, moreover, that Chinese children make a distinction between "living" and "having life" and that they apply the former more loosely than the latter to inanimate objects. These criticisms make apparent the need for a carefully standardized procedure with respect to (1) the items on which the questions are to be focused, (2) the framing of the questions, and (3) the interpretation of the questions from the standpoint of classification into developmental levels.

Grigsby [63] made an attempt to overcome the weaknesses of Piaget's procedure by a more careful wording and standardization of questions and by recording the answers verbatim so that they could be studied after the interview was over, by both the interviewer and others. However, most of the recent research has utilized a more elaborate standardization developed by Russell and Dennis.[64]

All the questions are focused upon twenty standard objects (stone, knife, mirror, broken button, comb, chair, broken dish, watch, etc.). The eight objects just mentioned are all in the room in which the test takes place. The other objects are referred to verbally, sometimes by pointing out of the window, as to a tree. Seated alone with the interrogator in a small room, the child is told: "We are going to play a game. I am going to ask you some questions and we will see how many you can answer. You know what living means? A cat is living but if an automobile runs over it, it is dead."

The criticism that the preliminary statement prejudices the outcome of further questioning was tested by comparing the responses of two comparable groups of children, one group with and the other without this statement. Since there was no difference in the content of the answers, the preliminary statement was retained in the standard procedure. It did have the advantage, at the outset, of producing more ready answers.

The subsequent procedure was as follows: The child's attention was drawn to the first item (stone) and he was asked, "Is the stone living or dead?" The comparable question was asked for each item in turn. Answers were recorded in detail. Two supplementary questions were used whenever the child's answer was of a certain nature. Suppose, for example, that a child said the stone was dead,

then added that this was because it didn't move. Would the child make a distinction between spontaneous (self-initiated) movement and movement imparted to the object by an outside force? To get at this, the following procedure was devised, to be used only when the child had himself raised the issue of movement: The questioner moved the stone and said: "Is the stone living or dead when it is moving?" If the child attributed life to it under these circumstances, and it was still not clear whether spontaneous or imparted movement was meant, the child was asked a further question: "Can the stone move by itself or does something move it?"

When Dennis and Russell applied this standardized version of Piaget's questionnaire to large groups of American school children, they obtained results in general agreement with those of Piaget. In most instances, a child at first attributed life to anything in good condition (but not to a broken button or dish); then to anything that moved; then to anything that moved spontaneously; and finally only to plants or animals. No definite age range could be assigned to each of these levels. A particular stage might be present at any age level. It was with respect to this point that these investigators failed to agree with Piaget.

Other judges, as well as Dennis and Russell, were in close agreement as to the reality of the four stages. Three independent judges, for example, showed 87 per cent agreement in their assignment of answers to a particular stage of animism. The test itself was shown to be fairly reliable, as indicated by a test-retest correlation of .81.

In subsequent research with approximately 1200 American school children, Russell [65] found the same stages and sequential development in urban, suburban, and rural children; in the two sexes; and also in children at every level of intelligence. In another study with feebleminded children, Russell, Dennis, and Ash [66] obtained essentially similar results. Using his own daughter as a subject, and questioning her at intervals over the period from two years and nine months until six years and two months, Dennis [67] found that adult concepts had been achieved at the latter age level. This is an unusually early age at which to achieve the mature concept. But the child had an I.Q. of over 150. She did, however, go through the same stages as other children in reaching this concept. A careful study of her reading and other sources of information suggested that development of animistic concepts is autogenous — that is to say, acquired through the child's own unguided observations.

Zuñi [68] and Hopi [69] children have animistic ideas like those found in France by Piaget and in the United States by Dennis and Russell. They also, according to these investigators, pass through the four stages found in other groups. Bruce,[70] using a somewhat different procedure — before Dennis and Russell had developed theirs — also found Piaget's four stages in white and Negro children in Virginia. Dennis [71] claims that "the earliest (animistic) ideas of children are uniform in all societies and are the product of universal child experiences and of mental immaturity." Russell claims that the results with children having different backgrounds (such as rural versus urban) support this belief in the universality of the sequence of animistic development. Huang and Lee,[72] as a result of their work with Chinese children, would not agree. It is possible that Chinese children, who seem to show relatively little animism, differ from children of other cultures in development of animistic concepts. But one could not be sure of this on the basis of Huang and Lee's experiment, which did not utilize procedures exactly comparable with those of the other investigators. Mead's [73] study of Manus children, in which she failed to obtain results like those reported by Piaget and later investigators, also involved a quite different procedure.

A rather surprising recent outcome of research in this field was the discovery by Dennis [74] that many college students have failed to attain a consistently adult concept of what it means to be alive. He found, for example, large percentages of students who maintained that a lighted match is living, that the sun has life, and that the ocean is alive. That they were not being whimsical in making such claims, or metaphorical, as when we speak of a "live" electric wire, is shown by statements like: "The match has flames which indicate life"; "The sun gives forth energy," hence is alive; and the ocean is alive because it "moves and makes a noise, and is powerful and changing." Like children, many students also attributed conscious processes to inanimate objects. The percentage of students expressing animistic concepts varied from around 50 for some groups to 12 for others. The latter percentage was found in a group studying biology.

The Dennis-Russell procedure, applied to a group of people 70 years old or over, yielded a higher incidence of animism than in older children and adults.[75] This is interpreted as "a return in senescence to childhood concepts." A similar procedure used by Werner and Carrison [76] with children who were both brain-injured and mentally retarded also produced higher-than-normal indices of animism. They attribute this outcome to brain pathology.

Although this extensive research has enlightened us concerning the nature of the concept of life and its prevalence in various groups and at various age levels, it is perhaps too early to reach a definite conclusion as to the universality of the concept and the degree to which it depends upon educational influences. While Dennis stresses its independence of formal education in one place, he shows the influence of a biology course in another. Bruce [77] questions whether the term "animism" is appropriate as applied to the children's answers. She prefers "evolution of the concept *alive*." Russell,[78] however, thinks that the term "animism" is appropriate. He found, for example, that a child who said that something was alive was also likely to regard it as having conscious processes like knowing and feeling.

There is reason to question any breaking up of the data into rigid stages, even though age ranges are not assigned a particular stage. One who was not biased by Piaget's original analysis into stages might discern a gradual transition. This might be especially true if, instead of testing large groups, he traced the development longitudinally in a few children over a number of years as Dennis did in the case of his daughter. The question of stages versus transition is that of saltatory as against gradual development. This problem, it will be recalled, came up in our discussion of motor development (p. 288).

Concepts and intelligence. The Terman-Merrill Revision of the Binet-Simon Intelligence Test, as well as several other tests of intelligence, gives age norms for certain kinds of concepts. For example, the average child of three years and six months should, according to the Terman-Merrill Revision, be able to indicate the *bigger* of two objects, as well as the *longer* of two sticks. The number concept of *two* is normally present by the fourth year. At four years and six months, the average child can indicate pictorial *likenesses* and *differences*. At the fifth year the number concept of *three* is normally present. The test for the seventh year indicates that a normal child should, at this age, have increased his number concepts to *nine*. Beginning with the test for year ten, ability to define certain *abstract* words is measured. *Similarity-difference* concepts of increasing complexity are found to be present at successive age levels from the age of $4\frac{1}{2}$ years on.

Thinking and Reasoning

Thinking is a form of activity in which, instead of manipulating objects and situations, one manipulates symbols. These, as we have previously noted (pp. 105, 303), are based upon modifications of the organism. They represent the stimuli which originally produced them. The activities based upon such modifications may be implicit (e.g., confined to the central nervous system) or they may be explicit (gestural, as in movements of the throat, limbs, and so forth). The explicit activities involved in thinking are themselves primarily under the control of symbolic central nervous mechanisms.

Implicit activities associated with thinking are beyond direct observation. They are inferred from behavior (verbal or otherwise) or from measurements of electrical activity within the brain (i.e., from electroencephalograms). Explicit thought activities are usually quite abbreviated. Delicate and elaborate apparatus is often necessary to disclose their presence.

Although external stimuli present at the time may be important in *initiating* thought processes, the most significant factors are substitutes (symbols) for *absent* stimuli. These substitutes are within the organism; probably within the central nervous system.

Differentiation of thought processes

Activities to which the term "thought" is applied are quite varied, and several types have been classified. Some of these, like reverie and fantasy, are akin to, if not identical with, imagination (see pp. 314–315). In the following discussion our attention is focused on reasoning. This is symbolic problem solving.

We are said to reason when, confronted by some problem, we attempt or achieve solution in terms of relevant past experience. As in sensorimotor learning, there may be overt trial-and-error activity prior to solution. In the case of reasoning, however, such activity is implicit, or, if explicit, very much abbreviated. Solution of the problems may involve some overt adjustment of the organism (such as obtaining food), or it may involve an implicit adjustment (such as the realization that one has the correct answer to a problem). When the problem is that of finding a general principle, or developing a concept or generalization, the reasoning process is sometimes referred to as *generalizing*.

Genetic investigations of reasoning

The reasoning process in children has been investigated extensively, and no useful purpose could be served by attempting to review all the pertinent research. We shall confine our discussion to a few typical experiments in which there has been a clear-cut genetic approach. In reviewing these experiments, our prime interest is in obtaining answers to such questions as: At what age does ability to reason first appear? How does reasoning ability develop as the child becomes older?

We have already (pp. 218–222) described the solving of certain problems by children. Some were solved by an overt trial-and-error attack. No evidence of reasoning was involved. A few children solved these and other problems by implicit processes. The presence of such processes is evidenced by (1) sudden solutions (suggesting the existence of insight), (2) "putting two and two together" in the solution of a novel problem, and (3) discerning and utilizing a principle. Such "higher processes" are probably related rather than distinct. It is certainly clear, however, that they are not much in evidence below the school age.

Children under five did not solve Maier's [79] reasoning problem, which called for the combining of past experiences in a novel way. A similar result was found by Harter [80] in the test (p. 220) requiring children to move pegs along a groove with as few moves as possible. Although children under five learned the problem, they did so on an overt trial-and-error basis, making many unnecessary moves. Older children sometimes "figured out" the moves beforehand, thus avoiding overt errors. These children were obviously reasoning.

The double-alternation problem, while it elicits much overt trial and error, cannot be solved except by reasoning. It thus represents, much more clearly than any other problem previously discussed, the transition from lower to higher learning processes. What the subject must learn is a principle (*right, right, left, left*). Then he must apply this principle.

He applies it in making the correct sequence of turns, not only in the original training situation but in a somewhat changed situation where a longer series is called for. The same principle is involved in the double-box test of double alternation. Here the boxes are opened in the order *right, right, left, left*, both in the original and in an extended series. It may be recalled that some of Gellermann's [81] four-year-olds solved the double alternation problem in a temporal maze and that two of Hunter and Bartlett's [82] three-year-olds solved the problem in the double-box situation. It was not until they were around four years old, however, that children verbalized the double alternation principle. Extension of the principle to a longer series did not occur until approximately five years.

The reasoning problems to be considered now involve pictorial material, and most of them place a great deal of emphasis upon verbalized solutions and their application. Some call for discovery of a relatively simple generalization. We shall proceed from the discussion of one such problem to the consideration of problems of increasing difficulty until we approach the sort of reasoning problems involved in formal logic.

The ability of children to discover and to apply to new situations the solving principle of a given problem was investigated by Roberts. [83] The problem was that of discovering which one of three colored doors in a toy house would release a colored aeroplane observable within. The aeroplane was red in one series of tests, blue in another, and green in another. The position of a particular colored door and aeroplane differed from trial to trial. Each child received the following instructions: "This house has three doors; all of them open, but only one makes an aeroplane fall. You open one door and see if you can make an aeroplane fall." Solution was achieved when the child observed that the door which released the aeroplane was always identical with it in color. The 43 subjects were from two to five years of age. There were 10 or more at each age level. After each child had solved the first series (say, that with the red aeroplane), he was asked, "Which door do you open to make the aeroplane fall?" While being questioned, the child could not see the house or aeroplane. Although all the children solved the problem, the youngest child who could give a verbal generalization was three years and four months old. The frequency of verbal generalization increased with chronological and mental age. Ability to apply the principle to new situations in which it formed an adequate solution was evidenced by all but the two-year-olds.

In Heidbreder's [84] investigation of reasoning the age range was from three years to adulthood. There were 10 subjects aged three years, 10 aged four years, 10 aged six to ten years, and 10 adults. Three problems which involved some general principle were used. In one problem-situation the subject was confronted by two boxes, one of which contained a doll. Although the right-hand box might be nearer than the left-hand at one trial and farther than it at another, it always contained the doll. Only one three-year-old solved this problem. It was solved by six four-year-olds and by all of the older subjects. The second problem, apparently the easiest one, involved plain and flowered boxes. A box with flowers on it, regardless of position or distance, always contained the doll. Two of the three-year group and all of the other subjects solved this problem. The third problem was much more difficult than the others. Two boxes were presented at each trial. Both possessed plain figures or they possessed figures with red dots on their perimeter. Sometimes a given box would be nearer and at other times farther than its partner. If plain figures appeared on the boxes, the doll was in the farther box. On the other hand, if dotted figures appeared the nearer box contained the doll. None of the subjects in the three-year group, one of those in the four-year group, and all of those in the older groups solved this problem. The number of trials required for solution of these problems decreased with age. None of the children of three years gave a "reason" (verbal general-

ization) for any of the solutions. Only 5 per cent of the solutions by four-year-olds were verbalized. Verbal generalizations were given in almost every case of solution by subjects from six years to adulthood. Older subjects gave more mature verbal generalizations than younger ones. Heidbreder says that the "reasons" reported by adults were more objective than those reported by children. Some children, when asked why they selected a green box, gave answers such as "because I like it."

Long and Welch [85] gave 15 children ranging from six to eight years a series of generalization tasks which went from simple problems involving identity relations to problems having a relatively high degree of abstractness. Typical of the simpler problems was one in which the child, confronted with three blocks, was shown that pressing a hexagonal key made the hexagonal block jump up and that pressing a triangular key had the same effect upon the triangular block. The child was then asked to indicate which block a square key would cause to jump up. Pictorial and verbal forms of this sort of problem were also used. Both the performance and the pictorial forms were easily learned, but the verbal variety was difficult. Once the principle of these problems had been learned, it was readily transferred to other situations in which it applied. Most children verbalized the principles involved.

A more difficult generalization problem required abstraction of certain causal relations, such as: candy is present whenever there are *two* objects and when the object is *round*. Ten out of the 15 children solved such problems within a set time limit and all but one of these verbalized the principle involved.

A still higher level of generalization was involved in a series of problems utilizing Mill's Joint Method of Agreement and Difference. Typical of such problems, as they were used in this age range, was that illustrated in Figure 113. If the combination AB turns on the light ($+$), the combination BC does not turn it on ($-$), and the combination AC turns it on ($+$), then which of the com-

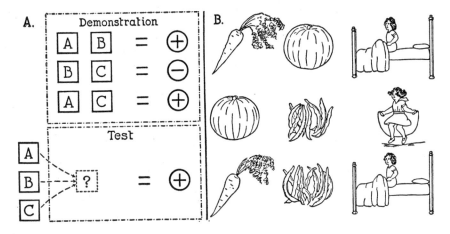

Figure 113. Reasoning Problems Involving Mill's Joint Method of Agreement and Difference

For description see text. (From L. Welch and L. Long, "Comparison of the Reasoning Ability of Two Age Groups," *J. Genet. Psychol.*, 1943, *62*, 67.)

bination ABC will turn it on? Likewise, in the pictorial form of such tests, if carrot and pumpkin make the child ill, beans and pumpkin do not make her ill, and carrots and beans make her ill, which vegetable had she better avoid eating? Only one child of the 15 solved such problems without hints. When these hints were given, all but two children achieved the solutions. In a later study with a group of four- to six-year-olds, Welch and Long[86] found that none of the 10 children solved these problems without hints and only one solved them with hints. On the simpler problems, however, there were no evident differences between the older and younger groups.

A more complicated form of the agreement-difference type of problem was given by Long and Welch[87] to 113 children arranged in three age groups: eleven, twelve, and thirteen years. Many such problems were presented, in increasing order of difficulty, as a pencil-and-paper test. One of the more complicated items was as follows:

Grouse	Lollipop	Corn flakes	Sherry	→ Sick
Clam	Coffee	Pear	Ketchup	→ Well
Shad	Oatmeal	Lemon	Spinach	→ Sick
Fudge	Cloves	Squash	Lamb	→ Well

Peanut brittle, Ham, Puffed rice, Lobster, Peach, Tabasco, Gingerale, Beet

What the child was required to indicate was which of the lower list of foodstuffs should be avoided by the individual affected as in the four lines above. The answer here is of course *Puffed rice*. Scores on this type of test increased with age, going from 64 at eleven to 92 at thirteen years.

Conceptual thinking may be classified in several ways. Welch and Long, in their research with children and in their subsequent theoretical discussions,[88] have made a distinction between what they call *horizontal* and *vertical* generalization. The former is illustrated when, for example, a certain red object is at one moment a *brick*, at another a *missile*, at another a *doorstop*, and so on. The latter is illustrated when a sparrow is called a *bird, an animal, living matter, matter* . . . and so on in classifications of increasing inclusiveness. In their investigation on the development of horizontal generalizations, Welch and Long[89] used tests like the following: There were two small blocks, one cubical and the other six-sided. In a bowling alley situation, both blocks were used as ammunition. In a drum-beating situation both became tips of a drum stick. In a balance situation both became weights. Each block had a different nonsense name in each situation, but the children learned the name appropriate to each situation with little difficulty. They learned, for instance, that the cubical block was CEF as ammunition, FEH as the tip of a drum stick, and QOB as a weight. They also learned that both blocks, while serving as ammunition were also XAT; while serving as tips were also KYH; and while serving as weights were also YOF. This is the sort of process which occurs when we learn that two different objects (a brick and a piece of lumber) are both of a certain broader class (building material). Learning such generalizations was not especially difficult for children within the ages of 66 and 83 months. Acquisition of vertical generalizations was, however, extremely difficult.

This type of problem is illustrated in Figure 114. Blocks of different shape were used, as illustrated. After the child learned to give the experimenter an MEF or a TOV upon request, he was asked to learn that either of these is also VIC. Likewise, after learning the separate names of YOP and ZIL, he was asked to learn that both are also DAX. Finally, he was asked to learn that all of these

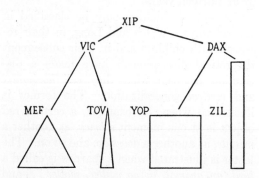

Figure 114. A Problem Involving the Vertical Type of Generalization

After learning the specific names for each block, the child then learns that MEF and TOV are both VIC, that YOP and ZIL are both DAX, and that all the VIC and DAX blocks fall under the broader classification, XIP. Control tests used blocks of different dimensions but the same general shape. (From L. Welch and L. Long, "The Higher Structural Phases of Concept Formation of Children," *J. Psychol.*, 1940, 9, 61.)

belong to the more inclusive classification, XIP. The initial level was relatively easy. Here all the child needed to do was hand the experimenter the block with a particular name. Out of 45 children, three failed to learn that, when asked for a VIC, they could give either an MEF or a TOV; or, when asked for a DAX, they could give either YOP or ZIL. The next step in the hierarchy was especially difficult to attain. Only 22 out of 45 children reached this level. A successful child could react as follows: To the request, "Give me all the XIPs" he could, from a large variety of blocks, push forth those illustrated. To the request, "Take back the VICs" he could retrieve MEF and TOV. To the request, "Hand me ZIL" he could present the block given this specific name. Solution of such problems, within the age range tested, was not related in any evident way to chronological age. However, a younger group of children aged from 19 to 23 months was studied earlier by Welch [90] and none of these children solved problems of this nature, even after six months of training.

We now turn to problems at a still higher verbal level. These involve syllogistic reasoning of the type with which students of logic are familiar. Moore [91] used 205 children ranging in age from six to twelve years and 105 college freshmen. His experiment dealt specifically with (1) verbal reasoning, (2) ability to discern autistic fallacies, and (3) ability to discern logical fallacies.* An example from the verbal reasoning tests is: "*If all horse-chestnut trees grow buck-eyes and my neighbor is going to plant a horse-chestnut in his yard, can I be sure that it will grow buck-eyes?*" The answer was regarded as correct if the child could explain that what is true of the class is true of the individual which belongs to it. Fourteen such tests are included. Ability to discern autistic fallacies was tested by four statements like the following: "*If one washes*

*Autistic fallacies involve wishful thinking as opposed to thinking in terms of reality. Logical fallacies involve thinking which violates logical principles.

Table 9. Development of Logical Ability as a Function of Chronological Age*

Type of test	Age							
	6	7	8	9	10	11	12	Freshmen
Reasoning......	23.1	24.8	32.1	43.1	51.1	56.0	63.2	88.0
Autistic fallacies........	0	0	1.25	4.0	3.05	14.2	23.1	83.0
Logical fallacies........	5.8	9.6	21.9	27.3	36.0	53.7	54.8	80.0

* From Moore. Figures give average value in terms of percentage of maximum possible score.

he cleanses himself from dirt. If one sins, he is dirty. If one washes he cleanses himself from sin." The subject was to indicate whether he considered the statement correct or incorrect, and why. Any answer which pointed out the difference between bodily uncleanliness and sin was considered correct. Ability to discern logical fallacies was measured by eight statements like, "*All automobiles have four wheels. Here is a vehicle with four wheels. Therefore it is an automobile.*" Again the individual was to indicate the correctness or incorrectness of the statement and the reason for his answer. The improvement in scores as a function of age is indicated in Table 9. One will observe that there was a steady improvement at almost every successive age level. A similar trend was obtained for data arranged in terms of school grade. Ability to detect autistic fallacies was just beginning to appear at the upper age level of the children's group. Moore recognized that inability to understand and answer the questions may in part be attributed to language difficulties.

Our review of typical research on reasoning in children suggests that ability to reason makes its appearance during the preschool period. No two-year-old has solved any of the problems involved in this research, but scores, as well as the complexity of the problems solved, have shown a more or less steady increase between the third year and later childhood. With increasing age there is also an increasing tendency to verbalize the principles involved in solution. Ability to solve purely verbal problems does not usually develop before the school age. It then develops gradually as a function of age and experience.

Thinking of children and adults

There is no doubt that reasoning ability, as studied by the various methods discussed in this chapter, shows a more or less steady improvement with age, and especially with the acquisition of linguistic processes. But suppose we should give the young child a demonstration of some physical event, like the displacement of water by a stone, and ask him to tell us why this phenomenon occurs. Then we should most likely find that his explanation is quite naïve. We might assume, from this, that the child's thinking is different from that of adults. Indeed Piaget [92] and Werner [93] have made this claim. Piaget emphasizes the absence of logical deductions and consistent explanations in the thinking of young children, who may, for example, claim that a stone displaces water because of its weight, yet say the next moment that the displacement results from the stone's size. Frequently a child's explanations are magical, like those which primitive peoples often give to natural events. Both Piaget and Werner have, in this connection, emphasized what they call the *syncretic* character of children's thinking. Werner points out that such thinking is characteristic, also, of primitive peoples. As defined in Warren's *Dictionary of Psychology*, syncretic thought is "a type of thinking, characteristic of young children, in which analysis based upon objective relations, as conceived by adults, plays little or no part; in the mind of the child, everything is connected with everything else but not in terms of adult conceptions of time, space, or cause."

It is one thing to say that children's explanations are inadequate, as judged by the standards of civilized adults, and still another to suppose, as Piaget does, that their thought processes are essentially different from those of adults. This alleged distinction between the thought processes of children and of adults has, however, stimulated a large amount of research, most of which is focused upon the explanations which children and adults give of simple demonstrations in physics and chemistry. This research shows that, while children often give inadequate explanations like those stressed by Piaget, such explanations may be attributed to a lack of relevant information rather than to poor reasoning ability.[94] Investigations by Oakes [95] and Hazlitt [96] have demonstrated, moreover, that adults without relevant information about the phenomena demonstrated also give childish explanations. Hazlitt says that, "Piaget's picture of a striking difference between adult and childish thinking is . . . due to an overvaluation of verbal expression as a measure of thinking, and an exaggerated view of the logicality of adult thought."

Summary and Conclusions

Symbolic activities are those in which external objects and situations are *represented by* modifications of the organism. These modifications are produced by the stimuli for which they substitute. Many symbolic activities are implicit. Others, like language, are explicit. Ability to acquire and use symbols is the most characteristic aspect of human intelligence.

The simplest and most fundamental symbolic process is memory for absent objects and situations. Memory of this type may be measured in terms of delayed reaction,

memory span, recall of narratives, and ability to report concerning events witnessed. Representative studies on each of these were considered. We observed some clinical evidence that delayed reactions are apparent as early as the third month. The interval between removal of a stimulus and successful delay increases gradually as the child becomes older. By the end of the second year this interval is fifteen minutes or more. In some preschool children it is as long as thirty-four days. The correlation between successful delayed reaction and age is positive and moderately high. The individual's memory span increases gradually with age. The upper limit is not reached until the teens. Ability to recall narratives and to make reports of past events also increases gradually with age. All tests of memory except the delayed reaction require use of linguistic responses. Hence the improved performance as an individual becomes older may in part be attributed to acquisition of language.

Evidence for imagery and imagination comes from verbal reports. Some children report imagery as early as the end of the second year. Whether it is present prior to this time is of course not known. Eidetic images, characterized by "hallucinatory clearness," are apparently peculiar to the period of childhood. Very few adults report their presence. On the other hand, it is estimated that approximately 50 per cent of children experience eidetic imagery. The vividness of these images is apparently greater in early than in late childhood. Various tests of imagination were described. During the preschool period there is evidence of increasing imaginative behavior as a function of age. Imaginative behavior beyond the preschool period has not been measured in such a manner as to disclose developmental trends.

Concepts are based upon the abstraction of common properties from otherwise diverse objects and situations. Several ways in which children acquire concepts have been discussed. Some concepts, like that of "triangularity" may be developed even before the one-year level. Some two-year-olds have learned such concepts as "roundness," "middleness," and with respect to number, "most," and "smaller." Ability to develop these concepts improves rapidly with age. Highly abstract concepts like "time" and "life" also improve with age, but many fail to develop fully mature concepts of this nature. The research on "animism" suggests that the individual's concept of what it means to have life goes through three phases (namely, anything in good condition is alive, anything that moves is alive, anything that moves by itself is alive) before he achieves the fully mature concept which attributes life only to plants and animals. Some college students, however, have failed to reach a consistently mature concept of "life." A particular phase of "animism" is not limited to any age level. Certain aspects of this research are highly controversial. Controversy centers primarily upon the view that such concepts warrant the designation "animism." The "phase" aspect is also questioned on the ground that development of the concept of life may develop gradually rather than in a saltatory fashion.

Some reasoning experiments with children are adaptations of procedures used with animals. Among these are Maier's problems, which call for novel combinations of past experience, and Hunter's double-alternation problem, solution of which involves the generalization that the correct temporal sequence of response is twice to the right and twice to the left. Performance on problems of this type yields no evidence of reasoning in children younger than three or four years. Children often solve such problems before they can give a verbal expression of the principle involved. Verbalized solutions become more frequent at successively higher age levels.

Most of the reasoning experiments with children have utilized performance, pictorial, or verbal problems in which the child is required to discover a principle. The performance and pictorial problems are solved at earlier age levels than the purely verbal ones. With increasing age, as might be expected, children achieve generalizations of increasing complexity. The horizontal variety of generalization (for example, stick, fishing pole, switch, pointer) can be developed at lower age levels than the vertical (for example, Fido, dog, animal, living matter).

Although children often give naïve and illogical explanations of physical events, this may be attributed to lack of relevant information rather than to poor reasoning ability, as such. Adults also reason naïvely when asked to explain physical events about which they lack relevant knowledge.

There is no doubt that reasoning ability in human beings is to a considerable extent related to language development. Although reasoning can take place in the absence of language (i.e., in animals), there is no doubt that language facilitates the recall and manipulation of past experiences which reasoning requires. Certain relations between language and the thought processes will be considered after we have discussed the development of speech in children. The chapter on development of intelligence during childhood will also have much in common both with this chapter and with that on language development. This is because intelligence tests designed for use with normal human beings are to a large extent reasoning and linguistic tests.

REFERENCES

1. Hunter, W. S., "The Delayed Reaction in Animals and Children," *Behav. Monog.*, 1913, *2*, No. 1.; and "The Delayed Reaction in a Child," *Psych. Rev.*, 1917, *24*, 75–87.
2. Hurlock, E. B., and R. Schwartz, "Biographical Records of Memory in Pre-School Children," *Child Development*, 1932, *3*, 230–239.
3. Bühler, C., and H. Hetzer, *Testing Children's Development from Birth to School Age*. New York: Farrar and Rinehart, 1935. The earlier

relevant publication was Bühler's *The First Year of Life*, New York: Day, 1930.

4. Hetzer, H., and S. Wislitsky, "Experimente über Erwartung und Errinnung beim Kleinkind," *Zsch. f. Psychol.*, 1930, *118*, 128–141.

5. *Op. cit.*, 1913.

6. *Op. cit.*, 1917.

7. Skalet, M., "The Significance of Delayed Reactions in Young Children," *Comp. Psychol. Monog.*, 1931, *7*, No. 4.

8. Allen, C. N., "Individual Differences in Delayed Reaction of Infants," *Arch. Psychol.*, 1931, *19*, No. 127.

9. Miller, N. E., "The Perception of Children: A Genetic Study Employing the Critical Choice Delayed Reaction," *J. Genet. Psychol.*, 1934, *44*, 321–339.

10. *Op. cit.*

11. Weinstein, B., "Matching-from-Sample by Rhesus Monkeys and by Children," *J. Comp. Psychol.*, 1941, *31*, 195–213.

12. *Op. cit.*, p. 30.

13. Emerson, L. L., "The Effect of Bodily Orientation upon the Young Child's Memory for Position of Objects," *Child Development*, 1913, *2*, 125–142.

14. Starr, A. S., "The Diagnostic Value of the Audito-Vocal Digit Memory Span," *Psych. Clin.*, 1923, *15*, 61–84.

15. Hurlock, E. B., and E. D. Newmark, "The Memory Span of Preschool Children," *J. Genet. Psychol.*, 1931, *39*, 157–173.

16. Stutsman, R., "Performance Tests for Children of Pre-School Age," *Genet. Psychol. Monog.*, 1936, *1*, No. 1.

17. Lumley, F. H., and S. W. Calhoun, "Memory Span for Words Presented Auditorially," *J. Appl. Psychol.*, 1934, *17*, 773–784.

18. Bronner, A. F., W. Healy, G. M. Lowe, and M. E. Shimberg, *A Manual of Individual Tests and Testing*. Boston: Little, Brown, 1927.

19. McElwee, E. W., "Further Standardization of Ellis Memory for Objects Test," *J. Appl. Psychol.*, 1933, *17*, 69–70.

20. Dewey, E., E. Child, and B. Ruml, *Methods and Results of Testing School Children*. New York: Dutton, 1920.

21. See the summary of this material in N. L. Munn, "Learning in Children," in L. Carmichael (ed.), *Manual of Child Psychology* (2d ed.), New York: Wiley, 1954, pp. 412–415.

22. Munn, *op. cit.*, p. 413.

23. Foster, J. C., "Verbal Memory in the Preschool Child," *J. Genet. Psychol.*, 1929, *35*, 26–44.

24. Stern, W., *Die Aussage als geistige Leistung und als Verhörsprodukt*. Leipzig: Barth, 1904.

25. Winch, W. H., *Children's Perception*. Baltimore: Warwick and York, 1914.

26. Ballard, P. B., "Obliviscence and Reminiscence," *Brit. J. Psychol., Monog. Suppl.*, 1913, *1*, No. 2.

27. A discussion of this research, as it pertains to children, will be found in Munn, *op. cit.*, pp. 425–430.

28. McGeoch, J. A., "The Influence of Sex and Age upon the Ability to Report," *Am. J. Psychol.*, 1928, *40*, 458–466.

29. Helson, H., "A Child's Spontaneous Report of Imagery," *Am. J. Psychol.*, 1933, *45*, 360–361.

30. Jaensch, E. R., *Die Eidetik*. Leipzig: Quelle and Meyer, 1925.

31. Jaensch, E. R., *Eidetic Imagery*. New York: Harcourt, Brace, 1930.

32. Peck, L., and R. Walling, "A Preliminary Study of the Eidetic Imagery of Preschool Children," *J. Genet. Psychol.*, 1935, *47*, 168–192.

33. Peck, L., *Child Psychology*. Boston: Heath, 1953, pp. 143–155.

34. Klüver, H., "Eidetic Images," in C. Murchison (ed.), *A Handbook of Child Psychology* (rev. ed.). Worcester: Clark University Press, 1933.

35. Markey, F. V., *Imaginative Behavior in Preschool Children*. New York: Columbia University Press, 1935.

36. Whipple, G. M., *Manual of Mental and Physical Tests*. Baltimore: Warwick and York, 1915.

37. Miles, W., "Age and the Kinephantom," *J. Gen. Psychol.*, 1934, *10*, 204–207.

38. Franz, S. I., *Handbook of Mental Examination Methods* (2d ed.). New York: Macmillan, 1920.

39. Street, R. F. A., "A Gestalt Completion Test," *Teach. Coll. Contrib. Educ.*, 1931, No. 481.

40. Eng, H., *The Psychology of Children's Drawings*. New York: Harcourt, Brace, 1931.

41. Johnson, B., *Child Psychology*. Baltimore: Thomas, 1932.

42. Andrews, E. G., "The Development of Imag-

ination in the Pre-School Child," *Univ. Iowa Stud.; Stud. Child Welfare*, 1930, *3*, No. 4.

43. See citation 35.

44. Ling, B-C., "Form Discrimination as a Learning Cue in Infants," *Comp. Psychol. Monog.*, 1941, *17*, No. 2.

45. Munn, N. L., and B. R. Steining, "The Relative Efficacy of Form and Background in a Child's Discrimination of Visual Patterns," *J. Genet. Psychol.*, 1931, *39*, 73–90.

46. Gellermann, L. W., "Form Discrimination in Chimpanzees and Two-Year-Old Children," *J. Genet. Psychol.*, 1933, *42*, 1–50.

47. Ray, J. J., "The Generalizing Ability of Dull, Bright and Superior Children," *Peabody Contrib. Educ.*, 1936, No. 175.

48. Smoke, K. L., "An Objective Study of Concept Formation," *Psych. Monog.*, 1932, *42*, No. 4.

49. Heidbreder, E. F., "A Study of the Evolution of Concepts," *Psych. Bull.*, 1934, *31*, 736. Although they deal only with development of concepts in adults, the later series of papers by Heidbreder are also relevant to the present discussion. The latest of these, which gives references to earlier papers in the series is: "The Attainment of Concepts: VII. Conceptual Achievements during Card-Sorting." *J. Psychol.*, 1949, *27*, 3–39.

50. Hull, C. L., "Quantitative Aspects of the Evolution of Concepts," *Psychol. Monog.*, 1920, *28*, No. 123. The quotation is from pp. 5–6.

51. See citation 48.

52. Long, L., "Conceptual Relationships in Children: The Concept of Roundness," *J. Genet. Psychol.*, 1940, *57*, 289–315.

53. Hicks, J. A., and F. D. Stewart, "The Learning of Abstract Concepts of Size," *Child Development*, 1930, *1*, 195–203.

54. Thrum, M. E., "The Development of Concepts of Magnitude," *Child Development*, 1935, *6*, 120–140.

55. See Warden, C. J., and J. B. Rowley, "The Discrimination of Absolute Versus Relative Brightness in the Ring Dove (*Tutor risorius*)," *J. Comp. Psychol.*, 1929, *9*, 317–338; C. J. Warden and C. N. Winslow, "The Discrimination of Absolute Versus Relative Size in the Ring Dove (*Turtor risorius*)," *J. Genet. Psychol.*, 1931, *39*, 328–341; T. L. McCulloch, "The Selection of the Intermediate of a

Series of Weights by the White Rat," *J. Comp. Psychol.*, 1935, *20*, 1–11.

56. Welch, L., "The Development of Size Discrimination Between the Ages of 12 and 40 Months," *J. Genet. Psychol.*, 1939, *55*, 243–268. See especially pp. 256–258.

57. Graham, V., T. A. Jackson, L. Long, and L. Welch, "Generalization of the Concept of Middleness," *J. Genet. Psychol.*, 1944, *65*, 227–237.

58. Long, L., and L. Welch, "The Development of the Ability to Discriminate and Match Numbers," *J. Genet., Psychol.*, 1941, *59*, 377–387.

59. Ames, L. B., "The Development of the Sense of Time in the Young Child," *J. Genet. Psychol.*, 1946, *68*, 97–125. Quotation is from p. 122. For a relevant study involving the understanding of clock time, see D. Springer, "Development in Young Children of an Understanding of Time and the Clock," *J. Genet. Psychol.*, 1952, *80*, 83–96.

60. Piaget, J., *The Language and Thought of the Child*, New York: Harcourt, Brace, 1926; *Judgment and Reasoning in the Child*, New York: Harcourt, Brace, 1928; *The Child's Conception of the World*, New York: Harcourt, Brace, 1930. Quotations are from the latter book, pp. 196 ff., 199, and 202.

61. Huang, I., and H. W. Lee, "Experimental Analysis of Child Animism," *J. Genet. Psychol.*, 1943, *63*, 71–121.

62. Huang, I., and H. W. Lee, "Experimental Analysis of Child Animism," *J. Genet. Psychol.*, 1945, *66*, 69–74.

63. Grigsby, O. J., "An Experimental Study of the Development of Concepts of Relationship in Pre-School Children as Evidenced by Their Expressive Ability," *J. Exper. Educ.*, 1932, *1*, 144–162.

64. Russell, R. W., and W. Dennis, "Studies of Animism: I. A Standardized Procedure for the Investigation of Animism," *J. Genet. Psychol.*, 1939, *55*, 389–400. Quotation from p. 392.

65. Russell, R. W., "Studies in Animism: II. The Development of Animism," *J. Genet. Psychol.*, 1940, *56*, 353–366.

66. Russell, R. W., W. Dennis, and F. E. Ash, "Studies in Animism: III. Animism in Feeble-minded Subjects," *J. Genet. Psychol.*, 1940, *57*, 57–63.

67. Dennis, W., "Piaget's Questions Applied to a

Child of Known Environment," *J. Genet. Psychol.*, 1942, *60*, 307–320.

68. Dennis, W., and R. W. Russell, "Piaget's Questions Applied to Zuñi Children," *Child Development*, 1940, *11*, 181–187.

69. Dennis, W., "Animism and Related Tendencies in Hopi Children," *J. Abn. & Soc. Psychol.*, 1943, *38*, 21–36.

70. Bruce, M., "Animism *vs.* Evolution of the Concept 'Alive,'" *J. Psychol.*, 1941, *12*, 81–90.

71. Dennis, W., citation 69, p. 35.

72. See citation 62.

73. Mead, M., "An Investigation of the Thought of Primitive Children with Special Reference to Animism," *J. Royal Anthrop. Instit.*, 1932, *62*, 173–190.

74. Dennis, W., "Animistic Thinking Among College and University Students," *Sci. Mo.*, 1953, *76*, 247–250.

75. Dennis, W., and B. Mallinger, "Animism and Related Tendencies in Senescence," *J. Gerontology*, 1949, *4*, 218–221.

76. Werner, H., and D. Carrison, "Animistic Thinking in Brain-Injured, Mentally Retarded Children," *J. Abn. & Soc. Psychol.*, 1944, *39*, 43–62.

77. See citation 70.

78. Russell, R. W., "Studies in Animism: IV. An Analysis of Concepts Allied to Animism," *J. Genet. Psychol.*, 1940, *57*, 83–91.

79. Maier, N. R. F., "Reasoning in Children," *J. Comp. Psychol.*, 1936, *21*, 357–366.

80. Harter, G. L., "Overt Trial and Error in the Problem Solving of Preschool Children," *J. Genet. Psychol.*, 1930, *38*, 361–372.

81. Gellermann, L. W., "The Double Alternation Problem: II. The Behavior of Children and Human Adults in a Double Alternation Temporal Maze," *J. Genet. Psychol.*, 1931, *39*, 197–226.

82. Hunter, W. S., and S. C. Bartlett, "Double Alternation in Young Children," *J. Exper. Psychol.*, 1948, *38*, 558–567.

83. Roberts, K. E., "The Ability of Pre-School Children to Solve Problems in Which a Simple Relationship Is Kept Constant," *J. Genet. Psychol.*, 1932, *40*, 118–135.

84. Heidbreder, E., "Problem Solving in Children

and Adults," *J. Genet. Psychol.*, 1928, *35*, 522–545.

85. Long, L., and L. Welch, "Reasoning Ability in Young Children," *J. Psychol.*, 1941, *12*, 21–44.

86. Welch, L., and L. Long, "Comparison of the Reasoning Ability of Two Age Groups," *J. Genet. Psychol.*, 1943, *62*, 63–76.

87. Long, L., and L. Welch, "Factors Affecting Efficiency of Inductive Reasoning," *J. Exper. Educ.*, 1942, *10*, 252–264.

88. Welch, L., "The Genetic Development of the Associational Structures of Abstract Thinking," *J. Genet. Psychol.*, 1940, *56*, 175–206; "A Behaviorist-Explanation of Concept Formation," *J. Genet. Psychol.*, 1947, *71*, 201–222; and subsequent references to Welch and Long.

89. Welch, L., and L. Long, "The Higher Structural Phases of Concept Formation in Children," *J. Psychol.*, 1940, *9*, 59–95; "A Further Investigation of the Higher Structural Phases of Concept Formation," *J. Psychol.*, 1940, *10*, 211–220.

90. Welch, L., "The Genetic Development of the Associational Structures of Abstract Thinking," *J. Genet. Psychol.*, 1940, *56*, 175–206.

91. Moore, T. V., "The Reasoning Ability of Children in the First Years of School Life," *Stud. Psychol. & Psychiat. Catholic University of America*, 1929, *2*, No. 2.

92. Piaget, J., *The Child's Conception of Physical Causality*. New York: Harcourt, Brace, 1930.

93. Werner, H., *Comparative Psychology of Mental Development*. Chicago: Follett, 1948. (Earlier printing was New York: Harper, 1940.) See especially Chapters X and XI.

94. See the review by I. Huang, "Children's Conception of Physical Causality: A Critical Summary," *J. Genet. Psychol.*, 1943, *63*, 71–121; M. E. Oakes, "Children's Explanations of Natural Phenomena," *Teach. Coll. Contrib. Educ.*, 1946, No. 926.

95. Oakes, M. E., "Explanations of Natural Phenomena by Adults," *Sci. Educ.*, 1945, *29*, 137–142; 199–201.

96. Hazlitt, V., "Children's Thinking," *Brit. J. Psychol.*, 1930, *20*, 354–361. The quotation is from p. 361.

SUGGESTIONS FOR FURTHER READING

Dashiell, J. F., *Fundamentals of General Psychology* (3d ed.). Boston: Houghton, Mifflin, 1949, Chapter 19.

English, H. B., *Child Psychology*. New York: Holt, 1951, Chapter 13.

Hall, G. S., "The Contents of Children's Minds," in W. Dennis, *Readings in the History of Psychology*. New York: Appleton-Century-Crofts, 1948.

Hunter, W. S., *Human Behavior*. Chicago: University of Chicago Press, 1928, pp. 66–67, and Part II, Chapter VIII.

Jersild, A. T., *Child Psychology* (4th ed.). New York: Prentice-Hall, 1954, Chapters 13–15.

Markey, J. F., *The Symbolic Process and Its Integration in Children*. New York: Harcourt, Brace, 1928.

Munn, N. L., "Learning in Children," in L. Carmichael (ed.), *Manual of Child Psychology* (2d ed.). New York: Wiley, 1954.

Peck, L., *Child Psychology*. Boston: Heath, 1953, Chapter 5.

Piaget, J., "Children's Philosophies," in C. Murchison (ed.), *A Handbook of Child Psychology* (2d ed.). Worcester: Clark University Press, 1934.

Thompson, G. G., *Child Psychology*. Boston: Houghton Mifflin, 1952, Chapter 6. While titled "Sensory and Perceptual Development," this chapter has a great deal of material on concept formation.

Vinacke, W. E., *The Psychology of Thinking*. New York: McGraw Hill, 1952. See especially the sections on thinking and concept formation in children.

12

Language

THE most characteristic attribute of human beings, as contrasted with infrahuman animals, is their possession of language. According to Langer,[1] "Language is, without doubt, the most momentous and at the same time the most mysterious product of the human mind. Between the clearest animal call of love or warning or anger, and a man's least, trivial *word*, there lies a whole day of Creation — or in a modern phrase, a whole chapter of evolution."

In our discussions of so-called trial-and-error learning, as represented by mastery of the maze, there was no gap between the objective aspects of the performances of men and animals. Where a difference was observed it was quantitative, such as in the number of trials, the time, or the number of errors involved. It was only when we turned to symbolic processes, as revealed in tests of insight, delayed reaction, and reasoning, that a somewhat different sort of divergence began to appear. Human subjects often exhibited insight where animals did not; and where animals gave evidence of insight, this was obviously limited as compared with that most evident in human subjects. In the delayed-reaction tests which were solved by animals as well as human subjects, the length of successful delay was usually greater in humans — even in children — than in animals. On

reasoning tests, also, there was usually a higher level of performance in humans than in animals. Human subjects, moreover, could go on to solve problems of far greater complexity than could be solved by animals. It will be recalled, too, that an increasing number of children at successively higher age levels verbalized the solutions of delayed reaction and reasoning tests.

The wide gap which so mystifies students of semantics and psychology and which seems to hide a "whole chapter of evolution" exists somewhere in this region of symbolic learning. Hunter[2] says that the symbolic processes of animals, and of infants who have not yet acquired linguistic responses, seem to have "all of the functions of language except the social characteristic of interstimulation and response." It is probable, he continues, "that true language ... grows out of the symbolic processes used by some animals in the solution of the types of problems represented in the delayed-reaction experiment." In order to have the functions of interstimulation and response, symbolic processes must of course become overt, or have overt correlates.

Language includes certain gestures as well as written and spoken symbols. A gesture is linguistic if it represents something other than itself. To function as language it should also convey meaning to others. It should communicate information and arouse in others symbolic processes comparable with those of the individual who makes it. The same is true of written symbols. Speech is more obviously symbolic and much more flexible than either gestural or written symbols. As a means of interstimulation and response it also has the advantage of functioning at a distance. It does not require that the symbols, whether gestural or written, be within range of the visual mechanisms.

But what of the gap between the highest symbolic performances of animals and the overt symbolization so characteristic of human behavior. Why is speech absent in animals yet so ubiquitous in human life?

Anybody who suggests that the use and understanding of speech is exclusively human is soon confronted with such questions as: "How about parrots? Almost everybody has heard them talk." "How about the talking crow on the radio?" "Don't mynah birds learn to talk?" "Didn't somebody recently teach a chimpanzee to talk?" Or, "Do you mean to say that my dog, who runs to the door every time we mention going for a ride, doesn't at least *understand* what we are saying?" Questions such as these can be answered only by considering so-called animal speech in some detail. Our discussion will also bring out, much more clearly than the above statement, what is meant by language. After that we shall point to some possible reasons why animals, even those closest to us in the evolutionary scale, do not possess speech or any other truly linguistic response.

The Question of Animal Speech

Many infrahuman animals, as is well known, assume postures and emit sounds which serve as stimuli for the reactions of other animals of their kind. Murphy and others[3] point out that the katydid, by its chirping, elicits similar chirping in other katydids. Craig[4] observes that the vocalizations of pigeons have a controlling influence over the behavior of other pigeons. For example, vocal responses serve to call the mate; challenge the enemy; inhibit various activities in which the mate is involved; proclaim the bird's species, sex, individual identity, and rights; and elicit various forms of spatial and temporal coordination. The books by Lorenz[5] and Tinbergen[6] offer many examples of comparable social control in other birds. Parrots, mynah birds, crows, and magpies may also be taught to repeat various words and phrases under certain conditions, some of which are discussed by Mowrer.[7] Mammals use gestures and sounds which serve to elicit mating, avoidance, and other responses. Alverdes[8] is a good source of relevant information on the signaling and other vocal responses of infrahuman mammals. Yerkes and Learned[9] describe the large vocal repertoire possessed by chimpanzees, most of which is, however, related to emotional excitement. These vocalizations are quite unlike those which appear in the human child while he lies undisturbed in his crib — a point to which we shall return later. Crawford,[10] it will be recalled, finds that a chimpanzee may elicit the cooperation of its partner by means of gestures and vocalizations which suggest to the human observer that it is *trying to say* "Help me do something."

Two apes have actually been taught to "say" something approximating words. Furness[11] trained an orangutan to say "papa" and "cup." Training it to say "papa" took six months. Furness says that "This word was selected not only because it is a very primitive sound, but also because it combined two elements of vocalization to which orangs and chimpanzees are . . . unaccustomed, namely: the use of the lips and an expired vowel sound" The word was taught by manipulating the lips and by the trainer himself making the desired sounds. When the word "papa" was learned, it was used appropriately, as in pointing to the trainer, patting him on the shoulder, and, in time of panic, saying it while clinging to him. The word "cup" was learned soon after mastery of the trick of pronouncing the *ka* sound.

Using somewhat similar methods, Hayes and Hayes [12] have more recently taught their female chimpanzee, Viki, to say the same two words and also "mamma." In her book, *The Ape in Our House*, Cathy Hayes [13] tells in some detail the difficulties involved in teaching a chimpanzee to talk. Her discussion brings to a focus some important differences between this "almost human" animal and a human infant.

At first Viki made the standard chimpanzee sounds. These are inborn and appear only during emotional excitement. They are referred to as Viki's "reflex sounds." Viki did not, like a human baby, come to play with syllables, or to babble. Except when emotionally aroused she usually made no sounds at all. Since she had no "urge to talk" it was decided to try to make Viki "speak" for her supper as a dog may be taught to bark for it. This was at first quite unsuccessful. When called upon to speak, says Mrs. Hayes, "She looked at the milk, and then at me, and of course said nothing. I waited for fifteen minutes and then rose to leave. As I moved away, worried little 'oo oo's' broke the silence and I quickly rewarded her for making the sound. The milk tasted good and Viki sputtered food barks which earned her a few more portions. Then as her appetite wore off, we spent more long moments gazing at the food and each other. I kept saying 'Speak!' and Viki kept saying nothing, but each time I rose to leave, she cried, and thus she earned her supper." Mrs. Hayes goes on to say that "Viki was not speaking *on command*. We were tricking noises out of her by arousing her emotionally in a way which automatically calls out chimpanzee reflex vocalizations." During five weeks, no progress was made except in bringing out reflex vocalizations. Then, quite suddenly, a strange new sound appeared. This "was like someone whispering 'ah' as loudly as possible and with great effort. When Viki said it her face contorted while her eyes assumed the tense preoccupied stare of a stutterer. From her lips burst this rasping, tortured 'ahhhhh!' She then confidently reached for the milk, so that we concluded she had at last gotten the idea of speaking for food." From this point on, Viki used the "ahhhh" sound when asked to speak. She also used it "to ask" for things.

Why was this sound so difficult for Viki to make? As the Hayes' considered this question they realized that, before their coaching, *"Viki had been completely unable to make any sound at all on purpose.* She made chimp noises, yes, but these were *beyond her control.* They were merely reflex expressions of her feelings ... except for the chimp noises, Viki had been voiceless!"

Training Viki to say "mama" at first involved pressing her lips together, as in Figure 115, then releasing them while she said "ahhh." After a while she inhibited the "ahhh" sound until the fingers were on her lips. She even helped the teacher get his hand in position. Later, her lips began to move without aid. Then only the finger tip needed to touch her lips. Within two weeks after this training began, Viki was saying "mama" by herself. The word "papa" came after she had learned to imitate a "Bronx cheer." Softer and shorter "p's" with relaxed lips were required, then the repetition of two "p's" in succession was accomplished and something approximating "papa" came out. The word "cup" was acquired suddenly after Viki had heard Mrs. Hayes repeat two favorite sounds "k" and "p." This word came to mean "I want a drink."

We see, therefore, that animals *do* use vocalizations, which may even have a signaling function, and that some apes may be taught to say a few words. Does this mean, however, that we are justified in speaking of animal language? We can discount the use of "words" by a bird, and by the orangutan and chimpanzee, on the ground that, without human aid and the verbal patterns set by human trainers, these animals would never have acquired anything approximating speech. Bierens de Haan,[14] in his excellent

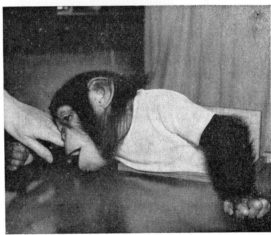

Figure 115. Teaching Viki to Say 'Mama"

As described in the text, the lips were first moved while Viki was making an "ahhh" sound. Then, as the lips began to move without aid, touching with a finger was sufficient. When the finger was removed Viki would put her lip to the trainer's finger, as illustrated, or touch the lip with her own finger while she spoke. (Photos courtesy The American Philosophical Society and Harper and Brothers.)

critical evaluation of the literature on animal language, raises a few issues that are of especial interest here. He points out that animals do not normally use their acquired vocalizations with communicative intentions. These responses are stereotyped and tied down rather definitely to the original conditioning situation. Dogs and parrots trained to "beg" or to "speak" for food repeat these responses only in the food situation and in the presence of human beings. No dog has ever been observed to "beg" or "speak" in order to obtain something from another dog. Nor has any parrot ever "talked" with another parrot. It is doubtful, also, whether Viki, if given the opportunity, would ever have "spoken" to other chimpanzees. Another limitation in so-called "animal language" is the failure of animals to combine words or phrases learned separately.

There is even less reason to attribute linguistic significance to the natural signaling responses of animals. As DeLaguna [15] says:

Speech offers a significant contrast to the cry in the relations it bears to the conditions which evoke it. Characteristic cries are called out . . . only by circumstances which have a direct affective value for the animal. Speech, on the contrary, is or may be evoked by things or events which have only the most indirect "interest" for the speaker, and to which he may remain affectively indifferent. Furthermore, the cry, so far as it "proclaims" at all, is able to announce only the general sort of situation — like "danger" or "prey" — while speech may *specify* and *analyze* the situation. The characteristic feature of human speech is that instead of being, like the cry, a response to a total situation having a direct affective value for the individual, it is a complex response, capable of discriminating the objective elements making up the situation, together with the relations these bear both to the individuals concerned, and to each, other. Instead of being limited, like the alarm cry to the mere proclamation of "danger," speech may announce, e.g., "There is a fire in the next block and the wind is blowing in this direction." So also, instead of proclaiming, like the animal cry, mere friendliness or triumph, speech may announce in advance the acts in which the speaker intends to show his friendliness, or it may relate the victorious deeds of the past. The correlation between the speech-response and its objective conditions is a correlation between independently variable elements of response and independently variable elements of the external situation, or of past or future events.

Even when infrahuman animals learn to make appropriate responses to human commands they are, as Bierens de Haan points out, merely responding to such aspects of these stimuli as pitch, intensity, or combinations of auditory stimuli *per se*. There is no evidence that they understand the words and phrases as these are understood by those who produce them. For example, Thorndike [16]

trained cats to climb upon a box for food whenever he said, "I must feed those cats." However, they climbed up just as readily when he said, "My name is Thorndike" or "Today is Tuesday." They were responding, apparently, to *vocalization* as such rather than to *what* was vocalized. Domestic animals are often trained to make differential responses to commands like "dead dog," "pray," "climb that tree," or "get that rat." An animal often differentiates between its "name" and the names of other animals. There is no reason for supposing, however, that such commands and names have any greater linguistic significance for the animal than would nonsense-syllables, sounds produced by tuning forks, or noises of various kinds, providing that the latter stimuli were associated in a more or less precise way with the requisite responses.

Despite the fact that some infrahuman animals are able to gesture and vocalize, to respond appropriately to human gestures and vocalizations, and to make sounds approximating human words, there is, as Bierens de Haan and others have suggested, no evidence that they ever develop anything even closely approximating the conventional symbols of communication which we designate as language. What accounts for man's marked superiority in this respect?

In order to develop into a talking animal man had to have a high level of insight, exceptional ability to respond to things in their absence, and great versatility in manipulating and combining symbols or, as Maier would say, "putting two and two together." Why did the higher apes evolve to a point approaching this level but get no further? The chimpanzee, as Langer [17] points out, "is conceptually not far from the supreme human achievement, yet never crosses the line." What, she asks, "has placed this absolute barrier between his race and ours?" She answers by supposing that

the ape has no instinctive desire to babble in babyhood. He does not play with his mouth and his breath as human infants do; there is no crowing and cooing, no "goo-goo" and "ba-ba" and "do-de-da" in his uproarious nursery. Consequently there are no sounds and syllables that please or frighten him by their sheer aesthetic character, as he is pleased, frightened, or comforted by purely phenomenal sights. Oddly enough, it is because all his utterances have *signification* — all are pragmatic or emotional — that none of them ever acquire *significance*.

This random, originally meaningless vocalization of human infants which Langer regards as so significant in accounting for the presence of language in man is attributed to "his descent from a vocalizing race — a genus of ape, perhaps, in which the rudiments of symbolic conception, that apparently are dawning in the chimpanzee, were coupled with an instinctive tendency to produce sounds, to play with the vocal apparatus." We observed (p. 388) that this absence of vocal play in Viki — and, indeed, her inability, without coaching, to utter sounds "intentionally" — was the major initial stumbling block in teaching her to "speak" for her dinner. Once she overcame this handicap, she soon learned to use the word "mama." With this step taken, it was easier still to learn "papa" and "cup."

Another difference between ape and man which may account for absence of language in the former — and which may even underlie the failure of apes to engage in spontaneous vocalizations — is the fact that man's cerebral cortex is larger and more complex and that it has a speech center. Absence of a speech center has been stressed by Furness,[18] Warden,[19] and other writers on human evolution — and Mowrer[20] thinks that this explanation is nearer the truth than Langer's.

Although differences in the vocal apparatus of apes and men have sometimes been mentioned as providing a possible basis for differences with respect to speech, this cannot be a crucial factor. Apes are handicapped, it is true, in imitating human vocal combinations, but they possess sufficient vocal range to have developed a speech of their own had the ability to do so also been present.

The Evolution of Language

The way in which language originated is not known. Although most theories deal with the origin of speech, the same principles might apply to gestures and, in some instances, even to writing. According to the *onomatopoeic theory* our primitive ancestors imitated the sounds of natural phenomena and used these imitations as symbols representing the phenomena in question. Examples would be *cuckoo, splash, buzz, bow-wow,* and the like. The same principle is said to apply when the child uses *bow-bow, choo-choo,* and *meow,* to represent the objects from which these sounds emanate. Another theory, the *interjectional,* supposes that language originated in the automatic exclamations or ejaculations of primitive man. Sounds like *oh, ah, pshaw,* and *ugh* are assumed to have served as symbols for the conditions which elicited them. According to another view, known as the *ding-dong* theory, various objects and situations in man's environment "rang out" unlearned or reflex gestures and vocalizations which served to represent them. The so-called *yo-he-ho* theory stresses rhythmical vocalizations presumably made by primitive men in the course of co-operative activities like pulling, shoving, and lifting objects. According to this view the sounds eventually became symbols for the objects and activities related with them.

Wundt[21] presents the view that language began with involuntary expressive movements. He points out that it is natural to represent something tall by raising the hand above the head, something short by placing the hand in a low position, something round by making movements which approximate a tracing of it, something straight by tracing a straight line, and so on. He points out, furthermore, that emotional expressions, both gestural and vocal, arouse in the percipient some idea concerning their cause. For example, observation of a wry face leads one to suppose that something distasteful has elicited it. Why? Because distaste is, in the percipient's own experience, associated with a wry face. Thus a wry face becomes the primitive linguistic symbol for something distasteful. It may represent the object which elicits the expression and it may become a surrogate for the idea of distaste in general. According to Wundt, various sounds may serve similar functions. He points out that something distant may be represented by a low sound, something intermediate in distance by a sound of middle pitch, and something near at hand by a sound of high pitch. Examples are cited to show how gestures and sounds at first representative of concrete objects may eventually serve to represent abstract ideas and relationships. In one primitive language the index finger is placed against the lips and then moved outward in a straight line. The gesture represents a truthful (straight) man, or even the concept of truth. Likewise, an angry sound may represent an angry person or, probably as a later development, anger in the abstract sense. De Laguna [22] and Pillsbury and Meader [23] follow Wundt in stressing the linguistic priority of emotional gestures and vocal expressions. Pillsbury and Meader present their own and De Laguna's view in regard to speech by saying that "language develops from the emotional expression as a cry that serves first to attract other members of the group, then becomes significant as a signal for approach or flight, and only later acquires a specific meaning as an indication of the presence of a particular object."

That chance, originally meaningless gestures and vocal expressions may assume linguistic significance has been pointed out by Judd and Thorndike. Judd [24] refers to the fact that children sometimes chance upon or invent certain terms and then use them to represent objects. A child was observed, for example, to call pebbles *pocos*. This term was not adopted by his elders because they already had the word *pebble* to designate the objects. However, in a group of children approximately his own age, especially if the inventor were the object of admiration, the word *pocos* might be adopted as a conventional

symbol for pebbles. In a like manner, according to Judd, primitive man may have chanced upon or invented, and then conventionalized, many gestural and vocal expressions. He says:

When the world was young, the opportunity for inventing new words must have been unlimited. Even in that far-away age, however, the inventor's task was less than half accomplished when he emitted the new sound. Before he could regard his task as complete, he must induce his neighbors to use the sound as he had used it.

Judd points out that prestige undoubtedly played an important role in the adoption of new expressions.

Thorndike's [25] theory is very similar to Judd's except that it places the emphasis upon chance associations between babbling sounds and objects rather than between invented sounds and objects. He says that "The human animal's miscellaneous play with his vocal apparatus and the articulate sounds he thereby produces and the associations he makes of these with things and events . . . deserve more attention from psychology and linguistic science than they have hitherto received." Thorndike assumes that the primitive speechless human would have had symbolic representations (images, ideas, expectations) of objects for which he as yet had no names.

Such a person would prattle while he worked or played much as a child of a year or two now prattles as he plays. If his making a certain sound became connected with his experiencing a certain object or act and having an image or expectation or idea of that object or act, he would have a language. The sound and the act of making it would mean that object or act to him.

Thorndike goes on to point out that, although this would be a narrow language and a private one, as yet of no use in communication, "it would be a valuable intellectual tool for its possessor, enabling him to replace the somewhat cumbrous and elusive images or expectations by sounds that he could make and arrange more or less at will." The chances of such associations occurring, especially in those of superior native intellect, are believed by Thorndike to be within the bounds of reason:

Consider a child of early man playing with a large shell. . . . Let us take the state of affairs least favorable to connecting the sound *ug* with that shell. . . . Let his prattling possibilities consist of a thousand syllables all equally likely to occur in any one situation or in any other. Then the chance that he will utter *ug* as he puts a pebble in the shell is 1 in 1000 if he prattles at all.

Even if he does make the sound *ug*, this connection will, as Thorndike points out, need strengthening. Otherwise some other sound, if any, may occur the next time the child drops a pebble in the shell. However,

there are forces which tend to cause progress away from purely miscellaneous vocal play. First of all the child who puts one pebble in the shell is likely to put another in then and there. His enjoyment of the act makes him repeat it, that is, strengthens its connection with the mental set in which he did it first. Now that mental set happened at that time to evoke also the vocal play of saying *ug*, and the confirming reaction which the enjoyment of the manual play set in action tends to spread or scatter so as to strengthen also the connection of the situation with the utterance. . . . In the second place, saying *ug* to the shell and pebble may be itself enjoyable and the connection may thereby be strengthened. Consequently, the probability that the child will drop a second pebble is substantial and the probability that he will utter *ug* therewith if he utters anything is far above 1 to 1000.

How words, once developed in such a "babble-luck" manner as this theory supposes, would be adopted by other members of the group, and would increase in number so as to provide linguistic means of communication, is still another problem. Thorndike deals with this at some length along lines already familiar from what we said about this aspect of Judd's theory.

One must recognize that the above theories, all of them unavoidably speculative to a high degree, have some possible basis in fact. On the other hand, none of these theories by itself seems adequate to account for all the characteristics of even the simplest known language. As Jesperson [26] pointed out, the only essential condition for the development of a new language is isolation of a group of individuals with no ready-made means of communication. One way or another, they will soon acquire means of communicating with each other. He cites cases of children who, when relatively isolated from adult linguistic influences, developed languages to suit their own communicative needs. It is also said that twins sometimes develop a speech which appears to be understandable to both, yet meaningless to their parents.

Whatever its origins, language changes markedly in course of transmission. This applies to gestural, spoken, and written language. Complex units are broken down into their elements, elementary expressions are combined in new ways, and eventually every symbol undergoes modification due to imperfect reproduction. Because of these factors a language may become so extensive and so complex as to belie its simple origins.

The prevalence of speech as a communicative tool is attributed to various factors. Some have pointed out that gestures, since they are useless in the dark and under other conditions where individuals are prevented from seeing each other, were soon relegated to a minor role in favor of speech. Paget [27] says that speech assumed greater significance than gesture when primitive man, becoming engaged in handicrafts, experienced difficulty in "talking" with his hands full. Another factor in favor of speech is undoubtedly its superior flexibility as a means of communication. Not only are the words which can be expressed almost innumerable, but different intonations of the same word may convey a variety of meanings. Of considerable significance, moreover, is the fact that speech requires much less effort than gesture.

Most writers agree that written language is a later development than either gesture or speech. It may have arisen as a means of leaving messages under circumstances where

personal contacts were prevented. Some believe that it arose merely as a form of amusement. In any event, the chief value of written
language is that it makes possible the transmission of cultural acquisitions in a manner
much more extensive and permanent than
that rendered possible by either gestures or
vocalizations, which depend, of course, upon
personal contacts.

The earliest written language comprised
pictures of the objects represented. Gradually these representations became more and
more sketchy. Then certain parts of the original drawings were used as representative of
the whole. Eventually, the characters became quite unlike the objects represented.
They became, in other words, increasingly
symbolic. Take, for example, the word
"dog" in Chinese. At first there was a picture
of the dog; then 犬, which has some resemblance to a dog; and finally 犬, which no one,
unless he knew its origins, would associate
with the pictorial representation of a dog.
Judd [28] draws attention to the fact that, as
man substituted symbols for the pictorial
representations of objects, he rendered possible a remarkable increase in linguistic flexibility. In early Egyptian, for instance, the
picture of an owl represented the bird alone.
Later, when a symbol in no way resembling
the owl was developed, it was used to represent night, silence, and wisdom as well as the
bird. Symbolism also facilitated the association of written characters with sounds. A
sound, which in no way resembled the object,
and a written symbol, which also failed to resemble it, were alike in representing it. Eventually the written symbol came to represent
not only the object but, by association, the
sound itself. The written symbol for eye, for
example, could represent both the eye and the
sound involved (or ī). The next step in the
evolution of writing was use of a separate
character to represent each sound in the vocal
representation of a word. Judd describes in
some detail how this development takes place.
The letter M has evolved, by the process described above, from the original Egyptian

pictorial representation of an owl. The sound
"M" is that with which the spoken name for
owl began. Now, after a long evolution, the
symbol for owl merely represents the sound
"M." The final step in the evolution of
written language was that of writing, in combination, the symbols which represent the
sounds in a spoken word.

The human child does not need to invent a
gestural, vocal, or written language as did his
remote forebears. His task is merely one of
acquiring the linguistic patterns already determined by the social history of his group.
As we shall observe later, every normal child,
regardless of race, nation, or social class, begins his linguistic development in the same
way and with comparable mechanisms. To describe how this linguistic acquisition occurs
is our aim in the following pages.

Ontogenesis of Gestural Language

Gestural activities are elicited in early infancy and, when they assume conventional
communicative functions, constitute the first
language responses. Many gestures acquire
a representative function for the child and, at
the same time, communicate his attitudes
and desires to others. Take, for example, the
grimace elicited by certain distasteful substances. Initially this reaction has no representative or communicative significance for
the infant. It is a reflex response elicited
only when certain substances are in the
mouth. By a process of conditioning, the
grimace becomes associated with the visual
characteristics of the distasteful substance,
or with the characteristics of associated
stimuli. The odor, tactual quality, and other
aspects of the substance may similarly serve
as bases for conditioned grimaces. We have
considered in a previous discussion (see pp.
201–210) how conditioning occurs.

Not only is the grimace elicited by previously neutral stimuli, but it assumes *representative* functions. In an abbreviated or
incipient form it serves as one of the symbols
involved in recalling or thinking about the

absent substance. Later still, the same expression is used to represent *anything* distasteful. In other words, it attains *conceptual* status.

A grimace has communicative significance to adults, for it indicates, in terms of their own conditioning, the child's distaste for objects and situations which elicit the response. The grimace assumes true linguistic significance *for the infant* only when he learns its meaning and how to use it as a means of controlling the behavior of others. Some gestures which achieve such a status during early childhood are head-shaking and nodding, smiling, reaching movements with one hand (meaning "give me," or the like), reaching with both hands (meaning "pick me up," and so on), shrinking motions (in response to strangers and to adverse suggestions), and waving "good-bye." All these gestures assume meaning for the child largely in terms of the responses which they elicit from others. Ability to interpret the more conventional human gestures is gradually acquired during infancy and early childhood. That gestures involved in emotional expression are often of limited communicative significance, even among adults, will be shown in a later discussion concerning the "language of emotion."

Acquisition of Speech

Speech involves manipulation of the *diaphragm, lungs,* and *muscles of the thorax,* which serve as bellows to blow air up the windpipe; the *vocal cords,* comparable, in a sense, with the reeds of a wind instrument, which provide tone or "voice"; the *chest, throat, mouth, nose,* and *head cavities,* which, acting as resonators, provide timbre or quality; and the *tongue, lips,* and *teeth,* the combined actions of which are involved in modification of vowels and production of consonants. While all these factors play a role in normal speech, a whispered speech is possible without involvement of vocal cords. We shall elaborate on this point presently. Figure 116 *A* shows the general characteristics and relative positions of the above-mentioned structures. In Figure 116 *B* the vocal cords are represented as viewed from above.

The vocal cords are two membranes stretched across the interior of a cartilaginous box-like structure known as the *larynx.* Air must pass through an opening between these membranes on its way up or down the windpipe. This opening, the *glottis,* is varied in size by means of a complicated system of muscles. Muscles also exert a delicate control over the tension of the vocal cords while these are in a given position across the larynx. When the glottis is but a small slit and the vocal cords are tightly drawn, passage of air elicits rapid vibration of the membranes. High tones are thus produced. Intermediate tones are produced when the glottis is larger and the vocal cords less tense. Passing of air through the wide-open glottis produces no tone. Under such circumstances one can speak only in unvoiced whispers. Similarly, when an individual's larynx has been removed without closing the air passage, his speech is confined to the unvoiced whispers produced by non-laryngeal vocal mechanisms.

During production of high tones, the entire larynx is raised. One can observe this by feeling his Adam's apple. Lowering of the larynx is associated with production of low tones. Tonal quality is modified by the various resonance cavities mentioned above and indicated in Figure 116 *A.* Sounds are referred to as chest, head, or nasal, depending upon the quality imposed by the respective resonance cavities. Intensity is determined by the strength of air blasts coming from the lungs and also by resonance factors.

Tones produced by vibrations of the vocal cords are weakened or amplified by, respectively, the soft and hard surfaces of the throat, mouth, and nose. Moreover, various surfaces and resonance cavities, owing to their positions and sizes, either damp or enhance overtones, thus changing tonal quality. Tonal changes are also effected by alterations in the relative positions of the epiglottis, tongue, hard and soft palate, teeth, and lips.

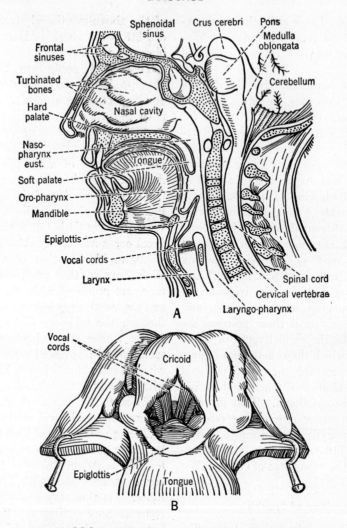

Figure 116. Diagram of Human Speech Mechanisms

A. A cross-section of the human head and throat.   *B.* The larynx viewed from above. (After Gerrish.)

Vowels are laryngeal tones which, while modified in the above-mentioned ways, have met with little obstruction. *Consonants,* on the other hand, result from various obstructions of expelled air. Fricative consonants like *th, f, sh, y,* and *z* are produced by friction resulting from certain related movements of the lips, tongue, teeth, and palate. The approximate positions assumed by these structures in production of fricative consonants may be ascertained by self-observation. Ex-

plosive consonants are produced by bringing two surfaces together and then separating them suddenly. Note, for example, the movements required in saying *p, t, ch,* and other explosive consonants. The resonating cavities of the nose impart a nasal quality to consonants like *m* and *n.* These are designated, accordingly, as nasal.

The motor activities involved in speech are controlled by neural mechanisms too complex for consideration here. These comprise certain of the cranial nerves and their cerebral connections. Important sensory components of speech are provided by the kinesthetic, tactual, and auditory receptors.

Initial vocalizations

The raw materials, as it were, out of which each individual builds his speech are the so-called "speech sounds" or "phonemes" made in early infancy. These are produced by air from the lungs and by unlearned or chance movements of the other vocal mechanisms. Children of all races and nationalities, and even those who are deaf, have a similar repertoire of prelinguistic utterances. This fact, in itself, is strong evidence that these vocalizations are unlearned.

Not all of the phonemes made by adults (and represented by the International Phonetic Alphabet) are present at birth, but Osgood,[29] when he made tape recordings of the vocalizations of a baby for ten minutes per week, found that all phonemes are to some extent present within the first two months. Within this period "may be found all of the speech sounds that the human vocal system can produce, including French vowels and trills, German umlaut and gutteral sounds, and many that are describable only in phonetic symbols." Eventually, in listening to those around him, and in making linguistic use of the sounds which predominate in his culture, the child fixates certain sounds and drops others which, however, may predominate in different languages such as German, Chinese, Aranda, or Choctaw.

Irwin and Chen[30] studied intensively the phonemes which appear between the time of birth and the age of 30 months. Their data comprised twice-monthly samplings of the vocalizations of 95 infants, 35 of whom were studied at successive intervals throughout most of the age range indicated. Each of their total of 1622 records was based upon vocalizations uttered in 30 respirations. Recording, in the symbols of the International Phonetic Alphabet, was done by the listener. The brevity of each sample and the intervals be-

tween samplings were such that only the most frequent sounds would have had much prominence in the data. This point is stressed by Osgood,[31] in view of the fact that during the first two months his child made many sounds which did not find a place in Irwin's records for this period.

Irwin and Chen report that within the first two months there are only eight distinctly different vocalizations, five vowels (like those in *cat, fit, set, up* and *food*) and three consonants (*h, l,* and the sound made by pressure of air against the closed glottis). Their data show a gradual increase in the types of vocalization to a total of 27 at around 30 months. This is 27 out of the total of 35 sounds which characterize adult English speech. Frequency of vocalization also increases.

Other studies by Irwin[32] bring out the relative prominence of vowels and consonants, as well as of different consonant sounds, at various age levels. The early vocalizations have no significance to the baby, and they have no significance for us unless we happen to interpret them, usually incorrectly (see Chapter 14), as indicating the existence of particular emotional states. The initial sounds, and combinations of them, do not acquire true linguistic significance until they become representative of objects, situations, or actions, and the infant uses them for communication. Before they are combined in meaningful ways, however, these sounds appear in a repetitive sequence well-known as babbling. Since this phenomenon involves factors of possible importance in the development of speech, we now consider it briefly.

Babbling

Somewhere around the age of five months, babies usually begin babbling, or "lalling." Shirley[33] observed "conversations" like the following: *uggle-uggle, erdah-erdah, oddle-oddle, a-bah-bah, hey-hey, bup-bup-bup* and *lul-lul-lah.* It seems, according to Osgood,[34] that "the mere discovery of a skilled movement is sufficient reinforcement for its own practice, and syllabic babbling has the important function of providing the child with practice on the part-processes that are later to be utilized in communicative speech." It is interesting to note, in this connection, that deaf babies do not babble. They only make weird sounds.[35]

Why is babbling so prevalent in normal babies? Various answers have been suggested. One is that babbling is an instinctive response; one which appears only in humans. This is the view stressed by Langer (pp. 340–341) as playing a key role in the phylogeny of speech. Another answer which has been stressed by many psychologists and philosophers is that the babbler is imitating himself. This is of course not a complete explanation, for one must explain self-imitation.

Holt's [36] reflex-circle concept places stress upon the fact that muscular reactions give rise to sensory impulses. Thus, when a nerve impulse causes a muscle to contract, this contraction stimulates kinesthetic receptors and sends resulting nerve impulses back into the central nervous system.

It is conceivable that impulses thus originating in the vocal muscles may, through a process of conditioning, give rise to impulses which again activate the same muscles. There are two facts which, however, make this theory of doubtful value as applied to babbling. In the first place, deaf children do not babble. Osgood [37] points out that these children should do so if Holt's reflex-circle theory, as applied to kinesthesis, were correct. The deaf child's vocal activity arouses kinesthetic impulses just as in any other child, yet these do not become conditioned to vocal reactions in such a manner as to produce babbling. In the second place, as suggested by Miller and Dollard,[38] Holt's theory assumes that the connections involved in babbling will become established through sheer temporal contiguity. They maintain that, although temporal contiguity is a necessary condition of learning, so also is reinforcement. For deaf children there could be no reinforcement of vocal responses such as babbling involves. In the case of hearing children, however, it is possible that reinforcement is in-

volved. This possibility has led Miller and Dollard to modify the reflex-circle theory, as applied to auditory-vocal associations, by showing what features of the total situation might serve to reinforce the temporal contiguity stressed by Holt.

In its original form, as applied to auditory stimulation, the reflex-circle theory assumed the following conditions: Saying "*da*," for example, provides auditory stimuli for the baby. He hears himself say "*da*." In the diagram below, we designate such auditory stimulation as *Aud S*. It is assumed that some unknown stimulus (*Un S*) first elicits the response "*da*." The auditory stimulus (*Aud S*) at first arouses no identifiable response. But every time that the child says "*da*" he stimulates himself. When conditioning has occurred, the response "*da*" is a conditioned stimulus (Aud S, Aud S[1] . . .) for eliciting the same response. So the child says "*da-da-da* . . ." as represented in the diagram.

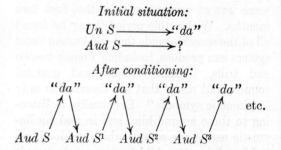

Initial situation:

$Un\ S \longrightarrow$ "*da*"
$Aud\ S \longrightarrow$?

After conditioning:

"*da*"   "*da*"   "*da*"   "*da*"
                                              etc.

$Aud\ S$ $Aud\ S^1$ $Aud\ S^2$ $Aud\ S^3$

This is the situation which takes account of temporal contiguity alone. According to Miller and Dollard,[39] however, the sound of the human voice has long since acquired secondary reward value. They point out that the mother, in ministering to the child's needs (for food, warmth, and so on), speaks to it. Thus the human voice, by being associated with primary reinforcement, could become a secondary reward. Through the process of stimulus generalization (p. 209), the child's own voice is assumed to acquire reinforcing properties like those of its mother. When this has occurred, "circular connections of the type described by Holt may be strengthened by the rewarding value of the child hearing himself produce a sound similar to that produced by his mother."

Why the babbler changes to other syllables, or stops altogether for a time, is an unanswered question. It could be, of course, that he becomes fatigued, that competing stimuli take over, or, as suggested by Miller and Dollard,[40] that repetition of a sound without primary reward extinguishes its acquired reward value.

Thus the child should shift to babbling with a different sound and eventually stop babbling altogether. After the passage of time, both the extinguished response of uttering the given sound and the acquired reward value of hearing that sound may undergo spontaneous recovery so that the child will return to uttering the sound. If the sound is again associated with primary reward, still more of its acquired reward value will be restored.

The beginnings of speech

Although babies normally babble by about the fifth month, it is not until they are nearing the end of the first year that they begin to speak. Their first words are usually rough imitations of something they have heard.

According to Mowrer, the child's first words are uttered because, whether made by himself or others, they sound good to him. This is in one respect an extension of the Miller-Dollard theory of babbling. Mowrer's [41] theory assumes that

the *first* stage of word learning is autistic; and by this is meant that a word, having been associated with satisfactions (drive reductions) provided by the parent . . . becomes satisfying in its own right, i.e. satisfying not only when uttered by another but also when uttered by the . . . baby itself. And from this it is but a short step to the conclusion that the capacity to utter the conventional noises called words develops because the organism is automatically, or "autistically," rewarded whenever it makes a noise somewhat like a word which has thus become satisfying. The organism is thus prompted to perfect this noise, with or without tutelage.

That words and wordlike sounds may in themselves have reward value for the child is an

assumption in keeping with reinforcement theories of learning. But another aspect of Mowrer's theory is more highly speculative than this, and completely without proof. He takes his cue from Langer,[42] who claimed that children speak "in order to bring something into their minds" instead of for the purely utilitarian purpose of bringing something into their hands. Mowrer supposes that the child, frustrated by the absence of his mother, speaks so as to recapture symbolically the satisfactions associated with her presence. Speech becomes, in this sense, a fetish. How such a theory could be substantiated is difficult to see.

A more parsimonious concept of how the first words occur is that of Allport,[43] who assumes that they are conditioned reactions elicited by the vocalizations of others, much as the babbling sounds of the child are set off by his own preceding vocalizations. Whether these reactions have been established through sheer temporal contiguity, or have involved implicit rewards such as the Miller-Dollard theory of babbling supposes, is of no particular consequence so far as the extension suggested by Allport is concerned. Suppose that the child has learned, on whatever basis, to repeat *"da"* when he hears himself say it. Now he hears someone else say *"doll,"* a sound which he has not yet learned to make. According to Allport's theory, the sound *"doll"* will elicit the nearest reaction to it, or *"da."* To use Allport's own words:

If the ear-vocal reflexes have been sufficiently established for the sound of a word to call forth the response of articulating it, it is no longer necessary that the child himself should speak the stimulating word. It may be spoken by another. The effect will then be that of the child repeating the sounds which he hears others utter. . . . It is, of course, assumed that only such speech responses as have been acquired through growth and practice will be evoked in this manner. The child does not imitate or duplicate the speech of his elders. There is evoked simply the nearest similar ear-vocal reflex which, with his present limitations of pronouncing, he has been able to fixate. The word "doll," spoken by the parent, would probably be repeated *da* (*a* as in *f*ather). In this manner whole phrases far beyond the learner's comprehension may be re-iterated rote fashion with as fair accuracy as the speech habits already acquired permit. It is essentially a parrot stage. In popular parlance it is known as "learning by imitation." The term "imitation" is however both inexact and misleading, for it suggests that the process is one of learning the speech reactions of others by voluntarily copying them; whereas it is really the touching off of *previously acquired* speech habits by their conditioning auditory stimuli.

Parents often adopt certain of the child's sounds, that is, indulge in "baby talk." They encourage such responses as "*dada*" instead of "*father*," "*mama*" instead of "*mother*," "*choo-choo*" instead of "*train*," "*tummy*" instead of "*stomach*," and so on. As a matter of fact, much "baby talk," including all the examples given above, has become conventionalized.* Jesperson [44] claims that the baby gets "pleasure" out of hearing his own vocalizations repeated by others, and that this encourages him to imitate even those sounds for which he has no ready-made response. It is perhaps true that the parental responses have some sort of reward value and thus encourage a less restricted form of acquisition than that indicated in the above quotation. Other motivating factors probably underlie a child's apparent attempts to copy the vocalizations of others. Much attention is lavished upon him whenever he produces a passable copy of the vocal patterns set for him. He is picked up, caressed, and rewarded in other ways. The advantages of being able to speak begin to make themselves apparent when the infant for the first time says something which sounds like "*ma-ma*" or "*pa-pa*." Later, when such attention is no longer forthcoming every time a new word is used, the child has already learned the value of language as a tool to facilitate social interaction. The infant seldom reproduces a very exact copy of the

parental vocalization. Hence, one cannot truthfully say that he imitates, except in the limited cases where the parental vocalizations are the same as his own babbling sounds. The important factor is that he eventually *tries to copy*. This introduces the motivation required for learning.

Ability to make combinations of sounds which closely approximate those of adults (*viz.*, "*doll*" instead of "*da*") develops gradually. There is no doubt that maturational factors are involved in this development.* Vocalizations produced by adults cannot be copied by the child until auditory-vocal mechanisms, including their cerebral connections, have sufficiently developed.** Nevertheless, it is obvious that children learn to speak just as they learn other manipulative habits. Saying the word "*doll*," for example, calls for a complex integration of lung, throat, mouth, and tongue movements in properly timed succession. The sound *d* is produced when the tip of the tongue is placed between the slightly open teeth in a certain way and air is expelled from the lungs. Saying *o* calls for an appropriate manipulation of lungs, vocal cords, tongue, and mouth as well as of resonance cavities within the throat and mouth. The *l* sound requires manipulation of lungs, vocal cords, tongue, and mouth. Saying "*doll*" in the adult way calls for a rather definite temporal patterning of these movements. Such patterns are gradually acquired. When ade-

---

* Strayer [46] presents evidence (gathered by the method of co-twin control) that a given amount of language training at 89 weeks of age is more efficacious than similar training at 84 weeks. The twin which at 89 weeks was still untrained acquired, within 28 days, a vocabulary which equaled that of the twin who had received five weeks of training previously. The results are interpreted as evidence for a maturational factor in language acquisition. However, the twin whose training began at 84 weeks slightly surpassed the other in vocabulary, pronunciation, and sentence construction at the end of the experimental period. Three months later this difference in favor of the earlier trained twin had largely disappeared.

** Jesperson [47] points out, for instance, that the jaw undergoes a rapid growth in length during the early acquisition of speech. He also indicates that certain necessary tongue movements do not seem possible until a given age has been reached.

---

* Jesperson refers to these responses, conventional or otherwise, as the "little language," a term also adopted by Latif.[45]

quately stimulated by his fond parents, and later by formal teachers, the child vocalizes in a trial-and-error fashion until he achieves the acceptable patterns. Thus, he learns to say "*doll*" instead of "*da*," "*stomach*" instead of "*tummy*," "*sugar*" instead of "*fugar*," "*light*" instead of "*yite*," "*elephant*" instead of "*fant*," and so on.

The meaning of words

We say that words take on meaning for the infant. It is said, furthermore, that meaning undergoes modification as the child grows older. What is the *meaning* of a word? In attempting to answer this question one must take into consideration the fact that, during the social history of an individual's group, given words have become conventional symbols (or substitutes) for certain objects, situations, relationships; in a word, phenomena. In the last analysis, therefore, the meaning of a word must be envisaged in terms of phenomena which the word conventionally represents. Words take on meaning for the child as he learns to make the conventional responses to them or to use them in conventional ways. In order to do either of these things he must learn what the words represent; what they are symbols for.

Words at first have an extremely limited meaning. The fact that a child responds to them in an appropriate manner does not indicate that they have the same representative significance for him as for the one who uses them. He may be in a position like that of Thorndike's cats. Moreover, the child's saying of a word, or of his best approximation to it, does not indicate that he has learned its representative significance. He may be repeating it in parrot fashion. It is quite evident, however, that words spoken by others elicit increasingly fine differential reactions as the child grows older. Similarly, the use of words becomes increasingly discriminative. Both of these trends indicate that, as the child grows older, words are, to him, taking on a *closer approximation to their fullest conventional representative significance as this has* developed during the social history of the group.*

Meaning varies not only with words as such, but with the inflection and context of a given word. The same word often has a somewhat different meaning in different situations. Furthermore, many words have diverse meanings for individuals who speak the "same" language yet live in different localities.

The meaning of a word may originate in peculiar individual experience as well as in the accumulated experience (culture) of the group. This is especially true of personal names. The word *Ruth* may have cultural significance but, in addition, it may mean sister, sweetheart, mother, wife, girl friend, or even baseball player. To use another example, the word *mother* has cultural significance, but much of its meaning to the individual is in terms of stimulation peculiar to his own mother.**

Children make certain appropriate responses to many words before they reproduce them overtly. To the extent to which they arouse appropriate reactions in the child, these words may be said to have meaning. In many instances, such meaning may be as limited as that of the words "I must feed those cats" for animals trained to jump upon a box

* Concerning the cultural meaning or significance of a word (its "potential" meaning for the individual who hears or says it), Gardiner [48] makes the following pertinent comments. He says: "Every word is a heritage from the past, and has derived its meaning from application to a countless number of particulars differing among themselves either much or little. When now I utter such a word, I throw at the listener's head the entire residue of its previous applications. ... In uttering a word, the speaker necessarily offers to the listener the whole range of its meaning." However, although offered the "whole range of its meaning," an individual attaches to a word (heard or spoken by himself) only as much meaning as that for which his training has prepared him. As his linguistic education covers a larger range, the child grasps, as it were, a greater part of the meaning offered him. It is doubtful, however, whether many adults realize the fullest meaning, even of common words.

** It is obvious that the meaning of a word is derived from contact with other individuals. However, such contacts may, to use Young's [49] term, be either *personal-social* or *cultural*. We are merely indicating that some of the meaning of a word may be derived from the cultural heritage and some from purely individual personal-social experience.

at such a signal. However, words become more meaningful as the child learns to speak; as he is controlled by words or uses them to control the behavior of others; and as he uses words implicitly in thinking.

How does the child learn to respond to and use words appropriately? In its initial stages, at least, the process seems relatively simple. It may be envisaged in accordance with the conditioned-response principles with which we are already so familiar. At the same time that an infant says "*da-da*," thus receiving kinesthetic and auditory stimulation as indicated in our previous discussion (pp. 348–349), he is frequently confronted with visual and other stimuli emanating from his father. This person may actually repeat "*da-da*," thus stimulating the child to reiterate. He may fondle the infant, pick it up, or stimulate it in other ways. Other men may provide somewhat equivalent stimulation. When the mother (or some other woman) is alone present during the response "*da-da*," and fails to react to it, the only associated stimuli are the kinesthetic and auditory ones produced by the child himself. There is no reinforcement such as the father provides. The response "*da-da*" is thus not associated with the mother, or a woman. On the other hand, stimuli emanating from the father (or other men), having reward value and being frequently associated with the "*da-da*" response and related kinesthetic and auditory stimulation, become conditioned stimuli for the arousal of this response. The process may be diagrammed as follows:

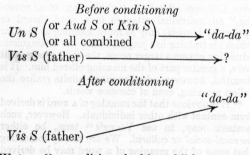

Before conditioning

$Un\ S \begin{pmatrix} \text{or } Aud\ S \text{ or } Kin\ S \\ \text{or all combined} \end{pmatrix} \longrightarrow$ "*da-da*"

$Vis\ S$ (father) $\longrightarrow$?

After conditioning

"*da-da*"

$Vis\ S$ (father)

Watson [50] conditioned his child to say "*da-da*" whenever a milk bottle was pre-

sented. Instead of petting the child every time he said "*da-da*," Watson merely gave him his bottle. Thus the bottle became "*da-da*" and "*da-da*" meant the bottle and the stimulation and responses associated with it.*

The use and meaning of many words is acquired while other persons are pointing at the things represented, giving objects to the child to play with or to use in some other manner, or associating actions with the appropriate words. The child is taught to speak at the same time as he is learning various habits of orientation and manipulation. He learns to speak while he is acquiring other aspects of the social heritage, such as learning to drink from a cup, to eat with a spoon, and to dress. Later on the meaning of many new words is learned through their verbal context (see p. 354). It is a case, as Ogden and Richards [53] have said, of "using language in order to learn language."

As the child grows older he learns that "*da-da*" is appropriate to one man and to no

---

* In this discussion we have passed over the problem of how words, gestures, and other signs or symbols are related to the objects or situations which they represent. This problem in semiotics is dealt with at length by Morris [51] and Osgood.[52] The latter presents several hypotheses, including his own. What he calls the "mentalistic view" assumes that the word *da-da*, for example, has in common with the father the *idea* which both arouse. The "substitution theory" supposes that the sign for the object, the father in our illustration, evokes the same reaction as the object itself. The view expressed by Morris is a modified substitution theory which supposes that the sign response, rather than being identical with the response to the object, "takes account of" this response. In other words, the connecting link is a "disposition" to make the response which the object itself (father) aroused. Osgood's own "mediation" hypothesis further modifies the original "substitution" hypothesis and the "disposition" stressed by Morris, by supposing that the sign "evokes in an organism a mediating reaction, this (a) being some fractional part of the total behavior elicited by the object and (b) producing distinctive self-stimulation that mediates responses which would not occur without the previous association of nonobject and object patterns of stimulation." Thus the word *da-da* is assumed to elicit in the child certain incipient responses anticipatory of those which might have been made to the father himself; for example, incipient arm movements and clutchings of the hands.

other. This is because his father alone continues to provide the stimuli associated with "*da-da*." Likewise, the child learns to be more discriminating in his use of other terms. Not only is meaning restricted in this way, but it is also generalized. Thus Lewis [54] describes how a child of about 18 months who had learned to say *fa* (flower) for hyacinths, later used the same word for tulips, irises, and a flowering cherry tree. At nearly 23 months she used this name for sugared flowers on a cookie and also for embroidered flowers on some slippers.

Many early words are used not as nouns, verbs, pronouns, etc., but as word-sentences or, to use Latif's term, holophrases. The expression "*da-da*" may mean "*da-da come here*" or "*da-da don't go*." Thus, during early linguistic development, a word may signify some general situation rather than a *specific* thing, act, or relation.

A child soon learns to use words as a means of asking for or talking about objects, situations, and relationships not actually present at the time. Similarly he acquires ability to use words in thinking about absent phenomena. Most of his concepts (pp. 315–324) are represented by words.

The first word

This landmark in the development of speech is of considerable interest to psychologists and parents, but the data concerning it are anything but reliable. Parents are prone to "recognize" as words what might not be so designated by others. As McCarthy [55] says, "they often read meaning into the child's early babbling which happens to coincide with the presence of certain persons, objects, or events in the environment." Suppose he utters *da-da* in his babbling and sometimes uses it in the presence of his father: when can one claim "that this is uttered to designate his father? If the criterion of using the word to mean only one person, and not using it in any other situation, is accepted, it is necessary to observe over a period of time,

to note consistency of usage, and to see that the sounds are not used in other situations."

Another difficulty with reports on appearance of the first word is that they differ widely as to the age when this normally occurs. Where the parents have been asked to indicate the age at which the first word was spoken they have given an age much lower than that reported by psychological observers. The median age reported by parents and recorded in the studies by Shirley [56] and Cattell [57] has been less than one year. However, the median age at which Shirley's 25 babies first spoke one word before the examiner was 60 weeks. Gesell and Thompson [58] report a median age of 52 weeks, but with some children speaking as early as the 28th week.

Despite such discrepancies, it is apparent that we can expect many children to be saying at least one word by the end of the first year. The data also show, however, that there are wide individual differences in the age at which the first word is spoken. According to Olson [59] the range in biographical studies is from about eight months to twenty months. Data summarized by McCarthy [60] suggest a positive relationship between the age at which the first word is spoken and the child's later intelligence. She cautions, however, that "the relationship is far from perfect, and the layman accepting such a generalization is quite likely to make serious errors in predicting a child's future mental development merely from a knowledge of the age at which he begins to talk." Although Terman's [61] gifted children, according to their parents, spoke at an average age of 11 months, some did not speak until they were from two to three years old. The feebleminded, on the other hand, are practically always slow in saying their first word. Few speak until they are from two to three years old and some idiots never accomplish anything beyond grunts and other noises. [62]

Even among children of the same native ability one would expect to find marked differences, not only in the first word spoken but in the age at which it appears. This is because, perhaps more than any other human characteristic, speech is sensitive to social conditions, which of course differ remarkably from one home to another.

Growth of the Vocabulary

There are two aspects to the development of a vocabulary. One is the ability to say words, and the other is the ability to understand the meanings of the words spoken by oneself or others. Learning to say the words which one hears may, as we have seen, occur partly through imitation and partly through something akin to a trial-and-error process. The representative significance of these words is to some extent given by the circumstances in which they occur. Objects are named, perhaps while someone is pointing toward them. Later still the words may be defined, as in formal education. Through conversation, and perhaps more so through reading, we also learn the meaning of words by their context. This method of acquiring word meanings was studied intensively by Werner and Kaplan,[63] who used a Word-Context Test in which artificial words were imbedded in sentences. Children between the ages of eight and thirteen were required, for example, to discover the meaning of the artificial word *corplum* through their reading of such sentences as: "A corplum may be used for support. Corplums may be used to close off an open place. A corplum may be long or short, thick or thin, strong or weak. A wet corplum does not burn. You can make a corplum smooth with sandpaper. The painter uses a corplum to mix his paints." When asked, "What is a corplum?" the child was expected to say a stick or piece of wood. Scores on this test increased at successive age levels.

The extent of the vocabulary at different ages has been studied by varied methods, each producing somewhat different estimates. Biographical studies, of which many have been reported, have used the longitudinal method. That is to say, they have followed the development of vocabulary in a particular child.

This has sometimes been done by noting every word spoken. At the beginning, this is relatively easy. But when the child begins to add words rapidly, as he usually does by the end of the second year, the task of noting every new word becomes increasingly burdensome, even for the fondest and most scientifically minded parent. Another method is to sample the vocabulary at intervals, perhaps noting stenographically every word said. The sample may comprise fifty consecutive verbal responses,[64] what was said in ten minutes,[65] or even in a whole day's conversation.[66] Most studies have utilized some sort of sampling approach, especially after the age at which the vocabulary becomes too large to follow it effectively in any other way.

Development beyond the early age levels of childhood has usually been studied by estimating the average extent of the vocabulary of successively older age groups. Words have been selected, at uniform intervals, from a dictionary or extensive word list, and a vocabulary test has been designed.[67] In one such study [68] the investigators used every twentieth word from Thorndike's list of 10,000 commonly used words. The number of these words understood by the child was then multiplied by 20 to estimate the extent of its vocabulary. This test yielded the data summarized in Table 10. However, another method of sampling [69] yielded much larger vocabulary lists. A large unabridged dictionary was used and the children were given easier methods of indicating whether they understood a word than were used in the above-mentioned study. Whereas the five-year-olds of the former study were credited with 2072 words, those of the latter were credited with 16,900 basic and 7100 derived words. It is thus clear that vocabulary lists should not be taken at their face value. The only finding common to all is that the child's vocabulary, however measured, grows slowly at first and then undergoes a marked spurt, after which words continue to be added as a function of age. The number of words actually spoken, or understood, or definable at

Table 10. Increase in the Average Size of Vocabulary (Words Understood) as a Function of Age *

Age in months	Number of children	Number of words	Gain
8	13	0	
10	17	1	1
12	52	3	2
15	19	10	16
18	14	22	8
21	14	118	96
24	25	272	154
30	14	446	174
36	20	896	450
42	26	1222	326
48	26	1540	318
54	32	1870	330
60	20	2072	202
66	27	2289	217
72	9	2562	273

* After Madorah Smith.

particular age levels cannot be stated with any degree of definiteness. Moreover, the actual words used by a child are so dependent upon that child's particular experience that no common vocabulary can be associated with a particular age level. Thus two children of the same age level who are using the same number of words may, to a large extent, be using different words.

Another point which emerges from vocabulary studies is that the various parts of speech differ in frequency of appearance. Not only is the first word usually a noun, but nouns continue to predominate. One investigator[70] sampled a child's vocabulary at three age levels. At 18 months 145 words were spoken, 79 per cent of which were nouns. At 36 months the number of words was 1205, of which 57 per cent were nouns. Of the 1870 words used at 48 months, 58 per cent were nouns. Next to nouns, the most prevalent parts of speech were verbs, with adjectives coming next. In a more extensive study, McCarthy[71] also found a predominance of nouns, but not proportionately as many as here indicated. All parts of speech increase

in frequency during the preschool years. But, as Young[72] has shown, the period of greatest change in their proportionate frequency is over before the child reaches the third year. McCarthy[73] points out moreover, that as soon as full and complete grammatically correct sentences are being used, the relative frequency of the various parts of speech is determined by the conventions of sentence structure. Thus a child who is using such sentences may, in a given sample of conversation, utilize a relatively small proportion of nouns.

Phrases and Sentences

Smith[74] claims that phrases are often as readily learned as words, but that the different words have, in such cases, no separate meanings. Her summary of the literature indicates that a vocabulary of from 100 to 200 words usually precedes construction of phrases or sentences. At the age of 24 months, Smith's subjects used, on the average, 1.7 words per phrase or sentence. At successive half-yearly periods the averages were as follows: 2.4, 3.3, 4.0, 4.3, 4.7, and 4.6 words. Later studies, which have been tabulated by McCarthy,[75] show somewhat similar results, despite differences in methods of observation.

An interesting discussion of early word-compounding is given by Watson,[76] whose child had 52 words at his command when he first put two of them together.

This occurred . . . at the age of 1 year, 7 months, 25 days. For a month prior to that date we had been setting a verbal pattern of two words for some time, such as "hello, mama," "hello, dada," without results. On this day his mother said, "Say good-bye to daddy." She set the pattern "good-bye da." He repeated after her, "bye" — then hesitation and five seconds later came the word, "da." This brought upon him a shower of petting, verbal commendation, and the like. Later in the day he said with the same long interval between the two sounds, "bye — bow wow." . . . Two days later, we got him to say "hello — mama," "hello — Rose," "ta-ta — Rose," "ta-ta — mama" ("ta-ta" means "thank you"). In each case the two-word stimulus had to be given before the response could be called out. He also said, "blea — mama" for the first time. Never up to this time could we get the two-word response without giving the two word stimulus. . . . [Nine days later.] He put two words together without any verbal stimulus from the parents; for example, he pointed to his father's shoe and said "shoe — da," and pointing to his mother's shoe, "shoe — ma." Then the next four days he used all of the above two-word responses at one time or another without any pattern being set, and some additional ones for which a two-word pattern had never been set, such as the following: "tee-tee bow-wow (dog urinates)," "bebe go-go" (when a little neighbor took his cart), "mama toa," "how-do shoes," "haa mama," "awri mama." Often when put back into his room for his sleep or his midday nap, he ran over these words and combinations again and again aloud in his room. . . .

As we have already observed, words and phrases which possess conceptual significance are acquired relatively late. The child does not learn the word *dog* as representative of *all animals possessing common properties* until long after merely verbal habits have been acquired. Abstract words like *life*, *liberty*, and *except* are acquired only after the child has achieved a high degree of generalizing ability (see pp. 324–329).

Conditions Which Influence Speech Development

Among the investigators of speech development there is unanimity on one point above all others. This is that such development is significantly influenced by socio-economic conditions as reflected in the home. The socio-economic differential is discernible even in the development of phonemes (p. 347), and it becomes much more evident later when words and sentences are considered. Irwin[77] found acceleration of phoneme development in infants from higher socio-economic groups (professional, business, clerical) as compared with infants from laboring groups. Young[78] sampled the speech of nursery school children

from self-supporting homes and from homes on relief. In the number of comprehensible words spoken and in the mean length of sentences used, the relief group was consistently behind the other.

These results are consistent with those reported by earlier investigators of socio-economic influences and are probably due to innate as well as environmental factors. The innate capacity to develop language, as well as other aspects of intelligent behavior (p. 373), is probably by and large superior in the higher socio-economic groups. Added to this is the fact that in such groups there is usually greater linguistic stimulation. McCarthy[79] says, in this connection, that "the occupational group differences which have been found so consistently in the larger scale studies may be due in some measure to the more restricted environment usually experienced by children of the lower socio-economic classes. Parents of children in the lower classes are presumably less gifted linguistically than parents of children in the upper classes, and hence not only afford a poorer example of language for a model, but also probably provide less verbal stimulation." In the upper socio-economic levels, on the other hand, there is a greater likelihood that parents will have a greater inclination and more time to converse with their children and to read to them. They are also likely to visit more with other families and to travel, thus providing a wider variety of linguistic experiences.

Only children, probably because of their more intimate contact with adults than is experienced by non-only children, are usually accelerated in speech development. Davis[80] found only children to be ahead of non-only children in such aspects of speech as length of sentences, extent of vocabulary, and talkativeness. The differences in favor of only girls was larger than in the case of only boys, a finding in agreement with the almost universally reported superiority of girls over boys in linguistic development. The acceleration shown by only children is doubtless due to the fact that they associate more with adults than with other children. McCarthy [81] found, in fact, that children who associated chiefly with adults were linguistically more advanced than those who associated chiefly with older children.

Being a twin is disadvantageous from the standpoint of early language development. Day [82] found that the number of words used in sentences by twins was significantly below that of singletons. Davis [83] found, however, that this difference disappears after the children enter school. McCarthy [84] mentions an unpublished study by Howard on a large number of triplets. This study revealed even greater retardation in length of sentences than had previously been observed in twins. Five-year-old triplets were about one year retarded as compared with Day's twins, and two years retarded as compared with McCarthy's singletons. Blatz and others [85] found the linguistic development of the Dionne quintuplets to be markedly retarded as compared with singletons.

The chief reason for speech retardation in children from multiple births is probably their relative isolation from normal adult contacts. They talk among themselves, and may even develop a "language" of their own (see p. 342). Such self-sufficiency reduces the amount of linguistic intercourse with older children and adults which other children normally enjoy.

Written Language

Writing involves a learned control of initially random arm and finger movements just as speech involves acquired coordinations of originally random vocal movements. Gesell and Thompson [86] have investigated the initial "paper and crayon" behavior of infants ranging in age from 36 to 56 weeks. They find:

At 36 weeks the initial response may be to the paper. The infant fingers it, picks it up, grabs it grossly, or slaps it. Rarely is the activity confined to the paper. Characteristically he picks up the crayon and puts it immediately into his mouth. He may mouth without further manipulation. Any marking of the paper which may occur is apparently adventitious. Even at 40 weeks he may give exclusive attention to the crayon (54 per cent). He may manipulate it with regard before putting it to the mouth, he may transfer it (38 per cent), or he may hit the crayon on the table top, and by the same drumming movement he may make staccato marks on the paper. But spontaneous combining is barely incipient and these marks too are by-products rather than end products.

Well-defined spontaneous combining of paper and crayon is not present even at 44 weeks. About one child in three combines by drumming, dragging, or dangling the crayon, which leaves faint meandering marks. This element of restraint making for delicacy of response should perhaps be regarded as a developmental increment rather than a personality characteristic. It may occur in association with vigorous hitting. It has already been noted in the cup and spoon situation.

At the three age levels, 48 through 56 weeks, spontaneous combining becomes increasingly well defined and rises in frequency from 42 per cent to 74 per cent. There is a corresponding trend toward prolongation and repetition of combining. The very intensity, number, and length of the strokes which the infant makes show some tendency to increase with age. Linear marks as contrasted with staccato show a significant increase at 56 weeks, rising from a frequency of 10 per cent to 74 per cent. Whereas at 52 weeks one child in three made staccato marks only, there were no such instances at 56 weeks. On the contrary one child in three made linear marks only at 56 weeks. This tendency toward linearity in spontaneous combining lies at the basis of the increasing responsiveness to the scribble demonstrations in the period from 48 weeks to 56 weeks. Considering the vigor and dominance of staccato marks at the earlier age levels, it is an impressive fact that after demonstration three-fourths of the 56-weeks-old infants made linear marks *only*.

Gesell and Thompson's data also indicate that the child's responsiveness to demonstrations of crayon-and-paper behavior increases with age. This responsiveness is, of course, an important prerequisite for acquisition of written language symbols. Freeman [87] and others have shown that the various activities involved in writing increase in ease of accomplishment with age.

Letter writing is achieved only after much trial and error. A study by Gates [88] shows that learning curves similar to those exhibited for other motor skills are evidenced in acquisition of letter-writing habits. From the standpoint of motor activity, of course, writing is merely drawing. How the "drawings" achieve conventional symbolic significance for a child is our chief interest. The principles discussed in connection with acquisition of vocal language apply here. As the child sees and learns to draw them, the various letters become symbols (that is, substitutes) for sounds. This is because sounds provided by the teacher, and later by the child himself, are frequently associated with the letters under reinforcing conditions. A given series of sounds and a given series of "drawings" thus become equivalent symbols for some object or situation. When the "drawings" achieve this significance they are written words and take their place, along with gestures and vocalizations, as linguistic symbols.

Learning to read these symbols, like learning to reproduce them, involves motor skill. Before he can read efficiently, the child must learn not only the meaning of written symbols, but also how to make appropriately coordinated eye movements.

Language and Thinking

There has been much discussion concerning the contribution of language to thought processes. Bain [89] said that thought is restrained speaking or acting. Many others, both before and after Bain, have presented a similar view. Watson [90] took over this view and gave it a cardinal position in his behavioristic system. He claimed that thinking is merely sub-vocal talking; in other words, that it comprises incipient or greatly abbreviated laryngeal activities. He later [91] presented the view that gestural as well as vocal symbols play a role in thinking, but that this process is not entirely dependent upon such conventional symbols. He says that, "Thinking at successive moments of time may be kinesthetic,

verbal, or emotional." Also, "We . . . think and plan with the whole body. But, since . . . word organization is, when present, probably usually dominant over visceral and manual organization, we can say that 'thinking' is largely *sub-vocal talking* — provided we hasten to explain that it can occur without words."

There is no doubt that, once linguistic activities have been acquired, thinking frequently, although not necessarily, involves words and symbolic gestures. Young children often "think aloud." However, social pressure of various kinds soon indicates the advantage of hiding one's thoughts. Watson [92] says that the deaf, dumb, and blind Laura Bridgman "talked to herself, using the finger language with great rapidity." This language had been taught her by the superintendent of the Perkins Institution and Massachusetts Asylum for the Blind. Thinking in terms of gestures is often quite evident. Movements made in writing may accompany thinking about what one intends to write. Ewert [93] has shown that eye movements similar to those made in reading are also involved in recall of the material read.

Linguistic activities are usually quite abbreviated when involved in thought. They may become so abbreviated that delicate instruments alone indicate their presence. Thorson [94] used a delicate lever system to record tongue movements associated with thinking. But her results disclosed no correlation between these movements and thought. However, Jacobson [95] found that action currents from the tongue and lips accompany silent counting and thinking. He presented his results as evidence that thinking involves inner speech. To say that inner speech and gestures of various kinds accompany, or are involved in, thinking is quite different from saying that thinking *is* implicit speech and gesture. So far, linguistic activities and thought processes have not been identified. One can merely say that language and thought are often found to be concomitant.

The fact that human infants and infrahuman animals, neither of which have a true language, are able to perform delayed reactions and develop simple concepts suggests that these processes are not solely dependent upon linguistic ability. Furthermore, some mammals exhibit reasoning ability despite the absence of a true language (see pp. 144–146). Children give no clear evidence of reasoning until after some language activities have been acquired (see pp. 324–329). This does not necessarily mean, however, that reasoning in the human being depends upon language. Delayed reaction, concept formation, and reasoning require use of symbols, but these need not be the conventional communicative ones which are alone designated as truly linguistic.

Many investigators have probed thought processes through the questions asked by the child and his answers to questions asked by the investigator. The discussion of animistic concepts (pp. 320–324) dealt with such data, as also did our consideration of the child's ideas of physical causality (pp. 329–330). Upon the basis of listening to children's conversations, Piaget [96] came to the conclusion that their thinking is at first largely egocentric. He says that

the child thinks for himself without troubling to make himself understood or to place himself at the other person's point of view . . .; these egocentric habits have a considerable effect upon the structure of thought itself. Thus it is because he feels no need to socialize his thought that the child is so little concerned, or at any rate so very much less concerned than we are, to convince his hearers or to prove his point.

Piaget says that socialized thought fails to appear until around the seventh year when, according to him, reasoning also begins. We have shown, however, that reasoning is evident as early as the third or fourth year (pp. 325–327), and McCarthy,[97] Day,[98] Johnson and Josey,[99] and Janus [100] have failed to substantiate Piaget's conclusion that the thinking of young children is largely egocentric.

It is true that young children use the pronoun *I* (and derivatives like *my* and *me*) with high frequency (as compared with *you, we, he, it* and *they*), but this does not mean that they are talking to themselves and thinking egocentrically. Jersild,[101] who summarizes the relevant data, points out that such predominance of the personal pronoun is to be expected, since

A child's own impulses and desires, activities, pleasures, and pains are more vivid and closer to him than is his comprehension of the personalities and concerns of other people. That the child's private and personal concerns stand uppermost in his first reactions to the world about him, insofar as these are revealed by his language, appears not only through his frequent use of "I" but also through the content and tone of his remarks, questions, and demands. However, from the time he begins to talk, the very fact that he expresses himself at all bespeaks a certain degree of sociability and adaptation to other persons . . . while a child's remarks are heavily studded with "I's," there also is a vein of sociability running through them, for they at least are usually addressed to another person.

Summary and Conclusions

Language is symbolic in a dual sense, for it represents absent objects and situations and at the same time it makes possible the communication of meaning. It is apparently an extension of the symbolic processes which have been found to mediate the higher learning functions of animals.

When left to their own resources, many infrahuman animals use sounds and gestures. However, these are unlearned; are not conventional, as are true language symbols; and are inseparably associated with emotional behavior. Some domesticated animals do, however, make certain appropriate responses to words and gestures and at times acquire these as a result of human tuition. Nevertheless, this does not constitute true language. Words stimulate animals merely in terms of their pitch, intensity, and temporal pattern. Conventional meaning is not conveyed. Even when a chimpanzee learns to say a few words, it does not apply them in an appropriate manner in new situations. Animals do not attempt to use their "speech" in communicating with other animals. Their failure to invent a language may depend upon the fact that they do not vocalize spontaneously, or babble, as human babies do. It may depend also on the (perhaps related) fact that their brains differ in certain marked respects from our own, especially in lacking a speech center. Nor do animals combine the separate "words" in a meaningful manner. Without human tuition they would have learned no "words" at all.

There is no clear evidence of the way language originated. We considered various theories and found that, although each theory has some basis in fact, none is in itself a sufficient explanation of linguistic origins. In common with other writers we stressed the view that man chanced upon or invented language, which then became a tool for facilitating social interaction. It is generally believed that gesture preceded speech as such a tool, and that writing was developed later than either gesture or speech. It is of course possible that gesture, speech, and writing originated concomitantly. Since writing has survived in concrete form, one can trace its development quite readily. The earliest writing comprised drawings of the objects represented. These drawings became increasingly abbreviated. Finally, they ceased to resemble that for which they served as substitutes. In other words, they became increasingly symbolic. This facilitated identification of a written symbol with a spoken one. Separate symbols (letters) then represented each sound made in speaking of an object, situation, or relationship. Finally, these symbols were combined to form words.

A child is not required to recapitulate the linguistic evolution of the group. He becomes heir to the whole past linguistic acquisition of his culture, and through social contacts receives the essential aspects of this within the early years of life.

The raw materials from which an individual's language develops are initially meaningless gestures, vocalizations, and scribblings. Gestural language develops first. Its acquisition is similar to that of other habits.

The mechanisms which underlie speech have been described. Although a whispered speech is possible without use of the vocal cords, these membranes normally play an important role. Modifications of tones produced by the vocal cords result from manipulation of the larynx as a whole, the tongue, teeth, and other structures of the throat and mouth. Various cavities serve as resonators. Under sensory and neural control these structures produce, during early infancy, all the fundamental sounds (phonemes) of speech. Acquisition of speech calls for an acquired manipulation of these structures. This acquisition is partly dependent upon maturation of sensory, neural, and motor mechanisms. The conventional patterns of sound which we designate as speech are learned gradually as the child interacts with other members of his group.

Reinforcement and temporal contiguity appear to play important roles in babbling and in later copying of the speech sounds of others. A degree of trial-and-error is involved in perfecting such vocalizations.

An infant's first words are usually nouns. Some early nouns, rather than being true parts of speech, are in reality holophrases, or word-sentences. The proportion of nouns to other parts of speech undergoes a change during the first three years. Other parts of speech gradually increase in frequency, so that nouns do not play as dominant a role as they did initially. As phrases and sentences come into use, a particular sample of verbalization includes still fewer nouns. This is because the use of the various parts of speech is dictated by conventionalities of sentence structure. Personal pronouns like "I," "me," and "my" are especially prevalent in early conversations. This does not mean, however, that the child's thinking is essentially egocentric. It is only natural that his own concerns should be uppermost at first.

The fact that he addresses himself to others implies a certain degree of sociability.

The growth of vocabulary has been studied in several ways, longitudinally and cross-sectionally and by a variety of sampling methods. Each procedure yields somewhat different findings both as to the age at which the first word is normally spoken and the extent of the vocabulary at different age levels. It is to be expected, however, that most children will be saying their first comprehensible word at around the age of one year, and that after this stage is reached words will be added rapidly. Although estimates differ, the average vocabulary probably jumps from a few words at around one year to two hundred or so a year later. According to one study, the three-year-old uses about one thousand words. The same study credits the six-year-old with more than twice the vocabulary of the three-year-old. Other studies give different figures for particular age levels. These studies all show, however, that once children begin to speak, they increase their vocabulary at a rapid rate. The combining of words into phrases and sentences usually begins after the child's vocabulary has grown to one hundred or more words. Such combinations increase in length and in adequacy as a function of age. Many two-year-olds are combining two words. By the age of five years the average number of words combined is between four and five.

The size of the vocabulary at any age level, as well as its actual word content and its use in sentences, reflects the child's level of intellectual development and his social experience. Verbal contacts with older children and adults are especially important. Only children, probably because of their intimate contacts with adults, usually show markedly accelerated linguistic development. Twins and triplets, compared with singletons, tend to be retarded linguistically. This may be because communicative self-sufficiency brings relative isolation from adults and older children, who would set more mature patterns than those which the twins or triplets find satisfactory for their own needs.

Linguistic development, in all of its aspects, is significantly influenced by the child's socio-economic status. Poor socio-economic conditions are associated with a relatively lower level of language development. This may result from a lower average level of innate ability in the children of laborers as compared with skilled workers and professional groups, and also from a lower level of linguistic stimulation than other children enjoy.

From the sensorimotor aspect, writing is a manipulative habit such as other forms of drawing. It is acquired very gradually, and the acquisition curve is similar to learning curves for other motor activities. When the drawings which constitute writing come to represent absent objects and situations, and especially the sounds which are themselves conventional symbols for objects and situations, they become linguistic. Conditioned-response principles account for acquisition of much, at least, of such linguistic significance. Reading is a motor skill as well as a symbolic activity. Efficiency in reading involves both skilled eye movements and understanding of written symbols.

There have been many attempts to identify thinking with abbreviated or implicit linguistic activities, and especially with internal speech. None of these attempts has been entirely successful. One may merely conclude that thinking and linguistic activities, once these activities have been acquired, are frequently concomitant. In cases of concomitance, the language responses are usually, but not always, implicit.

REFERENCES

1. Langer, S. K., *Philosophy in a New Key*. New York: New American Library, 1953. (Originally published in 1942 by Harvard University Press.) Quotation is from p. 83.
2. Hunter, W. S., *Human Behavior*. Chicago: University of Chicago Press, 1928, p. 329.
3. Murphy, G., L. B. Murphy, and T. M. Newcomb, *Experimental Social Psychology* (rev. ed.). New York: Harper, 1937, p. 181.
4. Craig, W., "The Voices of Pigeons Regarded as a Means of Social Control," *Am. J. Sociol.*, 1908, *14*, 86–100.
5. Lorenz, K., *King Solomon's Ring*. New York: Crowell, 1952.
6. Tinbergen, N., *Social Behaviour in Animals*. London: Methuen, 1953.
7. Mowrer, O. H., "On the Psychology of 'Talking Birds' — A Contribution to Language and Personality Theory," in Mowrer's *Learning Theory and Personality Dynamics*. New York: Ronald Press, 1950.
8. Alverdes, F., *Social Life in the Animal World*. New York: Harcourt, Brace, 1927.
9. Yerkes, R. M., and B. W. Learned, *Chimpanzee Intelligence and Its Vocal Expression*. Baltimore: Williams and Wilkins, 1925.
10. Crawford, M. P., "The Cooperative Solving of Problems by Young Chimpanzees," *Comp. Psychol. Monog.*, 1937, *14*, No. 2.
11. Furness, W. H., "Observations on the Mentality of Chimpanzees and Orang-Utans," *Proc. Amer. Phil. Soc.*, 1916, *55*, 281–290. Quotation from p. 283.
12. Hayes, K, J., and C. Hayes, "The Intellectual Development of a Home-Raised Chimpanzee," *Proc. Amer. Phil. Soc.*, 1951, *95*, 105–109; "Vocalization and Speech in Chimpanzees," 16mm. Sound Film, Psychological Cinema Register, State College, Penna., 1951.
13. Hayes, C., *The Ape in Our House*. New York: Harper, 1951. Quotations from pp. 64–66.
14. de Haan, J. A. B., "Animal Language in Relation to that of Man," *Biol. Rev.*, 1929, *4*, 249–268.
15. De Laguna, G. A., *Speech: Its Function and Development*. New Haven: Yale University Press, 1927, pp. 36–37.
16. Thorndike, E. L., *Animal Intelligence*. New York: Macmillan, 1911.
17. Langer, *op. cit.*, p. 94.
18. Furness, *op. cit.*, p. 281.
19. Warden, C. J., *The Evolution of Human Behavior*. New York: Macmillan, 1932.
20. Mowrer, *op. cit.*, p. 720.
21. Wundt, W., *Elements of Folk Psychology*. New York: Macmillan, 1916.
22. De Laguna, *op. cit.*
23. Pillsbury, W. B., and C. L. Meader, *The Psychology of Language*. New York: Appleton, 1928.
24. Judd, C. H., *The Psychology of Social Institutions*. New York: Macmillan, 1926.
25. Thorndike, E. L., "The Origin of Language," *Science*, 1943, *98*, 1–6. Also in *Selected Writings from a Connectionist's Psychology*. New York: Appleton-Century-Crofts, 1949.
26. Jesperson, O., *Language: Its Nature, Development, and Origin*. New York: Holt, 1921.
27. Paget, R., *Human Speech*. New York: Harcourt, Brace, 1930.
28. Judd, *op. cit.*
29. Osgood, C. E., *Method and Theory in Experimental Psychology*. New York: Oxford University Press, 1953, p. 684.
30. Irwin, O. C., and H. P. Chen, "Development of Speech During Infancy," *J. Exper. Psychol.*, 1946, *36*, 431–436. See also O. C. Irwin, "Infant Speech," in *Scientific American*, Sept. 1949, 22–24.
31. Osgood, *op. cit.*, p. 685.
32. Irwin, O. C., "Infant Speech: Consonantal Sounds According to Place of Articulation," *J. Speech Disorders*, 1947, *12*, 397–401; "Consonant Sounds According to Manner of Articulation," *ibid.*, 402–404; H. P. Chen, and O. C. Irwin, "Infant Speech Vowel and Consonant Types," *J. Speech Disorders*, 1946, *11*, 27–29.
33. Shirley, M. M., *The First Two Years: II. Intellectual Development*. Minneapolis: University of Minnesota Press, 1930.
34. Osgood, *op. cit.*, p. 687.
35. See the letter from Mrs. Zittzus (Perkins Institute and Massachusetts School for the Blind) quoted by Mowrer, *op. cit.*, p. 707.
36. Holt, E. B., *Animal Drive and the Learning Process*. New York: Holt, 1931. See especially pp. 37–38.

37. Osgood, *op. cit.*, p. 688.
38. Miller, N. E., and J. Dollard, *Social Learning and Imitation*. New Haven. Yale University Press, 1941. See Appendix I.
39. *Ibid.*, p. 277.
40. *Ibid.*
41. Mowrer, *op. cit.*, pp. 707–708.
42. Langer, *op. cit.*, p. 98.
43. Allport, F. H., *Social Psychology*. Boston: Houghton Mifflin, 1924, pp. 183–184. Allport gives credit to S. Smith and E. R. Guthrie for first presenting the essentials of this theory in their *General Psychology in Terms of Behavior*, New York: Appleton, 1923.
44. See citation 26.
45. Latif, I., "The Physiological Basis of Linguistic Development and of the Ontogeny of Meaning," *Psych. Rev.*, *41*, 55–85; 153–176; 246–264.
46. Strayer, L. C., "Language and Growth: The Relative Efficacy of Early and Deferred Vocabulary Training, Studied by the Method of Co-Twin Control," *Genet. Psychol. Monog.*, 1930, *8*, No. 3.
47. See citation 26.
48. Gardiner, A. H., *The Theory of Speech and Language*. London: Oxford University Press, 1932. Quotation from p. 35.
49. Young, K., *Social Psychology* (2d ed.). New York: Crofts, 1944.
50. Watson, J. B., *Behaviorism*. New York: Norton, 1930, pp. 228–229.
51. Morris, C., *Signs, Language, and Behavior*. New York: Prentice-Hall, 1946.
52. Osgood, *op. cit.*, p. 696.
53. Ogden, C. K., and I. A. Richards, *The Meaning of Meaning*. New York: Harcourt, Brace, 1923.
54. Lewis, M. M., *Infant Speech*. London: Routledge and Kegan Paul, 1936. Partially reproduced in W. Dennis, *Readings in Child Psychology*, New York: Prentice-Hall, 1951, pp. 268–278.
55. McCarthy, D., "Language Development in Children," in L. Carmichael (ed.), *Manual of Child Psychology* (2d ed.). New York: Wiley, 1954, p. 523.
56. See citation 33.
57. Cattell, P., *The Measurement of Intelligence of Infants and Young Children*. New York: The Psychological Corporation, 1940.
58. Gesell, A., and H. Thompson, *Infant Behavior: Its Genesis and Growth*. New York: McGraw-Hill, 1934.
59. Olson, W. C., *Child Development*. Boston: Heath, 1949.
60. McCarthy, *op. cit.*, p. 599.
61. Terman, L. M., *et al.*, *Genetic Studies of Genius: Mental and Physical Traits of a Thousand Gifted Children*. Stanford University Press, 1925.
62. See A. F. Tredgold, *A Text-Book of Mental Deficiency (Amentia)* (7th ed.). London: Bailliere, Tindall & Cox, 1949, pp. 132ff.
63. Werner, H., and E. Kaplan, "The Acquisition of Word Meanings: A Developmental Study," *Monog. Soc. Res. Child Devel.*, 1950, *15*, No. 1.
64. McCarthy, D., *Language Development of the Preschool Child*. Minneapolis: University of Minnesota Press, 1930.
65. Young, F. M., "An Analysis of Certain Variables in a Developmental Study of Language," *Genet. Psychol. Monog.*, 1941, *23*, No. 1.
66. Haggerty, M. E., "What a Two-and-One-Half-Year-Old Child Said in One Day," *J. Genet. Psychol.*, 1930, *38*, 75–100.
67. For a discussion of such tests and the markedly different results obtained from one test to another, see McCarthy, citation 55, pp. 527–536.
68. Smith, M. E., "An Investigation of the Development of the Sentence and the Extent of Vocabulary in Young Children," *Univ. Iowa Stud: Stud. in Child Welfare*, 1926, *3*, No. 5.
69. Smith, M. K., "Measurement of the Size of General English Vocabulary Through the Elementary Grades and High School," *Genet. Psychol. Monog.*, 1941, *24*, 311–345.
70. Nice, M. M., "The Development of the Child's Vocabulary in Relation to Environment," *Ped. Sem.*, 1915, *22*, 35–64.
71. See citation 64.
72. See citation 65.
73. See citation 64.
74. See citation 68.
75. See citation 64.
76. Watson, *op. cit.*, pp. 228–229.
77. Irwin, O. C., "Infant Speech: The Effect of Family Occupational Status and of Age on the Use of Sound Types," *J. Speech Hearing Disorders*, 1948, *13*, 224–226; "The Effect of Family Occupational Status and of Age on Sound Frequency," *ibid.*, *13*, 320–323.
78. See citation 65.

79. McCarthy, citation 55, pp. 587–588.
80. Davis, E. A., "The Development of Linguistic Skill in Twins, Singletons with Siblings and Only Children from Age Five to Ten Years," *Institute of Child Welfare Monog. Ser.*, 1937, No. 14.
81. See citation 64.
82. Day, E. J., "The Development of Language in Twins: I. A Comparison of Twins and Single Children," *Child Development*, 1932, *3*, 179–199.
83. See citation 80.
84. See citation 55, p. 590.
85. Blatz, W. E., M. I. Fletcher, and M. Mason, "Early Development and Spoken Language of the Dionne Quintuplets," in *Collected Studies of the Dionne Quintuplets. Univ. Toronto Stud., Child Development Ser.*, 1937, No. 16.
86. See citation 58, pp. 213–214.
87. Freeman, F. N., *The Handwriting Movement: A Study in the Motor Factors of Excellence in Penmanship.* Chicago: University of Chicago Press, 1918.
88. Gates, A. I., "The Acquisition of Motor Control in Writing by Preschool Children," *Teach. Coll. Rec.*, 1923, *24*, 459–469.
89. Bain, A., *The Senses and the Intellect.* New York: Appleton, 1879.
90. Watson, J. B., *Psychology from the Standpoint of a Behaviorist.* Philadelphia: Lippincott, 1919.
91. Watson, citation 50, pp. 267–268.

92. See citation 50, p. 241.
93. Ewert, P. H., "Eye Movements During Reading and Recall," *J. Gen. Psychol.*, 1933, *8*, 65–84.
94. Thorson, A. M., "The Relation of Tongue Movements to Internal Speech," *J. Exper. Psychol.*, 1925, *8*, 1–32.
95. Jacobson, E., "Electrophysiology of Mental Activities," *Am. J. Psychol.*, 1932, *44*, 677–694.
96. Piaget, J., *Judgment and Reasoning in the Child.* New York: Harcourt, Brace, 1928, p. 1. This is Piaget's summary of the findings of his former study, *The Language and Thought of the Child*, New York: Harcourt, Brace, 1926.
97. McCarthy, D. A., "A Comparison of Children's Language in Different Situations and Its Relation to Personality Traits," *J. Genet. Psychol.*, 1929, *36*, 583–591; also see citation 64.
98. See citation 82.
99. Johnson, E. C., and C. C. Josey, "A Note on the Development of the Thought Forms of Children as Described by Piaget," *J. Abn. & Soc. Psychol.*, 1931, *26*, 338–339.
100. Janus, S. Q., "An Investigation of the Relationship Between Children's Language and Their Play," *J. Genet. Psychol.*, 1943, *62*, 3–61. See also W. Dennis, "Mr. Janus on Children's Language," *J. Genet. Psychol.*, 1943, *63*, 183–185.
101. Jersild, A. T., *Child Psychology* (4th ed.). New York: Prentice-Hall, 1954, pp. 413–414.

SUGGESTIONS FOR FURTHER READING

Allport, F. H., *Social Psychology.* Boston: Houghton Mifflin, 1924, Chapter 8.
Barker, R. G., J. S. Kounin, and H. F. Wright, *Child Behavior and Development.* New York: McGraw-Hill, 1943, Chapter 7. An abridgement of McCarthy's monograph.
De Haan, J. A. B., "Animal Language in Relation to That of Man," *Biol. Rev.*, 1929, *4*, 249–268.
De Laguna, G. A., *Speech: Its Function and Development.* New Haven: Yale University Press, 1927.
Dennis, W., *Readings in Child Psychology.* New York: Prentice-Hall, 1951, Chapter 5. Selections from Lewis, Allport, Day, and Piaget.
Hayes, C., *The Ape in Our House.* New York: Harpers, 1951, Chapter 8.

Jersild, A. T., *Child Psychology* (4th ed.). New York: Prentice-Hall, 1954, Chapter 12.
Judd, C. H., *The Psychology of Social Institutions.* New York: Macmillan, 1926, Chapters 9 and 10.
Kuhlen, R. G., and G. G. Thompson, *Psychological Studies of Human Development.* New York: Appleton-Century-Crofts, 1952, Chapter 7.
Langer, S. K., *Philosophy in a New Key.* Cambridge: Harvard University Press, 1942, Chapter 5. Reprinted in New American Library (Mentor Books), 1953.
Latif, I., "The Physiological Basis of Linguistic Development and of the Ontogeny of Meaning," *Psych. Rev.*, 1934, *41*, 55–85, 153–176, 246–264.

McCarthy, D., "Language Development in Children," in L. Carmichael (ed.), *Manual of Child Psychology* (2d ed.). New York: Wiley, 1954.

Morris, C., *Signs, Language, and Behavior.* New York: Prentice-Hall, 1946.

Mowrer, O. H., *Learning Theory and Personality Dynamics.* New York: Ronald, 1950, Chapters 23 and 24.

Murphy, G., *Personality.* New York: Harper, 1947, Chapter 11.

Osgood, C. E., *Method and Theory in Experimental Psychology.* New York: Oxford University Press, 1953, Chapter 16.

Swanson, S. E., T. M. Newcomb, E. L. Hartley, *Readings in Social Psychology* (rev. ed.). New York: Holt, 1952, Part I-B.

Young, F. M., "Language Growth and Development," Chapter 9 in K. C. Garrison, *Growth and Development.* New York: Longmans, Green, 1952.

13

The Growth of Intelligence

THE criterion of intelligence in animals is flexibility of adjustment. We have emphasized the dependence of such flexibility upon learning, remembering, and "putting two and two together" in such a way as to solve problems and achieve relevant generalizations. From the standpoint of intelligence, evolution is more evident in the complexity of the problems which animals can solve than in the rate at which they learn relatively simple sensorimotor adjustments. As the human level is approached, the differences between one level and another, as well as individual differences on a particular level, are most evident in symbolic learning of the kind required in delayed reaction, conceptual discrimination, and double-alternation problems. Speech, as we have seen, is a symbolic process found only at the human level. Because it facilitates memory and the integration of past experience in such a way as to solve present problems, speech adds immeasurably to intelligence in human beings as compared with other organisms. As we shall observe in the following pages, individual differences in human intelligence are most evident through linguistic activities. We have non-verbal tests, but most of these are primarily for infants who have not yet acquired linguistic facility and for the illiterate and the feeble-minded. Most of our intelligence tests place a major emphasis upon symbolic versatility as revealed through verbal activities.

There are many definitions of intelligence, ranging from those which stress some capacity, such as the capacity to "carry on abstract thinking," to those which say merely that "intelligence is what the intelligence tests measure." By implication, the first type of definition denies intelligence to all animals below the primate level. This is unsound genetically, because there is, as we have seen, a more or less gradual transition from the relatively simple sensorimotor learning of lower animals to the higher types of symbolic processes exhibited by primates. The only clear evidence of a gap comes when language is added. It does not fairly represent the genetic data, therefore, to say that some animals are intelligent and others are lacking in intelligence. Actually, there are *degrees* of intelligence. To say that intelligence is what the tests measure is also unsound for our purposes. It is perhaps a good operational definition, with respect to human intelligence, but since most of these tests deal with linguistic processes, no cognizance is taken of lesser degrees of intelligence.

Intelligence is actually a logical construct, being inferred from individual differences in acquired behavior. A definition should therefore abstract from the many particular instances of "intelligent" behavior that feature which is discernible in all. The most clearly discernible feature in all instances of adjustment in which wide individual differences are also found is that of *flexibility* or *versatility*. This feature has been stressed by Edwards.[1] Among infrahuman mammals, as well as among children who have not yet learned to verbalize, individual differences in versatility are most evident in adjustments utilizing recall memory, generalization, and other non-verbal reasoning. Among older children and adults, however, verbalization is an important aspect of adjustment, and especially adjustment to new situations. At this level, therefore, individual differences in versatility are revealed most clearly by verbal tests of intelligence.

Our aim in this chapter is to trace the development of intelligent behavior from birth to maturity, paying especial attention to conditions associated with this development. The trend is most clearly discerned from normative test data.

A particular child's development may be indicated by his ability, at successive age levels, to perform tests comparable with those performed by the average child at his own and other age levels. At five, let us say, his performance corresponds with that of the average five-year-old, at six with that of the average six-year-old, and so on. If he is retarded, he may be a certain number of age increments behind; or if precocious, ahead of his age group. We shall see, however, that individual test performances at successive age levels are often subject to marked fluctuations. In cross-sectional studies, where large groups of children are represented at successive age levels, such fluctuations are not apparent, and in accordance with certain assumptions, it is possible to plot growth curves. The following discussion takes cognizance of individual as well as group trends and also considers possible causes of individual fluctuations in test performance.

Intelligence Tests

It is not our purpose here to attempt a definitive discussion of intelligence tests with their many ramifications. All that we need, prior to considering the development of intelligence, is a brief survey dealing with the main features of tests designed to gauge mental growth in children.

Infant tests

Tests of infant intelligence are in most respects very similar. At the lower age levels they focus primarily upon sensorimotor developments such as those considered in the chapters on sensory and motor development. At higher age levels, beginning at about one year, they include an increasing amount of symbolic material, including verbal items. A recently developed set of these tests comes from Northwestern University. It was standardized by Gilliland[2] for use between the ages of four and thirty-six weeks.* Tests which are primarily sensorimotor include adjusting the head when raised to a sitting position, grasping a ring, and responding in certain ways to a flash of light and a sudden sound. A few social items are included, like gazing into the examiner's eyes, changing facial expression upon the examiner's changing his tone of voice, responding to a mask, and attending while the examiner talks. One memory item is that of looking for a face which has disappeared. Age norms have been developed in terms of the number of items passed by the average baby at different age levels. All other infant tests go above the upper age limit involved in this one.

Several tests have been designed to cover the range from early infancy to the age at which verbal tests, like the Stanford-Binet, begin. Bühler's[3] baby tests were mentioned earlier (pp. 305-306). We pointed out that the items most predictive of later intelligence

* There are two forms, one for the age range of 4 to 12 weeks and another which goes from 12 to 36 weeks.

are those involving delayed reaction. Bayley's [4] test, developed at the University of California at Berkeley and used in her study of mental growth during the first three years, is like the others in that it begins with purely sensorimotor items. At the upper levels, however, this test includes items involving memory, imitation, and speech. Psyche Cattell's [5] Infant Intelligence Scale and the very widely used Developmental Schedule devised by Gesell and Amatruda [6] cover approximately the same age range as those already mentioned. According to the latter test, a normal two-year-old should be doing such things, under specified conditions, as turning pages in a book, imitating circular strokes, building towers with blocks, placing blocks in the appropriately shaped holes of a three-hole form board, adapting to reversal of the form board, identifying simple pictures, and playing that a teddy bear is alive by feeding it. Items like these merge, at lower levels, with those restricted more to sensorimotor activity. At higher levels they merge with items requiring a higher level of symbolic functioning. Here they overlap with the lower level of the Stanford-Binet test which, while it contains performance items at this level, becomes increasingly verbal at successively higher age levels.

Interest in baby tests is based upon the desire to know, as early as possible, what level of intelligence a child is likely to attain. Such information would be especially valuable to adoption agencies and to parents wishing to adopt children as young as possible, yet with some assurance that their ultimate level of intelligence will be satisfactory. In reality, however, such tests have been found of very limited value. The difficulty is that their results are not predictive of later intelligence, as measured with verbal tests. Consecutive tests, administered close together in time, correlate rather well with each other, but as the interval between tests increases, the correlation grows smaller, until it approximates zero.[7] According to Bayley's [8] results, the correlation between test scores obtained in infancy and those obtained during the school years is about zero.

There are various reasons for the limited predictive value of infant tests. In the first place, such tests, being primarily sensorimotor in content, overlap very little with the primarily verbal content of later tests. In the second place, it is possible that there is no correlation between sensorimotor and symbolic development. In the third place, the items in the infant tests which hold promise of being most highly predictive of later intelligence — the social and symbolic items — are difficult to score in a reliable manner. One cannot be sure, for example, that the child is actually looking into one's eyes. Whether or not the child misses an absent face, or something else that has been hidden, again involves subjective judgment, which lowers the reliability of the test. In the fourth place, mental growth, especially at early age levels, may fluctuate a great deal more than it does later. This would also lower the correlation between scores obtained during infancy and those obtained at later age levels.

It is apparent, therefore, that one can say very little of any value about the growth of individual human intelligence prior to the level at which predominantly symbolic processes, and those to a large extent verbalized, can be tested. What the infant tests show is that sensorimotor activities, social responses, and to some extent the elementary symbolic processes, increase in scope during infancy.

The Stanford-Binet Test

The best-known and most widely used individual * test of intelligence is the Revised Stanford-Binet, which was standardized in 1937 by Terman and Merrill [9] and further analyzed in 1942 by McNemar.[10] This test contains groups of items at age levels from two years to adulthood. Between two and five there are separate sets of items for each

* Group tests of intelligence are also widely used, both with school children and with adults, but we shall not consider them here. Some are referred to in a later discussion (pp. 379–381) on mental growth curves.

six-month period. The tests beyond five are in yearly groups through the fourteenth year. The items involved, the materials used, the procedures of administration, and the methods of scoring are carefully prescribed and only trained examiners are qualified to give the test and to score and evaluate the individual's performance.

The selection of items for each age level was not arbitrary, but based upon the *average* performance of representative individuals of that age level. After selecting items which suggested themselves as interesting to children and perhaps appropriate for testing intelligence at a given age, the investigators tried them out on individuals of that age and eliminated those items found to be too easy or too difficult. Thus, if the average five-year-old could perform an item, while the average four-year-old found it too difficult and the average six-year-old too easy, it was placed at the five-year-old level. It was also required that performance on this item correlate reasonably well with the performance of five-year-olds on the test as a whole. The entire test was standardized on a total of 3003 white native-born Americans ranging from two to eighteen years of age. These came from seventeen different communities in eleven states selected as representative of the country as a whole. The schools represented were judged to be average ones in their respective localities. Selection of subjects to be used in the standardization of the test was such that the various socio-economic groups were, as closely as possible, proportionally represented.

The various items at each age level in this test give a good idea of the kinds of performance considered indicative of average intelligence at that age level. Here are a few examples: The average three-year-old strings beads after watching a demonstration, responds to "What's this" by naming objects on a card, builds with blocks a bridge like the one demonstrated, recognizes an object which appears among others, makes a circle like one shown him, and repeats three digits

from memory. At the five-year-old level an average child completes the figure of a man, folds a triangle in imitation of the tester, defines certain common objects, makes a square like the copy, finds forms to match samples, and shows evidence of comprehension in answering certain "Why" questions. An average seven-year-old tells the examiner what is funny or foolish about certain pictures, in what way certain objects are alike, and what one should do under certain circumstances. He also draws a diamond like the sample, gives opposite analogies, and repeats five digits. At nine years the average child shows how a cut piece of folded paper will look when unfolded, points out certain absurdities in verbal statements, draws designs from memory, tells what words rhyme with the test words, tells how much change would be left if certain monetary transactions were carried out, and repeats four digits reversed. The average eleven-year-old draws from memory, points out certain absurdities which are more obscure than those used at earlier age levels, gives the definitions of certain abstract words, remembers sentences, tells why certain acts were performed, and points out the similarities in three things. An average thirteen-year-old suggests the plan to follow in looking for an object lost under certain circumstances, remembers words, shows how a folded and cut paper will look unfolded, explains incidents in a narrative, rearranges words to form sentences, and copies a complicated chain of beads from memory. At the level designed for the average adult, the individual defines twenty words, writes a given message in code, points out the differences between abstract words, reasons arithmetically, tells the meaning of certain proverbs, solves a verbalized problem requiring ingenuity, remembers long sentences, and tells in what way certain opposites are nevertheless alike.

The statement that these tests measure educational opportunity and achievement rather than *capacity* or *ability* is often made. This statement is based upon the obvious fact that many items (such as vocabulary) are learned in a school environment. However, there was an effort to eliminate any items which would depend upon conditions of *unusual* educational advantage. The theory is that, if the child of a given age has average ability, he will have acquired the symbolic behavior possessed by average children of that age. His *ability*, in other words, is measured in terms of group accomplishment. Thus, if a child just passes the tests performed by the average ten-year-old, he is said to have a *mental* age of ten years.

The general procedure used in determining mental age with the Stanford-Binet test is as follows: Suppose that we are to test a child who is seven years old chronologically and we guess that he is of approximately average intelligence. We begin with the tests one year below the seven-year level. If the child can perform the six tasks at this level he is credited with a mental age of six years, or seventy-two months. If he passes the six tests at the seven-year level, twelve more months are added to his mental age. At the eight-year level he may pass two tests. Since there are six tests for this age level, each valued at two months, the child is credited with four more months. At year nine, perhaps, he passes one test. This adds two months to his mental-age score. If he fails all tests at the next age level, the child is assumed to have covered the range of which he is capable. To summarize, the child's record is

		Months
Year VI	All tests passed	72
Year VII	All tests passed (basal year level)	12
Year VIII	Two tests passed	4
Year IX	One test passed	2
Year X	Failed all tests	0
	Mental age	90

His mental age is thus ninety months, or seven years, six months. The child is credited with intelligence six months in advance of that which characterizes seven-year-olds.

A mere statement of mental age does not indicate how intelligent an individual is with respect to his age level. The individual with a mental age of seven years may be five years old or he may be an adult. In the former instance he would be regarded as extremely bright and in the latter extremely dull. It is thus customary to report the ratio of an individual's mental to his chronological age. This ratio, when multiplied by 100 to remove decimals, is known as an Intelligence Quotient, or I.Q. It indicates the rate at which an individual has achieved his intelligence. The formula is

$$I.Q. = \frac{M.\,A.}{C.\,A.} \times 100.$$

Since the average child has a mental age approximately equal to his chronological age, the average I.Q. is around 100. The child whose test results were discussed above (mental age ninety and chronological age eighty-four months) has an I.Q. of 107.*

The Wechsler Intelligence Scale

Although it is relatively new and by no means as widely used as the Stanford-Binet test, the Wechsler Intelligence Scale for Children [11] is another test worthy of consideration in any discussion dealing with the growth of intelligence. This is an extension downward of the well-known and extensively used Wechsler-Bellevue Intelligence Scales, which are designed for adolescents and adults. The new test, however, has been separately standardized on 200 children — 100 boys and 100 girls — at each year between five and fifteen. This test differs from the Stanford-Binet in

* In calculating I.Q.'s for individuals older than 13 years, the actual chronological age is not used. The C.A. of a person between 13 and 16 years is calculated as 13 plus two-thirds of the additional months he has lived. Thus an actual chronological age of 14 years is counted as 13 years 8 months. The largest divisor used in calculating I.Q.'s for the Terman-Merrill Revision, regardless of the individual's true chronological age, is 15 years. The reason for thus disregarding actual age beyond 13 years is that yearly increments of mental age gradually decrease after this year. From the age of 15 on there is practically no further increase in mental age as measured by such tests.

several important respects. In the first place, both performance and verbal tests are used throughout the age range. The performance tests are designed to measure non-verbal symbolic processes. There are five such tests (picture completion, picture arrangement, block design, object assembly, and coding *or* mazes) and five verbal tests (general information, general comprehension, arithmetic, similarities, and vocabulary). In the second place, instead of the items being arranged in age groupings, with different materials at each age level, the same series is used throughout the test. On General Information, for example, there are 30 items. The individual, regardless of age, proceeds with these until he misses five in succession. A comparable procedure is followed with other items. Finally, there are no mental age norms. A child's I.Q. thus cannot be computed by dividing mental age by chronological age, as in the case of Stanford-Binet I.Q.'s. I.Q.'s are computed with the Wechsler Scale, but by comparing the child's raw score with that obtained by the average child of his own age. They are called "deviation I.Q.'s" because they indicate, in scaled units, how much the child deviates above or below the average child of his own age level. The child of five whose I.Q. is 100 has achieved a level of performance equivalent with the average score (total points) of the five-year group. One standard deviation above or below the average is set at 15 I.Q. points.* Thus the child whose score is one standard deviation above the average has an I.Q. of 115. With this test there are also percentile equivalents, as in the case of adult scales. Children with an I.Q. of 135 or more are, for example, in the 99th percentile. I.Q.'s derived with this test approximate those obtained with the Stanford-Binet.

* Readers unacquainted with the concepts of standard deviation and percentile ranks should consult the writer's *Psychology*, Dashiell's *Fundamentals of General Psychology*, or a text on elementary statistics. Statistical computations are not required of the tester. He uses tables to convert raw scores into I.Q.'s.

Hereditary and Environmental Contributions

A particular level of intelligence results from the interplay of hereditary and environmental influences, each of which would be ineffective without the other. It is thus meaningless to ask whether an individual's intelligence is of hereditary or environmental origin.

Although the I.Q. is an index of hereditary *and* environmental influences, fluctuations from time to time may be attributable to heredity, to environment, to variations in tests or test procedures, or to changes in the child's health, attitudes, and so forth. A particular child's heredity is constant, but there may be innately determined changes in his rate of growth. This possibility has been stressed by Bayley [12] in her report on the stability of mental growth from birth to eighteen years. The instability indicated in Figure 117 may have been innately determined to some extent, but it seems to depend more upon changes in health and in home and school conditions. Such extreme fluctuations are rare. The average change in a Stanford-Binet I.Q. from year to year is not more than plus or minus five points. [13]

Differences in I.Q. between one individual and another, or between one group and another, could stem from *either* hereditary or environmental influences, or from a combination of these. In the case of identical twins, however, any difference in I.Q. derived with the same test under the same conditions, would be attributable to divergent environmental influences. We have seen, in fact, that such differences in I.Q. do exist. Our earlier discussion (pp. 41–42) showed that the I.Q.'s of identical twins reared in the same home differ, on the average, by about five points and that the difference found for identical twins reared in different homes is about eight points. Among identical twins reared together, the range of I.Q. difference is 0–20 points; among those reared apart the range is 1–24 points. The I.Q.'s of identicals reared together yield a correlation of approximately .88; of those reared apart, approximately .77.

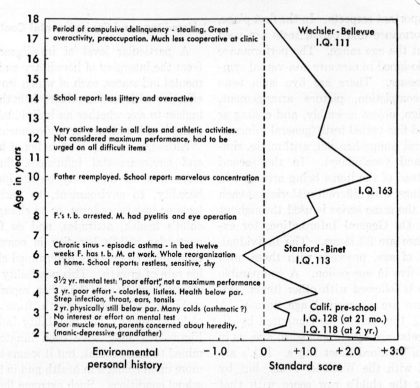

Figure 117. How the I.Q. of One Boy Fluctuated During a Period of Sixteen Years

Fluctuations of this magnitude are seldom reported. In this case we have information on what may have produced such instability of the I.Q. (From M. P. Honzik, J. W. Macfarlane, and L. Allen, "The Stability of Mental Test Performance between Two and Eighteen Years," *J. Exper. Educ.*, 1948, *17*, 320.)

Among fraternal twins reared together, there are greater differences in I.Q. than among identicals reared apart. The correlation between the I.Q.'s of fraternal twins is in the neighborhood of .63.[14] In identical twin pairs, we have a constant heredity; hence the indicated differences must be attributed either to variations in test administration or to differences in environmental opportunities.

What would happen were we to have a constant environment and hereditary variation, as in the case of rats (pp. 26–28)? This cannot be determined, with any degree of precision, at the human level. Even in the same home, or school, or neighborhood, human beings react differently to aspects of what appears to be the same environment. One child may attend to certain aspects and

not others. Different children may implicitly reconstruct the environment so that, psychologically, it differs for each. The closest we can come to equating human environments is to make them objectively equivalent, as by providing comparable homes and schools. But these may be far from equivalent psychologically. Thus, although we can discern which differences are environmentally produced in identical twins, and which are hereditarily produced in rats, we cannot say anything very precise about the hereditary contribution to human intelligence.

There are doubtless innately determined differences in the intelligence of human beings (as in the learning ability of rats) and there are doubtless environmentally produced differences (as in identical twins reared apart), but an I.Q. reflects both influences. It does this in a manner which, except in the case of identical twins, does not allow us to differentiate clearly the respective contributions of heredity and environment.

The I.Q. is merely a comparative index of test performance and the level of performance from which we derive it is a function of both heredity and environment. The level of intelligence, as defined earlier (p. 366), is inferred from the level of test performance. It seems best not to define it as a capacity *per se*. But many psychologists define intelligence not only as a *capacity*, but as an *innate capacity* to achieve the level of versatility which a test reveals. These psychologists overlook the important possibility that a capacity to achieve may have environmental as well as hereditary roots.

Contributions to intelligence considered as a capacity

Hebb [15] has pointed out that intelligence, as tested, has two different origins. There is, he says, "an *innate potential*, the capacity for development, a fully innate property that amounts to possession of a good brain and a good neural metabolism." In addition there is "the functioning of a brain in which development has gone on. . . ." He points out that the *capacity* to develop intelligent behavior, rather than being purely innate, may itself depend in part upon early experience. In terms of the above quotation, this means that the *early* "functioning of a brain in which development has gone on" may have a significant effect on later functioning, hence on the over-all capacity to achieve mature intelligence. Hebb perhaps has in mind the phenomenon considered earlier (pp. 137–138) as "learning how to learn." He cites certain experiments with rats which suggest that a "rich experience" during early growth may differentiate the later test performance of animals having similar heredity. His suggestion comes from the fact that rats with this "rich experience" were better able than their littermate controls to "profit from new experiences at maturity."

Theoretically, at least, the same sort of experiment could be done with identical twins, one of each pair being reared in an intellectually rich environment during the preschool period and the other in an intellectually impoverished environment. What we should need for the test of Hebb's hypothesis, however, is a more *extreme* difference than that experienced by the identical twins mentioned earlier (pp. 41–42). We should also need a difference which existed only during the first few years of childhood. One of each pair of identicals might be subjected to such an environment as the following: low socio-economic status, poorly educated foster parents, no other children to play with, and a home without picture books or other literature. The other member of each pair might be placed in a home of high socio-economic status, with well-educated parents, intelligent older children as playmates, and books of many kinds at his level of comprehension. His foster parents would not only be well educated but would read to him and answer his questions. Let us now suppose that both twins of each pair, when they reached school age, were brought together in an average home, sent to an average school, and treated identically in other ways. Suppose, in other words, that they were now reared under conditions comparable with those presupposed by the standardization of the Stanford-Binet test.

What could one predict about the subsequent mental development of these twins? It might be expected that the culturally deprived twin would have problems of adjustment not experienced, to such an extent, by the one from a rich cultural environment. It is almost certain that were they tested with the Stanford-Binet or Wechsler test at this time, the latter twin would have a higher I.Q. We could attribute this difference to the fact that neither child had previously had the *average* opportunities experienced by the theoretically average children on whom the tests were standardized. One had poorer than average, the other better than average opportunities. But what of future development in an "average" cultural environment? This is what, in the present state of our knowledge, we are unable to predict with any degree of certainty. According to those who say that the capacity to develop intelligence is purely innate, both twins would become more alike and eventually achieve the same level of test performance, hence have the same I.Q. According to Hebb's hypothesis, however, the twins would continue to differ in test performance and the one who was culturally deprived in earlier life would never achieve as high an I.Q. as the other.*

Situational aspects of differences in I.Q.

The I.Q. varies with educational and socio-economic group differences and also with differences in home and school situations, but the interpretation of these variations, with respect to heredity and environment, is by no means clear. One difficulty is that hereditary and environmental aspects are varied together — not independently, as is required for differentiation of their respective influences. Another difficulty is that certain situations, whether or not they really influence a child's capacity, or his level of intelligence, involve more test-like experiences than others. Thus a child subjected to these situations may test higher than another merely because he is more "test-wise," not because he has basically superior ability. In line with the difficulty just mentioned is the nature of the tests with which we attempt to measure the influence of different situations.

Unlike instruments for measuring physical traits, intelligence tests are contaminated, so to speak, by the factors whose influence we wish to measure with them. There is no way to measure "raw intelligence." An intelligence test is not something apart, like a yard-

---

* The failure of feral children to profit fully from later educational opportunities (as in the case of Itard's *Wild Boy of Aveyron*) is attributed by some to innate feeblemindedness and by others to a carry-over of the retarding effect of an early cultural impoverishment.

stick or a scale for weighing. It is, as we have seen, an instrument involving symbolic processes, and especially verbal symbols. No child, however superior in potential ability, could achieve a high mental age on these tests without an education which gave him the necessary linguistic skills. Since the tests are standardized on the basis of "average educational opportunity," a child with sub-average schooling would get a lower I.Q. than he should in terms of his potential ability. A child with much better than average schooling would, by the same token, get a higher I.Q. than he should in terms of his potential ability. Now, as we consider the influence of various environmental conditions upon the I.Q., we should remember that this is itself in part an index of environmental conditions — not alone of "raw intelligence" or "innate potential."

Parental education and occupation. There is a pronounced tendency for I.Q.'s to be higher the higher the level of parental education. The correlation between the I.Q.'s of children and the level of education achieved by their parents ranges from around .50 to .60, with the mother's level of education showing a higher correlation than the father's.[16] There is also a relation between the occupational level of fathers and the I.Q.'s of their children. The average I.Q. of the children of unskilled laborers is around 95 and there is an increase in average I.Q. from one socio-economic level to another until, at the professional level, an average I.Q. of 125 is obtained.[17] These findings on educational level and level of occupation are related in various ways. People in the upper socio-economic groups are usually better educated than those at lower levels. But what is especially interesting from our standpoint is the inextricable contribution of heredity and environment to these relationships. Individuals with relatively low innate ability are stopped at a relatively low rung of the educational ladder, whereas a large proportion of those with relatively high innate ability continue to the top rungs. A similar situation is to a considerable extent present with respect to socio-economic level. By and large, those with higher innate ability are likely to be better represented in the higher socio-economic brackets than are those with lower innate ability. Thus children of parents in the upper educational and socio-economic brackets must to some extent inherit the superior innate ability of their parents. But there is also the environmental contribution. People at the higher educational and occupational levels usually provide a superior cultural environment for their children. Quite frequently these children go to better schools than do the children of those at the lower educational and socio-economic levels. Many of them are likely to go to special schools, such as nursery and preparatory schools. The homes of the higher educational and socio-economic groups are characterized by books, good periodicals, music, and intelligent conversation. Children at these levels are thus more highly stimulated symbolically than are those at lower levels. Children at the upper levels are also likely to travel more, thus further increasing the range of experiences which contribute to high intelligence. The fact that many children rise above the educational and socio-economic levels of their parents may be taken to mean that there is much hidden capacity and that it sometimes manifests itself even under relatively adverse environmental conditions. Such capacity can of course express itself best in a society where educational and socio-economic opportunities depend upon capability rather than wealth or social prestige.

While there is no doubt that both hereditary and environmental influences play a role in determining the relationship between a child's I.Q. and the educational and occupational level of its parents, the question still remains whether one of these influences might not play a major and the other only a minor role. There is evidence, for example, that hereditary contributions such as we have mentioned outweigh the environmental. Jones[18] says that "Special interest attaches to the fact that the social differential in intelligence is well established as early as two or three years, and relatively constant in later childhood. If due chiefly to environmental effects acting directly, one would expect it to be small at two years but to increase gradually with age." As further substantiation of this view, he mentions certain studies which demonstrated that children removed from their homes in early infancy, and brought up in institutions, still differed in terms of the socio-economic status of their parents. Anderson[19] also favors this hereditarian interpretation of the data we have been considering.

Rural-urban residence and the I.Q. Several studies have shown that a child's I.Q. is to some extent dependent upon where he has been brought up. Studies of children reared in isolated mountain communities have yielded significantly lower average I.Q.'s than are found for the general population.[20] Moreover, the I.Q.'s of such isolated children become lower as they get older. One reason for the low I.Q.'s is of course the lack of average schooling presupposed by test standardization. These children, whatever their native ability, have not had an opportunity to acquire the skills and information which the average child in a normal community has acquired. Their I.Q.'s become lower as higher age levels are approached because their poor environment does not handicap them as much with respect to the relatively simple test items as it does with respect to the increasingly linguistic and more complicated test items at the higher age levels. As one might expect, improved school conditions produce a marked rise in the I.Q.'s of these children. It is possible, however, that hereditary selective factors are also implicated. The hereditary capacity of people who drift to isolated communities, or who remain in such communities while others get out, may be below average. Those who favor this view would argue that, even if given the best possible education, and placed in the most intellectually stimulating homes, the average

I.Q. for these children, although it rose to some extent, would still remain below the general average. Until these isolated communities are given such opportunities it is of course impossible to do more than speculate as to the outcome. Whatever happened to the average I.Q., there is no doubt that much hidden talent would be discovered among such isolated people. Some of them have "risen above their environment" in a remarkable manner, despite all the handicaps which now exist. This of course suggests the existence of superior innate ability in such individuals.

The average I.Q. of rural children is below that of those reared in urban and suburban areas. This difference in I.Q. averages between 5 and 10 points, with larger differences at the upper age levels of childhood.[21] Again we are confronted by various possible explanations. One of these is that there may be a hereditary differentiation of the rural and urban. Another is that the urban environment, with its better schools and intercommunication, may be conducive to development of a higher level of intelligence. Still another possibility is that children in the urban environment may be more familiar with the typical test items than children in the country. It is impossible to determine how much each of these possible influences contributes to the difference in average I.Q. between urban and rural groups.

Studies of foster children. Foster children come mainly from two sources, unmarried parents and married parents who, for various reasons, are unable to keep their children. Generally speaking, the illegitimate foster children have a higher average I.Q. than the others.[22] The homes in which foster children are placed are usually better than average, and in the case of legitimate children, these homes are almost always better than those of their own parents. Likewise, the intelligence of people who become foster parents is usually above average. In many instances it is far above average. From the standpoint of heredity and environment, three problems relating to foster children are of especial interest. One involves the correlation of the I.Q.'s of children and parents when (1) children are living with their true parents and (2) when they are living with foster parents. A second problem is that of discovering whether residence in a foster home raises the I.Q. above its original level, or above the level to be expected in view of parental origins. A third problem concerns the relation between the child's I.Q. and the kind of home in which he lives.

Correlation data relevant to the first problem have been reported in three extensive studies, two of them involving control groups of children living with their true parents. Burks [23] followed up 214 children placed in foster homes at an average age of three months. She found that their eventual I.Q's correlated .20 with the M.A.'s of their foster parents. In the case of children living with their true parents, however, the corresponding correlation was .52. Similar results were found by Leahy [24] in a study of 194 adopted illegitimate children placed before the age of six months. The adopted children's I.Q.'s correlated .21 with the adopting parents' mental test performance. The control children, living with their true parents, yielded a corresponding correlation of .60. In another investigation by Skodak and Skeels,[25] correlation data were obtained for 100 foster children placed before the age of six months. No correlations between child I.Q.'s and foster parent I.Q.'s are reported, but comparisons carried out after ten years showed no correlation between the child's I.Q. and the foster parents' level of education. The correlation between the foster children's eventual I.Q.'s and those of their true mothers, however, was .44. With true mothers' educational level, the I.Q.'s yielded a correlation of .32. Thus these different studies, one in California, one in Minnesota, and the third in Iowa, all point in the same direction. They show that the child's intelligence is correlated significantly with that of real parents and negligibly with that of foster parents. This suggests that the relative standing of foster children is related more with the relative standing of their true parents than with the relative standing of their foster parents.

What does this relationship mean with respect to the genetic problem? The answer is complicated by the fact that the children living with their true parents have a heredity and an environment which are themselves correlated. The parent who contributes a superior heredity also tends to contribute a superior environment, and both factors together account for the correlations obtained. But since there is little or no correlation between the test performance of foster parents and that of the children to whom they contribute only an environment, it appears that heredity is playing a major role in determining the child-parent correlations. Some elaborate statistical computations have been carried out in an effort to disentangle the respective influences of heredity and environment in foster studies, but the outcomes are not in general agreement.* However, as much as 75 per cent of the relationship between the I.Q.'s of children and their true parents is sometimes attributed to heredity.[27]

The fact that children's I.Q.'s are correlated with those of their true parents more than with those of foster parents does not mean that environment plays a negligible part in determining the level of a child's I.Q. The correlations deal only with *relative* status, not with the general level attained. Foster homes could conceivably raise the I.Q.'s above the level they might have attained had the children been in institutions, or living with irresponsible parents who failed to provide them with a normal home life. This could occur without affecting the magnitude of the correlation between the children's I.Q.'s and those of their foster parents. Skodak and Skeels[28] have shown, for example, that the I.Q.'s attained by children in foster homes

* It has been suggested by some that foster homes and foster parents show a very small spread as compared with true homes and true parents and that this factor may lower the correlation between children's I.Q.'s and those of their foster parents.[26]

average significantly above those of the true mothers. The average foster child's I.Q. was approximately 20 points above the average I.Q. of the real mother. Interpretation of this finding is of course complicated by the fact that the I.Q.'s of the fathers are not known. It is possible, therefore, that some of this apparent rise in I.Q. is not a true rise at all. The father's I.Q. might be far higher than the mother's, and only after both parents were taken into account could one know what the I.Q. of the child might have been under other circumstances. The child's own I.Q. may be higher after placement than before, but this finding is also difficult to interpret. Tests at early age levels are, as we have seen, unreliable and negligibly correlated with I.Q.'s determined years later.

Our third problem relates to the effect upon the I.Q. of the type of home in which a child is placed. Several investigations summarized by Anastasi and Foley[29] have shown that the I.Q.'s of children placed in institutions average lower than those of children placed in foster homes, a finding attributed to the fact that the foster home children get more affection and more intellectual stimulation than children in institutions. A factor which vitiates such studies, however, is selective placement. Perhaps the child of relatively superior parents is more likely to be adopted or placed in a foster home than the child who does not have such an advantage. The former might well have a better innate potential than the latter. This selective influence, rather than the superiority of the foster home, might to some degree account for the higher I.Q.'s of foster children.

Several studies summarized by Jones[30] have shown that children in foster homes rated as poor, average, and good tend to differ in I.Q. depending upon the rating of the home. In one such study, the respective average I.Q.'s were 91, 103, and 111. However, as Jones and others have pointed out such data are practically worthless from the standpoint of discerning the respective influence of heredity and environment. The reason for this is that placement agencies usually try to place a child in a home which corresponds with, or is better than, the sort of home environment which he might have had with his true parents. Thus the educational and socio-economic level of the true parents tends to produce a selective placement which prejudices the outcome of studies purporting to show how the level of the foster home in which a child is placed can influence his I.Q. With placement on a selective basis the results could hardly do otherwise than show that I.Q.'s tend to be higher the higher the educational and socio-economic level of the foster home. This result is undoubtedly due to the fact that, in general, children with superior heredity also benefit more from a superior home environment. The data summarized by Jones also show that, whether they are in foster homes rated as good, average, or poor, children still differ in terms of their true parental origin. In each group, for example, the illegitimate children have higher I.Q.'s than the legitimate ones.

Nursery school attendance. Does nursery school attendance raise the I.Q.? If so, does that mean that the I.Q. is determined by environment, or by environment more than by heredity? Here again we have a highly controversial issue. The controversy concerns both the facts and the interpretation of them. Some studies have shown no effect of nursery school education upon the I.Q. and others have shown an average rise of 7 points after one year of nursery school and 10 points after two years.[31]

The studies showing positive results have been criticized from various angles. In the first place, there is the criticism that I.Q.'s determined early in life are subject to wide fluctuations and do not correlate significantly with later I.Q.'s. Thus the gain, where it exists, may be illusory. Perhaps the most important criticism leveled at such studies is that which emphasizes the close similarity between nursery school experiences and the contents of the tests given at early age levels. The nursery school in which the average I.Q.

shows an increase after one or two years attendance may be one in which there is close cooperation with adults, in which many test-like situations are prevalent (like threading beads, building with blocks, listening to stories, and so on), and in which there is some advance in linguistic skills. Children subjected to these influences may, in a sense, become "test-wise," somewhat like a child who has been coached. In any event, the tests were not standardized on nursery school children. They were standardized on children in average schools, irrespective of whether or not the children had been to nursery school. The nursery school children thus constitute a special group, and it would not be at all surprising were they to make higher scores on the tests than other children without such a background. Such a rise, unless maintained years later under average conditions, could be regarded as an artifact of the test rather than as representative of a true rise in intelligence. Follow-up studies of small groups of children who attended nursery school have not revealed any satisfactory evidence that they retained their initial advantage in I.Q.[32]

Our discussion of hereditary and environmental contributions to intelligence has pointed out some of the difficulties inherent in research on this problem. The chief difficulties are: (1) that human environments are beyond adequate experimental control; (2) that the tests themselves are measuring relative performance, rather than intelligence as such; (3) that test items are contaminated by the very features of the environment whose influence we try to measure with them; (4) that the paternal heredity of foster children on whom we attempt to discover the influence of environment is often an unknown factor; and (5) that children in superior educational and socio-economic environments may also be superior in heredity, hence offer us no basis for differentiating the respective effects of heredity and environment. Despite such difficulties, certain conclusions are obviously justified. One of these is that heredity and environment are inextricably involved in the development of intelligence. Another conclusion is that the child's *relative* standing with respect to test performance corresponds more closely with that of his true parents than with that of his foster parents, a fact suggesting the strong influence of heredity. Still another conclusion, which is not at variance with the preceding, is that a good foster home raises the *level* of performance above what it would have been in a poorer environment. This suggests that, although the child's level of innate capacity tends to hold him to his relative position with respect to other children in his group, who are experiencing comparable opportunities, all are raised above what they would have been without such opportunities.

Although we can do nothing about the heredity of children once they are conceived, we can do a great deal to improve their general level of intelligence, as represented by performance in school and in everyday life. As English [33] has said, "The growth of intelligence depends pre-eminently upon the acquisition of the verbal tools of problem solving" and "whatever may be the contribution of one's innate capacity, intelligence must be learned." We may or may not be able to change the individual's capacity to learn (it may be purely innate or also influenced by early learning), but we can certainly improve his opportunities to acquire those skills which are necessary for intelligent behavior. If children in good homes and in good schools have an I.Q. which is significantly higher than it would have been if they had lived in poor homes and had received poor schooling, this represents an important environmental contribution to intelligence, even though it may not have changed their relative standing with respect to each other — something which, under comparable conditions, is more dependent on heredity than on environment.

Our best evidence on mental growth comes from intelligence tests like those described. Developmental trends may be inferred from the nature of the items found suitable for testing at successive ages or, in the case of a test like the Wechsler Intelligence Scale for Children, from the scores made at successive age levels.

Mental Growth Curves

Data from which mental growth curves are derived may be longitudinal or cross-sectional. We may test the same child at different age levels or we may test groups of children representing a succession of age levels. As suggested earlier, however, the growth curve for a single individual may show fluctuations not evident in group data. The average variation in I.Q. from year to year is about five points in either direction. If longitudinally obtained data are averaged for many children, or if the cross-sectional approach is used, the variations in one direction are balanced by those in the other and a smooth curve results.

The level of mental test performance normally increases with chronological age, but the rate of increase and the maximum eventually reached depends upon the general level of intelligence. That is to say, a normal child's M.A. increases at the same rate as his C.A. until it reaches its maximum somewhere in the late teens or early twenties. The M.A. of a subnormal child, on the other hand, increases more slowly than his C.A. and his relatively low upper limit is approximated quite early. Note from Figure 118, for example, that an idiot reaches his maximum M.A. in the early teens, whereas normal and superior children of the same age are still far from achieving their maximum.

Although there are some exceptions, children who show evidence of mental precocity in early life tend to maintain this position relative to other children. As Terman and others [34] have shown, the child with a superior I.Q. is usually superior in college and later in his everyday activities. Children with very low I.Q.'s also tend to maintain this relative standing in school and in everyday life.[35]

Opinions differ as to the age at which test performance reaches its upper limit. The

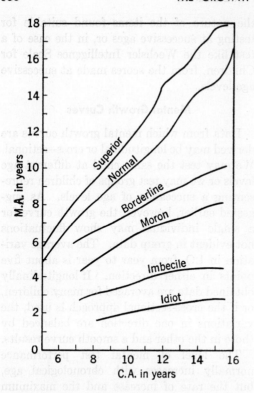

Figure 118.   Growth of Mental Age as a Function of Chronological Age and Maximum Level of Test Performance

The maximum I.Q. ranges would be approximately as follows: idiot, 0–25; imbecile, 25–50; moron, 50–70; borderline, 70–80; low normal (not represented), 80–90; normal, 90–110; superior, 110–120.   Children designated "very superior" have an I.Q. range of 120–140.   Those with 140 and over are usually designated "near genius."   A curve for these would start at M.A. 7 on the graph and would remain above the level of the "superior" curve.   (From F. D. Brooks, *The Psychology of Adolescence*, Boston: Houghton Mifflin, 1929.)

Stanford-Binet test, as we saw earlier, reveals no significant improvement beyond the age of 15 years.   Thorndike's [36] data, based upon group tests of intelligence, suggest that the upper limit is not reached until the age of from 18 to 20 years.   Using another group test, Miles and Miles [37] found that scores increased until the 18th year.   A study by Odom [38] demonstrated that scores were still increasing at the seventeenth year.   Wechs-

ler [39] found that scores on his adult test reached their maximum at about 20 years.

There is also lack of agreement concerning the *rate* at which intelligence scores increase with age before the upper limit is reached. According to Terman and Merrill [40] there is an approximately linear relationship between mental and chronological age from the second until around the thirteenth year. The mental growth curves presented in most textbooks exhibit a similar relationship.   They show, in other words, that for each increment in chronological age prior to the teens there is a rather uniform increase in mental age or in scores.   Thurstone [41] has pointed out, however, that such curves are inadequate, and for two reasons.   In the first place, we lack a satisfactory unit of growth.   An increase in mental age from three to four years and an increase from nine to ten years may not represent equal increments of *true* mental growth. Observe, for example, the different tests at the three- and nine-year levels in the Stanford-Binet.   Since the items at each level are so different, it is doubtful whether the mental age units between, say, three and four and nine and ten could be equal.   Thus one is not justified in representing mental age as a function of chronological age unless, like the units of chronological age, the successive mental units represent equal increments.   As we have seen, the data from which mental growth curves are plotted represent *average mental age* or *average scores* for each increment in chronological age.   Unless the groups from which the averages are derived are uniformly selected, another error is introduced.   Thurstone points out, in the second place, that zero intelligence is not represented in the usual curves of mental growth.   These curves begin with the age at which the tests are first given.

Thurstone believes that the first difficulty is overcome by plotting *absolute mean test performance*,* instead of mental-age or raw

* The details of this determination cannot be presented here.   The reader is referred to Thurstone [42] for detailed information concerning the determination of absolute mean test performance.

scores, against chronological age. The curve is drawn with the average test performance of the youngest tested age group as an arbitrary origin.

Determination of a statistical absolute zero is made possible when there is a uniform selection of individuals at each age level. With uniform selection of individuals at each level there is a linear relation between the standard deviation and the absolute mean test performance for the various age groups. The straight line fitted to those data is extended downward until it intercepts the base line (representing absolute mean test performance). The point of interception is taken to be *absolute zero*. As Thurstone [43] points out, "The absolute variability of test performance must be zero when the mean test performance is absolute zero because, in the nature of the case, variability cannot be negative." He says, furthermore, "The validity of the determination of absolute zero is subjected to a practical test by determining the age at which the mental growth curve passes through absolute zero. It is found that this happens at birth or shortly before." *

Using the above-mentioned method of determining theoretically equal scale units and of calculating absolute zero, Thurstone plotted mental growth curves for the data of various individual tests. The curves differed for different tests. Most of them approximated straight lines. Odom [44] used Thurstone's method in plotting mental growth curves for data from group tests. He found that most of the curves were negatively accelerated. Some curves, however, had a slight positive acceleration. Occasionally the curve approximated a straight line.

Using Stanford-Binet scores for 4208 individuals selected in an approximately uniform way at each age level, Thurstone and Ackerson [45] have presented what, in their opinion, is a representative curve of mental growth. Absolute scaling was used and zero test intelligence was calculated. The curve is shown in Figure 119. This curve is positively accelerated at earlier ages. Such a trend is contrary to that usually reported. This curve is believed to be more representative than other mental growth curves for two reasons. In the first place, it is based upon an unusually large number of cases uniformly selected at each age level. In the second place, its shape is similar to that of curves most often reported for biological functions. It is thus assumed to be more representative of the growth of intelligence as a biological phenomenon than curves most commonly reported.

For a further discussion of mental growth curves, the reader should consult Goodenough,[46] who expresses doubt concerning a generally acceptable growth curve but whose presentation includes an interesting exercise designed to illustrate the view that "one-half of an individual's ultimate mental stature has been attained by the age of 3 years."

Biological Bases of Mental Growth

Although it is generally conceded that the growth of intelligence (the innate potential aspect) is related to physical development, psychologists have achieved little success in discovering its fundamental biological concomitants. The problem has been approached in three general ways. (1) Intelligence, anatomical status, and physiological functions have been measured in large numbers of individuals at successive age levels, each individual being measured only once. (2) Measurements comparable with the above have been made on the same individuals at successive age levels. (3) Anatomical and physiological characteristics have been measured in groups representing widely separated levels of intelligence, such as the feebleminded, the normal and the superior.

The first two methods have yielded somewhat comparable results. They have shown that as individuals increase in age their

* This is especially interesting in the light of the fact that zero intelligence is sometimes assumed to exist in the fetus prior to achievement of motility. Of course, initial intelligence would be non-symbolic in nature. It might be similar to some early stage of phylogenetic intelligence.

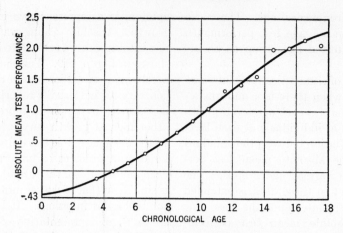

Figure 119. A Curve Representing the Growth of Stanford-Binet Test

Intelligence as a Function of Age

It will be observed that this curve is asymptotic to absolute zero and to the level of maturity.   There is an inflection point between ten and twelve years.   Thus the growth of
intelligence in terms of absolute mean test performance is positively accelerated up to
about eleven years and then negatively accelerated.   The level of maturity is not indicated
and could not be determined with the data available.   The individuals represented have
an average test score somewhat below normal.   However, this would not affect the shape
of the curve.   (From L. L. Thurstone and L. Ackerson, " The Mental Growth Curve for the
Binet Tests," *J. Educ. Psychol.*, 1929, *20*, 576.)

height, weight, skeleton, teeth, and brain exhibit development which to a certain extent
parallels the growth of test intelligence.
Physiological factors like blood pressure,
pulse rate, and vital capacity also show
changes correlated with chronological and
mental age.   When the influence of chronological age is ruled out,[*] however, such correlations become insignificant.[**]   Hence correlations between physical measurements and
mental test scores are due to the mutual
dependence of these factors upon chronological age.

Investigations in which the third method
has been used have shown, in general, that
gifted children (I.Q. 140 and over) are, as a
group, slightly superior to average children
in such traits as height, weight, breathing
capacity, and strength of grip.[49]   Within the

gifted group as in the average, however, there
are wide individual differences.   One could
not tell, upon the basis of physical measurements alone, whether a given child was gifted
or average.   Comparison of feebleminded and
normal groups shows, in general, that children who are subnormal in intelligence tend
also to be subnormal in physical development.[50]   Again, however, there are wide individual differences on each level, and physical development cannot in itself serve to indicate the intelligence of given individuals.

Paterson,[51] after summarizing the available
quantitative data on the correlation between
intelligence and physique, said that

prevalent notions regarding the intimacy of the relationship between physical traits and intellect have
been greatly exaggerated.   Search in the realm of
gross anatomy for a physical correlate of intellect
has yielded uniformly negative results.   It appears
that such structural characteristics as height and
weight are correlated only slightly with intelligence, narrowly defined.   Even measurements of

* Chronological age may be ruled out in two ways:
(1) by partial correlation and (2) by correlating physical status and intelligence on a *given* age level.

** This statement is based upon data reported by
Johnson [47] and Paterson.[48]

head size and shape are found to be relatively independently variable with respect to intellect, and skeletal development measured by precise X-ray photography yields either zero or low correlations with intelligence. The same may be said of dentition. Physiological development, measured in terms of pubescence, is found to be relatively unrelated to mental development and so are complicated morphological indices of body build.

The evolution of intelligent behavior in animals is, as we observed in Chapter 4, closely correlated with progressive changes in the central nervous system. Symbolic processes were found to depend upon cortical development. It is reasonable to suppose, therefore, that the development of intelligence in the individual is similarly related to neural growth. We have already intimated, however, that increases in skull capacity, as indicated by changes in the size of the head are not related in a causal manner to the growth of intelligence. Bühler [52] presents a curve, based upon data from Boyd, which indicates that the weight of the brain increases very rapidly during the years when intelligence is increasing. (See, also, the neural growth curve which appears in Figure 141.) Brain weight is more than doubled during the first year. By the third year it has trebled. At the nineteenth year the brain is approximately four times its birth weight. As in the case of gross physical characteristics, however, the increasing brain weight is a function of chronological age. When the chronological age factor is eliminated by comparing individuals at a given age level, it is doubtful whether brain weight will yield a very high correlation with intelligence scores. The average brain weight of females, for example, is lower than that of males, yet their intelligence is by no means inferior. Lapicque [53] believes that the ratio of brain weight to body weight is, both phylogenetically and ontogenetically, a significant correlate of intelligence. However, it is difficult to get adequate measures of brain weight in human beings.

The most significant correlate of intelligence may reside in the finer anatomy or in the physico-chemical constitution of the brain rather than in its mere size and weight. During the time that mental age is increasing, many subtle changes are taking place in the cerebrum. Pathways are myelinating, nerve-fibers are growing out to make new connections, and changes in the excitability of neurons are perhaps taking place. Paterson [54] says, "There is every reason to believe that improved methods of studying the functional relationship between nervous system and behavior will disclose the long-sought-for physical basis of intellect."

We observed in an earlier discussion (pp. 35–42) that an organism's physical growth is dependent upon heredity and environment, the two factors being integrally related. What is true of physical growth must be true of psychological, for although we have not discovered any precise biological correlates of higher levels of intelligence, such correlates undoubtedly exist, and the growth of intelligence must be concomitant with their growth, however produced.

Summary and Conclusions

Tests devised to measure infant intelligence are composed primarily of sensorimotor items and they fail to show any significant correlation with intelligence as measured with later tests, which have a high symbolic content. The most widely used intelligence tests for children are the Stanford-Binet and the Wechsler. These are designed to measure such symbolic processes as recall, imagination, concept formation, reasoning, and linguistic versatility. The Stanford-Binet test, which begins at two years, has some performance items, but it becomes completely verbal at the upper age levels. The Wechsler test, which begins at age five, includes performance and verbal items at each age level, but even the performance tests are such as to call for use of symbolic processes. I.Q.'s are determined with both tests, although the Wechsler uses standard scores instead of M.A.'s.

Intelligence has been considered from the

standpoint of versatility rather than of capacity as such. The capacity to develop the skills required for intelligent performance is undoubtedly dependent upon heredity, although this may be supplemented by an acquired capacity comparable with "learning how to learn." However, the skills are themselves undoubtedly learned, hence dependent upon environmental opportunities.

Since human intelligence depends upon the innate capacity to acquire symbolic skills, it is dependent upon both heredity and environment. When heredity is constant, as in identical twins, any differences in I.Q. are clearly attributable to environmental influences. But we cannot, except in animals like the rat, hold environment constant. And since objectively comparable environments are not comparable psychologically, it is impossible to say how much human beings would differ if their environments were constant. For this reason we are unable, with any degree of assurance, to say how much of a difference in I.Q.'s is dependent upon inherent factors and how much upon environment.

That there is an "inherent potential" or an "inherited capacity" to develop intelligence is no longer disputed. Evidence for such comes from the similarity of the I.Q.'s of identical twins, even when reared in different environments; from the fact that the I.Q.'s of foster children correlate more highly with those of their true parents than with those of their foster parents; and from the finding that children in institutional environments since early infancy show differences in I.Q. which correspond with the socio-economic levels of their parents, which levels are presumably dependent upon hereditary as well as environmental factors. The fact that objectively similar home and school environments produce I.Q. diversity rather than uniformity again suggests that differences in I.Q. are, at least in part, influenced by heredity.

Although hereditary differences undoubtedly play a role in producing differences in I.Q., the verbal and other skills which underlie

these differences are learned, hence dependent upon environmental opportunities. No matter what a child's innate potential might be, this could express itself only through what he learns. Nevertheless we cannot, in any particular instance, say how much the learned performance is dependent upon potential and how much on opportunity. The studies of foster children have suggested that, while the rank differences within a foster group do not change sufficiently to eliminate the correlation of the children's I.Q.'s with those of their true parents, the whole level of I.Q.'s may be raised, perhaps as much as 10 to 20 points, by the superior environments. However, this and related outcomes of research on environmental influences are subject to various interpretations. Children in foster homes have higher I.Q.'s than those in institutions, but this could, in part at least, be an outcome of selective placement. Children placed in foster homes from an early age have a significantly higher I.Q. than their true mothers. But this finding is difficult to interpret because of the fact that the I.Q.'s of the true fathers are not known. If the fathers were inherently brighter than the mothers, the expected average I.Q. of illegitimate foster children would be greater than that of their mothers, irrespective of the fact that their foster home environment may be better than they would have had if they had lived with their mothers.

Children reared in isolated communities have lower average I.Q.'s than children reared under average conditions. Here again, however, one cannot assess the degree to which this effect is environmental. It is possible that people living in isolated communities are, by and large, innately below average. The differences associated with rural-urban comparisons, educational level of parents, and socio-economic status are also vitiated by the fact that hereditary as well as environmental factors are so interwoven that one cannot assess their respective contributions.

Even when a child's I.Q. is obtained early in life and found to be higher after subjection to a superior environment, one is confronted with the unreliability of I.Q's derived at early age levels. We find that some nursery schools raise the child's I.Q. Here again one cannot be sure that the rise is to be attributed to the nursery school environment. It might have risen through greater than normal experience with the sorts of things involved in the tests, and it might not be permanent.

Thus, at every turn, our attempt to assess the respective contributions of heredity and environment is confused by such defects of scientific procedure as inability to hold human environments constant, the joint variation of heredity and environment in the populations studied, and the contamination of intelligence tests by environmental factors whose influence we wish to discover.

Nobody doubts that a superior environment is advantageous, and that children should be given the best possible homes and schooling, but there is as yet no satisfactory basis for predicting how much a child's intelligence will be increased as a result. There is every reason to suppose that those with superior heredity will make the most of such opportunities whereas those with inferior

heredity will be little affected by them. One should remember, however, that it is the environment which actualizes the hereditary potential and that the best possible environment should be provided if for no other reason than to reveal what might otherwise be a hidden capacity.

We have indicated some difficulties involved in the derivation of mental growth curves. The upper level of symbolic ability, as measured by intelligence tests, is reached somewhere within the late teens and early twenties. However, the shape of the mental growth curve prior to the point representing attainment of maximum ability depends upon the nature of the test and upon the method of plotting the curve.

Correlations between development of test performance and various aspects of physical growth become insignificant when the factor of chronological age is ruled out. The significant physical correlate of the growth of intelligence must, therefore, be some more subtle aspect of neural growth than has yet been measured. This correlate must reside in the finer anatomy or in the physico-chemical constitution of the brain.

REFERENCES

1. Edwards, A. S., "Intelligence as Capacity for Variability or Versatility of Response," *Psych. Rev.*, 1928, *35*, 198–210.
2. Gilliland, A. R., *The Northwestern Intelligence Tests*. Boston: Houghton Mifflin, 1949.
3. Bühler, C., and H. Hetzer, *Testing Children's Intelligence from Birth to School Age*. New York: Farrar and Rinehart, 1935.
4. Bayley, N., "Mental Growth During the First Three Years," *Genet. Psychol. Monog.*, 1933, *14*, No. 1.
5. Cattell, P., *The Measurement of Intelligence of Infants and Young Children*. New York: The Psychological Corporation, 1940.
6. Gesell, A., and C. S. Amatruda, *Developmental Diagnosis*. New York: Hoeber, 1941.
7. See the data summarized by F. L. Good-

enough, in L. Carmichael (ed.), *Manual of Child Psychology* (2d ed.), 1954, pp. 479–481.
8. Bayley, N., "Consistency and Variability in the Growth of Intelligence from Birth to Eighteen Years," *J. Genet. Psychol.*, 1949, *75*, 165–196.
9. Terman, L. M., and M. Merrill, *Measuring Intelligence*. Boston: Houghton Mifflin, 1937.
10. McNemar, Q., *The Revision of the Stanford-Binet Scale*. Boston: Houghton Mifflin, 1942.
11. Wechsler, D., *The Wechsler Intelligence Scale for Children*. New York: Psychological Corporation, 1949.
12. Bayley, N., *op. cit.*, p. 193.
13. Goodenough, F. L., *Developmental Psychology* (2d ed.). New York: Appleton-Century, 1945, p. 375.

14. Newman, H. H., F. N. Freeman, and K. J. Holzinger, *Twins: A Study of Heredity and Environment.* Chicago: University of Chicago Press, 1937. See also Woodworth, R. S., *Heredity and Environment,* New York: Social Research Council, 1941.

15. Hebb, D. O., *Organization of Behavior.* New York: Wiley, 1949. Quotations from p. 294.

16. Van Alstyne, D., "The Environment of Three-Year-Old Children: Factors Related to Intelligence and Vocabulary Tests," *Teach. Coll. Contrib. Educ.,* 1929, No. 366.

17. McNemar, Q., *op. cit.,* p. 38. See also W. S. Neff, "Socioeconomic Status and Intelligence: A Critical Survey," *Psych. Bull.,* 1938, *35,* 727–757.

18. Jones, H. E., "The Environment and Mental Development," in L. Carmichael (ed.), *Manual of Child Psychology* (2d ed.). New York: Wiley, 1954, p. 648.

19. Anderson, J. E., *The Psychology of Development and Personal Adjustment.* New York: Holt, 1949, p. 215.

20. Wheeler, L. R., "The Intelligence of East Tennessee Mountain Children," *J. Educ. Psychol.,* 1932, *23,* 351–370; M. Sherman, and C. B. Key, "The Intelligence of Isolated Mountain Children," *Child Development,* 1932, *3,* 279–290; M. Sherman and T. R. Henry, *The Hollow Folk,* New York: Crowell, 1933; A. S. Edwards, and L. Jones, "An Experimental and Field Study of North Georgia Mountaineers," *J. Soc. Psychol.,* 1938, *9,* 317–333.

21. Jones, H. E., H. S. Conrad, and M. B. Blanchard, "Environmental Handicap in Mental Test Performance," *Univ. Calif. Publ. Psychol.,* 1932, *5,* 80–83; Q. McNemar, *op. cit.,* p. 37.

22. Citation 18, p. 685.

23. Burks, B. S., "The Relative Influence of Nature and Nurture Upon Mental Development: A Comparative Study of Foster Parent-Foster Child Resemblance and True Parent-Child Resemblance," *27th Yearbook Nat. Soc. Stud. Educ.,* 1928, Part I, 219–316. Abbreviated in Barker *et al., Child Behavior and Development.* New York: McGraw-Hill, 1943, pp. 245–257.

24. Leahy, A. M., "Nature-Nurture and Intelligence," *Genet. Psychol. Monog.,* 1935, *17,* 235–308.

25. Skodak, M., and H. M. Skeels, "A Final Follow-Up Study of One Hundred Adopted Children," *J. Genet. Psychol.,* 1949, *75,* 85–125.

26. Anastasi, A., and J. P. Foley, *Differential Psychology* (rev. ed.). New York: Macmillan, 1949, p. 345.

27. Burks, B. S., "On the Relative Contributions of Nature and Nurture to Average Group Differences in Intelligence," *Proc. Nat. Acad. Sci.,* 1938, *24,* 276–282. See also citation 23, Barker *et al.,* p. 256.

28. Skodak and Skeels, *op. cit.,* p. 110.

29. Anastasi and Foley, *op. cit.,* pp. 362–367.

30. Jones, H. E. See citation 18, p. 685.

31. Wellman, B. L., "IQ Changes of Preschool and Non-Preschool Groups During the Preschool Years: A Summary of the Literature," *J. Psychol.,* 1945, *20,* 347–368; "Iowa Studies on the Effects of Schooling," *Thirty-Ninth Yearbook Nat. Soc. Stud. Educ.,* 1940, Vol. II, 377–399.

32. Anastasi and Foley, *op. cit.,* pp. 228–229.

33. English, H. B., *Child Psychology.* New York: Holt, 1951, pp. 310, 313.

34. Terman, L. M., and M. H. Oden, *The Gifted Child Grows Up.* Stanford University Press, 1947.

35. Minogue, B. M., "The Constancy of the IQ of Mental Defectives," *Mental Hygiene,* 1926, *10,* 751–758. On the later adjustment of people judged feebleminded in childhood, see D. C. Charles, "Ability and Accomplishment of Persons Earlier Judged Mentally Deficient," *Genet. Psychol. Monog.,* 1953, *47,* 3–71.

36. Thorndike, E. L., *The Measurement of Intelligence.* New York: Teachers College, 1926.

37. Miles, W. R., and C. C. Miles, "The Correlation of Intelligence Scores and Chronological Age from Early to Late Maturity," *Am. J. Psychol.,* 1932, *44,* 44–78.

38. Odom, C. L., "A Study of the Mental Growth Curve, with Special Reference to the Results of Group Intelligence Tests," *J. Educ. Psychol.,* 1929, *20,* 401–416.

39. Wechsler, D., *The Measurement of Adult Intelligence* (3d ed.). Baltimore: Williams and Wilkins, 1944.

40. Terman, L. M., and M. Merrill, *Measuring Intelligence.* Boston: Houghton Mifflin, 1937.

41. Thurstone, L. L., "Absolute Zero in Intelligence," *Psych. Rev.,* 1928, *35,* 175–179.

42. Thurstone, L. L., "A Method of Scaling Psychological and Educational Tests," *J. Educ. Psychol.,* 1925, *16,* 433–451.

43. *Ibid.*, pp. 196–197.

44. See citation 38.

45. Thurstone, L. L., and L. Ackerson, "The Mental Growth Curve for the Binet Tests," *J. Educ. Psychol.*, 1929, *20*, 569–583.

46. Goodenough, F. L., in L. Carmichael (ed.), *Manual of Child Psychology* (2d ed.). New York: Wiley, 1954, p. 479.

47. Johnson, B., *Child Psychology.* Baltimore: Thomas, 1932.

48. Paterson, D. G., *Physique and Intellect.* New York: Appleton-Century, 1930.

49. See L. M. Terman and B. S. Burks, "The Gifted Child," in C. Murchison (ed.), *Handbook of Child Psychology* (2d ed.) Worcester: Clark University Press, 1933, pp. 777–778. Also P. L. Boynton, *Intelligence.* New York: Appleton, 1933, pp. 117–126.

50. See R. Pintner, "The Feebleminded Child," in Murchison, *op. cit.*, pp. 315–316.

51. Paterson, *op. cit.*, p. 269.

52. Bühler, C., *The First Year of Life.* New York: Day, 1930.

53. Lapicque, L., "Le Poids du Cerveau et l'Intelligence," *J. de Psychol.*, 1922, *19*, 5–23.

54. Paterson, *op. cit.*, p. 269.

SUGGESTIONS FOR FURTHER READING

Anastasi, A., *Psychological Testing.* New York: Macmillan, 1954, Part II.

Anastasi, A., and J. P. Foley, *Differential Psychology.* New York: Macmillan, 1949, Chapter 11.

Anderson, J. E., *The Psychology of Development and Adjustment.* New York: Holt, 1949, Chapter 9.

Barker, R. G., J. S. Kounin, and H. F. Wright, *Child Behavior and Development.* New York: McGraw-Hill, 1943, Chapters VI (Nancy Bayley), IX (Freeman and Flory), X (Terman and Merrill), XIV (Wellman), XV (Burks), XVI (Skodak), and XVII (Terman).

Carmichael, L. (ed.), *Manual of Child Psychology* (2d ed.), New York: Wiley, 1954. See Chapters 8 (Goodenough), 10 (Jones), 16 (Miles), and 18 (Benda).

Dennis, W., *Readings in Child Psychology.* New York: Prentice-Hall, 1951, Chapter IV (readings from Goodenough, Honzik, Sherman and Key, Woodworth, Burks and Tolman, and Terman).

Goodenough, F. L., *Developmental Psychology* (2d ed). New York: Appleton-Century-Crofts, 1945, Chapter 15.

Goodenough, F. L., *Mental Testing.* New York: Rinehart, 1949.

Goodenough, F. L., and K. M. Maurer, *The Mental Growth of Children from Two to Fourteen Years.* Minneapolis: University of Minnesota Press, 1942.

Hartley, E. L., H. G. Birch, and R. E. Hartley,

Outside Readings in Psychology. New York: Crowell, 1950, Chapter XII (readings from Garrett, Klineberg, Axline, Kornhauser, Roberts, and Witty and Jenkins).

Kuhlen, R. G., and G. G. Thompson, *Psychological Studies in Human Development.* New York: Appleton-Century-Crofts, 1952, Chapters V and VI (readings from Honzik, Macfarlane, and Allen; Skodak and Skeels; Jones and Conrad; Garrett; Baller; Terman and Oden; and Bingham).

Newman, H. H., F. N. Freeman, and K. J. Holzinger, *Twins: A Study of Heredity and Environment.* Chicago: University of Chicago Press, 1937.

Paterson, D. G., *Physique and Intellect.* New York: Appleton-Century, 1930.

Schwesinger, G. C., *Heredity and Environment.* New York: Macmillan, 1933.

Stoddard, G. D., *The Meaning of Intelligence.* New York: Macmillan, 1943.

Thompson, G. G., *Child Psychology.* Boston: Houghton Mifflin, 1952, Chapter 10.

Valentine, W. L., and D. D. Wickens, *Experimental Foundations of General Psychology* (3d ed.). New York: Rinehart, 1949, Chapters VII and VIII.

Woodworth, R. S., *Heredity and Environment: A Critical Survey of Recently Published Material on Twins and Foster Children.* New York: Social Research Council, 1941.

14

Emotional Development

THE aim of this chapter is to offer an account of emotional behavior and how it develops. Some of the questions which we attempt to answer are: Does the newborn infant exhibit emotional behavior? What are the chief characteristics of early emotional responses? What is the role of maturation in emotional development? What part does learning play? What is the significance of social stimulation? In what ways are emotional responses modified? How does the repertoire of emotional responses change with increasing age? In what ways do emotions motivate? When can it be said that emotional maturity has been attained? As we proceed it will become evident that emotional development involves an integration of sensory, motor, and symbolic activities such as those considered in earlier chapters.

It seems advisable, before discussing the development of emotional behavior, to pause and consider the general characteristics of emotion as we observe it in adults. We all understand the general meaning of the term "emotional behavior," yet a simple definition to which all psychologists would give assent is not readily obtainable. The Latin word *emovere*, from which the term "emotion" is derived, means "to agitate," to "stir," "to shake up," "to move." With this derivation and behavior generally designated as emo-

tional in mind, some psychologists have defined emotion as "a stirred-up state of the organism," as "a temporary disorganization of response," as "a state of agitation," or as "a condition of shock."

We speak of fear, rage, love, and joy as "emotions" because it is convenient to do so. In reality, such terms refer to types of behavior. Strictly speaking, we should use them only as adjectives or adverbs. We should, for example, speak not of joy, but of joyful behavior or of behaving joyfully.

In some forms of emotional behavior, such as marked fear or rage, agitation is quite apparent. There is clearly a widespread disturbance of normal functioning. The individual, as we are prone to say, "goes to pieces." This "going to pieces" is apparent in overt behavior (expressions or postures) and also, when we are able to measure them, in internal physiological activities. The work of Cannon[1] has shown that violent emotional behavior involves marked physiological disturbances, some of which have an emergency function, as in preparing the organism for action. The sympathetic and parasympathetic nervous functions are thrown out of balance, adrenin is discharged into the blood stream, and various other physiological changes are thereby produced. These include increased respiratory activity, a more rapid heartbeat, heightened blood pressure, raising of the blood sugar level, cessation of gastric activity, and intestinal changes. This marked and diffuse disturbance of normal functioning is not, however, confined to overt and visceral responses. Emotional behavior has its symbolic components. These may be overt, as in swearing, calling names, and pleading, or they may be implicit. The individual undergoing the emotional disturbance may report, for instance, that he *experiences* agitation, shock, and so forth.

On the other hand, much emotional behavior like parental affection, sympathy, courage, self-respect, pride, aesthetic appreciation, and relief does not exhibit obvious "stirred-up" or "disintegrated" aspects. Postural and physiological changes may be present, to be sure, but these do not show the marked divergences from normal functioning which characterize such behavior as, for example, fear and rage. The individual's verbal responses also indicate that he feels no disintegration.

In some types of emotional behavior the postural and physiological concomitants are so abbreviated that our *only* evidence of emotion is the subject's report. Such abbreviation of activities is particularly characteristic of certain types of emotional behavior, but it may be present in any emotional responses of low intensity.

As Leeper [2] has pointed out, there is a tendency to attribute exaggerated importance to the more violent emotions and thus to the concept of emotional disintegration. As we grow older, these more violent emotional reactions occur only in crises. The milder emotions, however, provide an ever-present motivational undercurrent to all of our behavior, an undercurrent of which the individual himself may not be aware. These emotions have not received much emphasis in experimental and developmental studies of emotion, but this is only because their nature makes them difficult to observe.

Particular kinds of behavioral change which, in general, are classified as emotional have symbolic components which enable the individual who has acquired appropriate verbal and gestural responses to communicate something concerning their nature. He not only says that he is experiencing "an emotion," but he labels and, to a certain degree, describes his emotional experiences.

Gestures, including postures and facial expressions, communicate meaning to others and enable them not only to observe that the behavior is emotional but also to label it as fear, rage, or love. We thus have a language of emotional expression. Numerous experiments have shown that this gestural language of emotion has definite limitations.* When an observer is aware of the stimuli producing the altered expressions, his ability to label the particular emotional behavior as fear, rage, and so on is greatly enhanced. Sometimes the mere observation of a situation in which the individual is placed and of his resulting expressions is sufficient to arouse a somewhat similar emotional reaction in the observer. Later we shall note that individuals sometimes acquire emotional responses to given objects and situations in this way.

The precise changes in the internal and external responses of a person experiencing and expressing fear, for instance, may differ from moment to moment and from one situation to another. They may differ from individual to individual, even under the same external circumstances. Despite these differences, however, we name the various responses as *fear*. This is because all the situations which produce fear responses and all the responses involved in fear behavior of one kind or another possess certain common properties. All the situations, despite their variety, are such as to threaten the normal course of existence. Moreover, all the types of overt behavior labeled *fear*, although they are quite diverse at times, possess the common characteristics of avoidance, flight, or the like.

* See Ruckmick [3] for a discussion of the accuracy with which various emotional expressions may be labeled by experienced observers. We shall discuss later the accuracy with which observers of various ages interpret these expressions.

Also, they may have certain common internal characteristics, physiological and symbolic. Psychologists have had, as yet, little success in determining whether or not such common properties exist.*

What we have said concerning responses labeled collectively as *fear* is also true of the variety of responses labeled *rage* and *love*. It is apparent that the individual develops a *concept* of fear, of rage, or of love, and classifies under each of these terms many different types of implicit and overt activity.** This being the case, it is not difficult to see why psychologists fail to agree on a classification of emotional responses.***

Before concluding this discussion of the

* Cannon [4] failed to discover common physiological factors in different types of fear behavior which would differentiate it from rage and other violent emotional disturbances. Hunt [5] claims that the only common symbolic factor apparent in fear behavior of various kinds is the verbal report, "fear." He says: "In a series of twenty reports of 'fear,' the actual stimulus situation and the actual experimental materials present in consciousness may differ widely. The only constant factor comes in the issuing from these various causes of a common verbal report, 'fear.' This is simply saying that the individual's report is a conditioned verbal response that may be attached to varying and multiple factors, so that its appearance is no guarantee of a single constant stimulus."

** This point has been very aptly brought out by Hunt [6]. In attempting to ascertain the implicit *quale* of fear, for example, he asked his subjects to report their experiences. According to him, "when called on to introspect, the observer, on the basis of whatever raw experiential material may be present, performs an act of cognition (call it judgment, decision, comprehension, apprehension, as you will) the net result of which is the occurrence of an implicit verbal response. . . . The observer says to himself, 'I am afraid,' 'This is fearsome,' 'Fear is present,' 'Am I afraid? Yes!' This appearance of some implicit verbal response involving the concept 'fear' may then act as a stimulus to the overt verbal response 'fear.' Since the original experiential materials may be different, and the only common factor may be the implicit verbal materials aroused, is it not logical to identify the emotional *quale* with this implicit verbal response?"

*** Ruckmick [7] presents various classifications of emotional responses. The smallest number of differ-"emotions" mentioned in any classification is seven; the greatest number, over a hundred. Emotional responses are classified in terms of the situations which elicit them, the nature of overt responses, the reports of the individual experiencing them, and in terms of various rational criteria. Classifiers do not use exactly the same criteria.

general characteristics of emotional behavior, one more point needs to be mentioned. We have spoken as though emotional behavior were elicited only by external stimuli. It is common knowledge, however, that various internal processes may serve as the immediate "stimuli" for emotional responses. Chemical and neural changes, such as arouse hunger and pain may elicit emotional reactions. Furthermore, the individual may *think* of some past, present, or impending event and, as a result, be thrown into an emotional state. Even when external situations play the chief role in arousing emotional behavior, internal physiological and symbolic processes provide contributory "stimuli." One's physiological condition may determine whether or not a given situation is to elicit an emotional response. Moreover, we *interpret* the situation, and this interpretation is a symbolic factor in determining whether or not the aroused behavior will be emotional and, if so, its intensity and many of its precise characteristics.

The Question of Unlearned Emotional Reactions

It is generally conceded that at least some aspects of emotion are dependent on maturation rather than on learning. James,[8] in presenting his theory of emotional experience as the "feeling" of bodily changes elicited by emotion-provoking situations, assumed that these bodily changes are fundamentally instinctive. He also pointed out the difficulty of differentiating between instincts and emotions. "The only distinction one may draw," he said, "is that the reaction called emotional terminates in the subject's own body, while the reaction called instinctive is apt to go farther and enter into practical relations with the exciting object." McDougall [9] did not agree with James on all aspects of his theory, but he also regarded emotion as the "feeling" aspect of emotional experience. For each instinct listed by McDougall, there was alleged to be a corresponding emotional component.

Cannon's [10] theory differs from that of James in that it assigns the origin of bodily changes and affective experiences to activities of the hypothalamus. The hypothalamic theory assumes that the emotional experiences as well as the bodily changes are directly activated by hypothalamic functions. Emotional experiences are thus not assumed to be feelings of bodily changes such as James stressed.

There is much evidence for and against each of these theories, but this has been summarized elsewhere.[11] What is of especial interest to us here is the fact that the hypothalamic theory, like those of James and McDougall, also posits innate aspects of emotion. It assumes that some situations directly activate the hypothalamus in such a way as to arouse unlearned emotional responses. Masserman [12] has shown, in fact, that stimulation of the cat's hypothalamus with a needle electrode produces such responses as retraction of the ears, growling, back raising, and lashing of the tail.

One would infer from Cannon's theory that if emotional responses are present at birth, or if they develop later through the process of maturation, it is because of the existence at birth, or maturation after birth, of neural mechanisms within the hypothalamus. Likewise, any emotional responses found to depend wholly or in part upon conditioning could also be controlled through hypothalamic connections.* Cortical modifications based upon conditioning could elicit reactions to supplement, or even to some degree inhibit, those primarily dependent upon hypothalamic function. Cortical modification could also serve to control "voluntary" emotional expressions, that is, those affected by the individual.*

In general, the cortex exercises an inhibiting function on lower centers. Thus the anatomical or "functional" removal of the influence of the cortex (in brain operations or by alcohol) may release lower patterns which are otherwise masked or held in check.

Emotional Responses in Early Infancy

Before psychologists began to investigate the behavior of infants with scientific accuracy, it was assumed without question that man's many emotional responses are part of his "original nature." Watson and Morgan [16] were the first to question openly the existence of many different unlearned emotional responses or "emotions." They suggested that one go to the nursery, carefully observe the responses of infants to stimuli which produce emotional reactions in older children and adults, and determine how many of these reactions are really inborn. Various objects and situations which lead to emotional reactions in older children and adults were presented to large numbers of infants ranging in age from birth to a few months. Most of these stimuli were without effect. The results led Watson and Morgan to accept only three emotional responses as unlearned. They labeled these *fear*, *rage*, and *love*, but were careful to point out that, since the infants' emotional experiences were unknown, the responses might more appropriately be designated as reaction states *X*, *Y*, and *Z*. In other words, the investigators did not assume that experiences of fear, rage, and love underlay the observed responses.

The *fear* reaction, elicited by sudden loss of support and by a loud noise, was described as "... a sudden catching of the breath, clutching randomly with the hands (the grasping reflex invariably appearing when the child is

* Investigations by Culler and his collaborators [13] have demonstrated conditioning on a thalamic level in dogs deprived of the cortex or rendered functionally decorticate by means of curare. In the experiments with curare it was shown that conditioned responses (presumably dependent upon thalamic modification) disappeared when normal cortical function (cortical inhibition) was resumed. They reappeared upon further functional decortication. Such results may offer some indirect support to the thalamic theory.

* For other theoretical considerations on the ontogenesis of emotion, particularly from the standpoint of endocrinology and neurology, see Hebb [14] and Bousfield and Orbison.[15]

dropped), blinking of the eyelids, puckering of the lips, then crying." *Rage* behavior was exhibited when the infant's movements were hampered. The investigators said that

If the face or head is held crying results, quickly followed by screaming. The body stiffens and fairly well-coordinated slashing or striking movements of the hands and arms result; the feet and legs are drawn up and down; the breath is held until the child's face is flushed. In older children the slashing movements of the arms and legs are better coordinated and appear as kicking, slapping, biting, pushing, etc. These reactions continue until the irritating situation is removed, and sometimes do not cease then. Almost any child from birth can be thrown into a rage if its arms are held tightly to its sides: oftentimes even if the elbow joint is clamped tightly between the fingers the responses appear: at times just the placing of the head between cotton pads will produce them. Even the best-natured child will show rage if its nose is held for a few seconds.

What Watson and Morgan designated as a *love* response was elicited by stroking of the erogenous zones, tickling, shaking, gently rocking, patting, and turning the infant on its stomach across the knee. They found that "The response varies — if the infant is crying, crying ceases, a smile may begin, attempts at gurgling, cooing, and finally, in slightly older children, the extension of the arms which we should class as the forerunner of clasping in the narrowed sex act in coitus."

According to Watson [17] the complex emotional reactions of children and adults are acquired, these three responses providing an unlearned basis for such acquisition.* More recent research, however, has shown that Watson and Morgan were mistaken in positing the existence of even three emotional behavior patterns in the newborn. In attempting to verify the results of Watson and Morgan, investigators have uniformly met with failure.

* It appears strange that Watson and Morgan did not use needle-prick, electric shock, and the like to elicit emotional reactions. Although pain sensitivity is dull in newborn infants, sufficiently intense stimulation elicits withdrawal responses and crying, which observers interpret as emotional.

Sherman [18] failed to observe that loud noises and dropping universally elicited the responses reported by Watson and Morgan. Likewise, he found no evidence of a universal response to restriction of bodily activity or to stroking of the erogenous zones. Discussing these results in a later publication, Sherman and Sherman [19] say that

Any form of *sudden* stimulation such as dropping, loud noises, restraint, pain, or a rush of air on the face, produces in the young infant aimless activity of most of the musculature, accompanied by crying. The stimuli must be sufficiently strong, however, to produce a reaction. When an infant below four or five days of age is dropped one or two feet it frequently shows no perceptible response, except for vague movements of the arms and legs. The younger the infant the stronger must be the stimulus. This is also true for so-called "pleasurable" stimuli, such as stroking or petting, to which many newborn infants show no overt reaction.

As a result of these and similar observations, Sherman was led to investigate with what accuracy observers are able to name the "emotions" being expressed by infants subjected to various stimuli, including those used by Watson and Morgan. The observers were groups of graduate psychology students, medical students, and nurses. When they did not know the stimuli used, observers showed more disagreement than agreement concerning the interpretation of the infants' reactions. This was true whether the reactions were pictured on a film or whether they were observed directly, after removal of a screen behind which the stimulation had been given. Hunger reactions, for example, were labeled grief, discomfort, fear, anger, pain, colic, irritation, awakened from sleep, sleepiness, and hunger. These labels were attached indiscriminately, also to reactions elicited by dropping, by needle-pricks, and by bodily restraint. Even when the observers were given a list of the "emotions" supposedly involved (hunger, fear, rage, and pain) they were quite inaccurate in their judgments. Sherman [20] found, furthermore, that observers failed to agree when they heard crying elicited by the above-mentioned situations. The observers heard the crying, but did not know the nature of the situation eliciting it. When they could *see the stimulating circumstances* as well as hear the cry or see the reactions, the observers' judgments were in close agreement and conformed to those regarded as "correct" by Sherman. The Shermans [21] conclude, therefore, that

Most persons judge the emotional behavior of an individual in terms of the stimuli which have produced the reactions. They have learned the names of a number of emotions and have learned to evaluate various emotional responses in terms of the stimulating conditions which have aroused them. If the situation confronting an individual is estimated to be one which arouses an aggressive reaction, the resulting response is named "anger" but if it is considered dangerous to his welfare, the response will be called "fear." In this way the differentiation of emotions is based upon a knowledge of the character of the stimulating circumstances rather than upon differences in overt behavior.

Presumably Watson and Morgan, like Sherman's observers, classified the reactions of their infants as fear, rage, and love (or X, Y, and Z) in terms of the stimulating circumstances and their own experience rather than in terms of behavior as such. Unbiased witnesses would, according to Sherman, label the observed behavior in each situation as "aimless activity of most of the musculature." *

Irwin [23] also found that the fear reactions reported by Watson and Morgan are not typically elicited by loud noise or by dropping.

* Goodenough [22] takes exception to Sherman's experiment on the ground that the infants used by him were too young to have recovered from the shock of birth and were, for this reason, but slightly coordinated in their movements. Using still photographs of eight emotional expressions exhibited by an infant of ten months, she required 65 students to match each expression with a verbal description of an emotion-provoking situation. A choice of twelve situations was offered. The accuracy of matching was 47.4 per cent. This is almost six times greater than chance expectancy. These results are not, however, relevant to Watson and Morgan's experiment and Sherman's check on it. Watson and Morgan claimed that differential emotional reactions are present *at or soon after birth.*

The behavior observed by him is characterized as generalized or "mass" activity. This probably corresponds with Sherman's "aimless activity of most of the musculature," and Bridges' [24] "undifferentiated emotion of excitement." In Pratt, Nelson, and Sun's [25] investigation, restriction of bodily activity failed to arouse the "rage" reaction described by Watson and Morgan. More than half of the infants went to sleep. Very few of them continued their activity in response to the restraining situation.

Taylor [26] reports the results of an investigation which, in addition to offering a more thorough check upon Watson and Morgan's results than that of previous investigators, contributes a detailed description of infant responses to arm restraint, nose restraint, a sudden drop, and loud noises. There was, in this investigation, an attempt to duplicate Watson and Morgan's conditions as closely as possible. Taylor and another observer recorded the specific reactions of the infants. Forty normal infants ranging in age from one to twelve days were used. The stimuli were presented in the order indicated above. Questions specifically to be answered by this research were: Do the responses conform with those Watson and Morgan described? If they do not, what, if any, typical responses appear? Table 11 shows the frequency of various movements in response to the four stimulating conditions.

Examination of the data summarized in this table shows that marked differences in the nature of the responses to the various stimulating conditions were not exhibited. Statistical analysis disclosed no significant differences. Taylor concluded from these results that "it would be impossible to differentiate the responses instigated by the four stimuli as far as the percentage of segmental movements is concerned. He says furthermore that "any condition produces any and all responses." General observation, even with the inclusion of doubtful responses, still failed to verify the distinctions drawn by Watson and Morgan. Taylor says:

Table 11. The Number and Percentage of the Various Body Segment Responses Obtained for the Four Stimulus Conditions

	Stimuli											
	Arm Restraint				Nose Restraint				Drop		Noise	
	D. S.*		A. S.†		D. S.		A. S.					
	f	%	f	%	f	%	f	%	f	%	f	%
Arms..........	0	0	50	41.3	44	18.3	20	18.5	48	27.5	32	24.0
Legs...........	49	33.4	32	26.5	41	17.0	14	13.0	32	18.3	27	20.3
Trunk.........	29	19.7	10	8.3	54	22.4	18	16.7	19	10.8	22	16.6
Head..........	29	19.7	10	8.3	49	20.3	8	7.4	17	9.7	11	8.2
Facial..........	4	2.7	1	0.8	4	1.7	2	1.9	12	7.0	13	10.0
Vocal..........	11	7.5	7	5.7	20	8.3	23	21.3	19	10.8	8	6.0
Respiratory......	5	3.4	2	1.7	4	1.7	6	5.5	9	5.1	9	6.7
Sucking.........	20	13.6	9	7.4	25	10.3	17	15.7	19	10.8	11	8.2
Total	147	100.0	121	100.0	241	100.0	108	100.0	175	100.0	133	100.0

* D. S. = during stimulation. † A. S. = after stimulation.

Arm responses include all arm, hand, and finger movements. Leg responses include all leg, foot, and toe movements. Head movements include adduction, abduction, and rolling. Trunk movements are such movements as squirming, constricting, arching, shuddering, and the like. Because it is essentially a gross body response, and because the trunk is always involved, mass activity is classified as a trunk response. Facial responses include grimacing, eye blinking, eye opening and closing, mouth opening and closing, but not the lip movements made in sucking. Under vocal movements are found crying, sneezing, hiccoughing, and so forth. Respiratory movements, the most difficult to observe without mechanical assistance, are rough estimates of changes in thoracic and abdominal breathing. The sucking response was recorded when the tongue was placed between the lips and perceptible cheek movements were noted.

Because of the difference in stimulus conditions, responses under arm and nose restraint are divided into those occurring during stimulation (D.S.) and those occurring after stimulation (A.S.). The percentage of movement is computed by dividing the frequency of any segmental response by the total number of responses appearing under that type of stimulation. Referring to Table 11, it is shown that during arm restraint there were 147 movements recorded. Of these, forty-nine were leg movements. Hence, 33.4 per cent of all movements during arm restraint were leg movements.

It is clear that no matter how these data are treated they will fail to disclose any pattern response to the four stimulus conditions which were employed. This does not necessarily mean that there are no innate emotional responses. It does mean, however, that those conditions which Watson described do not initiate constant pattern responses in the infants used in this study; and since Watson's findings are considered basic to those who hold that emotional responses are innate, the entire theory is placed on the defensive.

Dennis [27] believes that those who attempted to repeat Watson's observations on the effect of restraint may not have used sufficiently intense and prolonged stimulation. His own motion picture records of restraint imposed upon a pair of twin infants (see pp. 194–197) show that about two-thirds of the responses accord with those described by Watson. These responses are not noticeably different, however, from those elicited by other intense non-restraining stimulation. Dennis also considers restraint from the standpoint of thwarting. That it does not always have this characteristic is shown by references to cultures where swaddling of infants is a general practice. According to Dennis,

The newborn and slightly older infant has no unique pattern of reaction to restraint. He reacts to all strong and persistent stimuli with restlessness and crying, a crude pattern of activity which is similar for all sorts of intense and enduring stimuli. The effective aspect of the stimulation employed by Watson, Sherman, Taylor, and ourselves was probably strong pressure or pain.

Clarke, Hunt, and Hunt[28] have analyzed slow-motion films of the responses to a revolver shot of 60 infants ranging in age from eight days to eighteen months. They failed to observe in all infants a fear response such as that described by Watson and Morgan. In very young infants the Moro reflex (Figure 120 A) appeared. This reaction has been regarded by some (see Pratt[29]) as a fear response. However, it is not universally accompanied by crying. Of 26 infants between birth and the third month, 10 failed to cry, 13 cried, and 3 varied crying responses which were present before the shot. There was a tendency for crying to increase in frequency with age.

Hunt, Clarke, and Hunt[30] found that at around the age of four months the Moro reflex begins to disappear and the "startle pattern" (Figure 120B) present in adults is simulated.* More recent work with a camera recording 700 to 1500 frames per second has enabled Landis and Hunt[32] to note that the startle pattern and the Moro reflex are both present in the youngest infants studied. They observed that the primary and apparently universal "startle pattern" appears and is then followed rapidly by the Moro reflex. The temporal succession of the responses is too short for unaided observation of the primary "startle pattern"; hence the Moro reflex masks the earlier response. Even the 64-frame speed of ordinary slow-motion photography (slowing the reaction one-fourth normal speed) is too slow to

* This pattern is described as follows: "Closing of the eyes, head movement, raising and bringing forward of the shoulders, abduction of the upper arms, bending of the elbows, pronation of the lower arms, clenching of the fists, forward movement of the trunk, contraction of the abdomen, and bending at the knees." Hunt, Landis, and Jacobsen[31] have found essentially the same response in monkeys and apes, some of which had brain lesions.

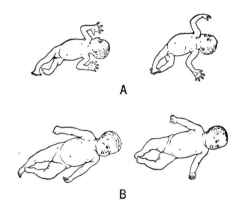

A

B

Figure 120. Moro Reflex and Startle Response Elicited by a Revolver Shot

A. Moro reflex in a very young infant. B. Startle response in an older infant. (Sketch of photographs from Hunt, Clarke, and Hunt.)

allow clear differentiation of the two responses. When, at around four months, the Moro reflex disappears, the "startle pattern" is clearly observed. The primary "startle pattern," which begins with an eye blink forty thousandths of a second after the shot and ends with movements of the lower extremities at from three-tenths of a second to one and a half seconds later, shows little change from the infant to the adult level. A few infants have failed to make the eye blink, whereas all adults manifest it. Infants exhibit a plantar reaction not present in older children and adults. In these respects the responses of infants correspond more closely with those of monkeys and chimpanzees than with those of adults. Hunt and Clarke[33] found that the amount of movement tends to be greater in children than in adults. Soon after the primary startle pattern appears, there is observed, in children and adults, a socialized, conventional, learned response which varies from individual to individual and changes with age. Hunt and Landis[34] suggest that the initial startle pattern is an unlearned reaction out of which all other emotional responses develop. They believe that it serves as "a basic indicator" of emotional response. Hunt and Landis would, apparently, substitute startle for the discredited "basic emotions" stressed by Watson and Morgan. Further research may determine whether startle is really basic to other emotional responses. There seems to be no doubt, however, that this response, in its fundamental aspects, is unlearned.

In summary, we may say that the "fear," "rage," and "love" responses described by Watson and Morgan do not appear in all or even in most young infants. The only unlearned response of emotional significance which appears in all normal infants as well as in all older children and adults is the "startle pattern." This pattern may eventually be found to underlie the "generalized response," the "mass activity," the "aimless activity of most of the musculature," and the "undifferentiated emotion of excitement" mentioned as primary by other investigators. At least it should, from the above discussion, be clear that very young infants fail to exhibit a variety of emotional responses recognizable to adults as such.

As the child becomes older he develops an increasing repertoire of emotional responses. Anger, fear, love, jealousy, delight, disgust, and joy are clearly evidenced. Furthermore, these responses come to be elicited by a wide range of objects and situations which were originally ineffective. The child may, for example, become afraid of darkness, of dogs, of snakes — objects and situations which at first failed to elicit emotional reactions. What factors underlie this emotional development? Some psychologists attribute a large influence to maturation, while others stress conditioning. We shall examine the data on maturation and then those on conditioning.

The Role of Maturation in Emotional Development

In considering the phylogenesis of unlearned behavior we observed that absence of a response at or soon after birth does not force us to the conclusion that its later appearance is due entirely to learning. Flying in birds,

copulation in rats, and accurate striking of grain in chicks are examples of activities which, while not present at birth, depend upon maturational processes for their development. It is quite possible that emotional reactions not present at birth also develop later as a result of maturation. The similarity of some emotional responses in man and infrahuman animals, a similarity stressed by Darwin, Spencer, and others, would support the view that, although these responses are absent at birth, their later appearance is due to maturation.

Discussions of the role of maturation in development of emotional behavior have dealt with two problems. One concerns the role of maturation in determining the nature of *emotional reaction patterns*. The other deals with the increasing *efficacy of various stimulating conditions* to arouse these responses as the child grows older.

Maturation of emotional reaction patterns

If the primary characteristics of emotional reaction patterns are due to maturation rather than to learning, they should appear in individuals deprived of the opportunity to learn them. Complete isolation of human individuals is out of the question. Probably the closest approximation to complete isolation from social stimulation, especially of the sort which might be important for learning of emotional responses, is to be found in those rare individuals who have been totally blind and totally deaf from birth. Such individuals could know of the emotional reactions of others only through actual contact. If no specific training in emotional expression were given, and yet emotional reactions developed as in normal individuals, one would be forced to conclude that social stimulation is not necessary for development of emotional behavior.

Goodenough [35] reports the only published observation of the emotional behavior of an individual totally blind and deaf from birth. She observed and took moving pictures of the emotional reactions of a ten-year-old girl who was thus afflicted. It had been found impossible to teach the child any form of language or even to teach her how to care for herself. She had, according to the mother, never been punished. The child was gentle and docile under ordinary circumstances. In order to observe her reactions to a situation involving frustration, Goodenough dropped a small doll down her neck.

The child's body, and especially the neck and shoulders, tensed and the mouth half-opened. The sightless eyes opened to their fullest extent and the eyebrows were raised. The left hand at once began to grope for the toy. Both the posture and the facial expression were suggestive of what we should ordinarily interpret as startled attention.* The child then began to search for the doll, but although she could feel it, the folds of her dress prevented withdrawal. The body tension relaxed; also the eye-muscles. The head was turned slightly to one side, the lips were somewhat parted. The expression was one of interest and attention but without the element of startled surprise. After several minutes of unsuccessful effort, she did not cry but made slight whimpering sounds. The head was dropped forward on her breast while the left hand picked at her nose — an unbeautiful but characteristic form of behavior when she was disappointed or displeased. Two minutes elapsed. Then, suddenly, as if struck by a new idea, she renewed the attack, this time from a different angle. Her behavior was very much more violent and took on the appearance of a struggle, determined in part by exasperation and mild rage. Her body writhed and twisted; the right hand impatiently beat the arm of the chair. When she got hold of the doll's head, its feet caught in her dress. At this her head was thrown back; the muscles of the neck and shoulders visibly tensed; the feet twisted about each other; and the retracted lips displayed clenched teeth. At the instant of success in extricating the doll she threw herself back into the chair with feet drawn up under her. Both the hand containing the doll and the empty hand were raised in an attitude of delight, which was further attested by peals of hearty laughter. The doll was clasped lovingly in both hands and she beat its head against her teeth

(a favorite method of securing vibratory stimulation). The exultant laughter faded to a smile of pleased satisfaction.

Goodenough also reports that this child danced although entirely untaught:

in an elaborate pattern of bows, whirls, bendings and posturings in which the head, arms, and entire body participate . . . ; the dance is clearly an expression of pleasure. It is usually accompanied by laughter and sometimes breaks up in wild peals of such violent laughter as to prevent her continuing. It may occur spontaneously when she is in good spirits, apparently as an expression of general *joie de vivre*, or it may sometimes be stimulated by giving her a bit of jelly or some other simple treat.

Marked thwarting produced temper tantrums. The child was also observed to express what would be interpreted as timidity, anger, and resentment. Goodenough [36] points out that the child's behavior corresponds very well with Darwin and Spencer's descriptions of emotional response in man and animals. She says:

This suggests that the primary forms of expressive behavior are determined by native factors. Although among persons with normal sensory equipment the original reaction patterns may become so overlaid with a veneer of socially accepted forms of behavior that it is difficult to distinguish the native from the acquired, nevertheless the essential similarity of many of the reactions of this child to those seen among normal children makes one willing to hazard a guess that the veneer is not so complete and not so impenetrable as many have supposed.

It is quite likely, in the light of evidence such as that presented by Goodenough, that the *primary overt characteristics* * of some emotional reactions are unlearned; that they have a phylogenetic origin as Darwin, James, McDougall, Cannon, and others have claimed. Experiments such as those of Landis and

* Speculation concerning the genesis of *experiential* aspects of these responses would be futile. Emotional experiences may, for all we know, have an unlearned *core*, as some have claimed. On the other hand, they may depend upon the acquisition of symbolic functions.

Hunt with slow-motion photography may eventually disclose, as in the case of startle, just what these primary overt characteristics are.

We have no clear evidence concerning the structures whose maturation underlies emergence of the unlearned aspects of emotional behavior. The James-Lange theory would stress maturation of visceral and postural mechanisms, while Cannon's thalamic theory would emphasize maturation of neural patterns within the hypothalamus. Emotional reactions related to the sex urge undoubtedly depend upon maturation of the gonads.

Changes in the efficacy of various stimulating conditions

If some emotional reactions are unlearned, what are the stimulating conditions which, prior to experience, serve to elicit them? One will recall that Watson and Morgan stressed sudden change for which the organism is unprepared (sudden loss of support and loud noise), thwarting of activity, and stroking of erogenous areas as the primary stimulating conditions for, respectively, fear, rage, and love.

Many specific objects and situations which fail to elicit emotional reactions in early infancy come to do so later. Watson and Morgan found that young infants are not afraid of darkness, of animals, of strangers, of grotesque masks, and the like. Watson has claimed that such objects and situations fail to elicit fear responses until the infant has been negatively conditioned with the primary stimulating circumstances providing unconditioned stimulation.

Some investigators have, however, argued that fear of specific objects and situations, rather than depending upon conditioning, may develop as a result of maturation. Valentine [37] observed that fear of various objects and situations appeared suddenly without evidence of having been learned. Until around the end of the first year, for instance, there was no fear of animals such as cats and dogs. Fear of darkness, of the sea, of the

"uncanny," and of various other situations also failed to appear during early infancy. English [38] has reported on the sudden emergence of fear responses to specific objects. According to Valentine there may be "lurking within, the germ of an innate fear, . . . not to ripen until ten or twelve months." But such a view, stressing fear of specific objects and situations, is reminiscent of the doctrine of innate ideas, long discarded by most psychologists.

Jones and Jones [39] have also argued for maturation as a factor in determining susceptibility to emotional stimulation of various kinds. Their interpretation of this maturation is, however, quite different from that of Valentine. These investigators observed the reactions of individuals ranging from fourteen months to adulthood when confronted by and asked to handle a snake. Altogether, 51 children and 90 adults were observed. Until the age of two years no fear of a snake was evident. By the age of three to three and a half years, the children were exhibiting caution and paying closer attention to the snake than hitherto. Definite fear behavior appeared frequently after the age of four. Such behavior was more prevalent in adults than in children. The investigators claim that the children could not have learned their fear of snakes through actual contact with them or through stories and pictures. They believe that development of emotional responses to specific objects and situations is related to general physiological development and a consequent increasing sensitiveness to aspects of the environment. The view that such responses depend upon "ripening of an innate fear of snakes" is given no credence. Speaking specifically of the fear responses exhibited in their study, Jones and Jones say that

Fear may be regarded as a response to certain changes in a total situation: changes requiring a sudden new adjustment which the individual is unprepared to make. The arousal of fear depends not only upon situational changes, but also upon the individual's *general* level of development. . . . As a child develops, his intelligence innately matures, and his perceptions become enriched through experience. New things startle him because of his keener perception of the fact that they *are* new and unusual. . . . *Fear arises when we know enough to recognize the potential danger in a stimulus, but have not advanced to the point of a complete comprehension and control of the changing situation.*

The chief maturational factors in development of emotional responses to given objects and situations are thus not specific to emotional behavior. They are the maturational factors which underlie sensorimotor and symbolic development. As the child grows older he becomes more receptive to the finer details of his environment, his susceptibility to conditioning increases, and he is able to acquire symbols and to use them in interpreting what he observes. These factors, and not the ripening of "innate germs," account for the child's increasing susceptibility to emotional stimulation by particular objects and situations as he grows older. In a later discussion we give further consideration to the situational aspects of emotional development.

We now consider the ways in which emotional reactions become, as it were, attached to objects and situations which at first fail to elicit them. How emotion-provoking objects and situations may be rendered ineffective is also considered.

Acquisition and Elimination of Emotional Responses to Specific Objects and Situations

Watson [40] claimed that the complex emotional life of adults is produced by compounding fear, rage, and love and the conditioning of each of these emotional responses to an increasing number of stimuli as the individual gets older. This view was based upon the following data. (1) Fear, rage, and love, as we have observed above, were identified as the only emotional responses of the newborn. (The fact that even three cannot be identified in newborn infants does not weaken Watson's argument for conditioning.) (2) Watson's observations had shown that young infants are not afraid of the dark, of strangers, of animals, and of various other objects and situations which elicit fear responses in older individuals. (3) Watson demonstrated that given emotional responses could be aroused by previously indifferent stimuli as a result of conditioning.

The reader may recall our earlier discussion (p. 209) of Watson and Raynor's [41] experiment on conditioned fear reactions. Albert, the nine-month-old subject of this study, was not afraid of a white rat, a rabbit, a monkey, a Santa Claus mask, and a mass of absorbent cotton when first confronted with these. However, a loud noise (produced by striking a steel bar behind the child's head) elicited obvious fear reactions. The experimenters then associated the loud noise and the rat in such a manner as to produce a fear reaction to the animal. When the rat was presented, Albert reached toward it. Just then the loud noise was produced. Albert reacted to the noise by starting and falling forward on his face. On the next presentation of the rat and noise, whimpering was added to the previous response. A week later the experiment was continued. After five further presentations of the rat followed by noise, the rat was presented without noise. This stimulus alone was now sufficient to elicit crying and withdrawal.

Was this fear response specific to the rat, or would it now be transferred to other objects having similar characteristics? To answer this question, Watson and Raynor substituted for the rat various objects somewhat similar to it. When a rabbit was presented, the child showed a fear response similar to that elicited by the rat. (See Figure 86, p. 209.) A dog aroused similar reactions. Withdrawal and crying were exhibited when a sealskin coat was presented. Absorbent cotton elicited a milder negative reaction than the other stimuli. Wooden blocks, used as control stimuli throughout the observation, failed at any time to elicit a fear reaction. Continued presentation of the substituted animals without a loud noise or the rat somewhat weakened the emotional reactions. This is what one would expect from the phenomenon of experimental extinction (p. 204). A month after the above observations Albert, who had been given no emotion tests in the meantime, was tested for retention of emotional responses to the rat, rabbit, dog, and fur coat. There was clear evidence of retention, although the intensity of the reactions had somewhat diminished.

Jones [42] has conditioned the galvanic reflex of infants between three and nine months of age. The reflex was elicited initially by slight electric shock, withdrawal of the bottle during feeding, confinement of normal leg and arm activity, and by loud sounds. Overt activity did not correspond with the implicit reaction. Using slight electric shock as the conditioning stimulus and light, sound, or tactual stimulation as the stimuli to be conditioned, Jones was able to obtain conditioned responses within four to fourteen associations. Repetition of the substitute stimulus alone usually led to rapid extinction of the response which, however, returned the following day without further conditioning (spontaneous recovery). One infant retained the conditioning over a period of four weeks and another over a period of seven weeks. Overt responses showed no correlated conditioning. The conditioned galvanic skin reactions exhibited phenomena essentially similar to those found in conditioning of overt sensorimotor activities. Jones says that

These results indicate that the C–R concept, as evolved by Pavlov and adopted in this country by Watson and others, is satisfactorily applicable to the modification of emotions in infancy. Emotional responses, in their inner as well as in their outward manifestations, do become connected to previously inadequate stimuli, and the circumstances of association and of subsequent inhibition are very similar to those which Pavlov has described in his experiments with the alimentary and defense reflexes of dogs.

Our discussion of the experiments of Marinesco and Kreindler (pp. 202–204) showed that overt reactions to electrical stimulation may also be conditioned during early infancy, and that such conditioning has the character-

istics described by Pavlov for salivary conditioning in dogs.

Watson and Raynor [43] suggested various ways in which an emotional reaction, once conditioned, might be unconditioned; in other words, eliminated. They did not, however, attempt such unconditioning. Mary Cover Jones, [44] working under Watson's direction, performed the experiment with children who had developed fear responses before coming under her observation. Attempts at eliminating fear of animals by keeping the animals away from the child for from two weeks to two months were without success. Verbal appeals, such as coaxing the child to touch the feared animal, were likewise without effect. Social ridicule was not very effective. Four other methods were, however, quite effective with certain children. One of these, designated as that of *adaptation*, consisted in leaving the feared object in the vicinity of the child until he became accustomed to it and found out that it would do him no harm. Godfried, one of the subjects of this experiment, was seemingly afraid that a rabbit would bite him. When, after continued association with the rabbit, this possibility was unrealized, the fear was overcome. Another method was that of *distraction*. When Arthur, who was afraid of a frog, wished to play with crayons, these were placed near the animal. The child picked up the crayons and, apparently, was temporarily unaware of the frog. Later he said: "I ran over there and got it (the crayon). He (the frog) didn't bite me. Tomorrow I'll put it in a box and take it home." The third method, *social imitation*, was successful in eliminating fear of a rabbit. A child lost his fear when he observed two other children playing with the animal. On the other hand, a child who was apparently unafraid of a rabbit became afraid when he observed a companion cry at the sight of it. Peter, a child whose case is reported in detail by Mary Cover Jones, [45] began to lose his fear of a rabbit by watching other children play with it over a period of several months. The fear was brought back to original strength, however, when the child was inadvertently frightened by a dog. Jones then tried the fourth, and most successful method. This was the method of *direct conditioning*. The child's reaction to food and candy was positive. This positive reaction was conditioned to the rabbit by presenting the animal while the child was eating. At first the rabbit was placed at a distance so that the negative reaction to it would not transfer to food. On successive days it was gradually moved closer. Finally the child played with it while eating his food. This positive reaction to the rabbit showed some transfer to other animals of which the child was previously afraid. Jersild and Holmes [46] asked mothers what methods were found most successful in preventing and eliminating fear reactions to specific situations. The techniques reported as most successful were (1) prompting the acquisition of skills helpful in coping with the feared situation, (2) leading the child by degrees into contact with and participation in the situation, and (3) giving the child an opportunity to become acquainted with the situation of his own accord.

The data of the above-mentioned investigations lend strong support to Watson's view that emotional reactions to specific objects and situations are habits developed by the process of conditioning. Sometimes the conditioning of a fear reaction is direct and obvious, as in the case of Watson and Raynor's experiment with Albert. Sometimes fear of a given object or situation, rather than being conditioned directly, is a transferred conditioned reaction based upon other similar objects and situations. This phenomenon of transfer may account for the apparent sudden "maturation" of certain fears. For example, fear of a dog, when the child has not previously seen or been negatively conditioned to one, may be transferred from some other object to which the child has developed a fear reaction. There is also evidence, as indicated above, that children acquire, as well as overcome, fear responses by observing others. Many emotional reactions are undoubtedly

acquired in this way from parents. Hagman [47] found that the nature and number of fears evidenced by children show a high correlation with those of the mother. Fear responses, as everyone knows, are also acquired symbolically. The parent, for example, tells a child that the policeman will get him if he doesn't behave, that God will punish him if he doesn't say his prayers, and so on. What we have said about acquisition of fear is probably true of other emotional responses not yet subjected to experimental investigation.

Some critics of Watson's view have argued that emotional reactions persist much longer than conditioned responses produced in the laboratory, and hence must be attributed to factors other than conditioning. The same argument has been used against the conditioned-response theory of learning. The chief answer is that unlike those acquired in the laboratory, the conditioned responses developed during everyday life are given support by many uncontrolled stimulating factors. Reinforcement of conditioned emotional reactions is offered by transfer of conditioning from other objects and situations than those to which the reactions were conditioned specifically. Peter's diminishing fear of a rabbit, for example, was strengthened after a fear-provoking encounter with a dog. Social stimulation (for example, from parents, other children, reading stories, seeing movies) provides constant reinforcement to conditioned emotional reactions. Symbolic rehearsal (imagination, imaginative play, and the like) also gives a certain degree of support to emotional responses already acquired.

The influence of age on the development of emotional responses may be investigated from various angles. One may observe the nature and frequency of specific responses (such as crying and kicking) involved in emotional episodes; he may observe the increasing repertoire of responses classified as fear, rage, joy, jealousy, and so on; he may observe changes in the nature and frequency of emotional responses to particular objects and situations; he may note how given responses such as

Table 12. Order of Appearance of Forms of Behavior During Emotional Episodes for All Five Children*

1–4 months	4–8 months	8–12 months	12–16 months	16–20 months	20–24 months
Crying Screaming Restless Struggling Starting					
	Refusing and resisting Holding out arms Throwing things Crying and calling				
		Stiffening Throwing self back Clinging and attempting to adapt			
			Running away		
				Hiding face Crying and saying no	
					Slumping Crying and asking

* From Blatz and Millichamp.

laughing, crying, and anger change as the individual grows older. We shall now consider the development of emotional behavior from each of these angles. Most of the studies of emotional development have, as we shall see, been confined to the period of early childhood.

Specific Reactions Involved in Emotional Episodes

This aspect of emotional development has been investigated by Blatz and Millichamp.[48] Their data were extracted from monthly records kept by parents especially trained for their task. The records consisted of complete accounts of the specific emotional activities of each child during three successive days each month. There was no attempt to evoke emotional behavior. Each child was observed while involved in normal everyday activities such as dressing, eating, and so forth. Observation began at ten minutes after midnight on the first day of the month and ended at midnight the third day. The first record was made when the infants were one month old. Observation continued for two years. The data on five children were sufficiently complete to serve as the basis of a genetic analysis. Blatz and Millichamp found that the genetic sequence for eighteen specific emotional reactions appearing within the first two years is more or less regular. Crying and restlessness appeared in every case as the most frequent responses during the first four months; screaming, starting, and struggling were present during the first four months, but infrequently; physical resistance and holding out arms appeared before the end of the first year; hiding the face, slumping, throwing things, crying plus trying to act in an adaptive manner, crying plus asking or saying "no," and running away made their first appearance in the second year. Early in the third year, for a few cases where observation continued, there was increasing evidence of verbalization in emotional episodes.

The data for five infants are summarized in Table 12. A response which appeared during a given four-month period usually continued to appear in succeeding periods. These responses are represented by a blank space at succeeding age levels. Although every item was not common to all subjects, each child exhibited an increasing repertoire which agreed with this general picture. One will observe the interesting fact that all of the responses reported in this study deal with what are generally called "unpleasant emotions" or "negative" responses. Smiling, laughing, and the like are missing from the list of activities. This may mean that such responses were infrequent in appearance, or it may mean that the observers were not impressed with their emotionality.

Some responses increased in frequency of appearance with age up to a certain period and then decreased. For example, struggling had its peak frequency between 12 and 16 months and crying plus indicating a desire between 16 and 20 months. Curves representing the average frequency of all emotional responses per day per month for one subject and for the five subjects combined are shown in Figure 121. One will observe that, despite the addition of new behavior items at successive behavior levels and the fact that some of these increased in frequency with age, the average frequency of emotional reactions shows a decrease with age. This is partly due to a decreasing frequency of emotional episodes. Irregularities in the curve are probably due to the small number of cases involved and to the fact that the situations present at the various age levels are themselves subject to considerable variation.

The addition of *new* emotional reactions at successive age levels is attributed to the individual's "developing motor and mental capac-

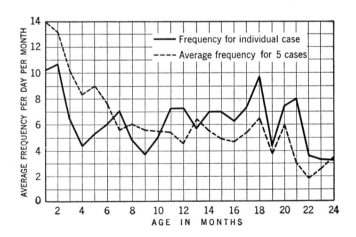

Figure 121. Average Frequency of Emotional Reactions Per Day Per Month
During the First Two Years

(From W. E. Blatz and D. A. Millichamp, "The Development of Emotion in the Infant," *University of Toronto Studies: Child Development Series*, 1935, No. 4, p. 15.)

ity." When the child is able to throw things, this response, although not in itself emotional, is added to the emotional repertoire. Likewise, when the child is able to run, running becomes a part of the emotional repertoire. When he has learned to speak, speaking is involved in emotional activity. This increasing complexity of emotional behavior is attributed to maturation and conditioning. According to Blatz and Millichamp, crying was the only specifically emotional reaction observed in their study.

Decreasing *frequency* of emotional reactions with age is attributed to an increasing ability to make adequate adjustments in emotion-provoking situations. Emotional activity, according to Blatz and Millichamp, exists only so long as there is "thwarting of directional impulse through inability to overcome the significant factor in the situation." They claim that when an individual is capable of overcoming thwarting situations as soon as they arise, emotional activity becomes less frequent. Many of the early emotion-provoking situations are alleviated by adult interference; hence the child soon learns the power of emotional behavior to control the reactions of others. Thus, according to Blatz and Millichamp, even though adjustment is possible, emotional responses may still occur for this reason.

Although they involve so few cases and do not go far beyond the period of infancy, Blatz and Millichamp's observations show very clearly that most of the activities involved in emotional episodes are not in and of themselves emotional. When emotionally aroused, the child uses his available repertoire of sensorimotor and symbolic activities. Thus emotional behavior becomes more complex as new sensorimotor and symbolic activities are added to the behavioral repertoire. Blatz and Millichamp's observations are also valuable in their demonstration of the fact that increasing ability to control the environment, except where emotional activity assumes a function of social control, goes with decreasing frequency of emotional behavior.

Appearance of Emotions

Practically all of the baby-biographers have reported that children exhibit a wider variety of "emotions" as they grow older. By "emotions" are meant, of course, the reaction patterns, complexes, or "syndromes" to which such terms as fear, anger, joy, etc., may be attached. As Sherman [49] has shown, these labels are applied in terms of emotion-provoking situations more than in terms of the observed behavior. Even in Goodenough's [50] investigation, which required the observers to match emotional expressions of a ten-month-old infant with various situations which might have elicited them, the accuracy of matching, while six times greater than chance, was only 47.4 per cent. We should keep in mind, therefore, that conclusions to the effect that a child of such and such an age exhibits joy, anger, or the like are situational as well as behavioral data. The specific emotional label is based upon one's interpretation of the observed situation and activities. Blatz and Millichamp avoided inferences concerning "emotions" by describing merely the specific activities of their subjects. While this is the most scientific procedure to follow, it is interesting to note the "emotions" inferred to be present at various ages.

Bridges [51] observed large groups of babies in order to note emotional changes associated with increasing age. Her subjects ranged in age from birth to slightly over two years. In some instances the same babies were observed daily for a period of four months. As was indicated in our discussion of unlearned emotional activity, Bridges concludes that the only recognizable "emotion" at birth is *undifferentiated excitement*. All other "emotions" are thought to be derived from this by differentiation resulting from maturation and conditioning. Her attitude is presented in the following quotation:

From birth onward there is a gradual evolution of the emotions taking place. The earliest emotional reactions are very general and poorly organized responses to one or two general types of situation. As weeks and months go by the responses take on more definite form in relation to more specific situations ... *in the course of genesis of the emotions there occurs a process of differentiation.* Coincident with the partial isolation of certain responses is a combining of the simpler reactions within the unit responses and the formation of bonds and association between these emotional situations. In this manner slowly appear the well-known emotions of anger, disgust, joy, love, and so forth.

According to Bridges, the initial excitement is soon differentiated to add distress and delight to the infant's emotional repertoire. Distress is believed to be exhibited by the end of the first month, delight by approximately the end of the second month. Then anger, disgust, and fear are added in rapid succession. Elation and affection are attributed to the period between approximately 9 and 12 months. Affection is, at about 13 months, thought to be further differentiable into affection for adults and affection for children. Jealousy, derived from distress, is, according to Bridges, added to the emotional repertoire at an age level of approximately 15 months. Joy is assumed to appear at around the 21st month. The origins and approximate age of appearance of these "emotions" are diagrammatically represented in Figure 122.

Bridges points out that because the children observed by her were in a foundling home, the ages indicated in the above figure might not be exactly representative of all infants. She says, however, that since the daily routine of infant care is quite similar whether the infants are institutionalized or not, the suggested inferences may have at least some general significance for infants brought up under other circumstances.

The chief significance of the above observations is their indication of the fact that as the infant grows older an increasing number of "emotions" may be inferred from his increasingly differentiated emotional responses to aspects of the environment. The exact classification of "emotions" is probably of little

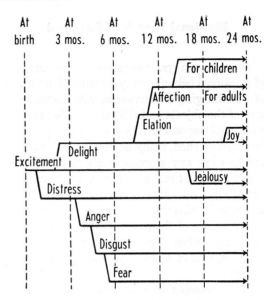

Figure 122. **Approximate Ages of Differentiation of Emotions in Early Childhood**

(Adapted by Dashiell from K. M. B. Bridges, "Emotional Development in Early Infancy," *Child Development*, 1932, *3*, 340.)

significance. It is doubtful whether other trained psychologists, unaware of the above classification, and yet observing exactly the same behavior as that witnessed by Bridges, would infer the same variety of "emotions." As a matter of fact, several observers of emotional behavior in infants have failed to mention all of the "emotions" of Bridges' list. Others have "observed," within the same age range, several "emotions" not mentioned by her. Bühler,[52] for example, reports the existence of anxiety and astonishment as early as the seventh month. Goodenough [53] includes obstinacy, dissatisfaction, and expectation in the list of "emotions" of an infant of ten months.

We have previously pointed out (p. 390) how classifications of adult "emotions" differ. Some classifications include as few as seven "emotions," others over a hundred. These classifications, unlike those based on infant behavior, are supported by reports of emotional experience. Even with such added refinement of data, inferences fail to agree.

Situational Aspects of Emotional Development

As we have already suggested, development of emotional behavior may be studied in terms of the changing effectiveness, with increasing age, of the objects and situations which evoke emotional responses. Until a certain age level has been reached, many objects and situations fail to elicit any emotional activity. These objects and situations, once they have assumed emotional significance, may increase or decrease in effectiveness as the child grows older. Some of them eventually become entirely ineffective. To illustrate, we shall refer to the results of a few representative investigations.

Our discussion of maturational factors in emotional development (p. 396) included some material on the problem which confronts us here. It will be recalled that Jones and Jones [54] found no emotional response to a snake in subjects younger than two years of age. There was an increase in the fear-provoking efficacy of the snake with an increase in the age of the subjects.

In her investigation of crying, Bayley [55] found that strangeness of an infant's surroundings assumed increasing emotional significance as a function of age. Strange situations failed to elicit emotional responses until the third month. In successive months, beginning with the third, the percentage of crying elicited by "strangeness" was 2.2; 5.0; 11.4; 9.9; 14.9; 17.0; 21.6; 26.1; 24.5; and 21.4. It will be observed that the highest frequency was attained at the tenth month. There was then a slight decrease. Had the investigation included older children, it is quite likely that crying in response to "strangeness" would have shown a steady decrease with age.

Jersild and others [56] found that strange objects and persons aroused fear in about 24 per cent of children between birth and 23 months, 8 per cent between 48 and 71 months, and less than 3 per cent beyond this age range. Fear of noise and agents of noise showed a similar trend. Animals, on the other hand, became increasingly effective with age as arousers of fear. Pratt [57] found that rural children feared animals more than any other objects or situations, but that fear of animals decreased with age. Had the above study included older children, as did Pratt's, a similar decline in fear of animals would doubtless have occurred. As Pratt points out, all such studies of fear, his own included, have limited significance in that they involve what children say they fear and not actual fear in response to the situations indicated.

The human face and voice increase in emotional effectiveness as a function of age. Spitz [58] carried on an extensive investigation of smiling in response to the human face and to face-like configurations. His subjects ranged in age from birth to over one year. One of the most interesting outcomes was the emergence of "indiscriminate" smiling between the second and the sixth month and the suppression of such smiling between the sixth month and one year. In this later period, instead of smiling indiscriminately, the child made a differentiation between faces, smiling at some and not at others. Evidence is presented which suggests that indiscriminate smiling is a response to face-like configurations without any implication that human qualities *per se* are perceived. Responses to a scolding and an affectionate voice were studied by Bühler,[59] who found no appropriately differentiated behavior (crying or smiling) until around the sixth month. Justin,[60] found that the efficacy of certain laughter-provoking situations increased up to the fifth year and then decreased. Situations involving greater subtleties, such as verbal jokes, would no doubt show an increasing effectiveness with age on into adulthood.

Blatz and Millichamp [61] have reported on age differences in the frequency of emotional responses to a large number of situations including physical discomfort, adult attention ended, adult seen or heard, adult care, being ordered to do something, being teased or laughed at, a change in routine procedure, interference with eating, inability to manipu-

Table 13. Frequency of Emotional Episodes Classified According to Divisions I, II, and III at Four-Month Intervals (5 Children) *

	1–4	4–8	8–12	12–16	16–20	20–24
I. Thwarting of non-specific attitudes						
(a) Discomfort............	288	267	116	105	87	44
(b) Attention ended........	161	82	61	49	69	28
Total............	449	349	177	154	156	72
II. Thwarting of approach						
(a) Social................	24	41	62	115	103	68
(b) Environmental.........	8	22	25	16	23	7
Total............	32	63	87	131	126	75
III. Thwarting of withdrawal						
(a) Loss of security						
(1) Sudden change......	10	15	25	21	29	14
(2) New situations......	4	15	16	11	9	6
(b) Learned withdrawal.....	5	18	4	5	4	3
Total............	19	48	45	37	42	23

I. Thwarting of non-specific approach and withdrawal attitudes
   (a) Physical discomfort and need of change. (b) Adult attention ended.
II. Thwarting of approach attitude
   (a) Social thwarting: adult is seen or heard; adult care (routine and non-routine); ordered to do something; refused a request; teased or laughed at; change in routine.
   (b) Environmental thwarting: interference with eating; unable to manipulate material; wanting some article, wanting to do something; physical restraint.
III. Thwarting of withdrawal attitude
   (a) Thwarting of immediate withdrawal, loss of self-security: (1) sudden changes (loud noises and loss of support; wakened by someone; physical hurt and falling); (2) new situations (unfamiliar physical environment; unfamiliar social environment; animals; physical inability to manipulate self). (b) Thwarting of learned withdrawal; discipline; forced feeding; involuntary evacuation.
   * From Blatz and Millichamp.

late material, physical restraint, loud noises, loss of support, being wakened by someone, physical hurt, unfamiliar surroundings, presence of animals, discipline, forced feeding, etc. All of the situations involved thwarting of some kind. Analysis of these situations leads the investigators to group them under three main headings with subclassifications as indicated in Table 13. This table gives the changing frequency of emotional episodes elicited by these general situations as the five subjects increased in age from the end of the first until the end of the 24th month. One will note that situations involving a thwarting of non-specific attitudes showed a marked tendency to decrease in effectiveness with an increase in the age of the subjects. Thwarting of approach became increasingly effective until the 16th month and then decreased in effectiveness. Thwarting of withdrawal reached a peak at the four- to eight-month level and then decreased. The fact that only five subjects were involved makes these results inconclusive. Their value is chiefly suggestive.

Blatz and Millichamp attribute their results to "genetic development of the individual's total response pattern" in particular situations. Both maturation and conditioning are regarded as fundamental to this development. As indicated in our discussion of maturation, general sensorimotor and symbolic development accounts for initial susceptibility to most forms of emotional stimulation. The infant must learn the significance of snakes, of "strangeness," of the human voice, and so on, before these objects and situations can assume emotional effectiveness. Such learning calls for sufficient development of sensorimotor and symbolic functions, whether produced by maturational or conditioning factors. An increase in the efficacy of situations to elicit emotional reactions as the individual grows older also functions. Decreasing effectiveness of an emotion-provoking situation may be attributed to the individual's increasing ability to adapt to the situation in a non-emotional manner. Blatz and Millichamp point out that as learning to adjust to a given situation progresses, emotional behavior in that situation tends to disappear. This is, of course, true of only those situations which, as in Blatz and Millichamp's investigation, involve thwarting.

There are many situations which continue to evoke both positive and negative emotional responses throughout life, sometimes with increasing effectiveness as the individual grows older. The individual's affection for his parents, for his brothers and sisters, his wife, and his family are of this type. Emotional receptivity to religious situations may increase throughout life. An individual's country, its flag, his personal property, and the like may assume a similarly increasing emotional effectiveness as he grows older. His dislike for foreigners and his other negative attitudes also change with age. When mild emotional reactions of various kinds become organized around some object or situation in this way we usually refer to the resulting emotional predisposition or attitude as a *sentiment*. Sentiments are abbreviated emotional responses in that symbolic rather than overt activities tend to play the predominant role. They may be thought of as emotionally toned symbolic habits.

Changes in Emotional Reactions

We have already observed the increasing number of behavior items which become involved in emotional episodes as the child grows older; we have noted that an increasing number of "emotions" may be inferred from the behavior of children at successively greater age levels; and we have discussed the emotion-provoking effectiveness of given objects and situations for children of various ages. In this section we shall describe how, as the child grows older, given emotional reactions and "emotions" exhibit changes in their nature and frequency.

As the child grows older, the differentiation of emotional states is increasingly discernible in his facial expressions as well as in more obvious reactions like crying, laughing, complaining, struggling, and running away. Facial expressions of emotion have been studied extensively in adults, but the data on children are only incidental.[62] An alert photographer often preserves expressions like those shown in Figure 123.

One of the most extensive investigations of crying is that of Bayley[63] on 61 infants. Observations were made during the first three days of life, and then at monthly intervals until the end of the first year. The crying was that elicited during routine administration of mental and physical tests. On the average, about 15 per cent of the time involved in each examination period was consumed in crying. Vehement crying was found to be very persistent, a slight whimper intermittent, and moderate crying of average persistency. These relationships, however, showed no significant changes as a function of age. Crying tended to decrease in frequency after the first month. It reached its lowest frequency at four months; thereafter, until the end of the year, its frequency increased. These changes in the total frequency of crying were related more

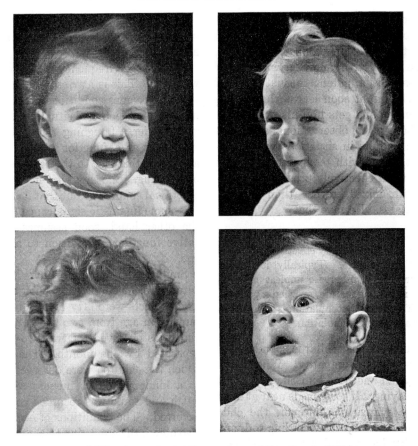

Figure 123.   Some Facial Expressions of Emotion in Children

Compare such expressions with the relative inexpressiveness of the face of an infant.
(Photographs from Armstrong Roberts.)

to the increasing, decreasing, and unchanging effectiveness of given situations than to age as such. In other words, crying in some situations (such as "strangeness," which we have already discussed) increased in frequency with age; in other situations (such as "colic") it decreased in frequency with age; in still other situations (such as "handling") it showed no significant change in frequency with increasing age.

Weeping (crying with tears) is rarely present at birth. Some investigators say that it fails to become prevalent until weeks after birth. Lund's [64] observations lead him to conclude that "unmistakable secretions resulting from an emotional upset did not appear, for the most part, until the second month." He says that the deeper emotional involvement of crying

becomes apparent in the secretion of tears and in the tendency to sob, a reaction induced by the spasmodic contractions of the respiratory muscles. In addition to the tears and the sobbing there is also a slight change in facial expression. The more decided contraction of the depressor muscles draws down the corners of the mouth, causing it to assume a squarish outline, and giving the face the pitiful expression associated with tears. These contractions are all involuntary and are not subject to conscious control. This absence of voluntary control is responsible for the quivering of the lips and the drooping of the mouth which are among the first signs of an approaching crying spell which the individual is trying to suppress.

Weeping soon becomes associated with various emotional behavior patterns. It is involved in temper tantrums, anger, fear, sympathy, and even in joy. Furthermore, crying, with or without tears, is a potent means of social control. The infant soon learns that crying brings attention and gets him his own way.

On the basis of his observational studies of children and adults in situations which normally elicit crying with tears, Lund believes that tears, when effectively produced, are associated with mixed, rather than specific, emotional states. He says that

Neither sorrow, dejection, joy, nor elation, when occurring in pure form, is very effective, if at all, in producing the discharge. Typically it appears when a depressing or otherwise unpleasant situation gains a redeeming feature, or when a period of tension with unpleasant stimulation is followed by pleasant or alleviating stimulation.

Lund points out that children soon learn to weep in response to sympathy. When alone a child may fall and hurt himself, yet get up and go on playing. If someone is near at hand and proffers sympathy, however, the child tends to burst into tears. According to Lund, adult weeping has a similar basis. Self-pity is mentioned as another basis of weeping which is acquired in early childhood.

Smiling and laughing

Washburn [65] investigated the development of smiling and laughing in fifteen infants during the first year of life. Standard situations were used to elicit these responses. Smiling to social stimulation appeared at eight weeks, laughing at twelve weeks. Peek-a-boo games first elicited smiling at eight weeks and laughing at sixteen weeks. Altogether, eleven situations of this general nature were used. Laughing in response to a given situation appeared later than smiling. Definite changes in the "smiling" pattern were observed to appear with an increase in age. Laughter, which was more stereotyped than smiling, exhibited no discernible age changes. Silent laughter was not observed in any of the subjects. Doubling of the body in laughter occurred after the seated position had been assumed.

The average frequency of smiling increased with age. This is attributed to the fact that smiling becomes conditioned to an increasing number of objects and situations as the infant grows older. Laughing failed to change in frequency as a function of age. Washburn attributes this fact to the relative stereotypy of laughing. She says that it is expressive of emotional conditions but that it does not tend to assume linguistic significance. Smiling, on the other hand, soon assumes a communicative function in addition to an expressive one.

Smiling and laughing have been investigated in older children by Ding and Jersild.[66] The subjects were fifty-nine Chinese children ranging in age from two to five years. Each child was observed for two two-hour periods separated by one month. The situation in which the children were observed was similar to a kindergarten or nursery school. Each laugh and smile was recorded as it naturally occurred. The conditions of occurrence were also noted, the aim being to obtain data which might have some bearing upon theories of laughter.

Smiles appeared to be associated primarily with social contacts and conversation, while laughter had its greatest frequency during motor activity. Both responses appeared more frequently in the presence of other children than when the child was alone. This fact is attributed to social conditioning of these responses. Smiling was seven times more frequent than laughing. Play situations involving physical activity elicited more smiles and laughter than all other situations combined. Three-year-old children laughed and smiled somewhat less frequently than children of two, four, and five years. Both responses occurred more frequently in the presence of relatives and friends than in the presence of strangers. There was no evidence to support theories of laughter other than those which regard this response as a motor outlet associated with other physical activities.

Resistance

Resistant behavior in test situations has been investigated by Levy and Tulchin, Goodenough, and others. Investigators regard resistance as a response associated primarily with anger. In some instances it is an anticipatory response associated with feared objects and situations. That is, if the child fears a given situation, he may manifest negativism whenever there are attempts to force him into it. In Levy and Tulchin's [67] investigation, which involved 983 children ranging in age from soon after birth until the 63d month, resistant behavior first appeared at the age of approximately 6 months. This behavior reached its highest frequency between 18 and 23 months in females and 30 and 35 months in males. After these ages, resistant behavior gradually decreased in frequency.

Goodenough's [68] study involved 1897 observations on 990 children ranging in age from 18 months to 6 years. Resistant behavior (negativism) in boys had a slight rise between 24 and 36 months, and then it decreased in frequency with increasing age. Resistant behavior in girls, on the other hand, showed a steady decrease throughout the whole age range. Since the youngest subjects were 18 months old, the age of greatest resistance for the girls in Levy and Tulchin's investigation, this result is not in conflict with that of these investigators. The results of Levy and Tulchin's and Goodenough's investigations are thus in close agreement on all points. Goodenough attributes the observed age differences in resistance to experience and training.

Age Changes in Typical Emotions

Several investigators have attempted to describe age changes in the nature and frequency of fear, rage or anger, jealousy, and other emotional reaction patterns. For reasons which are perhaps already apparent to the reader, such descriptions are of extremely limited value. Some of these reasons are as follows: Investigators fail to agree concerning the labels to be attached to the various reaction patterns.* When the situation is known, agreement increases. However, many different situations arouse behavior labeled, for example, as fear. A description of developmental changes in the "fear pattern" for one situation might not be adequate for other situations. This is especially true when, as we have previously observed, the situations themselves change in effectiveness as a function of age. The value of data on development of "emotions" is decreased by the fact that most of the investigations are of a questionnaire nature. Parents have been asked to describe the emotions of children of various ages, to report the situations which elicited them, and so forth. We have already (p. 276)) mentioned the inadequacy of data gathered by untrained observers. Even where the investigator has resorted to experimentally controlled observations, the subjects have been few in number and have only been observed over a short period of time. For these reasons we shall restrict our discussion to a few of the more representative studies in this field.

Goodenough [69] investigated the frequency of anger reactions in children of various ages. She asked mothers to fill out questionnaires concerning the anger outbursts of their children. Each child was observed by the parent for a month. Every observed anger response was recorded during this period. The parents also made descriptive comments. According to the data thus gathered, anger increased in frequency until the second year and then decreased. According to the descriptions reported, anger responses were more subtle in older than in younger children. Instead of throwing himself on the floor, stiffening his body, jumping up and down, holding his breath, and the like, the older child tended to

---

* As indicated earlier (pp. 388–390), it is even doubtful whether clearly differentiable emotional patterns exist. The writer uses the term "pattern" with a great deal of hesitancy for this reason.

make use of abbreviated and symbolic means to express his anger. He called names, made threats, argued, insisted, and so forth. Furthermore, in children at increasingly higher age levels there was an increasing tendency toward removal of the annoying circumstances and toward the use of retaliatory measures. Sulkiness, restlessness, resentfulness, and the like tended to follow an angry outburst more frequently in older than in younger children.

Jersild and Holmes [70] have, in a somewhat similar fashion, investigated the influence of age on changes in the nature and frequency of fear reactions. Questionnaire data from parents and from teachers indicated that the average number of fears per child tends to decrease after the second year. One fear which showed a steady increase with age and which was still increasing at six years, the upper age limit in the study, was fear of *imaginary* objects and situations. Holmes,[71] in an experimental investigation of children's fears, found that the percentage of subjects exhibiting fear of a dog, a strange person, a falling board, and a loud sound tended to decrease with age. On the other hand, the percentage of children showing fear of darkness, of snakes, and of being alone increased until approximately the end of the fourth year, then decreased.

Bridges,[72] as a result of her observations of fear in preschool children, describes fear responses as increasing in adequacy as the child becomes older. The earliest fear response is described as a "panic." As the child grows older, however, the initial panic gives way to running away, partial withdrawal, holding aloof, and avoiding the situation. Symbolic processes play an increasing role in fear as well as in anger as the child grows older. He says, for example, "It will bite me," "Take it away," "I don't want to go."

Fear often takes the form of worry or anxiety. That is to say, instead of being aroused by a present situation, fear is aroused in an internalized fashion by worry over what *has happened* or what *might happen*. Anxiety,

even in children, may have no apparent situational basis.[73]

In addition to psychoanalytic studies of anxiety in children,[74] there have been several investigations of the kinds of situations about which children say they worry. Jersild and others [75] asked fifth and sixth graders, "What do you worry about?" and they received replies which stressed school situations (like the possibility of having a poor report card) and non-school situations (like being scolded by a parent or losing one's friends). Pintner and Lev [76] gave their "worry inventory" to fifth and sixth graders, and found that these worried most about school and home situations.

A projective test designed to discern the presence of anxiety in children has been developed by Temple and Amen [77] and administered to nursery school children. It consists of pictured situations (See Figure 124) in which the faces of the individuals concerned are missing. The child indicates which of two faces, a happy and a sad one, applies to the particular situation. Dorkey and Amen [78] administered this test to nursery school children and found wide individual differences in the percentage of items revealing anxiety. Scores ranged from 7.1 per cent to 86 per cent, with an average anxiety score of 38 per cent. Older children had a higher average anxiety score than younger ones. The area of greatest anxiety was that of child-child relations and this remained true despite the fact that anxiety scores tended to decrease as a function of nursery school attendance. This decrease in anxiety is attributed by Dorkey and Amen to "development of the feeling of belonging to the group." Child psychologists who are interested in the practice of mental hygiene place much emphasis upon the child's need to feel that he belongs, that he is secure, and that he has the affection of those with whom he associates.

The coming into the family of a new member may represent a threat to the child's security, with resultant feelings of anxiety. Under these circumstances jealousy may arise. The behavior of jealous children at various

**Figure 124. Studying Anxiety by
a Projective Technique**

The child is asked to indicate which of the two expressions applies. He is asked, "What kind of face do you suppose this child will have, a happy face or a sad face? He (she) is using the bathroom." (From M. Dorkey and W. Amen, "A Continuation Study of Anxiety Reactions in Young Children by Means of a Projective Technique," *Genet. Psychol. Monog.*, 1947, *35*, 144.)

ages has been observed in several studies, two of which can be taken as representative. Foster [79] made a case study of 50 jealous as compared with 100 non-jealous children. Her descriptions indicate that jealous reactions are overtly like those of anger, but always directed toward another person, usually a child. In some instances the mother or father is the object of jealousy. In early childhood, jealousy may be evidenced by refusing to eat, feigning sickness, bed-wetting to get special attention, and striking or in other ways attempting to injure the individual

of whom the jealousy is felt. As the child grows older, however, jealousy may take the form of verbal quarreling, telling tales, or indulging in fantasy in which the object of jealousy is at a disadvantage. Most of Foster's jealous children fell within the age range of three and four years. There were twice as many jealous girls as boys. Sewell's [80] was also a case study. Of 70 preschool children who had younger brothers and sisters, 39 exhibited jealous behavior. Twenty-six of the jealous children had made attacks upon the younger sibling, two had ignored its presence, two had denied having a brother or sister, and nine merely evidenced various personality changes after the sibling was born. Preparation for the birth of the sibling did not appear to have reduced the incidence of jealousy. Differences in the age which separated the siblings was important in determining the presence or absence of jealousy. In two-thirds of the cases where jealousy appeared, the difference in age between the siblings ranged from 18 to 42 months. Differences greater or less than this produced only one-third the cases of jealousy. Various family conditions were related to jealousy. Jealousy occurred most frequently in situations where there was a decreased family income, family maladjustment, and inconstant discipline.

We have already (p. 389) referred to the very great motivational significance of the ever-present undercurrents from such "positive" emotions as affection, happiness, and sympathy. Despite the importance of such emotions, there is little developmental material other than that provided by general observation.

In recent years, a great deal of attention has been focused upon affection, but primarily from the standpoint of how much the infant needs to receive affection in order to develop a normal personality. This aspect is dealt with in the following chapters. How the child's own affections develop has not attracted so much attention. According to Bridges,[81] delight is present by the sixth month. This is shown (Figure 122, p. 405) as giving rise, within the next six months, to elation and affection. Affection is first attached to adults. By the fifteenth month, however, it is directed toward children as well as adults. Affectionate behavior is described in detail by Bridges.[82] The following is a sample:

Children smile and approach those who bring them pleasure. They sit close beside children or adults who show interest in them, or from whom they expect attention. They embrace their parents or guardians who minister to their needs and comfort them in distress, and sometimes they extend such affectionate embraces to teachers. . . . Some children frequently embrace others at school or kiss them spontaneously.

At later age levels affection takes the form of holding hands, using affectionate words, and hugging. Friendship and love, in the mature sense, emerge as the individual enters the period of adolescence. (See Chapter 17.)

Happiness has to some degree been dealt with in our discussions of smiling and laughter (pp. 410–411). We should like to call attention, however, to an unpublished study described by Jersild[83] in which individuals between the ages of six and eighteen years were asked to tell of their "happiest days." The tabulation given by Jersild provides a long list of the objects and situations that make children happy. What is especially interesting from the developmental angle, however, is the finding that "as children become older they less often mention days on which they had an especially happy time at play, or holidays, or festive occasions, and more often refer to happenings under such headings as 'self-improvement,' 'special successes,' and happenings such as the end of war." Children are not happy or unhappy all of their waking life. Even in older children and adults happiness and unhappiness show a certain amount of fluctuation.[84]

Sympathy in preschool children has been studied by Bridges[85] and Murphy,[86] but their data provide little information on developmental aspects. Murphy rated children for sympathy in spontaneous situations and in others designed to produce it. She derived diagrams showing who responded sympathetically to whom, and thus how much sympathy particular children received. In this respect there were large individual differences, with some children receiving little and others much sympathy. Sometimes the amount of sympathy received depended upon how loudly the child cried. There was a tendency for older children to exhibit sympathy more frequently and more effectively than younger children and to respond to a wider range of situations calculated to elicit sympathy.

Murphy points out, however, that a child's own personality is more important than his age in determining whether and, if so, how he reacts to distress in another child. One especially interesting outcome is the fact that the most aggressive children tend also to be the most sympathetic. This is shown by correlations between ratings of aggression and sympathy. Shifts from sympathy to aggression, and vice versa, are frequently noted.

Acquiring the "Language" of Emotion

An aspect of emotional development with which we have not yet dealt is acquisition of ability to discern the nature of emotional reactions in others. The genesis and development of ability to interpret facial expressions has been investigated by Gates and by Dashiell.

Gates[87] used six photographs of a face expressing, respectively, laughter, pain, anger, fear, scorn, and surprise. The photographs were from Ruckmick's series. They were selected for this study because adults have a high degree of success in differentiating them. The subjects comprised 458 children ranging in age from three to fourteen years. There were from eight to eighty-five subjects in each yearly grouping. The test was given individually. The child was shown a single expression and asked such questions as: "What is this lady doing?" "What is this lady thinking about?" "How does she feel?" The results indicate increasing accuracy as a function of age. About 50 per cent of the third-year group were able to name laughter. Pain was not named by 50 per cent of any group below six years. Anger was not correctly named by 50 per cent before the seventh year. Fear was first named by 50 per cent of the subjects at ten years of age. Surprise was not named by 50 per cent until the eleventh year. Scorn was not named by 50 per cent until the twelfth year had been reached. The expressions thus ranked, from the least to the most difficult, as follows: laughter, pain, anger, fear, surprise, and scorn. Dashiell,[88] feeling that improvement such as that observed in this test might be due merely to changes in vocabulary, used a markedly different method. He selected eighteen pictures of facial expression and arranged them in four series. Each series was shown during the telling of a story containing emotional incidents. At given places in the story, the child was required to point to the expression which would appear on the face of the person in the story. Dashiell's results are merely reported in an abstract, hence few details are available. He says, however, that there was in general an increase in ability to judge emotional expressions with increasing age. There were greater age differences in this than in Gates's study. The younger children showed a somewhat greater ability than older ones in differentiating the "subtler emotions."

Gates[89] has given a brief report concerning judgment of emotion from vocal expressions. The alphabet, spoken with expressions of happiness, unhappiness, anger, fear, scorn, surprise, defiance, pity, and suspicion, was recorded on a phonograph disc. Six hundred and twenty-seven children from grades three to eight listened to the record and attempted to discern the emotions being expressed. Increasing accuracy was correlated with age, grade, school experience, and intelligence. Judgment of vocal expressions was less accurate than that of facial expressions. Differences in the difficulty of the various vocal expressions are reported, but no details are given.

Emotional Maturity

One problem which confronts every parent and teacher is how to cultivate desirable emotions and how to eliminate or control those which, like anger, fear, anxiety, and jealousy, interfere with mental and physical health and prevent or render more difficult the child's everyday social adjustments, which are probably the most significant and the most difficult that the child is called upon to make. The emotionally adjusted adult is said to have achieved "emotional maturity" or "emotional stability." Emotional maturity has been defined as the "capacity for happy, full, and effective living, which consists essentially in a loosening and slipping away of attitudes and interests which are tolerable in children but fatal in adults."[90] Others have spoken of emotional maturity in terms of responding to anger-provoking situations in a "controlled, socially approved way," "expressing desirable effective response to esthetic situations," and being able independently to make "proper emotional choices."[91] There have been some attempts[92] to develop scales for measuring emotional maturity in children, but no generally acceptable scales have become available. Theoretically it should be possible for us to gauge emotional maturity as we do motor and mental maturity. Our failure to do so is doubtless related to the fact that emotional life is so varied, so effervescent, so dependent upon ever-changing situations, and, in short, so difficult to "pin down" for observation. Even at the adult level, there is only one scale which purports to rate emotional maturity, and this has not been generally accepted as a valid measure of it.[93]

General observation would suggest that, beyond the period of childhood, age has little to do with emotional maturity. Actually, some children are more emotionally mature than adults. Many persons fail to achieve emotional maturity at any age. In raising such issues we are of course going from the study of emotional behavior *per se* to that of social development and personality. These topics are dealt with in the following chapters, the last of which makes the transition from childhood through adolescence and adulthood to later maturity.

Summary and Conclusions

As preparation for our discussion of emotional development, we described some of the characteristics of emotional responses observed in adults. We pointed out that theories of emotion look upon fundamental emotional responses as phylogenetically derived, hence unlearned.

Our examination of data on unlearned emotional reactions in the newborn showed that clearly differentiable patterns such as fear, rage, and love are not universally present. Most investigators regard the initial emotional behavior of human infants as merely aimless activity of the entire musculature, mass activity, general excitement, or the like. In newborn babies the Moro reflex is elicited by sudden stimulation such as a revolver shot. Later, this response fails to appear. It thus has no continuing emotional significance. A "startle pattern" has been observed in infants from the time of birth on. This "pattern" is essentially like that of older children and adults. It may underlie the mass activity, general excitement, and so forth, which have been mentioned previously as fundamental. This response is observed in very young infants only when slow-motion photography is used.

Maturation and conditioning are both significant factors in the development of emotional responses after birth. There is evidence, based upon deaf-blind individuals, that some typical emotional expressions develop despite the absence of opportunities for learning them. Maturation of sensorimotor and symbolic processes appears to underlie some of the age changes in susceptibility to various emotion-provoking objects and situations. That emotional development is partly dependent upon conditioning has been demonstrated. After a few conditioning trials, fear responses

may be elicited by objects which were, as far as emotional behavior is concerned, previously ineffective. Furthermore, emotional reactions may be eliminated by conditioning procedures. We pointed out the fact, also, that social stimulation of various kinds is capable of arousing, and in some instances of eliminating, emotional reactions to given objects and situations.

At successive age levels, emotional episodes involve an increasing number of reactions, such as crying, screaming, restlessness, struggling, and refusing. Symbolic activities are added to this repertoire as soon as they appear. Most of the activities involved in emotional episodes are not in themselves emotional. When emotionally aroused, the child uses his available repertoire of sensorimotor and symbolic activities. His emotional behavior thus becomes more complex as new sensorimotor and symbolic activities are acquired. Emotional episodes tend to decrease in frequency as the child learns to adjust in a satisfactory manner to the emotion-provoking situations which elicit them.

As children grow older, an increasing number of specific "emotions" may be inferred from their activities in response to known situations. Bridges has given the most ambitious genetic classification of the emotions of children. According to this classification, until the end of the first month excitement is the only "emotion." By the age of three months, distress and delight have been added. At six months, according to this classification, the child manifests six different emotional reaction patterns; namely, fear, disgust, anger, distress, excitement, and delight. By the age of twelve months, elation and affection for adults are added to the above list. Jealousy and affection for children appear, according to Bridges, at around the fifteenth month. Joy is said to emerge at approximately the twenty-first month. We have pointed out that such classifications, while interesting, are merely suggestive of the growing complexity of the child's emotional behavior as it gets older. Observers do not agree concerning the nature and number of "emotions," or emotional reaction patterns, present at a given age. No generally accepted classification is available even for adults.

Emotional development may also be studied in terms of the increasing or decreasing emotion-provoking effectiveness of various objects and situations as the child grows older. We have shown how snakes, "strangeness," and other objects and situations change in effectiveness as a function of the child's age. Some objects and situations become less effective, while others increase in effectiveness. Smiling in response to the human face becomes more prevalent up to the age of six months, but it is indiscriminate. After that age, some faces arouse smiling responses and others do not. General sensorimotor and symbolic development appears to underlie such changes in the effectiveness of emotion-provoking stimuli.

Changes in specific emotional activities like crying, smiling, laughing, and resistance are evidenced with increasing age. Changes in the nature and frequency of given emotional reaction patterns such as anger, fear, anxiety, and jealousy have also been observed to occur as a function of age. The so-called positive emotions of affection, happiness, and sympathy also show such changes. The outstanding change in each emotion as the child grows older is the increasing involvement of symbolic activities. The study of particular "emotions" thus gives us a developmental picture similar to that observed in the case of emotional episodes or emotional outbursts regardless of precise characteristics.

As the child develops, he becomes increasingly capable of discerning the presence and nature of emotional reactions in others. This is shown in his ability to label the facial and vocal expressions associated with emotional behavior.

Emotional maturity is difficult to define and even more difficult to measure. It is apparent from general observation, however, that this characteristic, while it normally develops during childhood, is not always achieved, even by adults.

REFERENCES

1. Cannon, W. B., *The Wisdom of the Body.* New York: Norton, 1932.
2. Leeper, R. W., "A Motivational Theory of Emotion to Replace 'Emotion' as Disorganized Response," *Psych. Rev.,* 1948, *55,* 5–21.
3. Ruckmick, C., *The Psychology of Feeling and Emotion.* New York: McGraw Hill, 1936.
4. Cannon, W. B., *Bodily Changes in Pain, Hunger, Fear and Rage* (2d ed.). New York: Appleton, 1929.
5. Hunt, W. A., "Discussion: Professor Gray's 'Objective Theory of Emotion,'" *Psych. Rev.,* 1935, *42,* 395–397. Quotations from pp. 395, 396.
6. *Ibid.,* p. 396.
7. Ruckmick, *op. cit.*
8. James, W., *Psychology: Briefer Course.* New York: Holt, 1908, p. 373.
9. McDougall, W., *Outline of Psychology.* New York: Scribner, 1923.
10. Cannon, W. B., "The James-Lange Theory of Emotions: A Critical Examination and Alternative Theory," *Am. J. Psychol.,* 1929, *39,* 106–124; "Again the James-Lange and Thalamic Theories of Emotion," *Psych. Rev.,* 1931, *38,* 281–295.
11. See N. L. Munn, *Psychological Development.* Boston: Houghton Mifflin, 1938.
12. Masserman, J. H., *Behavior and Neurosis.* Chicago: University of Chicago Press, 1943, p. 35.
13. Culler, E., and F. A. Mettler, "Conditioned Behavior in a Decorticate Dog," *J. Comp. Psychol.,* 1934, *18,* 291–303; Girden, E., F. A. Mettler, G. Finch, and E. Culler, "Conditioned Responses in a Decorticate Dog to Acoustic, Thermal, and Tactile Stimulation,"

J. Comp. Psychol., 1936, *21*, 367–385; E. Girden and E. Culler, "Conditioned Responses in Curarized Striate Muscle in Dogs," *J. Comp. Psychol.*, 1937, *23*, 261–274.

14. Hebb, D. O., *The Organization of Behavior*. New York: Wiley, 1949.

15. Bousfield, W. A., and W. D. Orbison, "Ontogenesis of Emotional Behavior," *Psych. Rev.*, 1952, *59*, 1–7.

16. Watson, J. B., and J. J. B. Morgan, "Emotional Reactions and Psychological Experimentation," *Am. J. Psychol.*, 1917, *28*, 163–174. Quotations are from pp. 166 and 167.

17. Watson, J. B., *Psychology from the Standpoint of a Behaviorist*. Philadelphia: Lippincott, 1919.

18. Sherman, M., "The Differentiation of Emotional Responses in Infants," I. *J. Comp. Psychol.*, 1927, *7*, 265–284; II. *ibid.*, 335–351; *8*, 385–394.

19. Sherman, M., and I. C. Sherman, *The Process of Human Behavior*. New York: Norton, 1929, p. 145.

20. Sherman, citation 18, II.

21. Sherman and Sherman, *op. cit.*, pp. 142–143.

22. Goodenough, F. L., "The Expressions of the Emotions in Infancy," *Child Development*, 1931, *2*, 96–101.

23. Irwin, O. C., "Infant Responses to Vertical Movement," *Child Development*, 1932, *3*, 167–169; "The Latent Time of Body Startle in Infants," *Child Development*, 1932, *3*, 104–107.

24. Bridges, K. M. B., "A Genetic Theory of the Emotions," *J. Genet. Psychol.*, 1930, *37*, 514–527; *The Social and Emotional Development of the Pre-School Child*, London: Kegan Paul, 1931.

25. Pratt, K. C., A. K. Nelson, and K. H. Sun, *The Behavior of the Newborn Infant*. Columbus: Ohio State University Press, 1930.

26. Taylor, J. H., "Innate Emotional Responses in Infants," *Ohio State University Contrib. in Psychol.: Studies in Infant Behavior*. No. 12, 69–93. The quotation is from pp. 80–81.

27. Dennis, W., "Infant Reaction to Restraint: An Evaluation of Watson's Theory." *Trans. N. Y. Acad. Sci.*, 1940, *2*, 202–218.

28. Clarke, F. M., W. A. Hunt, and E. B. Hunt, "Incidental Responses in Infants Following a Startle Stimulus," *J. Gen. Psychol.*, 1937, *17*, 298–401.

29. Pratt, K. C., "The Neonate," in L. Car-

michael (ed.), *Manual of Child Psychology* (2d ed.). New York: Wiley, 1954, p. 238.

30. Hunt, W. A., F. M. Clarke, and E. B. Hunt, "Studies of the Startle Pattern: IV. Infants," *J. Psychol.*, 1936, *2*, 339–352.

31. Hunt, W. A., C. Landis, and C. F. Jacobsen, "Studies of the Startle Pattern: V. Apes and Monkeys," *J. Psychol.*, 1936, *3*, 339–343.

32. Landis, C., and W. A. Hunt, "Magnification of Time as a Research Technique in the Study of Behavior," *Science*, 1937, *85*, 384–385.

33. Hunt, W. A., and F. M. Clarke, "The Startle Pattern in Children and Identical Twins," *J. Exper. Psychol.*, 1937, *21*, 359–362.

34. Hunt, W. A., and C. Landis, "Studies of the Startle Pattern: I. Introduction," *J. Psychol.*, *2*, 201–205.

35. Goodenough, F. L., "Expression of the Emotions in a Blind-Deaf Child," *J. Abn. & Soc. Psychol.*, 1932, *27*, 328–333.

36. *Ibid.*, p. 333.

37. Valentine, C. W., "The Innate Bases of Fear," *J. Genet. Psychol.*, 1930, *37*, 394–420.

38. English, H. B., "Three Cases of the Conditioned Fear Response," *J. Abn. & Soc. Psychol.*, 1929, *24*, 221–225.

39. Jones, H. E., and M. C. Jones, "A Study of Fear," *Childhood Educ.*, 1928, *5*, 136–143. Quotation from pp. 142–143.

40. See citation 17.

41. Watson, J. B., and R. Raynor, "Conditioned Emotional Reactions," *J. Exper. Psychol.*, 1920, *3*, 1–14. Also J. B. Watson, *The Psychological Care of Infant and Child*. New York: Norton, 1928.

42. Jones, H. E., "The Retention of Conditioned Emotional Responses in Infancy," *J. Genet. Psychol.*, 1930, *37*, 485–598 (quotation is from p. 496); "The Galvanic Skin Reflex in Infancy," *Child Development*, 1930, *1*, 106–110; "The Study of Patterns of Emotional Expression," in M. L. Reymert, *Feelings and Emotions*, New York: McGraw-Hill, 1950, pp. 161–168.

43. Watson and Raynor, *op. cit.*

44. Jones, M. C., "The Elimination of Children's Fears," *J. Exper. Psychol.*, 1924, *7*, 382–390.

45. Jones, M. C., "A Laboratory Study of Fear: The Case of Peter," *Ped. Sem.*, 1924, *31*, 308–315.

46. Jersild, A. T., and F. B. Holmes, *Children's Fears*. New York: Teachers College, 1935.

47. Hagman, E. R., "A Study of Fears of Children of Pre-School Age," *J. Exper. Educ.*, 1932, *1*, 110–130.

48. Blatz, W. E., and D. A. Millichamp, "The Development of Emotion in the Infant," *Univ. Toronto Stud.: Child Development Series*, 1935, No. 4.

49. See citation 18.

50. See citation 22.

51. Bridges, K. M. B., "Emotional Development in Early Infancy," *Child Development*, 1932, *3*, 324–341. Quotation is from p. 324.

52. Bühler, C., *The First Year of Life.* New York: Day, 1930.

53. See citation 22.

54. See citation 39.

55. Bayley, N., "A Study of the Crying of Infants During Mental and Physical Tests," *J. Genet. Psychol.*, 1932, *40*, 306–329.

56. Jersild, A. T., F. V. Markey, and C. L. Jersild, "Children's Fears, Dreams, Wishes, Daydreams, Likes, Dislikes, Pleasant and Unpleasant Memories," *Child Devel. Monog.*, 1933, No. 12.

57. Pratt, K. C., "A Study of the 'Fears' of Rural Children," *J. Genet. Psychol.*, 1945, *67*, 179–194.

58. Spitz, R. A., "The Smiling Response: A Contribution to the Ontogenesis of Social Relations," *Genet. Psychol. Monog.*, 1946, *34*, 57–125.

59. See citation 52.

60. Justin, F., "A Genetic Study of Laughter-Provoking Stimuli," *Child Development*, 1932, *3*, 114–136.

61. See citation 48.

62. See P. T. Young, *Emotion in Man and Animal.* New York: Wiley, 1943. See especially Chapter VI, with expressions from the researches of Mrs. Nadie Kohts of the USSR.

63. Bayley, N., *op. cit.*

64. Lund, F. H., *The Emotions of Men.* New York: McGraw-Hill, 1930, p. 139. Second quotation from pp. 156–157.

65. Washburn, R. W., "A Study of the Smiling and Laughing of Infants in the First Year of Life," *Genet. Psychol. Monog.*, 1929, *6*, 397–539.

66. Ding, G., and A. T. Jersild, "A Study of the Laughing and Smiling of Preschool Children," *J. Genet. Psychol.*, 1932, *40*, 452–472.

67. Levy, D. M., and S. H. Tulchin, "The Resistant Behavior of Infants and Children During Mental Tests," *J. Exper. Psychol.*, 1923, *6*, 304–322.

68. Goodenough, F. L., "The Emotional Behavior of Young Children During Mental Tests," *J. Juv. Res.*, 1929, *13*, 204–219.

69. Goodenough, F. L., *Anger in Young Children.* Minneapolis: University of Minnesota Press, 1931.

70. Jersild, A. T., and F. B. Holmes, *Children's Fears.* New York: Teachers College, 1935.

71. Holmes, F. B., "An Experimental Study of the Fears of Young Children," in Jersild and Holmes, *Children's Fears.* New York: Teachers College, 1935.

72. Bridges, K. M. B., *The Social and Emotional Development of the Preschool Child.* London: Kegan Paul, 1931.

73. See the discussion and references cited by M. E. Breckenridge, and E. L. Vincent, *Child Development* (2d ed.), Philadelphia: Saunders, 1949, pp. 100–123; and also L. Kanner, "Behavior Disorders of Childhood," in J. Mc.V Hunt, *Psychology and the Behavior Disorders,* New York: Ronald, 1944.

74. See, for example, A. Freud, "Psychoanalysis of the Child," in C. Murchison (ed.), *Handbook of Child Psychology,* Worcester: Clark University Press, 1931; and M. Klein, *Psychoanalysis of Children,* New York: Norton, 1932. Also see the sections which deal with psychoanalytic concepts of anxiety in children in Rollo May's *The Meaning of Anxiety,* New York: Ronald, 1950.

75. Jersild, A. T., B. Goldman, and J. J. Loftus, "A Comparative Study of the Worries of Children in Two School Situations," *J. Exper. Educ.*, 1941, *9*, 323–326.

76. Pintner, R., and J. Lev, "Worries of School Children," *J. Genet. Psychol.*, 1940, *56*, 67–76.

77. Temple, R., and E. W. Amen, "A Study of Anxiety Reactions in Young Children by Means of a Projective Technique," *Genet. Psychol. Monog.*, 1944, *30*, 59–114.

78. Dorkey, M., and E. W. Amen, "A Continuation Study of Anxiety Reactions in Young Children by Means of a Projective Technique," *Genet. Psychol. Monog.*, 1947, *35*, 139–183.

79. Foster, S., "A Study of the Personality Make-up and Social Setting of 50 Jealous Children," *Ment. Hygiene*, 1927, *11*, 53–77.

80. Sewell, M., "Some Causes of Jealousy in Young Children," *Smith Coll. Stud. Soc. Work,* 1930, *1,* 23–40.

81. See citation 51.

82. Citation 72, p. 150.

83. Jersild, A. T., *Child Psychology* (4th ed.). New York: Prentice-Hall, 1947, pp. 318–319.

84. Iisager, H., "Factors Contributing to Happiness Among Danish College Students," *J. Soc. Psychol.,* 1948, *28,* 237–246.

85. See citation 72.

86. Murphy, L. B., *Social Behavior and Child Personality.* New York: Columbia University Press, 1937.

87. Gates, G. S., "An Experimental Study of the Growth of Social Perception," *J. Educ. Psychol.,* 1923, *14,* 449–461.

88. Dashiell, J. F., "A New Method of Measuring Reactions to Facial Expression of Emotion," *Psych. Bull.,* 1927, *24,* 174–175.

89. Gates, G. S., "The Role of the Auditory Element in the Interpretation of Emotion," *Psych. Bull.,* 1927, *24,* 175.

90. Willoughby, R. R., "A Scale of Emotional Maturity," *J. Soc. Psychol.,* 1932, *3,* 3.

91. Millard, C. V., *Child Growth and Development.* Boston: Heath, 1951, pp. 310–311.

92. Chambers, O. R., "A Method for Measuring the Emotional Maturity of Children," *J. Genet. Psychol.,* 1925, *32,* 637–647; A. J. Mitrano, "Preliminary Construction of a Schedule of Emotional Stability for Children," *Am. J. Orthopsychiat.,* 1939, *9,* 360–368.

93. Willoughby, R. R., "Willoughby EM (Emotional Maturity) Scale." Stanford University Press, 1931.

SUGGESTIONS FOR FURTHER READING

Anderson, J. E., *The Psychology of Development and Personal Adjustment.* New York: Holt, 1949, Chapter 11.

Barker, R. G., J. S. Kounin, and H. F. Wright, *Child Behavior and Development.* New York: McGraw-Hill, 1943, Chapters XIX (Jersild), XX (Lois Murphy), XXIII (Levy), and XXV (Keister).

Bridges, K. M. B., *The Social and Emotional Development of the Pre-School Child.* London: Kegan Paul, 1931, Part III.

Carmichael, L. (ed.), *Manual of Child Psychology* (2d ed.). New York: Wiley, 1954, Chapter 14 (by Jersild).

Dennis, W., *Readings in Child Psychology.* New York: Prentice-Hall, 1951, Chapter VII. Readings by Watson and Morgan, Sherman, Dennis, Goodenough, and Jersild.

Goodenough, F. L., *Developmental Psychology* (2d ed.). New York: Appleton-Century, 1945, Chapters VIII and XIII.

Jersild, A. T., *Child Psychology* (4th ed.). New York: Prentice-Hall, 1954, Chapters 9–11.

Landis, C., and W. A. Hunt, *The Startle Pattern.* New York: Rinehart, 1939, Chapter V.

May, R., *The Meaning of Anxiety.* New York: Ronald, 1950. Especially pp. 87–96 and sections on anxiety in children.

Pearson, G. H., *Emotional Disturbances in Children.* New York: Norton, 1949.

Prescott, D. A., *Emotion and the Educative Press.* Washington: American Council on Education, 1938.

Reymert, M. L. (ed.), *Feelings and Emotions.* New York: McGraw-Hill, 1950, Part VII. Articles on various aspects of emotional development by Gesell, van der Horst, and Anderson.

Thompson, G. G., *Child Psychology.* Boston: Houghton Mifflin, 1952, Chapter 8.

Valentine, W. L., and D. D. Wickens, *Experimental Foundations of General Psychology* (3d ed.). New York: Rinehart, 1949, Chapter 12.

Young, P. T., *Emotion in Man and Animal.* New York: Wiley, 1943, Chapter IV.

15

Development of Social Behavior

THE individual is said to behave socially when his own behavior is influenced by, and, in turn, influences, the behavior of others. A newborn baby, however, is *asocial*. It fails to differentiate between human and non-human stimuli and it makes no apparent attempt to influence the behavior of those around it.

Initially, the mother's voice, her smile, the warmth of her body, and her caresses could have no more meaning for the newborn infant than any non-human representation of such stimuli. It is only as such human stimuli come to have *human significance* that the infant can be said to respond socially to them.

The baby is, to be sure, a social stimulus for its parents and others, but in this respect it plays a merely passive role. Its actions do not develop a truly social significance until they are used by the infant as a means of controlling the behavior of others. Crying to be picked up, smiling to elicit a smile, and waving in order to produce a wave in return are elementary examples of such social behavior. As the child grows older, gestures, speech, and written words become media for social interaction. Now he not only responds to the linguistic behavior of others but stimulates them linguistically in return.

Earlier discussions dealt, more or less incidentally, with certain aspects of social behavior in children. We considered the motivational significance of social recognition, rivalry, praise, and blame; the role of imitation in learning, especially in relation to babbling and the early stages of linguistic development; the influence of social environments on the development of intelligence; various social contributions to the development of language; and socially significant aspects of emotional development.

As we turn now to social development, our prime concern is with complex integrations out of which the processes considered in previous chapters were, so to speak, abstracted. In its social perceptions and in its interactions with others, the child is utilizing sensory, motor, emotional, and linguistic processes whose development was traced in earlier chapters. And we should add that these processes, at any particular stage of development, were to some extent themselves products of earlier social perceptions and interactions. Moreover, in considering social development, we are heading into an area which, in many respects, could just as well be designated that of personality. This is because the most characteristic feature of personality traits is their social reference.

For convenience in discussion we are considering social development from the standpoint of social perception and interaction without particular reference to individual differences, which are to a large extent end-products of social influences. In the following chapter, on the other hand, our attention is turned to that *unique* integration of physical and social characteristics known as personality.

We shall examine the development of social behavior first from the standpoint of social perception and then from that of social interaction. These processes are of course interdependent, but the justification for separating them in this way is that it is convenient, for purposes of discussion, to do so.

The data on interaction deal with such phenomena as social play, competition, aggression, cooperation, friendship, leadership, and sympathy. If adequate information were available, one could trace the development of each such process from its inception until it had attained a mature level. There have, however, been few longitudinal studies upon which such a discussion could be based. Research, for the most part, has focused on particular forms of interaction in, say, a nursery school, a classroom, or a boys' club. Even though play has been studied at different age levels, it has been with groups, with specific play activities, and with methods which are far from comparable. Accordingly, our discussion is organized along cross-sectional lines. It deals with social activities which characterize each of the three fairly well-defined periods of childhood, namely, infancy (first two years), the preschool period (three to five), and the school period (up to the level of adolescence, which is considered in the final chapter). After considering the relevant data from this standpoint, we examine some attempts to measure social competence in children and also attempt to find out what these reveal about social development.

Growth of Social Perception

An infant is usually about two months old before it differentiates between the human and non-human aspects of its environment. In a study of 126 infants between the ages of birth and five months, Hetzer and Tudor-Hart [1] used such stimuli as a singing human voice, a kind voice, an angry voice, handclapping, a whistle, knocking sounds, and noises made with a spoon. Until the age of two months, the infants reacted indiscriminately to such stimuli. At about that age, however, they began to smile more in response to the voice and they exhibited greater acuity for this sound than for the others.

As indicated in our discussion of emotional reactions, diverse adult expressions are gradually differentiated by the growing infant. At first there is no apparent discrimination of kind from scolding tones. The same is true of smiling versus angry faces and inviting versus threatening gestures. Bühler and Hetzer [2] found that the infants studied by them were from five to seven months old before they showed signs of differentiating these diverse expressions. At this age the unfriendly expressions elicited crying and the friendly ones smiling or laughing. Spitz [3] observed that smiling in response to human smiles and moving masks appeared at around two months and became more prevalent with age. But this smiling was indiscriminate. *Any* moving mask or face was adequate to produce it. After the age of six months, however, only the familiar face elicited smiling. Other faces produced expressions of solemnity or fear.

During his first year an infant learns to differentiate mother from father, parents from mere visitors, adults from children, and brothers from sisters. He also learns to distinguish between his own voice and that of others, between tactual stimulation produced by his own activities and that produced by others, and between self-produced and other-produced visual stimulation. We know nothing about the subjective aspects of this perceptual development. The best we can do is to make inferences based upon observations of differential reactions to social stimuli. Gesell and Ilg,[4] through their extensive observations of infants, have been led to such inferences as the following:

In a few weeks he "sees" a "face" hovering over him. The experience is not a personalized perception of a personal face, but it contains the germ of a sense of *someone else.* In due time through sheer association combined with more matured perceptual power this face will become identified with food, play, and ministering care. It will take many months before the face is apprehended in its true features and in its relationships as to head, neck, arms as part of a personal physique. Even the perception of the physical aspect of other persons takes shape by sketchy stages. . . . As the infant matures, his discernment of the anatomy of other persons becomes increasingly particularized. At the same time he learns to interpret the meaning of the nodding face, of the beaming eyes, the smiling mouth, the approaching hands. . . . Somehow or other the experience of these meanings . . . becomes organized into a complex of emotional reactions, which at last is sufficiently elaborate to be called a sense of another self. In its early stages this sense is so uncritical and so piecemeal that little distinction is made between a face, a false face, a parent, a nurse, a visitor, or a mirror image. The baby smiles more or less indiscriminately at all of these varied stimuli; but by the middle of the first year he begins to distinguish between a familiar person and a stranger; between a frowning and an approving face. His extraordinary ability to read facial expressions is an impressive developmental phenomenon. He distinguishes delicate variations in posture, gesture, and countenance. . . Sensitivity to the posturings of facial features and to the postural attitudes of other persons lies at the very basis of his acculturation.

This sensitivity to cultural impress is so great that he acquires a sense of other selves before he acquires a clear sense of his own self. . . . He is aware of the incoming and outgoing hand of his mother before he becomes acquainted with his own hand as it travels in and out of his field of vision. . . . Likewise he makes no distinction in the beginning between his own voice and that of others. He probably hears his mother's voice before he identifies his own vocalizations as his own. . . .

Gesell and Thompson's [5] tabulation of social behavior during the first year includes data from 107 infants observed at intervals from the fourth to the fifty-sixth week. Examination of Table 14 shows that most of the responses elicited in this age range are relevant to our present discussion since they involve perception of social stimuli rather than actions designed to produce responses from others. Observe that items 1–12 are all perceptual in nature. The percentage of subjects exhibiting a given response is indicated. One will note that this percentage usually increases with age. Thus, "knows mother" is evident in only 3 per cent at four weeks, 21 per cent at six weeks, 39 per cent at eight weeks, 81 per cent at twelve weeks, and 92 per cent at sixteen weeks. Most items show such age increments. Notice, however, that the item "accepts strangers" shows a marked decrease after sixteen weeks. This is of course an index of differentiation. The three final items suggest interaction which, from the infant's standpoint, is more than merely perceptual. Some infants seem, at about 32 weeks, to try to get attention. Somewhat earlier than this a few play pat-a-cake and peek-a-boo. The percentage of the group exhibiting such responses is not large at any age before the end of the first year. [6]

When Bühler [6] placed pairs of infants of about the same age together in a crib, there was, until the fourth or fifth month, no evidence that one infant noticed the other. At this age an infant might look at the other, perhaps smile at him, or he might cry when the other received attention.

It seems apparent that the earliest social development of infants is largely in their perception of social stimuli. Interaction with others, in which they play an active part, is relatively late in appearing. As will become apparent in later discussions of social interaction, this aspect of development is not prominent until the second half of the first year.

Our social perception continues to grow and it is basic to all social interactions. Beyond the period of infancy, however, little attention has been given to this aspect of social development except for perceiving the meaning of emotional expressions and certain physical differences between racial groups. We have already (pp. 408–415) discussed the percep-

Table 14. Social Behavior During the First Year

Behavior items	Age in weeks														
	4	6	8	12	16	20	24	28	32	36	40	44	48	52	56
1. Responds to smiling and talking	8	62	63	—	—										
2. Visually pursues moving person	12	69	74	—	—										
3. Knows mother	3	21	39	81	92										
4. Sobers at strangers	0	3	4	35	56										
5. Turns head on sound of voice	0	3	26	42	50	100									
6. Accepts strangers	100	100	100	100	80	61	52	59	41	39	39	26	18	18	14
7. Withdraws from strangers	0	0	0	0	19	8	24	16	47	42	19	48	44	30	9
8. Adjusts to words					0	8	12	16	47	68	75	94	82	89	73
9. Responds to "bye-bye"					0	3	3	3	13	35	53	65	38	59	27
10. Adjusts to commands					0	0	0	3	22	23	31	55	56	73	50
11. Responds to inhibitory words					0	0	0	3	25	23	28	45	44	52	23
12. Responds to "So big"					0	0	0	0	6	7	8	26	18	34	—
13. Elicits attention					0	0	0	0	9	16	14	26	27	53	50
14. Plays pat-a-cake					0	0	3	6	19	23	25	42	27	50	9
15. Plays peek-a-boo					0	6	6	0	9	13	11	13	9	25	9

* From A. Gesell and H. Thompson, *Infant Behavior: Its Genesis and Growth*, New York: McGraw-Hill, 1934.

tion of pictured and vocalized emotional expressions, showing that accuracy increases with age between the ages of three and twelve years.

In studying perception of racial differences the general procedure has been to have children select pictures (photos or line drawings) in such a manner as to reveal whether they differentiate themselves and their own race from other persons and other races. Horowitz [7] found that about one-half of the 24 two- to five-year-old white and Negro children studied by her were able to make racial differentiations. When shown two or more pictures, some of animals as well as of white and Negro children of about their own age, these children could indicate "Which one is you?" and "Which one is ... ?" (name of subject). In another part of the study they were shown a series of pictures, one at a time, and asked "Is this you?" and "Is this ... ?" Identifications were primarily on the basis of color. A child would say, for example, "That's a black boy." One partial exception is particularly interesting. A white girl with curly

hair had been identifying on the basis of color until shown a picture of a Negro child with curly hair. She picked this girl as being "herself" despite the difference in skin color. This was apparently no increasing awareness of racial differences with age, but this may have been due to the smallness of the group and the narrow age range involved.

Several studies patterned after that of Horowitz, but with larger groups, have been reported by Clark and Clark. [8] In one study, involving 150 segregated Negro preschool children, the percentage identifying themselves with pictured Negro children increased with age. The percentage of such identifications was about 32 at three years and 63 at five years. In another of these studies, the investigators arranged their subjects into groups on the basis of whether they had light, medium, or dark coloring. One outcome of this study was that whereas the light-skinned identified themselves with Negro children in only 36.5 per cent of their selections, the medium and the dark-skinned chose Negro pictures more than 50 per cent of the time.

Again there was evidence of increasing differentiation of white and dark as a function of age. This was further supported by another investigation in which 253 Negro children between the ages of three and seven years selected white or colored dolls in answer to such requests as "Give me the doll that looks like a colored child," "Give me the doll that looks like a white child," and "Give me the doll that looks like you." The relevant data are summarized in Table 15.

All the above studies dealt with Negro-white discriminations, but an investigation by Springer [9] involved Orientals and whites in Hawaii. Awareness of racial differences was studied by using colored portraits of Chinese, Japanese, Caucasian, and racially mixed children. The subjects were 207 Oriental or racially mixed and 80 Caucasian preschool children. In this "picture-choosing game," each subject was asked to select, from five pictures of children of about the same age and sex, that picture which looked like himself. He was then asked why the picture looked like him. Oriental children selected Oriental pictures with a great deal of accuracy. Chinese children confused themselves with Japanese, but 78 per cent of their choices were either Chinese or Japanese. Japanese children responded similarly. Part-Orientals identified about equally with Oriental and Caucasian. Non-Orientals, on the other hand, identified 89 per cent of the time with non-Orientals. When asked to indicate the children with whom they would like to play, most of the children preferred playmates of their own racial group. When they were asked

to tell why the selected picture looked like them, the non-Oriental children referred to such physical features as color of hair and eyes, whereas the Oriental children emphasized the appearance of the hair and the shape and size of the eyes.

There is no doubt that differentiations like the above are influenced by what the children have learned from listening to adults and from watching adult reactions to individuals of different races. Radke and others [10] used a projective picture test to study the religious and racial attitudes of 250 children in kindergarten and the first two grades. Such attitudes were apparent in the youngest groups and did not depend upon actual contact with Negroes and Jews. The investigators conclude that these perceptions "develop out of adult values and the status quo." With increasing experience of this nature, as well as their own observations, children probably become more aware of the differences between themselves and others of different races. Data reported by Horowitz [11] concerning the growth of attitudes toward Negroes show that prejudice, whatever its bases, increases markedly between kindergarten and the eighth grade. The indicated rate of increase differs, however, depending on how the extent of prejudice is tested.

Our discussion of social perception has dealt with it from the standpoint of the child's awareness of his social environment and of socially significant differentiations, as between himself and others, and as between his own and other races. With increasing age he also becomes aware of differences in social and

Table **15.** Racial Color Identification with Increasing Age *
(per cent correct identifications)

Request	3 years	4 years	5 years	6 years	7 years
For white doll	77	86	94	97	100
For colored doll	77	83	94	96	100
For doll "like you"	36	66	48	68	87

* From data reported by Clark and Clark in Swanson, Newcomb, Hartley, et al., Readings in Social Psychology, rev. ed., New York: Holt, 1952, p. 554.

economic status, in religion, in morals, and in other aspects of the culture in which he is reared. All such distinctions assume increasing significance from the standpoint of social interactions, but they also color the child's further social perceptions. We are referring to what MacLeod [12] calls the "social determination of perception." "In everyday life," he says, "we do not always perceive things as they really are. Within wide limits we perceive them as we want them to be, as we expect them to be, or in terms of an unconscious bias ... our wants, expectations and biases are in large measure socially determined." This aspect of social perceiving need receive brief mention here, not because it is unimportant, but because we have very little relevant information on such perceiving in children. Even when poor children make larger overestimations, from memory, of the size of coins than do children from wealthy backgrounds, we know only that one's economic environment may influence his judgments. We know nothing about the developmental aspects of such influences.[13] There is no doubt, from general observation, however, that our earlier experiences with persons make us especially attentive, or "reaction sensitive," to their characteristics and their actions. Thus those who, for various reasons, have come to hate or dislike members of a certain race or religion or national group are quicker to notice their "faults" than to recognize such faults in members of their own classification. It is said, in the same sense, that we "overlook" the faults of our friends.

The problems of "perceiving the social" and of the "social determination of perceiving" are interrelated, as MacLeod suggests. Thus it is not at all far-fetched to suppose that a child who has been brought up to like Negroes will be less prone to observe physical differences between a Negro child and himself. And a child reared in an environment prejudicial to Negroes may be expected to "perceive" so-called "racial" characteristics in addition to the more obvious ones of skin color and hair texture. The same principle applies not only to racial stereotypes but also to those concerning religious, economic, and other aspects of our social environment.

The Beginnings of Social Interaction

One of the earliest indications that a baby is learning to influence the behavior of others occurs when he cries to be picked up. That he is crying for this purpose is inferred from the fact that, whereas crying previously continued after the infant was picked up, it now stops. Bühler,[14] who regards this as the first evidence of social behavior, places it in the second month. Other early social interactions observed by Bühler in testing a group of 69 infants, and the ages at which they normally appeared, are as follows.

Between the *first and second months* at least 60 per cent of the infants returned the glance of an adult with smiling, were quieted by touching, became restless when spoken to, and cried when an attending grownup left. Between the *second and third months* smiling back at a grownup, exhibiting disturbance when approached, and returning an approaching glance by lalling were added to the repertoire. Infants between the *third and fourth months* exhibited "displeasure" at losing the glance of an adult, and were quieted by caressing. Disturbance at the sight of people and neglect of play upon meeting the glance of a grownup were added between the *fourth and fifth months*. No new social reactions are reported until between the *seventh and eighth months*. At this time the infants "strived for attention" by lalling, stretched hands toward a grownup, and cried when a grownup stopped talking. In the *ninth month* two new responses were added. These were "striving for attention by movements" and pulling on the grownup's clothes. At around the *tenth month* the infant offered the grownup an object, imitated movements, and engaged in organized play activity. The only further response during the first year is reported as appearing at approximately the *eleventh month*. Bühler says that at this age 60 per cent of her infants looked at a grownup "amazed" because of some incident. Since so few infants were involved, these results can be considered no more than suggestive. Several of the other "baby tests" (see pp. 367–368) include social items like these. Three such items (elicits attention, plays pat-a-cake, and plays peek-a-boo) are included in Table 14 (p. 424). Such items begin to appear between six and eight months, but do not become prevalent until the end of the first year.

An infant's earliest and most persistent social contacts during the first year are with adults. Other infants usually play an insignificant role in its social development. One finds it interesting, however, to consider the reactions of infants to others of approximately their own age. Two investigations are of particular relevance here, one by Bühler and the other by Maudry and Nekula. Bühler [15] placed babies of about the same age in a crib and observed the characteristic interactions which appeared at various age levels. We have already (p. 423) mentioned one outcome of this study — the finding that one infant failed to give evidence of noticing the other until the age of four to five months, at which time it might smile at its crib mate or cry when the latter received attention. Nothing of special interest from the standpoint of social interaction was evident until between the eighth and ninth months, when one child might offer the other a toy, lall to it, or imitate its activities. Between the ninth and tenth months there was resistance to having the other infant take away a toy. There was also evidence of organized play with the partner. Beginning between the tenth and eleventh months, one child might attempt to get the other's attention, exhibit ill-humor when it moved away, and put down a plaything and turn toward the other.

Maudry and Nekula's [16] investigation, carried out at Bühler's suggestion, offers a more carefully controlled experimental setting for the study of infant interactions and a more detailed analysis of the responses than existed in the pioneer study which we have just described. There were 92 children between the ages of six and twenty-four months. Each child was observed in a play situation, within a play-pen, with a partner who was not more than three months older or younger than himself. One investigator arranged the play situation, according to a standardized procedure, while the other observed and kept a detailed record of the behavior of the children. The procedure was as follows: Four minutes after the children were placed in the pen, each was offered a cube and a third cube was placed on the floor between them. Four minutes later the cubes were removed and one child was given a bell. After another four minutes the bell was removed, a drum was placed between the children, and they were offered a drumstick apiece. Four minutes elapsed, and after the drum and drumsticks had been removed, the children were shown how to roll a ball, which was then given to one of them. After having the ball for a period of four minutes the children were taken back to their cribs. The experimenter left the room after making each of the indicated changes. All observations were made from behind a one-way vision screen. Thus the children were alone while being observed. Reactions were dealt with in terms of an inventory too detailed for presentation here. The tabulations show the percentage of the total number of inventoried items which appeared at each of four age levels, 6–8 months, 9–13 months, 14–18 months, and 19–25 months. Some of the items which showed age changes are represented in Figure 125, which is derived from the tabulations in Maudry and Nekula's report.

The period from 6 to 8 months was characterized by the impersonal way in which interactions occurred. Except that he might receive a friendly smile, the partner was treated pretty much as play material. Even fights were impersonal, consisting of blind attempts of one child to get something held by the other. Between 9 and 13 months fighting became more frequent and more personal, but it was more pronounced when one child had a plaything and the other did not. There was no evidence of hostility toward the

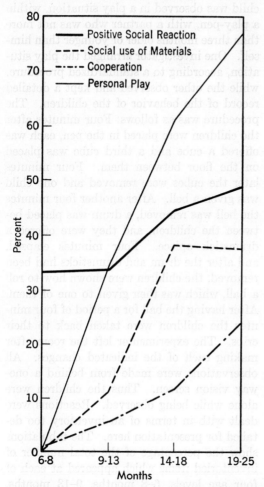

Figure 125. Some Aspects of Social Development in the Reactions of One Infant to Another in a Play Situation

The situation was a play-pen in which two infants differing in age by no more than three months were placed together and given certain play materials, as described in the text. These curves are for a few social items in which more or less steady growth was apparent. Some items, like negative social reactions, increased in frequency between the first two age groups and then decreased. Other items, like handling the same object and interference without social intention, showed a decline with age. (Based upon data reported by M. Maudry and M. Nekula, "Social Relations Between Children of the Same Age During the First Two Years of Life," *J. Genet. Psychol.*, 1939, *54*, 193–215.)

partner as such. On the positive side, this period was marked by giving of special attention to the partner and the first signs of cooperation and social use of material, such as rolling a ball toward the other. From 14 to 18 months there was a decided shift of interest from the material to the partner. There was less conflict, and except where one partner was deprived of play material, there was an evident friendly attitude toward the other. Cooperation and social use of play materials were becoming more evident.

In the period between 19 and 25 months there was much more social contact and more friendliness toward the partner regardless of the placement of play materials. At this age range, according to the investigators,[17] "Positive social reactions predominate in which cooperation has become as important as the more primitive forms of looking, smiling, and grasping; games show a considerable increase in frequency and length. The play is personal, i.e., both children modify their behavior in adjustment to the partner's activity; the material is no longer a hindrance but a means for establishing social relations as social use of it has become an important feature of the game."

Social Interaction in Preschool Children

Until the age of two or three years, a child is apparently not capable of maintaining active contact with more than one individual at a time. When three infants are placed together, active social contact at a given time is between only two of them. This statement is based upon Bühler's[18] summary of several German investigations, some of them unpublished. Reininger found that groups of children develop spontaneously at about the middle of the second year, and that at this age a child begins responding to two others simultaneously. When Klein and Wander placed two-year-old children together in groups of three, 8 per cent of the subjects had no social contact with the others, 67

Figure 126. Situation Used to Study Cooperative Behavior in Preschool Children

Food was placed in a cup at the end of the lever, which was arranged so that if the child in *A* pulled the string, the child in *B* could reach the cooky. Subjects alternated in *A* and *B*. The crucial test of cooperation came when the child who was in a position to pull was prevented by a screen from seeing whether or not the cup contained food, the experimenter sometimes faking its placement. The worker could then pull on appropriate occasions only if his partner gave him proper instructions. (After J. J. B. Morgan, *Child Psychology*, 3d ed., New York: Rinehart, 1942, as adapted from the description by Wolfle and Wolfle of their experimental situation.)

per cent made social contacts with only one other child, and only 25 per cent kept up contact with two at a time. During the later preschool period, according to Bühler, groups of three predominate. Furthermore, with increasing age there is a decrease in the incidence of solitary children. Bühler claims that the chief factors which lead children to associate are helplessness and need, desire for companionship in play, common interest in some material or toy, and the quest for information.

Cooperative behavior

We have already suggested that cooperative behavior between two children increases with age. This trend continues in the preschool period and is greatly facilitated by development of language. The role which language can play in this connection is interestingly revealed in an experiment by Wolfle and Wolfle.[19] The subjects were monkeys and preschool children, and the situation for each

was comparable with that illustrated in Figure 126. The subject in *B* could receive his cooky only if the one in *A* pulled the string. On alternate trials the subjects changed places as workers and receivers. All subjects, animal and human, learned to pull food to the partner. The greatest test of cooperation came when food was present on some trials only and the subject who was to do the pulling was prevented by a screen from seeing whether or not a cooky was in the food cup. The monkeys did not solve this problem. They pulled just the same whether food was present or not.* Nor was the problem solved by the youngest children (two years, six months and two years, eight months), who had insufficient communicative facility to make appropriate requests; their partner's pulling had nothing to do with whether or not a cooky was present.

* It is interesting to note, in this connection, that recent research at the University of Wisconsin suggests that monkeys have a "manipulatory drive" which induces them to pull strings and manipulate other devices even though no extraneous reward is given.

These children made such inadequate verbalizations as "See that thing," "Look at that," "I want my cake," and "Jump it to me." The older children were much more explicit, saying such things as "Pull me that cooky," "Will you give me the cooky if I pull it in?" or "Pull that string." The older children also made "deals," like offering the worker the legs of the animal cracker if he'd only pull it in.

Cooperative participation in play activities develops gradually during the preschool period and is preceded by various other forms of participation which Parten [20] has designated as *solitary play, looking on, parallel play,* and *associated group play.* She and three assistants kept detailed records of the play activity of 22 boys and 20 girls between the ages of two and five years. An observational sampling method was used. It involved one-minute samples taken during a free-play hour in a nursery school. The behavior of a particular child was sampled at different times during the play hour so as to control for fatigue, boredom, and the like. Symbols were used to designate the classification to which the particular sample of behavior belonged. Comparisons of the records made by different observers suggested that the data had high reliability. An idea of the kind of information

revealed by this procedure may be provided by the following example: Child J4 was observed a total of 33 times. In none of these periods was he unoccupied. In 6 per cent of them he was engaged in solitary play, in 15 per cent in looking on, in 27 per cent in parallel play, in 27 per cent in associative play, and in 25 per cent in cooperative play.

Few of the children, even in the lowest age classification, were ever found to be unoccupied. *Solitary play* involved playing alone and independently, with different toys from the others, and within speaking distance of them, yet without attempting contact. This sort of play became less frequent with age, as suggested in Figure 127. *Onlooking behavior* may involve verbal participation or merely an interest in watching the others play. It is not very frequent at any age level and shows no particular growth trend. *Parallel play,* which involves using the same toys as others, but playing beside rather than with others, is the most frequent of all at the earliest age levels. It declines with age. The other two forms of play, associative and cooperative, both show some increase with age, but greater changes occur in the latter and would doubtless continue were observations carried beyond the preschool period. In *associative play,* as here designated, the children play together, bor-

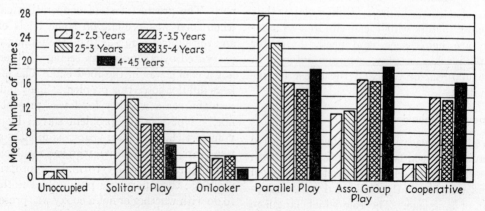

Figure 127. Mean Number of Times Each Activity Was Observed at Different Ages

For definitions of the various terms used to differentiate levels of social participation, see the discussion in the text. (From M.B. Parten, "Social Participation Among Pre-School Children," *J. Abn. & Soc. Psychol.,* 1933, *27,* 260.)

rowing, lending, using similar or different toys, and perhaps making attempts to control others, but with each for himself regardless of any possible group interests. In *cooperative play*, however, "The child plays in a group that is organized for the purpose of making some material product, or of striving to attain some competitive goal, or of dramatizing situations of adult or group life, or of playing formal games. There is a marked sense of belonging or not belonging to the group. The control of the group situation is in the hands of one or two of the members who direct the activity of the others. The goal as well as the method of attaining it necessitates a division of labor, taking of different roles by the various group members and the organization of activity so that the efforts of one child are supplemented by those of another." [21] Play coming within this category, as compared with associative play, is illustrated in Figure 128.

Composite scores for social participation increased as a function of age and yielded a

Figure 128. A Comparison of Associative and Cooperative Play

In associative play (above), as defined by Parten, the children play together, but with each following his own interests. Cooperative play (right) is characterized by organization for some end result, with leadership and a division of labor. (Photographs from Devaney and Keystone.)

correlation of .61. Investigation showed that there was an insignificant correlation between social participation and length of time that the child had been in the nursery school; thus the correlation with age was not due to the fact that older children had received more nursery school experience. The correlation with I.Q. was positive, but of doubtful reliability.

The same investigation included observations of leadership, but very little true leadership in which the child directs others occurred at this age level. What leadership was present, however, showed an increase with age. The correlation between composite leadership ratings and age was .67. But there was a similar correlation between height and leadership. Between social participation and leadership the correlation was .97. This high correlation came from the fact that leadership can hardly occur unless there is social participation. There was a positive correlation, although of doubtful reliability, between I.Q. and leadership rating.

Sometimes, as Hanfmann [22] has shown, a leadership hierarchy develops, even at the preschool level. One child may lead (or dominate) several others. However, the hierarchical position of a child may differ, depending upon the kind of play activity involved. The child who dominates all others in destructive activities, for example, may be dominated by others when he participates with them in some constructive endeavor.

Bossing others becomes increasingly evident during the preschool period, as Hattwick and Sanders [23] found from their analysis of teachers' ratings of various aspects of social behavior. Looking for praise and seeking attention follow a similar trend. Some of these characteristics are considered in the next chapter as aspects of personality.

Social facilitation and related interactions

We say that social facilitation is present if there is an increment in the frequency or intensity of behavior when an organism is working in the presence of others, as compared with when it is working alone. Where such facilitation occurs it is usually assumed to result from competition, or rivalry. That this phenomenon occurs in preschool children is shown in an experiment by Leuba,[24] who observed the putting of uniformly colored pegs into a form board when the children were working alone and when they were working in pairs. Thirty-two children between the ages of one year, nine months and six years served as subjects. Under both conditions (alone and paired) the children worked while the adult who was in the room occupied himself with something else nearby. There was no attempt to induce rivalry. Another person observed the children through a one-way vision screen and recorded their responses, verbal and otherwise. The youngest group (two years) paid little or no attention to the child working at the same task. No rivalry was evident, and all but two who were nearing three years of age made approximately the same number of placements alone and together. In the three-to four-year group, however, there was a good deal of social interaction, but of a nature which lowered output in the together situation. Little rivalry was apparent. All but one of twelve five-year-old children gave unmistakable signs of being motivated by rivalry, and nine of these (two spilled the pegs) increased their output in the together situation.

The following verbal reactions are characteristic of those found at the upper age level; both children are working on a square.

M.B. finishes it first and says, "I did." After working for a while V.E. gets ahead and says, "Look how much I have done." They keep informing each other of the progress they have made. M.B. says, "I am going to beat you, though." V.E. says she is not. They are very close. M.B. has adopted V.E.'s method. ... V.E. finishes first and says, "Ha, ha, I win."

Greenberg [25] also found an increase in competitive behavior with age. Her subjects were Viennese children between the ages of two and seven years, and the situation in which competition was studied involved block building.

Efforts were made to stimulate competition. For example, when two children had finished their constructions they were asked to stand at the side of the experimenter and to observe what they had built. They were then asked, "Whose is prettier?" Sometimes the experimenter said, "Let me see who can build bigger." The two- to three-year group gave no evidence of competition. These children seemed merely interested in the materials. Of the next age group (three to four), about 43 per cent showed competitive behavior. This age group had a better understanding of the idea of excelling, but the social relationship between the children seemed more important than competition as such. About 70 per cent of the four- to five-year group were competitive. The percentage increased to 86 per cent at the upper age level. In these upper levels there was not only more competitive construction, but the children became increasingly critical of each other's work.

One type of interaction which often occurs in situations like those discussed is imitation, as when M.B. of Leuba's experiment adopted V.E.'s procedure. The scale used by Bridges [26] to rate children for social development includes various imitational items like copying another child's actions (jumping off the bottom step when the other child does), mimicking another's words (saying "Here we go Lubin-Loo" after the first child), and laughing because another child has laughed. This sort of behavior, once considered innate in the sense of being automatic or reflexly elicited, is now generally regarded as a learned response. Elsewhere (pp. 349–350) we have discussed its role in the development of early aspects of language.

Miller and Dollard [27] made a special study of learning to imitate. Their experimental subjects were first graders. However, there is no doubt that such learning as they observed begins in the preschool period and that their results would have been similar had preschool children been used. Two boxes were placed in a room and the child to be imitated was told which one to open in order to get a piece of candy. There were two pieces in the box, the second of which was to be left there. The second child (imitatee) got the second piece of candy if it opened the box which it had seen the other child open. On the first trial there was only a slight tendency to imitate, perhaps because the potential imitatee thought the first child had all the candy. Within a few trials, however, all children were imitating. Most of them continued to imitate in a new situation involving four boxes, thus generalizing what they had learned. In a similar manner, children were taught to be non-imitators and to generalize this non-imitative tendency. The investigators point out that in everyday life children soon learn to imitate certain people and not others, or certain actions and not others. Their report includes several case studies of preschool children which are illustrative of the point that learning to transfer from one model to another is difficult for the child. One of these, a three-year-old, had been eating when his younger brother ate. Now there was difficulty in getting him to forego eating with his brother and to eat at a later hour with his parents instead.

Social conflict and aggression

Most of the studies of conflict and aggression in preschool children have been made in nursery school situations. This is apparently a good setting in which to study such behavior, for according to Jersild and Markey,[28] children's fights and quarrels increase in frequency when they attend nursery school. One should hasten to point out, however, that this is no indictment of nursery schools. Jersild and Fite [29] attribute the high incidence of conflict in this situation to increased contacts and social activity; not to an increase in "sheer combativeness." Several investigations summarized by Anderson and Anderson [30] have shown, moreover, that although nursery school is a good setting in which to study conflict, it is also a good one in which to observe friendly contacts. The data show that, by and large, "Children are more friendly than unfriendly by our current measures." We shall discuss conflict and aggression now and friendships later. Aggressiveness and friendliness as personality traits are considered in the following chapter. Here we are more concerned with interacting children than with the individual child and his characteristics.

Jersild and Markey,[31] for the purposes of their own investigation, defined conflict as "Any instance in which one child attacks another's person or by word or deed interferes with the person, activities, or possessions of another, or threatens by word or gesture to do so, or endeavors by force or verbal demands to possess another's belongings, or to direct another's activities in opposition to the apparent desires of the child against whom the aggression is made." Physical aggression or defense centering around material, space, or activities included such acts as: snatching, knocking down, tampering, intentional collision, and teasing by withholding another's playthings. Physical attacks centering upon the other child's person included hitting, pushing, holding down, and various other forms of interference. Verbal aggression took such forms as commands to "Give me," "Get out of my way," or "Get out of here"; claims such as "That's mine"; temporizing as in saying "You can have it later"; epithets like "Cry baby"; teasing such as is involved in "Bronx cheers" and in laughing at another's misfortune; and threats like "I am going to hit you," or "I'll tattle to the teacher." Emotional reactions, which either the aggressor or the victim might use as a means of social control, included screaming, sobbing, temper tantrums, and running to the teacher.

Each of the 54 children of this study was observed for ten 15-minute free-play periods by two observers, who wrote running descriptions of what occurred. Groups of at least four children were involved in each observation. The data relevant to our present discussion, which is focused upon developmental trends, show that the frequency of conflicts declines, although somewhat irregularly, with increasing age; that emotional concomitants like screaming and calling for help decrease in frequency with age; and that verbal attacks gradually increase in frequency.

In this, as in all other studies of social interaction, there are marked individual differences, some children being quite aggressive and others not. Moreover, a child who is aggressive with one child may not be so with another. Not only this, but he may be aggressive with the same child at one moment and friendly with him at another. Indeed Murphy,[32] in her investigation of sympathetic contacts between preschool children, found that the most aggressive children were also, under somewhat different circumstances, the most sympathetic. This was especially when they were not themselves the aggressors.

Several studies of preschool conflicts have sought an answer to the question of what sorts of interactional situation are conducive to conflict. H. H. Anderson [33] and Muste and Sharpe [34] found that aggression and domination of one child by another tend to be circular in that aggression incites aggression and domination incites domination. Anderson [35] paired children in various ways and rated them for dominative behavior. He found correlations ranging from .68 to .85 between the domination scores of the paired children. One child's domination or aggression tended to increase that of its partner. High correlations were also found between one child's integrative interaction and that of the other. Integrative interaction is defined by Anderson [36] as "a relationship in which individuals may come closer and closer together in their understandings and in their actions and still remain different" and in which they work together without evidence that one is in any way dominating the other. Both Brewer [37] and Anderson [38] have found that the actions of teachers, in their classroom contacts with children, may elicit dominative or integrative behavior. Resistance and non-cooperation between children, between parents and children, and between teachers and children are assumed to stem in large measure from whether the one who leads in this relationship is dominative or integrative in his approach.

Sympathetic interactions

The free-play situation in nursery school is conducive to arousal of sympathetic as well as aggressive behavior. Much of the sympathetic contact which does occur is found in situations involving conflict. Non-participants in the conflict may sympathize with either the aggressor or the victim. Later they may themselves be the aggressors, and as suggested earlier, the children who most frequently express sympathy tend also to have high scores for frequency of aggression.

Murphy's [39] data on sympathy were obtained during systematic observations of nursery school children engaged in free play. Each child was rated on a five-point scale, and data showing the number and kinds of contacts which each child gave and received were also noted. Sympathetic responses were evident when, for example, one child helped another in a situation involving distress, when he sided with the other in a conflict, when he provided comfort with pats, embraces, or verbalizations, or when he reproved the aggressor. There was no clear increase in the frequency of such behavior as a function of age, partly because individual differences overshadowed those associated with age. Nevertheless, older children were more prone than younger ones to show sympathy and to discern the proper occasions for its expression. The latter was especially true when pictures, stories, and experimental situations calculated to arouse sympathy were presented to the children. Another outcome of this study is the observation that children differ a great deal with respect to how much sympathetic attention they give and receive. Here again we make a transition from social interaction as such to individual differences, hence to personality.

Our discussion of typical interactions at the preschool level has by no means exhausted the topic. Other aspects, like recreational activities and friendships, might have been included in our discussion were it not for the fact that such aspects of social interaction have been studied more extensively at the school level, where they assume greater significance than at earlier ages. Before leaving the preschool level, however, it is well to bear in mind that interactions such as we have considered are reflections of a particular situation and a particular set of cultural influences. The particular situation has been a nursery school or kindergarten. Studies in a home environment which involved several children might have had somewhat different outcomes. Comparable studies carried out in certain other cultures would almost certainly have yielded different findings. This is borne out by general observations of child behavior in cultures in which the climate is either less competitive and less individualistic than our own (Zuñi, Arapesh, Samoan) and those in which it is more so (Mundugumor, Dobuan, Kwakiutl).[40] We have not, therefore, been considering forms of social interaction which, through a process of maturation, inevitably emerge in young children. Increasing maturity (physical and intellectual) are of course aspects of social development, but patterns of social interaction depend upon the social environment in which the child is developing — upon the nature of his contacts with older children and parents and teachers, through whose own behavior and admonitions the cultural influences are conveyed. The large individual differences which exist in this behavior, in any society, show that it reflects nurture to a much greater extent than nature.

Several investigations on preschool social development have dealt specifically with the impact upon the child of different kinds of parents and teachers and different social settings and cultural influences. The emphasis in these studies, however, has been on the resulting characteristics of individual children. We shall therefore reserve further discussion of them until personality as such is considered.

Social Activity in Children of School Age

Entrance into the school environment seldom involves fundamentally different forms of social contacts than those of the preschool period. As indicated above, most children have learned to play with others long before entrance into school. Furthermore, most of them have engaged in some forms of organized play. They have already learned something about rules of the game: loyalty to their own group, the need for fair play, and so forth.

The teacher-pupil relationship has to some extent also been experienced before the school age. Such experience has been derived from parental instruction of a more or less informal type, from contact with other children, and perhaps from Sunday school, nursery school, and kindergarten. When the average child enters school, he has acquired certain of the cultural habits of the group. He may not be able to read and write, but he has learned the elementary techniques of gestural and vocal communication. He has already, through stories, commands, prohibitions, and the like, learned something of the *codes* which regulate the activities of his group. In going to school, the child merely associates with larger groups of children, is subjected to teacher-pupil relationships more formal than hitherto, and continues his contacts with various aspects of the social heritage.

Investigations of social interaction in children of school age have dealt especially with such phases as recreational activity, various organizational relationships which exist in so-called "gangs" and "cliques" as well as in more formal clubs, and personal attachments of greater intimacy, as in friendships. Much of our information about social interests and activities during this period of childhood has come from questionnaires and general observations by teachers, camp counselors, and sociologists of childhood.

Recreational activities

Lehman and Witty [41] made a study of recreational activity in 6886 individuals ranging in age from seven to nineteen years. A Play Quiz comprising 200 items and spaces for the addition of items was checked by each individual. The subjects were instructed to indicate any activities engaged in "during the past week just because you wanted to."

Although Lehman and Witty's results are influenced by seasonal variations in play, by regional peculiarities, by the possible unreliability of some children's reactions, and by the fact that cultural changes have appeared within the years since the study was made, they suggest the nature of important non-institutionalized social contacts made by the growing child. The results show that boys of eight years most frequently engage in such social activities as playing catch, running and romping, and running races. By the tenth year, automobile riding and going to the movies have assumed a high frequency. By the twelfth year, baseball and football come within the group of most frequently reported social activities. Basketball and watching athletic contests achieve a high frequency by the age of fourteen. With the exception of having "dates" and social dancing, there is little change in the nature of recreational social contacts beyond this age.

At the age of eight years girls tend most frequently to engage in social recreational activities like jumping or skipping rope, listening to stories, playing house, and playing hide-and-seek. Riding in an automobile is a frequent activity by the tenth year. Going to the movies is frequently reported by the twelfth year. Visiting and entertaining company is frequent by the sixteenth year. Having "dates" and social dancing are increasingly prevalent from the sixteenth year until the adult level. Today the latter activities frequently occur before the sixteenth year.

Lehman and Witty's data show that the average number of recreational activities engaged in by boys and girls decreases with increasing age. As shown in Figure 129, the average number of social activities also decreases. There are, however, large individual variations at each age level. The amount of

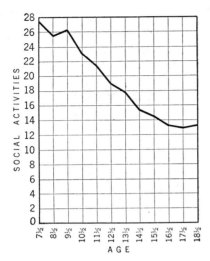

Figure 129. Average Social Recreational Activities Reported by 6886 Individuals Classified According to Chronological Age

Data for both sexes are combined. (From P. A. Witty, "A Study of Deviates in Versatility and Sociability of Play Interest," *Teachers College Contrib. to Educ.*, 1931, No. 470, p. 19.)

variability decreases in successive age groups. Older children tend to engage in closely related activities more than do younger children. There is no evidence of discrete stages of play activity, such, for example, as an individualistic and a social stage. The greatest sex difference occurs between the ages of $8\frac{1}{2}$ and $10\frac{1}{2}$ years. The most frequent recreational activities which do not involve direct participation of others are reported to be: looking at the "funny papers," reading the newspapers, reading short stories, and reading books.* Such activities, while not social in the sense of direct participation of others, are social in the last analysis. The "contacts" which children make with historical and fictional characters in this way are of undoubted significance in their social development. Indeed, such "contacts" sometimes change the whole course of further social relations.

* Were this study done today, we should no doubt find "looking at comics" and "watching television" among such activities.

Children's organizations

By the time he reaches school, the average child has already begun the slow process of achieving independence from his family group. From this time on, he becomes increasingly dependent upon contacts outside of the home. As Ojemann [42] puts it, the child between six and twelve years

leans more and more heavily on the attention and emotional support of his age-mates. Acceptance and approval by his group may become even more important than approval by his family or his teacher. The widening of the circle is a gradual one, of course. As he moves outward from family-centered interests and needs to those of his own age group, the child "shops around" from one group to another until he finds one that can make him feel wanted and needed.

Thus the influence of the "peer group" supplants, in a sense, that of the family group.

The earliest organized activities are found in play. Children build things together. Later they play such games as follow the leader, "cops and robbers," "cowboys and Indians." Dramatization of the sort so well depicted in Figure 130 is common among boys, and also among girls in their less spectacular activities involved in playing nurse, housekeeper, or school teacher. At the upper school ages, especially among boys, games requiring more organization and individual specialization come to the fore. In this country, of course, such games are often baseball, football, basketball, and ice hockey. As Anderson [43] points out, the tendency to specialize increases steadily until "By thirteen or fourteen years a boy, when asked if he plays baseball, will say, 'Yes, I'm a catcher,' indicating that he both understands and performs special duties and responsibilities."

At about eight or nine years there is a decided tendency, which thereafter increases with age, for boys and girls to play in separate groups. They often form group organizations which are confined to one sex. These, for want of a better name, are referred to as "gangs" in the case of boys and "cliques" in

Figure 130.   An Illustration of Dramatization in Children's Play

(By Amos Sewell. Courtesy *Saturday Evening Post*.)

the case of girls. According to Brown [44] and other sociologists who have studied these organizations, the emphasis at this period shifts from individual to group motivation. Through initiations, acceptance of the leader, and identification with the group and its expressed purposes, the child is made to feel that his own wishes must be subordinated to those of the organization. Such gangs and cliques are not necessarily destructive and antisocial. Many might better be called clubs. There are hiking clubs, stamp or coin clubs, and the like. Some such groups soon break up; others persist on into adolescence. Fraternities at the college level and adult fraternal organizations, despite their greater sophistication and widespread organization, are similar in many ways to the gangs and cliques found at earlier age levels.

In our society a large proportion of school-age children belong to nationally organized groups like the Cubs or Brownies and the Boy or Girl Scouts. Programs associated with such organizations are arranged sequentially to correlate with the child's physical, social, and intellectual development. If we were to discuss the impact of these organized social activities upon the growing child we should be led too far afield. We may note here, however, that such programs have a marked influence upon the child in helping him to adapt to the standards of our primarily Christian culture, but that their effects are variable, depending on those who administer them and on the personality of children who come under their influence. A good discussion of what such organizations try to accomplish from the standpoint of social development will be found in Breckenridge and Vincent.[45]

Experiments on social interactions in school children are conspicuously few in number. The most noteworthy are those of Lewin and his associates on democratic, laissez-faire, and autocratic boy's clubs. Groups of ten-year-old boys were established as clubs so that questions like the following could be answered: What underlies such differing patterns of group behavior as rebellion against authority, persecution of a scapegoat, apathetic submission to authoritarian domination, or attack upon an outgroup? [46] In the *authoritarian group*, all determination of policy was by the leader, who also dictated the group projects and the procedures to be used. He criticized the work, but remained aloof so far as active participation was concerned. The *laissez-faire group* had complete freedom, as did the individual members. There was no true leadership. The "leader" gave information only when asked. He did not participate in projects and he made no comments unless questioned. In the *democratic group*, all policies were discussed by the group.* The leader suggested possible goals and procedures, but the group made final decisions. The leader participated as a member of the group and his comments were "objective" or "fact-

* The terms used to designate these groups are not, of course, entirely related to social structures thus designated in the adult world.

minded." The groups were equated and each boy served, at different times, as a member of five democratic, five authoritarian, and two laissez-faire situations. The leaders sometimes played the autocrat and sometimes the democrat. Observers kept detailed records of a large number of interactions, including verbal.

Some of the most important outcomes of these experiments were as follows: The authoritarian groups generated 30 times as much expressed hostility as occurred in the democratic groups. In both the authoritarian and the laissez-faire groups there was much more irritability and aggression than in the democratic group. In some of the authoritarian situations the boys were apathetic. That this apathy was caused by the repressive influence of the autocratic leader was suggested by the following observations: there were outbursts of aggression on "days of transition to a freer atmosphere"; there was an increased aggression when the autocratic leader left the room; there was no smiling and joking in these groups as compared with others; and the boys expressed a much greater liking for other leaders than the autocratic ones. Aggression which occurred in these experiments was attributed to "tension, restricted space of free movement, rigidity of group structure, and style of living (culture)." [47]

Although these experiments were not designed to bring out developmental trends (all boys being the same age) they are of interest to us here because they show the possibility of experimentation on group interaction in children of school age and because they suggest that the interactions which characterize children's societies and the personality characteristics of the individual members may be influenced in an important manner by different "social climates."

Interpersonal relationships

Several investigations have focused upon the person-to-person relationships within classrooms and other groupings of school-age children. One procedure, developed by Moreno [48] and known as "sociometry," requires each child to say which member of the group he would like as his partner in some project.* A plot based upon such data is known as a "sociogram." As illustrated in Figure 131, a sociogram shows that some children are chosen much more often than others. Some may not be chosen at all. Children who were popular in such choices were found by Bonney [51] to possess to a high degree such characteristics as: health and vigor, conformity and group identification, dependability, cooperative attitudes, and behavior which aroused admiration in others. The unpopular children, on the other hand, tended to be inadequate in these respects.

According to J. E. Anderson, [52]

Sociograms are of practical value in working with children's groups as they clearly point out isolated and overlooked children who need attention. But there is some question about their contribution to science.... Moreover, there is always some question about the generalizations that can be drawn, since they are relative to the particular group on which they are obtained. Despite this, sociograms, when used at various age or grade levels, have revealed interesting developmental trends and have confirmed results obtained by other methods of studying social behavior.

The developmental trends to which Anderson refers are those shown by particular children who become increasingly or decreasingly popular as a function of age and social experience.

Children's friendships have also been widely investigated, the usual procedure being to ask a child to write the names of his best friends in rank order. By asking him to repeat this procedure after an interval, say, of two weeks, one is able to obtain some indication of the stability of friendships. When they obtained such information on boys and girls ranging in age from 11 to 18 years, Thompson and Horrocks [53] found a trend suggesting greater stability of friendships as a function of age. Friendship is in large measure

* Various procedures may be used in gathering such data. See especially the research by Koch [49] and the critical discussion by Thompson, Bligh, and Witryol. [50]

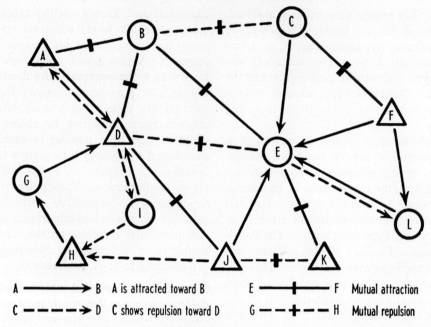

A ——————→ B   A is attracted toward B   E ———+——— F   Mutual attraction

C ------→ D   C shows repulsion toward D   G ---+--- H   Mutual repulsion

Figure 131.   A Sociogram

These are third-grade children.   Triangles represent boys, and circles girls.   Each child had
been asked: "Which boy(s) or girl(s) would you like (not like) to work with?"   (After
Moreno, from J. F. Dashiell, *Fundamentals of General Psychology*, Boston: Houghton
Mifflin, 1949, p. 503.)

determined by propinquity. Being in the same classroom, riding the same school bus, or living close together in the same neighborhood are important factors. According to data obtained by Austin and Thompson,[54] sixth-grade children choose their three best friends predominantly on such bases as frequent association, similarity of interests and tastes, cheerfulness, and friendliness. Frequently-given reasons for changing friends over a two-week interval are: lack of recent contact, a quarrel, and becoming friends with another child.   Thompson[55] says that "Although children are originally drawn together by physical proximity and similarity of interests and tastes, the prolongation of friendly relations is largely due to the complementary nature of their behavioral dispositions."

Social Maturity

As the child learns to perceive the presence of others, to differentiate between persons, to discriminate differences in gestures and verbal expressions, to cooperate with other children and adults, to develop recreational interests involving others, to form stable friendships, and to become less dependent upon his home and parents, he is developing in the direction of what is often referred to as "social maturity."   Several normative studies have been carried out, and scales developed, with a view to gauging the level of social development attained at different age levels.   One such scale was devised by Bridges[56] for use with children from two to five years old.   Relations with children and with adults were rated separately, as indicated in Table 16, which suggests the nature of some of the 85 behavior items involved in this scale.   One will observe that the children were scored in terms of whether or not they exhibited the behavior in question.   The greater the number of points obtained, the greater the presumed level of social development.   This scale thus provided a rough index of the social maturity of a child's reactions to other children and adults. The results reported by Bridges showed an increase in average social scores from around 54 at two to around 79 at five years. Scores

Table 16. Selected Items from a Social Development Scale for Recording Social Reactions of Preschool Children to Other Children and to Adults *

SECTION I. RELATIONS WITH CHILDREN (age 2 to 5 years)

The child *has* or has not:

Often spoken to other children

Originated new play activity with another child

Joined group of children in play

Sought another child's approval

Asked another child for help

Always given up toys at fair request

Pointed to others' errors

Tried to help others

Stopped work to aid another child

Comforted another in distress

The child has *not* or has:

Usually stayed out of group marching or games

Claimed others' toys

Interfered with others' work

Created disorder in group or led others into mischief

Frequently pulled or pushed others

SECTION II. RELATIONS WITH ADULTS (age 2 to 5 years)

The child *has* or has not:

Often spoken to adults

Asked help when needed

Always found occupation for self

Usually put away materials before taking out more

Told own experiences to adult

The child has *not* or has:

Frequently refused to do what adult asked

Usually resisted adult suggestions

Persistently refused to eat dinner

Sought help by passively waiting

Waited to be fed at table

* From Bridges.

also increased as a function of preschool attendance.

Bridges points out that her results fail to support specific conclusions concerning the age at which various items are exhibited and the score characteristic of each age level. The behavior observed is a function of ever-changing conditions both within and around the child. Furthermore, the scoring of the responses calls for a certain amount of interpretation by the observer. The behavior observed in the McGill University Nursery School, moreover, might not be characteristic of that appearing in other situations. Nevertheless, Bridges believes that some very general conclusions concerning the social development of her subjects are warranted. In summarizing her observations on reactions of children to other children she [57] says,

. . . between the ages of two and five years children in a nursery school progress from being socially indifferent infants, through the stages of self-assertiveness and interference with the liberties of others, to a stage in which they show consideration, sympathy, and kindness for others. They then delight in group play and cooperate with one another for mutual enjoyment. They show real concern for the approval and disapproval of others, and express their own appreciation or disapproval in words rather than in actions. Not all children reach this high degree of social attainment within the pre-school period, while, on the other hand, some children under three show advanced social development. There are very noticeable individual differences. Moreover, children do not progress from stage to stage in a uniform manner. They regress at times to earlier forms of behavior or develop new anti-social reactions. But, when all aspects of social behavior are considered together, most children show progress during the nursery school period.

The development of social behavior in response to adults is summarized as follows:

. . . children between the ages of two and five years progress through three roughly defined stages of development in their social relations with adults. In the first or dependent stage the child is somewhat passive and relies upon the adult for assistance and attention. The second stage, which reaches its height between two and a half and three years, is one of resistance against adult influence and striving for power and independence. The behavior of the child then gradually changes from being resistive or obstinate to being cooperative and friendly. The desire to win approval and avoid disapproval grows. Conversation develops, and topics change from protests and wishes to descriptions of events or actions of mutual interest between child and adult. Thus the third stage, reached usually between the fourth and fifth year, is one in which the child shows self-reliance, trustworthiness, and friendly cooperation with adults.

Bridges points out that each child varies in social behavior from time to time. During fatigue, sickness, and emotional upset there is frequently a relapse to former, less social, modes of response.

Doll,[58] whose Vineland Social Maturity Scale is widely used to assess the social development of children, looks upon social maturity as "the extent to which the person progressively dominates his environment and creates, demands, or justifies his own freedom of action as age increases." The Vineland Social Maturity Scale is a rating device which, in the hands of a skilled examiner and interviewer, yields a social age from which a social development quotient (S.Q.) may be derived. The scale is so arranged and used that the average S.Q. is 100. It is used over the age range from early infancy to eighteen years.

Many items in this scale are not in themselves social. They are similar to items earlier referred to as indices of sensorimotor, linguistic, emotional, and intellectual development. Other items are more obviously social. They stress group activities and independence from adult supervision. Social development expected at different age levels gives some indication of this emphasis. Thus, by the time a child has reached four years he is expected to be taking part in various group activities, including games and parties. Before he reaches six he is playing simple table games with others in which he follows the rules and does little squabbling. Moreover, he is going to school unattended, but often accompanied by friends. The average child of eight years is engaging in group play with other children — such activities as unorganized baseball, follow the leader, and hiking. Girls of this age are playing house, school, nurse-doctor, or otherwise imitating aspects of adult social life. Between the ages of twelve and fifteen both boys and girls are usually taking part in games that require skill and are played according to rules. The boy may be an active member of an athletic team. Parties, dances, and other such social activities are placed within this age range.

The Fels Research Institute at Antioch College has made extensive use of the Vineland Social Maturity Scale. Patterson[59] reports the data obtained. Figure 132 compares the average raw scores at each six-month age period with scores reported by Doll. One will observe that scores increase more or less regularly with age. The Antioch scores are higher than those reported by Doll, but the two curves are quite similar in trend. Patterson reports that scores on this scale correlate highly with chronological and mental age, but only poorly with I.Q. It is thus concluded that "the scale measures an aspect of maturity, presumably social, which overlaps with mental maturity through the common influence of chronological age, yet is not identical with intelligence." Children with high S.Q.'s are found to be "independent and self-sufficient." The Vineland scale thus provides an index of emancipation from adult supervision with respect to certain simpler aspects of social behavior. It does not deal with the personality trait generally referred to as "sociability."

Summary and Conclusions

This chapter has dealt with two aspects of social development: social perceiving and social interaction. Emphasis has been on social processes rather than on the effect of these upon the individual — upon personality.

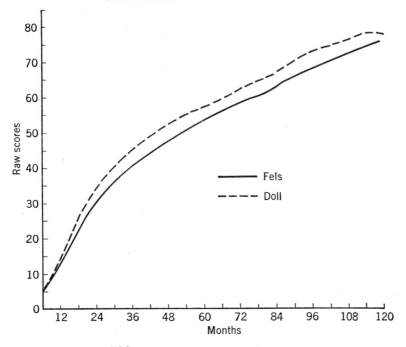

Figure 132. **Social Maturity as a Function of Age**

The Fels means were based upon interviews with the mother. Rating was by two examiners. Doll's S.Q.'s are given for comparison. (From C. H. Paterson, "The Vineland Social Maturity Scale and Some of Its Correlates," *J. Genet. Psychol.*, 1943, *62*, 276.)

The infant's earliest responses to social stimuli as such occur during the second month. Among these responses are smiling at an adult, ceasing to cry when picked up, and differentiation of human from non-human sounds. Differentiation of familiar from unfamiliar individuals also appears during the early months. It is not until the middle of the first year that babies characteristically differentiate between friendly and unfriendly vocalizations and gestures. Smiling in response to the human face is at first indiscriminate. Discrimination between familiar and unfamiliar faces begins at around six months. Part of the infant's early perceptual development involves differentiation of itself from others. Perception of racial differences (as between Negro and white) begins early, being quite prevalent at two years, and it increases with age.

When infants younger than four or five months are placed together in the same crib,

they fail to respond to each other. At about the fourth or fifth month they give evidence of noticing each other. Actual interaction such as offering a toy to the other child, copying its actions, and the like, fails to appear until several months later. Pairs of children placed together in a play-pen at first treat each other impersonally, as play material. Beginning at about nine months, interactions become more personal — such as fighting over the same plaything, or rolling a ball toward the partner. Early in the first year, interest shifts from playthings to the partner, and social use of material is more common than before. Cooperation, as in playing games, increases with age, as does the unbroken duration of play.

Infants under a year old are apparently unable to make social contact with more than one other infant at a time. By the end of the second year a few children keep up contact with two others simultaneously. It is only in the later preschool period that groups of three interacting children are very prevalent.

Cooperative behavior continues to increase in frequency during the preschool period, and it is greatly facilitated by the development of language. Between two and five, play tends to go through various stages, beginning with solitary activity and culminating in cooperative endeavors. Social participation and leadership in play are correlated with chronological age, but not to any significant degree, apparently, with I.Q. Social facilitation, as evidenced by greater output when working with others than when working alone, is evident in preschool children. It becomes increasingly apparent as rivalry emerges. This is prevalent by the age of five years. Another aspect of social interaction is imitation. The child learns to imitate certain actions (or persons) and not others.

Social conflict is common among preschool children engaged in free play, although friendly contacts are also prevalent. There is a tendency for physical conflict to decline as the child approaches school age. Verbal attacks, on the other hand, increase in frequency with age. Aggression varies a great deal from one child to another, but certain situations seem more conducive to its appearance than others. There is a tendency for domination and aggression in others to arouse aggressive behavior in return. Some parents and teachers act in such a manner as to make children more aggressive (and resistant) than they would otherwise be. The data on sympathetic contacts among preschool children show that perception of the occasions for sympathy increases with age, as does the frequency of sympathetic behavior. There is a tendency for the most aggressive children to be sympathetic when they are not themselves the aggressors. Individual differences in sympathy (as well as in other processes involved in interaction) often overshadow age differences. The point was made, moreover, that the interactions studied in preschool children might differ considerably if children from other cultures than our own were observed under otherwise comparable conditions.

Social activities of school-age children have not been studied as widely, from the genetic standpoint, as those of preschool children. Interest has centered especially upon recreational activities, organizations such as "gangs" and clubs, and friendly relationships as when a child chooses those with whom he would like to carry out certain projects. Recreational activities change considerably, both in nature and frequency, as children grow older. One notable trend is the decreasing frequency, with age, of activities involving participation with others. What this amounts to is that, although some social activities persist, the older child engages in fewer such recreational activities in relation to solitary ones, like reading. As the growing child comes to participate in groups outside of the home (gangs, cliques, clubs) he gradually leans more heavily upon contacts with his peers and is accordingly less dependent than formerly upon those within the home. Identification with peer groups becomes increasingly important. Investigations of social interaction in experimentally arranged clubs of ten-year-olds have shown that democratic organization is less conducive to aggression and other undesirable interactions than authoritarian and laissez-faire organization. Sociometric procedures have been used to study differences in the popularity of children and also the characteristics which make for such acceptability. Children's friendships, studied by asking children to indicate their best friends, become increasingly stable as adolescence is approached. Frequency of association and similarity of interests rank high among factors conducive to friendly relationships.

Efforts have been made to measure social maturity by rating children for various kinds of interaction with others. Scores increase with age. The Vineland Social Maturity Scale, which covers the range from infancy to adolescence, places stress upon development of self-reliance. No cognizance is taken of sociability as such. The scale appears to be rating something which differs from intelligence, as represented by the I.Q.

REFERENCES

1. Hetzer, H., and B. H. Tudor-Hart, "Die Frühesten Reactionen auf die Menschliche Stimme," *Quellen und Studien*, 1927, *5*, 103–124.
2. Bühler, C., and H. Hetzer, "Das erste Verständnis von Ausdruck in ersten Lebensjahr," *Zsch. f. Psychol.*, 1928, *107*, 50–61.
3. Spitz, R., "The Smiling Response: A Contribution to the Ontogenesis of Social Relations," *Genet. Psychol. Monog.*, 1946, *34*, 57–125.
4. Gesell, A., and F. L. Ilg, *Child Development: An Introduction to the Study of Human Growth.* New York: Harper, 1949. Quotation from pp. 31–32.
5. Gesell, A., and H. Thompson, *Infant Behavior: Its Genesis and Growth.* New York: McGraw-Hill, 1934.
6. Bühler, C., *The First Year of Life.* New York: Day, 1930.
7. Horowitz, R. E., "Racial Aspects of Self-Identification in Nursery School Children," *J. Psychol.*, 1939, *7*, 91–99.
8. Clark, K. B., and M. K. Clark, "The Development of Consciousness of Self and the Emergence of Racial Identification in Negro Preschool Children," *J. Soc. Psychol.*, 1939, *10*, 591–599; "Skin Color as a Factor in Racial Identification of Negro Preschool Children," *ibid.*, 1940, *11*, 159–169; "Social Identification and Preference in Negro Children," in Swanson, Newcomb, Hartley, *et al.* (eds.), *Readings in Social Psychology* (rev. ed.), New York: Holt, 1952, pp. 551–560.
9. Springer, D. V., "Awareness of Racial Differences by Preschool Children in Hawaii," *Genet. Psychol. Monog.*, 1950, *41*, 215–270.
10. Radke, M., H. G. Trager, and H. Davis, "Social Perceptions and Attitudes of Children," *Genet. Psychol. Monog.*, 1949, *40*, 327–447. Quotation from p. 444.
11. Horowitz, E. L., "Development of Attitude Toward Negroes," *Arch. Psychol.*, 1936, No. 194. An abridged version is to be found in Swanson, Newcomb, Hartley, *et al.* (see citation 8).
12. MacLeod, R. B., "The Place of Phenomenological Analysis in Social Psychological Theory," in J. H. Rohrer, and M. Sherif, *Social Psychology at the Crossroads.* New York: Harper, 1951. Quotation from p. 229.
13. See J. S. Bruner and C. C. Goodman, "Value and Need as Organizing Factors in Perception," *J. Abn. & Soc. Psychol.*, 1947, *42*, 33–34; and L. F. Carter and K. Schooler, "Value, Need, and Other Factors in Perception," *Psych. Rev.*, 1949, *56*, 200–207.
14. Bühler, C., *op. cit.*, Table III, p. 56.
15. *Ibid.*, Table IV, p. 57.
16. Maudry, M., and M. Nekula, "Social Relations Between Children of the Same Age During the First Two Years of Life," *J. Genet. Psychol.*, 1939, *54*, 193–215.
17. *Ibid.*, p. 214.
18. Bühler, C., "The Social Behavior of Children," in C. Murchison (ed.), *A Handbook of Child Psychology* (2d ed.). Worcester: Clark University Press, 1933.
19. Wolfle, D. L., and H. M. Wolfle, "The Development of Cooperative Behavior in Monkeys and Young Children," *J. Genet. Psychol.*, 1939, *55*, 137–175.
20. Parten, M. B., "Social Participation Among Preschool Children," *J. Abn. & Soc. Psychol.*, 1932, *27*, 243–269; "Leadership Among Preschool Children," *Ibid.*, 1933, *27*, 430–440; "Social Play Among Preschool Children," *ibid.*, 1933, *28*, 136–147; (with S. M. Newhall) "Social Behavior of Preschool Children," in Barker, *et al.*, *Child Behavior and Development*, New York: McGraw-Hill, 1943.
21. *Op. cit.*, 1932, p. 251.
22. Hanfmann, E., "Social Structure of a Group of Kindergarten Children," *Am. J. Orthopsychiatry*, 1935, *5*, 407–410.
23. Hattwick, L. A., and M. K. Sanders, "Age Differences in Behavior at the Nursery School Level," *Child Development*, 1938, *9*, 27–47.
24. Leuba, C., "An Experimental Study of Rivalry in Young Children," *J. Comp. Psychol.*, 1933, *16*, 367–378.
25. Greenberg, P. J., "Competition in Children: An Experimental Study," *Am. J. Psychol.*, 1932, *44*, 221–248.
26. Bridges, K. M. B., *Social and Emotional Development of the Pre-School Child.* London: Kegan Paul, 1931.
27 Miller, N. E., and J. Dollard, *Social Learning*

and Imitation. New Haven: Yale University Press, 1941.

28. Jersild, A. T., and F. V. Markey, *Conflicts Between Preschool Children.* New York: Teachers College, 1935.

29. Jersild, A. T., and M. D. Fite, "Children's Social Adjustment in Nursery School," *J. Exper. Educ.*, 1937, *6*, 161–166; *The Influence of Nursery School Experience on Children's Social Adjustment*, New York: Teachers College, 1939.

30. Anderson, H. H., and G. L. Anderson, "Social Development," in L. Carmichael (ed.), *Manual of Child Psychology* (2d ed.). New York: Wiley, 1954.

31. Jersild and Markey, *op. cit.*, pp. 152–153.

32. Murphy, L. B., *Social Behavior and Child Personality: An Exploratory Study of Some Roots of Sympathy.* New York: Columbia University Press, 1937.

33. Anderson, H. H., "Domination and Social Integration on the Behavior of Kindergarten Children and Teachers," *Genet. Psychol. Monog.*, 1939, *21*, 287–385.

34. Muste, M. J., and D. F. Sharpe, "Some Influential Factors in the Determination of Aggressive Behavior in Preschool Children," *Child Development*, 1947, *18*, 11–28.

35. Anderson, H. H., *op. cit.* Tabulated, with additional data, in L. Carmichael (ed.), *Manual of Child Psychology* (2d ed.). New York: Wiley, 1954, pp. 1191–1192.

36. Citation 30, p. 1185.

37. Brewer, H. M., and J. E. Brewer. The dissertations of these investigators are discussed by H. H. Anderson in "Domination and Socially Integrative Behavior," in Barker *et al.*, *Child Behavior and Development.* New York: McGraw-Hill, 1943.

38. Anderson, H. H. Research described in citation 37.

39. Murphy, L. B., *op. cit.*

40. On the Zuñi and Dobuans, see R. Benedict, *Patterns of Culture*, Boston: Houghton Mifflin, 1934; the Arapesh and Mundugumor are discussed in M. Mead, *Sex and Temperament in Three Primitive Societies*, New York: Morrow, 1935; Mead discusses Samoan Culture in her *Cooperation and Competition Among Primitive Peoples*, New York: McGraw-Hill, 1937; on the Kwakiutl, see F. Boas, *35th Annual*

Report of the Bureau of American Ethnology, 1921, Part II.

41. Lehman, H. C., and P. A. Witty, *The Psychology of Play Activities*, New York: Barnes, 1927; P. A. Witty, "A Study of Deviates in Versatility and Sociability of Play Interest," *Teach. Coll. Contrib. Educ.*, 1931, No. 470.

42. Ojemann, R. H., "The Child's Society — Clubs, Gangs, and Cliques." Booklet published by Science Research Associates, Chicago, 1953. Quotation from p. 26.

43. Anderson, J. E., *The Psychology of Developmen and Personal Adjustment.* New York: Holt, 1949, p. 348.

44. Brown, F. J., *The Sociology of Childhood.* New York: Prentice-Hall, 1939.

45. Breckenridge, M. E., and E. L. Vincent, *Child Development* (2d ed.). Philadelphia: Saunders, 1949.

46. Lewin, K., R. Lippitt, and R. K. White, "Patterns of Aggressive Behavior in Experimentally Created 'Social Climates,'" *J. Soc. Psychol.*, 1939, *10*, 271–299. Quotation from p. 271.

47. *Ibid.*, p. 299.

48. Moreno, J. L., *Who Shall Survive? Foundations of Sociometry, Group Psychotherapy and Socio-drama* (rev. ed.). New York: Beacon House, 1953.

49. Koch, H. L., "Popularity in Preschool Children: Some Related Factors and a Technique for Its Measurement," *Child Development*, 1933, *4*, 164–175.

50. Thompson, G. G., H. F. Bligh, and S. Witryol, "A Critical Examination of Several Methods of Determining Levels of Social Status," *J. Soc. Psychol.*, 1951, *33*, 13–32.

51. Bonney, M. E., "Popular and Unpopular Children, a Sociometric Study," *Sociometry Monographs*, 1947, No. 9.

52. Anderson, J. E., "Methods of Child Psychology," in L. Carmichael (ed.), *Manual of Child Psychology* (2d ed.). New York: Wiley, 1954, p. 26.

53. Thompson, G. G., and J. E. Horrocks, "A Study of the Friendship Fluctuations of Urban Boys and Girls," *J. Genet. Psychol.*, 1947, *70*, 53–63.

54. Austin, M. C., and G. G. Thompson, "Children's Friendships: A Study of the Bases on which Children Select and Reject their Best

Friends," *J. Educ. Psychol.*, 1948, *39*, 101–116.

55. Thompson, G. G., *Child Psychology: Growth Trends in Psychological Development.* Boston: Houghton Mifflin, 1952, p. 470.

56. See citation 26.

57. *Ibid.*, pp. 85 and 88.

58. Doll, E. A., *The Vineland Social Maturity Scale.* Vineland, N. J. 1936. See also Doll's *The Measurement of Social Competence.* Minneapolis: Educational Test Bureau, 1953.

59. Patterson (Peterson), C. H., "The Vineland Social Maturity Scale and Some of its Correlates," *J. Genet. Psychol.*, 1943, *62*, 275–287. Quotation from p. 287.

SUGGESTIONS FOR FURTHER READING

Anderson, H. H., and G. L. Anderson, "Social Development" in L. Carmichael (ed.), *Manual of Child Psychology* (2d ed.). New York: Wiley, 1954.

Barker, R. G., J. S. Kounin, and H. F. Wright, *Child Behavior and Development.* New York: McGraw Hill, 1943, Chapters XX (L. B. Murphy), XXVII (H. H. Anderson), XXVIII (Lippitt and White), XXIX (Parten and Newhall), and XXX (Jennings).

Biber, B., L. P. Woodcock, L. B. Murphy, and J. S. Black, *Life and Ways of the Seven-to-Eight Year Old.* New York: Basic Books, 1952.

Bossard, J. H., *The Sociology of Child Development.* New York: Harper, 1948, Part VI.

Breckenridge, M. E., and E. L. Vincent, *Child Development* (2d ed). Philadelphia: Saunders, 1949, Chapters 5, 6, and 13.

Bridges, K. M. B., *Social and Emotional Development in the Pre-School Child.* London: Kegan Paul, 1931, Part II.

Brown, F. J., *The Sociology of Childhood.* New York: Prentice-Hall, 1939.

Bühler, C., "The Social Behavior of Children," in C. Murchison (ed.), *A Handbook of Child Psychology* (2d ed.). Worcester: Clark University Press, 1933.

Dennis, W., *Readings in Child Psychology.* New York: Prentice-Hall, 1951, articles by Lewin and Jersild.

Doll, E. A., *The Measurement of Social Competence.* Minneapolis: Educational Test Bureau, 1953.

English, H. B., *Child Psychology.* New York: Holt, 1951, Chapter 14.

Isaacs, S., *Social Development in Young Children: A Study of Beginnings.* New York: Harcourt, Brace, 1933.

Jersild, A. T., *Child Psychology* (4th ed.). New York: Prentice-Hall, 1954, Chapters 6–8.

Kuhlen, R. G., and G. G. Thompson, *Psychological Studies of Human Development.* New York: Appleton-Century-Crofts, 1952, Readings 19 (Baldwin), 42 (Radke-Yarrow, *et al*), 46 (Maudry and Nekula), and 47 (Greenberg).

Murphy, L. B., *Social Behavior and Child Personality.* New York: Columbia University Press, 1937.

Swanson, G. E., T. M. Newcomb, and E. L. Hartley (eds.), *Readings in Social Psychology* (rev. ed.). New York: Holt, 1952, articles by Moreno, Jennings, Lippitt and White, Horowitz, and Clark and Clark.

Thompson, G. G., *Child Psychology.* Boston: Houghton Mifflin, 1952, Chapters 11 and 12.

16

The Growth of Personality in Children

In our discussion of sensory, motor, symbolic, emotional, and social processes we concentrated upon one aspect of development at a time. Consideration was given to the growth of vision, hearing, motor skills, memory, reasoning, language, emotional reactions, and social interactions. However, the fact that these processes, individually and as a group differ in expression from one individual to another received little attention. We were interested in them abstractly, *as processes;* not as interrelated aspects of the behavior of *particular* individuals. We did not consider the unique pattern of such processes which each individual possesses.

When our interest turns to personality it ceases to be abstract. The focus of attention goes from processes as such to individual variations in the expression of these processes. Moreover, we are concerned not so much with individual variations of theoretically separate processes as with the diverse integrations of these processes which may be observed in different individuals and in the same individual at various stages of development.

Personality may be defined as the most characteristic integration of an individual's structures and activities. The integration is characteristic in a dual sense. Because of its uniqueness, it *differentiates one individual from another*. It is also fairly consistent, representing the *customary integration of a given individual's structures and activities*.

If all babies were identical in appearance and exhibited exactly the same behavioral repertoire, we should, in speaking of babies, have no use for the term "personality." There are, however, clearly discernible differences in the structure and behavior of newborn individuals. These differences become increasingly great throughout life. The conditions which produce changes in personality as the individual grows older also differ in nature and potency at various age levels. Structural and behavioral integrations of the newborn are attributable entirely to hereditary and to non-social environmental conditions. Social factors have played no part in their determination. A month or so after birth, as indicated in the preceding chapter, the infant begins to respond to other individuals, and its behavior is modified accordingly. From this time on, social conditions become increasingly important in the shaping of its personality. This does not mean, however, that hereditary influences cease. They continue to play an important role, especially in the manner in which learning takes place.

Two individuals who are practically alike in physique, sensorimotor abilities, and symbolic abilities, and in every trait of significance for the acquisition of behavior, may exhibit increasingly different personalities as they grow older. In other words, the increasing influence of social conditions produces divergent personalities despite similarity in basic structures and behavioral processes. Take identical twins, for example. At birth they are practically indistinguishable in terms of either physique or behavior. As they grow older, the twins may, as far as many personality traits are concerned, differ as much as unrelated individuals. Such differences appear even when identical twins are reared in the same home. Even in Siamese twins, whose heredity is identical and who must of course live in the same objective environment continually, there are large differences in personality. Koch [1] studied such a pair of Siamese twins and found that, on the Pressey X–O test, one had a higher worry score and a higher score for wrongs crossed out, and underlined a much longer list of pleasures than her sister. The sister made quite superior intelligence test scores, was more talkative, had a greater speed of movement, and exhibited a higher per cent of common associations on the Kent-Rosanoff test. In all other measured traits the twins were remarkably similar. The work of Newman, Freeman, and Holzinger [2] shows that while identical twins have, on the average, quite similar intelligence, their personality traits often differ markedly. This is especially true when their home environments are widely different, as in certain identical twins reared apart.

A large portion of any treatise on personality must of course take cognizance of the individual's social perceptions and his participation in social interactions like those discussed in the previous chapter. Moreover, every discussion of social behavior, except when it focuses on the processes of interaction as such, is concerned a great deal with personality. Many psychologists identify personality with individual social behavior. Allport,[3] for example, says that "with the exception of a few traits, personality may be defined as the individual's characteristic reaction to social stimuli, and the quality of his adaptation to the social features of his environment." It is undeniable that as the individual develops and acquires various motor skills, concepts, emotional tendencies, interests, and so forth, his personality becomes increasingly identifiable with socially integrated activities.

We begin this chapter by considering some methods of studying personality in children. Our chief interest is in what these reveal concerning the growth of personality We then outline some significant aspects of personality development in individuals at various age levels ranging from birth through childhood. Much attention is given to biological and situational factors which influence this development. Our final chapter traces such development from the period of adolescence until later maturity and old age.

Methods of Investigating Personality Development

Several methods have been devised for the study of personality in children and adults. These methods assume genetic significance when they offer information concerning the biological and situational factors which underlie development of personality, and when, by applying them to individuals at various age levels, one obtains some indication of developmental changes in personality. The chief general methods of studying personality are as follows: the *case-history* method, the *psychoanalytical* method, use of *projective tests*, *observation of behavior in standardized situations*, and use of *questionnaires, rating scales*, and *standardized pencil-and-paper tests*. The various methods are not mutually exclusive. A particular study of personality might involve one or all of them. In addition to describing these methods we shall examine the kind of data made available by their use.

The case-history method

This method is used to obtain information on the origin of personality characteristics which have already developed. Along with other clinical methods, the case-history ap-

proach is most often used in an effort to discover the causes of some abnormality of behavior, such for example as excessive timidity,
delinquency, unusual fears, and sex perver-
sion.

In using the case-history method, an investigator gathers all available data concerning the individual's past. He or his social
workers attempt to obtain a record of the
subject's forebears (information on their intelligence, mental or other diseases, socio-
economic status, educational attainments,
criminal records, and the like); a record of his
personal history (the nature of birth, whether
or not birth injuries were present, health,
childhood interests and behavior tendencies,
eventful experiences, nature of friends, formal
education, and so on); and a record of his
home environment (number of brothers and
sisters, birth order, relations with parents,
socio-economic status of home and neighborhood, and other relevant information). As
an example of the type of data gathered by
this method, the following summarized case
history by Rogers is reproduced: [4]

Edward is a tall, blond youngster, with a great
scar on the left side of his head which even the
physician calls "unsightly." He was brought to
the clinic by his parents, who feel they cannot manage him. The behavior picture obtained by the
worker shows he has difficulties in school, out of
school, and at home. He is very restless, even in
his sleep, and sucks his thumb a great deal. He
teases other children, especially smaller ones, hits
and bullies them. He has no close friends. In
school he upsets the whole class. At times he
crawls around the schoolroom on his hands and
knees and barks like a dog. During a visit to his
classroom made by the worker, Edward hit another
child with a ruler, but when the other child slapped
back at him he screamed, put his hands to his head,
ran out of the classroom and out of school. The
teacher says she has to stand beside him to make
him study. She considers him subnormal. Other
teachers describe him as "impossible," and mention
his "queer look." In school he is always unprepared, slovenly, late. He "gets sick" whenever he
has to do work he dislikes. At home he has been
an enuresis problem since the age of three. He pays
no attention to his parents. He has taken pennies
from his mother and pencils from children at school,
though the teacher thought he did the latter primarily to annoy the children rather than to get the
pencils. When he is with adults, Edward is very
forward about breaking into the conversation. He
enjoys reading and the movies. At times he sits
and stares, evidently daydreaming.

The father is a boastful, "sporty" man of thirty,
who was once arrested for carrying a blackjack.
He believes in carrying on discipline with a big
stick. He seems intelligent and is anxious to talk
about himself. For seven years he has been a milk-
wagon driver. His wife is thirty-two. She has
always had to work hard, and began living with
Edward's father two years before they were married.

Edward is said by the parents to have been a
wanted child. He was a healthy infant, and rather
"wild" as a youngster. At the age of four an automobile accident injured his head severely. There
was no fracture, but a very large scalp wound, exposing and scratching the skull. There is no hair
on the large red scar.

There are two other children, a boy of five and a
baby girl. Both of them are quiet, attractive children. Both suck their thumbs. The parents continually compare Edward with the five-year-old
boy, always to the advantage of the younger child.

The psychological examination showed Edward
to be a boy of superior intelligence, with a mental
age of 11–4. He showed inferior abilities in handling concrete material. In spite of this lack of
manual skill he daydreams about mechanical projects. He confided to the examiner that he had
plans for a great invention, saying, "The kids say
I'm crazy. If I get that invention made they'll all
flock to me."

Some of his other attitudes may be gleaned from
these comments, made to teachers, psychiatrists,
and others. He says he had no friends because of
the scar on his head, and because the children call
him crazy. He once said that his father and
mother hated him. "There is not a person in this
whole world to love me. If somebody would love
me, I would be good." The psychiatrist asked him
what his father thought about his fighting with
other children. "Father says 'I wish they would
kill you'" he replied. He says the children call him
"Crazy Eddie." He cannot fight with them, so he
picks up a stick. Then they call him a coward.
When asked if his cowardice was due to a fear that

something might happen to his head, he burst out crying, and said, "Yes." He said that the scar bled if it was hit. He consistently blames other children and other people for his misbehavior.*

In commenting on this case, Rogers [5] says in part: "Here is a remarkable illustration of the far-reaching effects of an obvious physical deformity. Not only does it make Edward feel sensitive about his appearance, but it makes him appear cowardly; and thus it starts a social isolation which brings him, at the age of nine, to the nickname 'Crazy Eddie.'" Other case histories could be cited, some of them showing personality defects due to abnormal parental attachments, others due to poverty, still others resulting from disadvantageous friendships, and so forth.

The chief advantage of the case history over other methods of obtaining data on the growth of personality lies in the scope of the information obtained. The chief disadvantage is that case-history data are somewhat unreliable. One usually obtains much of his information from the subject himself, his parents, relatives, neighbors, friends, school teachers, and perhaps the minister. It is obvious that such factors as poor memory, exaggeration, response to suggestion, the desire to protect or to injure the individual, and similar factors may color the information gathered. A good social case worker uses every possible means of avoiding these vitiating influences.

The psychoanalytic method

This method, like the one just considered, is used most often with unusual individuals. Likewise, it is very broad in its scope, dealing with every possible relevant fact concerning the past history of the individual. However, the typical psychoanalytic technique differs from the case-history method in one significant respect. *All data are customarily obtained from the individual whose personality is being investigated.*

* Rogers combined testing and case-study methods. Only part of the case history of Edward L. is quoted here.

Two specific methods of obtaining information are widely used among psychoanalysts. One, the method of *free association*, requires the individual to assume a condition of relaxation and then to tell everything that comes to mind. After a series of seances during which the subject is encouraged to recount everything, trivial, shameful, and even apparently meaningless, about his past experiences, his life history is theoretically laid bare for observation and interpretation by the analyst. The second specific method of obtaining information concerning the individual's history is that of *dream analysis*. The subject describes his dreams. These are then interpreted as wish-fulfillments; as symbolic and disguised representations of desires frustrated in the usual course of existence. Through dream analysis the psychoanalyst attempts to discern fundamental motives, "depth factors," not evidenced in more direct ways.

The psychoanalyst does not approach his information impartially. Rather he interprets it in terms of a system. If he is a Freudian, he is prone to see in the individual's past activities a struggle between instinctive sexual impulses (the *id*) and the inhibiting or repressing influences of polite society (represented by the *superego*). As we shall observe later, this conflict is believed to begin in the early days of infancy and to continue in various forms throughout life. Anna Freud,[6] Klein,[7] and Freud again in association with others [8] have given especial attention to the practical and theoretical aspects of child analysis.

Should the analyst be a follower of Jung, he will give somewhat less emphasis to sexual interpretations than is given by the Freudians. Moreover, he will seek evidence of withdrawal of interest from the external environment. If he is a follower of Adler, the analyst will interpret his results in terms of *inferiority feelings*. He will look for and stress physical, intellectual, or cultural disabilities. If he is a so-called Neo-Freudian (a follower of Kardiner, Fromm, or Horney) the analyst will look for evidences of social maladjustment. Interpretations will be based upon conflicts between the person and aspects of his social environment as focused in the family and school; little attention will be given to instinctive urges. The various psychoanalytic concepts of personality development are discussed later in this chapter.

Most criticisms of psychoanalysis are pointed at the interpretative rather than the purely methodological aspects. Our chief interest here, however, is in the psychoanalytic method of obtaining information. If this method discloses significant factors in the development of personality, it is of value to the genetic psychologist. However, the reliability of psychoanalytic data is frequently questioned. The subject often knows something about psychoanalytic theories, and his "free" associations may thus be distorted.* The type of questioning used by a psychoanalyst may lead the suggestive subject to "remember" experiences which never occurred, or to give distorted representations of actual experiences. It is not customary for the psychoanalyst to check, by case study or other techniques, the accuracy of what the subject (patient) tells him.

The two general approaches to personality so far discussed are, so to speak, retrospective. In using these methods the investigator attempts to *reconstruct* the growth of personality characteristics after they have already reached a given level of development. In so far as they are used developmentally the remaining methods measure personality characteristics in process of formation. Applied at successively greater age levels, these methods allow one to follow the growth of personality more or less directly. They also allow us to investigate the influence of various conditions upon personality traits.**

Projective tests

Projective tests have much in common with psychoanalytic procedures in that the investigator attempts to reveal hidden features of personality, the so-called depth aspects — like repressed aggressive tendencies, tensions, and anxieties. It is assumed that the subject's arrangement of test materials, his interpretations of ambiguous items such as inkblots and poorly structured pictures, and his creative activities as in finger painting and drawing will reflect his "inner person." In this sense the test performances are regarded as projections of personality. In another context (see pp. 314–315) such performances would be considered as evidences of imagination.

Projective tests have long been used for diagnostic purposes at the adult level, but they are now coming into wide use with children, both to diagnose behavior disorders and to study personality.

Some projective tests designed for use with children are like the behavior tests discussed in a later section, except that instead of taking the behavior at its face value, the tester here looks for hidden meanings. The doll-play techniques are used in this way. Their particular value, as we shall see, is the fact that they induce the young child to express feelings and attitudes which he could not verbalize even if he were aware of them. Other tests, used at higher age levels, require verbal responses, although not the verbalization of feelings and attitudes as such. These are adaptations, for use with children, of inkblot (Rorschach) and thematic apperception tests.

---

* Estabrooks [9] found, for example, that students tended to give sexual or non-sexual "free" associations depending upon what they thought the experimenter expected of them. Almost everybody knows that Freudians stress sex experience.

** A given personality trait is not something either present or absent in an individual. Like intelligence, other personality traits are distributed in accordance with the normal curve. Irritability, for example, is present to some degree in all. However, very few are greatly irritable, and very few of low irritability. Most individuals exhibit an intermediate degree of irritability. Woodworth [10] points out that personality traits are "dimensions" of behavior in which individuals differ. Using factor analysis of test results, psychologists have tried to discover how many really different traits go to make up what we call personality. So far there is no generally accepted classification of such traits.[11]

Doll-play techniques. Doll play has been used for diagnostic purposes, as a form of psychotherapy, and as a means of investigating child development. The literature is extensive.[12] In this discussion, however, we can do no more than suggest uses which are relevant to genetic psychology.

In one of the pioneer studies from this standpoint, Murphy [13] and her associates encouraged preschool children to play with miniature toys representing furniture, people, and animals. Most children dramatized their play, arranging the objects spatially and naming the "persons" involved. They talked as they played and the tester sometimes questioned them by asking, for example, "Does the mother do nice things for the little girl?" or "What does her daddy do when she does that?" A detailed description of the spatial arrangements and comments was kept.

Such behavior can be recorded with a high level of objectivity, even reproduced on film and magnetic tape if desired. But to be used projectively it must be interpreted. This is where subjective factors inevitably enter. Murphy [14] interpreted the doll play as revealing

conflicts and problems rooted in family relations of the child. . . . What kind of mother is his image of a mother, what kind of image is his image of a father. . . . The life space . . . the world he has unconsciously selected as significant, awareness of which he carries about with him; the objects, space relations, relations with people, of his objective world as experienced, interpreted, assimilated by him. . . . His life space . . . . its own dimensions, its own geometry, created by the child's perceptions of his own size, strength, and what he counts for in his world. . . . sharp boundaries created by consistent taboos, or fuzzy boundaries created by inconsistent taboos, or no perceptible boundaries, as in the case of children who move freely through space in accordance with limits of which they are constantly unconscious.

According to Sears,[15] "the child's doll-play performance carries an almost overwhelming aura of revelation to a sensitive observer."

At first the child explores, then arranges the furniture and persons in customary ways.

But suddenly the observer realizes there has been a change, not a quick or easily detectable one, but one that has taken several minutes and has just now reached the observer's threshold. The child is more intent on the dolls, less reactive to the observer, and he is living strangely in this new fantasy world. He begins to tell stories that have no immediate parallel in his real life; he makes the family people behave as family people virtually never do. There are fantastic punishments and catastrophic accidents, social roles are reversed, and a few routines like toileting may exclude all the rest of ordinary everyday activity. . . . and then the observer has a feeling that blinds have gone up, and he is seeing the inner person of this child. It is as if the child were making him see this family world as the child himself sees it — or, perhaps, as he would like to see it. There are nuances and subtleties that cry out for interpretation.

One great difficulty is that interpretations, unless standardized and validated, may vary with the observer, perhaps as projections of his own "inner world." Another difficulty is that the play materials, the administrative procedures, and the methods of recording and measuring responses have not been standardized. This makes it impossible to repeat the observations of different investigators. However, an investigation by Bach,[16] carried out under Sears's direction, has suggested how the above shortcomings may, at least to some extent, be eliminated. Bach used a stylized doll house representing the layout of the child's own preschool. School furniture and fixtures, two teacher dolls, and six preschool children dolls were provided. Figure 133 shows part of the general layout with three dolls in use. It also shows what one child did in this situation.

The procedures, including the themes suggested to the children and the methods of recording their reactions, were carefully prescribed and set forth in an observer's manual. The reliability of the observations was examined by finding the per cent of agreement between two independently recording

Figure 133.   An Example of Projective Doll Play

Thus is an instance of what Bach characterizes as "Hostile Fantasy Aggression." One teacher is "burning" on the stove, another's head is pushed into the toilet, and a boy is squeezed under a wash basin.   (From G. R. Bach, "Young Children's Play Fantasies," *Psych. Monog.*, 1945, *59*, 21.)

observers. Depending upon the items recorded, agreement ranged from 71 to 97 per cent. This degree of objectivity was made possible only by placing certain restrictions on the themes considered (fantasy affection, fantasy aggression, etc.) and, further, by restricting the nature of the items to be recorded (doll is made to hide, sexual regions are investigated, etc.). Such restrictions made it possible to quantify the data. Bach could then report, for example, that doll manipulations denoting sexual curiosity averaged 7 per cent of non-stereotyped fantasies; hiding-escaping, 19 per cent; commanding and ordering about, 11 per cent; and so on. Teacher's ratings of behavior in comparable real-life situations showed various degrees of correspondence with the doll-play data.

This general approach to doll play has since been used to study the effect of various home conditions on children's fantasies. Using a situation stimulating the child's home, Bach [17] compared the father fantasies of 20 children whose fathers were away from home with those of 20 control children whose fathers were home. He found that the former children had an "idealistic and feminine fantasy picture of the father" whereas the latter "elaborated the father's aggressive tendencies." A somewhat comparable study by Sears, Pintler, and Sears [18] on fantasy aggression in children between three and five years of age led them to conclude, among other things, that boys from father-absent homes portray much less fantasy aggression than boys from father-present homes, and that boys show greater aggression toward the doll father than toward the doll mother. Some age trends are also reported in this study, but few are consistent. One consistent trend, however, is a rise in the mean frequency of total fantasy aggression toward the father in boys whose fathers are absent. In the three-year group, this mean was 9; in the four-year group, 18; and in the five-year group, 26.

The Rorschach Test. Rorschach's [19] Inkblot

Test is the most widely used projective device at higher age levels and it is now coming into widespread use with children, even at the preschool level. The ten inkblots of the Rorschach series are so well known as to need little description here. Some are merely black and white while others are wholly or in part colored.

In Ford's [20] research with children, an inkblot was shown and the child was asked "What could this be?" If no answer was forthcoming, the tester said, "Tell me all about it. What could this be?" If the child responded and then stopped, the tester said, "Yes? Can you tell me more." Finally she said, "Is that all? When you finish, give it to me and I'll give you a new one." The responses, as is customary, were scored in four principal categories: manner of apperception, quality of response, content of response, and degree of originality. Responses were scored with the usual symbols, such as W (to figure as a whole), D (to frequently selected details), F (to form as the sole determinant of interpretation), M (indicating experience of felt movement), C (color as sole determinant), A (animal), H (human), and so forth. In this study there were approximately 25 children at each of the yearly age levels from three to seven.

Curves are presented showing the mean frequency of given response as a function of age. These curves are compared with those derived from an earlier study by Klopfer, Margulies, and others [21] on children from two to six years. The two studies agree with respect to some responses but not others. Of particular interest to us here are interpretations of such responses and what they are alleged to suggest concerning the growth of personality.

According to the Rorschach theory, the ratio of M responses (felt movement) to C-sum (the sum of color responses) is indicative of introversive or extratensive tendencies. A predominance of M responses in relation to C is alleged to indicate a balance in the direction of "introversive" living, or

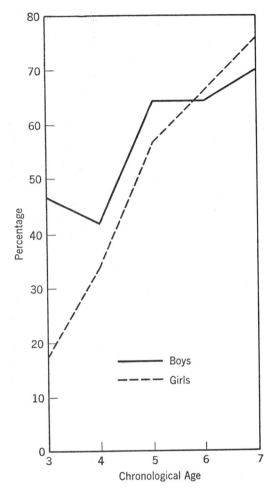

Figure 134. Rorschach Response as a Function of Age

This represents the percentage of boys and girls revealing introversive tendencies as inferred from the $M:C$-sum ratio ($M > C$-sum) on the Rorschach Inkblot Test. For interpretation, see text. (From M. Ford, *The Application of the Rorschach Test to Young Children*, Minneapolis: University of Minnesota Press, 1946, p. 79.)

introversion.* A greater C response, on the other hand, is assumed to imply sensitivity to external stimuli and a consequent "extratensive" or extravert tendency. As illus-

---

* Extreme introverts may be characterized as self-centered, reflective individuals. They have relatively little interest in external events and are not outwardly expressive. Extreme extraverts show the opposite tendencies. (See also p. 457.)

trated in Figure 134, Ford observed that introversive response (M greater than C-sum) increased with age, in both boys and girls. The extratensive tendencies (M less than C-sum) decreased with age. With a view to discovering the validity of such alleged indices of introversiveness, Ford had 30 of the children rated on Marston's behavior test of introversion-extraversion (see pp. 457–459). The agreement between Rorschach and Marston ratings was sometimes above and sometimes below chance expectancy, depending upon the formulas used. The investigator interprets the various comparisons as denoting "fair agreement." There was also "fair agreement" between level of emotional adjustment (as measured by C responses) and the emotional adjustment of the children as rated by teachers. In general, Ford's analysis suggests that child norms for the various responses will be needed if these responses are to be of value in diagnosing personality in children. The more recent investigation by Ames [22] and others is a step in the direction of providing children's Rorschach norms. It is based upon the testing of 50 children at each half-yearly interval from two through $5\frac{1}{2}$ years and at yearly levels thereafter up to age 10. Changes in the commonly reported determinants are given for each level and a concluding statement characterizes the typical personality changes as a function of age. The cross-sections suggest that ups and downs in personality integration are more evident than a steady trend. There is, as in Ford's study, the suggestion of increasing introversion up to age 10.

Thematic apperception tests. Murray's Thematic Apperception Test [23] is a series of pictures about each of which the subject makes up a story. He tells what events have led up to the event portrayed, what the characters are thinking and feeling, and what the outcome will be. This test has been used extensively with adults, and there is evidence that their themes reveal something of inner personality structure. As in the case of other projective techniques, however, the interpretations to be placed upon particular responses are difficult to standardize and validate. An apperception test similar in principle to Murray's, but adapted for use with children from three to ten years of age, is Bellak's [24] in which the pictures are of animals in various situations of significance for children. For use at the adolescent level, Symonds [25] has arranged a series of pictures different in content but similar in principle to those of Murray's Thematic Apperception Test.

There is no doubt that these and the many other projective tests do reveal aspects of personality not otherwise apparent. One value is that they catch the individual "off-guard." This is especially true if he knows nothing about the real purpose of the tests. He reveals what he might otherwise try to keep hidden. The weakness of all such tests, however, is the difficulty of obtaining dependable scores and interpretations. Some testers decry the effort to quantify data; saying that the overall intuitive judgments of experienced clinicians are more valuable than scores which lend themselves to quantification. Nevertheless, as indicated in the above discussion, efforts are being made to standardize, quantify, and validate the tests. Until these efforts are successful, such tests will continue to be of limited usefulness in research on the growth of personality.

Observation of behavior in standardized situations

Some previous discussions of behavior in standardized situations (pp. 426–428) have dealt with situations arranged to reveal the nature of social interactions, such as participation in play, leadership, dominance, aggression, cooperation, and sympathy. Had we emphasized the reactions of individual children, we should have been studying personality traits such as aggressiveness, cooperativeness, and so on. Here we discuss the use of certain standardized situations as personality tests. These are in some respects like the doll-play situations already considered, but the data are taken at their face value rather than being interpreted projectively.

Shirley,[26] in her study of personality in 25 babies, used this approach: She scored the incidental responses of infants to anthropometric,* physical, and psychological test situations which were applied at frequent intervals during the first two years. Irritability, vocalization, manipulation, attempted escape, attention, and certain other responses were recorded. At each presentation of the test situations the infant was scored in terms of the number of times it exhibited the activity in question. The total number of opportunities for a given activity to be exhibited was also noted. The percentage of the total possible score was then derived for each baby. Non-scorable and incidental items were also noted. Furthermore, a personality sketch (case history) was obtained for each individual. From her data Shirley was able to obtain information concerning the characteristic pattern of behavior exhibited by each baby, the degree of difference from baby to baby, and the development of given traits as the babies grew older. Figure 135 shows how the data of such an investigation may be arranged to indicate personality differences and developmental trends. It is significant that in this investigation the *same* infants were tested at successive age levels.

In Marston's [27] introversion-extraversion experiment each child was placed in standard situations and his behavior recorded. A description of two of these situations will sufficiently illustrate the nature of the experiment. The child was playing in a room when the experimenter was suddenly revealed sitting with a toy in his hand. At first he ignored the child. At the end of sixty seconds he looked at the child. After a further period of thirty seconds he smiled. Thirty seconds later he said, "Do you like to teeter-tauter?" After a further period of thirty seconds he said, "Would you like to play with this?" Thirty

seconds later, if the child had still failed to approach and play with the toy, the experimenter said, "You may. Come on and play with it." Refusal was met with further persuasive comments. Scoring of reactions was in terms of the degree of extraversion exhibited. Persistent refusal to play and running from the room were scored zero. If much persuasion was needed, but the child eventually approached and played with the toy, it received a score of one. A slightly more ready positive response to the experimenter's persuasions was scored two. When a child played with the toy without urging, he received three points. Children who made advances to the experimenter as soon as the latter smiled at them were scored four. A score of five was given when the child approached the experimenter as soon as the latter appeared.

The locale of the other experiment which we are selecting for illustration was the natural history portion of a museum. Each child was observed closely, and his reactions scored in a manner comparable with that of the above experiment. A low extraversion score was given the child who paid little attention to the exhibits and was slow in moving along. The child who showed great spontaneous interest, going rapidly from one exhibit to another, was given a high extraversion score. The following descriptions of the behavior of two subjects illustrate extremes. J. K., rated as an introvert, "walked around and around the center section of the museum. He moved slowly and quietly, observing the exhibits with casual interest, seldom stopping to examine them closely. He retraced his course several times and did little exploring. The environment failed to attract him, and although he was undoubtedly bored, he would not ask to return to the school but continued his monotonous walking." B. G., who was judged to be an extravert, "ran about the room, commanding the experimenter to follow and plying him with questions about the exhibits which greatly interested him. He was easily distracted, however, and for a time

---

* Anthropometry involves measurements of parts and proportions within the human body — *anthropo* = human; *metric* = measurement.

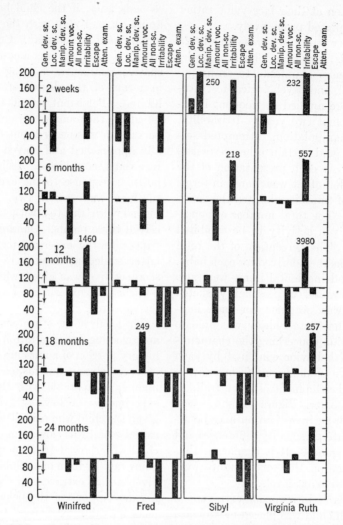

Figure 135. Personality Profiles of Four Infants at the Ages of Two Weeks
and Six, Twelve, Eighteen, and Twenty-Four Months

The items measured are indicated at the top of the figure. They represent data derived
directly from tests as well as from scorable and non-scorable personality traits exhibited
during administration of tests. The point of origin of each bar is the median score of the
group. The length of a bar shows the percentage of the median score represented by the
score of the individual baby. A bar above the median line means that a greater than
median score was obtained whereas a bar below means that a lower than median score was
obtained. Note the characteristic profiles for each infant, changes in some items as a baby
grows older, and the persistence of certain other items throughout successive age levels.
(From M. M. Shirley, *The First Two Years: A Study of Twenty-five Babies.* Vol. III,
Personality Manifestations. University of Minnesota Press, Minneapolis, Minnesota,
1933, p. 54.)

eagerly followed the janitor about the hall. His behavior was determined by an objectively directed but shifting interest. He was ready to leave the museum after eleven and a half minutes." A graphic representation of differences in activity exhibited by introverted and extraverted children is given in Figure 136. In Marston's experiment, each of the two- to six-year-old objects was tested once. Hence, instead of having data for a given individual at successive age levels, Mar-

ston obtained data on groups representing each age level.

Free-play situations may be arranged to reveal aspects of personality. Barker, Dembo, and Lewin,[28] for example, allowed children to play with certain objects while observers rated their activity for constructiveness. The children were then given an opportunity to play for fifteen minutes with some highly enticing toys. At the end of this period the preferred toys were removed to a place where

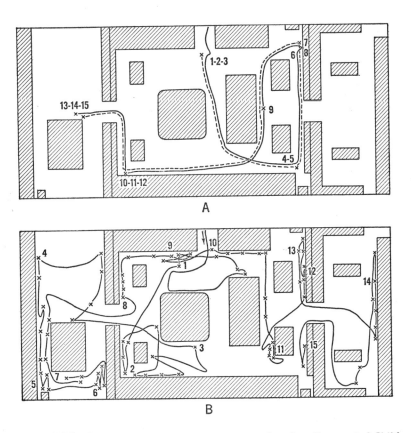

Figure 136. **Different Behavior of an Introverted and an Extraverted Child in the Museum**

A. The path of an extremely introverted child in the museum. This child refused to move without the experimenter, whose path is represented by the broken line. Crosses indicate stops. Shaded areas represent exhibits. The figures indicate the child's position at the close of each minute.

B. The course of an extremely extraverted child through the museum. The long distance traveled and the stops are characteristic of the extravert. (From L. R. Marston, "The Emotions of Young Children," *University of Iowa Studies: Studies in Child Welfare*, 1925, *3*, 68 and 71.)

they could be seen but were inaccessible. In subsequent play with the less desirable objects, some of the children regressed to a lower level of constructiveness. Among 30 preschool children subjected to such frustration, 22 regressed, 3 did not change, and 5 were more constructive than before.

Hartshorne and May's [29] investigations involved a still further modification of the general method of measuring personality in standard situations. Only two specific techniques will be discussed. For our first example we select one of the deception experiments. Each child was given a sheet containing ten circles varying in size and position. At a signal from the experimenter he was to *close his eyes* and write a given figure in as many circles as possible. The test was repeated five times. Finally the child recorded as his score the total number of circles in which figures had been placed. The average number of circles numbered by subjects who were prevented from peeping had already been determined. Thus the child who made a score far higher than the average of those with eyes closed was revealed as a cheat.

Our second example is taken from the tests of service or altruism. Each child was handed a kit containing ten articles such as eraser, pen, and drinking cup. The teacher, in giving out the kits, announced that they had been donated by a friend of the school. After each child had examined his kit for ten minutes, the teacher passed on "a suggestion from the principal." This was to the effect that many school children are deprived of objects such as those in the kits. The pupils were then given an opportunity to denote the entire box, or separate objects, to less fortunate children. The teacher added, "It is quite all right for you to keep any or all of the kit if you would rather. The kit belongs to you." Donation of a penholder, an object readily accessible to each child and hence most readily given up, was scored two points. On the other hand, donation of an eraser, which few children ordinarily possessed and with which few were willing to part, was

scored five. Thus each altruistic act was scored in terms of the valuation placed by the children upon the object donated.

The value of measuring responses to standardized situations such as the above resides in the objectivity of the results. We do not, for instance, ask what the child *would do*, if given an opportunity to cheat, but we give him an opportunity and determine whether he does cheat. Despite the objectivity of the standard test as such, a certain degree of subjectivity often enters into scoring of responses. For example, in a given case, irritability may be reported by one observer and not by another. Training of the observers often achieves a partial solution of such differences in judgment. The administration and scoring of Marston's tests of introversion-extraversion also involve subjective factors which may be reduced to a minimum by practice.

The chief disadvantage of the objective tests used to measure personality traits is that they are greatly restricted in scope. The situations involved are not broadly representative of the constantly varying circumstances in which an individual finds himself from time to time. Hence they measure very restricted aspects of the personality as a whole. Furthermore, while these tests may be used with young children they are of little use with more sophisticated individuals.

Questionnaires, rating scales, and pencil-and-paper tests

The most widely used approach to the study of personality is that of using printed material which asks questions, requires the individual to rate himself or others, requires him to indicate choices among possible alternatives, or to mark true-false statements concerning his characteristic reactions to a large variety of situations.

Questionnaires. Data such as those involved in a case history are often obtained by use of questionnaires. The individual whose development is being considered may be asked such questions as "Were you ahead of or behind your grade in school?" "As a child, were you made to feel inferior?" "Did your parents punish you?", and so on. Another person, such as a parent or an acquaintance, may be asked similar questions about the individual. Sometimes a questionnaire is filled out by children of various age levels or by observers of them. Such questions as the following may be asked: "If you could only play three games, which ones would you choose?" "Which do you like best as chums, boys larger or smaller than yourself?" "Do you want things that you cannot have?"

Questionnaires are useful in obtaining information from large numbers of individuals concerning aspects of personality not readily measured by more objective means. If the psychologist seeks information on interests and attitudes, a questionnaire is frequently the most convenient means of getting it. Lehman and Witty's data on recreational interests were obtained in this way. The only other means of getting such information would be to observe and record actual recreational activities. This would entail so much labor as to make but a small amount of information available.

The questionnaire method has been subjected to the following criticisms: The questions are often ambiguous or suggest the most "desirable answer." There is no check on the truthfulness of the answers. Prejudices of the person who answers the questionnaire color his responses. In most instances many questionnaires are sent out but only a small proportion returned. This introduces a selective factor. Those who return questionnaires may not, in other words, be representative of the whole group. When the questions are unambiguously framed and avoid suggesting the answers, when the subjects know that they can respond truthfully without fear of identification (for example, when no names are attached), and where a representative sampling can be obtained, questionnaires often yield valuable data not obtainable by other means.

Rating scales. Rating scales may be used by an individual to rate himself on some personality trait or they may be used by others who observe his behavior. Such scales are sometimes used as a means of recording the reactions of individuals to standardized situations. A rating scale was used by Bonham and Sargent [30] in their studies of personality development. A portion of Bonham and Sargent's scale is reproduced on the next page. This scale was used to rate the same infants at the ages of 24 and 30 months. Most of the situations were standardized.

Although detailed rating scales like that of Bonham and Sargent are more useful than a mere indication of the presence or absence of responses, or a more detailed verbal report of the infants' activities, they undoubtedly involve a certain degree of subjectivity. The rating depends upon an individual's judgment of what is taking place. Furthermore, babies particularly liked by the investigator may receive higher ratings on "desirable" traits than those toward whom indifference is felt. However, the reliability of rating scales may be determined by having the individual rated by two or more observers and then comparing results. A high correlation between ratings by different observers indicates that the behavior is being measured reliably. Averages of ratings by different observers are frequently used. These are usually much more reliable than ratings by a single individual.

Standardized written personality tests. Many such tests are merely standardized questionnaires and rating scales. They are utilized more widely in measuring personality differences among adolescents and adults than in measuring the growth of personality. Their standardization is, in general, somewhat as follows: After deciding upon the trait to be measured, an investigator devises questions or statements which in his opinion are related to this trait. For example, if introversion-extraversion is to be measured, questions such as "Do you like to play with others?" and "Are you happier when alone?" may be involved. Sometimes the subject rates his own behavior by indicating whether he *often, infrequently,* or *never* talks to himself; whether he *often, infrequently* or *never* goes out of his

Typical Items from Bonham and Sargent's Rating Scale

Behavior to be Rated by Observer	Absent	Very slight	Slight	Average	Marked	Very marked	Extreme	Was Your Judgment		
								doubtful	fairly certain	very certain
1. Reaction to examiners.......										
Runs away.............										
Comes forward...........										
Hides face.............										
Refuses to talk..........										
Talks................										
Cries................										
3. Does he tease other children? .										
10. Does he suck his fingers?.....										
17. Is he noisy in eating?........										
22. Has he a tendency to argue? . .										
23. Does he have tantrums?.....										
26. Does he try to open examiner's packages?................										
32. Does he try to find out how mechanical toys operate?.....										
35. Does he say "please" or "thank you"?..............										
39. Is he cheerful when toys are taken away from him?.......										
41. Does he climb for objects?....										
44. Is he obedient to parents?....										
47. Does he show sympathy when mother feigns weeping?......										
56. Has he good looks?.........										

way to play with others; and so on. After the statements or questions are tentatively decided upon, the test is usually criticized by other psychologists and, as a result, items are eliminated or added. The test is then given to a large number of individuals, and norms as well as data on reliability and validity are obtained.

There are many different standardized personality tests. Apart from anthropometric and general intelligence tests, tests have been devised to gather information on such aspects of personality as introversion-extraversion, ascendancy-submission, neurotic tendency, will-temperament, suggestibility, emotional maturity, values, fairmindedness, social in-

telligence, social beliefs or attitudes, interests, personal adjustment, character, moral judgment, radicalism-conservatism, happiness, speed of movement, drive, femininity-masculinity, sociability, and sense of humor. The chief general criticism of such tests is that they merely get at surface aspects of personality. This criticism comes especially from those who favor psychoanalytic and projective approaches. By elaborate statistical techniques known as "factor analyses," investigators are seeking to discover how many distinctive personality traits (see p. 452) actually exist. It has been found that many of the "traits" indicated by separate labels in the above list are identical. There is much overlapping among others. Allport and Odbert [31] list 17,953 terms that have been used to designate personality traits. A recent factor analysis of children's questionnaire responses by Cattell and Beloff [32] suggests the existence of only 16 really different traits, some of which are: will control, emotional sensitivity, anxiety level, and superego strength. There is, however, little agreement among psychologists as to the number or names of personality traits. Even if other investigators, going over Cattell and Beloff's data and using their method of factor analysis, agreed that there are 16 factors, it is almost certain that some of the factors would be given different names. This comment is not to be construed as disparagement of factor analysis, but only as indicating some of the difficulties involved in such an approach to personality.

The growth of personality is influenced by biological conditions and also by the economic and social situations in which the individual develops. Biological aspects include glandular functioning and physique. Situational influences include the culture, the home, the parents, siblings, friends, and teachers, as well as the economic conditions which pervade the social environment. Interactions between the child and aspects of his social environment, and the frustrations associated with such interactions, play an important role in making personality what it is.

Biological Contributions to Personality

Most of the biological contributions are, in the last analysis, hereditary. We inherit our glands and to a considerable extent our physique, including our facial characteristics. There is no doubt, moreover, that the normal growth and functioning of our body depends upon endocrine secretions (or hormones).

The endocrines

Most of what we know about endocrine contributions to personality comes from observing what happens when malfunctioning occurs. Endocrinologists are concerned primarily with physiological disturbances as such and have little or nothing to say about personality. When one of them does mention personality he is prone, like Hoskins,[33] to say that "A genuinely satisfying discussion of the relationship of the endocrine glands to personality cannot yet be written," and that by and large "the problem remains for future solution." The little that is known about the relation of the endocrines to personality can be briefly outlined.

The pituitary. We know that the key gland is the *pituitary*, whose position in the body and in relation to the other glands was illustrated in Figure 75 (p. 170). This is a dual gland, or in reality two separate glands. The *posterior* lobe is concerned with certain metabolic processes. Its relation to personality would be very indirect. The *anterior* lobe, on the other hand, is extremely important not only for bodily and mental health, but for life itself. This is because its own hormones, of which there are several kinds, provide necessary stimulation for other important endocrine glands, as illustrated in Figure 137.

Some of the hormones from this "master" gland work directly on the body, as on general growth. The dwarfs and giants seen in circuses illustrate what inadequacy or superfluity of growth hormones may do when present during early development. Overactivity of the anterior pituitary in adults may produce the grotesque enlargement of features and extremities known as *acromegaly*.

The greatest importance of the anterior pituitary resides, however, in its stimulation of the thyroid, adrenal cortex, testis, and ovary. Such stimulation normally causes these glands to secrete their respective hormones. The hormone ACTH,* for example, stimulates the adrenal cortex, which then secretes cortisone, a hormone associated with salt metabolism and other physiological processes. When a metabolic upset suggests that there is adrenal insufficiency, ACTH may be

* Adrenocorticotropic hormone (the hormone which stimulates the adrenal cortex).

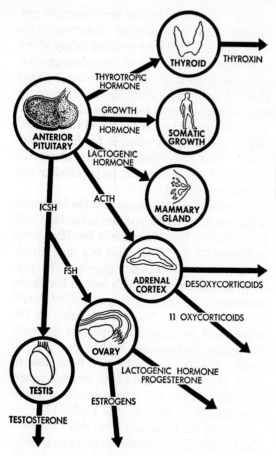

Figure 137. The Anterior Pituitary and Its Functions

This so-called "master gland" secretes several hormones, some of which work on the body directly and some of which stimulate other glands as illustrated. (From C. H. Li, "The Pituitary," in *Scientific American Reader*, New York: Simon and Schuster, 1953, p. 393.)

administered to stimulate the adrenal cortex. If this fails, it may mean that the adrenal cortex itself is defective and cannot be stimulated. In this event, cortisone is administered. Somewhat similar relations exist between the anterior pituitary and the other glands illustrated in Figure 137. Thus aspects of personality attributed to functions of a particular gland may be due, in the last analysis, to pituitary stimulation of that gland.

Some like Berman[34] have claimed that the pituitary gland plays a more direct role in personality than we have indicated. Rowe[35] and others have attributed certain aspects of delinquency to pituitary functions. Endocrinologists like Hoskins,[36] however, are skeptical of such claims. Even where glandular therapy does seem to produce favorable outcomes, these may be due to the psychotherapy associated with administration of hormones rather than to the hormones themselves.

The sex glands. The gonads (testes and ovaries) secrete hormones (androgens and estrogens) which markedly affect sexual development, hence the different physique and, possibly to some extent, the different strength and temperament of males and females. Human beings from whom the gonads have been removed in childhood fail to develop normal secondary sexual characteristics. Distinctly feminine characteristics are absent in females, and males are neutral in appearance. Glandular injections, if started early, can remedy these defects.

In the early stages of development the embryo is asexual. Rudiments of ovaries and testes are present. Under the influence of their different sex chromosomes, however, males and females come to have predominantly male or female gonads. It sometimes happens, although rarely, that both ovaries and testes develop in the same person. We then have what has been known since ancient times as *hermaphroditism*. Thus a "male" may look and act very much like a woman, or a "woman" like a man. It is sometimes possible, operatively, to "change" the person's "sex" in the dominant direction. The large majority of homosexuals, on the other hand, are not hermaphrodites. It is not clear, even, that their sex gland secretions are any different from those of heterosexuals. The data summarized by Hoskins,[37] Kinsey,[38] and Beach[39] lead to the conclusion that the alleged relation between sex hormones and homosexuality, such as that male homosexuals have an excess of estrogenic hormone, has not been proved. It is apparent that homosexuality is difficult to define, that individuals often change from homosexual to heterosexual behavior or vice versa, and that childhood contacts and experiences play a large role in its etiology, quite independent of possible glandular biases.

The thyroid. Complete thyroid deprivation in infancy is associated with the condition known as *cretinism.* In addition to exhibiting bodily deformities like dwarfism, pot belly, and retarded genital development, the cretin is always of low intelligence (idiot or imbecile), generally sluggish in reactions, and relatively unemotional. Treatment with thyroxin, if started sufficiently early, may remedy this condition within a few months. But treatment must continue. Hypothyroidism in adults is associated with general physical and mental sluggishness. Hyperthyroidism, on the other hand, produces nervousness, irritability, and overactivity. It has often been claimed, but without proof, that the alert and aggressive person has a superabundance of thyroid secretion.

The adrenals. Here, as in the case of the pituitary, we have in reality two glands, the adrenal cortex and the adrenal medulla. The *adrenal cortex,* as we have already pointed out, secretes cortisone when stimulated by ACTH. Its removal, without hormone replacement, leads to various bodily and psychological symptoms which shortly culminate in death. Among these symptoms are loss of appetite, lethargy, general weakness, irritability, and loss of sexual desire.

Overactivity of the adrenal cortex in early childhood is associated with precocious sexual development. Girls thus affected may menstruate and show other evidences of sexual maturity as early as three years.[40] A boy of six years had a moustache and the sexual and general bodily development of a fourteen-year-old.[41] Overactivity of the adrenal cortex after puberty may produce excessive masculinity. Women thus affected often develop masculine proportions, a deep voice, and excessive hairiness.

The *adrenal medulla* secretes adrenalin during emotion. Except for this connection with emotion, where it may have an emergency function, giving the organism increased energy with which to meet emotion-provoking situations, adrenalin has no known relation to personality.[42]

The other endocrine glands need not concern us here. There is little or no evidence that their functions contribute specifically to personality.

Much research is at present being focused upon glandular functions in the mentally ill. Thyroid, adrenal, and pituitary functioning may be seriously disturbed in patients with schizophrenia and possibly other psychoses. But no definite causal relation has yet been established. Hoagland,[43] writing about schizophrenia as recently as 1953, says that "it is still uncertain whether [adrenal] abnormalities are a result or a cause of the psychosis."

Physique and personality

Does the possession of a particular physique predetermine the sort of personality one will have? Since ancient times the answer to this question has been rather generally affirmative. It has been assumed, for example, that the fat person will be jolly, the thin one reserved, and the excessively muscular one dynamic. Such body typing seems to be simple until one attempts to put it on a quantitative basis. He then discovers that the so-called types are merely extremes and that most physiques fall, by indiscriminable steps, somewhere between these extremes. If the types dissolve in this way, then what of the personality traits alleged to be associated with them? It seems that, here also, gradations rather than discrete characteristics are the rule. This does not mean, however, that there is no relation between variations in physique and variations in personality. One does not need clear-cut types to find correlations. Height and weight, for example, show quantitative gradations rather than discrete steps, yet there is a high correlation between them.

Recent studies of physique have failed to support Kretschmer's [44] contention that there are three distinct types,* but they have suggested that there may be three distinctive *dimensions* along which physiques differ. Sheldon [45] photographed large numbers of male college students from various angles and then derived anthropometric measurements from the photographs. His measurements led him to conclude that there are three dimensions of variation: *endomorphy* (abdominal prominence), *mesomorphy* (muscular prominence), and *ectomorphy* (prominence of fragile structures, such as bones). He somatotyped each individual on a seven-point scale in each of these dimensions. Thus a person at the upper extreme of endomorphy would have a somatotype like 7-1-1 and the person at the upper extreme of ectomorphy would be typed as, for example, 1-1-7. An extreme mesomorph might be typed as 1-7-1. Thus this scheme finds a niche into which every individual may be fitted. The use of quantitative data and the ability to find a place for everybody is a decided advance upon the Kretschmer scheme, but there are skeptics who say that perhaps someone else using Sheldon's data would have found four dimensions, only two, or perhaps only one. To refute such skepticism one would need a correspondingly elaborate study, along similar lines, which revealed comparable somatotyping. No such study has yet been undertaken.

Arranging individuals quantitatively with respect to physique is only preliminary to the discovery of a possible correlation between physique and personality. The next step is to devise tests from which quantitative personality ratings can be derived. Sheldon devised such tests. Through a factor analysis of the results, he came to the conclusion that there are also three dimensions of temperament **

* Pyknic (fat, rotund), asthenic (tall, thin), athletic (muscular, well-proportioned).

** The term "temperament" embraces such aspects of personality as emotionality (joviality, melancholia, calmness) and general vigor or activity level.

which, as in the case of physique, lend themselves to representation on a seven-point scale. He called these dimensions of temperament *viscerotonia* (characterized especially by such traits as amiability), *somatotonia* (need for action), and *cerebrotonia* (shyness, thoughtfulness, and the like). It is perhaps not surprising, since Sheldon himself was responsible for both somatotyping and devising the temperament scale, that dimensions of physique and dimensions of temperament were highly correlated, yielding a coefficient of .80. He admits the possibility of bias, but discounts the possibility that it could have produced such a correlation. Again the need for independent investigations is evident.

The data so far available are certainly suggestive of a relation between physique and temperament, but they provide little or no justification for predicting, upon the basis of physique, what personality traits will go with a particular physique. Even if a high correlation were established, and predictions justified, the following questions would remain unanswered: Is the body type itself somehow responsible for the traits of temperament? Are both body type and temperament produced by a third factor, say glandular constitution? It is probably true that physique and temperament are to some degree jointly determined by inheritance of a certain glandular constitution. But one needs to add that the possession of a certain physique, especially some extreme, might influence the reactions of other people to us and that these reactions might in turn influence our reactions to them. Some aspects of temperament might have such an origin. The fat man's temperament, assuming that there is a relationship such that fatness and a particular temperament go together, could be contingent to some extent upon the way people react to fat men. But even such a statement as this involves the assumption, which may or may not be correct, that fat men elicit reactions peculiar to themselves.

Childhood Experience and Personality

Some aspects of our personality are to a large degree determined by what happened to us as children. About this there can be no doubt. But what happenings of childhood are influential in molding personality? What situations are conducive to the development of particular traits? On these and related questions there has been plentiful discussion and little agreement. Here we consider a few of these issues and the relevant theories and factual data.

Motivation and frustration

Like any other of the higher organisms, the human child has certain physiological needs which, if he were perfectly free and able to do so, he would satisfy in animal-like rather than "civilized" human ways. He soon learns, however, that the "approved" ways of satisfying such needs are quite often different from what Frank [46] has called "naïve" ways. When the child acts in non-acceptable ways, he is punished. Physical and verbal restrictions are imposed. Attempts are continually made to channel his activities in directions other than those which they would otherwise take. Such thwarting and channelizing is necessary if the individual is to develop characteristics which will enable him to get along with a minimum of social friction in later years. His helplessness in infancy, together with his high degree of plasticity and retentivity, make the human child especially susceptible to such social conditioning. Thus most children soon come to know the mores, the group codes. They know how their basic needs are to be satisfied. Bladder and bowel actions are anticipated and controlled. Hunger is alleviated at the proper time, in the approved ways, and with the customary foodstuffs. Violent emotions are restrained more or less. Sex organs are hidden from the gaze of others. The child stops playing with his genitals and he inhibits other overt sexual activities — or he develops guilt feelings when he breaks such taboos.

This process of changing "naïve" responses in such a manner as to produce a "civilized" personality has been stressed in recent years by sociologists and psychologists, but the general viewpoint stems more directly from Freudian psychoanalysis. The following digest of this viewpoint, some aspects of which have already been mentioned (pp. 451–452), is paraphrased from a discussion by Anna Freud.[47]

The child is dependent entirely upon the parents for survival. This places the latter in a position where they are able to impose their own codes of conduct upon the helpless individual. Since, in the early weeks of life, food plays a major role, the mouth becomes the most important part of the body. The infant gets "pleasant sensations" from sucking his mother's breast. These "oral sensations" become important in their own right, that is, they cease to be associated with food-getting alone. By sucking his fingers, his fists, and various objects around him, the infant gains a large amount of "oral enjoyment." This enjoyment is soon rudely interrupted by the parents. Sucking, except in relation to food, becomes a "naughty habit" to be engaged in only surreptitiously.

When the child is trained to control his excretory activities in the interests of cleanliness, another frustrating situation arises. He continues to defecate and urinate long after voluntary control has been acquired. Desire for "anal pleasure" is said to be associated with these activities. Later, when the child is finally made subservient to adult influences, playing with dirt, chalk, and in general smearing activities are *sublimations*, or indirect socially approved means of satisfying the thwarted desires.

At a little later stage, according to this view, the child delights in hurting things. He has an instinctive urge to tear living things apart. Direct suppression of these *sadistic* tendencies is usually short-lived, for adults soon suppress the activities in question. The urge remains, however, and is expressed in sublimated ways.

Interest in the sex organs is said to develop next. The child obtains great pleasure, it is claimed, by playing with and exposing the sex organs. Again, adults suppress the overt manifestation of these activities. According to Anna Freud, the obvious sexual stage is reached at the fourth or fifth year.

This and the preceding stages are all assumed to originate as expressions of sexual energy; that is, of the *libido*.

The child's closest companion, and the one who has been associated for some time with his oral activities, is soon forced to deny him further pleasures. Furthermore, he often learns that other children are usurping his place. Various jealous activities are said to result from this frustration. Later still the boy observes that his father can associate with the mother in ways denied him. The father can go out with her whenever he desires, can sleep with her, etc. When the child reaches this stage, according to Freudian psychoanalytic doctrine, the *Oedipus complex* arises. The boy becomes sexually jealous of his father. He loves his mother and hates and fears his father. The girl is assumed to develop an *Electra complex*, loving the father and resenting the mother's intimacies with him.

According to Anna Freud, these and similar frustrations have been met and various associated complexes developed during the first five or six years of life. When the child goes to school further thwarting occurs. The conflict between sexual tendencies and the thwarting activities of the group continue. It is assumed that the child will, if normal, eventually transfer the expression of his desires from the parents to others of his own sex (homosexual stage), and finally to the opposite sex (heterosexual stage). All preceding stages of development are believed to have left their marks upon his personality. It is said that because of their unpleasant nature, the experiences associated with frustration of libidinous expressions are forgotten, that they become *unconscious*. According to Freudian belief, these forgotten experiences are important determining factors throughout life. They constantly strive for conscious expression, but are inhibited by the *censor*, which is synonymous with socially conditioned inhibitions.

As the individual passes from infancy to adulthood his *ego*, identified with his own pleasure-seeking tendencies, is said to be partially superseded by the *superego*, the inner voice or conscience which parental inhibitions have developed. Now, even though the parents, teachers, and other inhibiting agents are no longer present, the individual obeys their will, as represented by the conscience, or superego. "Thus the old relationship between the child and the parents continues within the child, and the severity or mildness with which the parents have treated the child is reflected in the attitude of the superego to the ego."

According to Freudian psychoanalysis, many of the maladjustments of later life are due to a carry-over of infantile complexes. Other anomalies of personality are said to result from regressions to infantile modes of response. Thwarting is regarded as the precipitating factor.

The importance of thwarting for development of personality was not generally recognized until Freud brought it to the attention of psychologists. Nor was sufficient recognition given to the significance of early childhood experiences in later life.

All psychologists would agree that frustration constantly confronts the relatively helpless child, especially during the early years of life. They would also agree that the effects of frustration are carried over into later life in the form of self-imposed inhibitions.

Aspects of the Freudian position other than those mentioned above are not generally accepted. Malinowski [48] has shown that the Oedipus complex, regarded by the Freudians as instinctive, fails to appear among the Trobriand Islanders, a Melanesian group having a quite different culture from ours. These "complexes" are believed by him to be of cultural origin. There is no evidence, even, that they are universal within our own civilization. Stagner and Drought,[49] using a specially devised attitude scale, found no statistically reliable difference in the attitudes of over one hundred male and one hundred female college students toward either parent. They conclude that there is no universal Oedipus complex. Simpson [50] found that both boys and girls tended to show a greater mother than father preference.

Freud's emphasis upon sex, and especially his broad application of the term, led Adler, Jung, and many other psychiatrists and psychologists to break with him.

We have no reliable evidence concerning the child's pursuit of oral, anal, and sex-organ "sensations," or of the sequential development of oral, anal, genital, sadistic, homo-

concepts and principles

sexual, and heterosexual interests. Hollingworth[51] points out that the Freudian concepts and principles have not received scientific verification and that, rather than being descriptions and explanations, they are mere figures of speech. He says that "all the facts which these notions seek to explain are at least just as readily understood in the light of ordinary descriptive psychology — though not perhaps in so entertaining a fashion."

Jung[52] and Lewin[53] place special emphasis upon the significance of frustration in the development of personality. Their approach is, however, markedly different from that of Freud. Jung's view concerning introversion is well known. He points out that continual thwarting leads to a "turning inward of the libido."* The thwarted individual may, in other words, turn his interest from outer to inner spheres, becoming self-centered and reflective rather than overtly expressive. The same type of reaction is, as we shall see, often assumed by individuals given an inferior status by reason of physical defect.

Lewin's view, while fundamentally like Jung's, stresses the concept of valences, or, attracting and repelling forces of the environment. These "forces" are not physical in the physicist's sense, but may be conceived of as having attracting or repelling power consonant with their relation to the individual's past experiences. A certain object will, for example, "attract" — that is, elicit approach — if it has in the past been associated with favorable end results. Stimuli to which the child has been negatively conditioned will, to use Lewin's concept, tend to "repel" it. He conceives of the individual as surrounded by a field of such attracting and repelling forces, or vectors. Response results from a resolution of these "forces." According to Lewin, if the repelling forces predominate or if the differential becomes too finely drawn, the individual will tend to encapsulate or insulate

himself from the environment. In Jung's terminology, he may become introverted.

One is constantly confronted by many conflicting possibilities of action. There is a so-called "conflict of motives," or of "selves." As a result each of us is called upon to choose between patterns of behavior which are mutually incompatible. James[54] puts the situation very neatly when he says:

I am often confronted by the necessity of standing by one of my empirical selves and relinquishing the rest. Not that I would not, if I could, be both handsome and fat and well dressed, and a great athlete and make a million a year; be a wit, a *bon vivant* and a lady-killer, as well as a philosopher; a philanthropist, statesman, warrior, an African explorer, as well as a "tone-poet" and saint. But the thing is simply impossible. The millionaire's work would run counter to the saint's; the *bon vivant* and philanthropist would trip each other up; the philosopher and the lady-killer could not well keep house in the same tenement of clay. Such different characters may conceivably at the outset of life be alike *possible* to a man. But to make any one of them actual, the rest must more or less be suppressed.

The alternatives selected by the individual under such circumstances undoubtedly depend upon his early training, upon acquisition of "values." How the rejected "motives" shall be treated also depends to a large degree upon modes of reaction acquired in earlier frustrating situations.

Horney,[55] while differing in several respects from Freud and the other psychoanalysts whom we have mentioned, also stresses the influence of early conflict and resulting frustration and anxiety. For her, however, the conflict is primarily social. In discussing how a neurotic personality develops, she says:

The combination of many adverse environmental influences produces disturbances in the child's relation to self and others. The immediate effect is what I have called the basic anxiety, which is a collective term for a feeling of intrinsic weakness and helplessness toward a world perceived as potentially hostile and dangerous. The basic anxiety renders it necessary to search for ways in which to

* The libido for Jung is the "life urge." The sex drive plays a lesser role than that assigned to it by Freud.

cope with life safely. The ways that are chosen are those which under the given conditions are accessible.

Horney goes on to say that neurotic trends develop a compulsory character, since they shield the person from potential dangers and are avenues of reaction involving the least anxiety. But

The security they offer is always precarious; the individual is easily subject to anxiety as soon as they fail to operate. They make him rigid. . . . Invariably he becomes entangled in contradictory strivings . . . the neurotic trends further alienate the individual from himself [and] contribute to a further impairment of human relationships. The main reasons for this are that they help to increase dependency on others, and that they precipitate various kinds of hostile reactions.

The role of frustration in development of personality has also been stressed by Adler,[56] but his approach is different still from those already considered. The frustration stressed by him comes from physical defect and associated feelings of inferiority. Adler assumes that the basic drive is a striving for superiority and that physical (or social) inferiority thwarts this "drive." Some individuals acquiesce and continue to maintain an inferior status throughout life. The case of Edward L. (p. 450) is a good example. Others make capital of their deformities by showing what they can do *in spite* of them. Helen Keller's life exemplifies this reaction to physical inferiority. Others compensate for their inferiority along different lines from those in which they are handicapped. The cripple may, for example, become a great artist or a great political leader. A beautiful "dumbbell," finding herself thwarted along intellectual lines, may compensate by making amatory conquests. Sometimes, as Adler indicates, compensation takes symbolic rather than overt expression. The weakling may live in a world of fantasy, dreaming that he performs great feats of strength; the physically unattractive girl may dream of her male conquests; and the child subjected to continued physical indignities by his parents may devise a world of fantasy in which he, a prince, was snatched from his real parents by gypsies.

One view which relates specifically to what we have discussed above is worthy of more detailed consideration. It is the view that each individual finds his "role" early in life and that this is a persistent guiding factor in all further development. Adler[57] says, "Early in life, in the first four or five years, a *goal* is set for the need and drive of physical development, a goal toward which all its currents flow."

It is obvious that an individual with marked defects is often made aware of his status quite early. Of especial importance in this connection are the attitudes of others. The late H. C. Warren, an outstanding psychologist, who from the age of eighteen months suffered marked disfigurement due to burns, writes in his autobiography that this had a great influence upon the whole course of his life, leading him to be an introspective dreamer and causing him, at first, to shun social intercourse. Professor Warren[58] says:

Two tendencies, due to my unusual appearance, were of importance in directing the lines of intellectual development. One was a habit of rigid emotional repression, the other a decidedly introvertive attitude. I was very sensitive as a child about my scarred face and hand. These peculiarities were far more marked than later in life. People in the streets or the cars were constantly turning to look. I came to feel that everyone's eyes were fixed upon me. It was a tremendous ordeal to sit facing a group of people. I could not bear to turn around in our pew at church. Gradually I learned to suppress any emotional manifestations in these situations and to conceal my trepidation. Eventually this practice of emotional control became an ingrained trait.

A word lest all this be misinterpreted. The attitude of others was never unkind; only once do I recall ridicule, and that from a group of children. Very rarely, either, were there impertinent inquiries from strangers. The turning to look was quite automatic. It was the *invariability* of the act that led to the shrinking and introversion.

Further, I do not believe my attitude indicates

an inferiority complex in the Freudian sense; certainly it was not pathological. My atypical appearance was obvious to myself. This knowledge, though distressing, led to no chronic neurasthenic symptoms; on the contrary, the shock effects of the accident and operations gradually wore off.

This example merely indicates *one* direction which reaction to physical defect may take. The age at which a child begins to develop such reactions is probably an individual matter. That early reactions to defect tend to persist is further substantiated by studies like those of Landis and Bolles [59] and Barker, Wright, and Gonick [60] on the personality of people suffering from physical handicaps.

The kind of reaction developed by an individual afflicted with physical defects will depend, as Adler himself suggests, upon the nature of the anomaly, the constitution of the afflicted individual, and the reactions of parents, other children, and teachers to his condition. Adler and various other writers have also pointed out that social inferiority, due to lack of skill or poverty, may elicit feelings of inferiority and compensatory reactions like those often associated with physical defect.

Personality as a function of infant care

It is not surprising, in view of their stress upon oral-anal-genital functions, that Freudian psychoanalysts, and others influenced by them, regard infant care as a significant factor in the development of personality. Ribble [61] claims that one of the "rights" of infants is to be fondled and petted and that when such "needs" remain unsatisfied there are dire consequences both for physical and psychological development. If the infant's own mother is not available to cuddle it, rock it, and provide the "needed" stimulation, Ribble feels that others should substitute for her. The chief evidence for postulation of such needs is the fact that institutional children given no more than perfunctory attention are often retarded in physical and emotional development. A recent textbook of psychology [62] shows an institutionally reared child with an extremely emaciated appearance. A

second photograph, taken after affectionate maternal care in a home, shows a well-developed and apparently happy child.

Ribble's ideas have received a great deal of favorable attention, but a note of skepticism has been introduced recently by Orlansky. [63] To those of our cultural background it seems only humane that babies should be given as much affection and related stimulation as possible, and this regardless of whether or not such stimulation contributes favorably to their physical growth and personality. This feeling is perhaps also influenced by the pleasure which the parent herself may get out of mothering a helpless infant. What Orlansky criticizes, however, is the absence of convincing proof in favor of the view that the child's personality reflects the sort of mothering it has received. Contrary evidence is seen in the fact that children in other cultures than our own survive absence of such mothering as Ribble prescribes and without apparent harm to bodily development or personality. Orlansky also points to Dennis' experiment (pp. 194–197) as refutation of Ribble's claims. This is the experiment in which two children were reared under restricted conditions yet without suffering any apparent physical or psychological defects as a result. Conclusive evidence on this issue could come only from well-designed experiments in which there were two large groups of otherwise comparable infants, the members of one group "mothered" as Ribble claims they should be, and the members of the other group given everything needed for survival except "mothering." The further development of these children under controlled conditions would need to be studied and tests used to discover any possible differences in their personality. Until such an experiment is done we should regard Ribble's pronouncement concerning the "needs" and "rights" of infants as an interesting hypothesis needing verification.

There are many other interesting hypotheses concerning the influence of parent-infant relationships and the subsequent development of personality. Among these is the idea that the characteristic personality traits (pugnacity, individuality) of certain peoples is related to the way individuals are suckled, carried, and otherwise treated during infant care. Mead,[64] for example, regards the characteristic hostility and aggressiveness of the Mundugumor of New Guinea as possibly dependent, in part, upon frustration associated with the suckling situation. She says:

Mundugumor women suckle their children standing up, supporting the child with one hand in a position that strains the mother's arm and pinions the arms of the child. There is none of the mother's dallying, sensuous pleasure in feeding her child that occurs among the Arapesh. Nor is the child permitted to prolong his meal by any playful fondling of his own or his mother's body. He is kept firmly to his major task of absorbing enough food so that he will stop crying and consent to be put back in his basket. The minute he stops suckling for a moment, he is returned to his prison. Children, therefore, develop a very definite purposive fighting attitude, holding on firmly to the nipple and sucking milk as rapidly and vigorously as possible. They frequently choke from swallowing too fast; the choking angers the mother and infuriates the child, thus further turning the suckling situation into one characterized by anger and struggle rather than by affection and reassurance.

Whiting and Child [65] made a cross-cultural study in which judges rated the severity or leniency, in various cultures, of practices related to weaning, toilet training, sex, and independence and aggression. The ratings were then correlated with ratings of such aspects of personality (characteristic of the culture) as guilt feelings and fear of others. These correlations were used to test certain Freudian-oriented hypotheses about the relation between child-rearing practices and personality. The details of such procedures cannot be considered here; nor can we deal with the outcomes in detail. It is sufficient to say that some hypotheses received a certain amount of support while others did not. Orlansky,[66] in commenting upon the cross-cultural approach of Whiting and Child says that "The effort to objectify their procedures

is commendable, but it runs the risk of substituting a cultural bias for a personal one — i. e., all American raters or all American psychologists may agree in weighting a particular discipline as 'severe' or 'lenient' in terms of our values; Chinese or Hopi observers, however, might weight the same disciplines differently."

Those who claim that infant care marks personality for life find it incumbent upon themselves to show how such modification occurs at this early age, when social perceptions (pp. 422–425) cannot be demonstrated.

We have barely touched upon the extensive literature dealing with child-rearing practices and personality. For further information, Orlansky's excellent critical survey (150 references) is recommended. There is no more appropriate way to terminate this discussion than to quote with approval Orlansky's general conclusions. He rejects the thesis that "specific nursing disciplines have a specific, invariant psychological impact upon the child" and favors the view that "the effect of a particular discipline can be determined only from knowledge of the *parental attitudes* * associated with it, *the value which the culture places upon that discipline*, the organic *constitution* of the infant, and *the entire sociocultural situation in which the individual is located*." He believes that "personality is not the resultant of instinctual infantile libidinal drives mechanically channeled by parental disciplines" but is instead "a dynamic product of the interaction of a unique organism undergoing maturation in a unique physical and social environment." This view, as Orlansky points out "is in substantial agreement" with views held by Horney [67] and Fromm.[68]

Birth Order and Onliness

It is rather generally believed that first-born children have a personality which differs markedly from that of intermediate and last-

* Italics ours.

born individuals. This viewpoint is to some extent supported by psychoanalysts. Adler [69] says, for example:

After a few years another child comes along and the situation of the older is not so pleasant. He is no longer the center of the scene. . . . The older child feels dethroned. . . . He is always striving in a thousand ways to recapture his old situation of power and importance with his family. Feeling the obstacle in his way, he wants to overcome it by fighting. Unless he can overcome in the struggle for supremacy in his universe he is apt to become depressed, peevish, more or less hopeless, and will show his hopelessness later in life if confronted by problems. He is very likely to be conservative, to understand power and to agree with it. If he is strong enough he becomes a fighting child.

As for the second child, he is never alone, but is always confronted by the older child. This constant picture before him of an older and bigger child begets in him a sense of rivalry. He has a pacemaker in his older brother. . . . If successful, he is an excellent type, but if defeated, for instance, if he is not able to compete successfully with the older child in work and in play, he loses hope, becomes depressed, and has a bad time of it.

When the third or youngest child comes along he is in a different situation from the first child and the middle child. But his condition is somewhat similar to the second child in that he also has a sense of rivalry with his older brothers or sisters. He has to fight for his place in the sun so far as they are concerned, but he has no successor. This gives him a great sense of power, and if he is capable he often overcomes the older children in the family by his sense of importance. If he is not capable he perhaps hides behind the fact of being spoiled, and becomes lazy, escaping from tasks, wasting time, and making excuses.

Anna Freud [70] claims that the coming of the second child creates an emotional crisis for the first-born, often making him realize for the first time that he cannot have his mother to himself. She intimates that jealousy is indubitably aroused in this situation. The older child, in turn, is said to act, along with the mother and father, as a repressing agent. In other words, according to this view, the older sibling aids in forcing the younger individual to repress his oral erotic, anal erotic, and other tendencies which run counter to the codes of polite society. (See pp. 467–468.)

Statistical studies, of which over eighty are summarized and critically evaluated by Jones, [71] fail to show any definite effect of birth order upon intelligence and other aspects of personality. One cannot, on the basis of these studies, make any generalizations such as those indicated above. However, as Jones and others have pointed out, mass statistics on this problem may involve many factors which mask the true influence of birth order. The child with an older sibling is placed in a situation having factors which *may* precipitate jealous behavior and related difficulties. That jealousy does not always occur in such situations is shown by Sewell's [72] investigation of jealousy. Of her 70 subjects, only 39 appeared to be jealous of the sibling. The nature of personality disturbances in two children who exhibited jealousy is apparent in the following case reports:

(a) When Myron Conway was five years old, his baby sister was born. At this time Myron had whooping cough and was told by the doctor not to cough near the baby "or else she will get sick and then you won't have a baby sister any more." Several times after this, the mother found Myron coughing into the baby's face . . . and on another occasion he pushed the bassinet over. One day his mother taught him to pat the baby's face. He did this, and when his mother's back was turned, he slapped the baby hard and bit her finger.

(b) Rachel Levine had been the only child for two and a half years when Harry was born. Her behavior following the birth of her brother was of such a nature as to cause her parents and other people to suspect mental retardation. . . . Previous to the birth of Harry, Rachel had been a very "good girl," easy to manage. . . . Her mother told of Rachel's present behavior in a tone of mingled censure, apprehension, and discouragement. She said Rachel refuses to feed herself. . . . She likewise refuses to try to dress or undress herself. . . . Her spells of temper are becoming more frequent and more severe. She is very negativistic and impudent toward her parents. At no time has she expressed her jealousy of her brother by attacking him. She goes rather to the other extreme —

whenever anyone asks her about her brother she denies having one. As soon as the problem of jealousy was recognized and dealt with, the behavior difficulties began to grow less and finally disappeared.

Obviously it is not the mere fact of having a baby brother or sister which creates such personality disturbances. Whether or not jealousy will appear depends upon how adequately parents foresee and handle the social situation. Sewell's study shows that previous knowledge of the impending arrival had no effect in preventing jealousy. There is, however, no evidence concerning the specific ways in which the parents of the jealous and non-jealous children prepared them for arrival of the new member of the family. Even such knowledge as this might not tell us a great deal. Children who differ in intelligence, temperament, interests in and out of the home, and so on, would probably react in different ways to the same kind of preparation.

The whole problem of birth order is merely a *potential* one. Whether or not a given birth order shall have given effects depends upon such factors as age differences, the personality of the child when the new situation arises, the way in which parents react to the situation, the reactions of other children (if more than two siblings are involved), the presence of other adults in the home, the socio-economic status of the family, how much attention the children normally receive from the parents (they may be attended to primarily by maids), whether parents are separated, the marital happiness of the parents, and so on.

What we have said about birth order is, in general, also true of the "onliness" problem. Widespread opinion has it that "only" children are always problem cases. One hears it said that they are spoiled, selfish, neurotic, sissy, and so forth. Brill [73] presents his view of this problem as follows:

It is due to the undivided attention and abnormal love that the only child gets from his parents that he develops into a confirmed egotist. He is never neglected in favor of sisters and brothers, he is the sole ruler of the household, and his praises are constantly sung. It is, therefore, no wonder that the only child becomes vain and one-sided and develops an exaggerated opinion of himself. In later life he is extremely conceited, jealous, and envious. He begrudges the happiness of friends and acquaintances and he is therefore shunned and disliked.

Statistical investigations and case studies do not support such a generalization. In studies by Goodenough and Leahy,[74] Fenton,[75] and Hooker [76] there was no clear evidence that "only" children are thus differentiated from children reared with siblings. Hooker matched "only" children with "not-only-children" for school grade, sex, chronological age, nationality, family organization (such factors as number of other persons and broken home), and I.Q. Thirty pairs of children were matched in this way. Personality tests and ratings were then administered. The results indicated that 42 per cent of not-only and 57 per cent of only children were well adjusted; 41 per cent of not-only and 40 per cent of only children had minor behavior difficulties; 3 per cent of both not-only and only children presented extremely difficult behavior problems. There was a difference of but 3 to 4 per cent in the Woodworth-Mathews Questionnaire rating of only and not-only children. Ratings of children by their school teachers showed, when statistically analyzed, that only children are slightly *less* likely to be "neglectful, forgetful, or irresponsible in duties"; that they are *less* likely to become "sulky or sullen"; that they are *less* likely to be "rude, impolite, or impudent"; that they are *less* likely to be nervous ("unable to control themselves muscularly"); and *less* likely to be dishonest. They are *more* likely to "show signs of being sissies or tomboys." Significant differences failed to appear in other traits. Hooker says that "according to the results obtained in this study, only children at school as a group probably differ little, if at all, from those with siblings." The results of other research on this problem have led to similar conclusions.

It appears that onliness is merely a potential problem. Most intelligent parents realize the potential problem and forestall it by seeing that their children get opportunities to associate with other children, that they do not receive undue attention, and so forth. In summary we may say that one cannot predict the personality traits of a first-born, last-born, or only child. Numerous factors may overcome potential dangers in birth order and onliness.

The Constancy of Personality Traits

Are infant personality traits retained? Several investigators have given special attention to this problem. Moore and Bonham and Sargent in an unpublished study summarized by Murphy and Murphy [77] obtained personality ratings of children at birth and then at the ages of twenty-four and thirty months. Although the investigation began with 120 babies, only 38 were available for study at later ages. The Bonham-Sargent rating scale was used at the upper age levels. It included items rated at birth by means of the Moore personality inventory. The only item which showed a consistently significant positive correlation with the birth rating at both twenty-four and thirty months was "good looks." The correlation between the birth rating and the rating at twenty-four months was .42 ± .14. A correlation of .44 ± .14 was obtained between the rating at birth and that at thirty months. There was a correlation of .93 ± .02 between "good nature" at birth and the same trait at twenty-four months. However, the correlation between the birth rating and the rating at thirty months was − .15 ± .16. Other traits which evidenced a slight degree of constancy were pride, nervousness, sucking of fingers, and sociability.

Shirley's [78] investigation, although it involved but 25 babies, was much more extensive than that of Bonham and Sargent. The infants were observed and tested at frequent intervals under standardized conditions such as those described in our discussion of methods. Each infant was scored in terms of the percentage of possible responses exhibited. Its scores were interpreted on a point basis and in terms of their relation to the trends manifested by the group as a whole. A total of twenty behavior items were recorded for each baby. Some of these were indicated in Figure 135, p. 458.

According to the results of this investigation, babies consistently exhibit certain characteristics and vary from age level to age level in the manifestation of others. Developmental scores (locomotor ability, manipulatory ability, and general development) evidence the greatest constancy at the various age levels. Each baby tends to maintain its relative position in the group with respect to these. The traits which show least constancy are irritability and sociability. Traits of intermediate constancy are talkativeness and linguistic skill. These data and others not susceptible to quantitative treatment lead to the conclusion that certain aspects of personality are inborn and persist from age level to age level. According to Shirley,[79]

Both constancy and change characterize the personality of the baby. Traits are constant enough to make it plausible that a nucleus of personality exists at birth and that this nucleus persists and grows and determines to a certain degree the relative importance of the various traits. Some change is doubtless wrought by environmental factors, but this change is limited by the limitations of the original personality nucleus.

Washburn [80] found that the characteristic emotionality of infants, as indicated by tests of smiling and laughing, tended to persist from the early months of life into the second year. Bayley [81] reports similar consistency for the relative frequency of crying in infants.

Studies of behavior constancy at various age levels within the preschool period have been reported by Arrington [82] who, with three assistants recorded such characteristics as overt activity, use of materials, talking to others, talking to self, social contacts, laughing and crying. The subjects were in a nursery school. A child's score for some responses was the average number of seconds per five-minute period spent in the activity in question. In other instances rating was in terms of the average number of times a response appeared during a period of five minutes. A large number of five-minute observations were made in obtaining a subject's score. These were taken at the same time daily over a period of four months. Sixteen children were scored in the nursery school on two occasions separated by a year. The scores at the two age levels were then correlated. Rank difference correlations between the scores obtained one year apart varied from − .22 ± .17 to .62 ± .11. The highest correlation was for "talking to persons." "Talking to self" yielded a test-retest correlation of .46 ± .14.

Consistency may not be characteristic of a group yet be present in indivuduals. When data for individuals are combined, a consistent child may have his consistency concealed by inconsistent children in the group. Individual cases may thus be more significant than group data. Profiles for individual children showed varying degrees of consistency. The nature of the results, as indicated by profiles, is illustrated in Figure 138.

In Jersild's [83] study, eleven children from Arrington's investigation were observed while in kindergarten one year later. Arrington's method of recording was used. Case-study data were also obtained. Correlations between nursery school and kindergarten scores ranged from − .25 to .94. The median correlations for given items ranged from .10 to .37. On the whole, little behavior constancy is indicated by the quantitative group data. Jersild [84] says,

Apart from the observational technique, many similarities and some differences could be discerned in the behavior of the S's as compared with their behavior of the previous year. One S who was so aloof and unenterprising in the nursery school as to be quite a distinguished character appeared to be a changed creature a year later in the kindergarten. Where once he mumbled softly to himself he now conversed freely with others, where previously he played alone, carrying in his hand a little stick or button, he was now energetic in the use of equipment and in joining in the play of others. In contrast to his marked change, several S's showed characteristics which were observable the previous year. One S who frequently played the part of a ringleader in the nursery school continued to initiate group activities in the kindergarten. Other S's who seldom took the lead in initiating projects or in influencing the activities of others in the nursery school continued to play a rather inconspicuous and insubordinate role in their new environment. One S who was active and alert but quite independent in her activities in the nursery school continued her solitary enterprises the following year in the kindergarten.

Investigations of the consistency of personal-

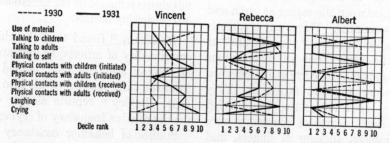

Figure 138. Graphs Showing Decile Ranking of Three Children According to Mean Duration or Frequency of Activities for Equivalent Periods of Observation Separated by One Year

Note that Vincent is extremely inconsistent. Albert shows much greater consistency. (From R. E. Arrington, "Interrelations in the Behavior of Young Children," *Child Development Monograph*, 1932, No. 8, p. 137.)

ity traits at age levels beyond the preschool period have seldom been reported. The reason for this is undoubtedly the difficulty of carrying out longitudinal research. Subjects tested earlier are often not available for long-time study. There are, however, three studies which followed the same children from the preschool period into later years. McKinnon [85] observed eight boys and eight girls over a five-year period beginning at an average age of around four years. Dominant behavior trends such as conformity, withdrawal, and caution were rated on the basis of school records, conferences with teachers, and data obtained by direct observation. Five children were rated as predominantly conformist at the earliest age level, and three of these were similarly rated at the age of eight to nine years. Of five first characterized as invasive (forcible use of materials, active approach, infringement on other's rights, physical and verbal attack), two were so characterized at the upper age level. Three characterized by withdrawal persisted in this trait throughout the period. Three were first rated as cautious, and two of these were still categorized as cautious at the end of the period. Thus, although changes in characterization occurred in some cases, consistency predominated.

Neilon [86] made a follow-up study after fifteen years of 15 of Shirley's original group of 25 babies. Shirley had written personality descriptions for each child, based upon her two years of experience in testing them. Without referring to Shirley's descriptions Neilon wrote sketches based upon her own experience with the same children as adolescents. This experience included test data, ratings, and interviews with the children and their mothers. Judges were then given the task of matching the infant sketches with those of the adolescents. Individually and as a group the judges (5 to 10 in number) matched with better than chance accuracy. Some subjects were more easily identified than others. The infant and adolescent sketches for one girl were matched by ten

judges, for another girl they were matched by nine judges. One adolescent, however, was identified by none of the judges. Neilon believes that some individuals have a "greater uniqueness of personality pattern" than others and that the persistence of this is what enabled the judges to identify them from their infant sketches.

Arkin [87] used case-history data to compare the personality traits of individuals five to eight years of age with their personality traits when twenty-five to forty years old. Forty cases were studied. It is reported that 100 per cent of the men were equally "emotional" at both age levels. Only 67 per cent of the women, on the other hand, were judged to be as emotional between twenty-five and forty as between five and eight years. Intellect, special endowment, social attitude, and initiative were judged to be consistent in 67 to 100 per cent of the cases. Constancy of personality traits is undoubtedly greater after than before adult status has been achieved. We shall give more attention to this point when adult personality is considered.

From the data summarized above it is apparent that constancy is exhibited in different degrees by individuals and that some traits are more constant than others. The most constant characteristics are, in general, those associated with physical development, intelligence, and temperament. The most variable traits from one age to another tend to be those which to a high degree involve social relations. Some of the inconstancy of these traits may be attributed to the fact that social situations are themselves constantly varying. The child whose behavior is observed in the same nursery school at periods a year apart may actually be reacting to quite different social situations on the two age levels. The child's own experiences during the interval may make the nursery school psychologically a different situation at different age levels. Playmates at the two ages may not be identical. Even if they are the same children as those involved in earlier observations, attitudes may have changed considerably during the interval. As Goodenough [88] has pointed out, the only adequate method of measuring personality in children is to obtain data concerning reactions to the widest possible number of social situations. Personality characteristics (apart from physique, intelligence, and emotionality) are so specific to given social situations as to make any narrow sampling an inadequate measure of personality traits at a given level.*

Although she recognizes that both hereditary and environmental factors are involved in its development, Shirley [92] has stressed the hereditary basis of the "personality nucleus." Gesell [93] points out that variability at different age levels is constantly channelized by the influence of hereditary factors. Differences in certain aspects of personality undoubtedly have a hereditary basis. Newman, Freeman, and Holzinger [94] have shown that identical twins reared in different environments are still remarkably similar in traits which can be measured anthropometrically. In intelligence, as we have indicated previously, they differ more than in physical traits. Correlations based upon scores on the Pressy Emotions Test, the Kent-Rosanoff Associations Test (to measure peculiarities of association), the Woodworth-Mathews Personal Data Sheet (measuring neurotic tendencies) and the June Downey Will-Temperament Test (said to measure speed and flexibility, forcefulness and decisiveness, and carefulness and persistence of reaction) were not significantly higher for identical twins (reared together or apart) than for fraternal twins. Despite what correlations indicate, however, there is remarkable similarity in the personality profiles of identical twins reared apart. For ex-

* Researches by Hartshorne and May [89], Hartshorne, May, and Maller [90], and Newcomb [91] show that there is much inconsistency of personality traits from one social situation to another. In a given situation individuals tend consistently to be honest, altruistic, introverted, and the like. When they are observed in different situations, however, individuals may swing from introvert to extravert tendencies, from honesty to dishonesty, and so on. Relatively few individuals maintain a consistent degree of introversion, honesty, etc., in all situations.

ample, in five of the nineteen cases of identical twins reared apart the will-temperament profiles are almost identical. Ten are similar in most respects. Scores on other personality tests show a greater difference than did scores on will-temperament. Newman, Freeman, and Holzinger, like Shirley, suggest that a "nucleus of personality" persists in different environments, but that it nevertheless shows clear evidence of environmentally produced variations. They conclude that "forms of behavior exist which are determined largely by the original character of the organism. None of these forms of behavior is impervious to influence, but some of them may actually not be greatly modified because they have not, as a matter of fact, been incorporated into an organized system of behavior."

Investigations on animals lend some support to the idea that hereditary factors underlie differences in temperament. Several investigators have demonstrated that such factors as wildness, timidity, and savageness vary, in a constant environment, as hereditary factors are varied. Stone [95] observed not only hereditary differences at a given age level, but persistence of these differences in later life. We have already observed (p. 28) that the general activity level and emotionality of rats varies in accordance with the assortment of hereditary factors. There are good reasons for believing that differences in such factors as bodily vigor and temperament are related to differential glandular functions (see pp. 463–465). These differences undoubtedly have a hereditary basis.

Summary and Conclusions

Personality is the integration of structure and activity which characterizes an individual. Every child is at first asocial. As he grows, and as his behavior is modified by social interactions, the child's personality becomes increasingly identifiable with socially integrated behavior.

Various methods of investigating personality have been considered, such as: the case history method; psychoanalytic interviews and dream analysis; projective procedures like doll play, the Rorschach inkblot test, and thematic apperception; studying behavior in standardized situations; and methods involving questionnaires, rating scales, and pencil-and-paper tests. Although each of these approaches has certain limitations, each yields data of value to students of personality and especially to those concerned with its growth. Certain aspects of personality revealed by each method have been described.

Personality is the resultant of two major sets of influences — the biological and the social. Biological contributions include secretions of the endocrine glands. Although one cannot as yet point to any specific influence of the endocrine glands in determining a particular personality trait, it is apparent that their integrity is essential for possession of normal health and the development of a normal physique. Sexual motivation is of course directly related to endocrine secretions. The anterior pituitary holds a key position in the endocrine system. It has a direct influence upon growth processes and an indirect influence (through its stimulation of the thyroid, adrenal, and sex glands) upon metabolic and sexual functions.

Physique is another biological aspect of personality. There is a strong suggestion that physique and temperament are somehow related, but the evidence pointing in this direction is not conclusive. Such a relationship, if established, might result from endocrine contributions to both physique and temperament. It could also depend, to some degree, upon social interaction. This is because our reactions to others might depend upon how they react to our physique. The fat boy might have his temperament determined, in part at least, by how other children react to fat boys.

Psychoanalysis has entered our discussion in many ways. Its concepts have been highly stimulating to students of personality. The concept that personality is influenced by the early thwarting (or frustration) of sexually motivated acts has been considered in detail. Both the Freudian and the Neo-Freudian positions have been discussed. Confirming and conflicting lines of evidence have received attention. No single approach seems completely adequate in itself, although each serves to highlight certain significant features of personality as well as factors possibly contributing to its development. Thwarting of activities not sanctioned by the group begins early and continues throughout life. As one grows older, actual thwarting is replaced by self-inhibitions. Actions come to be guided in accordance with group codes, even though others may not be present to enforce them. The Freudians of course emphasize the sexual aspects of this process of acculturation. Others, like Jung, Adler, and Horney, place less emphasis upon sex (and physiological motivation in general) and more upon aspects of personal-social (or interpersonal) relations. Each child is confronted early in life with mutually incompatible possibilities of action. How he resolves these conflicts has a great deal to do with the characteristics of his developing personality. Conflicts associated with physical defects seem especially important in this connection. How the person reacts to his defects (hence what they do to his personality) is largely dependent upon how other people react to them.

Another question related to psychoanalytic theory has to do with the effect upon personality of certain infant-care practices. It has been claimed, for example, that infants need the sensual stimulation associated with "mothering" and that inadequate satisfaction of this "need" interferes with normal physical and psychological growth. The evidence, however, is not completely convincing, especially since infants in certain other societies appear to develop normally without such mothering as babies in our culture usually receive. The claim that cultural differences in disciplines associated with suckling and toilet training are to some degree responsible for the adult personality traits present in various cultures is also tenuous. More evidence will be needed before such views can receive general acceptance. Even if such a relationship between infant care and later personality traits were established, there would still be the question as to its basis. From what we know at present, the infant's perceptual ability is poor at the age level at which modification of personality associated with infant care is supposed to occur. It is possible, in any event, that the constitution of the particular child and the persistent attitudes of the parent toward it are more significant than infant care as objectively envisaged.

Birth order and onliness are of *potential* significance for personality, but their actual effect, if any, depends upon individual circumstances. In other words, one is unable to predict personality traits in terms of birth order or onliness as such. Investigations have demonstrated conclusively that, as groups, only, first, second, and third children are no different from children of equal socioeconomic status, intelligence, and so on, selected without regard to onliness or birth order.

Some personality traits show a certain degree of consistency. Others change with age. Individuals differ in consistency. The relatively persistent traits are physique, appearance, intelligence, and possibly temperament. These seem less susceptible to social modification than such traits as introversion-extraversion, values, attitudes, and interests. There is no doubt that inheritance accounts for a certain amount of consistency. Perhaps early experience, although not necessarily that associated with infant care, provides part of the "nucleus of personality" around which other traits are formed. The culture itself, through the pressures placed upon the child, may foster a certain degree of consistency, especially with respect to values.

REFERENCES

1. Koch, H. L., "Some Measurements of a Pair of Siamese Twins," *J. Comp. Psychol.*, 1927, *7*, 313–333.
2. Newman, H. H., F. N. Freeman, and K. J. Holzinger, *Twins: A Study of Heredity and Environment.* Chicago: University of Chicago Press, 1937.
3. Allport, F. H., *Social Psychology.* Boston: Houghton Mifflin, 1924, p. 101.
4. Rogers, C. R., "Measuring Personality Adjustment in Children Nine to Thirteen Years of Age," *Teach. Coll. Contrib. Educ.*, 1931, No. 458, pp. 65–67.
5. *Ibid.*, p. 67.
6. Freud, A., "Psychoanalysis of the Child," in C. Murchison (ed.), *A Handbook of Child Psychology.* Worcester: Clark University Press, 1931.
7. Klein, M., *The Psychoanalysis of Children.* New York: Norton, 1932.
8. Freud, A., *et al.*, *The Psychoanalytical Study of the Child.* Vols. I–VIII. New York: International Universities Press, 1945–54.
9. Estabrooks, G. H., "The Effect of the Attitude of the Operator on Responses in Free Association," *J. Abn. & Soc. Psychol.*, 1930, *24*, 480–481.
10. Woodworth, R. S., *Psychology* (3d rev. ed.). New York: Holt, 1934.
11. See especially R. B. Cattell, *The Description and Measurement of Personality*, Yonkers: World Book Co., 1946; and D. W. Fiske, "Consistency of the Factorial Structures of Personality Ratings from Different Sources," *J. Abn. & Soc. Psychol.*, 1949, *44*, 329–344.
12. Good summaries of this literature are to be found in J. E. Bell, *Projective Techniques*, New York: Longmans, 1948, and in H. H. Anderson and G. L. Anderson, *An Introduction to Projective Techniques*, New York: Prentice-Hall, 1951.
13. Murphy, L. B., "Experiments in Free Play," in E. Lerner, L. B. Murphy, L. J. Stone, *et al.*, "Methods for the Study of Personality in Young Children," *Monographs of the Society for Research in Child Development*, 1941, *6*, No. 4.
14. *Ibid.*, p. 4.

15. Sears, R. R., "Influence of Methodological Factors in Doll Play Performance," *Child Development*, 1947, *18*, 190–197. Quotation from pp. 190–191.

16. Bach, G. R., "Young Children's Play Fantasies," *Psychol. Monog.*, 1945, *59*, No. 2.

17. Bach, G. R., "Father-Fantasies and Father-Typing in Father-Separated Children," *Child Development*, 1946, *17*, 63–80.

18. Sears, R. R., M. H. Pintler, and P. R. Sears, "Effect of Father Separation on Preschool Children's Doll Play Aggression," *Child Development*, 1946, *17*, 219–244.

19. Rorschach, H., *Psychodiagnostik*. Bern: Bircher, 1921. For discussions of Rorschach general procedures and data, see especially Bell, Anderson and Anderson (citation 12), and L. E. Abt and L. Bellak, *Projective Psychology*. New York: Knopf, 1950.

20. Ford, N., *The Application of the Rorschach Test to Young Children*. Minneapolis: University of Minnesota Press, 1946.

21. Klopfer, B., H. Margulies, L. B. Murphy, and L. J. Stone, "Rorschach Reactions in Early Childhood," *Rorschach Res. Exch.*, 1941, *5*, 1–23.

22. Ames, L. B., J. Learned, R. W. Métraux, and R. N. Walker, *Child Rorschach Responses*. New York: Hoeber, 1951.

23. Murray, H. A., *The Thematic Apperception Test*. Cambridge: Harvard University Press, 1943.

24. Bellak, L., and S. S. Bellak, *Children's Apperception Test*. New York: C. P. S. Co., 1949.

25. Symonds, P. M., *Adolescent Fantasy: An Investigation of the Picture-Story Method of Personality Study*. New York: Columbia University Press, 1949.

26. Shirley, M. M., *The First Two Years:* Vol. III. *Personality Manifestations*. Minneapolis: University of Minnesota Press, 1933.

27. Marston, L. R., "The Emotions of Young Children: An Experimental Study in Introversion-Extroversion," *Univ. Iowa Stud.: Stud. in Child Welfare*, 1925, *3*, No. 3.

28. Barker, R. G., T. Dembo, and K. Lewin, "Frustration and Regression: An Experiment with Young Children," *Univ. Iowa Stud.: Stud. in Child Welfare*, 1941, *18*, No. 1.

29. Hartshorne, H., and M. May, *Studies in the Nature of Character*. Vol. I. *Studies in Deceit*. New York: Macmillan, 1928.

30. Unpublished, but see G. Murphy and L. B. Murphy, *Experimental Social Psychology*. New York: Harper, 1931.

31. Allport, G. W., and H. S. Odbert, "Trait Names: A Psycho-Lexical Study," *Psych. Monog.*, 1936, *47*, No. 211.

32. Cattell, R. B., and H. Beloff, "Research Origin and Construction of the I.P.A.T. Junior Personality Quiz," *J. Consult. Psychol.*, 1953, *17*, 436–442.

33. Hoskins, R. G., *Endocrinology*. New York: Norton, 1941, p. 364.

34. Berman, L., *The Glands Regulating Personality*. New York: Macmillan, 1928.

35. Rowe, A. W., "A Possible Endocrine Factor in the Behavior Problems of the Young," *Am. J. Orthopsychiat.*, 1931, *1*, 451–475.

36. Hoskins, R. G., *op. cit.*, p. 186.

37. *Ibid.*, pp. 215ff.

38. Kinsey, A. C., W. B. Pomeroy, and C. E. Martin, *Sexual Behavior in the Human Male*, Philadelphia: Saunders, 1948. With P. H. Gebhard, *Sexual Behavior in the Human Female*, Philadelphia: Saunders, 1953.

39. Beach, F. A., *Hormones and Behavior*. New York: Hoeber, 1948. Also (with C. S. Ford) *Patterns of Sexual Behavior*. New York: Hoeber, 1951.

40. See Hoskins (citation 33); and A. Gesell, "The Influence of Puberty Praecox on Mental Growth," *Genet. Psychol. Monog.*, 1926, *1*, No. 6.

41. McClure, W. E., and B. Goldberg, "A Clinical Study of 'Toledo's Strong Boy,'" *J. Abn. & Soc. Psychol.*, 1932, *27*, 159–167.

42. Cannon, W. B., *The Wisdom of the Body*. New York: Norton, 1932.

43. Hoagland, H., "Schizophrenia and Stress," in *Scientific American Reader*. New York: Simon and Schuster, 1953. The quotation is from a footnote (1953) to the article written in 1949.

44. Kretchmer, E., *Physique and Character*. New York: Harcourt, Brace, 1925.

45. See W. H. Sheldon, S. S. Stevens, and W. B. Tucker, *The Varieties of Human Physique;* W. H. Sheldon and S. S. Stevens, *The Varieties of Temperament*; and W. H. Sheldon *et al.*, *Atlas of Men*. New York: Harper, 1940, 1942 and 1954, respectively.

46. Frank, L. K., "Physiological Tensions and Social Structure," *Publ. Amer. Sociol. Soc.*, 1928, *22*, 74–82. Also see Frank's "Cultural

Control and Physiological Autonomy," in C. Kluckhohn, H. A. Murray, and D. M. Schneider, *Personality in Nature and Society.* (2d ed.). New York: Knopf, 1953, 119–122.

47. Freud, A., *Introduction to Psychoanalysis for Teachers.* London: Allen and Unwin, 1931.

48. Malinowski, B., *Sex and Repression in Savage Society.* New York: Harcourt, Brace, 1927.

49. Stagner, R., and N. Drought, "Measuring Children's Attitudes Toward Their Parents," *J. Educ. Psychol.,* 1935, *26,* 169–176.

50. Simpson, M., "Parent Preferences of Young Children," *Teach. Coll. Publ. Psychol.,* 1935, No. 652.

51. Hollingworth, H. L., *Abnormal Psychology: Its Facts and Principles.* New York: Ronald, 1930.

52. Jung, C. G., *Contributions to Analytical Psychology.* New York: Harcourt, Brace, 1928. Also see F. Fordham, *An Introduction to Jung's Psychology.* London: Penguin Books, 1953 (with a foreword by Jung.)

53. Lewin, K., *A Dynamic Theory of Personality.* New York: McGraw-Hill, 1935.

54. James, W., *Psychology,* Vol. I. New York: Holt, 1890, pp. 309–310.

55. Horney, K., *New Ways in Psychoanalysis.* New York: Norton, 1939. Excerpts are from pp. 277–279.

56. Adler, A., "Individual Psychology," in C. Murchison (ed.), *Psychologies of 1930.* Worcester: Clark University Press, 1930.

57. *Ibid.,* p. 399.

58. Warren, H. C., in C. Murchison (ed.), *A History of Psychology in Autobiography.* Worcester: Clark University Press, 1933, p. 445.

59. Landis, C., and M. M. Bolles, *Personality and Sexuality of the Physically Handicapped Woman.* New York: Hoeber, 1942.

60. Barker, R. G., B. A. Wright, and M. R. Gonick, *Adjustment to Physical Handicap and Illness.* New York: Soc. Sci. Res. Council. Bull., 1946, No. 55.

61. Ribble, M., *The Rights of Infants.* New York: Columbia University Press, 1943.

62. Dashiell, J. F., *Fundamentals of General Psychology* (3d ed.). Boston: Houghton Mifflin, 1949, p. 620.

63. Orlansky, H., "Infant Care and Personality," *Psych. Bull.,* 1949, *46,* 1–48.

64. Mead, M., *Sex and Temperament in Three Primitive Societies.* New York: Morrow, 1935. Part II. Quotation from pp. 196–197.

65. Whiting, J. W. M., and I. L. Child, *Child Training and Personality: A Cross-Cultural Study.* New Haven: Yale University Press, 1953.

66. Orlansky, *op. cit.,* p. 25; second quotation from p. 39. Permission to quote granted by American Psychological Association.

67. See citation 55, p. 70.

68. Fromm, E., *Escape from Freedom.* New York: Farrar, 1941, p. 286.

69. Adler, A. "Characteristics of the First, Second, Third Child," *Children,* 1928, *3,* No. 5, p. 14.

70. See citation 47, pp. 502–503.

71. Jones, H. E., "Order of Birth in Relation to Development of the Child" in C. Murchison (ed.), *A Handbook of Child Psychology.* Worcester: Clark University Press, 1931.

72. Sewell, M., "Some Causes of Jealousy in Young Children," *Smith Coll. Stud. Soc. Work,* 1930, *1,* 23–40.

73. Brill, A. A., *Psychoanalysis.* Philadelphia: Saunders, 1913, p. 258.

74. Goodenough, F. L., and A. M. Leahy, "The Effect of Certain Relationships upon the Development of Personality," *J. Genet. Psychol.,* 1927, *34,* 45–71.

75. Fenton, N., "The Only Child," *J. Genet. Psychol.,* 1927, *34,* 45–71.

76. Hooker, H. F., "A Study of the Only Child in School," *J. Genet. Psychol.* 1931, *39,* 122–126. Quotation p. 123.

77. See citation 30.

78. See citation 26.

79. *Op. cit.,* p. 56.

80. Washburn, R. W., "A Study of the Smiling and Laughing of Infants in the First Year of Life," *Genet. Psychol. Monog.,* 1929, *6,* 397–539.

81. Bayley, N., "A Study of the Crying of Infants During Mental and Physical Tests," *J. Genet. Psychol.,* 1932, *40,* 306–329.

82. Arrington, R. E., "Interrelationships in the Behavior of Young Children," *Child Development Monograph,* 1932, No. 8.

83. Jersild, A. T., "The Constancy of Certain Behavior Patterns in Young Children," *Am. J. Psychol.,* 1933, *45,* 125–129.

84. *Op. cit.,* p. 128.

85. McKinnon, K. M., *Consistency and Change in*

Behavior Manifestations. New York: Teachers College, 1942.

86. Neilon, P., "Shirley's Babies After Fifteen Years: A Personality Study," *J. Genet. Psychol.,* 1948, *73,* 175–186.

87. Arkin, E., "The Problem of the Stability of the Human Organism," *J. Genet. Psychol.,* 1933, *42,* 228–236.

88. Goodenough, F. L., "Interrelationships in the Behavior of Young Children," *Child Development,* 1930, *1,* 29–47.

89. See citation 29.

90. Hartshorne, H. H., M. May, and J. B. Maller, *Studies in the Nature of Character.* Vol. II. *Studies in Service and Self-Control.* New York: Macmillan, 1929.

91. Newcomb, T. M., "The Consistency of Certain Introvert-Extrovert Behavior Patterns in 51 Problem Boys," *Teach. Coll. Contrib. Educ.,* 1929, No. 382.

92. See citation 26.

93. Gesell, A., "Some Observations of Developmental Stability," *Psych. Monog.,* 1936, *47,* 35–46.

94. Newman, H. H., F. N. Freeman, and K. J. Holzinger, *Twins: A Study of Heredity and Environment.* Chicago: University of Chicago Press, 1937.

95. Stone, C. P., *et al., Studies in the Dynamics of Behavior.* Chicago: University of Chicago Press, 1932.

SUGGESTIONS FOR FURTHER READING

Allport, G. W., *Personality.* New York: Holt, 1937.

Axline, V. M., *Play Therapy: The Inner Dynamics of Childhood.* Boston: Houghton Mifflin, 1947.

Barker, R. G., J. S. Kounin, and H. F. Wright, *Child Behavior and Development.* New York: McGraw-Hill, 1943. Selections from Barker, *et al.,* Dennis, Erikson, Escalona, Levy, Macfarlane, L. B. Murphy, and Sanford.

Bell, J. E., *Projective Techniques.* New York: Longmans, Green, 1948.

Carmichael, L. (ed.), *Manual of Child Psychology* (2d ed.) New York: Wiley, 1954, Chapters 12 (Mead), 13 (Vernon Jones), and 15 (Lewin and Escalona).

Dashiell, J. F., *Fundamentals of General Psychology* (3d ed.). Boston: Houghton Mifflin, 1949, Chapters 20 and 21.

Dennis, W., *Readings in Child Psychology.* New York: Prentice-Hall, 1951, Chapters 8 and 9 (readings from Reynolds, Olson, Axline, Neilon, J. E. Bagby, Anderson, Malinowski, Mead, Havighurst, Lewin, *et al.*)

Freud, S., *An Outline of Psychoanalysis.* New York: Norton, 1949. A brief account of Freud's later views.

Hartley, E. L., H. G. Birch, and R. E. Hartley, *Outside Readings in Psychology.* New York: Gardner Crowell, 1950. Readings 8 (L. K. Frank), 86 (Murphy and Jensen), and 87 (W. B. Wolfe).

Horney, K., *New Ways in Psychoanalysis.* New York: Norton, 1939.

Hunt, J. McV. (ed.), *Personality and the Behavior Disorders.* New York: Ronald, 1944, Chapters 20 (Ribble), 21 (L. B. Murphy), 23 (Babson), and 25 (Kanner).

Jersild, A. T., *Child Psychology* (4th ed.). New York: Prentice-Hall, 1954, Chapter 19.

Kluckhohn, C., H. A. Murray, and D. M. Schneider, *Personality: In Nature, Society, and Culture* (2d ed.). New York: Knopf, 1953.

Maier, N. R. F., *Frustration.* New York: McGraw-Hill, 1949. See especially the discussions of childhood frustration.

McClelland, D.C., *Personality.* New York: Dryden, 1951.

Murphy, G., *Personality.* New York: Harper, 1947.

Ribble, M., *The Rights of Infants.* New York: Columbia University Press, 1943.

Stagner, R., *Psychology of Personality* (2d ed.) New York: McGraw-Hill, 1948.

Whiting, J. W. M., and I. L. Child, *Child Training and Personality.* New Haven: Yale University Press, 1953.

17

Changes in Personality from Adolescence
until Senescence

Our discussion of psychological processes has surveyed their development from lower organisms to man, and in man from conception until later childhood. After childhood no essentially new psychological processes develop, and most of those already considered do not undergo much further development before maturity is reached. The most important changes which appear after a child enters the teens are in certain aspects of personality. These changes take place under the impact of new physiological and social conditions which make childish adjustment inadequate and call for readjustment. The chief physiological changes calling for readjustment are those which have their onset at puberty and usher in the period of adolescence. This is also an important period socially because it involves a certain degree of emancipation from parental authority and the assumption of relatively independent status, with all of its responsibilities.

In 1904 G. Stanley Hall gave adolescence a major place in psychological literature by writing his monumental two-volume treatise entitled *Adolescence: Its Psychology and Its Relations to Physiology, Anthropology, Sociol-ogy, Sex, Crime, Religion and Education.* Since then adolescence has been the focal point of extensive investigations from all the angles suggested in Hall's subtitle. Most departments of psychology now offer courses on adolescence, and many textbooks are available. It is a field to which several disciplines contribute. Anthropologists study various cultures with such questions in mind as: Is the onset of puberty given social recognition, and if so, how? Is adult status assumed abruptly or gradually, as in our society? Sociologists focus upon such aspects as the adolescent "peer culture," family conflicts, community relationships, and juvenile delinquency. Physiologists are primarily interested in glandular and metabolic changes associated with the onset of puberty. Anatomists give their attention to skeletal, muscular, and other aspects of bodily development. Educators investigate various aspects of adolescent education. The role of the psychologist in this area has been many-sided. Some psychologists have done work which in no way differs from that of investigators in other fields. They have studied adolescents in cultures other than our own, the roles assumed by adolescents in our own society, the incidence of delinquency among adolescent youth, basal metabolism and other physiological concomitants of puberty, skeletal and muscular growth through the adolescent period, and various educational problems confronting the adolescent in our society. Usually, however, adolescent psychologists have concentrated upon more obviously psychological problems, like intelligence, emotionality, and, in general, personality and social adjustment of adolescents. Much information on adolescence is also derived from cross-sectional studies covering the whole range from childhood to old age.

Following the example set by Hall, textbooks on the psychology of adolescence attempt to integrate the relevant data from all of the above-mentioned sources. All that we attempt here is a brief epitome of what is known about this broad area; one which lays particular stress upon the growth of personality beyond the point at which we left it in the preceding chapter. Some attention is given, in this connection, to underlying physiological changes as well as to peculiarities of adolescent social behavior.

When adult status is fully attained, the individual enters upon a period which is, in some respects, like a long plateau in the growth curve. It is characterized by consolidation and application more than by growth of fundamental psychological functions. After later maturity, however, the effectiveness of behavior in coping with the environment usually undergoes a decline. This decline is associated with physiological changes, including the menopause in women, and possibly something akin to it in men. The decline is also in many instances associated with changing social responsibilities. Our discussion of adulthood concentrates upon personality in relation to physiological and social events.

Around the late fifties or early sixties the decline which was hardly more than hinted at before, becomes more pronounced, in some cases even precipitous. Such negative developments are often paralleled by noticeable personality changes. As in the case of adolescence, this is an area on which there is an extensive literature, covering various cultural, physiological, and social, as well as directly psychological aspects. All we can do here is delineate some of the alterations in personality which are often associated with the period from later maturity to senescence.

Recent and more extensive treatises on adolescence and old age are referred to in the references for further reading at the end of this chapter.

Adolescence

The term *adolescence* is derived from the Latin *adolescere*, meaning to approach maturity. Adolescence begins with the onset of puberty and ends when adult status is attained. In many primitive societies a sort of rebirth or resurrection is believed to occur at puberty. Elaborate ceremonies mark the event.[1] Following the pubic ceremony an individual frequently takes his place as a full-fledged member of the tribe. In so-called "civilized" society, however, the period of adolescence is artificially, as it were, extended far beyond the onset of puberty. Even though the adolescent is frequently capable of it, there is no sudden assumption of adult status.

Puberty

The age of pubescence varies with such factors as sex, race, climate, living conditions, and intelligence. In females it is marked by the onset of menstruation. Observational data summarized by Shuttleworth[2] show that the average age at which menstruation occurs in the white population of the United States is around 13 years. Kinsey *et al.*[3] report an average age of 13.1, which is the age at which the women of their sample recalled having menstruated for the first time. Other observational data summarized by Kinsey from a wide variety of sources also suggest 13 as the average age at which menstruation

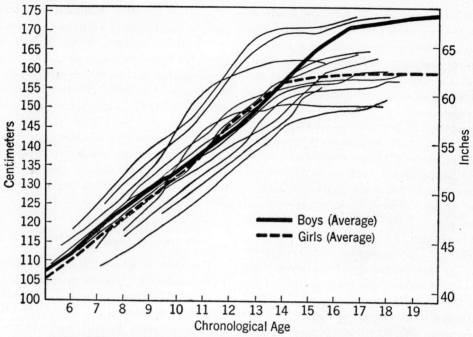

Figure 139. Individual Growth Curves of Standing Height for 12 Boys

The average curves for both boys and girls are given for comparison.   (Derived from data of the Harvard Growth Study as reported in W. F. Dearborn and J. W. M. Rothney, *Predicting the Child's Development*, Cambridge: Sci-Art, 1941, p. 313, Fig. 79; and F. K. Shuttleworth, "The Physical and Mental Growth of Boys and Girls Aged Six Through Nineteen in Relation to Age of Maximum Growth," *Monog. Soc. Res. Child Develop.*, 1939, *4*, No. 3, Fig. 248–249.)

first occurs. This is often preceded by the appearance of pubic hair and noticeable breast development.

In boys the age of pubescence is not so readily determined as in girls. This is because there is no readily observed event, like the menses, which marks the transition from childhood to adolescence. Kinsey *et al.*[4] regard the time of the first ejaculation as the most significant single event marking the onset of adolescence in boys. But it is difficult to obtain observational data on ejaculation. One method is of course to examine specimens of urine, especially the first morning sample, for evidence of sperm. The most extensive data available at present are those based upon memory, as reported by Kinsey. According to data from the whole sample of over three thousand cases, the average age is a little under 14. This is of course almost a year

later, on the average, than when menstruation occurs in girls. It is in line with the general observation that girls are ahead of boys in achieving sexual maturity. Pubic hair usually precedes ejaculation; change of voice usually follows it.

The data on both males and females show a wide age range. It is also well to note that, while the menarche and ejaculation are taken as crucial evidences of the transition from childhood to adolescence, the changes leading up to and following this "climax" are usually quite gradual.

Aspects of adolescent growth

When the average height or weight of successive age groups is plotted, there is apparently a more or less gradual increase with age. The change at adolescence is not especially pronounced. But when *increments* of

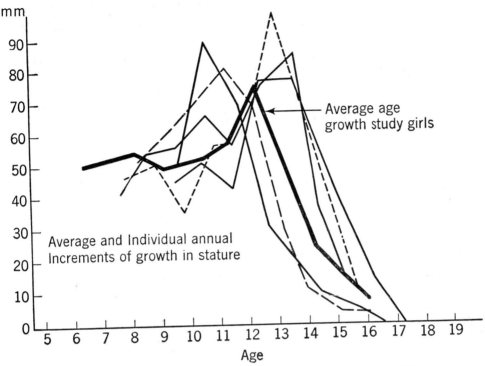

Figure 140.   Average and Individual Increments of Height in Girls

The curves show that some girls exhibit a growth change before and others after the average, and that some fall above and others below the average increments in the magnitude of change. (Based upon data for girls from the Harvard Growth Study as reported in W. F. Dearborn and J. W. M. Rothney, *Predicting the Child's Development*, Cambridge: Sci-Art, 1941, p. 314.)

growth are plotted, it becomes quite evident that a sharp acceleration usually occurs around the time of puberty.[5] Physical growth curves for individuals differ considerably, some individuals growing at a fairly steady rate while others show a marked spurt. Some of these comparisons are shown in Figures 139 and 140. Pronounced spurts in general bodily growth are the exception rather than the rule. When sudden atypical changes do occur, they may be quite disconcerting to the individual involved — not because of the physical growth *per se*, but because the person's physique represents, to a high degree, his image of himself.[6] Atypical changes are all the more disconcerting when they make the adolescent the topic of conversation, the butt of jokes, or the isolate in a social group, like the fat or tall girl who cannot get a dancing partner.

Some structures do undergo a pronounced spurt at adolescence in most individuals. These are of course the genital organs. The lower curve in Figure 141 represents the growth of the testes, ovaries, and related structures and shows the sharp increment at puberty, as compared with the increments for aspects of the body as a whole and the nervous system. At about the same time as this change occurs, the secretions from the gonads also change, as illustrated in Figure 142. We see that estrogens are secreted in about equal amounts by boys and girls prior to puberty but that at this period, the girls secrete these hormones to a sharply increased extent while boys show little change. On the other hand, we see that the boys increase their androgenic output so that it exceeds that of the female by a much larger amount than before.

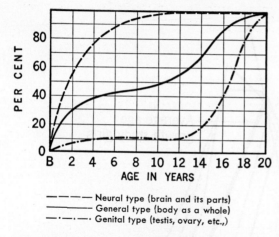

- - - - Neural type (brain and its parts)
———— General type (body as a whole)
—·—·— Genital type (testis, ovary, etc.,)

Figure 141. A Graph Showing the Major Types of Postnatal Growth of the Various Parts and Organs of the Body

The curves are drawn to a common scale by computing their values at successive ages in terms of their total postnatal increments (to twenty years). (After R. E. Scammon, "The Measurement of the Body in Childhood." In *The Measurement of Man*, by permission of the publisher, University of Minnesota Press, Minneapolis, Minnesota, 1930, p. 193.)

These changes in sexual physiology doubtless underlie the increasing sexual sensitivity and motivation which makes its appearance following puberty. Very few males and females of Kinsey's [7] study reported that they had sexual outlets (such as petting and masturbation) at 10 years. Shortly thereafter, the per cent of subjects reporting all forms of sexual outlet showed a marked increase. More than 80 per cent of males and 40 per cent of females reported that they experienced such outlets by the age of 15 years. Eighty per cent of both sexes reported that petting was an outlet between 17 and 18 years.

There are many other adolescent physiological changes than those already mentioned. Some of these were studied by Shock [8] with 100 teen-age boys and girls. The same subjects were studied at intervals over a seven-year period; thus individual as well as group trends became evident. Some aspects of physiology (such as pulse rate) dropped

steadily in both sexes throughout the seven years. Others, like systolic blood pressure, went up, but more so for boys than for girls. These were group trends. Some individuals, however, showed marked fluctuations. This was especially true in basal metabolism.

Changes in strength and in general motor ability are also associated with the adolescent period. Data reported by Jones [9] show that marked deficiencies in these respects among boys may have a decidedly unfavorable impact upon personality and social adjustment. The measures used in this study were strength of grip, of pull, and of thrust. Strength improved with age in both boys and girls, but much more so in boys, most of whom showed a spurt at the time of puberty. In the case of boys there was a correlation of .50 between strength and the Espenschade [10] measures of motor skill. Jones [11] reports that "Among boys at 17.5 years, total strength was shown to correlate about .5 with weight, about .3 with height and with mesomorphy, zero with endomorphy, and negatively with ectomorphy.* The multiple correlation of strength with these five factors is .866, indicating that constitutional factors (as contrasted with experiential or training factors) are of primary importance in determining individual differences in strength."

From the standpoint of personality, data on strength in relation to social prestige are of particular interest. Low but significant correlations (.30 and .39) were obtained between indices of strength and rated popularity. Such relationships became more evident when the 10 strongest and 10 weakest boys were compared. The former not only had good physique and general physical fitness, but they were high in social prestige and in general level of adjustment. The latter tended to be asthenic in physique, to have poor general health, to be unpopular, to have feelings of inferiority, and to show other personal maladjustments. In commenting on the relation between strength and social status among adolescents, Jones [12] says that the "positive

* See pp. 465–466.

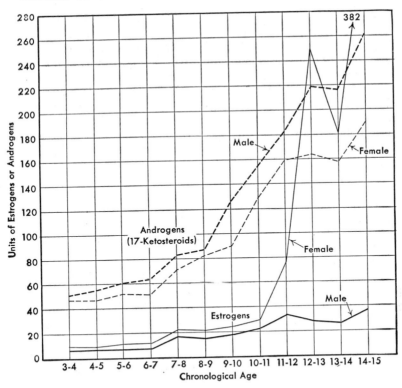

Figure 142.   Excretion of Sex Hormones

These results are derived from urinary assays. Note that the curve for estrogen secretion in males flattens during adolescence while that for females undergoes a precipitous rise. The androgen curve, however, tends to flatten for females while it continues to rise for males. Androgens (17-Ketosteroids) are also produced by the adrenal cortex. (After Nathanson, *et al.*, from N. W. Shock, "Physiological Changes in Adolescence," in *43rd Yearbk. Nat. Soc. Stud. Educ.*, Part I, 1944, p. 75.)

relationship of strength to 'prestige traits' (among boys) . . . may be regarded as evidence of the role of physical prowess in the adolescent value system. Superior strength is a part of a complex of physical characteristics valued highly in the preadult culture; the absence of these characteristics is a handicap which can be overcome only by strongly compensating personal traits in other areas which are also highly valued."

Individual differences in certain aspects of physique and in physiological processes such as strength and muscular skill are thus seen to be potentially important for personality. When sufficiently marked as to make the person conspicuous, they may affect his social status and his attitudes toward himself. We say that differences in this region are "potentially" important because the atypical adolescent is not inevitably at a disadvantage. As the quotation from Jones suggests, certain avenues of compensation are sometimes available. Some adolescents exhibit no remarkable change in the rate of growth, in any direction, while others change rapidly, sometimes in one direction and not in others. Some of the latter take these changes in their stride, even joining others in laughing at themselves. Others become embarrassed, and perhaps withdrawn. It is thus not particularly enlightening to speak of the "typical adolescent" from the standpoint either of growth or of how adolescents react to it. The following cases from Averill [13] amplify this conclusion.

Tom shot up amazingly fast from the height of five feet, four inches to six feet, three inches. His trouser cuffs did not reach nearly to his ankles, and his wrists dangled from his coat sleeves in a most amusing fashion. His walk became an awkward shuffle. He bumped into most articles of furniture that he passed. He joggled everything within joggling distance. He seemed to care nothing at all about his personal appearance. His hair was always uncombed, his nails and hands dirty, his linen, in spite of his mother's persistent efforts, was spotted and grimy, and his shoes were never shined. Besides all this, his voice was changing. He would initiate a conversation in a deep tone and conclude it in a high falsetto. Surprisingly enough, he was not embarrassed by this occurrence, but seemed to enjoy it and would laugh heartily over it with another lad of his acquaintance who frequently did the same thing. The two of them even held contests to see which voice changed the oftener in a single sentence!

John, on the other hand, developed gradually and evenly. One was almost unconscious that he was developing at all, it was so inconspicuous. He just grew up. He was never particularly awkward or unkempt. His voice change was quite unnoticed. His clothes never became misfit, for his growth was never anything but gradual. Although he did not attain the great height that Tom did, he has grown up into a stalwart young collegian.

Hall [14] claimed that adolescence is characterized by growth varying in magnitude for different physical processes, and he believed that the unequal development of rapidly growing structures tends to disrupt earlier modes of adjustment, making the individual awkward and, as a result, extremely self-conscious. Some adolescents like Tom (above) are awkward, but even when such awkwardness occurs, it may result from social rather than, or in addition to, anatomical and physiological influences. This possibility is stressed by Goodenough as well as several later writers on adolescence. Goodenough [15] says:

It is easy to see . . . why some children do show an increased motor awkwardness at this time. Changes in their appearance are so marked that people are always commenting on it, often in rather tactless fashion.

"Gracious, how John is stretching out! And look at the size of his feet!"

"My goodness, don't tell me this is little Mary! Why, she used to be such a dainty little girl. I never in the world would have known her."

Daily exposure to remarks of this kind can hardly help but embarrass and annoy a sensitive child, even though no unkindness is intended. Often the adolescent member of a large family is made the butt of a great deal of chaffing about his appearance. His clothes are perpetually too short, his hands and feet, which are made doubly conspicuous by protruding so far out of his outgrown garments, his voice with its unexpected growls and squeaks, all come in for their share of banter. Even though he takes it good-naturedly, some degree of self-consciousness is almost certain to be the result, and as most of us know from experience there is nothing like self-consciousness for disturbing one's motor control. It is an exceptional golfer whose drive cannot be interfered with by remarks about his personal appearance, particularly if he knows them to be true. The adolescent who is so clumsy and awkward that disaster seems to follow wherever he goes may show surprising dexterity of hand in his workshop when no one is watching him and splendid bodily control on the athletic field. His awkwardness in public is not due to lack of motor skill but is the result of embarrassment and self-consciousness.

Growth of psychological processes during adolescence

Basic psychological processes do not change so obviously during adolescence as those already discussed. Brooks [16] reproduces growth curves for speed of tapping, control of eyewink, precision of movement, speed of handwriting, quality of handwriting, reading, speed of cancellation, threshold for pain, weight discrimination, color discrimination, sustained voluntary attention, effect of divided attention, memory, and reasoning. Each curve shows a rather steady rise. We have already presented curves showing the steady growth of general intelligence prior to and during the adolescent period. All such curves lack the spurt which sometimes appears in aspects of anatomical and physiological growth. Marked individual variations are sometimes shown for I.Q. and other indices of mental growth, but these occur at any time. They are not particularly related to the period of adolescence.

Hall [17] promulgated the notion that adolescence is a period of emotional instability. On *a priori* grounds one might expect adolescents to be emotionally unbalanced. Maturation of sexual functions, with emergence of associated lustful inclinations, could conceivably cause an emotional crisis in the life of the individual, making him subject to fears, worries, and general emotional disturbance. There is little evidence, however, that such emotional unbalance is characteristic of adolescents. Mathews [18] and Brooks [19] tested the theory of adolescent instability by having a total of almost three thousand boys and girls between the ages of 12 and 19 fill out the Woodworth-Mathews Personal Data Sheet. The questions, to be answered "yes" or "no," refer to common complaints, worries, fears, and so on. The combined results of these investigations show no clear evidence of a greater than normal number of unfavorable responses during adolescence. However, Pollock and Malzberg's [20] data on the incidence of mental disease during adolescence may be interpreted as lending some support to Hall's view. Both males and females show an incidence of less than ten cases of mental disease per 100,000 population at the beginning of adolescence. By the age of 20 years the incidence for males has increased to eighty and that for females to about sixty.

Individual adolescents frequently exhibit characteristics suggestive of emotional instability. Their "crushes," their worry about sexual functions, their subjection to sudden impulse, and the like, are the bases of the generalization concerning emotional instability. However, as in the case of alleged saltatory growth and awkwardness, emotional instability is by no means characteristic of all adolescents. Some individuals are unstable at adolescence and others not. Even where emotional instability does exist, it is more reasonable to credit inadequate social adjust-ment than some characteristic inherent in emotional growth as such. As Horrocks [21] points out, "We find the adolescent experiencing considerable emotional upset when his peer relations are not satisfactory. As a child he has strong emotional attachments — usually to his parents. With broadening social interests and greater physical-space mobility the child develops new needs and transfers his emotional attachment to other persons — and becomes upset if they do not respond."

The changes in interests which in our society come with adolescence have been studied intensively. We have already (p. 437) reproduced a curve from Lehman and Witty [22] showing how the average number of social activities decreases as a function of age. As he approaches adolescence, the average child becomes more discriminating and more individualistic in his choice of recreations. Kuhlen [23] reports unpublished data gathered by Pressey on the changing frequency with age of several particular interests. Items like "social affairs," "dancing," and "clothes" continue to rise, and do so more sharply beginning with adolescence than before. This is true for both sexes. Other interests like "bicycling," "roller skating," and "fishing" tend to decline with age. A large amount of information on other interests of various kinds has been summarized by Kuhlen.

Problems of adolescent adjustment

Some problems of adolescent adjustment are related to growth changes, especially when, as we have seen, the changes are atypical. Others are related to the emergence of strong sexual impulses. Still others have to do with changing social relations and responsibilities. Some of the more important of these problems are here considered briefly. More extensive discussions appear in books on the psychology of adolescence such as those cited at the end of this chapter.

Control of sexual impulses in accordance with the group codes is, for the adolescent in our society, an important aspect of adjustment. Difficulties reside in the fact that we do not sanction any overt sexual outlets until some years after sexual maturity has been attained. Non-sanctioned outlets occur in most males and in a large proportion of females, as the Kinsey reports have shown. There is no evidence that the most frequent of these outlets are harmful to later adjustment except when feelings of shame are associated with them or when they become fixated in such a way as to hinder or prevent heterosexual adjustments later on.

Anthropologists find that the problems of sexual adjustment are peculiar to particular cultures. Malinowski[24] found that children of the Trobriand Islands engage in sex play from an early age and that parents encourage them in the "copulation play." Mead[25] has also written about the sexual freedom of the Samoans and how the transition from childhood to adolescence is consequently much smoother than in our society. The great variations in sexual customs in various societies are discussed by Ford and Beach.[26] It is quite common, in societies other than our own, for copulatory activities to occur at puberty, if not before, and thus the delay sanctioned by us, with its resultant problems, does not exist. There is, however, a universal taboo against incest. The difference between our own society and others, with respect to sex mores, is of course related in part to the socio-economic complexity of our own as compared with primitive societies.

Our religious tradition is against preoccupation with sex, and there are many who feel that it is possible to refrain from reproductive activities without endangering either health or personal happiness. It is often maintained, too, that a great deal of the drive toward "constructive effort" which characterizes societies like our own comes from the fact that reproductive activities are to a large degree restrained. This may be true, but we should not assume that other peoples who lack our sexual inhibitions are necessarily preoccupied with sex. Nor should we assume

that it is because of their different attitudes toward sex that they are behind us in constructive effort. As indicated in a previous discussion, (p. 472) cross-cultural comparisons are likely to be biased by our own prejudices. Who is to be the judge of what constitutes "constructive effort"? An unbiased judge might regard many of our present-day efforts as destructive.

As a member of our society approaches adulthood and begins to assume social and economic independence, the problem of "psychological weaning" arises. This is often, although not necessarily, a difficult time for all concerned. There is, as Zachry[27] reports, a great deal of ambivalence on the part of both adolescents and their parents. She says that

most adolescents have mixed feelings about becoming adult; they want to be grown-up at times, but often feel inadequate and then wish to enjoy childhood protection for a little while longer. Frequent swings between the two occur before a more mature pattern is finally established. Difficulties are intensified because the adolescent's parents are similarly ambivalent about his growing up. At one moment they talk with pride about their growing son who will soon be attending medical school; at the next, they bemoan the fact that they are losing their baby. Unfortunately the adolescent and his parents seldom have their moments together. When the adolescent is asserting himself, his mother and father will be pulling him back into childhood status; when his feeling is infantile, they are wishing for a young adult upon whom they may lean.

A large portion of the literature on adolescence deals with the sorts of things which produce conflict between parents and children. As one can well imagine, the "bones of contention" change with the times. Use of the family car replaces use of the family buggy; radio programs are superseded by television shows; and so on.

Allied with the struggle for emancipation from adult control is the strong hold which the peer group comes to have over most adolescents. They identify strongly with this group, and their activities within it are often a source of conflict with parents and, all too often, with the law. Horrocks [28] says that

the peer group is one of the greatest motivating forces of adolescence. The relation of an adolescent to his peers and his participation in their activities is usually one of the most important things in his life. His ego-involvement is often such that exclusion can be a major tragedy, while acceptance brings feelings of security and happiness.

The cliques, crowds, and gangs which make up adolescent groups; the nature of their activities, social and antisocial; their linguistic and other affectations; and the characteristics of their leaders have been dealt with extensively in all recent texts on adolescence, and the reader is referred to these for relevant details.

As the adolescent in our society approaches adulthood, the problem of choosing a vocation confronts him. At one time there was no choice. The boy normally followed his father's trade, and the girl, except in rare instances, became a housewife and nothing more. Today, however, there is not only the problem of finding out what one can do, and preparing for it, but also that of actually being able to earn a living. Competition is so keen that many are unable to assume economic independence from their families or from the state. Then, too, in times of international crisis there is for male adolescents the problem of military service, with a consequent further delay in education and economic independence. Such problems, like those of sexual adjustment and psychological weaning, are of course artifacts. They result from nothing that is inherent in adolescence as such, but stem from the organization of our society. Needless to say, the primitive adolescent knows no such problems.

Some indirect indication of how individual adolescents view the world about them and their relations to it are provided by projective tests (pp. 452–456). Symonds [29] administered a special form of thematic apperception test to teen-age boys and girls. Each was shown the pictures and asked to make up stories about them. The stories of course differed a great deal depending upon the picture; and for the same picture, depending upon the individual adolescent. Fantasies took as many forms as there were individuals, but recurring themes dealt with aspects of aggression and love.

Adolescence is a time of moral and religious adjustment, but the characteristics of such adjustment change with the times. At the turn of the century, Starbuck [30] found a high incidence of conversion and assumed that conversion took place so frequently in this period because of the storm and stress experienced by the adolescent, with a consequent need for some belief around which personality could be integrated. Thirty years later, Clark [31] found sudden conversion to be a rare phenomenon, only about 7 per cent of his sample of 2000 college students reporting it. This shows very clearly that conversion is a function of culture rather than of physiological or psychological processes as such. Kuhlen and Arnold [32] have made an extensive study of age changes in religious beliefs and practices, and Kuhlen [33] presents an extensive discussion of these and other findings in this area. He says:

The available evidence regarding religious views suggests that definite changes occur during the teens with respect to views held, the trend being toward more abstract concepts and greater intellectual freedom. Adolescents appear to have a great number of general religious problems, want help on these problems, but find many church programs unsatisfactory. There is a decline in church attendance with age. There is little evidence available regarding philosophy of life. Although not consistent, anecdotal evidence suggests a fair amount of concern with such issues in the teens.

Adult Personality

Although there is no marked change in development before and after the beginning of adolescence, the menses of females and the seminal emissions of males are convenient differentiating phenomena. There is, however, no event which separates termination of adolescence and assumption of adult status. The term adult is derived from *adultus*, the past participle of *adolescere*. It thus means "full grown" or "mature." Individuals attain maturity at different ages, and reach it earlier for some processes than for others. It is generally agreed that achievement of physical and psychological maturity occurs, on the average, during the late teens or early twenties. However, adulthood has social as well as psychological implications. The individual may be designated an adult as soon as the social responsibilities of men and women are assumed. In some societies this is at or soon after puberty. Assumption of adult status in a civilized community varies from one group to another. We can thus make no generalization concerning the age at which adulthood begins.

It may be said, at least, that the individual in his early twenties is usually an adult in both the psychobiological and the social sense. What are the distinguishing characteristics of adult personality? Recognizing that personality is peculiarly an individual phenomenon, we may say that, by and large, the personality of adults is characterized by greater consistency than that of children and adolescents; that it tends to be markedly channelized in the direction of family, vocational, and avocational interests; and that conservatism is the rule. The three factors just mentioned are by no means distinct. Consistency and conservatism are, in a sense, synonymous. They may, furthermore, be attributed to channelization of interests. We shall discuss each of them very briefly.

Watson [34] makes the following very pertinent comment concerning the relative consistency of adult as compared with adolescent personality traits:

Personality changes most rapidly in youth when habit patterns are forming, maturing and changing. Between fifteen and eighteen a female changes from a child to a woman. At fifteen she is but the playmate of boys and girls of her own age. At eighteen she becomes a sex object for every man. After thirty personality changes very slowly owing to the fact . . . that by that time most individuals, unless constantly stimulated by a new environment, are pretty well settled in a humdrum way of living. Habit patterns become set. If you have an adequate picture of the average individual at thirty you will have it with few changes for the rest of that individual's life — as most lives are lived. A quacking, gossiping, neighbor-spying, disaster-enjoying woman of thirty will be, unless a miracle happens, the same at forty and still the same at sixty.

It is doubtful whether really fundamental changes in personality normally occur during the period of adulthood prior to senescence. Sometimes the alleviation of glandular malfunction, toxic conditions, and the like may effect some change in the temperament and general attitude of an individual. Sometimes, also, marriage, a change of mates, the coming of children, assumption of new economic or political responsibilities, and other variations in social relationships lead to some change in certain aspects of personality. However, as Watson indicates, the fundamental behavioral integration of the adult is normally quite constant from year to year. Witness, for example, a wife's allegedly futile efforts to change the premarital habit patterns of her spouse.

Adult interests differ somewhat from those of the child and the adolescent. If the adult is married, and especially if he has children, his fundamental interests tend to center around the home. His every action may be evaluated by him in terms of what it will mean to his loved ones. The vocational interests of the adult are usually determined before marriage. Change from single to married status may involve, in the case of males, more intense application along vocational lines. For the woman it once meant giving up all thought of a vocation outside of the home. Today it may mean anything from giving up a vocation to seeking one in order to provide for the added expenses of keeping up a household. In most primitive societies there is no choice. The woman who is married follows well-defined codes concerning extramarital activities.

The adult period is of course that in which most people reach their maximum level of achievement. According to data reported by Lehman,[35] outstanding accomplishment in most physical skills comes in the early adult period (boxing, 23; baseball, 28; bowling, 30; and so on). In literary and professional skills, the period of maximum performance is nearer 35. This is somewhat earlier than in former generations.[36] When it comes to positions of outstanding responsibility, however, the age level is raised considerably. United States Senators, for example, had an average age of 65 in 1925, when Lehman compared them with those of 1799, whose average age was nearer 45.

Most older people, when asked to cite the happiest period of their lives, mention the early adult years.[37]

Avocational interests may be no different in adulthood than in childhood and adolescence. As Lehman and Witty's[38] studies have shown, however, greater conservativeness characterizes the recreational activity of adults as compared with that of children and adolescents. Adults usually exhibit a few generally accepted forms of avocational interests rather than individualistic ones. Their recreational interests tend, in other words, to be channelized in accordance with custom.

The relative conservatism of adults as compared with children and adolescents requires little comment. The conflict between age and youth is proverbial. Even here, however, one is not safe in making broad generalizations. In our day and society many an adult is extremely radical and many a youth just as extremely conservative. When it is said that adults are more conservative than youths, emphasis is of course placed on general trends rather than on individual cases. Conservatism is often attributable to the fixity of personality traits and the channelization of interests. The adult often fears that familial, economic, and other interests will suffer from social change. It is well known that, by and large, the most radical adults are those who have little to lose as a result of change. Conversely, the more an individual has in the way of wealth and social status, the more conservative he tends to be.

One of the most important adjustments of the late adult period is that associated with the cessation of sex hormone secretion. This problem is especially evident in women. The menopause occurs at an average age of 45. It is marked by various physiological symptoms, the most obvious of which is irregularity, and finally cessation, of the menstrual flow. Since the ovaries stop secreting the estrogenic hormones, a general glandular readjustment must occur. Many women go through this change with relatively little discomfort, physical or mental. Some others have such disturbing symptoms as "hot flashes" and nervousness. A few become so disturbed mentally that psychiatric attention is needed. A small percentage of these women develop the psychosis known as "involutional melancholia." One characteristic, which gives this psychosis its name, is severe psychological depression.

Some physicians try to produce physical and mental readjustment by replacement therapy — by administration of ovarian hormones — but the efficacy of such treatment is in doubt. Even when it seems to succeed, there is a question as to how much of the improvement is through suggestion. In one experiment, for example, the results were no different when the subjects really got the hormone injection than when they got a sterile solution of oil.[39] Endocrinologists and psychiatrists emphasize the personality of the patient more than the physiological changes as such. Thus English and Pearson[40] say,

During the period of menopause some women become panicky with the thought that the energy which leads to sexual pleasure, romance, children and motherhood is leaving them, and believe it can be replaced artificially by an injection. This feeling is true to the extent that the body has been producing a vital ovarian substance since the age of twelve and is now ceasing to produce it. But if a woman has not found love, romance, a happy marriage, enjoyment in her children and interests to have made life worthwhile before she reaches forty-five, she is not likely to get these satisfactions from an injection of a glandular substance now.

What is usually advocated in such cases is psychotherapy rather than hormone replacement. Sexual enjoyment is not necessarily impaired after the menopause. Kinsey's data [41] suggest that in many cases it may even be improved, partly because there is no longer any fear of becoming pregnant.

There is some question whether men go through a "change of life" in any sense comparable with that experienced by women. The change in men is gradual, and not marked by any obvious physiological sign such as women experience. Nevertheless, some men in middle life feel that their powers are waning and seek replacement therapy. As in the case of women, it is doubtful whether such replacement (either in the form of testicular grafts or injections) has more than a psychological effect. Often, there is not even that. To quote English and Pearson [42] again,

One of the inconsistencies of human nature is that man erects many anxieties, fears, prohibitions, and prejudices, and deprives himself (or herself) of happiness until he is forty-five, and then, finding it disappearing, runs around madly trying to find a doctor with a syringe who will inject the means of happiness into him. If he has not found happiness and romance before forty-five, his chances are much more limited of finding them after.

There is of course no sharp transition between adulthood (usually considered to range up to 60 years) and old age. Both physiological and psychological capacities begin their decline in the thirties, at first slowly and imperceptibly, then somewhat more rapidly as old age approaches. Some of these changes will now be considered in relation to over-all changes in personality during old age.

Changes in Personality from Later Maturity to Senescence

. It is common knowledge that marked changes in certain aspects of personality are often associated with old age. Clinical data abound with evidence of personality disintegration in the aged. Psychologists, however, have only recently begun to make a systematic study of psychological changes during late maturity and senescence.

One reason for our current interest in old age is the marked increase in the number of old people among us, an increase largely due to medical advances. The earliest systematic investigation of personality changes during old age was that of G. Stanley Hall.[43] He sent a questionnaire to a "few score" of "mostly eminent and some very distinguished" old people. Among the questions asked were the following: "How and at what age did you first realize the approach of old age?" "Are you troubled with regrets for things done or not done by or for you?" "What temptations do you feel, old or new?" "In what do you now take your greatest pleasure?" "Did you experience an 'Indian summer' of revived energy before the winter of age began to set in?" "Do you think or worry about dying or the hereafter more or less than formerly?" Hall presents no tabulation of replies. He does, however, present a general discussion of the responses obtained. Probably the most significant result is a clear indication of the fact that no formula can be applied to the senescent individual. While forty was frequently reported as the time at which old age appeared imminent, there were great individual differences. Old age began to be felt quite early by some and quite late by others. Some were filled with regret; others not. Some experienced rearousal of youthful temptations, while others led a perfectly serene existence. Some were interested only in the past; others in the future. Some experienced an "Indian summer" and others not. Responses to the question concerning death and the hereafter showed the "utmost diversity." Of the changes which mark the onset of old age, Hall [44] says:

The first sign of baldness, the first touch of fatigue at stated tasks, lapse of memory for names, waning potency in men; and the first gray hairs, wrinkles, fading of complexion, and change of figure, etc., in women are often specified in our returns. Such and many other signs usually gave the first sad recognition that the meridian of life was being crossed and that gradual decline was just ahead.

Changes in personality during later maturity and senescence are attributable, among other things, to general physical and psychological decline. Some of the physical changes which occur during late maturity are general glandular involution, smoothing of cerebral convolutions, impairment of sense organs, hardening of arteries, and wasted musculature. The psychological concomitants of these changes are, as recent research has indicated, a general decrement in sensory, motor, and symbolic function.

Sensorimotor decline

Miles [45] reports that visual, auditory, and tactual acuity decreases gradually from the twenties until the late sixties. It then drops precipitously. Wide individual differences are observed. The general trend for visual acuity is a drop of 5 per cent below normal in the late twenties, a 24 per cent drop below normal by the seventieth year, and a drop of 54 per cent below normal between seventy and ninety years. Other senses exhibit a somewhat similar decrement. As several investigators have indicated, the declining visual and auditory acuity of many old people often leads them to withdraw from active participation in what is going on around them. In effect, many of them become extreme introverts. To use Lewin's term, they tend to encapsulate themselves.

Studies on strength,[46] speed of reaction,[47] motor dexterity,[48] and various manual skills [49] all agree in showing a maximum in the twenties or early thirties and then a decrement with age.

Learning ability also declines with age. Several investigators [50] have shown that the decrement in the learning function is most marked for complex learning which calls for new kinds of adjustment.

One of the most thorough studies on skill is that of Welford et al.[51] This involved complex learning tasks and provided for separate recording and later analysis of different aspects of the total performance. Most of these investigations were carried on in the laboratory, but some involved practical industrial situations and operations.

Where an age decrement was found for relatively simple skills, it was usually at the receptor end. Anything which required the subject to integrate complex incoming stimuli (as in tracking a stimulus which moved unpredictably) was likely to show marked age increments. It seemed that this was because, in performing such tasks, the subject's actions needed to conform to stimulus patterns beyond his control. Where implicit guidance was importantly involved, and the subject could thus control the timing and integration of his own reactions, the age decrement was not so apparent. But what would happen if the receptor aspect were relatively simple (such as a light to be turned off) and the effector aspect closely constrained (as in complex coordinator tests like those used during the war with prospective flyers). Under these conditions, would the effector integration also break down in old age? To answer this question a coordination test was devised in which, as lights appeared one after the other in serial order, the subject was required to learn the sequence of key-pressing which would, without error, turn out each light as it appeared and turn on the next one. The results are shown in Figure 143. Although there were only ten subjects at each age range, the errors, time scores, and trials to learn showed a consistent increase with age. Variability also increased with age. The standard deviations for time were, at successive age levels: 20, 37, 36, 86, and 153. There was a somewhat comparable increase for other criteria. Age decrements were also found for later recall and relearning of the response sequences. Thus it was demonstrated that an age decrement is to be expected when *either* the receptor or the effector integration

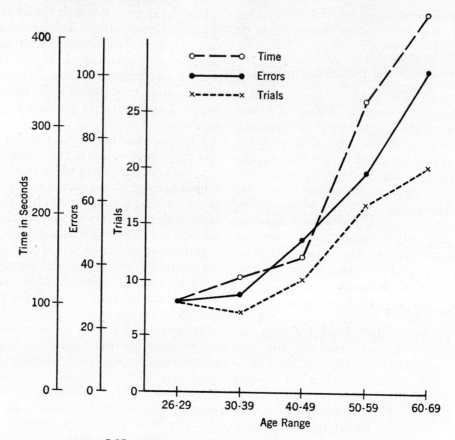

Figure 143. Learning a Complex Skill as a Function of Age

The scales on the ordinate have been arranged to make the scores for the 20–29-year group coincide.   (From A. T. Welford *et al.*, *Skill and Age: An Experimental Approach*, London: Oxford University Press, 1951, p. 113.)

is closely constrained by the situation. This, as Welford points out, is perhaps because opportunities for compensatory activity are thus minimized.

Most investigators have observed that an older person, by compensating for certain deficiencies, is often able to equal or even exceed the performance of a younger individual. The older person may compensate by working more cautiously than the younger one, by slowing down, or by putting forth greater effort. As Welford [52] says, however,

the extent to which these conditions occur is largely dependent upon the extent to which the method and timing of the task are under the subject's own

control. Where such control can be fully exercised, compensation is likely to occur, but where the performance is narrowly constrained in either the form or timing of the constituent reactions, compensation will be virtually impossible. It can be readily seen that receptor functions, in so far as they deal with events of external causation impinging upon the subject, are essentially less under his control than effector processes initiated by his own central mechanisms, and therefore permit less compensation for deficiencies of ability, and are likely to break down sooner. Where rigid constraints are placed upon effector processes, as they were in our learning experiment by the requirement to learn a definite serial order of actions, effector functions are likely to break down just as rapidly as receptor.

Memory defects

One of the most obvious concomitants of advanced age is defective memory. Jones, Conrad, and Horn [53] have found such defects even for recall of what has been witnessed in a moving picture. Recall scores ranged from an average of 52 in their youngest group (19–24) to an average of 45 in their oldest group (45–54). The age decrement is not so marked here as in many other tests of memory, but the oldest subjects were young as compared with those of investigations about to be considered. In Shakow, Dolkert, and Goldman's [54] experiment, for example, the upper age level was 90 years. One will observe from Figure 144 that recall of new material underwent a marked decrement. The least decrement was found for vocabulary, a finding in conformity with data from several other studies of vocabulary in old people.[55] Patients diagnosed as arteriosclerotic and senile had poorer recall and vocabulary scores than normal people of the same age level.

Of the several studies on memory in old people, Gilbert's [56] is also worthy of special attention. This is because she matched her younger and older groups (174 subjects in each) for initial intelligence level. On the face of it, this seems impossible unless one can dig back into records and get the original I.Q.'s, which of course are not available for old people. It has been demonstrated, however, that vocabulary shows little or no decline before the seventies, and that at early age levels it correlates highly with I.Q. Gilbert therefore gave Terman's (1916) vocabulary test of 100 words to both the younger group (20–29 years) and the older group (60–69 years). When she subsequently selected her two groups, matched on the basis of vocabulary scores, she assumed that they were also equivalent with respect to intelligence level — the present level for the younger group and the maximum, before general decline set in, for the older group. Memory was tested with eleven tests, ranging in difficulty from memory span to learning (and

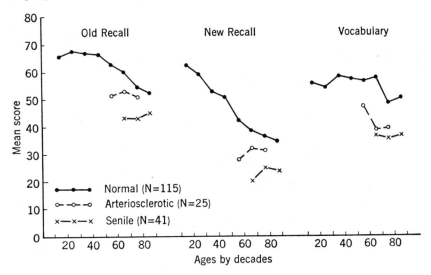

Figure 144. Memory and Age

A revision of the Wells memory test was used. This provides an index of ability to recall past events (old recall) and material learned recently such as figures, sentences, and ideas presented during the test (new recall). Note that even though ability to define words (vocabulary) holds up through most of the age range, it shows a precipitous decline at around 70 years. (From D. Shakow, M. B. Dolkert, and R. Goldman, "The Memory Function in Psychoses of the Aged," *Dis. Nerv. Syst.*, 1941, *2*, 43–48).

later recall) of paired associates. In every comparison the average scores of the older group were significantly lower than those of the younger. This discrepancy grew larger and more reliable as the tests became more difficult. The brighter sixty-year-olds showed a smaller age decrement, on every test, than the less bright. When comparison was based upon the bright young and the bright old group, there was still an age decrement, but smaller than for the entire older group. The bright sixty-year-olds were behind the entire younger group on only four tests — the most difficult ones. On some tests they did better than the younger group. Gilbert concludes that

older persons on the average show relatively little decline in ability to receive new impressions but suffer greatly in their ability to form the new associations necessary to the learning of new material. Their learning process seems to suffer from their decreased flexibility and adaptability. They can and do learn new material, but the learning is laborious and the results less satisfactory than when they were young and at the peak of their efficient functioning. The brighter they are to begin with, the better they tend to retain the efficiency of their learning process; while the real cause can only be conjectured, it may bear some relation to the greater flexibility of the bright persons and their continued activity in the intellectual field.

Intelligence-test performance

Studies of intelligence-test performance during later maturity and old age show that a decline begins in the twenties and continues throughout life. Miles and Miles [57] found that the decrement is at first gradual. Beyond the seventieth year, however, there is a sudden decline. Jones and Conrad,[58] Mrs. Miles,[59] and Wechsler [60] obtained similar results. The same general trend is present for men and women and for groups of individuals with different degrees of education. The college group usually starts at a higher level and declines less than the general population. The two age curves are, however, approximately parallel. When individuals are given

unlimited time to complete the tests, the decline is still present, though it is not so steep as when time limits are involved. In commenting on this work, Miles [61] points out that intelligence tests, since they are standardized on young people, may not be fair to the old. He believes that tests devised for the specific purpose of testing the whole age range from 25 to 95 will show the peak of performance to occur later than is indicated at present.

Fox and Birren [62] summarize and extend the information on Wechsler-Bellevue performance in old age. They give particular emphasis to the differential age decline revealed by subtests. Several studies in addition to their own show least decline for the vocabulary test. The information and comprehension tests also show little decline. Most decline is revealed by the block design, picture arrangement, and digit-symbol tests. We have just commented upon the absence of a marked decline in vocabulary prior to an average age of 70 years. The subjects of the above report were in their sixties.

Emotional reactions

Hollingworth [63] and others have mentioned that old age is partly characterized by dulled emotionality. Hall,[64] however, takes exception to this view. He says:

They say our emotional life is damped. True, we are more immune from certain great passions and our affection is very differently distributed. But what lessons of repression we have to learn. If the fires of youth are banked and smouldering they are in no wise extinguished and perhaps burn only the more fiercely inwardly because they cannot vent themselves, as even the James-Lange theory admits for repressed feelings, inhibition of which really only makes them more intense. We get scant credit for the self-control that restrains us from so much we feel impelled to say and do, and if we break out, it is ascribed not to its true cause in outer circumstances but to irritability thought characteristic of our years. Age has the same right to emotional perturbations as youth, and is no whit less exposed and disposed to them. Here, as everywhere, we are misunderstood, and are such a feeble minority that we have incessantly to renounce our impulsions.

Rorschach responses give support to the view that old age often brings restricted emotionality. The most extensive of several studies is that of Ames et al.,[65] which involved 200 subjects ranging in age from 70 to 100 years. Comparison of Rorschachs within this age range showed no consistent difference between the 70-, 80-, and 90-year-olds. Within each age grouping, however, a few gave responses which were indistinguishable from those of normal adults, a few gave responses indicative of senility, and most gave responses suggesting presenility. The detailed reactions to the Rorschach and questions concerning its validity need not concern us here. It is interesting, however, to examine the description of presenile personality which the investigators feel they are justified in deriving from Rorschach details. The presenile individual, they say,[66] "is uncertain of self and suspicious of others. There is a vagueness of both perception and expression." Despite egocentricity, he "shows considerable interest in other people. Though vague and uncertain much of the time, he is at other times extremely certain, definite and rigid." Also noted is "marked restriction of both intellectual and emotional processes, though most are more introversive than extratensive. Though given to easy laughter and ready tears, these individuals do not seem to be the victims of or even the possessors of strong emotions." Subjects characterized as senile showed a further decrease in emotionality. The senile is "extremely restricted, unproductive, stereotyped, intellectually and emotionally impoverished, uncritical and insecure. Little interested in those about him, his interest gradually narrows down to a complete concern with self and bodily parts and functions, particularly a concern with eliminative functions. . . . There appears to be rather marked emotional lability but no deep emotion."

In general, Ames and her collaborators[67]

conclude that as people get older their Rorschach responses show regression. They say that the "changes which commonly take place as any subject proceeds from normal through presenile to senile responses may be characterized as in many respects exactly the reverse of the changes which take place from childhood to adulthood." One may recall, from an earlier discussion (p. 323), that Dennis and Mallinger[68] observed an increase in animism during senescence and were also led to conclude that their senescent subjects had in this respect reverted to childhood ways.

Banham (Bridges)[69] has extended her well-known schema of emotional development in infancy (Figure 122, p. 405) so that it represents what is, in her opinion, the transition through the whole life span from birth to senescence. She regards the emotions of the senescent person as restricted, perseverative, and often regressive. The "emotions" cited as especially evident during senescence are: grief, worry, self-pity, guilt feelings, querulousness-depression, irritability, boredom, mystical ecstasy, possessive satisfaction-content, benevolence, and gustatory sensuousness. Apathy and passivity are regarded as generally representative of emotional life at this period. There is no implication, however, that all old people show a predominance of such emotion.

Other aspects of personality

Miles[70] reports some data, obtained incidentally during the Stanford Later Maturity Research project, which show that individuals, as they become older, are increasingly aware of disabilities and handicaps. He says: "If the adult age range is divided into four periods, 20–29, 30–49, 50–69, and 70–89, the percentages of handicap for each succeeding age group for the women are 16, 32, 41, and 56; for the men these are 22, 19, 35, and 44 respectively." Mrs. Miles[71] gave the Bernreuter Personality Inventory to 154 men and 174 women ranging in age from 25 to 95 years. Correlations between age and neurotic tendency, self-sufficiency, and introversion were negligible. There was a small negative correlation between dominance and age. Pollock and Malzberg [72] present statistics which indicate that both males and females become increasingly susceptible to personality disorders as they grow older. There is a rapid increase in the incidence of mental disease after 55.

Studies of the interests and attitudes of individuals in late maturity and old age have been reported by Strong,[73] Thorndike,[74] and many others whose findings are summarized by Kuhlen.[75] These studies show, in general, a declining interest in activities which call for physical and psychological skill and for change in habitual modes of response. There is an increasing interest in sedentary pursuits as individuals grow older. After 50 there is apparently little change of interests. Strong attributes this to diminution of learning ability. He also points out that individuals approaching old age tend to develop a pronounced dislike of any change.

It should be remembered that the data on sensory and motor ability, learning, memory, perception, intelligence test scores, neurotic tendencies, mental diseases, interests, and so on, are representative of *group* trends. Every investigator has observed marked individual differences in the characteristics of old people. Such differences are especially evident in such fields as economics, politics, and science. Some individuals produce their best work in youth; others during old age. Some are incapacitated early, while others continue to participate in social affairs until a ripe old age.

One can find no more fitting conclusion to this discussion of old age than a quotation from Miles, who, through his direction of the Stanford Later Maturity Research, has had more intimate over-all contact with the psychological problems of the old than has any other psychologist. He [76] says:

The loss in accommodation power of the aging person's eyes typifies the total individual's decrement in capacity to accommodate in a rubber-like manner with advancing age. But accommodation ability as such is really more important in the early developmental stages of life where the organism has chiefly to work out its ecological status. When the individual life has found or fitted itself into what is both convenient and comfortable as an environmental situation, then relative constancy and sticking power become more useful than the great elasticity necessary at a younger age. Older persons became systematized in complex habit constellations and points of view as younger ones are in the process of doing in the field of motor skills. When society asks for rapid changes, e.g., modified production methods in industry, the older person is at a disadvantage, while the younger adult on the average does not show up so well where consistency and devotion are the valued qualities. Facing the total picture for the influence of age on man beyond maturity, we see, from the experimental results so far achieved, that decline appears earlier and is more prominent and regular in the purely anatomical and physiological functions, and is considerably less evident in those that are predominantly psychological. Biologically this is what we might expect, because mind remains the most plastic adaptive mechanism. Of the ancient pillars of mind — memory, imagination, and judgment or common sense — the first, as a result of aging, undoubtedly shows less readiness to retain new material. But decline in imagination and judgment if it occurs before senility can to a large extent be compensated or perhaps more than compensated for by enrichment of experience, with the result that the total functioning intellectual organism has a more ample base for socially effective operation. In the later years considerable decrement on the physical side, even where it encroaches on the psychological, can still be compensated for by persisting powers of imagination and judgment. All individuals, and particularly older ones, to some extent learn the use of mental strategy in marshaling their forces for purposes of private and public life. We strive to put forward our best ideas as well as our best foot; and we have many more ideas than we have feet from which to select. Advancing age puts a premium on mental organization, and we must not forget that the long-lived tend to be the stronger minded.

Summary and Conclusions

Adolescence is generally assumed to begin at puberty, when the female begins to menstruate and the male has his first ejaculation.

The average age at which these events occur is around 13 for girls and a year later for boys. There are, however, large individual differences.

The idea that adolescence is necessarily a time of storm and stress due to changes in growth processes is largely erroneous. Group averages show that most body structures, as well as strength, skill, and psychological functions, undergo a rather steady growth before, during, and after adolescence. Although increments of growth tend to be somewhat larger during the adolescent period, these are usually not so large as to cause adjustment difficulties. Where the rate of growth does show an unusual spurt, the individual suddenly becoming fat or tall, difficulties such as awkwardness and self-consciousness are not inevitable. If they exist it is usually because the individual's self-concepts have changed or he has received undue attention from others. Such difficulties are ultimately social in origin and not direct resultants of growth changes.

The sex organs and related structures normally show a marked increment of growth at puberty. There is a concomitant change in sex hormones. Estrogens and androgens are present in both males and females. Around the time of puberty, however, there is a very great increase in female estrogenic secretion. Estrogenic secretions in boys show little or no change. At the same time that the estrogen output in females undergoes such a spurt, the androgen output in boys shows a somewhat similar spurt. Associated with such changes in the sexual structures and hormone secretions are changes in sexual interests and activities. The sexual frustrations which are associated with this period in our society do not exist in primitive societies. Primitive adolescents are thus usually free from the sexual conflicts which cause so much trouble for many in our own society. It is sometimes maintained, however, that sexual restraint is conducive to constructive effort.

Adolescents in our society are especially influenced by what has been called their "peer culture." Identification with peers is characteristic as they begin to break away from parental control. The social peculiarities of many adolescents in such matters as jargon and dress can often be understood only in terms of peer-group influences. The transition from parental control to independence is often characterized by ambivalent attitudes in both parents and adolescents. Use of projective tests suggests that adolescent fantasies are often characterized by themes of aggression and love.

The interests and attitudes of adolescents have been studied extensively. Interests tend to be more discriminating than at earlier ages and to be narrowed to relatively few. Religious interests, which at one time made the adolescent period one of conversion or "religious awakening," have changed with the times so that such "awakening" is no longer regarded as characteristic of adolescence.

The personality characteristics of adults have a relatively high degree of constancy. They tend to remain throughout life. Adult personality is also characterized by channelization of interests along domestic, vocational, and avocational lines. It is obvious that adult personality represents the culmination of all the factors, phylogenetic and ontogenetic, which were considered earlier in this book. The adult human being is what he is by reason of his animal ancestry; the previous development of his fundamental sensory, motor, and symbolic functions; and the integration of structure and behavior under the influence of the various social conditioning factors considered in this chapter. This is the period in which the most outstanding achievements occur. Early adulthood is usually cited, in retrospect, as the happiest period of life. Later, at around age 45 for women, the climacteric occurs and often brings problems of adjustment. Psychiatrists feel that these have their genesis in earlier life and cannot be blamed upon the menopause as such. The glandular change in men is slower than in women and not marked by any obvious event.

There is no sharp transition between adulthood and old age, although the latter is usually assumed to begin at around the age of 60. During later maturity there is a tendency for the fundamental physical and psychological functions to decline. This decline continues and becomes more precipitous with advanced age. In most functions the precipitous decline usually comes in the seventies. There are, however, large individual differences. Some people show a decline earlier than others and some, even though they live to an advanced age, do not show it at all. Many old people compensate so as to cover up deficiencies which might otherwise be obvious.

Skills which require complex integrations of sensory data, or which place rigid constraints upon the integrations required for performance, show the most decrement with advanced age. This is because these skills prevent the subject from working at his own (centrally controlled) pace and in ways which allow him to compensate for sensory and motor deficiencies.

Generally speaking, the learning of new skills places the older person at a disadvantage. This is also seen when symbolic skills are involved. Memory declines with age, but the decline is much greater when new material must be learned and recalled. An interesting outcome of research in this field is the observation that mnemonic deficiencies do not develop as early in bright people as in those of average or low intelligence. In some kinds of memorizing, bright old people are no poorer than average adults.

Analysis of intelligence test performance in later maturity and old age shows that, while the general level declines with age, vocabulary shows little or no decline until the seventies. Information and comprehension (as tested by the Wechsler-Bellevue Intelligence Scale) also resist the encroachments of old age.

One aspect of the personality change in old age is the tendency toward restricted emotionality. Rorschach data suggest that such restriction is only notable in subjects rated as presenile and senile. Others, up to their nineties, evidence normal emotionality. Rorschach responses in the presenile and senile show regression to a childish level. Such regression has also been found in studies of animism. In old age there is usually a marked restriction in interests and in social participation. Mental illness becomes more prevalent than at earlier age levels.

It should be emphasized that in every aspect of old age which psychologists and others have studied, there are exceptions to group trends. Some persons begin to show decrements early and some, despite advanced age, show relatively little psychological deterioration.

REFERENCES

1. See Ford, C. S., and F. A. Beach, *Patterns of Sexual Behavior*. New York: Hoeber, 1951, pp. 174–178.
2. Shuttleworth, F. K., "The Adolescent Period: A Graphic and Pictorial Atlas," *Monog. Soc. Res. Child Develop.*, 1938, *3*, No. 3.
3. Kinsey, A. C., W. B. Pomeroy, C. E. Martin, and P. H. Gebhard, *Sexual Behavior in the Human Female*. Philadelphia: Saunders, 1953.
4. Kinsey, A.C., W. B. Pomeroy, and C. E. Martin, *Sexual Behavior in the Human Male*. Philadelphia: Saunders, 1948.
5. See the data in Shuttleworth (citation 2).
6. Horrocks, J. E., *The Psychology of Adolescence*. Boston: Houghton Mifflin, 1951, pp. 258–260.
7. See citation 3.
8. Shock, N., "Some Physiological Aspects of Adolescence," from *Texas Reports on Biology and Medicine*, 1946, *4*, 289–310. Reprinted in J. M. Seidman, *The Adolescent: A Book of Readings*. New York: Dryden, 1953.
9. Jones, H. E., *Motor Performance and Growth*. Berkeley: University of California Press, 1949.
10. Espenschade, A., "Motor Performance in Adolescence," *Monog. Soc. Res. Child Develop.*, 1940, *5*, No. 1.

11. *Op. cit.*, p. 166.

12. *Ibid.*, p. 167.

13. Averill, L. A., *Adolescence*. Boston: Houghton Mifflin, 1936, pp. 47–48.

14. Hall, G. S., *Adolescence: Its Psychology and Its Relations to Physiology, Anthropology, Sociology, Sex, Crime, Religion, and Education.* New York: Appleton, 1904.

15. Goodenough, F. L., *Developmental Psychology* (2d ed.). New York: Appleton-Century-Crofts, 1945, pp. 474–475.

16. Brooks, F. D., *The Psychology of Adolescence.* Boston: Houghton Mifflin, 1929.

17. Hall, G. S., *op. cit.*

18. Mathews, E., "A Study of Emotional Stability of Children," *J. Delinquency*, 1923, *8*, 1–40.

19. Brooks, *op. cit.*

20. Pollock, R., and B. Malzberg, "Expectation of Mental Disease," *Mental Hygiene*, 1929, *18*, 132–163.

21. Horrocks, *op. cit.*, p. 95.

22. Lehman, H. C., and P. A. Witty, *The Psychology of Play Activities.* New York: Barnes, 1927.

23. Kuhlen, R. G., *The Psychology of Adolescent Development.* New York: Harper, 1952.

24. Malinowski, B., *Sex and Repression in Savage Society.* New York: Harcourt, Brace, 1927.

25. Mead, M., *From the South Seas: Studies of Adolescence and Sex in Primitive Societies.* New York: Morrow, 1939.

26. See citation 1.

27. Zachry, C. B., "Problems of Adolescents." From *Bulletin of the Menninger Clinic*, 1940, *4*, 63–73. The quotation is from p. 68.

28. Horrocks, *op. cit.*, p. 129.

29. Symonds, P. M., *Adolescent Fantasy: An Investigation of the Picture-Story Method of Personality Study.* New York: Columbia University Press, 1949.

30. Starbuck, E. D., *The Psychology of Religion.* New York: Scribners, 1899.

31. Clark, E. T., *The Psychology of Religious Awakening.* New York: Macmillan, 1929.

32. Kuhlen, R. G., and M. Arnold, "Age Differences in Religious Beliefs and Problems During Adolescence," *J. Genet. Psychol.*, 1944, *65*, 291–300.

33. See citation 23, p. 456.

34. Watson, J. B., *Behaviorism* (rev. ed.). New York: Norton, 1930, p. 278.

35. Lehman, H. C., "Chronological Age vs. Proficiency in Physical Skills," *Am. J. Psychol.*, 1951, *64*, 161–187.

36. Lehman, H. C., "Man's Most Creative Years: Then and Now," *Science*, 1943, *98*, 393–399. See also "The Creative Years: Oil Paintings, Etchings and Architectural Works," and the references cited there in *Psych. Rev.*, 1942, *49*, 19–42; *Age and Achievement*, Princeton: Princeton University Press, 1953.

37. These findings are summarized by E. B. Hurlock, *Developmental Psychology*, New York: McGraw-Hill, 1953, pp. 481–484.

38. See citation 22.

39. English, O. S., and G. H. J. Pearson, *Emotional Problems of Living.* New York: Norton, 1945, p. 391.

40. *Ibid.*, p. 392.

41. Citation 3, p. 737.

42. *Op. cit.*, p. 392.

43. Hall, G. S., *Senescence.* New York: Appleton, 1923.

44. *Ibid.*, pp. 322–323.

45. Miles, W. R., "Age and Human Ability," *Psych. Rev.*, 1933, *40*, 99–123; "Age and Human Society," in C. Murchison, (ed.), *A Handbook of Social Psychology*, Worcester: Clark University Press, 1935.

46. The research on strength, as well as other characteristics of old age, has been summarized by W. Dennis, "Age and Behavior. I: A Survey of the Literature," *American Institute for Research*, Pittsburgh, 1952.

47. See especially the data of W. R. Miles, "Measures of Certain Human Abilities Throughout the Life Span," *Proc. Nat. Acad. Sci.*, 1931, *17*, 627–633. Reprinted in R. G. Kuhlen, and G. G. Thompson, *Psychological Studies of Human Development.* New York: Appleton-Century-Crofts, 1952.

48. Barker, R. G., "The Relation of Age of Human Adults to Some Aspects of Ability to do Fatiguing Muscular Work: Age Range, Twenty-Five to Ninety Years," *Psych. Bull.*, 1934, *31*, 606–607. Also see Miles, *op. cit.*

49. Welford, A. T., *Skill and Age.* London: Oxford University Press, 1951.

50. Hollingworth, H. L., *Mental Growth and Decline*, New York: Appleton, 1930; E. L. Thorndike, *Adult Learning*, New York: Macmillan, 1928; F. L. Ruch, "The Differentiative Effects of Age upon Human Learning," *J. Gen. Psychol.*, 1934, *11*, 261–286; F. L. Ruch,

"Adult Learning," *Psych. Bull.*, 1933, *30*, 387–414; and Welford, *op. cit.*

51. See citation 49.

52. *Ibid.*, p. 123. Quotation courtesy of Oxford University Press and the Nuffield Foundation.

53. Jones, H. E., H. S. Conrad, and A. Horn, "Psychological Studies of Motion Pictures: II. Observation and Recall as a Function of Age," *Univ. Calif. Publ. Psychol.*, 1928, *3*, 225–243.

54. Shakow, D., M. B. Dolkert, and R. Goldman, "The Memory Function in Psychoses of the Aged," *Dis. Nerv. System*, 1941, *2*, 43–48.

55. See J. C. Raven, "The Comparative Assessment of Intellectual Ability," *Brit. J. Psychol.*, 1949, *39*, 12–19.

56. Gilbert, J. G., "Memory Loss in Senescence," *J. Abn. & Soc. Psychol.*, 1941, *36*, 73–86. Quotation from p. 86, with the permission of the American Psychological Association.

57. Miles, W. R., and C. C. Miles, "The Correlation of Intelligence Scores and Chronological Age from Early to Late Maturity," *Am. J. Psychol.*, 1932, *44*, 44–78.

58. Jones, H. E., and H. S. Conrad, "The Growth and Decline of Intelligence: A Study of a Homogeneous Group between the Ages of Ten and Sixty," *Genet. Psychol. Monog.*, 1933, *13*, No. 3.

59. Miles, C. C., "Influence of Speed and Age in Intelligence Test Scores of Adults," *J. Gen. Psychol.*, 1933, *10*, 208–210.

60. Wechsler, D., *The Range of Human Capacities* (2d ed.). Baltimore: Williams and Wilkins, 1952, Chapter IX.

61. Miles, W. R., citation 45, 1935.

62. Fox, C., and J. E. Birren, "The Differential Decline of Subtest Scores of the Wechsler-Bellevue Intelligence Scale in 60–69-Year-Old Individuals," *J. Genet. Psychol.*, 1950, *77*, 313–317.

63. Hollingworth, H. L., *Mental Growth and Decline.* New York: Appleton, 1927.

64. Hall, G. S., *Senescence.* New York: Appleton, 1923, p. 383.

65. Ames, L. B., J. Learned, R. W. Métraux, and R. N. Walker, *Rorschach Responses in Old Age.* New York: Hoeber, 1954.

66. *Ibid.*, p. 207.

67. *Ibid.*, p. 207.

68. Dennis, W., and B. Mallinger, "Animism and Related Tendencies in Senescence," *J. Gerontology*, 1949, *4*, 218–221.

69. Banham, K. M., "Senescence and the Emotions: A Genetic Theory." *J. Genet Psychol*, 1951, *78*, 175–183.

70. Miles, W. R., "Age and Human Society," in C. Murchison (ed.), *A Handbook of Social Psychology.* Worcester: Clark University Press, 1935, p. 642.

71. See citation 59.

72. See citation 20.

73. Strong, E. K., *Change of Interests with Age.* Stanford University Press, 1931.

74. Thorndike, E. L., *Adult Interests.* New York: Macmillan, 1935.

75. Kuhlen, R. G., "Age Differences in Personality During Adult Years," *Psych. Bull.*, 1945, *42*, 333–358.

76. Miles, W. R., citation 45, p. 642.

SUGGESTIONS FOR FURTHER READING

Cattell, R. B., *Personality.* New York: McGraw-Hill, 1950, Chapter 20.

Cavan, R. S., E. W. Burgess, R. J. Havighurst, and H. Goldhamer, *Personal Adjustment in Old Age.* Chicago: Science Research Associates, 1949.

Cole, L., *Psychology of Adolescence* (4th ed.). New York: Rinehart, 1954.

Gilbert, J. G., *Understanding Old Age.* New York: Ronald, 1952.

Havighurst, R. J., and H. Taba, *Adolescent Character and Personality.* New York: Wiley, 1949.

Horrocks, J. E., *The Psychology of Adolescence.* Boston: Houghton Mifflin, 1951.

Horrocks, J. E., "The Adolescent," in L. Carmichael (ed.), *Manual of Child Psychology* (2d ed.). New York: Wiley, 1954.

Hurlock, E. B., *Developmental Psychology.* New York: McGraw-Hill, 1953, Chapters 1, and 7–14.

Jones, H. E., *Development in Adolescence.* New York: Appleton-Century-Crofts, 1943.

Kaplan, O. J., "Gerontology," in D. Brower and L. E. Abt, *Progress in Clinical Psychology.* New York: Grune and Stratton, 1952.

Kuhlen, R. G., and G. G. Thompson, *Psychological Studies of Human Development.* New York: Appleton-Century-Crofts, 1952, Readings 3 (Kallman and Sander), 5 (Sollenberger), 6 (Jones and Bayley), 7 (Espenschade), 8 (Walter Miles), 17 (Simmons), 22 (Jones and Conrad), 23 (Lorge), 29 (Bingham), 31 (Dennis and Mallinger), 37 (Stone and Barker), 39 (Strong), 48 (Kuhlen and Lee), 50 (Cavan, Burgess, Havighurst, and Goldhamer), 63 (E. S. Jones), 65 (Lehman), 67 (Healy and Bronner), and 71 (Morgan).

Lansing, A. I. (ed.), *Problems of Aging.* Baltimore: Williams and Wilkins, 1952.

Kuhlen, R. G., *The Psychology of Adolescent Development.* New York: Harper, 1952.

Lehman, H. C., *Age and Achievement.* Princeton: Princeton University Press, 1953.

Seidman, J. M., *The Adolescent: A Book of Readings.* New York: Dryden, 1953.

Shock, N., "Gerontology (Later Maturity)," in C. P. Stone (ed.), *Annual Review of Psychology,* Vol. 2, 1951.

Symonds, P. M., *Adolescent Fantasy.* New York: Columbia University Press, 1949.

Wechsler, D., *The Range of Human Capacities* (2d ed.). Baltimore: Williams and Wilkins, 1952, Chapter IX.

Index of Authors

Italicized page numbers refer to bibliographies.

Index of Subjects